Treasures of
THE BLOODSTOCK BREEDERS' REVIEW

Treasures of The Bloodstock Breeders' Review

Compiled by
Leon Rasmussen and Miles Napier

J. A. ALLEN
London

First published in Great Britain by
J. A. Allen & Co. Ltd
1 Lower Grosvenor Place, London SW1W 0EL
1990

British Library Cataloguing in Publication Data
Treasures of the bloodstock breeders' review.
1. British thoroughbred horses
I. Rasmussen, Leon   II. Napier, Miles   III. The Bloodstock
breeders' review
636.1320941

ISBN 0-85131-502-X

Designed by Alan Hamp
Typeset by T & S Typesetting, Hewish, Avon BS24 6RW
Printed and bound by
Bath Press, Lower Bristol Road, Bath BA2 3BL

Acknowledgements

The compilers are indebted to Susan Cameron for her ready co-operation with this project, to Guy Wilmot of W. W. Rouch & Co., who tirelessly searched his files for long-forgotten photographs, to Mr J. A. Allen, for his help and encouragement, to Jane Lake for devoted attention to acres of proofs, to Caroline Burt for unceasing attention and assistance in getting this book into print, and lastly, to T & S Typesetting who kept working to schedule despite power cuts and part of their roof being blown off in the gale of 25th January 1990.

Contents

PART 2 - RACEHORSES

PART 3 – OWNERS

PART 4 - TRAINERS

PART 5 - JOCKEYS

PART 6 - BETTING

PART 7 - BREEDERS

PART 8 – STALLIONS

PART 9 – MARES

PART 10 – BREEDING THEORIES AND THEORISTS

List of Photographs

xv

About The Compilers
A Foreword
to a Foreword

When *The Bloodstock Breeders' Review* became a financial casualty in 1979, it was a very sad time for racing and breeding adherents throughout the thoroughbred world. Started as a quarterly in 1912 before subsequently becoming an annual, the *Review*, from the outset, had an international mission. 'Where the thoroughbred is to be found, thither will it travel, conveying information calculated to be of interest and value to breeders. . . . It is our aim to make this *Review* an indispensable adjunct to every breeders' library.'

The *Review* may not have found its way into every breeder's library, but the more the pity! When this observer first became acquainted with the *Review* around 1950, he was so impressed that he promptly became a subscriber – and, proudly, a contributor for some years – and went to considerable effort to acquire every issue which had been published. This personal 'mission' was finally accomplished, although several copies have been photostatted.

From the time of the *Review*'s demise until retirement in 1987, this Turf writer always had one persistent thought and purpose in the back of his mind: save the best of *The Bloodstock Breeders' Review* for those who never knew it existed, for those who found out about it too late and were unable to experience the glories of its earliest editions, and for those who may have known about it but didn't realise what unique and enduring literary treasures were to be found there. Hence, this anthology: *Treasures of the Bloodstock Breeders' Review.*

The authors hope that it will be considered the finest reference book on worldwide thoroughbred racing and breeding. We may say this in all modesty because we have only selected and saved what others, more

1

knowledgeable and closer to the events, have written, adding a 'precede' here and there along the way to try and bridge the gaps in time.

It is our sincerest hope that *Treasures* will not only be unequalled as a source of information in its field, but also unequalled as a source of entertainment. Along with the presentations of breeding theories, pro and con, and other very serious matters which have attached themselves to the Turf throughout its existence, thousands of recorded facts have been furnished – some amusing, some outright humorous, some personal, some anecdotal, some tremendously serious, some tender, some sorrowful, some inspirational, some just chatty, but always absorbing and always with the thought that the reader would enjoy knowing about them.

Indeed, there is the sanguine hope and firm expectation that a person, looking for a specific piece of information, may become so interested in what else he or she finds in the book that, like a stirring, enthralling novel, it will be hard to put down.

In 1932, when giving Major Fairfax-Blakeborough's book, *The Turf's Who's Who*, a favourable review in its 'The Library Shelf' department, the *Review* said of the Major: 'He is an indefatigable newsgatherer, and has rescued from oblivion much useful and interesting information pertaining to the Turf of bygone days.' What the *Review* said about Major Fairfax-Blakeborough must also be said about the *Review* during its lifetime. It was always the 'indefatigable newsgatherer' and it certainly rescued and saved from oblivion much useful and interesting information pertaining to the Turf, not only of bygone days but also of all the days of its existence wherever the thoroughbred raced.

The *Review* was never lazy or haphazard about anything. It believed in thoroughness and went to all ends to present the complete story. For example, when Vahren, the dam of The Tetrarch, died, the history of her family was given. The *Review* noted:

'For many of the details that are about to be set forth we are indebted to breeders and others who at one time or another owned members of this thoroughbred family. We constantly have occasion to beg for information of this sort, and gladly acknowledge the assistance which is almost invariably given willingly. Without such aid it would, of course, be impossible to present anything like a complete narrative. Is it not rather unfortunate that the rescue from oblivion of facts of this kind is dependent upon private initiative? There have been periods in the past, and there may be others in the future, when nobody has felt, or will feel, a call to undertake the task. However, we will venture to give an undertaking that so long as the *Review* is alive the duty will not be neglected.'

Dedicated to that promise and refusing to be unfaithful to it, the *Review* was responsible for much of the finest writing on the many facets of racing and breeding, including many memorable personal touches that are not to be found in most books of reference. It is our fervent desire that *Treasures* will transcend such an objective.

Edward Moorhouse, a superlative writer with an innate feeling for thoroughbred racing and all that it means to many of us, was with the *Review* from its beginning. In 1933, twenty-one years after it all began, Mr Moorhouse wrote:

> 'When each autumn we review the results of the season's classic races, they frequently seem to have been fairly obvious. If we recall the problems that confronted us as each of the events approached it may, perhaps, be with a feeling of surprise that the solutions seemed so difficult to find.
>
> 'At the present time most followers of racing are inclined to let this year's "dead past bury its dead", but there will come a day when we shall desire to remind ourselves of the facts and incidents, doubts and fears, jubilations and disappointments associated with these big events. That is why the stories related year by year in *Review* become more and more interesting as time goes on.'

So, time has gone on, and the day, we believe, has come 'to remind ourselves of the facts and incidents, doubts and fears, jubilations and disappointments associated with the big events' which have transpired through the triumphant and tumultuous, and always exciting and engaging, years of the Turf.

That is the purpose of this book – *Treasures of the Bloodstock Breeders' Review* – to rescue and preserve the heritage of the Turf.

LEON RASMUSSEN

Foreword
to the First Issue, 1912

SIX MONTHS ago the Breeders' Bureau was founded as a branch of the British Bloodstock Agency Ltd. Its purpose and aim are to supply members with information collected from all quarters of the globe. That the Bureau met a want felt in breeding circles was proved by the steady flow of applications for membership. The number of names already registered actually exceeds the limit that was provisionally fixed.

The working of the Bureau has demonstrated that breeders of thoroughbreds are greatly in need of some means whereby they can acquire knowledge of events and movements occurring in distant parts of the world. Frequently, of course, the information they require is of personal rather than general moment. In that case the Bureau exactly meets their needs. There are, however, many happenings and developments which are of consequence to the general body of breeders. How could we help them?

One of the members of the Bureau, in forwarding his subscription of two guineas, sent an accompanying letter in which, after heartily approving the scheme, he wrote: 'I think it would be better if you increased the subscription to five guineas and gave us a periodical dealing with matters pertaining to the thoroughbred. If you will adopt this suggestion, you will, believe me, be doing breeders a great service.' There is the germ of the idea which has resulted in the publication of the first number of *The Bloodstock Breeders' Review*. It has not been deemed necessary to increase the Bureau subscription, but the suggestion that, by means of a magazine, the work can be considerably extended was so happy we decided to act upon it.

Such, then, is the genesis of the *Review*. This, the first quarterly number, cannot be allowed to go forth without a word or two of explanation of its scope. There might be the less to say if its wanderings were to be confined to the British Isles, the home of the thoroughbred. The *Review* has, however, an international mission. Copies of this and every succeeding issue will cross the wide seas and find student readers in far-off lands. It is to be a cosmopolitan magazine in every sense of the word. Where the thoroughbred is to be found, thither will it travel, conveying information calculated to be of interest and value to breeders.

We have set our hands to an ambitious undertaking. Most accomplishments of any value involve hard work, patience and perseverance. It is hoped that our labours will often be lightened by the kindly assistance of our readers. Their help will always be welcome. As time goes on we trust they will realise that they have a personal interest in the *Review*. The breeding industry is essentially one in which the co-operative spirit should be given a place. If that spirit is to have full play there must be a centre from which its beneficient influence can radiate. Are we overleaping ourselves when we venture to entertain the hope that this journal may come to be regarded as the bond of union?

We live in a scientific age. Searchers after the truth are probing deeper and deeper, thrusting ruthlessly aside old-standing beliefs founded mainly on tradition. Each year brings to light some new discovery which opens out a new vista to those who can look beyond the obstacles that have accumulated for generations. What have the scientists to tell us about horse-breeding? As yet it may not be very much. Very few of them are applying their investigations directly to the horse. But as each fresh fact bearing on the law of heredity is brought to light, its association with the equine species is being carefully tested by experts. The sum of the knowledge thus acquired is already very considerable, but many steps have yet to be taken before it will be possible to present the truth in a form that will compel the sceptics to capitulate.

Scepticism is deep rooted in the minds of most breeders. This is hardly surprising. Again and again have they had theories and ideas placed before them which, when subjected to a practical test, have utterly failed to substantiate themselves. All these schemes have been at variance with the Law of Nature. It is by a right understanding of that mysterious law that we shall make progress.

Mendel pulled the scales from our eyes. His experiments led to the discovery that nature works in well-defined grooves and with marvellous mathematical precision. The dominants and the recessives, whose behaviour is unalterable, are met with in all heritable characters. There is no known exception to the Mendelian law. That is a great and outstanding fact. It enables us to apply it with absolute confidence. A few months ago a breeder triumphantly informed an apostle of Mendel that he could produce for inspection a bay colt by a chestnut horse out of a chestnut mare. Now, according to the Mendelian law, chestnut is a recessive colour, and so chestnut crossed with chestnut is bound to produce chestnut. The student of Mendelism was in no way dismayed. Hearing that the mare had been sent to a farm to be served, he suggested that the owner of the mare should boldly accuse the proprietor of the establishment to which she was sent of having used some horse other than the chestnut stipulated for. The plan was adopted, and, sure enough, it was admitted that the presumed fraud had been committed. The culprit is still wondering how his misfeasance was discovered. In the *General Stud Book*, there are numberless alleged exceptions to the chestnut rule. Every case that has been investigated – and every possible case has been inquired into – has been proved wrongly described, either owing to sheer carelessness, or to perplexity at the time the return was made.

It is, then, by the persistent application of science, and by following up the clues which that application reveals, that we must hope to make headway towards a higher standard of excellence, a higher ideal. In this *Review* it will be our privilege as much as our duty to keep our readers in close touch with developments as they arise. There is no boasting on our part when we state that we are placed in a peculiarly favourable position for obtaining tidings of the progress of events in scientific circles.

This, however, will be but one feature of the journal we are now launching. The breeder will naturally want information likely to be of immediate assistance to him in the working of his stud. When he turns to these pages his search will not be in vain. In this, the first number, he will find much valuable and interesting matter, presented in a concise form. It is our aim to make this *Review* an indispensable adjunct to every breeder's library. If it finds its way to the water-paper basket its mission has sadly failed.

We propose in each number to reproduce, in summarised form it may be, articles bearing upon the thoroughbred which appear in English and foreign publications. In this way our readers will be kept *au courant* with the thought of the day. This survey cannot fail to appeal to a wide circle. It should interest even many who are not actual breeders of bloodstock, but who, nevertheless, wish to familiarise themselves with the trend of events in breeding circles.

Lastly, attention may be drawn to the 'Diary', an instalment of which appears in the present issue. This section of the *Review* will enable us to present a chronological record of happenings of interest and importance.

The entries will often be more than a mere formal catalogue of incidents; the governing idea is that it shall develop into a section to which readers can turn again and again for guidance and entertainment. A diary of this sort acquires an added value as the years roll by.

Here then, broadly, we have outlined the object and *raison d'etre* of *The Bloodstock Breeders' Review*. We submit the first number in the expectant hope and belief that it will meet with acceptance and appreciation. Doubtless it has its faults. May we ask readers to favour us with their criticism? We shall heartily welcome friendly suggestions that make for improvement.

Edward Moorhouse
1868-1939

In every personal venture, although the undertaking may seem of importance only to the person devoting himself to the enterprise, there is, or was, almost invariably, an inspiration which ignited the project. When this individual discovered The Bloodstock Breeders' Review *and with it the genius of Edward Moorhouse, its joint-founder and editor from its inception in 1912 until his death in 1939, the inspiration was conceived, although it was to remain dormant until the demise of the publication itself in 1979.*

Then, as the years swept by, came the reality that the 'best' of the Review *must be saved for those deserving people who never had the opportunity to appreciate its historic significance in helping to keep the fascinating romance of the Turf forever alive and available. The writings of Mr Moorhouse in the* Review *were the inspiration for this publication,* Treasures of the BBR. *Once one found Mr Moorhouse's incomparable knowledge of the thoroughbred interwoven with his incredible literary talent, the idea that such precious writings could be allowed to sink without trace became unthinkable. When Mr Moorhouse was alive he was an inspiration to his contemporaries, and when he passed away he became an inspiration to those who followed him and that inspiration carried through for another forty years of the* Review.

As far as this admirer is concerned there was no one like him before nor has there been anyone like him since. In his chosen profession he was the 'Eclipse' whose renown will never be transcended. The following tributes, written by his staunch friend and joint Review *founder, Mr E. E. Coussell, shortly after his death, say as much – and more.*

Edward Moorhouse.

IT WAS with a profound sense of personal loss that we announced the death of our friend and colleague, Edward Moorhouse, in February, 1939.

Moorhouse, together with the writer, conceived the idea of a *Review* devoted to the British thoroughbred. From 1912 until the day of his passing, *The Bloodstock Breeders' Review* was Moorhouse's chosen life's work; moreover, it was a labour of love. Thus the *Review* may be justly regarded as a memorial of Edward Moorhouse.

The first twenty-seven volumes of the *Review* reveal the calm character and wise judgement of events and horses made in his writings by the friend with whom we were privileged to be associated for almost thirty years.

As it was felt that the continuance of *The Bloodstock Breeders' Review* was essential to the thoroughbred breeding interests of the country, the appreciated aid of Captain David Livingstone-Learmonth and Captain V. R. Orchard was enlisted to supply the special contributions so long featured by Edward Moorhouse.

His successors are only too well aware of his unique qualities and vast knowledge in that connection, for Moorhouse always retained close in mind the worldwide appeal of the *Review*.

It will be our aim and endeavour to continue and maintain the high standards and fine traditions established ever since Edward Moorhouse wrote the 'Foreword' to the first issue of the *Review* in April, 1912.

* * *

The news of the passing of Moorhouse, as he was familiarly known to hosts of friends in thoroughbred breeding circles, came as a great shock. It was not even known he was unwell. Moorhouse died on February 11th, after three days' illness. He passed peacefully away in his sleep, in his seventieth year.

It was in December, 1932, that Moorhouse suffered the amputation of a leg, which for many long years had caused him much pain, about which he was always silent. His numerous activities thereafter greatly curtailed. From the time of his retirement in the spring of 1924 until 1933, Moorhouse, next to his life's work – the production of *The Bloodstock Breeders' Review* – found very much happiness in daily tending the beautiful flower garden which surrounded his home in Guernsey. The loss of his limb he regretted only from the fact that he could no longer play golf or walk much in the beautiful lanes or along the cliffs that he loved so well.

Edward Moorhouse was born at Leeds on February 22nd, 1868. He came of a Quaker family. Obviously he was not expected to fit himself for and adopt a career which eventually led him to be regarded as one of the world's great authorities on the breeding of the thoroughbred.

An incident occurred in 1881, while spending a holiday with his grandmother and two maiden aunts, very sedate and religious ladies. One morning they drove to Eaton Hall. Passing through the Park, the coachman pointed with his whip to a group of buildings, and said, 'That is where "Bend Or" is now.'

' "Bend Or",' exclaimed his grandmother, 'what *is* "Bend Or"?'

With a look of pained surprise on his face, the man explained that 'Bend Or' had won the Derby the previous year.

'Oh!' was all the response he got.

That incident was the first that associated Mr Moorhouse's mind with the thoroughbred.

When he left school three years later he began to take interest (in a surreptitious way) in racing. Then came an illness lasting for months. During his convalescence he began to write stories in which a racehorse always figured. From the age of ten the urge to write was uppermost in his mind. When he recovered from that illness he applied for a young reporter's position on the *Leeds Mercury*. To his great joy he became a member of the staff of that newspaper. Steadily he made progress, not, however, on the sporting side, for it did not exist. Moorhouse, however, took a particularly keen personal interest in the history of the great racehorses bred at the famous stud farms in Yorkshire.

Meanwhile the editorial direction of the *Leeds Mercury* had changed. Great was the astonishment of the readers of that then old-fashioned journal when a couple of columns of racing news were added. That section speedily became one of its most popular features.

It was in 1901 that Edward Moorhouse joined the staff of the old *Pall Mall Gazette*, whose offices were then in Charing Cross Road. Within a short time Moorhouse accepted the Turf editorship of the *PMG*. He quickly gained great prestige as a writer of remarkable ability on Turf matters. All the time he was making weekly contributions to the *Sunday Chronicle*, Manchester, and a little later on to the Sunday *Observer*. Then even he strongly advocated the adoption of *pari-mutuel* betting, and the concentration of racing. Another five years had passed, when he became Special Commissioner of *The Sporting Life*. His brilliant descriptions of stud farms, their inmates and owners, speedily brought him into close and happy personal contact with most of the then great personages of the British Turf.

It was in 1908 he wrote his famous *History and Romance of the Derby*. This work in two large volumes, profusely illustrated, immediately took its place as one of the most valuable works in the literature relating to the thoroughbred. It has long been out of print. Many times Moorhouse considered bringing his book up to date, but he never felt quite at liberty to do so. He accumulated much material of essential interest to that end, and then finally relinquished his idea. The reason was he then felt that he could make such a better book if he entirely re-wrote it.

Moorhouse retained his position on *The Sporting Life* until he resigned in 1913, but continued his other journalistic connections, to which were added regular contributions on Turf matters to the great South American newspaper *La Nacion*, Buenos Aires, with which he was connected until his death. At odd times he contributed to the *Dictionary of National Biography*.

It was in August, 1911, that Edward Moorhouse joined the writer in founding the British Bloodstock Agency. Before the turn of that year numerous happy conversations ultimately led to the idea of issuing a quarterly *Review* devoted to the thoroughbred. Thus *The Bloodstock Breeders' Review* was founded. Its object and its policy were clearly set forth by Moorhouse in the first number. He was gratified that within a very few years the *Review* came to be regarded as *the* reliable recorder of the world's thoroughbred interests. The first issue appeared in April, 1912. Two years later broke the World War. It was a great struggle to keep the *Review* going. Thanks, in the main, to the unceasing work and ability of Moorhouse, this was achieved. Then he wrote all the articles, even those dealing with American, Australian and New Zealand events. Indeed, he did so for nearly twenty years – so cleverly, that friends from those countries visiting us could not believe the articles were written by someone in London. The quarterly issues of the *Review* were abandoned at the end of 1918. Thenceforward *The Bloodstock Breeders' Review* became an annual. It was in 1916 that Moorhouse paid a visit to the United States, visiting the chief stud farms in Virginia, Kentucky and New York, gathering material for his memorable article on the 'Renaissance of the American Thoroughbred'. He was never in full sympathy with the terms of the rule governing the entry in the *General Stud Book* of animals bred in other countries.

From the early numbers of the *Review*, Moorhouse concentrated upon the opening section. He aptly entitled it *The Racing Year*. Each season Moorhouse's views and opinions were eagerly perused by sporting journalists in almost every country in the world, at first greatly to his astonishment, for he never thought to write himself into an international figure. His calm judgment and wise summing-up of the possibilities of famous horses were almost universally accepted and adopted. Moorhouse, however, took endless pains to be certain of his facts.

In 1918, as he then expressed it, not being exactly overwhelmed with work, due to war-time conditions, he wrote another very valuable book, *John Porter of Kingsclere*. Like all Moorhouse's work, it is extremely interesting, authoritative, and full of painstaking and valuable facts, only gleaned from a close personal contact with that great master of his profession.

During the war, Moorhouse assisted in the purchase of two horses destined to achieve great fame as stallions. They were My Prince and Limond. They cost 100 guineas each! Moorhouse also paid 45 guineas for a mare named Silver Grey. Mated with Limond she produced a really smart two-year-old colt named Limosin, the only horse ever to carry Moorhouse's colours. A bad 'go' of 'heel bug' ruined the subsequent career of Limosin. Still he did enough to attract much attention to his sire, with the result that Limond was sold for 4,000 guineas to the New Zealand breeder, Mr G. M. Currie. He became one of the greatest sires of modern times in the Dominion and in Australia, for up to date Limond has sired the winners of £273,500. Many of his offspring won classic races. Earlier on, Moorhouse had assisted in the sale of Absurd, also to Mr Currie. He also developed into an outstanding stud success, for the offspring of Absurd won nearly £294,000 in New Zealand and Australia. He was the leading sire in the Dominion five times.

It was during the Great War that Moorhouse played a very energetic part in the foundation of the Thoroughbred Breeders' Association. He was the Secretary from 1917 to 1924. During that period he put forward numerous suggestions for improvements in the value of racing stakes, increased added money, reduction of entries, more convenient entry and forfeit dates for classic races. Many were eventually adopted.

As hinted, Moorhouse was always a most ardent advocate of the *pari-mutuel* form of betting on racecourses. Again and again in his bi-weekly articles he returned to the subject. Not unnaturally, then, many disapproved of his advocacy of something they considered revolutionary. Moorhouse was undaunted. Powerful people became interested. Finally the Customs and Excise decided to examine the possibilities of the 'Tote' with reference to a betting tax. What happened is Turf history. It was after the famous 'bookmakers' strike' at Windsor, in November, 1926, there began a very careful consideration of the necessary legislation to enable the Tote to be erected on racecourses. Moorhouse's only comment was – it was a reform long overdue!

It would require much space to mention the names of many horses, then famous, or who later became renowned, whose sales were negotiated by the British Bloodstock Agency while Moorhouse was a director. About the first sale of importance was that of Aboyeur, the Derby winner of 1913, for 13,000 guineas to the Imperial Racing Society of Russia. Bronzino went to Australia, to which country Rossendale and Buckwheat followed; Absurd and Limond to New Zealand. To the United States were sent Wrack, Light Brigade, Brown Prince, Stefan the Great, Chacolet (won nearly $100,000), Royal Canopy and Craigangower. Parth and Florist went to France. Many head of bloodstock, including Maiden Erlegh, were lost by enemy action in the Atlantic when the *Minnehaha* was sunk in 1918.

Moorhouse has left a memory of steady, painstaking work in *The Bloodstock Breeders' Review*, which radiates his personality. He had a true sense of value and proportion, as well as versatility in his subject. For twenty-seven years Edward Moorhouse contrived to write large sections of the *Review*. The many invaluable statistics were based upon his ideas of the right and clear manner in which such essential facts should be presented.

Moorhouse was a man with a strict sense of honour, reflected in his life and his writing. Moreover, he was one of the kindest and most generous men it was possible to meet. Still a few years before his death, when he paid his last visit to Newmarket, he was really disappointed to discover so many familiar faces were missing. His own disability added to his difficulty. He left the December Sales feeling he was saying good-bye to the Newmarket he had loved so deeply, for he would always tell Colonial and foreign visitors they had never seen *real* racing until they had visited Newmarket. Still with a sigh he would add – they could make there the greatest round course in the world.

In 1924 Edward Moorhouse disposed of all his shares and interests in The British Bloodstock Agency Ltd, to 'Jock' Crawford. He then retired to Guernsey to enjoy many years of great happiness. It is so sad to recall that one of the finest tributes Moorhouse ever wrote was to the memory of 'Jock' Crawford, whose tragic death occurred a few days over twelve months before Moorhouse himself passed on, ere the last volume of the *Review* he prepared had been issued, for he did not live to see it in print. His very last task was the compilation of the Index. He had a fluent pen, a masterly yet simple style of presenting facts, comments and opinions. For more than forty years Edward Moorhouse's devotion was unswerving to his life's interest – the true enhancement of the prestige of the British thoroughbred.

Part 1

THE RACECOURSE

What Events Interest Us?

WHAT EVENTS and incidents in the past history of the Turf interest, or, to keen lovers of the thoroughbred, enthrall us? I think the truthful answer is to be found in the words of the Psalmist: things 'which we have heard and known and such as our fathers have told us.' I am singing the words, as I write them, to the glorious old four-fold chant. Whenever possible go to a church where there is good singing on the fifteenth evening of the month, and if you can sing the whole seventy-three verses of the 78th Psalm through without a break you may consider yourself a stayer of the first water, and top weight in the Cesarewitch won't stop you!

In Support and Vindication of Racing

'IT IS the chief stronghold of our hypocrisy to feel delight in judging one another.' So wrote Milton. The cranks who are for ever girding at racing should take the rebuke to heart.   BBR–1918

THUS WROTE Lecky: 'Injudicious suppression of amusements that are not wholly good, but which afford keen enjoyment to great masses, seldom fails to give an impulse to other pleasures more secret and probably more vicious.'   BBR–1918

THE DEAN of Durham considers that, of all human vices, betting or gambling is the most difficult of outright condemnation.   BBR–1921

BC Tipster!

IN A recent number of the *Racing Specialist* 'Nick o' Lincoln' wrote: 'I wonder if many people know that there is a tipster's advertisement on the walls of one of the buried suburbs of Herculaneum? The translation runs roughly, thus: "For the smallest reward Elvius the charioteer will tell all factions the name of the winning chariots in the races of Rome, and this before the day of the contest. At Crocus the wine-seller's near the Gate of Augustus sits Elvius with his secrets".'

'Nick' imagines Elvius soliloquising the day after the races: 'And what did I give yer? Two secon's and a third! And if Pontius Appolinans the charioteer had been trying a cubit he'd have come 'ome alone! Instead of which he was standin' in with Judas of Jerusalem, the perishin' book-maker. These thievin' charioteers ought to be warned orf!'

The Oldest Horserace

WHAT IS claimed to be the oldest horserace is that for the Kiplingcote Stakes. It originated in 1519 and the present course has been used since 1664. The starting point is near Kiplingcote Station on the railway line from York to Hull and runs for four miles on an old Roman road. The race has been run in unbroken sequence for 269 years. The conditions read: 'For a horse race to be observed and ridd yearly on the third Thursday in March open to horses of all ages to carry horsemen weight 10 stones exclusive of saddle and bridle to enter at ye post at 11 o'clock on ye morning of ye race. The race to be run before two.' Competitors have to be at the post at 11 a.m. and pay an entrance fee of £4 5s. Formerly there was a gold cup for the winner which could be won outright. As there is now no such trophy the winner often receives less than the second, for he gets £8, the interest on £464 invested in Consols, whereas the rider of the second gets the entrance fee, less small expenses. Six years ago the race was run through a heavy layer of snow. These details are taken from an article that appeared in *The Times*.

The Kiplingcote Stakes is still run at Beverley. It was contested on April 22nd 1989 as a selling race, run in two divisions.

The Classic Races

WHEN each autumn we review the results of the season's classic races, they frequently seem to have been fairly obvious. If we recall the problems that confronted us as each of the events approached it may, perhaps, be with a feeling of surprise that the solutions seemed so difficult to find. At the present time most followers of racing are inclined to let this year's 'dead past bury its dead', but there will come a day when we shall desire to remind ourselves of the facts and incidents, disappointments associated with these big events. That is why the stories related year by year in the *Review* become more and more interesting as time goes on.

The Historic Derby of 1913

Even at this place in time, it is certain there has never been an Epsom Derby providing such historic and perplexing events as the renewal of 1913. Not only did it result in an unheard-of disqualification and a

mistaken placing of another runner, but this was the year when a
suffragette was fatally injured while rushing on to the track to bring
down the King's horse. It also stamped Craganour, first past the wire,
as one of Turfdom's all-time unfortunate horses. It was Craganour
who had 'lost' the Two Thousand Guineas to Louvois although the
general concensus was that the judge had erred and that Craganour had
been best by half a length.

But the Review's *peerless journalist, Edward Moorhouse, was*
there, and it was his stirring account of this unbelievable happening,
reprinted here, that should forever ward off any comparisons with other
runnings.

HISTORIC! It is scarcely an adequate appellative. The dictionary
would, however, be searched in vain for one conveying all that it is
desired to express. There have been many Derbys which could
truthfully be described as sensational. That of 1913 must be added to the
group. It was not only sensational; it was very nigh to being a travesty of
a contest the chief purpose of which is supposed to be that of testing the
merits of our leading three-year-olds. For nearly an hour after the race
was over there prevailed a state of affairs bordering on chaos. Hardened
campaigners were almost stricken dumb with astonishment and
chagrin. They left the course in mournful mood because they had lived
to see a winner of the Derby disqualified.

Craganour, who started a strong favourite, was first 'home'. He
finished a head in front of Aboyeur, a colt against whom odds of 100 to 1
were offered at the fall of the flag. Crowded together within a couple of
lengths of the two leaders there was a group of half a dozen competitors.
The spectacle had thrilled the onlookers. Until the judge had given his
decision in favour of Craganour nobody was quite sure what had won,
and the hoisting of the favourite's number was hailed with a shout of joy
by the assembled thousands. But many who would gladly have
contributed their share of the cheering refrained from so doing. They
instinctively felt there was trouble brewing. Before the judge had issued
his decree I heard someone exclaim: 'If Craganour has won he is sure to
be disqualified.'

When, therefore, Craganour in due course made his way back to the
weighing-room enclosure, led by his proud owner, Mr Bower Ismay,
and accompanied by his clever trainer, W. T. Robinson, there was a
cloud of doubt overhanging him. The moments that followed were
charged with anxiety. We saw Reiff, the rider of Craganour, with the
saddle over his arm, step briskly into the weighing-room. Presently

someone shouted, 'All right!' Never, surely, has that cry, so familiar to the frequenters of race meetings, created a greater feeling of relief, and the feeling was intensified when we saw the red flag bearing the words 'All Right' fluttering in the breeze from the top of the pillar of the number board. The glad news was thus officially confirmed.

Craganour was about to leave the little enclosure when an emissary of the Stewards rushed out from the weighing-room and shouted to the colt's attendant, 'Come back!' What did it mean? Reiff had drawn his weight. Piper, the rider of Aboyeur, had, it was said, declared there had been no irregularities which justified him in formally lodging an objection. The Stewards thought otherwise. They had hurriedly resolved to hold an inquiry. A few more minutes elapsed and then the 'All right' flag was hauled down, and a blue one, bearing the ominous word 'Objection', was substituted.

In the meantime the bookmakers had been settling with their ready-money clients. One of them paid out over £200 before he heard the arresting call, 'Don't pay!' What could be the matter? So lightly did the bookmakers regard the 'objection' whatever it might be for, that they tried to do business by offering odds of 4 to 1 against Aboyeur getting the race. Of course they could well afford to tender this rate, because very few of them had previously laid a penny against the outsider who had given such an astounding performance. Nevertheless, had they known the Stewards had taken action on their own initiative it is hardly likely they would have adopted so sceptical an attitude. The moment the Stewards interfered the position of Craganour became perilous in the extreme, for it was obvious they would not have taken so unusual a step, especially in connection with a race like the Derby, unless they were convinced there was an absolute necessity for investigation.

The inquiry was forthwith held. Evidence was obtained from some of the jockeys who had ridden in the race; also from the judge and from the Clerk of the Scales, who was with him in the box. The Stewards, further-more, had the evidence of their own eyes to assist them in arriving at a conclusion. It was perfectly plain that, when about two furlongs from the winning post, Craganour twice bumped Aboyeur, and that, in consequence, the chance of Shogun, who was trying to get through on the rails, if not that of Aboyeur himself, had been seriously prejudiced. This much proved, the disqualification of Craganour became inevitable, and it followed as a matter of course that Aboyeur was declared the winner of the Derby.

Although the decision had been very generally anticipated its promulgation caused something like stupefaction. The public had hoped against hope that the Stewards would discover a method of exercising their authority short of depriving Craganour of the honours he had gained, and thereby visiting upon the innocent owner and trainer of the favourite the dreadful blow they must experience if the extreme penalty was enacted. We may be sure the Stewards – Lord Rosebery, Major Eustace Loder and Lord Wolverton – would eagerly have taken advantage of any loophole that had presented itself. They could find none, and so the highly distasteful duty of disqualifying the winner was thrust upon them.

When the public had had time to realise the full meaning and effect of Craganour's deposition, a storm of criticism broke over the heads of the Stewards. For the most part the condemnation of their action was of an indiscriminate character; much of it was based upon a false foundation. In many quarters it was wrongly assumed that Craganour had been 'put down' for misdemeanours committed in the neighbourhood of the winning post. We were therefore told that Aboyeur was as guilty as his rival. There was a flood of testimony, both from jockeys and onlookers, that at the finish there was a scrimmage worthy of a Rugby football match. One of the jockeys decared that he and his confreres might have been taking part in a bull fight! It was all very unsatisfactory, not to say disgraceful. At that stage of the race there was, however, no blame attaching to any particular horse or rider. They were all equally involved.

Three days after the Derby, or just twenty-four hours too late, Mr Bower Ismay sent to the Clerk of the Course a notice of appeal against the decision of the Stewards. It is understood that he was anxious to ascertain whether, before the inquiry was held, all the needful formalities required by the Rules had been complied with. Inasmuch, however, as the notice was out-of-date, it had to be ignored. It may be pointed out that the appeal would, if in order, have come before the Stewards of the Jockey Club, two of whom are Major Loder and Lord Wolverton, the third being Mr F. W. Lambton.

A fortnight later Mr Ismay set the law in motion with a view to obtaining an injunction restraining the stakeholders from paying over the Derby Stakes to the owners of Aboyeur, Louvois and Great Sport. An interim injunction was actually granted. On June 18th, however, Mr Ismay instructed his solicitor not to proceed further with the action – a decision which was in sporting circles regarded as a very wise one.

A few words more before I pass on to other details of the ever-memorable race which resulted in this deplorable upset. It is no exaggeration to say that the sympathies of everyone, including the three

Stewards, were with Mr Bower Ismay and his trainer, Robinson, in their hour of distress. For a moment Mr Ismay brushed aside his own trouble and, going up to his trainer, who was bravely but ineffectually trying to hide the grief he was suffering, he patted Robinson on the back and chivalrously said, 'Never mind, we shall win the Derby again some other day.' That was the action of a true-hearted sportsman – an action which illumined an occasion that was depressing in the extreme.

The fifteen competitors lined up in bright sunshine behind the barrier at the starting point with commendable punctuality, and, giving hardly any trouble, they were very quickly dispatched on their momentous journey. It was an excellent start, though Agadir, who had drawn the berth next to the rails, was slow to get into his stride, and was, in consequence, a few lengths behind the others for half a furlong or so, but before a quarter of a mile had been covered he was near to the leaders.

Going up the hill to the City and Suburban starting post – that is to say while traversing the first two furlongs – Aldegond led for a while, but when the field had fairly settled down Aboyeur went to the front and was soon three or four lenghts clear of Craganour, behind whom came Aldegond, Nimbus, Sun Yat, Louvois, Shogun, Prue and Agadir. Seven furlongs from home Aldegond dropped back and Day Comet drew into third place behind Aboyeur and Craganour, with Shogun and Louvois fourth and fifth.

The Suffragette incident, Tattenham Corner. Jameson and Sandburr are the two horses behind the fallen Anmer.

In this order they came down the decline to Tattenham Corner. After the first ten horses had passed at this point a woman suddenly came from under the rails and, eluding the police who were guarding the course, rushed on to the track right in front of Agadir. By a dexterous movement Earl managed to make his horse swerve out of the woman's way. Unfortunately the strain on Agadir's forelegs instantly caused slight lameness, and thence forward he was a mere 'passenger'. Behind Agadir came the King's horse, Anmer. The woman, who turned out to be a Miss Davison (of Morpeth, Northumberland), a militant Suffragette, made a dash for Anmer's reins. Before the startled onlookers had had time fully to grasp what was happening they saw the woman, Herbert Jones (the rider of Anmer) and the horse on the ground. Jones and the woman were both unconscious. Another horse that suffered interference as the result of Miss Davison's mad behaviour was Nimbus. His jockey, Milton Henry, afterwards asserted that he lost ten lengths, but that was perhaps an exaggerated estimate. Still, whatever the number was, it made a very serious difference, as will be shown presently.

This dreadful mêlée had scarcely been noticed by the spectators on the stands. Their attention was all the while riveted on the great struggle that was now taking place between the leaders. Three furlongs from the winning post Craganour drew up alongside Aboyeur, the latter having the inside berth, and the pair came on with Shogun, near the rails, at their heels. When another furlong had been covered Wootton (Shogun's jockey) made for the space between Aboyeur and the rails, which he afterwards said was wide enough for a waggon to pass through. Here again, no doubt, there was a little exaggeration. Be that as it may the path of Shogun was suddenly obstructed. Aboyeur was bumped over towards the rails by Craganour. Wootton, on Shogun, shouted to Piper (Aboyeur's jockey) to keep his horse straight. The latter called back that it was not his fault. Presently Wootton again saw his way clear to get through on the rails, but just as he drew up to Aboyeur's quarters there was another bump from Craganour, and once more Shogun had to be momentarily eased to avoid a collision. That, at any rate, is the version of what occurred subsequently given by Wootton, and his story has not been contradicted.

In the meantime Craganour and Aboyeur were rapidly drawing near to the goal. When about 300 yards away the favourite spurted and gained a half-length advantage, but a moment later he dropped back until level with Aboyeur. Then again he led by a neck only to falter once more. All this while several of the other competitors were steadily gaining on the leader. Louvois and Day Comet, who had passed

Shogun, were making headway near the rails, while Great Sport and Nimbus were coming along on the stand side. It was at this stage that there was the scrimmaging to which reference has already been made. Every second there seemed to be a re-shuffling of the colours like that which occurs with every turn of a kaleidoscope. When all was over almost every man who had looked on at this amazing scramble freely confessed that he had but a hazy notion of what he had seen. If a score of witnesses had been summoned to give evidence at an inquest on the subject there would most assuredly have been a score of depositions each varying in many particulars from the others.

Had Craganour won? Or had Aboyeur headed him on the post? Or was it a dead heat? A momentary hush prevailed until the judge made known his decision. Up went No. 5; Craganour had prevailed. There was great cheering. Aboyeur was second, beaten a head; Louvois was placed third. The judge said he was a neck behind Aboyeur.

Great Sport was given the fourth place; he finished about a head in front of Nimbus. *There can, however, be no doubt whatever that Day Comet was one of the first four to pass the winning post.* This is conclusively proved by the photographs which accompany this article. Look first of all at the picture of the horses coming head on. The horse on the extreme right, nearest to the rails, is Day Comet. Next to him, in the front line, is Louvois. Both have a big star on the forehead and a blaze right away

Nearing the winning post in The Derby. Left to right: Nimbus, Great Sport, Craganour, Aboyeur, Sun Yat, Louvois, Shogun, Day Comet.

Finish of The Derby, 1913. Left to right: Sun Yat, Nimbus, Great Sport, Shogun, Craganour, Aboyeur, Louvois, Day Comet.

down to the nose. Now turn to the photograph which was taken from the stand side of the course from a point just beyond the judge's box. There are four horses whose heads appear to be practically level. The nearest one is Craganour, next to him Aboyeur, beyond whom is Louvois. But what of the fourth horse next to the rails? The markings on his face show, do they not, that it is Day Comet. Moreover, the cloth bandage on his foreleg is clearly to be seen. *None of the other horses among the leaders wore bandages.* Hidden as he was by the other three the judge did not see Day Comet. And very few other people saw him either; at any rate they did not realise that he was so close up. A large original print of this photograph was inspected on the Press Stand the day after the Derby. No one could explain it. There was a consensus of belief that Craganour, Aboyeur and Louvois were the only horses that came into the argument, and the suggestion was made that in some mysterious way Louvois' head had been duplicated by the camera! It is only when the two pictures of the finish are examined together that the truth is revealed. Reports of the·race place Day Comet sixth, behind Great Sport and Nimbus. He was, of course, known to be among the leaders. As the judge did not put him in the first four, and as Nimbus was obviously only a few inches behind Great Sport, the reporters were compelled to assume that Day Comet must be sixth. Never, surely, has there been greater confusion over the result of a race, and it would certainly appear that Day Comet received far less recognition than was his due.

Then came the Stewards' inquiry, ending in the disqualification of Craganour for not keeping a straight course and for bumping Aboyeur. Before this was over we learned particulars of the accident at Tattenham Corner. Jones, with a number of abrasions on his face and bruises all over his body, was brought to the stands on a stretcher and taken to the ambulance room, where he presently recovered consciousness. It was possible to remove him to an hotel in London the same evening, and the following day he was happily well enough to return home to Newmarket. The woman, Davison, had a badly fractured skull. She was conveyed to Epsom Cottage Hospital in a motor car. On the Friday she underwent an operation but, gradually sinking, died on the Sunday without having recovered consciousness. The following Saturday the Suffragettes escorted their misguided comrade's body through London, seeking thereby to gain the utmost possible advertisement out of an appalling incident. There can be little doubt that it was by the merest chance that Miss Davison brought down the King's horse. When she rushed out from the rails on the near side she could not possibly have known what horses were yet to pass. In all probability her original intention was to get in front of the whole field and so ruin the race. Had she carried out that purpose we should to a certainty have beheld a ghastly tragedy. A merciful Providence ordained that she alone was to suffer the fate she had intended others to endure with her.

Although for many years Desmond has been one of our leading sires he has often been slightingly referred to as a stallion incapable of begetting a son or daughter good enough to win a classic race. After the judge's decision that Craganour and Aboyeur had finished first and second we were confronted with a peculiarly piquant situation. Both colts are by Desmond. They were, moreover, the only Desmonds in the field!

There is no need to dwell on the racing career of Craganour. His brilliant achievements as a two-year-old brought him into such prominence that everyone must be familiar with his record. As to his erratic behaviour in the Derby, the only feasible explanation that has been offered is the one that he found the distance rather beyond his compass. Towards the finish of the race he had lost his wonderful action. His staccato movements at the crucial stage of the contest were probably occasioned by his inability properly to inflate his lungs. Whatever his shortcomings may have been, it cannot, however, be charged against him that he showed a lack of courage. Distressed though he was, he 'slogged on'. Though he will not go down in history as a 'Derby winner', none can deprive him of the honour of having been first past the post. A strange fatality has pursued him this season. First of all there was his defeat at Liverpool by Flippant, a colt vastly his inferior. Then came the verdict in the Two Thousand, 'beaten' a head by Louvois, although there is a substantial body of evidence to the effect that he actually won by half a length. And lastly the Derby fiasco. Verily he will be remembered as a brilliant but unlucky horse.

A Sorry Spectacle!

'A SORRIER spectacle surely has never been seen at Aintree.' That was the way the *Review* of 1913 reported the running of the 4 miles, 856 yards Grand National Steeplechase when only three horses finished. The margins were 'a distance; a similar gap between second and third'. 'There was,' continued the *Review*, £70 awaiting the horse placed fourth by the Judge, but none could claim the money. When Glenside won the Grand National in 1911, he alone completed the course without meeting mishap, but three of his opponents were remounted and ridden 'home'. This year Covercoat and Irish Mail were the only two competitors (twenty-two started) who did not fall or get rid of their riders. Carsey (remounted) was running second to Covercoat when he blundered at the last fence but one and threw his jockey out of the saddle.'

A Leisurely Pursuit

RACING was a leisurely pursuit in 1822. In a summary of the proceedings the third day of the Ascot Meeting that year we read: 'Soon after one o'clock the King arrived, in a plain carriage and four, and proceeded to the grant apartment. . . The King left the ground immediately after the colt race (the third) for his cottage in Windsor Great Park. The races were not over till nearly seven o'clock.' The programme consisted of only six events, but there were no trains to catch in those days!

A Memorable Return

May 30th – RACING at Belmont Park, New York. It is the first meeting held in the 'Empire' State for nearly three years! The racecourses had to be closed because of the passing of a law by the State Legislature rendering managers of meetings liable to imprisonment, without the option of a fine, if any people were found betting on premises under their control. A recent decision in the courts to the effect that it was not illegal for one man to bet privately with a friend greatly altered the position, and it was decided to hold this meeting at Belmont Park, due precautions being taken by the employment of a small army of detectives to prevent anything in the nature of systematic betting. Arrangements were made for an attendance of 15,000. The actual attendance was estinated at 35,000. When the bugle summoned the horses to the post for the first race the band played 'Auld lang syne'. Whisk Broom, recently returned to his native land from England, won the Metropolitan Handicap, the principle event on the card.   BBR–1913

Prince Palatine and Tracery – An Unsatisfactory Result

PRINCE PALATINE and Tracery, the St Leger winners of 1911 and 1912, opposed each other, for the first time, in the race for the Ascot Gold Cup. A great tussle between them was anticipated, though public opinion greatly favoured Prince Palatine, on whom odds of 7 to 4 were laid while backers of Tracery could get 6 to 1. The French horse, Predicateur, also had a substantial following. After passing the Stands, Jackdaw made the running for nearly a mile and a half and was then headed by Tracery. At that stage, Prince Palatine, going easily, was laying fourth, about twenty lengths away. Four furlongs from home Tracery suddenly disappeared from view. It was afterwards learned that a man of independent means, named Hewitt, had rushed on to the course flourishing a Suffragist flag in one hand and a fully loaded six-chambered revolver of an old-fashioned type in the other. He shouted to Whalley, the rider of Tracery, to stop. The next instant, Hewitt was bowled over by Tracery and lay on the ground unconscious, and badly injured. The man was obviously copying the dastardly action of Miss Davison, at Epsom, on Derby day, but subsequent enquiries showed that he was not associated with the 'Votes for Women' campaign.

Tracery fell and Prince Palatine had to jump over him. Whalley fortunately escaped with a bad shaking. When Tracery came down Jackdaw was left in front with Gorgorito (a French candidate) in close attendance. Immediately after entering the straight, Prince Palatine challenged Jackdaw, and, quickly gaining the mastery, won in a canter from Stedfast and Aleppo. There was afterwards many an argument as to whether the favourite would have beaten Tracery if the latter had not been interfered with. Opinions differed sharply, and they must continue to do so until the two horses are afforded another opportunity of settling the matter in a practical way. All are agreed, however, that Prince Palatine accomplished a very fine performance. He covered the $2\frac{1}{2}$ miles in the record time of 4 mins. 22 3-5 secs.   BBR–1918

The Resolution to Prohibit the Use of Assumed Names

A debate on the use of assumed names took place in official Jockey Club circles in October of 1913. In a 'tight fit' it was voted to keep them available. This is how the Review *reported the proceedings.*

October 29th – ON THE 15th inst., the Jockey Club, on the motion of the Stewards, passed a resolution, the effect of which was to prohibit the use of assumed names for the purposes of racing. When, today, the proposal was submitted for confirmation, it was rejected by fifteen votes to fourteen – a most unusual procedure. It may be said, however, that outside official circles, opinion is in accord with the views of the majority. In the course of the debate which took place when the motion was adopted, Mr F. W. Lambton, the Senior Steward, said that he and his colleagues (Major Loder and Lord Wolverton) felt it was not wise or right that the Jockey Club should have anything to conceal, or that the atmosphere of the Turf should be tainted in any way by the slightest breath of suspicion. Suspicion might exist where they had secrecy, for as Dr Johnson said, 'Where secrecy or mystery begins, vice or roguery is not far off.' Was there any gentleman in that room who, in his private capacity, would aid and abet a businessman to deceive his clients, or who would aid and abet a son to deceive his parents? What a gentleman would not do in his individual capacity it was wrong for a body of gentlemen like the Jockey Club to do. Those were the grounds on which the Stewards asked the Club to rescind the rule permitting the use of assumed names. He took it that the reason for an assumed name could only be for two purposes – either concealment or deception. An assumed name implied one of two things: either that the Turf was not good enough for a man's name, or that a man's name was not good enough for the Turf. Either of these propositions was insulting, but they accepted the registration fee of £30 and swallowed the insult. They wanted racing to be above board and perfectly pure.

W. S. Vosburgh's Comments on Handicaps

William Spencer Vosburgh, an able and distinguished participant in the Turf affairs of the US during most of his long and productive life, was a champion of the handicap race. When he died at nearly eighty-four years of age in 1938, he was revered as the dean of American racing officials. For many years he had served in the difficult role of handicapper for the New York Jockey Club, achieving international respect. Because of his consuming interest in racing and breeding, along with his marvellous mentality and writing ability to match, he left a bountiful legacy of worthwhile observations for ensuing generations of racegoers to enjoy and benefit from. Mr Vosburgh's writings, fortunately, made regular appearances in the Review, *which always knew a good thing when it saw one.*

Aware of the differences then (and now) existing between English and American racing, Mr Vosburgh, in 1914, wrote a piece on the value of handicaps, which first appeared in The Thoroughbred Record *and was then picked up by the* Review. *In it, Mr Vosburgh not only offers some excellent handicap pointers which are valid to this day, but also makes a good argument for the handicap races which are a way of life in America as opposed to the weight-for-age races which are a way of life in England and most of Europe. To wit:*

OUR AMERICAN racing public has been badly educated as regards racing generally and in no respect more so than in respect of handicaps. They seem to be possessed with the idea that the topweight alone has any right to win. We all know the intent of a handicap is so to equalise the horses by means of weights, that the poorest racer has an equal chance with the best. But if a light-weighted horse wins, the public rather resent his success, and then it is suddenly discovered that he was 'thrown in', 'pitch-forked' and other expressions of ill-temper. Of course this is because they have not backed him – you never hear complaints except from losers – and this illustrates the fact that the interests of racing and betting are not always identical.

Moreover, the American idea of handicapping seems based on the assumption that racing is an exact science – which it is not. We have read articles on handicapping in which so many pounds are allowed for so many lengths, half lengths or heads. If this were true, it would only need a mathematician to make the weights – he need never have seen a race or a racehorse. As a matter of fact, a length may mean 1 lb or 12 lbs – it depends upon how the horses finish. We often read in reports of races that a horse 'won easily' when in fact not one race in ten is won easily. The natural tendency is to exaggerate, to exalt the winner. He may be 'all out' at the finish, but he is recorded as having 'won easily' and this causes many who credit such reports to lose their money the next time such horses start.

There are people who sneer at handicaps and clamour for weight-for-age races. But it is impossible to interest the public in one-sided races such as weight-for-age races usually produce. Hence, the handicap becomes the only means of equalising horses and insuring better contests – particularly when racing is catering for the patronage of the public. Comparisons with the sport in England do not apply. There they have a large number of owners who are men of wealth, and who are willing to race for their own money. They are not so dependent upon public support as we are here, and the willingness of their owners to make many and heavy subscriptions, enables them to offer weight-for-age races of such great value that horses are prepared specially for those races.

Nor from the standpoint of the 'improvement of the breed of horses' are weight-for-age races to be preferred to handicaps – except in the case of two-year-olds or spring events for three-year-olds. A horse which wins an important handicap with high weight conceding many pounds to his field, has a better certificate of merit than one which at weight-for-age has beaten two or three horses 25 lbs his inferiors – a mere procession in which he has never been called upon to extend himself.

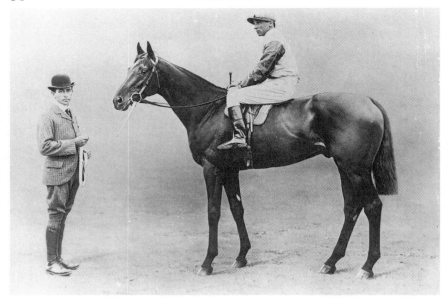

Rock Sand. Brown horse, by Sainfoin–Roquebrune, by St Simon.

The Epsom Derby is the greatest of all weight-for-age races. Yet, in the past twenty-three years only one winner of the Derby (Rock Sand) was sired by a previous winner (Sainfoin). There have been 133 winners of the Derby and only 24 were sired by Derby winners. It is about the same with the St Leger – in twenty-three years only four winners were sired by previous winners. Thus, as a breeding standard (the ridiculous Figure System, for instance) the Derby and St Leger will not stand the test when carefully looked into, for certainly the Derby and St Leger winners when they enter the stud are better patronised both as to number and quality of the mares sent to them than any class of horses.

On the other hand, some of England's most celebrated sires have won their credentials to fame in handicaps. Isonomy won the Cambridgeshire, the Manchester Cup and the Great Ebor – all handicaps. Sterling won the Liverpool Cup and was second in one of the best Cambridgeshires on record. Bend Or won the City and Suburban. Rosebery won both the Cesarewitch and the Cambridgeshire. Hampton won the Northumberland Plate (and sired more Derby winners than any modern Derby winner). Master Kildare won the City and Suburban and Liverpool Cup. Marco won the Cambridgeshire. Amphion won the Jubilee Handicap. Minting won the Jubilee Handicap. Melton won the Liverpool Cup. Vedette won the Ebor Handicap. Barcaldine won the Northumberland Plate. Adventurer won the City and Suburban. Sundridge was twice winner of the De Warrenne Handicap (the last time with 137 lbs). These horses have completely outbred the Derby winners of recent years.

In conclusion, it will be seen by reference to the races quoted that a really high-class horse is capable of conceding a vast amount of weight to an inferior horse over the middle distances (which constitute the real test). Over longer distances, weight will tell with greater effect, for there the inferior one having less nerve force, or speed, is able to rate along until the weight begins to tell on the 'crack'. Of course, racing is not an exact science – there are too many incidents in a race to permit of its being so – the slightest incident will upset the most carefully prepared handicap; yet, the handicap is the nearest approach to scientific racing that has been devised as it enables us to prove the difference between horses which at weight-for-age is only a guess.

The European War

WE HAVE been face to face with epochal events during the past two months. The most gigantic conflict of arms the world has ever known is at this moment being waged. Vast tracts of land, seared by the tramp of hosts of combatants, lie derelict and devastated. In France, Germany, Russia, Austria-Hungary, Belgium, Serbia and Montenegro every able-bodied man of fighting age is with the colours. The United Kingdom of Great Britain and Ireland has sent thousands of her soldiers across the Channel to aid France and Belgium. Already there has been a terribly heavy toll of lives. Untold, and as yet unheeded, millions of money have been squandered by the warring nations. Throughout the world finance, commerce and credit have been thrown into a state of chaos. In the remotest corners of the globe the effect of this appalling war has been severely felt. And the end of it all seems still a long way off.

Do we, who are so deeply interested in the British thoroughbred, realise that the prosperity breeders have enjoyed in recent years has, in a large measure, been due to the preparations made for this mighty life-and-death struggle of the great nations of Europe? France and Russia, Germany and Austria, have all laid out huge sums of money in the purchase of thoroughbreds in order that their cavalry should be well mounted and their guns efficiently horsed. It was the late Count Lehndorff who set the pace towards the goal of perfection. There is a somewhat bitter irony in the fact that the troops forming the British Expeditionary Force had their task made all the harder because the foe was aided by the descendants of stallions and mares sold by English and Irish breeders to the Prussians. It is too soon to discuss whether the

British cavalry regiments were as well horsed as their opponents, and this is not the moment when criticism and recrimination should be indulged in.   BBR–1914

When Racing Returned to New Orleans

When the anti-betting crusade began to abate in the US, New Orleans, which city had been without its winter meetings, resumed again on January 1st, 1915. This event was reported by the Review *and the account prompted some chuckles. Anyone reading this and comparing it with what is going on in the States today could not help but find it most humorous.*

January 1st – AFTER BEING in abeyance for several years, racing was on this date revived in New Orleans. The suppression of the winter seasons there came about at the period when the anti-betting crusade brought racing to a standstill in most of the States of the American Union. Following the lead given in the State of New York, the supporters of the Turf are gradually resuming operations, though not quite on the old lines. Betting on the races has to be conducted under severe restrictions, some of which are of an amusing character. The New Orleans *Times Picayune*, gives the following description of the backer's procedure at the local meeting:

'After paying $1.50 admission fee, the first procedure necessary to make a bet is to purchase a numbered badge for $1.00, which entitles the holder to enter the Palm Garden and Paddock. In the Palm Garden those desiring to make a bet walk up to the small tables at which are seated the official stakeholders, about whom are gathered the men who will bet. When a bet is made – say $2.00 on Lady Moon'et at 2 to 1 to win, and her number on the program is No. 1 in the first race – the man who takes the odds places his $2.00 on the table and it is covered by the $4.00 by the man laying the odds. The $6.00 is then picked up by the official stakeholder and placed in an envelope. The official stakeholder then writes on the outside of the envelope the number of the race, the number of the horse on the program, the position the horse is bet to finish, and the number of the badge of the man accepting the odds. After the race the individual winning the bet goes to the official stakeholder, who wears a blue cap with a number on it, and shows him the number of his badge. The stakeholder then goes through the pile of envelopes until he comes to the number corresponding with the winner's badge number, and the envelope is handed over to him.'

It is beyond understanding that a free and enlightened people like the Americans can tolerate all this circumlocution. If betting is allowed, common sense decrees that it should be conducted in the simplest way that can be devised. However, American sportsmen appear to be, for the time being, and perhaps, quite naturally, well satisfied that they have got the ball rolling once more.   BBR–1915

Some Notable Dead-Heats

In 1944, Brownie, Bossuet and Wait A Bit dead-heated for first place in the Carter Handicap at the old Aqueduct racetrack in New York. It remains the most famous three-horse dead-heat in the history of American racing. But England had a more unusual one way back in 1855, when four of the five starters dead-heated for first place in a £10 sweep-stake at Newmarket. An article describing a triple dead-heat for first place at Sandown Park on April 23rd, 1915, recalled some other notable ties in English racing.

April 23rd – THAT EXTREME rarity, a dead-heat between three horses for first place, occurred today in a contest for a two-year-old selling plate over five furlongs at Sandown Park. The youngsters concerned were Mr F. Phillip's colt by Littleton out of Portia; Mr L. McCreery's filly Kitty O'Hara, and Mr B. Parr's filly Somali. They were respectively ridden by E. Gardner, J. Clark and S. Donoghue, and were practically inseparable while traversing the final furlong. A 'run off' was not, of course, allowed for it is prohibited by Rule in the case of two-year-olds. At the subsequent sale by auction Somali made 300 guineas, Kitty O'Hara 360 guineas and the Portia colt 370 guineas.

At Lewes in 1880, Scobell (Tom Cannon), Wandering Nun (J. Goater), and Mazurka (Fordham) dead-heated for first place in the Astley Stakes, and a head behind them came Cumberland (Archer) and Thora (Luke) who also dead-heated for what, we suppose, must be described as fourth place. There was a memorable dead-heat for the Cesarewitch of 1857 between Prioress, El Hakim and Queen Bess. A deciding heat resulted in favour of Prioress. Two years before that, in a £10 sweepstake decided at Newmarket, four of five runners dead-heated for first place. A dead-heat between three horses took place at Haydock Park in 1902. This had a curious sequel, for after the deciding heat had been run the winner was disqualified for crossing. In the 'nineties there were triple dead-heats at York and Derby, and Sandown Park was the scene of one in 1882 between Marden, Gerald and Leonora. Marden won the decider easily. It was discovered subsequently, but too late to be of any avail, that Marden carried 5 lbs more and Leonora 5 lbs less than their proper weights, according to the conditions of the race.

BBR–1915

The Virtues of the American Thoroughbred

THE CONSIDERABLE number of races which imported horses have won in America this year has attracted a good deal of attention and led to some discussion of the relative merits of foreign and native-bred stock. Very properly the American thoroughbred has its champions. One of them who, unfortunately, preferred that his name should not be mentioned, gave his views to *The Thoroughbred Record*. We select the following extracts from the interesting statement he made:

'I would regard Hourless as a phenomenal horse, perhaps as good as any that has appeared in this country for many years, while for wear-and-tear qualities Omar Kayyam has seldom been equalled. They are a wonderful pair of colts, but because they are foreign-born is no reason why we should forget the home-breds that have shown class during the past season, nor those which have achieved distinction for us in the past both at home and abroad.

'It is largely a matter of accident. Some years we have several performers which surpass their fellows, while in other seasons no great superiority is evident. The Ascot Meeting represents what is unquestionably the acme of English racing. There isn't a selling race on the programme. Any British Turfman that wins a single one of the events at that meeting considers himself recompensed for the expense and worry of a season. Yet what do the records show? During the Whitney-Lorillard-Keene invasion some years ago Americans won at least one race a day at Ascot, while on the closing day they captured no fewer than four events. It created a sensation.

'During the Saratoga meeting (I think it was the day that Sun Briar won the Hopeful) I quite lost patience with a man who was deploring the decadence of the American thoroughbreds and saying what a splendid thing it was that we were able, because of the war, to replenish our supply of blood. Now, while I am willing to admit that we have secured many desirable thoroughbreds of English and French lineage I am also of the opinion that we have had quite a lot of inferior animals marketed in this country in the past few years. The importation of the Joel and Sledmere yearlings by Messrs Macomber and Coe respectively was a ten-strike, and the benefit to the American thoroughbred of the future cannot be over-estimated. Englishmen are still lamenting their departure from their shores, but I have heard no lamentations over the taking of some of the other stock which must ultimately be assimilated in this country.

'I couldn't resist the temptation after the gentleman had held forth for some time to call his attention to the fact that American blood had played a prominent part in the few racing tests which had been held on the Continent during the past summer. He was surprised to learn that Brume, the dam of Brumelli, Mr W. K. Vanderbilt's good filly, which had won the substitute for the French Derby, was out of Duella, by Bramble, the mare that carried the Whitney colours on the flat and over the hurdles in this country some years ago; and he was still further surprised when I told him that Frank Hitchcock's Sandy Hook, which ran second to Brumelli, and which had also scored in several races over a distance of ground at Chantilly, had for a grandam the American mare Hand-spun, by Hanover, and the next dam the immortal Spinaway by Sensation. When his attention was called to the fact that San Gennaro, winner of the Austrian Derby, had for his grandam Meta II, by Sensation, my friend capitulated, and was willing to acknowledge that the United States still had strains of blood that were potent.

'Mind you, I am strong for foreign blood of the proper sort, and we must have it if we are to keep up with the other nations in the development of the horse of blood; but I am not saying that it is the only thing in the world that makes for excellence. Mingled with our stout American strains, it produces results that are satisfying. The best of foreign blood, however, is what we want, and the wisdom of securing it has been demonstrated in striking fashion in the experience of Marcus Daly and James R. Keene in the past; and in our own day of August Belmont. Let us take Mr Belmont as a concrete example because of what Hourless and other horses of his breeding have done. Hautesse, by Archiduc, the grandam of Hourless, cost Mr Belmont $17,500, and I do not think he regrets her purchase any more than that of Fairy Gold, for which he gave $20,000, and which produced for him such great horses as Friar Rock and Fair Play, besides mares which are breeding on and will be a powerful factor in the development of the Nursery Stud.'

BBR-1917

Death of a Great Race

IN THE April number of the *Review* we referred to the reduction of the distance of the race for the King's Plate at Melbourne (formerly the Champion Stakes) from three miles to two miles, and pointed out that this step was in keeping with the policy Australian racing authorities had been pursuing in recent years. We suggested that the AJC and the VRC could well afford to encourage the training of real stayers and urged that it would be a thousand pities if the principal jockey clubs in the Commonwealth gave colour to the idea that they regarded stamina in the racehorse as a quality of less importance than it was formerly considered.

Mr William Reid writes in the *Leader*:

'Racing men in Victoria, especially those of the old school, will cordially endorse the above. Prior to the recent w.f.a. reduction, most of us thought this class of race, at all events, at two miles and under, had been cut down to the bone, but we were mistaken. The Champion became unfashionable, not so much because of the distance, but the miserable stake provided for so trying and important a race. Who, in these days, would run a valuable horse under w.f.a., three miles, for £1,000, with – unless he galloped like blazes all the way – the chance of only getting half the money? As a sign of the times and the general trend of the Turf, it is a significant fact that the winner of the Newmarket Handicap, our principal sprint race, is paid at the rate of just about £420 per furlong, while the winner of the Champion, before that race became extinct, only received about £40 per furlong for galloping three miles at his top. However, the Champion is dead and buried. He was the finest old oak in the forest, of whom we were proud, and lived for well nigh sixty years. Apparently we have now no more use for such sterling winners as The Barb, Fireworks, Richmond, First King, Grand Flaneur, Commotion, Abercorn, Carbine, Portsea, Wallace, Newhaven, La Carabine, Wakeful, Dividend, Tartan, Trafalgar, and many others perhaps equally good. Although the race itself is no more, the genuine stayers that took part in it will live in history long after the ruthless axemen who cut it down have been forgotten.'

In another part of his article Mr Reid states:

'Australia is under the disadvantage that almost all our racehorses are bred for sale as yearlings. The public breeder knows his business, and is rarely given to philanthropy. If early two-year-olds and sprinters are in most demand, he will breed and rear them accordingly. If stayers are the most marketable, he will do his best to supply them. Buyers can get what they require, and in these days the craving is for phenomenal speed. Whether we have good horses or bad, sprinters or stayers, all depends upon our race programmes. These depend upon our race clubs, while they in turn depend upon the gate. Here we come right back to the best and worst in our thoroughbreds. If the sprinter is to be the Australian horse of the future, well and good, nothing could be more gratifying than the strides we have made, and are making, towards his perfection and establishment. On the other hand, if the substantial stayer is best in the general interests of the country, then the whole boiling of us should be sent to Pentridge for our criminal neglect.'   BBR–1917

Moorhouse's 'The End of the War'

Edward Moorhouse expressed himself with an eloquent directness on any subject on which he wrote, whether it was a horse, a race, a horseman or such a universal experience as the ending of a great war. Racing and breeding will forever be the richer because of Moorhouse's association with the BBR *from its very beginning. When World War I ended late in 1918, Moorhouse set down the following. Could any one else have written it with such an artistic and yet such a sincere feeling? It is doubtful.*

THE GUNS are silent. A semblance of peace prevails. Millions of armed men are resting, impatiently awaiting the order to go home. Although it is now nearly two months since the fighting stopped we find it difficult to realise that the War, which has dominated the lives of nations and of individuals for over four years, is practically at an end. Humanity is still, as it were, gasping for breath after emerging from a struggle of unimaginable severity. The titanic effort has resulted in the triumphant vindication of the great principles on behalf of which the British Empire entered the War. Despotism has perished for ever – perished by reason of its unbridled and over-reaching ambition. Deluded victims at last saw the beacon of freedom beyond the choking fog of deception and tyranny, and with irresistible impulse pressed forward, brushing aside the worm-eaten idols by whom they had been hypnotised.

The thrilling, awe-inspiring period of destruction is ended. We are about to begin the work of so-called reconstruction. It is likely to be a stern task, testing man's genius and powers of organisation to the utmost. We stand on the threshold of a new era in the history of the world. The War has wrought tremendous changes. We can even no longer be sure of what we used to regard as eternal verities. Many of our ideals have gone into the crucible, to be fashioned anew so that they may conform to the requirements of a regenerated universe. For a time it will be hard to grasp the real significance of the upheaval we have witnessed, and still harder to adjust our actions to the altered conditions. The difficulties have, however, to be faced resolutely, and with a clear, unfettered mind. Old prejudices must ruthlessly be jettisoned if the best use is to be made of the opportunities that now present themselves.

The Racing Year – A Survey of Events in 1919

The following is presented, in part, because of Mr Moorhouse's great talent in portraying the way it was in 1919, the first full season of racing in England after World War I and how 'with occasional bad patches, we managed to rub along'.

SHORTLY after the Armistice had been arranged with the Germans on November 11th, 1918, the Stewards of the Jockey Club announced that during the ensuing season the racing programme would be restored to a pre-war footing. That decision was taken after a consultation with the War Cabinet, and it undoubtedly gave much pleasure to a very natural and widespread desire to be rid, once and for all, of the shackles which had hampered the sport since the spring of 1915. It may be assumed, however, that the consequences of so sudden and so complete an emancipation were not appreciated, even if they were considered. Be that as it may, they quickly became manifest. The past racing season was still in its infancy when Clerks of Courses became painfully aware that there were not enough horses in training to satisfy requirements. It was often difficult, and sometimes impossible, to secure an adequate number of entries; it was occasionally still more difficult to persuade owners and trainers to run their horses. Then, again, transport troubles were encountered, the railway companies being either unable or unwilling to grant anything resembling pre-war facilities for the movement of race-horses.

For these and other reasons it became obvious as time went on that the Stewards of the Jockey Club would have been well advised to proceed rather more cautiously. In 1918 we had 53 days' racing in Great Britain; this year's schedule provided 277 days' racing, although the number of horses available was sure to be much smaller than the normal total. This could be deduced from the fact that whereas in 1913 the two-, three-, and four-year-old horses that raced numbered 2,743, the number in 1917 was only about 930. Having regard to the pressure brought to bear on owners and trainers in 1918 still further to reduce their racing studs, it was hardly likely there would be an appreciable accession of strength in 1919.

However, the best was made of the situation created. Fortunately there was no lack of two-year-olds, and three-year-olds were fairly plentiful. More races than usual were set apart for the latter, and in one way or another, with occasional bad patches, we managed to rub along. The public as it happened were wonderfully complaisant: they did not bother their heads much about the character of the racing. Never in the long history of the British Turf have such enormous crowds attended race meetings as those seen during the past season. They were often of embarrassing dimensions, and the resulting inconvenience and discomfort would have subjected the patience of Job to a severe test.

The shortage of horses in training had also another consequence which cannot be ignored in this general survey. Numberless races could be won so easily that the demand for sound horses with a shred of form became very strong, and prices went soaring to a height that would have seemed ridiculous in pre-War days. Winners of selling races were, of course, embraced by this development, so that after a time owners were often reluctant to allow their horses to compete in that class of event. Now and again a selling race, and other races too, had to be declared void because none of the horses entered had turned up to run. It was, indeed, an altogether abnormal season, and perhaps we shall have to wait until 1921 before we again see racing re-established on its old footing.

Going to Epsom for the 1921 Derby

The road to Epsom in 1921 was a scene so richly documented in the BBR *that it must be preserved. A time 'for gaiety, raillery and hilarity' with a lot more thrown in for good measure.*

THE TRAFFIC along the roads leading to Epsom, more especially those from London, was stupendous. It began very early in the morning. Maybe we shall never see the like of it again. At any rate, we may venture to hope so. Elaborate arrangements had been made by the police for controlling the traffic. They even called to their aid a monster airship, which hovered over the more crowded routes and, by means of wireless messages, reported congestions. Whether or not this auxiliary was of much practical value is a matter of no consequence. It provided a spectacular element, and, by reason of its novelty, may have had some psychological influence. Certain it is that the unbroken streams of vehicles, mostly motor-driven, moved towards their destination with astonishing smoothness and celerity. There can be very few, if any, persons now living who remember the Derby days of the pre-railway era. We, however, read of the lovely scenes witnessed along the roads from London to Epsom in those far-off times. They were this year reproduced, though in a very different form. The lordly coach and the humble coster's cart had been replaced by the luxurious Rolls-Royce, the juggernautish motor-coach, and the nimble taxi. The former made for gaiety, raillery and hilarity, the latter gave no time for such triflings. On this occasion the roads were lively in a twentieth-century sense, and it is not a picturesque or romantic one.

Flagging Attendance Figures in 1922

Observant of the flagging attendance figures throughout England in 1922, the BBR of that year blamed it on this 'rampart of stubborn stupidity' which had 'spragged' the wheels of progress and left England woefully behind in providing comfort and accommodations for the fans as had been done so energetically in other racing countries. There was no ambiguity about these remarks.

THERE WERE unmistakable indications during the past season, more particularly during the latter part of it, that the post-War 'boom' in racing had spent itself. Except on special days, like the Derby at Epsom and the Cesarewitch at Newmarket, attendances at meetings were nothing like so great as those which for three years had caused much embarrassment to executives. Occasionally, indeed, they were noticeably meagre. This reaction was almost bound to come sooner or later. Its arrival was hastened by the severe depression of industry. When there are over a million men subsisting on a weekly unemployment dole, luxuries such as racing are compelled to suffer. The pursuit of racing is, in England, a very costly business. It is far more costly here than in any other country, and the public get less in the way of accommodation and comfort than in most other countries. The policy that produces this state of things is a fatuous one. It is based on traditions that ought to have been scrapped long ago. Satisfactory progress will not be achieved until they are scrapped. All who are anxious to see a thorough reform of the Turf, root and branch, realise, however, that they quickly come up against a solid, inert mass of prejudice, which, so far, has resisted all attempts to remove it.

But the time will come when this rampart of stubborn stupidity will be torn down. Progress will then be amazingly rapid. The Turf is as sound as a bell, awaiting the opportunity to develop in the way some of us can visualise. The vision is the clearer and more definite because we know what has been accomplished in other parts of the world, where the wheels of progress are not spragged by tradition and vested interests.

BBR–1922

When is a Derby not a Derby?

The English do not consider the Kentucky Derby a 'true' Derby and such an opinion was expressed in the **BBR** *of 1926:*

'There is now a swarm of Derbys in the United States. Every racecourse promoter seems to think it desirable that the title should be associated with his mushroom track. The Kentucky Derby, run at Louisville, is, however, and seems likely to continue to be, the only one that makes a nationwide appeal. Even this great event is not a Derby in the real sense of the word, because the course on which it is decided measures only ten furlongs. There is a woeful dearth of stayers in America. The system of racing there is very different from the one we have in England, and still further removed from that adopted in France. A horse that keeps sound is, generally speaking, requested to take part in from twenty to thirty races in the course of a season. This is the chief reason why races over greater distances than ten furlongs are so few and far between. The few there are receive but little support. It would, therefore, be a mistake to blame the Kentucky Jockey Club for not transforming their Derby into a real Derby by lengthening the distance to a mile and a half.'

A Plea for More Geldings

In a letter to the **BBR** *in 1926 discussing 'sundry affairs of the Turf', a Mr J. Reid Walker made a pointed reference to geldings when he wrote:*

'I cannot help thinking that racing would be even more interesting than it is if more horses were added to the list than at present. Geldings retain their temper, soundness and form much longer and are more useful for leading work, whereas the entire in many cases loses his temper altogether, and requiring, as he does, more work, there is a greater strain on his legs. Also he is frequently a source of difficulty to the starter, and an instrument of danger to those who frequent the paddock. Even if retained as a stallion and sent to stud, he is, unless a high-class horse, generally a drug in the market, and frequently sold for an old song.'

An Observation

An observation: The BBR, *well before it happened, editorially expressed the opinion that 'mechanical betting will tend to purify the atmosphere of the Turf.'*

The Derby Lunch, 1927

At the customary Derby Luncheon in 1927 held at the London Press Club a few days before the event, Lord Birkenhead (Secretary of State for India and an ex-Lord Chancellor), was a guest. He had this to say of what he had just heard from the various owners of Derby horses as well as the great jockey Steve Donoghue:

'As a tip-giving entertainment this has been one of the most ghastly failures in which I have ever taken part. We have heard a lot of nonsense about everyone wanting the best horse to win. They do not want the best horse to win. They want their own horse to win. They do not care a brass farthing whether it is the best or the worst – neither do I. That one should go away from a lunch – adorned by all the brains of Fleet Street, enriched by the presence of four more disappointing owners, adorned by one or two not inconsiderable jockeys – with less information than that with which one arrived is, I confess, a moving illustration of the folly of human hope. I feel rather like that Shah of Persia who, on a visit to this country, was asked whether he would like to see the Derby, and replied: "I am very conscious one horse must win, and I do not care which".'

An Irish Wake

In 1926 the BBR *quoted the following strange story from the* Daily Chronicle *of March 17th:*

'An Irish "wake" was held yesterday around the corpse of Cannon Ball, a famous Connemara pony sire, who was parent of many of the best ponies in Ireland and had an unbeaten record in country race meetings. He died on Monday in his thirty-eighth year. As soon as his death was announced large numbers of people visited the owner, Mr H. O'Toole, of Leam, Connemara, who was as much affected as if he had lost a near relative. Neighbours had the body taken into the kitchen, where it was laid out on an improvised bier. A half-barrel of porter stood in the corner of the room, and the pony was "waked" as if it had been a human being.

'Soon after midnight the body was placed on a large stable door, which had been taken off its hinges, and was carried by ten stalwart peasants to a grave lined with hay on the owner's farm. There, at the dead of night, the burial took place, and a local bard read the following verse:

> Sleep, brave old pony, thy race is run,
> No more with earthly kin you'll mingle;
> Dream of racecourse tracks you've won,
> Of noble steeds and epic deeds,
> And bookies left without a jingle.

Cannon Ball was probably the last pure-bred Connemara sire in the country, for in recent years the mating of the Connemara with other types has resulted in the pure Connemara strain becoming extinct.'

Salvator's Tirade Against Juvenile Racing

The debate over the advisability or inadvisability of two-year-old racing has raged on and on. It is ageless. Perhaps the key adjective is 'inordinate'. The amount of two-year-old racing continues to accrue, as do the purses. After all, through 1989 only one winner of the Kentucky Derby had not raced at two and most classic winners everywhere did have some experience as juveniles. So the following comments which appeared in the BBR of 1927 are not reprinted because of any contribution they may make in solving the problem, but because of the scolding diatribe penned by that famous American turf writer, John 'Salvator' Hervey. He had a way with words and much of what he wrote should be preserved. This is an example.

IN AN article he wrote for *Daily Racing Form* in August, the veteran racing journalist, 'Salvator', in wrathful mood, mercilessly denounced the 'inordinate' racing of two-year-olds in the USA from January to December.

'Why,' he asked, 'are the three-year-olds such a poor lot? Why is it that so many of them, beginning brilliantly, curl up like frost-bitten foliage ere the campaign has progressed beyond mid-season? Why do they display the most glaring inconsistency, running alternate brilliant races and races of which a selling plater with a shred of self-respect should be ashamed? Why do they beat each other back and forth in the most disconcerting manner? What is the explanation of all these and many similar charges that validly may be brought against them?'

The chief cause in 'Salvator's' opinion is the over-racing of two-year-olds, and the lack of a period of rest between seasons. He goes on to say:

'The managers of the winter meetings are naturally desirous of attracting "the stars" if possible; the result being stakes of dazzling values run when the snow lies deep north of Mason and Dixon's line and it may be below zero in Kentucky, where the majority of our thoroughbreds are born and reared. Owners succumb to these temptations, as is only to be expected.

'How many "Derbys" – so-called, at least – had been run in the USA in 1927 before the English Derby – which, in prestige and actual importance, means more than all of them put together – had been contested? Who today can even bother to burden his memory with their details or has more than a hazy idea what won them? "Out of sight, out of mind" – scarcely are they raced off but they are, to all intents and purposes, forgotten. For which one potent reason has approved itself – namely, that the horses that win them are for the most part not worth remembering. How many of them can be expected to win two races in succession, to say nothing of two "Derbys"? Let echo answer.'

Of course, 'Salvator' exaggerates in order to drive home his point. During the past season the three-year-olds were, it is true, consistent only in their inconsistency. It does not, however, follow that this was the effect of any precise cause. There are occasional seasons in other countries when the leading three-year-olds show very variable form. This is almost bound to be the case when there are several horses of almost equal merit at the top of the handicap, because the least thing will tip the scale now one way, now the other. That is what happened in the USA during the past season. There was no superlatively good three-year-old.

BBR–1927

The Kentucky Derby of 1928

The 1928 Kentucky Derby was won by Mrs John Hertz' Reigh Count over one of the worst tracks in the history of the classic at Churchill Downs in Louisville, Kentucky. Five inches of rain had converted the oval into 'liquid mud'. This served Reigh Count well and he only had to feel the whip once to score handsomely by three lengths. Reigh Count, who was also going to win The Jockey Club Gold Cup, was not a sire of great magnitude, but he did sire Triple Crown winner and champion sire and champion broodmare sire, Count Fleet, and a daughter of his, Countess Time, bred the surprising Kentucky Derby winner Gallahadion. For a time it seemed the male line of Sundridge, grandsire of Reigh Count, would survive, as Reigh Count's son, Count Fleet, sired consecutive Horses of the Year in 1951 and 1952 when Counterpoint and One Count each accounted for both the Belmont

Reigh Count

Stakes and The Jockey Club Gold Cup. He also sired the Kentucky Derby winner Count Turf. However, none of these classic winners could carry on in tail-male. Nonetheless, Reigh Count's name does live on in quality pedigrees through Count Fleet's many important contributions as a sire of quality broodmares.

But, in all truth, the 1928 'run for the roses' should perhaps be just as memorable for the fluent, Ciceronian oratory of Kentucky Governor Sampson in presenting the winner's trophy to Mrs Hertz:

AFTER REIGH COUNT had been duly weighed in, Mr Sampson, the Governor of Kentucky, who had watched the race from the Stewards' Stand with the Mayor of New York and other celebrities, handed the Gold trophy to Mrs Hertz, and made the customary flowing speech. He said:

'At this moment, around the world is sounding the name of a horse, Reigh Count, a Derby winner. He has contended, he has achieved, he has made glorious history. His name shall be emblazoned eternally in the hall of fame among heroic horses and go down the ages as the proud winner of the Kentucky Derby of 1928. The race was like a beautiful poem, an epic, picturesque in setting, in surroundings and in execution.

'Instituted as an event, more than half a century ago, the Kentucky Derby is the classic sporting event of America today, and brings to both the conqueror and the concourse a new and more vivid thrill of triumph, of victory and of pulsating delight, than in all past time. There is and can be no sporting contest more colourful, more tense, than the triumph of a thoroughbred horse in a well-conducted race. Man's innate fondness for the horse, the animal next to humans, intensifies his interest and multiplies the subtleness of the sporting delight which emanates from the sight of fervid contest. So has it been in this grand old Commonwealth of song and story, of entrancing beauty and soul-stirring shrines, of untold natural wealth and waiting opportunity, of tradition, romance, courage, sentimentality and life since "Aristides," the little red horse, was acclaimed the king of thoroughbreds at the first Kentucky Derby in an ancient day.

'To the owner we present the trophy, a beautiful gold cup in testimony of the excellence of her skill and accuracy of judgment. We salute the gallant rider of the winner as a true horseman, and felicitate the owner and trainer upon the marvellous results of their efforts to produce the best horse.

'Amid the acclaim of the countless throng of lovers of clean and honourable sport, gathered from every clan and clime, upon historic Churchill Downs, made sacred to Turfdom by the flying feet of many renowned Derby contenders, we in one voice proclaim and declare Reigh Count the stoutest of heart, the fleetest of foot, the champion of all horsedom, and crown him with a garland of American beauty roses as the winner of the Kentucky Derby, the King of the American Turf. May horseracing, the sport of kings, crowned and uncrowned, ever remain fair and clean, and may the best horse always win.'   BBR-1928

Some Pre-St Leger 1928 Comment

While it was true that the Fates plotted against Fairway in the Derby, in which he was tormented by his own admirers, he never lost his appeal because he lost that race. Indeed, he was once again made the choice in the St Leger, and this time he won with aplomb. Some of the goings-on prior to the 1928 renewal appeared in the BBR *of 1928. To wit:*

AS BEFORE the Derby, so just before the St Leger, the question was eagerly discussed: Can Fairway stay the course? It was almost universally conceded that if he could, and if his nerves did not again give way, he was practically certain to win. But for the doubt he would probably have started an odds-on favourite because, in the matter of class, he seemed to dominate his opponents. Now there was, of course, nobody who knew more about Fairway than Mr George Lambton, the manager of the Stanley House Stable, and it is worthwhile recording here an extract from an article he wrote for the *Evening News* shortly before the St Leger. Here it is:

'I expect Fairway to stay well enough to win the race. He is continually written about as a very temperamental horse, in my opinion without due reason. With the exception of the Derby, he has been a most consistent horse in all his races, and, personally, I have little fear that the preliminaries or the big crowd of the St Leger day will upset him, but until it is proved there must be a doubt about his staying the last two furlongs. He has shown no signs of tiring in his gallops, but the horses at Stanley House are not good enough to find out a horse of his great speed. In appearance there is no doubt that he is a greatly improved horse.'

There was a judicious blend of confidence and caution in that statement. In the case of many of the runners it was very necessary to be cautious. There were, in fact, only two whose ability to stay the fourteen and a half furlongs could safely be assumed – Cyclonic and Flamingo. Palais Royal II had, however, to be regarded as a competitor probably endowed with the necessary stamina.

This year's St Leger was staged in a wonderful setting. There was the customary mammoth crowd, drawn from all parts of the country, but mainly, of course, from the mining districts and industrial centres of the West Riding of Yorkshire and Southeast Lancashire. There was, it may be mentioned, more money taken at the turnstiles than either last year or the year before. The weather was perfect, and it may safely be asserted that never in its long history – it was first run in 1776 – has the great event been favoured with conditions more ideal. Though the race track was hard, it was covered with a rich growth of grass, which minimised the risk to the horses.   BBR–1928

Lord Derby's Presentation to William Woodward

When William Woodward's home-bred Gallant Fox captured the 1930 Kentucky Derby, 'It was indeed,' explained the BBR, 'a race which provided nothing in the nature of a thrill.' Gallant Fox, the favourite, won by two lengths but, 'in all probability he would not have had to exert himself unduly to win by twenty.' As a result, the two things to remember about this running were the congenial remarks made at the presentation of the Derby trophy to Mr Woodward by England's Lord Derby and the scathing remarks 'Salvator' made about the quality of the field following the race. To wit:

LORD DERBY was invited to present to Mr Woodward the Gold Cup, worth $5,000, associated with the Derby Stakes, the winner's share of which amounted to $50,725, the second getting $6,000, the third $3,000, and the fourth $1,000. The owners of the horses entered contributed $10,725 and the executive $50,000. When making the presentation Lord Derby said:

> 'I came 5,000 miles to see this Derby. One's expectations are hardly ever realised; more rarely are they surpassed. In this case I had the unique experience of having enjoyed myself far in excess of my highest expectations.' He expressed appreciation for the hospitality shown him in Kentucky. The love of good horses manifested in Kentucky, he declared, reminded him of his own country. He described himself as 'deeply touched' when the band played 'God Save the King' at his entrance. 'It was an honour which I shall not soon forget. I was pleased to see a good horse win,' he said, handing the trophy to Mr Woodward. 'Furthermore, I like to see a good horse like yours increase its reputation. I congratulate you, I congratulate your jockey, and last, but not least, I congratulate your horse.'

In an article published in *Daily Racing Form*, 'Salvator', one of America's leading authorities on Turf affairs, made some caustic remarks about the horses that opposed Gallant Fox in the Kentucky Derby. He wrote:

> 'They were supposed to be the flower of America's three-year-old contingent, with the exception of a few not named for the event. Practically everything, with these exceptions, in the entire country believed to be of high caste had been nominated and the field represented the residue remaining after the process known as the 'survival of the fittest' had pursued its course. The exhibition that they made was dismal. Gallant Fox had them, in the language of the street, 'too dead to skin,' after he had galloped a mile in 1 min 40⅘ sec, and from then on Sande was just letting him loaf along as he liked without allowing him to destroy all pretense of a contest by, as it were, running away and hiding from them. At the finish they came staggering and reeling along in the wake of the jaunty winner, whose ears were pricked as if he was merely amusing himself.'

'Salvator' suggested that, for the purpose of history, it was necessary only to record that Gallant Fox won and that the Earl of Derby was present. As for the rest, 'let there be silence'.   BBR–1930

Emergence of Japan

Since World War II, Japan has emerged as one of the most progressive racing and breeding countries in the world. For years the country has been purchasing a great deal of the finest bloodlines in the world. Racing is extremely popular, with crowds often exceeding 100,000 not that uncommon. Its racetracks are spacious and marvellously appointed. There is wagering on and off the tracks and restraint in betting is not a Japanese virtue. It was a different story in Japan in 1929, although then, as now, the government supervised the sport. The following account appeared in the Review of 1929.

The export of horses like Priory Park and Shian Mor to Japan has aroused curiosity regarding horse breeding and racing in that country. According to Mr B. B. McManus, who last winter took some mares from Kentucky to Japan, thoroughbreds are not allowed to race there until they are three years old, and then not over distances shorter than a mile. They must have been bred in Japan. Both breeding and racing are supervised by the Government, whose sole aim is to obtain good cavalry horses. Thoroughbred colts are never castrated, but a stallion cannot be used unless it has been approved by a departmental committee. A correspondent of *The Times* states that a day's racing at Tokyo begins at nine in the morning and ends at dusk. There are eleven events on the card. A penalty is carried for every race won, and after winning fifteen times a horse must be retired from racing. No horse over six years old is allowed to race. Betting is conducted with a totalisator. No one may have more than one bet on a race, and that bet must be one of £2. When an outsider wins his backers are paid no more than £20 (9 to 1), the surplus, sometimes amounting to hundreds of pounds, going to the race club. These regulations aim at checking anything in the nature of gambling, and keeping the poorer people away from racecourses.

My, what changes time has wrought!

When is a Generation Moderate?

When a generation is truly contentious and a number of classic winners emerge, should that be an indictment that it is a 'moderate' generation? Without a standout, that is often the opinion of the media and of knowledgeable horsemen as well, but is it right? The following commentary, which appeared in the BBR *of 1928, suggests that 'a judgment of this sort betrays a lack of imagination. Great weight attaches to recorded results, but the testimony they furnish is not necessarily conclusive.' It also doesn't take into consideration the fundamental concept of 'improving the breed.'*

IF FAIRWAY had won the 'triple crown' we should have had him hailed as a great colt; because he merely won the St Leger he is just so-so. A judgment of this sort betrays a lack of imagination. Great weight attaches to recorded results, but the testimony they furnish is not necessarily conclusive. Fairway may be an exceptionally good horse. As to that, we are likely to be considerably wiser before another year has gone by.

The writers referred to are disposed to indulge in lamentations when an Ormonde or an Isinglass does not emerge from the mass of three-year-olds. It is good to see horses of that type, but if they were forth-coming every season we might find them rather tiresome, for the classic races would be utterly spoilt as spectacles. Far better is it, from the sporting point of view, that we should have a group of three or four horses, any one of which has a reasonable chance of gaining classic honours.

Why should it be assumed that the members of such a group are necessarily moderate? We prefer to believe that during the present century our breeders have wrought a remarkable improvement in the class of bloodstock they send to the Turf. There has been a levelling up, more especially in the higher ranks. The reason for this state of things is, we should say, the importance attached, and attention given, to the credentials of the broodmares now to be found at our leading studs. The fierce competition witnessed whenever a high-class mare comes up for sale is not capricious; it is the result of the adoption of a definite and sound policy. The consequences of that policy are already apparent, and will become still more obvious in the years to come. There is no occasion to bemoan the rarity of 'triple crowned' heroes.

The foregoing had been written when we came across a statement William Halsey (one of the leading jockeys of his day, and later a trainer) made to a journalist shortly before the Derby. He declared that the horses of the present day are unmistakably superior to the horses he rode in his time, and attributed the improvement, as we do, to the fact that they are more scientifically bred. He further asserted that we now see more good horses in one season than were to be seen in four or five years at the beginning of the century, so that it had become increasingly difficult to win the Derby.   BBR–1928

When is a Guineas Winner not a Guineas Winner?

THE BELIEF, often expressed, that Claremont, and not Camballo, won the Two Thousand Guineas in 1875 is categorically endorsed by Mr William Allison, who writes: 'Camballo was the first Two Thousand Guineas winner I ever saw, and I am quite sure he did not win it, Claremont being the easy winner, on the far side of the course, right under the judge's box, which used to be on that side. All the rest of the field finished on the stand side, with Camballo in front, but the judge never saw Claremont. I am quite sure of this, because I was on the far side of the course, on the hill, from which one can see over the judge's box, and I know that Claremont won, as also – from the fact he was unplaced – that the judge never saw him. He knocked up against Galopin in the Derby, but he beat the Two Thousand Guineas form by many a length.' Many of us are quite sure that Craganour (who also finished right under the judge's box), and not Louvois, won the Two Thousand Guineas in 1913.   BBR–1928

Tattenham Corner Misplaced?

An Epsom resident wrote the following in the Review *of 1929:*

'From old documents it appears that, about the time of the Stuarts, a member of the Tottenham family bought a tract of land in the parish of Banstead, which remained in the possession of the family for many years, and which came to a point at the spot where the present five-furlong course joins the Derby course, abutting on the road from Epsom to Walton. The corner at the point of this land became known as 'Tottenham's Corner', which was corrupted to 'Tattenham's Corner'. It is thus incorrect to talk of horses coming 'round Tattenham Corner', as the corner is on the opposite side of the course.'
BBR–1929

Whom to Believe?

'A tablet was recently placed in a room at the Red Lion Hotel, Doncaster, bearing the inscription: "A gathering of noblemen and gentlemen was held in this room in 1778, at which was instituted the celebrated race known as the Doncaster St Leger Stakes",' notes the *Review* in its 1928 edition. However, the *Review* begged to differ. 'The accuracy of this statement is doubtful,' it explained. 'There is another story, fairly well authenticated, that the dinner took place at Warmsworth Hall, which Colonel St Leger was renting at the time, and that Lord Rockingham suggested that those present should subscribe to a sweepstake and institute a race to be called after their host.'

New Zealand-bred Runners in Australia

The long-standing success of New Zealand-bred runners in Australia's most prestigious and glamorous staying classics has been an unwelcome irritation to Australians for best-be-forgotten decades. 'This lack of good class stayers' was sourly noted in the Review *of 1929. To wit:*

IT IS the opinion of most people (states the *Australian*) that fewer stayers of calibre are being bred these days than at any other time in the history of the Australian Turf. Worse still, there is no assurance that the decline has stopped. In his opinion the principal causes of this retrogression have been too much racing of two-year-olds before January in each season (the season begins August 1st); too much money allotted during the season for two-year-olds and not enough for three-year-olds; insufficient inducement by subsidiary clubs for the breeding of stayers by their catering too liberally for speed; and the use of a large number of stallions unfitted to maintain stamina and staying ability in our bloodstock. In this respect the worst aspect is the craze for imported sires simply because they are imported. Except for a very small percentage, those which have been used in Australia in the last twenty years have been English culls, mostly unsound, and not many above selling plate or welter form in England. *A pedigree, be it ever so fashionable, without the horse is worse than useless – it is a menace.*

A Silly Rule

IN MAY the members of the Jockey Club were asked by the Stewards to pass a Rule that 'No horse shall run un-named'. Unfortunately the motion was rejected. The proposed change would only have affected two-year-olds because several years ago it was decreed that no horse three years of age or older should run un-named. The refusal to extend this regulation to two-year-olds is based on the excuse that, as there is not an unlimited supply of good and appropriate names, it is a pity to waste any of them on horses that disappear from the Turf before they are three years old.   BBR–1930

Superstitions Involving the Derby

There is no disavowing the fact that a great many people involved in racing are superstitious. Even if they are not, they are made aware of such mumbo-jumbo by those who are. Take the 1934 Epsom Derby for example. After Colombo secured the Two Thousand Guineas, there was some mention made that perhaps the 'spell' or 'hex' that the trial fixture, the Craven Stakes, had over the winners of that event, had been broken. But when Colombo failed as one of the hottest Derby favourites in many years and the race was won by Windsor Lad, the BBR of 1934 brought up the seeming witchcraft of the Craven Stakes once again as well as the divine (?) prophesy of the gipsy sorceress, Gipsy

*Lee. It is all part and parcel of the magnetism and romance of the Turf.
Who would want it otherwise?*

THE COMFORT of the countless thousands of people who wended their
way to Epsom Downs on Derby day was marred by showers. This was
the more aggravating because there had been no rain in the London
district for more than three weeks, and because, also, the little that
descended was of no use in the way of improving the state of the course,
which was inevitably hard, though fortunately there was a good
covering of grass. The King and Queen were there, together with the
Prince of Wales and other members of the Royal Family.

Was there any horse in the field capable of beating Colombo? That
was the question uppermost in everybody's mind. If the opinions of the
multitude could have been collected they would undoubtedly have
revealed an almost unanimous belief that the favourite had the great
prize at his mercy. Followers of racing reck little of the past, and the fate
that overtook Orwell in the Derby two years ago was probably forgotten
in the excitement of the moment. The careers of Colombo and Orwell
had run on almost parallel lines; practically the only difference was that
Orwell had been unexpectedly beaten in his first race, whereas Colombo

Colombo.

had a clean sheet when he went forth to run for the Derby. Both horses won the Two Thousand Guineas, Orwell the more easily, and both won a preliminary race, Orwell the Greenham Plate at Newbury and Colombo the Craven Stakes at Newmarket.

The Craven Stakes! To quote a passage from the 1930 volume of the *Review*:

> 'This is an event which no superstitious owner desires to win with a horse he believes to have a chance in the Guineas or the Derby. It is one of the recognised "trial" races for classic horses, but we have to go back to the year 1898 to find a "Craven" winner that also won the Derby. That phenomenon was the gigantic Jeddah, who staggered humanity when he scored at Epsom. Among present-day owners none has greater cause than Lord Astor to be disquieted when he sees his colours first past the post in the Craven Stakes. Last year his colt Cragadour won the race and was then beaten a head in the Two Thousand by Mr Jinks, and finished seventh in the Derby, for which he started a strong second favourite. In 1924 his St Germans finished second in the Derby, after winning the Craven Stakes, and in 1919 Buchan, also a "Craven" winner, was beaten a neck in the Guineas by The Panther and half a length in the Derby by Grand Parade. In 1928 Captain Gough's Royal Minstrel won the Craven Stakes, and was beaten a head in the Two Thousand, while in 1925 Picaroon, a few days after winning the "Craven" was "down" with the illness which prevented him running in the Guineas and Derby, both of which he would probably have won had he remained fit. It is, of course, nonsensical to suppose that there is a "hoodoo" attaching to the Craven Stakes, but its winners do seem to be pursued by bad luck. In Buchan's case it extended to the day when he won the Ascot Cup only to be disqualified for boring Tangiers.'

Nobody has ever accused Lord Glanely of being superstitious; he does not look the sort of man who would be. In any case, Colombo defied the Fates when he won the Guineas, and it seemed extremely probable he would defy them again by winning the Derby. And 'right here' allusion may be made to another occult mystery. Sixty-six years ago a woman of the Romany tribe named Gipsy Lee, who posed as a prophetess, was asked by a nobleman who passed her on his way to see the Derby what she thought would win. She was wearing a blue dress and replied, 'Look at my gown'. Not understanding her tip, the nobleman handed the woman his racecard and a pencil and asked her write the name of the horse. When the card was given back to him he saw the words "Blew Gown." After Sir Joseph Hawley's Blue Gown had won, the nobleman again saw Gipsy Lee, and, giving her a sovereign, suggested she should learn to spell correctly. The woman was intensely annoyed by this 'impertinence', and in her anger prophesied that so long as she lived no horse whose name began with a W would win the Derby. Strange to say, none did. Gipsy Lee died last year, and the gipsy colony gathered on

Epsom Downs for this year's Derby was feverishly excited. The only runner in the big race whose name began with a W was Windsor Lad, and every man and woman of them backed him – or so it is said.

The First Running of the Santa Anita Handicap

Santa Anita Park, near Los Angeles, opened on Christmas Day, 1934. By the time its first meeting had closed in the Spring of 1935, it was an extraordinary success, 'winding-up the year with a profit, after paying all fixed charges as well as the cost of construction'. People able and willing to pay $5,000 a share to the Los Angeles Turf Club, owners of the track, became wealthy practically overnight. This started a gold rush mined from pari-mutuel *machines that would have made successful prospectors from the gold rush days of 1849 blush with shame. A charming track of architectural splendor nestled at the base of the usually purple San Gabriel Mountains, Santa Anita has gone from strength to strength. Today, it is generally accepted as being the world's centre for quality racing in the winter and spring. Its founder, the former dentist from San Francisco, Dr Charles H. Strub, taught America how to stage a race meeting. He revolutionised the sport not only in California but throughout the continent and, subsequently, throughout the world.*

It was at the first meeting that the track presented the first running of the $100,000-added Santa Anita Handicap at one and a quarter miles – the first $100,000-added feature ever presented in the US.

Because of its historical significance and the fact that the race is now being renewed (1989) at a million dollars a copy, the BBR*'s account of the initial Big 'Cap at Santa Anita, won by the surprising Irish-bred cast-off, Azucar, is reprinted here.*

ONE OF the sensations of the year was the unexpected victory of imp. Azucar in the Santa Anita Handicap, the richest prize, from the winner's standpoint, ever run for in the racing history of the world. The Futurity of 1929 grossed more than the Santa Anita Handicap of 1935, but Azucar's portion of the stake was $2,000 more than Whichone earned. The Los Angeles Turf Club, which controls Santa Anita Park, has decided on improvements involving an expenditure of $275,000. The initial investment was a million and a quarter dollars.

The Santa Anita Handicap was run at Santa Anita, Arcadia, California, February 23rd. It was the most highly advertised race for years. The distance was ten furlongs, and $100,000 was added. It attracted a field of twenty. Equipoise was top weight with 9 st 4 lb and started a hot favourite coupled with High Glee. Twenty Grand carried 9 st, Mate and Faireno 8 st 8 lb, Time Supply 8 st 6 lb, Azucar, Ladysman, Head Play and Gusto 8 st 5 lb, Riskulus 7 st 13 lb, the others less than 7 st 12 lb. Equipoise, Twenty Grand, Faireno, Ladysman, Head Play and Gusto were patched-up cripples, Azucar's underpinning was under suspicion, Mate was all 'washed up', and the balance lacked class, with the exception of Top Row, 7 st 11 lb, and Time Supply. Ted Clark led for a mile and then faltered, as did Time Supply, the runner-up. Shortly after the mile, George Woolf on Azucar slipped through on the inside rail, saving several lengths, and after a furious duel with Ladysman went away to win by two lengths. Ladysman was a length in front of Time Supply, who beat Top Row two lengths for third place. Mate was sixth, Equipoise seventh, Gusto eighth, and Twenty Grand tenth. The race netted the winner $108,400.

The winner is owned by Mr Fred M. Alger, Jr, of Detroit, Michigan, was trained by Alexis Wilson and ridden by George Woolf, who rode Gallant Sir to victory in the Agua Caliente Handicap in 1933, and later rode Top Row in several of his races; he is regarded as an exceptionally good 'money rider'. Prior to the Santa Anita Handicap Azucar won the New Year's Handicap at Santa Anita, January 1st, beating Mad Frump, Faireno, Top Row, Head Play, Riskulus and five others. This race was worth $4,750. Azucar has not won another race, although he started in five. Discovery made mincemeat of him in Detroit, beating him some fifteen lengths. Azucar was unquestionably the luckiest horse that ever stood on plates when he won the Santa Anita Handicap, as there were at least fifteen horses through the season that would not have experienced the slightest difficulty in defeating him at level weights. Mr Alger gave Mr Widener $8,000 for Azucar as a jumper in the spring of 1934. However, he discovered the horse still possessed ability on the flat, with the result that Azucar won four races and ran second twice for his young owner, who thereupon decided to enter him in the big handicap at Santa Anita.

Foaled in 1928, Azucar was bred at the Straffan Station Stud, County Kildare, by the executors of the late Mr Edward (Cub) Kennedy, and purchased as a yearling by Capt. Cecil Boyd-Rochfort on behalf of Mr Joseph E. Widener for 1,050 guineas. He ran in England when two and three years old. At two he was out eight times, won the Gosforth Park Biennial Stakes worth £703, was second to Pomme d'Api in the Fulbourne Stakes, and third in the Woodcote Stakes. When three he ran

five times without winning, his best effort being his third in the London
Cup to Nitsichin. Shipped to the United States, he was developed into a
steeplechaser, won his first race, then finished second and was twice
unplaced. He won other steeplechases in the next two seasons, and in
August, 1934, was sold to Mr Alger for $8,000. He was returned to flat
racing, and for his new owner won the Washington Handicap, ten
furlongs, value $8,025, and finished second to Faireno in the Havre de
Grace Handicap. Azucar is a chestnut gelding by Milesius out of
Clarice, by Picton out of Clarilaw, by Persimmon. His fifth dam is
Thistle, who produced Common, Throstle and Goldfinch.

The Prix de l'Arc de Triomphe of 1935

*The Prix de l'Arc de Triomphe of 1935 holds historical interest
because of two unusual developments: fillies filled the first three places
and it marked the only defeat in France of the adored French champion
Brantôme.*

RUN AT Longchamp on October 6th over a mile and a half, this race
proved full of exciting interest. It was the fourteenth start of the French
champion Brantôme – hitherto unbeaten in his land of birth. The field
also comprised Peniche, winner of the French Oaks, Corrida, the best
two-year-old filly of 1934, Assuérus, William of Valence, Ping Pong,
Pampeiro, the best juvenile of the previous season, Astrophel, Sa
Parade, Admiral Drake, Samos, and Kant. As the formal result shows,
the contest proved a triumph for three-year-old fillies, which filled the
first three places. The other filly in the race, Sa Parade, was unplaced.

M. E. de Saint Alary's b. f. **Samos**, by Brûleur – Samya, 3 yrs –   W. Sibbritt   1
Baron E. de Rothchild's gr. f. **Peniche**, by Belfonds – Caravelle, 3 yrs P. Villecourt 2
M. Marcel Boussac's ch. f. **Corrida**, by Coronach – Zariba, 3 yrs –   C. Elliott   3
Baron E. de Rothschild's b. c. **Brantôme**, by Blandford – Vitamine, 4 yrs –
                                                         C. Bouillon   4

Also ran: Admiral Drake, 4 yrs (fifth); Pampeiro, 3 yrs (sixth); Assuérus, 5 yrs; Astrophel,
4 yrs; Sa Parade, 4 yrs; Kant, 3 yrs; William of Valence, 3 yrs; Ping Pong, 3 yrs.

Won by a neck; same second and third; length and a half third and fourth. Time:
2 min 42$^{64}/_{100}$ sec. Winner received 402,000 francs; second 80,000 francs; third and
breeder of winner, each 40,000 francs. Winner bred by owner; trained by F. Carter, at
Chantilly.

Brantôme and Péniche were coupled favourite at 2 to 1 on. At the start,
Péniche took the lead followed by Kant. At the top of the hill Ping Pong
joined the leaders. In the rear were Brantôme with Samos and Assuérus
behind him. Nearing the turn into the straight, Bouillon endeavoured to

make headway with Brantôme, but the response was slight. The spectators were dumbfounded, for the French champion had become almost an idol. The finish was thrilling. Villecourt, when he realised that Brantôme was out of the race, did his best to secure the victory for Péniche, but was beaten a neck by Samos. Corrida was only another neck away. A further length and a half came Brantôme. Various reasons were advanced to account for the defeat of the son of Blandford. No doubt he was affected by his escapade in breaking away from his attendant on Oaks Day just before he was sent to Ascot to compete in the Gold Cup, in which he was defeated. In the race under review, it was stated that Brantôme struck one of the stakes which mark out the course, and this caused him to lose his position and affected his speed. However this may be, Brantôme has run his last race and has gone to the Haras de Meautry, at Toques, not far from Deauville, where he was bred.

Getting the Most Out of Life

Here is an extract from the Sunday Times, *dated April 27th, 1834:*

On the death of Lady Penrhyn, in 1816, six of her horses had pensions assigned to them of £45 per annum each. The first five died at the respective ages of twenty-eight, twenty-nine, and thirty-one, the executors having paid for the pension of this one horse, £810.

The Death of King George V

The year 1936 was one of emotional turmoil in Great Britain and her colonies. Their revered king, George V, passed away to be succeeded by his son, King Edward VIII who, before the year was out, abdicated in favour of his brother, the Duke of York, who thus became King George VI. At the same time, frowning, trouble-filled clouds were gathering on the irascible international scene.

Mr Edward Moorhouse, with his literary skill and sense of history, told it as it was in those threatening and dreary times in the BBR. It is well worth repeating.

AT 9.38 ON the night of January 20th we heard over the air the sad, though not unexpected, announcement, 'The King's life is moving peacefully towards its close.' This was repeated every quarter of an hour until, at midnight, there came the news that His Majesty King George V had died at 11.55 p.m. No section of the community mourned the dead monarch more deeply and sincerely than that allied with the Turf.

HM King George V congratulating Mr Jarvis after Limelight had won the Newbury Spring Cup in 1933. On the right of the picture is Queen Mary.

Throughout his reign of twenty-five years he had, notwithstanding much discouragement, perseveringly maintained the association with racing and breeding which characterised the careers of many of his forbears, more especially that of his beloved father, King Edward VII.

Within a few weeks of his accession to the throne, Edward VIII made known his desire that his and the nation's bereavement should be allowed to interfere as little as possible with everyday affairs. A striking example of his concern for the welfare and happiness of his people was the expression of his wish that the great Ascot meeting in June should not be shorn of its customary brilliance by any display of mourning. This thoughtfulness was inspired not only by a desire to enhance the happiness of the public but also to serve the interests of those who minister in various ways to the needs of visitors to the Royal meeting. Ascot, therefore, provided the usual grand spectacle, though the King's Stand was, of course, unoccupied.

The new monarch's connection with racing had been mainly on the National Hunt side of the sport – the side on which he played an active part for a time as a rider in steeplechases. A doubt was entertained in some quarters as to whether he would maintain the breeding stud at Sandringham and the racing stable at Newmarket established by his grandfather and fostered by his father. At the end of January any such doubt was, however, resolved by a statement Lord Derby issued to the Press. It read, in part, as follows:

'His Majesty the King was graciously pleased to give me an interview this morning, at which he confirmed an arrangement previously come to between General Tomkinson and myself whereby I lease the late King's horses now in the possession of his present Majesty. The procedure that will be adopted is precisely the same as when I leased his late Majesty's horses when he succeeded King Edward. They will remain at Egerton Lodge under Jarvis, and they will be managed by Brigadier-General Tomkinson. They will be kept entirely apart from my own stable, and will run quite separately. . . . This arrangement will continue till the end of the racing year. His Majesty was good enough to give me permission to state that he has every intention of continuing the Royal connection with the Turf both as regards his racing stable and as regards the stud. Both will be subject to such alterations as his Majesty may, after consideration, find necessary and advisable, but the connection which has lasted now through so many generations in the Royal family will be effectively maintained.'

This statement was received with the utmost satisfaction in racing circles.

Towards the end of March it became known that the King has decided to close the paddocks at Sandringham which had for about half a century been tenanted by thoroughbred mares, foals and yearlings, and remove the bloodstock to paddocks at Hampton Court, near London, which formed part of the Royal Stud farm until the long reign of Queen Victoria was nearing its close. This migration from Sandringham did not involve any change at the nearby stud at Wolferton, where the stallions and visiting mares had for so long been accommodated. The paddocks there will still be used as hitherto. It was at Hampton Court that Springfield was located and in those paddocks were bred the Derby winner Sainfoin as well as that great mare La Flèche.

Followers of racing have derived much pleasure and satisfaction from the achievements during the past season of several horses leased by His Majesty to Lord Derby. The filly Feola finished second in the One Thousand Guineas and won the Midsummer Stakes at Newmarket in July, while Fairey was an easy winner of the Waterford Stakes at Ascot. Another leased horse was the four-year-old Marconi. He made his debut as a fencer in a steeplechase at Birmingham in February, and defeated a big field by twenty-five lengths. Marconi was bred at Sandringham.

The foregoing matter was ready for the press when, on December 10th, King Edward sent a message to the Speaker of the House of Commons announcing his irrevocable decision to renounce the throne in favour of his brother the Duke of York. For more than a week the people of the United Kingdom and of the Dominions had greatly feared His Majesty would take this step because the Governments at home and overseas found themselves unable to facilitate a marriage he contemplated. The news that the step had definitely been taken caused profound regret and sorrow. The new King was formally proclaimed on December 12th.

On December 15th it was officially stated that HM King George VI will maintain the Royal racing stable and stud on the same lines as his late father, King George V. The welcome news gave great satisfaction to everyone interested in racing and breeding. Thus King George VI will, as King Edward had intended, continue to maintain the association between the throne and the greatest of our national sports which has existed for so long a period.

A year ago we were able to record the fact that, notwithstanding political and economic disturbances abroad, the racing season of 1935 pursued its course unruffled by such troubles. This year, again, the situation on the Continent has occasioned great anxiety. The old order is changing. Traditions are being uprooted. The ideals that will replace them have yet to be found and fashioned. Great nations are being re-born, and the process has quickened the spirit of aggressive nationalism. The motto 'All for each and each for all' has become old-fashioned. Dictatorships have swept democracy away. It is with the chaos thus created that we are confronted. Great Britain is steadfastly preparing to meet effectively any emergency that may have to be faced, but in the meantime lets the world know that we are, with equal assiduity, carrying on 'business as usual'.

Again, therefore, the affairs of the Turf have, during the past season, been conducted with unabated zeal and with conspicuous success. The country as a whole is prospering. This means that there is more money available for the pursuit of pleasure and entertainment, and racing has received its share of attention. Attendances at race meetings have been appreciably larger, and the betting turnover, a very reliable indication of the public's financial stability, has increased considerably. For the moment, all is well.

Fillies

After the 1936 season was over, it was the opinion of the BBR that 'the three-year-old fillies have turned out to be just an average collection. There is none of outstanding merit.' Nothing is more accurate than 20-20 hindsight, but in light of what the first two finishers in the One Thousand Guineas did as producers, the chronicler might have been less harsh in his appraisal.

The winner was Lord Derby's Fairway filly Tide-way by a length and a half over Lord Derby's Feola, a daughter of Friar Marcus on lease from the King.

Tide-way, 'somewhat lacking in substance', was produced by Drift, by Swynford. Among Tide-way's foals was Hyperion's son Gulf Stream, champion two-year-old of 1945 and third best three-year-old of 1946 when he ran second in the Derby and secured the Eclipse Stakes. Exported to Argentina he became one of that country's leading classic sires.

Feola, who 'has good size and is very shapely', was also third in the Oaks. Her foals included the Yorkshire Oaks winner Angelola, dam of champion older horse and outstanding sire, Aureole; the winner Knight's Daughter, dam of Round Table, for many years the world's leading money winner and subsequently a champion sire; Starling, dam of the Argentine Oaks winner Siderea as well as the champion Argentine sire, Sideral; the Yorkshire Oaks victress Above Board, dam of the stakes winners and sires Doutelle and Above Suspicion, and the One Thousand Guineas heroine and stakes producer Hypericum.

An expansive book could be written on Feola's ramifying family alone.

And, oh yes, one might mention Lord Astor's Traffic Light who might have been closer than fourth had she not tossed her head into the air at the start, losing several lengths. The daughter of Solario bred the major stakes winner Amber Flash and the latter, in turn, produced Ambiguity, the daughter of Big Game who captured the Oaks of 1953.

Well done for 'an average collection'.

The line of Feola was further strenghtened by Nashwan, the 1989 winner of the Two Thousand Guineas, the Derby, the Eclipse Stakes and the King George VI and Queen Elizabeth Stakes. Nashwan is out of Height of Fashion, the winner of the Princess of Wales's Stakes, who is out of Highclere, the winner of the One Thousand Guineas and Prix de Diane, who is a grandaughter of Hypericum. Nashwan possesses an additional line of Feola through his dam, who is by Bustino, himself out of a Doutelle mare.

The Dream Match That Never Was

War is an on-going series of monstrous tragedies which, by comparison, rob the things of seeming importance in normal, everyday living times, of any significance. So it was in September of 1939 when the world, once again, was plunged into global conflict. That was the year Lord Rosebery's Blue Peter, a son of Fairway, captured the Two Thousand Guineas before proving a dominant winner of the Derby and then adding the Eclipse. In France, Pharos' son, Pharis, took both the French Derby and the Grand Prix de Paris. Thus, this pair, champions in their respective countries, were poised to settle the supremacy of Europe in the St Leger when just a few days earlier hostilities broke out. Pharis II was already on the scene. Therefore, an event which would have excited the entire thoroughbred world never took place and few people, at the time, had the time to worry about it. Blue Peter, for his part, was denied a chance to join that illustrious list of Triple Crown winners and Pharis and the French were denied another chance to avenge Waterloo.

If the winner of this 'might-have-been' dream match were to be decided on how each of them performed at stud, the edge, perhaps, belongs to Pharis II. He sired such classic winners as Ardan (French Derby and Prix de l'Arc de Triomphe); Asterblute (German Derby); Scratch (French Derby and English St Leger); Stymphale (French St Leger); Auriban (French Derby) and Philius (French Derby). Also his daughter, Corejada, best in the French One Thousand Guineas and Irish Oaks, bred Apollonia, successful in both the French One Thousand Guineas and Oaks, and Macip, an Ascot Gold Cup and French St Leger winner.

As for Blue Peter, his only two classic winners were Ocean Swell, a Derby and Ascot Gold Cup hero, and Botticelli, who swept the Italian Triple Crown and also made an incursion into England to snare an Ascot Gold Cup. Blue Peter's daughter, Glen Line, produced an Eclipse winner in King of the Tudors and a Two Thousand Guineas winner in Our Babu.

So, it was a reasonably close thing on paddock performance and it probably would have been on the racetrack as well.

Breeding, Racing and Public Opinion During War-time

If the world today was plunged into another war-time crisis and racing was continued in the afflicted countries, the situation would be applauded by some and disparaged by others. 'Obstinacy's ne'er so stiff as when 'tis in a wrong belief.' Samuel Butler said it first, but who is right and who is wrong? Both contemporary views were given space in the press during those dire times and examples were reprinted in the BBR of 1940, including one from one of racing's staunchest spokesmen, the Hon. George Lambton.

IT WAS inevitable that the carrying-on of racing in war time should have aroused a certain amount of questioning. Criticism was voiced in certain sections of the Press and, on one or two occasions, in the House. Much of it was unjustified, and some of it was so uninformed as to call for no comment.

None of the criticisms were original; they had all been voiced in the war of 1914-1918. Mostly they took the form of complaints that petrol was being unnecessarily wasted, that war-time racing was in bad taste, and so on; towards the end of the year there were complaints that food was being used for racehorses which was needed for human consumption!

Extracts from a considerable volume of correspondence in the Press – mostly in *The Times* – are given below. Leading articles in the news-papers, many of them regrettably misleading, are not re-printed; greater value is attached in any case to correspondence published in the Press, representing as it did the views of all classes of the community. The first extract, therefore, is from a letter addressed to the Editor of *The Times*, from Trinity Hall, Cambridge, and dated May 21st, 1940:

> Sir, – I cannot believe that I am alone in feeling a sense of shame that, at a time when the whole world must be listening in to British broadcasts, when the life of France, of our own Army in France and of all nations who love liberty seems to hang by the slenderest of thread, our news bulletins should be associated with racing results. It is easy to imagine the feelings of any of our French, Norwegian, Dutch, or Belgian allies who should happen to be listening in, and I am certain that those feelings must be shared by millions of our own countrymen.
>
> If indeed an appreciable number of Englishmen still exist who require racing results to satisfy their craving for excitement at the present time, then at least let us keep the deplorable fact out of the limelight instead of following broadcast news from France with news from the Turf.

This was followed by a letter to the same journal from an address in Dulwich:

> Sir, – The following announcement appears in today's issue of *The Times*: 'As at present advised, no interruption in racing next week is anticipated.'
>
> We, as workers for the nation, are asked by the Government and prominent members of Parliament to work seven days a week for our King and country and the lads at the Front; and also to contribute our hardly earned savings to pay for the war. Many of us are willingly doing this for the sake of our country and the cause we are fighting for. But is it right that at the same time money should be spent and time wasted by able-bodied men who are still allowed to seek their pleasure on the racecourse, dog track, and in other forms of sport which entail the use of railways and other means of transport, involving the consumption of coal, petrol, and man-power, and also a large expenditure on the production of newspaper reports? . . . . Is this inequality of effort fair to our Fighting Forces and those of our Allies?

On May 25th *The Times* published six letters, under the heading: 'Are We at War?' One complained of BBC broadcasts of racing results, 'nicely calculated to make our Allies feel that we are not taking the war seriously'. The next ended by saying, 'if the Government does not stop racing of all sorts . . . its demands on the life, labour and property of all citizens will hardly be taken seriously.' A third complained of greyhound racing and football pools. Only one of the series was in favour of carrying on sport. The correspondence continued, for and against, but mostly against, until May 29th, when Mr Lambton picked up his pen and wrote a vigorous defence of war-time racing. It is only possible, unfortunately, to publish extracts from his letter:

Sir, – It requires a man of some moral courage to stand up and take the odium that would be thrown at him of being so lost to any sense of decency that he could give his mind to horseracing while his country is in the throes of such a desperate struggle, but my brother Lord Durham, although he himself never set foot upon a racecourse during the war (1914-18) wrote a letter to *The Times* setting forth plainly the reasons for continuing racing and showing that the complete stoppage of racing would mean the ruin of an industry in which Britain was supreme. There were letters from the late Lord Rosebery and Lord Derby to the same effect. These carried great weight and had much to do with changing public opinion, and it was not very long before the Government recognised the true position. One of the arguments used by those who thought that racing should stop was that the men who were fighting in France were strongly opposed to it. I believe this to have been an absolute fallacy. I certainly never met one man of the fighting forces, officer or private, who held that opinion, and I was in constant touch with them. I was frequently asked whether I would show parties of men who were on leave round Lord Derby's stable, more especially men of the overseas forces, Australians, Canadians, New Zealanders, and Americans.

Again on one occasion I went to France to see my brother, General Sir William Lambton, who had been terribly injured and whose life was in great danger. He was in a clearing station, close to Arras and near the firing line. Before I had been in the camp a couple of days I found officers, Tommies, doctors, and nurses all talking and asking me about racing, and the racing and sporting papers were all studied with the greatest interest. . . .

I will quote some lines in a leading article in your issue of today: 'The courage to go on quietly doing one's job to the very height of capacity and endurance is a courage which the civilian need not be ashamed to range in support of the shining bravery of those who fight for him.' My job is racing and I am not ashamed to carry on, and if when we have won this war I have left something for a younger generation to build up again I shall be content. We have in our Labour Minister, Mr Ernest Bevin, a great man and one who is like Mr Lloyd George in 1914, ruthless in his prosecution of the War. So long as limited racing has his sanction those who are in doubt may also be content.

I am, Sir, yours faithfully,
GEORGE LAMBTON
Mesnil Warren, Newmarket, May 29

Mr Lambton's letter had a very salutory effect, for it virtually wound up the debate for the time being.

A War-time Diary

From the first full year of World War II, 1940, until 1945, 'the most eventful year in recorded history', Mr V. R. Orchard wrote 'A War-time Diary' annually for the BBR. *It was a marvellous contribution as it not only chronicled the sub-plot of what was transpiring in racing and breeding during this brooding, trying time, but also presented a continuing account of the terrible reality of the conflict itself. Typical of Mr Orchard's dexterity in weaving the two together was the following, appearing in the* BBR *of 1940:*

JUNE 4th, a Tuesday, was chosen by the Prime Minister, Mr Winston Churchill, for a review of the European situation and for a classical declaration of Britain's determination to see the war through. His words: 'We shall fight on the beaches . . . in the fields and in the streets; we shall fight in the hills; we shall never surrender' earned a permanent place among the great orations of history. He recited the splendid story of Dunkirk and the nation knew for the first time how the miracle of the evacuation had been accomplished. On the following day, Germany's major offensive was launched and, nine days later, German motorised forces entered Paris. The Italian Government meanwhile had declared war on the Franco-British Allies and, on the 15th-16th, the French Government, now in Bordeaux, resigned. Marshal Petain, M. Reynaud's successor, immediately sought an armistice and his envoys signed the dictated terms in Compiègne on the 22nd.

So much for the major events. In face of such tragedy it seems incredible that racing was carried on without interruption from June 1st to June 18th. Large crowds saw the Derby and the Oaks at Newmarket and, on the very day that the Prime Minister had told the House of the final stages of the French debacle, *The Sporting Life* issued a list of the probable starters for the substituted Ascot Gold Cup, due to be run on the following Friday. Whether the Government had been too busy to stop racing, or whether it was deliberately allowed to go on to allay possible panic among the less informed section of the community, is a matter which need not be discussed here. Suffice it to record that circumstances of a military nature precluded the holding of the 'Ascot' meeting. Racing was presently shelved and there was a hiatus which lasted nearly three months.

Thus passed a not uneventful month in matters affecting breeding and racing. Sixteen months of war had shaken the industry to its foundations. But the foundations were secure, whatever the condition of the

War Time Derby at Newmarket, 1940.

superstructure. It is not the function of the diarist – at any rate of the racing diarist – to draw morals or to look ahead. It might, none the less, be permissible to record that the more responsible persons associated with the bloodstock industry looked forward with confidence, not perhaps to the year 1941, but to the years which would follow the dictation of the peace terms by the Imperial Government and its Allies. There is an old racing saying that: 'he will come back to his horses'. Time will show that the world, when peace and order are restored, will come back to England, the home of the thoroughbred, to replenish and improve the stock and breed of the thoroughbred.

Part 2

RACEHORSES

Could Whisk Broom Stay?

Whisk Broom II, a chestnut foal of 1907, by Broomstick from the Kentucky Oaks winner Audience, by Sir Dixon, had been sent to England during the racing blackout in the US by his owner, H. P. Whitney. He enjoyed considerable success there and was being readied for the Grand Jubilee Stakes at Kempton Park when Mr Whitney ordered his trainer, A. J. Joyner, to return him to the States where racing was under-way again. This was in 1913 when Whisk Broom was aged six. He raced but three times in his native land, winning three of the most respected handicaps in the nation – the Metropolitan, Brooklyn and Suburban. These races are now known as the Handicap Triple Crown. He was the first to score this hat trick and it was not done again until forty years later in 1953 by the magnificent champion Tom Fool.

Whisk Broom's triumph under 139 lb in the Suburban remains one of the most legendary races of all time. Not only because of his hefty impost in which he gave 27 lb to the second horse and 20 lb to the third, but because the official clocking for the $1\frac{1}{4}$ miles was 2 minutes exactly, a new world and American record. The official clocker was the only one to catch Whisk Broom going that fast, the next fastest being 2:01 min 3/5 sec. Nevertheless, the record was Whisk Broom's to keep for many years – indeed, for nearly a half-century in the US.

Whisk Broom sired a Kentucky Derby winner in Whiskery and a Preakness winner in Victorian, but his influence has survived most significantly through his daughter Broomshot, dam of the champion racehorse and highly successful sire Double Jay.

COULD WHISK BROOM STAY? – Andrew Joyner, who trained Whisk Broom in England for Mr Whitney, has been giving his views concerning the merits of the horse. He declares that the son of Broomstick and Audience would have held his own with 'any man's horse in any country', up to ten furlongs. Whether Whisk Broom would have gone further he cannot say, because he did not try to develop his staying powers to the utmost.

'When,' added Joyner, 'I was training Whisk Broom, I used to send Iron Mask, a sprinter of rare speed, with him for threequarters of a mile and then make him pick up Borrow for another half. He never experienced the least difficulty in galloping Iron Mask to defeat and, although he could not actually beat Borrow the extra half, he always made Borrow stretch his neck. Borrow, as every one knows, was a good horse in Great Britain and has done pretty well over here (America).

'I was readying Whisk Broom for the Kempton Park Great Jubilee Stakes, when Mr Whitney ordered me to send him back to the United States. I believe he would have won too. Mr Whitney wrote me after I had shipped Whisk Broom, that he was sorry to interfere with my plans, but that there were so few horses of good class in this country he felt he owed it to American racing to bring Whisk Broom home.'

BBR–1917

Oaks Winner Owned by Sir Winston Churchill's Father

It is quite well known that Sir Winston Churchill was always a stalwart defender of English racing and breeding and even owned some worth-while runners during his lifetime. However, there are probably far fewer who recall that his father, Lord Randolph Churchill, owned the filly L'Abbesse de Jouarre, heroine of the Oaks in 1889 and, subsequently dam of St Simon's talented racing son, Desmond, who became a leading sire in 1913. Bought for a dismissive 300 guineas, L'Abbesse de Jouarre won other major fixtures and her only three foals also included Desmond's own sister, Festa, a modest winner but the dam of three classic winners in Germany and of five significant stakes winners in all. Desmond's influence has also been enduring. His son, Charles O'Malley, sired Malva the dam of Blenheim; his daughter, Ayn Hali, produced the important sire Sir Cosmo and another daughter, Molly Desmond, foaled two Irish Derby winners and is one of four daughters of Pretty Polly to have kept the latter's name a cherished one in the finest pedigrees.

THE *DAILY TELEGRAPH* related that Lord Randolph Churchill, father of the Right Hon. Winston Churchill, was a frequent visitor to the London Library. He asked for Renan's work, 'L'Abbesse de Jouarre', and it was his admiration for this drama, it was stated, that caused Lord Randolph thus to name his filly, who won him the Oaks in 1889.

The filly, a black, bred in 1886, was sired by Trappist, who was gifted with great speed and won twenty-four races. She was out of Festive, by Carnival, a very moderate horse, by Sweetmeat. As Festive had won only one race, £100, and bred one winner of small class before her Trappist filly was sold at Doncaster, little wonder it realised 300 guineas.

As a two-year-old she ran eight times, winning twice at Newmarket and once at Pontefract. She ran five times at three years old. Her only success was in the Oaks when, starting at 20 to 1, she defeated the favourite, the One Thousand Guineas winner, Minthe, by a neck. Next year the filly won the Manchester Cup, 1¾ miles, carrying 8 st 8 lb, beating seventeen others. She also won good races at Doncaster and Sandown. At five years L'Abbesse de Jouarre started twice, winning the Hardwick Stakes, 1½ miles, Ascot, under 9 st 9 lb, and giving 9 lb to Martagon. Her total winnings amounted to £10,050.

L'Abbesse de Jouarre lives in modern pedigrees through her famous son Desmond, who was a really high-class stallion, and possibly the only one who, as stated by his Irish manager, sired 'two Derby winners at once'. He was referring to Craganour and Aboyeur. The former, after winning the 1913 Derby, was disqualified and the race awarded to Aboyeur.

A sister to Desmond was named Festa. She went to Germany, and there established a line of powerful sons whose influence upon German bloodstock was incalculable. They were Fels, by Hannibal; Festino, by Ayrshire; Fervor, by Galtee More. Festa, the first foal of her dam, was not much account as a racehorse, for she won a couple of races over five furlongs. She had bred two winners here before she was sold for 1,000 guineas to Germany. How great winners were her sons is obvious from the fact that the produce of Festa won over £70,000.

L'Abbesse de Jouarre died on March 6th, 1897, when foaling to Isinglass. She had bred three foals. Her second was named Cowl. That son of Galopin ran several times, and could not win a race. He was tried, but failed at the stud. The third and last foal of the Oaks winner was Desmond. He forced his way to the front rank, for when he went to the stud breeders looked askance at him. He began his stud career at a fee of £24 10s. What really settled Desmond's reputation as a racehorse was that when a three-year-old he was an 11 to 10 favourite for a handicap at Newmarket. Sloan was his rider. The colt was in a most ugly mood. He refused to start, and was left at the post. Yet at the time of his death in 1913 the fee of Desmond was 250 guineas. He was eighteen years old when he died; his sire, St Simon, and his grandsire, Galopin, were both twenty-seven years old when they passed away. It was only thirty-one days before his death that his sons were Derby winners. The first yearling by Desmond sold at auction was at Limerick, when the gelding out of Zoraida made two guineas! Before his end, prices like 5,000 guineas and 6,000 guineas were paid in the sales for Desmond's yearlings.

BBR–1942

Tracery's St Leger Victory

Tracery made one of the most unusual debuts in the history of racing. His first appearance on a race track was at Epsom in the Derby of 1912 'and it was with some little astonishment that the crowd saw him finish third to Tagalie and Jaeger – the position being gained after a hard and prolonged tussle with the King's horse Pintadeau,' noted the Review. *After that portentous start, it is not surprising that Tracery was held co-second choice for the St Leger, which he won, quite handily, by five lengths with Sweeper II, the Two Thousand Guineas winner, and the filly Tagalie, best in the One Thousand Guineas and Derby, both out of the frame. The* Review *reported:*

'Tracery, a son of Rock Sand, bred in America and owned by Mr August Belmont, President of the New York Jockey Club, won the St Leger. Any chagrin which the victory of a "foreigner" may have occasioned was, however, modified by the knowledge that his pedigree is English through and through. His sire, Rock Sand, when the property of the late Sir James Miller, who bred him at Hamilton Stud, Newmarket, won the Guineas, Derby and St Leger in 1903. Rock Sand had had but one season at the Stud in England when Sir James Miller died. That was in the winter of 1905-6. The son of Sainfoin remained here for another season, but in the spring of 1906 he was sold to Mr Belmont for £25,000 and went to America, There he remained until recently, when he was leased to a French syndicate.'

During his brief stay in the US, Tracery sired but one stakes winner of note, Cirrus, a Brooklyn Handicap winner in 1920. However, he became a proven breeding talent in Europe. His male line did not carry on. It appeared for a time that it would through his son Copyright, the winner of the Gold Vase who sired the exceptional Argentine-bred Congreve, one of the all-time leading sires in Argentina. Tracery also sired that inimitable Cup mare, Teresina, a superior producer whose influence is still an eloquent presence in many splendid pedigrees. The Review *also commented on:*

'The international flavour that has characterised this year's classic races is a point worthy of notice. Sweeper II is by Broomstick, an American horse, but was foaled in France, and was ridden by Maher, an American, when he won the Two Thousand Guineas. Tagalie, the One Thousand Guineas and Derby winner, is out of the French-bred mare Tagale. She was ridden in the Guineas by Hewitt, an Australian, and in the Derby by John Reiff, an American domiciled in France. Mirska, the Oaks winner, though bred and trained in England, is owned by a French sportsman, and was ridden by Childs, an Anglo-French jockey. And now we have Tracery, owned by an American, bred in America, by an English horse out of an English mare, trained at Newmarket, and ridden by Bellhouse, a native of Birmingham, but who has done all his riding in France.'

The Death of Carbine

Carbine, who died at the Duke of Portland's Welbeck Stud in 1914 at the age of twenty-nine, was bred in New Zealand and became 'the Pride of All Australasia' with his many exceptional performances in Australia, including a victory in the Melbourne Cup Handicap in the then record time for the 2 miles under a ponderous impost of 145 lb. When he was imported he was considered 'the best horse that ever came to England from the southern hemisphere.' That expansive recognition probably still applies, although he probably has to share pride of place as the greatest racehorse ever to be exported from the southern hemisphere with the mighty Phar Lap.

CARBINE, who had attained the patriarchal age of twenty-nine, was on June 10th mercifully 'put away' at the Duke of Portland's Stud, Welbeck, where he had been a resident since 1895. An opportunity thus presented itself for reviewing the career of the best horse that ever came to England from the southern hemisphere.

Carbine would, in all probability, have proved himself a great race-horse even if he had been foaled in England and passed his active life on the Turf in this country. Bred, born and reared in New Zealand, he was destined to do all his racing in Australasia, and there he revealed himself a veritable champion. Regarded as a whole, his achievements showed him to be not only a high-class but also a splendidly consistent performer. He took part in forty-three races and won thirty-three of them. Once only did he fail to finish first, second, or third.

One at least of Carbine's victories raised him far above the normal plane of excellence. We refer to his memorable triumph in the contest for the Melbourne Cup Handicap in 1890, when he was a five-year-old. In the corresponding race the previous year, he carried 10 st, and finished second to Bravo, whose weight was 8 st 7 lb. Showing him no mercy, the handicapper called upon Carbine to carry 10 st 5 lb in 1890. Carbine not only won, but won easily by three lengths from 38 opponents. To Highborn, who finished second, he gave 4 st all but 3 lb, and he traversed the two miles in 3 min. 28¼ seconds, which at the time constituted a record, though it is one which has since been beaten on several occasions, though only by a second or so. This was the greatest of Carbine's many great performances. It is the one with which he always has been, and always will be, chiefly associated. It has been stated, and we have not seen a contradiction, that for some time before he ran that race, Carbine was suffering from a split hoof. The mischief re-asserted

Carbine.

itself during the contest, but not until he was nearing the winning post. For several days afterwards the condition of the hoof was such that it was feared Carbine's racing days were over. The injury, however, was quickly repaired, and he not only won again that season, but was successful in ten races the following year.

Bred by the New Zealand Stud Company in 1885, Carbine was by Musket out of Mersey. Both sire and dam were bred in England and exported to New Zealand. Mersey, who was out of Clemence (believed by some to have been the dam of Bend Or), was a product of the Eaton Stud. Carbine was her first foal, and when a yearling he was sold to Mr J. O'Brien for 620 guineas. He did all his racing as a two-year-old in New Zealand. His score as a juvenile was five victories, and he was unbeaten. The following season he was sent over to Australia, the immediate purpose of his going thither being the fulfilment of his engagement in the Victoria Derby at Melbourne. In that race he was unluckily beaten a head by Ensign, his defeat being universally attributed to bad jockeyship. An opportunity of avenging his downfall was denied him, because a day or two later Ensign broke a leg and had to be destroyed.

Having reached Australia, Carbine remained there until 1895, when he came to England. We will not weary our readers by enumerating the thirty-three races he had won when he retired from the Turf to the stud. It is sufficient to say that the value of the prizes he captured was £29,476. No other horseracing at the Antipodes has been able to amass anything like so big a total. The nearest approach to it is that of £19,496 standing to the credit of Poseidon. Wakeful comes third with £16,690.

During the greater part of his career on the Australian Turf, Carbine was a tremendous favourite with the public, who called him 'Old Jack'. With regret they saw him leave the racetrack for the stud, after he had been in hard training for five seasons; with lamentations they received the news that he had been bought by the Duke of Portland for 13,000 guineas, and was to come to England. That was in 1895, the year in which his Australian-bred stock made their first appearance on the Turf.

Owing to the hard work Carbine had done while in training, his owner decided that it would be judicious to 'go slow' the first season the son of Musket spent at the stud. In accordance with this determination, Carbine was allowed only three mares in 1891. But one of them was Melodious, and the result of her mating with 'Old Jack' was Wallace, who is probably the best of Carbine's sons, the achievements of Spearmint notwithstanding. Wallace was a very good racehorse; he has proved himself a great stallion. Other successful offspring of Carbine in Australia were Charge, winner of the A.J.C. Derby, and Amberite, who won both the Sydney and Melbourne Derbys.   BBR–1914

Defrauded of the Real Thing – Pommern's New Derby Victory

THE VICTOR'S performance was unquestionably a very convincing one. He defeated his rivals in effortless fashion, and proved that we have at least one high-class three-year-old colt. The time he took to cover the mile and a half was exceptionally fast. It beats the Epsom Derby record (held by Lemberg) by 2 3/5 seconds. It has generally been supposed that twelve furlongs at Newmarket affords a severer test of stamina than twelve furlongs over the Epsom gradients, but Pommern's achievement tends to negative that idea. By securing second place on his merits, Let Fly demonstrated afresh that his running in the Two Thousand Guineas was misleading. The three French horses – Florimond, Le Melior and Chickamaugwa – made no show at all. The Vizier (third in the Two Thousand) handicapped himself by beginning slowly. There was some clapping of hands when Pommern entered the unsaddling enclosure in the paddock, but we sadly missed the fervour and excitement always associated with the Derby at Epsom. In short, it was borne in upon us that, interesting and important though the New Derby was, we had been defrauded of the real thing.   BBR–1915

Obituary of Man o' War

No thoroughbred in the history of American racing has inspired such lasting adoration as Man o' War, a foal of 1917. Beaten but once in twenty-one starts and then through unfortunate circumstances by a colt appropriately named Upset, Man o' War was never truly tested through-out his other starts. He captured the hearts, the respect and the imagination of America's devoted race-goers without dissent. And although racing in America has loved and lauded and revered such great champions as Man o' War's own son, War Admiral, Seabiscuit, Challedon, Whirlaway, Count Fleet, Armed, Citation, Tom Fool, Native Dancer, Nashua, Swaps, Bold Ruler, Round Table, Kelso, Buckpasser, Damascus, Dr Fager, Forego, Seattle Slew and, yes, Secretariat, and that magnificent old gelding, John Henry, that aura of immortality, of being the best of the best has never left Man o' War. Indeed, it is doubtful if time will ever erode one iota his exalted place in the history of the American Turf.

MAN O' WAR, one of the great figures in the history of the American Turf, died on November 1st, at the age of thirty, at Faraway Farm, Lexington, Kentucky. Since 1943 he had been retired from stud service because of a severe heart attack. Shortly before his death, recurrent attacks of colic seriously weakened his stout heart until sedatives were finally administered to make his final days easy.

One cannot compare horses of different times or countries with the complete satisfaction of arriving at a concrete result. Those who knew Man o' War, saw him race, studied his stud record, declared him the best racehorse they ever saw, probably the most powerful single genetic influence of the century in thoroughbred breeding. Strong praise? – to Americans he was the embodiment of the perfect horse, a horse for which no excuses were needed.

In brief, his record on the racecourse was twenty-one starts, twenty wins, one second, and his earnings totalled $249,465. In the stud he became the first sire in the world whose get won over $3,000,000, despite the fact that he was never bred to more than twenty-five mares in a single season, that his foals raced largely during the depression years of the 1930s, and that the mares to which he was bred were less distinguished than those sent to any other outstanding stallion of our times.

Man o' War was foaled at Major August Belmont's Nursery Stud, near Lexington, Kentucky, on March 29th, 1917. He was a chestnut, by Fair Play – Mahubah, by *Rock Sand. Fair Play, a great sire even without Man o' War's contribution, was a son of the terrible-tempered Hastings, a great-grandson of West Australian. Fair Play was out of *Fairy Gold, from whom have come in tail-female line such horses as Zariba, Dark Legend, Goyescas, Corrida, Coaraze, Abjer, *Goya II, and others. Man o' War's dam, Mahubah, produced to the cover of Fair Play, the good stakes winner, My Play (also sire), the stakes-winning mare Masda, the dam, and grandam of a group of more than useful stakes horses, including Assault, leading three-year-old of 1946.

	Hastings	Spendthrift	*Australian Aerolite
		*Cinderella	†Tomahawk Manna
Fair Play (Ch, 1905)			
MAN O' WAR (Ch. 1917)	*Fairy Gold	Bend Or	Doncaster Rouge Rose
		Dame Masham	Galliard Pauline (9)
	*Rock Sand	Sainfoin	Springfield Sanda
		Roquebrune	St Simon St Marguerite
Mahubah (B, 1910)			
	*Merry Token	Merry Hampton	Hampton Doll Tearsheet
		Mizpah	Macgregor D. of Underhand

Family. No. 4

Breeder   MAJOR AUGUST BELMONT
Owner   SAMUEL D. RIDDLE

Man o' War was recognised from the beginning as a good horse, but nothing as extraordinary as he turned out. Major Belmont felt that he was the best yearling in the 1917 crop and when, due to war work, he decided to sell his 1917 yearling crop, he thought for a time of holding Man o' War. He had been named by this time by Mrs Belmont. However, less than a month before the yearling sales at Saratoga he wrote his farm manager, Mrs Edward Kane, that he 'had decided to add Man o' War to the sale.' Man o' War and the rest of the Nursery Stud yearlings went under the hammer at Saratoga Springs, New York, on August 17th.

Louis Feustel, who had worked with the Belmont Stable as a youngster during the days of Fair Play, wanted his employer, Samuel D. Riddle, to buy a Fair Play yearling. Before the sales he looked over the Nursery Stud yearlings at Lexington, liked Man o' War, thought some of the others might be better. Recalling his first sight of Man o' War, he afterwards said, 'Very tall and gangling, he was thin, and so on the leg as to give the same ungainly impression one gets in seeing a week-old foal.' Mr Riddle was dubious on seeing Man o' War, but thought he would make a good hunter. Mrs Riddle, however, pointed out that Feustel had to train the horses. She had a great deal of influence on the purchase. Mr Riddle made the final bid on Man o' War, $5,000, the greatest bargain ever made in an auction ring anywhere. His bid topped that of Robert L. Gerry's, who was looking for a hunter prospect! The $5,000 bid was the third highest paid for any of the Nursery Stud yearlings, was the fifth highest for the Saratoga Sales of 1918.

Yearling trials revealed to Feustel that Man o' War was something 'extra'. In early spring training in Maryland as a two-year-old, Man o' War was running over other horses. By the time he made his first start on June 6th, 1919, in a maiden race at Belmont Park, he was so well regarded that he started at 3 to 5. With Johnny Loftus up, Man o' War won his first race by six lengths, five furlongs in 59 seconds.

Three days later he won the Keene Memorial against On Watch, Ralco and others. He did not go to the front until the stretch, then won by three lengths easily on a sloppy track. Track conditions made no difference to 'Big Red'. By this time Feustel was convinced that he had the best two-year-old of the season. The easy wins which followed in the Youthful, Hudson and Tremont Stakes solidified this conviction.

In the meantime Man o' War had taken care of *Golden Broom, a son of *Sweeper and the highest-priced yearling at the Saratoga Sales the previous year. He had been bought by Mrs Walter Jeffords, niece of Mr Riddle, for $15,600. In a yearling trial *Golden Broom beat Man o' War at a quarter-mile, although the latter was gaining at the end. Mike Daly, who was training *Golden Broom, suggested to Feustel that they split up the stakes. Feustel thought that since he had the best, there was not much point to that. A private match at three furlongs was arranged. Man o' War ran each of the three furlongs in 11 seconds, beat *Golden Broom by a length. Mr Riddle was now convinced that he had a champion. A little later veteran horsemen were wondering if Man o' War was the best since Sysonby.

At Saratoga Man o' War won the United States Hotel Stakes, and then started in the Sanford Memorial Stakes on August 13th. For the

Man o' War

first time he was meeting *Golden Broom in open competition. Both carried 9 st 4 lb. There was also Upset at 8 st 3 lb, and four others. Man o' War broke fifth in a straggling start, *Golden Broom and Upset went to the front. Jockey Johnny Loftus, who rode Man o' War in all his races at two, was conscious of the lost ground, and sent him to the inside going into the far turn. In the stretch *Golden Broom was in front, but was stopping; Upset was on the outside and Man o' War was boxed in the rail. When Loftus realised that he was not going to get through on the inside, he swung Man o' War to the outside a furlong from home, losing lengths. The more lightly-weighted Upset went to the front, and had just enough left to outlast Man o' War by little less than half a length. The well-named Upset was never to get near Man o' War again. In the course of time legend placed the blame of Man o' War's defeat on Jockey Loftus or Starter Pettingill. Legend reports that Loftus never rode again, but he was up on Man o' War for the rest of his races at two. Sometimes it has been reported that Man o' War was facing the wrong way at the start!

In his next start Man o' War met Upset again. 'Big Red' started at 11 to 20, gave 5 lb to Upset, led all the way to win by a length, easing up. Upset was second. In the Hopeful Stakes Man o' War held up the start for 12 minutes, then won by four lengths galloping. His last start of the year was in the Futurity at Belmont Park. He carried top weight of 9 st 1 lb, gave John P. Grier 10 lb, Dominique 5 lb, with Upset, the mare Cleopatra, On Watch, Paul Jones, and others in the field. John P. Grier and Dominique led for half the distance, and then Man o' War passed them and won as he pleased by 2½ lengths. Man o' War was sent to winter quarters at Berlin, Maryland.

He was not entered in the Kentucky Derby but was saved for the Preakness, which he won easily by killing off the late challenge of Upset and Wildair, the H. P. Whitney entry.

Eleven days later Man o' War won the one-mile Withers Stakes at Belmont by two lengths, in new American record time of 1:35 4/5. Man o' War had worked six furlongs in 1:11 for the Withers, and on the morning of the race a furlong in : 10 1/5.

The Belmont Stakes was hardly a contest. With only one other starter, *Donnacona, Man o' War won by 20 lengths in 2:14 1/5 for 1⅜ miles. Major Belmont, who had bred Man o' War, no longer insisted that Tracery was the best horse he had ever bred. This was followed by an easy win in the Stuyvesant Stakes, with Yellow Hand the only other starter, getting 33 lb and an eight-lengths' beating.

The Dwyer Stakes of 1920, Man o' War's next start, is now recorded as one of the most famous races in the history of the American Turf. In this race Man o' War carried 9 st, John P. Grier, the only other starter, 7 st 10 lb. They got away together, matched stride for stride, neck and neck. Inside the final furlong pole John P. Grier got his head in front. It was only for a moment, for Jockey Clarence Kummer hit Man o' War, and the red champion leaped away to win by a length and a half in the last 70 yards. It was a new American record – 1:49 1/5.

That was the last of any really serious competition. Man o' War cantered to an easy win in the Miller Stakes at Saratoga, and then won the Travers Stakes in 2:01 4/5 after running John P. Grier into the ground in the first six furlongs in 1:10, the mile in 1:35 3/5. He equalled the track record. The Lawrence Realisation at 1⅝ miles was no contest. Man o' War won by a quarter mile from Hoodwink in 2:40 4/5, a new American record, although Man o' War was cantering at the finish. The weight-for-age Jockey Club Stakes at 1½ miles was another two-horse race. Man o' War set another new American time record of 2:28 4/5 with Damask, the other starter, beaten fifteen lengths. The 1 1/16-mile Potomac Handicap, at Havre de Grace, was Man o' War's next start. He carried 9 st 12 lb, gave 30 lb to Wildair, and beat him a length and a half in 1:44 4/5 a new track record.

Man o' War's final race was a special match race at Kenilworth Park in Canada, with Sir Barton, one of the handicap stars of the year. It was not a good race, just a great spectacle. Man o' War ran in front all the way, won by seven lengths in 2:03, a new track record. The record he broke was 2:09 2/5. Man o' War won $75,000 plus a $5,000 Gold Cup. A special $50,000 race against Exterminator was declined, and so was an offer to race in England.

Man o' War was shipped back to Glen Riddle Farm, Berlin, Maryland, and then to Miss Elizabeth Daingerfield's Hinata Farm, Lexington, for his first stud season in 1921. In May of 1922 Man o' War moved to his owner's newly-acquired Faraway Farm, near Lexington, which was his home until his death in 1947.

At the time of Man o' War's death he had been retired from the stud for four years. A heart attack in 1943 decided Mr Riddle that his great horse would not be bred to any more mares. Therefore at the time of Man o' War's death practically his entire stud career can be accounted for. In twenty-two seasons he had sired 386 foals, 220 winners of $3,382,652. Only one year did he lead the American sire list; on twelve other occasions he was among the leading twenty. This is not the record of a failure, nor is it a record of an outstandingly brilliant sire, such as St Simon, Lexington, Hyperion, and others like Foxbridge in New Zealand.

Man o' War was handicapped at the start of his stud career. Mr Riddle had to go out and buy mares, a difficult feat in the early 'twenties when racing was expanding in America. It was easier to get mares in Europe. With the help of the late William Allison, the English writer and pedigree expert, a group of mares was quickly assembled. Those purchased by Mr Allison contributed greatly to the early successes of Man o' War.

One of these mares – *Lady Comfey, by Roi Hérode – was the dam of Man o' War's first outstanding horse, American Flag, from the first crop. American Flag won the Belmont, Dwyer, and Withers Stakes in 1924. The second crop left no question as to Man o' War's success; included were Crusader (best three-year-old of 1925, won $203,261), Mars (winner of $128,786), and the good stakes-winning filly, Edith Cavell. Best of the third crop was Scapa Flow, who died after eighteen starts and won $93,955. Next came Bateau, one of the outstanding race mares of her time, and Genie, winner of $84,190. Man o' War's first Kentucky Derby winner was in his fifth crop – Clyde Van Dusen, winner of $122,452.

His first five crops constituted his 'banner' years in the stud. Thereafter his best produce were scattered, some years failing to register anything outstanding. In 1927 came Battleship, winner of the Grand National at Aintree. In 1934 War Admiral was foaled; he became the outstanding three-year-old of his year, perhaps Man o' War's best son. War Relic was foaled in 1938. There were others that were good, but not outstanding.

As has been stated before Man o' War was never bred to more than twenty-five mares in any one season. Very few outside mares were accepted. In Man o' War's last seven years of his stud life, he was bred to only a dozen mares which had previously distinguished themselves either on the race tracks or in the stud.

War Admiral appears to be Man o' War's son with the best chance of carrying on this famous American male line. He led the American sire list in 1945 with three crops to race; has been prominent ever since. None of the others has been of top rank.

His daughters have been outstandingly successful in the stud. Despite their few numbers, they have placed Man o' War consistently near the top of the broodmare sire list for the past fourteen years. He has been second since 1942. Man o' War produced only 198 fillies, while among those which have foals old enough to race several years, about a third have produced stakes' winners on the flat. His daughters have produced such performers as Pavot, Vagrancy (dam of Black Tarquin), Level Best, Dauber, High Fleet, Firethorn, Cravat, Thumbs Up, Snow Goose, Equestrian (sire of Stymie, world's leading money-winner) and others.

Man o' War was described by his groom, Will Harbut, as the 'mostest horse'. It is a fitting epitaph!   BBR–1947

Roamer

Roamer was one of the first thoroughbreds to gather the acclaim of American racing fans once the blackout on racing had been lifted in New York in 1913. A foal of 1911, this venerable gelding had a great fondness for Saratoga and in his seventh year set a new American record for the mile from a running start. It was the last such record for a popularly run distance established in a race against time. All subsequent marks were made in actual competition. Roamer was the result of a mating between a blind mare and the 'teaser' for Star Shoot, who was not mated with Roamer's dam as he also was blind. What Roamer's trainer and rider had to say about him in the BBR of 1918 makes the memory of that grand old warrior all the fonder.

EARLY IN THE autumn Roamer was retired for the season, and an announcement was made that in all probability Mr Andrew Miller would pension him off without requiring further service. The horse has well earned a luxurious ease for the rest of his life. From first to last he has run in 91 races, won 38, finished second 23 times, and third eight times, leaving a balance of 22 races in which he was out of the money. The total value of the stakes he captured is £19,354. As recorded in the last number of the *Review*, Roamer, at Saratoga in August, covered a mile, with a flying start, in 1 min 34 4-5 secs and so established a new American record for that distance.

Roamer is a seven-year-old bay gelding by Knight Errant out of Rose Tree, by Bona Vista. In Vol. VI of the *Review* we related the circumstances under which Rose Tree came to be mated with Knight Errant, a sire deemed of little account. The mare was blind, and it was, in consequence, desired to keep her at home. Colonel E. F. Clay, her owner, therefore put her to Knight Errant, the only horse he had available, and Roamer was the result of this chance alliance. Mr Miller bought Roamer privately for £700, and the second time the horse carried Mr Miller's colours he won the Saratoga Special. It is said that Roamer has made more track records than any other horse that has raced in America. Here is what his trainer, Goldsborough, had to say about him in a talk with a representative of *Daily Racing Form*:

'He can't be handled like an ordinary horse. You must set him down – flatten him out – or he isn't worth a quarter. In his preparation for his Saratoga campaign this year he ran three times in two weeks at Empire City. Before going to Saratoga he got a mile and a quarter in 2.06½. The day after he arrived there I worked him in the mud a mile and a quarter in 2.09. He then went out and won the Saratoga Handicap. That amount of work would have cooked any ordinary horse, but it only put Roamer on edge and he got it hot and heavy up to two days before he lowered the mile record. He has never weighed over 1,000 lbs and as a younger horse I had the greatest difficulty getting him to eat six or seven quarts of oats a day. He was given this at night and you never saw a poorer hay eater. He wouldn't eat a mash until recently, and I don't know where he got his vitality. His action is what makes him great. I never expect to see another like him.

'The old fellow is unlike any other horse I ever rode. When he was younger he wanted to dive into his bit and stand his opponents on their heads the first half mile. Now, as he grows older, I have to ride him nearly all the way. He likes a fast hard track and on that kind of footing you would think you were in a rocking chair. When the track is soft or cuppy he shortens his stride and is a choppy mount. He is as smart as they come, but is as honest as the day is long. He will give up to the last ounce of speed he has on tap and it was for this reason I begged Mr Miller to have no pacemaker at Saratoga when he beat the mile record.'

BBR-1918

A Classic Speech

*When Commander John Kenneth Leveson Ross's Sir Barton, described
at the time by one expert as 'the biggest little horse ever seen', captured
the 1919 Kentucky Derby en route to becoming the first winner of the
American Triple Crown, the* BBR *of that year felt that its coverage of
the American classic should include the post-race speech of Kentucky's
Governor Stanley. In its own way, it is a classic, too.*

BEFORE LEAVING the Kentucky Derby we cannot forbear to reproduce
a report of the speech which Governor Stanley addressed in public to
Commander Ross immediately after the race. As an example of flowery
diction it is very precious. The Governor spoke as follows:

'It is peculiarly fitting that the lovers of this kingly sport should make this
commonwealth their mecca. Courage, grit, a fine and aspiring spirit that does
not brook defeat, are the common heritage of the Kentuckian and his horse. The
martial state reviews with commendable pride those old and illustrious families
who in Virginia and in Kentucky have produced statesmen, sages and heroes, but
the scion of the proudest race on the continent must doff his hat before the shining
victor in this contest. Antedating the Crescent and Cross, back in the twilight of
time when the ancestors of Charlemagne were pirates and forebears of the Cæsars
dwelt in caves, beyond them all he traces his ancestry without a break to the swift
and docile companion of the sheik in his tent. The horse is the only animal worthy
to share the perils and glories of heroes. Alexander and Bucephalus, Lee and
Traveler, share a common immortality, and the Corsican conqueror comes down
to us as "the man on horseback". Civilisation but yesterday was saved by the
courage of the hero and the endurance of his horse. An army without its cavalry is
lacking in inspiration as if its banners were furled and its music were silenced. The
charger's ancestor is here. These swift and exquisite creatures, miracles of
endurance and grace and strength, in the hour of peril are as essential to the
nation's security and its honour as fleet or fortress of frowning guns. I felicitate you
upon a prize nobly won. Second only to the warrior's laurels is the coveted crown
of the winner of a Kentucky Derby.'

A few days after making the foregoing oration Mr Stanley relinquished
the office of Governor in order to represent Kentucky in the Senate at
Washington.   BBR–1919

The Match Between Zev and Papyrus

*The Turf world was all agog in 1923 because of the Match Race
which had been arranged between the Epsom Derby winner Papyrus
and the Kentucky Derby winner Zev. An estimated 60,000 fans
assembled at Belmont Park for this event which 'will live in Turf*

history'. Mr Sydney Galtrey (Hotspur), Turf writer for London's Daily Telegraph, *crossed the Atlantic to cover 'the greatest venture of its kind' and the* BBR *of 1923 picked up his 'graphic narrative'.*

'Papyrus, immensely admired, looked, as he always does, a gentleman of quality, though there was not the slightest doubt that he was not a perfectly-trained horse as we understand the term in England. The crowd, however, was most generous in cheering him wherever he went, and it was beyond question that his cause had enlisted extraordinary sympathy.

'Our horse was cool, even stolid. It would have been better had he been more on his toes. Zev could have spared him some of his exuberance. . . . Nothing could have been sharper in the way of contrasts than the sight presented by the two combatants. Papyrus quiet and subdued almost to the point of indifference; Zev excited and immensely highly-strung. Yet Zev looked the most efficient. If ever a horse was roused to the last point of nervous energy then he was. He was sweating, too, about the middle piece and flanks and, indeed, his appearance was almost that of a distraught horse. When his jockey mounted him he could only prance, every nerve seeming to be desperately on edge. . . . Once on the track, Zev was far too crazy to walk. He seemed over-anxious to get on with the dance, while Papyrus . . . was probably too much unconcerned. When he got upon the mud he sank into it up to his fetlocks, and the boy leading him slithered about to his own considerable astonishment. The surface looked like nothing so much as a thick layer of French mustard, both as regards colour and greasiness. . . .

'The starter did not detain them. If anything, he gave an advantage to Papyrus, for when the break took place Papyrus and Donoghue were ready, whilse Zev was slightly caught unawares. Papyrus was drawn on the outside, but, because of what happened, had he chosen, could have gone right into the lead next the rails. But he deliberately refused to accept what the gods had sent him. Finding himself in front, Donoghue checked his horse. In a flash Zev had gone past to the inside position. It happened so quickly that Donoghue had no chance to dally. From easing he instantly passed to urging, and so they settled down.

'It had been expected that Zev would show, beginning speed as to draw right away, and when he did not one felt that if Papyrus could so live with his rival at the outset he would come up to the highest expectations.

'So they ran round the first two turns and began the length of the back stretch. Papyrus was going all right close to the other's quarters. Donoghue thereby revealed his tactics, which were to wait, and then go on to win, because of the supposed better stamina and proved speed of Papyrus. He was destined, however, to learn something, and with something of a shock, too. Earlier than might have been expected, with five or six furlongs to go, including two more turns, Sande gave Zev his head. It was just a perceptible movement, but not so Zev's response. That was given whole-heartedly, and so in a stride or two Donoghue found himself two lengths behind. Then he too called upon the English Derby winner.

'Just for a stride or two Papyrus answered, but feebly, to the point of fading right away. And as he did so he seemed to be lost in the going. Could this be the horse we had seen win the Derby at Epsom? It was indeed hard to believe so, and I imagine that many Americans looking on would be given at that moment a dreadful idea of the requirements demanded of an English Derby winner.

'The adventure of Papyrus to America collapsed at that moment with the completeness of a pierced bubble. He was not destined even to make a fight of it. Donoghue urged him with hand and heel, but the gap began to widen. Then he drew his whip which he had to use, though it was a case of flogging a beaten horse. Zev had Papyrus licked as they turned into the home stretch, and with our horse tiring to nothing, Zev was left to win by five lengths, with Donoghue easing up his horse. He surrendered before the winning post was reached, which made the win of the American horse appear all the more spectacular and complete.

'Zev did not really look like one that had been racing at Newmarket, but as for Papyrus and his jockey – well, they gave one the idea that they had been in a mud bath. The horse had mud in his eyes, ears, nostrils and mouth. He was smothered in it. He was a lifeless, exhausted mud-larker. Zev, however, was still full of pep after weighing in, and one cannot doubt that he was a much better horse on this day, and in such weird conditions.'

Papyrus.

In a word, the splendidly-staged drama degenerated into a paltry farce. That overnight deluge may have been a contributor to the fiasco, but it was not wholly responsible. The mud had not begun to play its part when the critics noted the stolidity, listlessness and indifference of Papyrus. That was his state before he stepped into the quagmire. What was the cause? Why was there 'not the slightest doubt that he was not a perfectly-trained horse?' The change of climate had begun to affect him, as most of us knew it was bound to do. 'He was not the same horse I had ridden in England,' said Donoghue immediately after the race, and the statement gives us the whole thing in a nutshell.

From private sources in America we received many comments on the Match. Every correspondent, like every writer for the Press, attributed the defeat of Papyrus to the way he was shod. 'I backed Papyrus a little, but against my own judgment,' writes one of our friends, 'because I had been told that he was shod smooth. The fact is he did not run well enough to beat a selling plater. Indeed, a selling plater ran the following race faster than Zev did. I had a firm opinion that Zev was not at his best, and I think the race bore that out. He is, however, very much helped by mud, and there is no doubt that on the day and track he was better than Papyrus.'

Another correspondent, who holds a responsible position on the American Turf, writes: 'We were all disappointed with Papyrus's race. I doubt if anyone believes that it represented any approach of his real form, for two days before the race he did a trial in such style that made him favourite in the betting taken in conjunction with Zev's sudden skin trouble. Had Papyrus been shod with 'clips' he would, no doubt, have performed differently, but shod as he was he had no footing. . . . In appearance, as well as in manners, he was a gentleman, and he reminded me of Leamington, only not so large and lighter-waisted. Basil Jarvis made friends wherever he went, and all regret that his horse was not shod as Zev was. Papyrus's race was too bad to be true.'

Much has been made of the good form shown by Papyrus in his gallop two days before the race, and there is a tendency to assume that had the track remained dry he would have reproduced that form in the race. Perhaps he would, but perhaps not. We have often heard of races being left on the training ground. Papyrus may have lost his there. If there was debilitation due to the change of climate the force he expended in the fast training gallop would, one supposes, considerably lower his vitality.

One of the correspondents quoted just now refers in his letter to having seen Chacolet (a mare by St Amant out of Martial Note, by Carbine) win the Kentucky Special at Latonia. 'She has,' he states, 'improved into a real good distance mare, and in my opinion could win a pretty fair race anywhere in the world. I have made a careful study of the matter, and believe that *it takes two years to get a mare from England thoroughly acclimatised.*' Papyrus had been at Belmont Park three weeks when he met with his sad discomfiture.

We are reluctant to enlarge further on this Papyrus–Zev affair. So much space has been devoted to it because it is the greatest venture of its kind that has ever been organised. That it will live in Turf history is beyond question; that it is the forerunner of other similar enterprises is open to doubt.   BBR–1923

Pharos and Epinard

Beyond question the best racehorses make the best sires. However, in the course of breeding history there have been some notable exceptions and, perhaps, Pharos qualifies as being among the most notable. Not that he was an ordinary performer; he won a Coronation Cup, he was second to Papyrus in the Derby, among other quality efforts, but, using the 1923 Cambridgeshire as a measure, Pharos, the most influential son of Phalaris and the sire of Nearco and his living dynasty, was, according to the BBR, *'only a moderate colt'.*

The BBR *commented that the nine-furlong Cambridgeshire 'was undoubtedly* the *handicap of the year. It will be forever known as "Epinard's Cambridgeshire", although he was beaten a neck by Lord Coventry's filly Verdict.'*

Epinard, carrying 9 st 2 lb (128 lb), was giving Verdict, also a three-year-old, 18 lb and no less than 37 lb to the three-year-old Dumas, who was third. Pharos was in fourth position while in receipt of 9 lb from Epinard. Said the BBR:

Our insular pride is somewhat humbled when we reflect that though getting 9 lb from Epinard, Pharos was only fourth. With the French horse out of the way, he would have been third, and we should have praised him for a good show. As it was, he had to be looked upon as being, after all, only a moderate colt, for a horse that is a stone (14 lb) behind one of his own age cannot be anything but moderate.

Lord Derby, his owner and breeder, must have had a prescient feeling about Pharos because 'during that summer (he) received, but refused to entertain, the offer of a substantial sum for Pharos, made on behalf of the Australian breeder Mr Sol Green.

Imagine no Nearco, no Nearctic, no Northern Dancer, no Nasrullah, no Royal Charger, no Turn-to, no Hail to Reason, no Never Bend, no Mill Reef, no Riverman – and the list rolls on. No, it is beyond imagination!

Michael Beary, who rode Verdict, embossed the magnificence of Epinard's performance in his post-race quotes:

> 'He set us a terrific pace. So fast was he going that I was convinced, great horse though I knew him to be, that he could not keep it up and was sure to crack. I expected this to happen by the time we reached the Bushes at the latest. Without driving Verdict too hard, I kept her within striking distance and gradually went to him. To my surprise Epinard was still going at the same tremendous pace after we had reached and passed the Bushes. No other horse so weighted could have lived so long. Nevertheless I was not frightened, for I knew that no three-year-old could take the hill at Epinard's pace with so much weight up. Though I had been riding Verdict hard from the Bushes, I had scarcely gained any ground when we reached the Dip. Then I called on the mare for a still greater effort. She gave it. We drew up to Epinard's quarters, for he had come over to the Stand side. Then for a few strides we gained inches only. It was the last twenty yards that beat Epinard.'

Epinard's superiority over Pharos on the racetrack did not reflect itself in the breeding shed. Epinard sired a number of quality winners, including Rodosto, best in both the French and English Two Thousand Guineas, as well as Epithet, a winner of the Hopeful Stakes in the States.

So, here is another example where the 'form' in breeding can be as 'formless' as in racing itself. Which is, after all, quite a good thing or all the fresh eggs would be in the same baskets.

Pharos

The line-founding Phalaris was a brilliant performer, surely the best of his era at distances under a mile while carrying incredible burdens. His most influential son, Pharos, sire of Nearco, won fourteen races and was classic-placed but did not attain a champion's mantle until age four when his victories included the Champion Stakes. Even then his crown was restricted, as reported in the BBR *of 1924.*

TWO WEEKS LATER the result of the race for the Champion Stakes again raised the question of the relative merits of the four- and three-year-olds. This contest over ten straight furlongs was won by Pharos, who finished an 'easy' length and a half in front of Parth. A similar distance away, Salmon-Trout was third. Verdict and Polyphontes, the only other runners, were fourth and fifth. There could be no excuse this time that Polyphontes was not well suited. His complete failure can only be accounted for by the theory that he had gone stale on his long work for the St Leger and the Jockey Club Stakes. As for Salmon-Trout, the ten-furlong course was of no use to him. By his brilliant victory in the Duke of York Handicap at Kempton Park three days previously, Pharos became an automatic favourite for the Champion Stakes, and it was a moral certainty that he would win. If the distance had been extended to twelve furlongs there would have been no such confidence in his ability to defeat his opponents. Many would have esteemed the chance of Parth more highly. If, however, the contest had been decided over the last mile and threequarters of the Cesarewitch course, we may perhaps assume that both Pharos and Parth would have gone down before Salmon-Trout. That Pharos is the best horse of his time over ten furlongs cannot, surely, be disputed; but that admission does not prove that four-year-olds are better than three-year-olds. Titans, among the latter will, perchance, be discovered next season.

Prince Rose's Racing Record

Superior sires are not expected to be found in Belgium. Prince Rose was an exception. As the following item in the BBR *of 1931 explains, he was the best of his age in that country at both two and three. Once at stud he sired three outstanding runners and sires in Princequillo, Prince Bio and Prince Chevalier – certainly enough to fortify the Persimmon branch of the St Simon male line for generations to come.*

DR H. COPPEZ'S Prince Rose, a bay colt, by Rose Prince (by Prince Palatine) out of Indolence, by Gay Crusader, was the best two-year-old in Belgium in 1930, when he won four races and 131,550 francs. He was the best three-year-old of the past season, and won 1,115,000 francs in his unbeaten seven starts in that country. His wins included the Grand Prix de Bruxelles, the Grand Prix d'Ostende, and the Grand International d'Ostende. In the latter race he met Amfortas and the brilliant French filly Pearl Cap, and defeated the latter by a length. In October Prince Rose was sent to compete in the Prix de l'Arc de Triomphe, and there met with defeat at the hands of Pearl Rose and Amfortas, finishing a length and a half and a length behind these two. Prince Rose was bred by the late Lord Durham, and sold as a foal at the Newmarket December Sales in 1928 for 260 guineas.

Swynford as a Racehorse

When, in 1923, Swynford, a classic-winning son of John o' Gaunt from the Oaks victress, Canterbury Pilgrim, by Tristan, secured his first and what was to be his only sire championship, the BBR *of that year was considerate enough to reprint an article by his trainer, Mr George Lambton, on Swynford's career as a racehorse, which had appeared in the* Weekly Dispatch *the previous summer. Considering Swynford's profound impact on the breed, particularly through his son, Blandford, this very personal account brings an intimate freshness to a great name now found only in the deeper recesses of important pedigrees.*

IN ONE of his interesting articles published last summer in the *Weekly Dispatch*, Mr George Lambton, who trains for Lord Derby, told the story of Swynford as a racehorse. He states that as a yearling he was a great, plain, rather flat-sided colt, but he had a big, lean, game head, good legs and feet, and, when he chose to extend himself, he was a fine galloper. When he went into training he was a very ugly customer, 'all legs and wings'. However, when the breaking tackle was put on he soon showed that he was as strong as a bull, full of courage, and very good-tempered. He was given plenty of time to develop, and it was not until July of his two-year-old days that he had his first strong gallop.

Swynford's first race was the Exeter Stakes at Newmarket. He completely mastered his jockey, Maher, and ran himself to a standstill before he had gone five furlongs. He then threw out the worst through-pin Mr Lambton ever saw, and did not run again that year.

Coming to his three-year-old career, Swynford was, says his trainer, a good doer in his stable, quiet and sensible out of it, and although he would pull very hard when alongside another horse, he would follow on at any pace desired. He made no show in the Derby, but there was a good reason, because he was struck into and the skin was taken off the back of his leg from the hock to the fetlock joint. It was the nearest thing in the world he was not ruined for life. However, he was soon all right again. At Ascot he was expected to win the St James's Palace Stakes, but finished a bad third after rolling all over the course, but on the Friday he cleverly won the Hardwicke Stakes when receiving a lot of weight. By that time Mr Lambton's confidence in Swynford was much shaken.

Then came the Liverpool Summer Cup, and at last the son of John o' Gaunt did what was expected, for he won, pulling up, by many lengths. His next race was the St Leger. In his preparation for that event he went better with every gallop, and wore out nearly all the horses in the stable.

Swynford.

But he was not a very 'taking' goer to watch, for he had an enormous stride and went very wide behind. A man who was told by Mr Lambton to back Swynford for the St Leger asked another trainer at Newmarket if he thought the colt had a chance of beating Lemberg. 'Yes,' was the reply, 'he has a chance – about the same as my hack would have.' At Doncaster Mr Lambton told Maher, who was riding Lemberg, that Swynford would probably beat him. 'No doubt,' said Danny, 'yours is a good horse, but he is not in the same class as Lemberg.'

Mr Lambton had an idea that Lemberg was not a great stayer, so he told Frank Wootton, who was on Swynford, to make the pace as hot as he could from the start. Coming to the Red House, Lemberg moved up to Swynford and got to the latter's quarters, but Swynford went away again.

Maher, continues Mr Lambton, was following dead in Swynford's track. Although he was sitting still, so well did I know Danny's riding that I was certain his horse was tiring, and I said to Bob Vyner, who was beside me in the stand: 'I've got him; we shall win!' Frank Wootton was but a boy at the time, riding 7 st 4 lb, and by this time he was a passenger on Swynford, who was hanging away from the rails, where the Yorkshire crowd were shouting and waving their racecards according to their usual custom. There was plenty of room for Lemberg to come up on the inside had he been good enough, but he was not – his bolt was shot. As it was, Bronzino, a horse of Mr Jimmy Rothschild's, came with a tremendous rush in the last 100 yards, nearly catching my horse on the post, but the head was the right way. You can see from the picture of the finish that the jockey was far more beat than the horse, but it was a marvellous performance for a boy of that weight to ride such a big, heavy horse at all. His father, Dick Wootton, told me that the night after the race Frank kept talking in his sleep and crying out: 'I won't let you up, Danny; you shan't get up.' My description of this race I know entirely differs from what was the general opinion. This was that Maher rode a chocking race and ought to have won.

The following day Maher told Mr Lambton that Lemberg would never beat Swynford in any race of the St Leger distance run at the pace the St Leger was. In describing the race to him Maher said: 'When I first went up to Swynford I did so easily but he kept going away from me again, and each time I had to ask my horse to go after him the response was weaker, and two furlongs from home I knew that unless an accident happened he had me beat.'

The performances of the two horses the following year bore out, Mr Lambton claims, Maher's contention. In a slow-run race for the Coronation Cup at Epsom, Lemberg beat Swynford three-parts of a length. Frank Wootton for the first, and last, time waited with Swynford instead of letting him stride along, and that, in Mr Lambton's opinion, lost him the race. They afterwards met in the Prince of Wales's Stakes at Newmarket and the Eclipse Stakes at Sandown, when Swynford made all the running and won easily.

With all due deference to Mr Lambton, and to Danny Maher, dead and gone, we feel bound to state that we cannot agree with his story of the St Leger. We have a very vivid recollection of the finish of the race as seen from the Press Stand right up over the winning post. Maher got hopelessly bunched in close behind the leaders while traversing the last furlong. He had waited too long for an opening on the rails. When, as Mr Lambton says, Swynford swerved away from them, Lemberg instantly made for the gap, but before he quite got there Swynford went back again, and Maher had to snatch Lemberg up to avoid a collision. No other chance presented itself. The impression most of us obtained was that, with a clear run, Lemberg would have won the race, because the alacrity with which he made for the momentary opening indicated that he was anything but an exhausted horse.

While he was being trained for the Jockey Club Stakes as a four-year-old, Swynford, while doing a half-speed gallop, 'smashed his fetlock joint to atoms'. Fortunately he was a good patient, and so was saved for the stud. And here we have him at the head of the list of stallions.

The Unbeaten Tiffin

There have been few fillies in English Turf history more beloved than Tiffin, a foal of 1926 by Tetratema from Dawn-wind, by Sunstar. Unbeaten in eight starts at two and three when forced to retire due to an injury of her own folly, Tiffin, while not having done enough to merit comparison with the likes of Pretty Polly, Sceptre and La Fleche, 'was certainly a marvel in her own particular line,' according to the BBR of 1929. The following review of her high-gear career, highlighted by her scant victory over the older Royal Minstrel, deserves to survive in time.

AS A two-year-old Tiffin was an unbeaten winner of five races. Her brilliance was revealed the first time she ran, for in the contest for the Wilbraham Stakes at Newmarket in the spring, she gained an eight lengths' victory over twenty-eight opponents. That the amazing form she produced that day was merely a reproduction of the form she had been showing on the Beckhampton training ground may be inferred from the fact that, huge though the field was, she started a strong favourite at 5 to 2. We did not see Tiffin again until the latter part of July, when, receiving 7 lb, she easily beat Mr Jinks (the favourite) in the National Breeders' Produce Stakes at Sandown Park. There and then the daughter of Tetratema was acclaimed the best of her age, and she confirmed her right to be so regarded by winning the Ham Stakes at Goodwood, the Convivial Plate at York, and the Cheveley Park Stakes at Newmarket. All these victories were gained easily or comfortably, and when the Two-year-old Free Handicap made its appearance she was placed at the top.

Her first outing this year was in the Fern Hill Stakes at Ascot, a five-furlong race. When stripped she was seen to have gained height during the winter, but to have retained her refined lines and excellent quality. No trace of her recent illness, which had so nearly proved fatal, was visible. She had ten opponents, but none of them gave her the slightest trouble, and at the finish she was two lengths ahead of the Aga Khan's colt Le Phare, who was placed second. Le Phare had recently won two races, and was thought to have a good chance of beating Tiffin, as the betting return shows, odds of 7 to 4 being laid against the filly and 11 to 4 against Le Phare.

Then came the race for the July Cup at Newmarket. This is run over the six-furlong Exeter Course. Except for a few yards near the winning post, the final furlong is a sharp decline. There were only three runners, Le Phare being one. He was of no account on this occasion, attention being concentrated on the other two, Tiffin and Royal Minstrel, who, to all intents and purposes, were engaged in a match. The present generation has seen few contests of this character invested with greater interest and a keener sporting spirit. The value of the prize was only £295, so it is hardly necessary to say that the mercenary motive was entirely eliminated. By the victories he had gained in the Victoria Cup (seven furlongs) at Hurst Park, and the Cork and Orrery Stakes (six furlongs) at Ascot, the four-year-old Royal Minstrel had shown that he was endowed with exceptional speed, and it appeared to everybody that, at weight-for-age, he and Tiffin were well matched. Tiffin was backed at

Tiffin.

even money, while odds of 11 to 10 were laid against Royal Minstrel. Offers of 25 to 1 against Le Phare were practically ignored. Both Tiffin and Royal Minstrel had incurred a 12 lb penalty; the filly received the usual 3 lb sex allowance. Royal Minstrel, therefore, carried 10 st 3 lb and Tiffin 9 st 2 lb.

When the barrier went up Tiffin was off like a flash, and for half a mile led Royal Minstrel by about a length. Then the latter drew closer, and at the top of the slope, a furlong from home, got his neck in front of the filly. It now looked good odds on the colt, and his success seemed absolutely assured until just before he reached the bottom of the hill. He then checked himself in order to change legs. This procedure brought about his downfall, for it enabled Tiffin to get her head in front again. Royal Minstrel had barely recovered his balance when he reached the winning post, beaten the shortest of short heads. Many hundreds of people had left the stands and gathered in the hollow to see this finish. There was tremendous excitement while the colt and filly charged down the slope, and an almost painfully tense feeling during the few moments the crowd awaited the judge's decision. There would have been no surprise or quibbling if the verdict had been a dead heat. When Tiffin's number was displayed there was a mighty shout. The result was undoubtedly in accordance with the desires of the majority, but we may be sure there would also have been a storm of cheers for Royal Minstrel if he had won. Verily it was a thrilling business. Childs, who rode Royal Minstrel, is convinced that his horse would have won if the final furlong had been the one approaching the further winning post, for that is a rising gradient. The colt still has the excessively high action in front which he displayed last year. When coming downhill he begins to feel for the ground, and that, it is assumed, is why he changed his legs near the end of his encounter with Tiffin. We need only add that the race for the July Cup was run in 1 min 12$\frac{1}{5}$ sec, believed to be the fastest time in which the Exeter Course has ever been covered.

At Goodwood, a month later, Tiffin enlarged her sequence of successes to eight by winning the King George Stakes, another six-furlong race, in a canter by three lengths from Lord Derby's filly Pladda, who was receiving 9 lb. Third, another four lengths back, was Mr J. B. Joel's five-year-old gelding Tag End. It was now announced that Tiffin's next race would be that for the Nunthorpe Stakes (five furlongs) at York. Royal Minstrel also was pointed for that event, so there was the pleasurable prospect of a 'return match'. Unfortunately, an accident to Tiffin not only prevented her going to York, but brought her racing career to an abrupt close. In the last volume of the *Review* reference was made to the filly's playful, but alarming, habit of suddenly jerking her rider out of the saddle when out at exercise. One morning last August she performed this trick once more. Having secured her freedom she scampered away and, when crossing a road, slipped and badly damaged a knee. The mischief was of such a character that it seemed futile to contemplate the possibility of preparing her for another race, so she was turned out of training and sent to Lord Ellesmere's stud. Her achievements on the Turf cannot, of course, stand comparison with those of mares like Sceptre, Pretty Polly and La Flèche, but in her own particular line she was certainly a marvel. The eight races she won were worth £16,516.

BBR–1929

Portrait of Diolite

Diolite, winner of the Two Thousand Guineas of 1930, sold as a yearling for 480 guineas – 'not since Col Eustace Loder gave Sir Tatton Sykes 300 guineas for Spearmint in 1904 has a winner of one of our classic races been sold under the hammer for a figure so contemptuous' – was described as follows by George Lambton in an article for the Sunday Express *and reprinted in the* Review.

'In appearance he does not in the slightest degree resemble his sire, Diophon. Neither is he built on the same lines as his famous great-grandsire, Isinglass, but he has apparently inherited one valuable trait from that wonderful horse – a happy temperament which only wakes up to brilliance when on a racecourse.

'This was also a characteristic of his grandsire, Rock Sand, to whom in some respects Diolite perhaps bears most resemblance. A dark brown horse, standing about 16 hands, he is slightly on the leg, and narrow behind, a characteristic of many a good stayer. He has plenty of length underneath him, yet with a short back, not one atom of extra lumber to carry, and clean legs of good quality.

'Still there is nothing grand about him, and in his clothes you might easily pass him by without special notice; but, like many other good horses, when he is stripped and with a jockey on his back, he looks a real racing machine. In movement, he is all that could be desired, but again without any fireworks.'

That delightful word-picture concerns one of the first English classic winners to be exported to Japan. This happened in 1935, five years after his Two Thousand Guineas triumph. Diolite became a very significant sire in Japan where racing, then, as now, is religiously protective of homebreds and thus diminishes the opportunities of such horses to become permanently influential internationally in improving the breed.

But, during his stay in Japan, Diolite sired the Nippon and St Leger winner St Lite and the Emperor's Cup winner Hirosukura, while his daughters produced the Derby winners Bostonian and Hakuchikara, the Oaks heroine O-hayabusa as well as the Emperor's Cup winners Hakuryo, Kuripuro, Kurihide and Takamagahara.

Derby winner Hakuchikara, also winner of an Emperor's Cup, has probably the most unique distinction in the annals of Japanese breeding.

Without a rival in his own country, Hakuchikara, produced by Diolite's daughter Noborishiro, was sent to California in 1958 for comparison purposes. On February 23rd 1959 at Santa Anita Park he accounted for the major fixture, the Washington's Birthday Handicap at $1\frac{1}{2}$ miles over soft turf. He won! This shocker was all the more shocking as Round Table, 1958's Horse of the Year and destined to be the world's leading money winner for many years, was in the beaten field, finishing last of sixteen when suffering one of the few injuries of his long and fabulous career of forty-three victories in sixty-six starts.

Thus, Diolite became the maternal grandsire of the first and still the only Japanese-bred horse to capture a major stakes race in North America (or Europe for that matter!).

The 1930 Derby Won by Blenheim

For many reasons, best left told in the following account by the BBR, the Epsom Derby of 1930 was one of the most memorable runnings of this historic race. The last two furlongs provided the material and the BBR's description of what took place did that material absolute justice.

BUT THIS enthralling contest had not even yet reached its climax. While attention had been concentrated on the short but sharp tussle between Iliad and Diolite, the Aga Khan's second string, Blenheim, almost unobserved, had been making a long, sustained run well away from the rails. By the time Iliad had gained his seemingly decisive lead, Blenheim had become noticeable, but, as he was still behind Diolite, there was scarcely a likelihood that he would deprive the favourite of second place, much less trouble Iliad. This complacent view of the situation was suddenly shattered. Gathering momentum with every stride, Blenheim collared and beat Diolite, and then, travelling faster, ever faster, also collared and beat Iliad. With still a few strides to go, this apparition had won the Derby. Blenheim finished a length in front of Iliad, who had Diolite, third, two lengths behind him. Less than a length away, Silver

Flare came in fourth, with Trews and Seer near at hand, and, after a gap, followed Noble Star and Ballyferis.

The result was astounding. There were many palpitating hearts when all was over. The race home from Tattenham Corner had produced a succession of thrills: the first when Rustom Pasha collapsed, the second when Iliad overcame Diolite, and the greatest of all when Blenheim swooped down on Mr Tattersall's colt to snatch the verdict almost on the post. We can recall no Derby that provided a finish similar to this one. Everybody became almost blind with excitement. For quite an appreciable time there was, as the saying goes, a silence that could be felt. It was not broken until the smiling owner of the winner appeared on the course, walking along to meet Blenheim and lead him back to the weighing-room door. The Aga Khan, bare headed, had watched the race from the little stand adjoining the winning post on the far side of the course, a primitive structure which serves as a reminder of the days, not so long ago, when all the fitments at Epsom looked centuries old. From his viewpoint he could see nothing of the race until the leaders came round Tattenham Corner into the straight. Then, if his hands were steady enough to focus his binoculars on the rapidly approaching colours, he would have observed that his own were in the van – his own without the distinguishing cap, so that the bearer was Rustom Pasha. His happiest dream was at last to come true. He was surely about to win a Derby with a horse bred by himself. Alas, it was a mirage. The picture vanished. Rustom Pasha was not there at all – only Diolite and Iliad, with some phantoms behind them. Perhaps the Aga Khan was wondering how many more years he would have to wait before he really did win the Derby, when Blenheim came from the back of beyond to revive his shattered hopes. The emotions he experienced while the next few seconds were ticked off cannot easily be imagined. They must have been almost overwhelming in their intensity. No mirage this time! A vivid living scene, with his own horse the outstanding figure. 'It seems like a dream,' he exclaimed, when friends gathered round to offer congratulations. 'I can hardly believe it to be true, and I do not suppose I shall do so until I actually see it in print. It is impossible to say how glad I am to have won the greatest race in the world.'

If the crowd forgot to cheer when Blenheim passed the winning post, there was a striking demonstration of enthusiasm when the Aga Khan, hat in hand, and laughing like a happy schoolboy, led the colt through a lane of humanity to the unsaddling enclosure, whence he was presently summoned to the presence of the King and Queen. In the meantime there were condolences distributed in appropriate quarters. Mr

Tattersall was entitled to a liberal share, and received it. His experience was most vexatious. It may be the idea still prevails that he would have been agreeably surprised if Iliad had won. That is not the case. The splendid performance of his colt did not surprise him at all. The only horse he feared was Diolite, and the fear was qualified by the suspicion that the favourite might not stay on to the end. When, therefore, Diolite did in fact fail to sustain the great effort he made until two furlongs from home, and Iliad took the lead, Mr Tattersall, far from being surprised, must have congratulated himself on his successful, if daring, forecast. But, like most people, he had underrated Blenheim, and, again like most people, he certainly was surprised when the son of Blandford came along to rob Iliad of what had seemed an assured triumph.

Jim Dandy Upsets Gallant Fox in the 1930 Travers

New York's Saratoga, the 'grande dame' of America's racetracks, has another less beguiling sobriquet – the 'graveyard of favourites'. Indeed, perhaps the biggest upset in a classic or semi-classic race in the US took place there in 1930 when Jim Dandy, not considered within 30 pounds of Gallant Fox and offered at 100 to 1, captured the Travers Stakes over 1¼ miles of heavy going after Gallant Fox and Whichone, the choices among the four starters, fought a private duel which found Whichone breaking down and Gallant Fox having nothing left for the stretch run. It was Gallant Fox's only loss that season which found the champion becoming the first horse in history to earn over $300,000 in a single year. Thirty-four years after his stunner, Saratoga honoured Jim Dandy with a race of his own, a graduate fixture for three-year-olds at 1⅛ miles. Coming into the Travers, Jim Dandy had been twice third in nineteen starts. Curiously, the Travers wasn't the first time Jim Dandy had staggered the summertime fans at the Spa. The previous year he had been the rankest outsider in the field of eleven when securing the Grand Union Hotel Stakes at 50 to 1. This is how the BBR of 1930 reported that upset of upsets in American racing.

THE $64,750 GALLANT FOX won by his success in the classic increased his total to $274,980, so that it was now only $38,659 below that of Zev's. Those associated with him hoped and believed that the greater part of this sum would be secured by a victory in the Travers Stakes at Saratoga, Gallant Fox's next objective. True, he would again have to account for Whichone, but in view of what happened in the contest for the Belmont Stakes, there was every reason for supposing he would again beat the Whitney champion. In a mile handicap made by Mr Vosburgh at the beginning of August, Gallant Fox was at the top with 5 lb more than the weight allotted to Whichone.

The Travers was due to be run on August 16th. Gallant Fox was prepared for it on the training track, but Whichone was, in part, trained by 'sweating for t' brass'. In other words, the son of Chicle won the Saranac Handicap and $9,050 on August 6th; the Whitney Stakes and $7,100 three days later, and the Miller Stakes and $4,475 on August 12th, scoring easily each time. This series of successes greatly heartened his admirers, who now somewhat confidently expected he would prove a thorn in the side of Gallant Fox. Little did they or anybody visualise the fiasco that loomed ahead.

There were only four runners for the Travers – Gallant Fox and Whichone (both carrying 9 st), Jim Dandy (8 st 8 lb), and Sun Falcon (8 st 5 lb). The race was run over ten furlongs, on a heavy track. Odds of 2 to 1 were laid on Gallant Fox, 8 to 5 against Whichone, 30 to 1 against Sun Falcon, and 100 to 1 against Jim Dandy. Gallant Fox got quickest away from the barrier, but Whichone was slightly in front at the first turn. Side by side, the two favourites began to leave the other pair. Going along the back stretch, Gallant Fox had his head in front again, but no more than that, for Workman, riding Whichone, was evidently determined that Sande, up on Gallant Fox as usual, should not get away. Both jockeys were, in fact, behaving as if the race were one over five or six furlongs. Going round the far turn, Jim Dandy spurted and got within two lengths of the two leaders – a move that was to have remarkable consequences. When turning into the straight Whichone moved away from the rails and compelled Gallant Fox to follow suit. Thus presented with an opening, Jim Dandy made the most of it. While the two favourites were unbalanced, he dashed to the front, and, with only two furlongs to go, was leading by three lengths or more. It soon became apparent, indeed, that he was certain to win. Gallant Fox and Whichone struggled on, head to head, until a furlong from home. The Whitney colt then collapsed; the tendon of his near foreleg had bowed. For a little while longer Sande persevered on Gallant Fox, but ceased to do so when he realised that Jim Dandy was unbeatable, and the latter reached the winning post eight lengths ahead of the bearer of the Belair Stable's red-spotted jacket. Whichone limped home six lengths farther back.

This amazing result stunned the great crowd of witnesses. It was, indeed, ludicrous. Not for the first time were there puckered brows at

Saratoga in consequence of Jim Dandy's impudence. When he won the
Grand Union Hotel Stakes there last year he was, with 50 to 1 offered,
the rankest outsider of the eleven runners. From that day until he
staggered everybody by winning the Travers he had taken part in
fourteen races without showing a semblence of form better than that of a
third-rate plater; not once did he get his head first past the post.

In searching for an explanation of the downfall of Gallant Fox, an
examination of the times recorded is helpful. He and Whichone ran the
first three furlongs in $34\frac{4}{5}$ sec, and the first six in $73\frac{3}{5}$ sec. Earlier in the
afternoon Mrs Hertz's smart filly, Risque, won the Spinaway Stakes, a
six-furlong race, and had to strive her utmost to do so. She took $76\frac{3}{5}$ sec
in covering the distance. These figures suggest very strongly that Sande
and Workman, riders of the Travers' favourites, displayed judgment
unworthy of such experienced jockeys. All followers of racing are aware
of the frequency with which, in a three-horse race, the least fancied of
the runners wins. Over the last half-mile the Travers was a three-horse
race. Regarding Jim Dandy with contempt, Sande and Workman were
so intent on beating each other that they pursued tactics which resulted
in the discomfiture of both. Their horses were ridden into the ground. It
was all very deplorable because Gallant Fox was robbed of the honour of
having an unbroken sequence of victories as a three-year-old. This is, of
course, assuming that, with Jim Dandy out of the way, he would have
beaten Whichone. If the latter's breakdown was bound to have
happened in any event, Gallant Fox must have won. Possibly, however,
it was the extra effort called for when Jim Dandy obtained his lead that
caused Whichone to go lame. Assuming he had remained sound, would
Gallant Fox have beaten him? In all probability he would. Mr
Woodward's colt had his neck in front when Whichone collapsed, and
had had a similar advantage all the way up the straight.

Poor Whichone, beset by so many troubles during his brief Turf
career, was, so far as the remainder of the past season was concerned,
down and out, and it hardly seems likely he will be able to race again.
During the period he was in training he ran fourteen times. He won ten
races, was second twice and third once. His stake total is $192,705, more
than half of which he earned when he won the Futurity at Belmont Park
last year.

Just a word or two about the now notorious Jim Dandy. He is a
chestnut colt by Jim Gaffney (son of the Bend Or horse Golden Garter)
out of Thunderbolt, by Star Shoot (son of Isinglass) from Grace G.
(winner of twenty-seven races), by imported Albert, by Albert Victor.
He was bred in Kentucky by Colonel W. S. Dudley, who won a race

with him in the spring of last year, and then sold him to his present owner, Mr C. Earl, a Californian. Jim Dandy has not run since he won the Travers Stakes.

The Death of Phar Lap

One of the most disconcerting deaths in the history of international thoroughbred racing occurred in 1932 when that superlative Australian champion, Phar Lap, died from a colic attack, caused by poisonous vegetation, at Menlo Park, California, just seventeen days after his stirring victory in the Agua Caliente Handicap on his North American debut. Many Australians could not believe it was accidental and there have been strained relations in some quarters down through the years. But the Americans were as devastated by this cruel twist of fate as were the Australians. The BBR of 1932 recounts some facts on that equine tragedy. At the end of the article it is mentioned that Mr J. H. Whitney purchased Phar Lap's own sister, Nea Lap, for breeding purposes. She had several winners in the US, including the Brooklyn and Widener Handicap winner, Four Freedoms, but her several daughters failed to carry on in tail-female, although a full sister, Raphis, became the second dam of the Australian classic winner Monte Carlo.

PHAR LAP, the Australasian wonder, arrived in California in the middle of January. Two months later he triumphantly accomplished his mission by easily winning the Agua Caliente handicap in which, carrying 9 st 3 lb (129 lb), he gave from 9 lb to 39 lb to his opponents. By this victory he earned $50,500 (£10,000 at par). Agua Caliente is in Mexico, close to the Californian border. The meeting there is run by Americans who have to 'go foreign' because of the restrictions on betting in California.

So great was the reputation Phar Lap took with him to America, and so well did he shape in his preparation for the Agua Caliente Handicap, unorthodox though it seemed to American trainers, that he started a 3 to 2 favourite. Only two of his ten opponents were believed to have backable chances of beating him. One was Spanish Play who, following other victories, had won the New Orleans Handicap eight days previously; the other, Reveille Boy, who had been trained for the event by racing at Agua Caliente, and was a recent winner. Spanish Play was at 3 to 1 and Reveille Boy at 7 to 1. The distance to be traversed was ten furlongs.

After running under restraint for about half a mile, Phar Lap was allowed to stride along, very quickly went to the front, and for another three furlongs was three lengths ahead of Reveille Boy. For a little while Spanish Play was lying third, but he was beaten before entering the home straight. Coming round the far turn Phar Lap was given a 'breather', and the onlookers became greatly excited when they saw Reveille Boy creep up and actually get to the favourite's head. The winning post was then about a furlong away. Phar Lap's jockey, W. Elliott, now got busy again, and in effortless fashion the Australian horse sailed away from the challenger to beat him two lengths, and receive a great ovation from the crowd. Although he had been ridden without any thought of creating a time record Phar Lap did, as a fact, cover the ten furlongs in the fastest time associated with the track, namely, 2 min 2⅘ sec.

From Agua Caliente, Phar Lap retired to Menlo Park in California, the intention being that he should remain there until a decision had been made with regard to his next race, plans being already afoot for him to show his paces in the Chicago area and elsewhere. On April 6th, seventeen days after he had secured his victory at Agua Caliente, came the startling announcement that he was dead. He succumbed to an attack of colic believed to have been caused by his picking some poisonous vegetation while exercising in a field. It was a sore blow to those immediately associated with the son of Night Raid, and great regret was felt all over America, the followers of racing throughout the States having become greatly interested in the horse.

Phar Lap's heart was sent to Australia. In an article he contributed to the *Sydney Referee*, Dr Stewart McKay stated that he and Professor Welsh had carefully measured the thickness of the wall of the left ventricle and found it to be 4.2 centimetres (about one and seven-tenths of an inch) or twice as thick as the wall of the left ventricle of another horse's heart they dissected. Dr McKay believes the thickness of the wall of Phar Lap's heart gave him an enormous advantage over his adversaries because of its great tractile power.

Mr J. H. Whitney has acquired for his stud Phar Lap's sister, Nea Lap, now five years old. She was a winner of four races, but of moderate class.

Hyperion at Two Years Old

Hyperion became a double classic winner in 1933 when winning the Derby and St Leger. Subsequently, he was England's champion sire

*five times. He was a good two-year-old, but considered inconsistent.
The* BBR *of 1932 thought the Lord Derby colt had a name befitting a
Derby winner and also ventured to say that his Dewhurst triumph
suggested he had the talent as well. Because of his place in racing and
breeding history, the* BBR*'s 'before the fact' assessment of Hyperion
becomes something to save and savour.*

THIS COLT, bred and owned by Lord Derby possesses a name that
would look well in the list of Derby winners! And who dare say that it
will not be tacked on to the list next June? Before he won the Dewhurst
Stakes many would have dared, but that success, which was not in the
least expected – odds of 16 to 1 were laid against him – compelled us to
regard him with great respect. If he were a little bigger his prospects
would be even brighter than they are, but what there is of him is first rate
and, so far as quality and perfection of conformation are concerned, he
compares favourably with the most attractive of his rivals.

Hyperion is another of the Gondolette tribe. Assuredly, Lord Derby
had a happy inspiration when he decided to buy Gondolette from Lord
Wavertree, for to that acquisition he has been indebted for many of his
more notable achievements on the Turf during the last fifteen years or
so. From Gondolette herself he obtained the classic winners Ferry and
Sansovino; from her daughter Serenissima another classic winner in
Tranquil, together with Bosworth and Selene; from Selene, who won
over £14,000, have come Pharamond, Sickle, Hunter's Moon, and now
Hyperion. This is a record that will take some beating. Hyperion
appeals the more strongly because he is apparently going to be a stayer,
as are so many of Gainsborough's offspring. It was his stamina that
enabled him to win the Dewhurst Stakes, for the going was so holding
that the seven furlongs took a lot of 'getting'.

When not thoroughly 'wound-up' Hyperion ran fourth in his first
race at Doncaster in May, but he started second favourite for the New
Stakes at Ascot and won easily, beating the filly Nun's Veil (giving him
4 lb) three lengths. Odds were laid on his winning the Prince of Wales's
Stakes at Goodwood, and it was somewhat disconcerting to his admirers
when he only managed to run a dead heat for first place with the filly
Stairway. Matters looked worse still – much worse – when, in the race
for the Boscawen Stakes at Newmarket at the end of September,
Hyperion finished third, beaten eight lengths by Manitoba. His form
that day was evidently hopelessly at variance with his 'home'
reputation, but it accounted for the long odds laid against him in the
Dewhurst Stakes. It will be seen, therefore, that his record is not remark-

able for its consistency, but when at his best he is a very good colt. He is credited with a stake total of £5,105 as the result of the two-and-a-half races he has won.

Hyperion's 1933 Derby Victory

Hyperion was certainly one of the most celebrated and revered thoroughbreds in history. A horse of 'generous courage', he passed that vital attribute on to a high percentage of his offspring. In 1944, an Englishman with the nom de plume *of 'The Briton' wrote as follows in Kentucky's weekly magazine,* The Blood-Horse: *'He seems to be an institution, rather than a blood horse. Maybe you criticise your President or your Prime Minister, or General Motors, or Ford, or our own ICI, just as we may criticise some or all of them, in reverse. But neither you nor we can criticise Hyperion.'*

Hyperion was always a great favourite with this contributor to this anthology. In the book Hyperion, *published by J. A. Allen, edited by the late, exalted Turf writer, Clive Graham, with an Introduction by Lord Derby, I wrote the section on Hyperion's influence in North America. I was also permitted to express my feelings for him in that book as follows: 'This devotee, who had read of Hyperion's fabulous record at stud and of the affection he immediately inspired in people, had to wait until 1958 to make his pilgrimage to Woodlands Stud and visit the little horse. It was a day and a visit never to be forgotten. Although his back was swayed and massive dark circles were under his eyes because of damaged tear ducts, the personality was there. It was an intangible thing, but it was real. One could feel the magnetism of his being. At twenty-eight he was delightfully alert and interested in all about him. He showed some displeasure as Alcide was paraded about the yard, but all was well again when he strutted before this individual who had waited so many years to say "hello" and quietly tell him in person how much he was admired. Hyperion, I believe, sensed this, and I shall always tell myself it was so.'*

The BBR *account of his most famous victory, that in the 1933 Derby, follows.*

THIS YEAR'S Derby was run under ideal conditions. The weather was delightful, and the atmosphere free from haze. Then, too, the course, thanks to recent showers, afforded splendid going, if slightly on the firm side. There was, as always, an enormous throng, and in the Royal Box were the King, Queen, Prince of Wales, Duke and Duchess of York,

Princess Royal (Countess of Harewood) and Prince George. The race produced the following result:

DERBY STAKES of £100 each; £50 forfeit if declared by Tuesday of the week before running, £25 if declared by the last Tuesday in March, 1933, or £5 only if declared by the first Tuesday in July, 1932, with £3,000 added. For colts and fillies three years old; colts 9 st, fillies 8 st 9 lb. The winner received £9,836½, the second £1,169 (10 per cent of the whole stake), and the third £584½ (5 per cent of the stake). The winner's breeder (Lord Derby) received a premium of £500. The race closed November 3rd, 1931, with 304 entries, but one was withdrawn under Rule 108. The £5 forfeit was declared for 117, that of £25 for 100, and that of £50 for 60, leaving 26 to pay £100 each. One mile and a half. Run at Epsom, May 31st.

Lord Derby's ch. c. HYPERION, by Gainsborough–Selene T. Weston	1
Sir Hugo Cunliffe-Owen's b. c. KING SALMON, by Salmon-Trout–Malva H. Wragg	2
Mr Victor Emanuel's br. c. STATESMAN, by Blandford-Dail B. Carslake	3
Lord Durham's b. c. Scarlet Tiger, by Colorado–Trilogy A. Wragg	4
Lord Derby's b. or br. c. Thrapston, by Gay Crusader–Bythorne S. Donoghue	5
Sir Abe Bailey's b. c. Raymond, by Gainsborough–Nipisiquit G. Nicoll	6
Count John McCormack's ch. c. Franz Hals, by Gainsborough–Needle Eye T. Burns	7
Sir Frederick Eley's b. c. Solar Boy, by Solario–Najmi J. Collins	8
Maj. C. Behrens' b. c. Light Sussex, by Galloper Light–Wyandotte P. Donoghue	9
Mr Edward Esmond's br. c. Interlace, by Hurry On–Straitlace E. Smith	10
Mr W. Barnett's b. c. Harinero, by Blandford–Athasi C. Ray	11
Mrs G. H. Drummond's b. c. Melfort, by Colorado–Caltha W. Johnstone	12
Sir Alfred Butt's br. c. Young Lover, by Son-in-Law–Tryst R. Perryman	13
Mr E. J. Marshall's b. c. Happy Call, by Call Boy–Happy Girl K. Gethin	14
H.H. Aga Khan's gr. c. Gino, by Tetratema–Teresina M. Beary	15
Lord Carnarvon's b. c. Madagascar, by Blandford–Madawaska T. Bartlam	16
H.H. Aga Khan's b. c. Felicitation, by Colorado–Felicita E. C. Elliott	17
Miss Dorothy Paget's b. c. Tuppence, by Spion Kop–Waffles H. Beasley	18
Mr W. H. Gull's b. c. Blue Grass, by Phalaris–Blue Ice F. Fox	19
Mr H. Crum Ewing's ch. c. Caymanas, by Papyrus–Eagle's Eyrie F. Lane	20
Lord Woolavington's b. c. Manitoba, by Manna–Berystede G. Richard	21
Mr W. M. G. Singer's b. c. Myosotis, by Phalaris–Scarlet Martagon R. A. Jones	22
Mr D. Crossman's br. c. Lovers Walk, by Arcade–Queen of the May J. Childs	23

Col. F. J. Lundgren's br. c. Coroado
   by Colorado–Trustful
            D. McGuigan   24

Winner bred by owner; trained at Newmarket by the Hon. George Lambton.

BETTING

	Book Odds	Approximate Tote Odds
Hyperion	6 to 1	$7\frac{1}{2}$ to 1
Manitoba	13 to 2	$7\frac{1}{4}$ to 1
King Salmon	7 to 1	$5\frac{3}{4}$ to 1
Tuppence	10 to 1	28 to 1
Young Lover	100 to 8	8 to 1
Scarlet Tiger	18 to 1	15 to 1
Felicitation	20 to 1	$19\frac{1}{4}$ to 1
Statesman	20 to 1	15 to 1
Harinero	22 to 1	$25\frac{1}{2}$ to 1
Light Sussex	22 to 1	$17\frac{3}{4}$ to 1
Thrapston	25 to 1	$22\frac{1}{2}$ to 1
Gino	25 to 1	$23\frac{1}{4}$ to 1
Happy Call	25 to 1	$24\frac{1}{2}$ to 1
Interlace	28 to 1	$24\frac{3}{4}$ to 1
Franz Hals	28 to 1	$47\frac{1}{2}$ to 1
Melfort	33 to 1	$71\frac{3}{4}$ to 1
Raymond	33 to 1	46 to 1
Caymanas	40 to 1	77 to 1
Madagascar	50 to 1	$125\frac{1}{4}$ to 1
Myosotis	50 to 1	$45\frac{1}{2}$ to 1
Lovers Walk	66 to 1	38 to 1
Blue Grass	100 to 1	67 to 1
Coroado	100 to 1	125 to 1
Solar Boy	100 to 1	$120\frac{1}{2}$ to 1

TOTALISATOR POOLS

Win	145,892	2s. units	£14,589	4s.
Place	123,614	2s. units	£12,361	8s.

Hyperion won by four generous lengths; one length between second and third. Time: 2 min 34 sec, a record for the race, the previous best time being 2 min 34 2/5 sec, made by Call Boy in 1927, and by Felstead in 1928.

After a brief delay caused by Felicitation, Captain Allison got the runners away from the 'gate' in good alignment. Donoghue at once took Thrapston to the front. Up the hill to the ten-furlong post Coroado and Light Sussex – the latter from Malton in Yorkshire, and much fancied – were lying second and third, just in front of Hyperion, whose immediate followers were Blue Grass, King Salmon and Manitoba. At the end of the second furlong Coroado dropped back, and presently Hyperion drew up to the girths of Light Sussex, Raymond then being fourth and King Salmon fifth. Hereabouts Manitoba began to fade out, and Scarlet Tiger, who had dwelt a little at the start, to move forward.

Six furlongs from home Hyperion raced up to Thrapston, attended by Light Sussex, King Salmon and Scarlet Tiger. Rounding Tattenham Corner, with half a mile still to go, Hyperion, next the rails, was level with Thrapston, and went to the front directly after entering the straight. King Salmon and Statesman were now third and fourth, with Solar Boy, Light Sussex, and Raymond close up. Light Sussex, however, was eased after swerving and colliding with Raymond. Three furlongs from home Hyperion was out 'on his own', and obviously had the prize at his mercy. He continued to gain ground with every stride, and before he reached the winning-post, Weston was patting his neck. King Salmon was second on his merits, for he had been the master of Statesman, Scarlet Tiger and Thrapston most of the way down the straight. Scarlet Tiger finished a length and a half behind Statesman, and a like distance in front of his stable companion Thrapston. Thus it came about that three of the first five horses were from the Stanley House stable at Newmarket. It was a fine training feat on the part of Mr George Lambton, one only surpassed in recent times by Frank Butters, who, at

Hyperion

Doncaster last year, saddled four of the first five in the St Leger, all owned by the Aga Khan. Mr Lambton, unfortunately, could not saddle his trio at Epsom, for, as already stated, he was at home nursing a sprained leg. He had, therefore, to get the exciting and comforting tidings by listening to the running commentary on the race broadcast by the BBC. Matthew Dawson had no such consolation when he was unable to go to Epsom to see Ladas win the Derby for his patron Lord Rosebery.

Hyperion is Lord Derby's second Derby winner, his first being, of course, Sansovino, hero of the 1924 renewal. When he led the son of Gainsborough to the unsaddling enclosure, he, his horse and his jockey, were loudly cheered. Congratulations were showered on the proud and smiling owner. And how thoroughly they were deserved, for, of the present-day pillars of the Turf, Lord Derby is the acknowledged chief. From the day he inherited the peerage and its appurtenances from his father, he has seen to it that the Stanley House stables, together with the breeding studs that feed them, should be conducted on the highest-class lines. The reward has been justly great.

When the announcement that Hyperion had won by four lengths appeared on the number board everyone was astonished. If the verdict had been one of eight lengths, most people who saw the finish would have accepted it as approximately correct. That it should have been more than four is certain, as photographs prove. When questioned the following day, the judge, Mr Malcolm Hancock, admitted that he might have made a more liberal estimate, but he did not feel inclined to go beyond five lengths. It is a detail of little consequence. Whatever the number of lengths may actually have been, there would have been more to add if Weston had persuaded Hyperion to extend himself to the utmost. As it was, by running the course in 2 min 34 sec, the colt had established a new Derby time record, beating as it did that made by Call Boy and equalled by Felstead by two-fifths of a second.

Just after Hyperion had taken the lead from Thrapston at Tattenham Corner, Weston drew his whip and 'showed' it. 'I did that,' he explained, 'only to remind him that because he was in front he must not think he could go to sleep. I shall never again,' added Weston, 'be so certain that I have won the Derby as I was when I passed Coroado and Light Sussex, and tracked Thrapston down the hill to Tattenham Corner.' Lord Derby expressed to Steve Donoghue his heartfelt thanks for the readiness with which he agreed to ride Thrapston as a mere pace-maker, and for the able manner in which he performed his subsidiary duty during the race.

Manitoba was lost in the crowd long before the race was half over. Talking to a Pressman, Gordon Richards whimsically described his experience by saying: 'There may have been Hyperion and Manitoba in it for three furlongs, but then there was only one, and it was not mine!' That Manitoba might fail to stay the twelve furlongs had been the inference many drew from his running at Birmingham, but that he would make so poor a show was unimaginable. Fred Darling felt confident Manitoba would not be beaten in the Derby for want of stamina. On what he had done at home he should, anyhow, have made a 'show' in the straight. Verily, racehorses are at times 'queer cattle'.

King Salmon ran true to his form. It was bad luck for Sir Hugo Cunliffe-Owen that his horse had to contend against a superlative opponent like Hyperion, for, with the latter out of the way, he would assuredly have been able to rejoice in the possession of a second Derby winner, Felstead being his first. The son of Salmon-Trout lacked the finishing speed he required to cope with Hyperion when the latter began his half-mile run home, and so, for the third time in successive big events, he had to be content with second place. Statesman presented a more racing-like appearance than on Guineas day. If his good performance surprised many people, his trainer, Duller, was not amongst them. Well as Scarlet Tiger ran, he might have done even better if there had not been that steep descent to Tattenham Corner, while Young Lover would probably have shown to greater advantage had the turf been softer.

The day after that on which the Two Thousand had been decided, we had occasion to send an account of the race to the Buenos Aires paper *La Nacion*, and informed the readers of that journal that if Hyperion was not good enough to win the Derby we'd be hanged if we could name a colt worth backing to do so. Why, after he had won that twelve-furlong race at Chester, he did not become and remain an outstanding favourite for the Derby was astonishing. In some quarters Hyperion was regarded with suspicion because, forsooth, he happened to have four white feet. The superstition on which this ridiculous attitude was based was in days long gone by embodied in rhymes, a few of which were published in the correspondence columns of *The Times* before and after the Derby. One of them runs:

> One white foot, ride him for your life.
> Two white feet, give him to your wife.
> Three white feet, give him to your man.
> Four white feet, sell him – if you can!

Here, however, is another which emphasises opinions of a very different order:

> One white foot, keep him not a day;
> Two white feet, send him soon away;
> Three white feet, sell him to a friend;
> Four white feet, keep him to the end.

One can only suppose that the simpletons who allowed Hyperion's four white feet to prejudice their views concerning his chance of winning the Derby will in future mutter the second of the two jingles we have quoted when they feel it necessary to pay heed to foot markings. Or it may be they have come to the conclusion that 'there is nothing in it'.

Hyperion Wins the 1933 St Leger

Hyperion went on to capture the 1933 St Leger as comfortably as he had won the Derby. However, there was some concern before that happened, as reported in the BBR.

EARLY IN July there came an announcement that he had slipped his patella (the bone corresponding to the human knee-cap) when, it was supposed, he had risen awkwardly from a recumbent position. The bone was replaced and the colt had had walking and trotting exercise for a few days when the same thing happened again. There was, in consequence, much perturbation in places where they bet, and odds of 20 to 1 were offered that he would not win the St Leger. According to some folk, it was any odds he would not run at Doncaster. This scare was based on ignorance. As 'Mankato', a veterinary surgeon, informed his readers, hundreds of horses partially or completely slipped the patella bone of the stifle, and, after it has been replaced, gone on with their work as if nothing had happened. After the second 'slip' there was no more trouble, and early in August Hyperion was in training again. He was then quoted at 5 to 1 in the St Leger betting. About that time Lord Derby was presiding at a meeting at Chester, and, having listened to the expression of a hope that his colt would follow up his victory in the Derby by winning the St Leger, told the audience that Hyperion was very fit. He caused laughter by adding: 'That is not a tip, because I remember a Lord Mayor of Liverpool saying, "If I can get away from a public function at which Lord Derby is present without his giving a tip, I am a much richer man."'

Hyperion's trainer, Mr George Lambton, had intended to use Highlander as a pacemaker for the son of Gainsborough-Selene, by Chaucer, in the St Leger, but decided against it as that colt hated hard ground. However, he would have been an unnecessary sacrificial lamb in any case as Hyperion was fully capable of doing his own 'donkey work' as the post-race comments of his rider, T. Weston, as expressed to 'Ajax' of the *Evening Standard* so well explain.

> 'Being so sure of my mount's stamina, I did not want any hanging around. The other jockeys probably also knew I wanted a good gallop, and they were not out to help me. As soon as we jumped off I could see it would be a crawl unless I took matters into my own hands, so I immediately went to the front and set a pace to please myself. When we had got settled down Sans Peine came along and joined me, but we did not start to race in earnest until we had actually got into the straight. I then decided to give the others a chance to catch me if they could. Without any trouble I went into a lead of several lengths, and my little colt kept galloping so smoothly that I knew I had the race won a long way from home. I have seldom felt so confident of victory such a long distance away, but the truth is that the others were not in the same class. I was so far in front a furlong from the winning-post that I could afford to take matters easily. He is the best little horse I have ever ridden, and a great stayer.'

From 'The Londoner's Diary' in the *Evening Standard*, we cull the following:

> 'A literary friend with a taste for racing points out to me today that Hyperion is the first horse named after a god to be successful in any classic race. Four years ago Horus ran third in the St Leger and Polyphontes occupied the same position in 1924. Keats evidently had a prophetic vision of yesterday's race. In the second book of the 1820 version of Hyperion I find the following lines:
>
> > *Victory might be lost or might be won,*
> > *And be ye mindful that Hyperion,*
> > *Our brightest brother, still is undisgraced –*
> > *Hyperion, lo! his radiance is here.*'

It is rather a curious fact that Hyperion was the only chestnut-coloured horse in the St Leger field.

Commenting on the performance of his mount, Felicitation, Beary said:

> 'It was only my colt's stamina which got him into second place. I was in a good position, not far behind the leaders, rounding the turn, but when they quickened up I was soon left astern. A furlong in the straight, I did not look like being in the first ten, but gradually most of those in front began to tire, and my colt kept on like a true stayer. It was in the last few strides that I beat Scarlet Tiger for second place.'

Butters, the trainer of Felicitation, expressed the opinion that the colt would probably have run even better if the ground had not been so hard.

The firm going no doubt also handicapped other contenders, Young Lover for one.

The bookmakers had cause to view the victory of Hyperion with wry faces. They were all losers over the race; some of them lost heavily. They had, however, only themselves to blame. 'Laying the favourite' is their habitual method of trying to make money, and more often than not it is successful; but in the case of Hyperion they took undue liberties. Why they opposed him so persistently, not to say recklessly, after he had overcome the stifle trouble, is difficult to understand. If his supporters had been asked to lay odds they could not have complained.

Needless to say, Lord Derby was delighted. He is not an owner who contrives to hide his pleasure behind a stolid countenance. When there is occasion to rejoice he does so heartily and unaffectedly. He had to hold a reception outside the Weighing Room because of the desire of so many of his friends to congratulate him. Mopping his brow while talking to a Pressman, he said: 'I have been away for a thinning cure, but, believe me, this is far more effective and much cheaper.'

Hyperion is the fifth winner of the St Leger bred and owned by Lord Derby. The others were Swynford (1910), Keysoe (1919), Tranquil (1923), and Fairway (1928). Fairway was trained by Frank Butters, but Mr George Lambton has the proud satisfaction of having prepared and saddled the others. In the St Leger roll Lord Archibald Hamilton is given as the owner of the winners in 1786, 1787, 1788 and 1792. The winners in 1808, 1809 and 1814 are credited to a Duke of Hamilton. After Hyperion had won, the belief was entertained that by furnishing the winners of five St Legers, Lord Derby had created a record, but an investigation showed that Lord Archibald Hamilton and the (ninth) Duke of Hamilton were one and the same person. Lord Derby must persevere.

Famous American Horses

When Walter S. Vosburgh died within a few weeks of his eighty-fourth birthday in 1935, he was remembered as one of the most revered, capable and distinguished racing officials in American Turf history. The intervening years have not dimmed that recognition.

The Review *always had the highest respect for Mr Vosburgh's opinions and therefore it is not surprising that when he gave some of his views on the best American horses he had seen during his long career in the American Turf publication,* The Daily Racing Form, *the* Review *of 1917 was quick to reprint those views. For many years he thought:*

LONGFELLOW the best he had seen. 'A horse of gigantic stature, he had a stride such as I have never seen equalled; but in heavy ground it was his drawback. . . . Longfellow, in appearance, was different from any horse I can remember, and what is most remarkable was that for so large and long-striding a horse he was as quick as a cat at the post. Gathering himself for a spring, he leaped to the front at the start with a pace that carried his opponents off their stride at the outset. He always made the running, never trying to win by waiting.'

TOM BOWLING was one of the most exquisitely beautiful of all the horses Mr Vosburgh can remember, and repeatedly demonstrated his superiority over the horses of his day, but he was cursed with a temper that often caused him to lose races by refusing to start. Tom Bowling would catch rats like the most approved terrier, leaping upon them in his box and stamping them to bits.

DUKE OF MAGENTA, the last of the really great sons of Lexington, was a plain horse, coltish and even 'cobby' as a two-year-old, but at three no colt could live his pace.

LUKE BLACKBURN was probably the most heavily-muscled horse that has appeared within the last forty years. Only a moderate two-year-old, at three he was invincible, winning all the stakes of his class, and then won the Grand Union Prize, for all ages, at Saratoga.

HINDOO, who succeeded Blackburn as the hero of the hour, was completely his opposite. A racing machine in appearance, but with a long weak-looking back, he never did nore than his jockey asked him, while Blackburn nearly pulled McLaughlin out of the saddle.

SPENDTHRIFT, when he won the Lorillard Stakes, gave an exhibition of speed similar to Lord Clifden's in the St Leger, coming from far behind and beating his field in the last furlong; but he had tender feet and, sent to England, he turned 'roarer', and the Turf knew him no more.

MISS WOODFORD was undoubtedly the superior of any horse of her time, and most people will claim we never saw her equal in her own sex. She was a great, coarse mare, so masculine as to deceive the casual observer as to her sex.

BEN BRUSH, a plain demure little horse, was quite the best of his era, and at two years old could, in Mr Vosburgh's opinion, have conceded his year in weight to any three-year-old of that season.

HENRY OF NAVARRE was not an impressive horse to look at, but it is doubtful if a better one had been seen up to the date of his appearance. Domino was his master up to a mile, but beyond that Henry could outrun anybody's horse. He raced four seasons and met and defeated the best horses of those four seasons – that is a fact that should be remembered.

HERMIS was the quickest starter seen in many a day; a small horse, but so perfectly adjusted, that he tired less under weight than horses usually do. He also met a better class of horses than some champions have had the luck to meet, and his Suburban, with 127 pounds, beating The Picket and Irish Lad, left no doubt of his right to class with the giants of racing history.

SYSONBY was one of the most powerful as well as one of the speediest horses that has ever carried a silk jacket. His race for the great Republic Stakes at Saratoga, when, after being almost left at the post, he outran his horses in the first quarter of a mile, was an exhibition such as few people have even seen equalled. His race for the Annual Champion, when he ran away from Oiseau and Broomstick, proved him a stayer as well as a sprinter. He evidently held safe any horse of his era from a quarter of a mile to three miles, and the power of his heart and lungs must have been far beyond the ordinary.

Which of the foregoing great racers was the greatest is a question Mr Vosburgh declared he cannot answer. He gets over the difficulty by declaring that 'it is only a matter of opinion, after all.'

Windsor Lad's Final Race

While it was a pity that France's fine champion Brantôme and England's splendid champion Windsor Lad, clearly the best four-year-olds in Europe in 1935, were not able to decide the question of superiority on the racetrack, Windsor Lad was able to say he exited a winner, whereas Brantôme suffered his first and only loss in France in his final race, the Prix de l'Arc de Triomphe. With Windsor Lad it was 'all's well that ends well', as, despite a sulky-like pace, he turned back Theft and Fair Trial in the Eclipse Stakes. He retired with an enviable record. After being out of the frame in his first two starts at two, Windsor Lad won his third and only other start as a juvenile, scoring in the Criterion Stakes.

In his next ten career starts, six at three, and four at four, he was returned the winner each time, excepting a third in the Eclipse as a three-year-old, a loss he adequately compensated for in his grand finale as a competitor.

THE KING and Queen went to Sandown Park to see the race for the Eclipse Stakes, as they usually do. It was a dull day and inclined to be showery, but the weather had been dry for some time, and the course was on the hard side. Had the going been normal, Hairan would have accompanied his stable companion to the post. He was withdrawn at the last moment.

Windsor Lad disliked racing in front and it was, therefore, unfortunate that he could not have the services of a pacemaker, for the jockeys riding his four opponents took good care that he should have no assistance from them. It was, of course, Charlie Smirke's business to see that the favourite's staying power was brought into play as much as possible so, willy nilly, he had to take the lead right away. While the straight five-furlong stretch to the turn was being traversed it was, however, manifest that the pace was slow, and the onlookers began to wonder whether Windsor Lad would meet with trouble when the speed merchants, Fair Trial and Theft, got busy after entering the line for home.

Windsor Lad came into the straight, half a mile from the goal, followed by Bondsman, Adept, Fair Trial, and Theft. The last-named had been 'whipper-in' from the start. He and Fair Trial were obviously being reserved for a final sprint. Before another two furlongs had been covered, Fair Trial, ridden by Gordon Richards, became second. Presently Gordon left the rails to get a clear run on the favourite's near side, and, having obtained the position he wanted, made his challenge. Great was the excitement when Fair Trial drew alongside Windsor Lad, and there was a frenzied shout when the Beckhampton colt was seen to be leading the favourite by about a neck. For a few seconds the issue hung in the balance. If Fair Trial could maintain his effort the situation seemed fraught with peril for Windsor Lad, but those who already imagined he was doomed to suffer defeat did him less than justice. The sudden advent of the 'apparition' on his left roused the fighting spirit within him. Smirke too was undaunted. The jockey let Windsor Lad see

Windsor Lad (C. Smirke up).

his whip, and as he did so the horse swerved slightly towards Fair Trial, but fortunately there was no collision. Those were tense moments during which Windsor Lad, revealing once again the courage and resolution that had often served him so well, regained the lead. When he had done so, Fair Trial's stamina quickly gave out, and the crowd's attention became focussed on Theft. After entering the straight, Perryman had left the rails and directed the Aga Khan's colt along a line far from them, for he had earlier in the afternoon discovered that the going there would favour the son of Tetratema. All the way up the hill Theft had been steadily drawing closer to the leaders, so that when Fair Trial was beaten he was less than a length behind Windsor Lad. By this time, however, the favourite was revelling in his job and running so strongly that if there had been another furlong or two to go he would probably have won easily. When he reached the winning post he was, however, only three-quarters of a length in front of Theft, who had Fair Trial another three-parts of a length behind him. Adept finished fourth.

It was not surprising to find that it took Windsor Lad 2 min 13⅘ sec to run the ten furlongs. Last year King Salmon covered the course in time 7 seconds faster, and had Windsor Lad only a length behind him. King Salmon's time is the 'record' for the event. The slow pace at which the race was run this year placed Windsor Lad at a great disadvantage and favoured Theft and Fair Trial. If the favourite had been beaten it would have been a horrible fluke. However, all was well, much to the delight of the crowd, who cheered lustily when Windsor Lad reached the goal triumphant.

Mr Benson's horse had taken with him to the stud a splendid record of achievements on the Turf. Here is a complete list of them.

WINDSOR LAD'S TURF RECORD

TWO YEARS OLD, 1933

	£
Unplaced Two-Year-Old Sale Stakes (5 f), Newmarket	—
4th Richmond Stakes (6 f), Goodwood	—
Won Criterion Stakes (6 f), Newmarket	665

THREE YEARS OLD

	£
Won Chester Vase (1½ m)	1,605
Won Newmarket Stakes (1¼ m)	1,790¾
Won the Derby (1½ m), Epsom	9,352
3rd Eclipse Stakes (1¼ m), Sandown Park	—
Won Great Yorkshire Stakes (1½ m), York	1,754
Won the St Leger (1 m 6½ f), Doncaster	10,401¾

FOUR YEARS OLD

	£
Won Burwell Stakes (1½ m), Newmarket	520
Won Coronation Cup (1½ m), Epsom	1,560
Won Rous Memorial (7½ f), Ascot	1,040
Won Eclipse Stakes (1¼ m), Sandown Park	7,569

£36,257½

BBR–1935

Brantôme's Sensational Failure in the Gold Cup of 1935

If the 'disappointment was deep and widespread' when the English champion Windsor Lad and the French champion Brantôme failed to meet in the Ascot Gold Cup of 1935, imagine the disappointment, particularly in France, when Brantôme, unbeaten in eleven races in his homeland, kept his Ascot engagement only to be soundly beaten. Like England's darling, the previously unbeaten Pretty Polly, who had journeyed to France in 1904 only to have her copybook blotted in the Prix du Conseil Municipal at Longchamp, Brantôme met his Waterloo at Ascot. Both had their excuses: Pretty Polly had to endure a terribly rough Channel passage while Brantôme had barely managed to survive a very frightening runaway escapade just eleven days before the Cup. In another oddity, or at least coincidence, both lost their last race, that of Pretty Polly being in the same Gold Cup which ended Brantôme's win skein, while Brantôme's other loss came in the Prix de l'Arc de Triomphe, a classic he had won the previous season at age three.

Despite these two career defeats, Brantôme rates high among the finest thoroughbreds ever bred in France. He also enjoyed quite a successful career at stud, although the sobriquet, 'France's Hyperion', appears to have been quite an exaggeration.

ONE SUNDAY in the autumn of 1904 the staggering news reached London from Paris that Pretty Polly had suffered defeat in the race for the Prix du Conseil Municipal at Longchamp. She had gone to France an unbeaten winner of fifteen races, including the One Thousand Guineas, Oaks and St Leger; that she would return home still unbeaten was taken so much for granted that the announcement of her downfall could scarcely be believed. Last June, Brantôme came to Ascot from Chantilly an unbeaten winner of eleven races in France, to compete for the Gold Cup. French sportsmen regarded him as highly and as invincible as we had regarded Pretty Polly. When they received the tidings that the colt had not only been beaten, but failed to finish in the first three, they were incredulous. Some actually telephoned to London to ask whether the news was true.

At the end of May, three weeks before the race for the Cup was due to be run, three English-owned horses that had seemed to have backable chances of tackling Brantôme at Ascot had been withdrawn from the event. They included Felicitation, who won the Gold Cup last year and was kept in training this season solely to give him the chance of repeating the victory. Mention has been made of the fact that in the contest for the Chippenham Stakes at Newmarket at the beginning of May he finished a bad third to Tai-Yang and Tiberius. He was then nothing like fit. Three weeks later he easily won the Yorkshire Cup over two miles at York, carrying 9 st 7 lb and giving 12 lb or more to his opponents. Those who saw the performance came to the conclusion that Brantôme would need all the merits claimed for him to be able to get the better of Felicitation at Ascot. Unfortunately, the Aga Khan's horse won the race at York at the expense of a strained tendon. He could not, therefore, be further trained for the Ascot Cup and his owner quickly decided to retire him to the stud.

Sir Abe Bailey's four-year-old colt Tiberius, a son of Foxlaw who won the Ascot Cup for Sir Abe in 1927, now became the most formidable candidate that could be pitted against Brantôme. What were his credentials? When two years old he ran four times for two 'seconds' and two 'thirds'. Last year he took part in nine races, to win four – the Hastings and Payne Stakes in the spring, and the 'St Legers' at Newmarket and Liverpool in the autumn. He ran fourth in the Derby, and second in the St Leger at Doncaster. In the Free Handicap for three-year-olds he was placed 8 lb below Windsor Lad. Though he might not be a top notcher, he had certainly shown he was a good stayer. Before he went to Ascot last June he had, since running second to Tai-Yang, easily won the Queen's Plate over two miles at Kempton Park. Judged by his public form, Tiberius did not appear to have a great chance of beating Brantôme, France's 'horse of the century'. Reports were, however, coming from Manton, where the son of Foxlaw was being trained by Joe Lawson, that he was 'going great guns' and sure to reveal himself a much better horse than he had even done before.

Meanwhile, Brantôme, a son of Blandford, bred and owned by Baron Edouard de Rothschild, was lengthening his unbroken series of victories. On May 1st, at Le Tremblay, he won over 2 miles 3 furlongs,

Brantôme

and eleven days later romped away with the Prix du Cadran, the distance of the race being 2½ miles less about 30 yards. In the latter event his opponents included Admiral Drake and Cadmus, winners last year of the Grand Prix de Paris and the Prix du Conseil Municipal. Brantôme ran the course in the record time of 4 min 23⅖ secs.

These achievements convinced Brantôme's legion of worshippers he was as good as ever, and more than that they did not desire. A month later, June 9th, eleven days before the date of the Ascot Cup, there was consternation in the camp. While being led to the racecourse at Chantilly, to run for the Prix de Dangu (2½ m), Brantôme broke away from his attendant, scampered off along a road dodging motor cars, and had covered, it was said, several furlongs before he was re-captured. During this escapade he cast three plates and cut himself. For four days he was given no work and received an anti-tetanus injection. When he did resume exercise on the training ground it was apparent that he was not quite himself, and the idea of abandoning the trip to Ascot was seriously considered. However, after his work on the Friday before the race his owner decided, though not without some hesitation, that the colt should meet his engagement at the Royal meeting. It was a bold and sportsmanlike gesture, not to say a risky one. The horse was rushed from

Chantilly to Ascot, making the journey in a day with a short rest at Folkestone.

There were only six runners for the Gold Cup. The four who accompanied Brantôme and Tiberius to the post were M. Boussac's Denver II (from France), Mr Crum-Ewing's Caymanas, Mr Woodward's Alcazar, and Lord Astor's Bright Bird. The last-named, winner last year of the Princess of Wales Stakes, was started to make a good pace for the benefit of his stable companion Tiberius. When the race began the betting was: 13 to 8 on Brantôme, 100 to 30 against Tiberius, 100 to 8 Denver II, 100 to 6 Caymanas, 20 to 1 Alcazar, and 33 to 1 Bright Bird. The appearance of Brantôme when he came under examination in the paddock caused surprise. By comparison with Tiberius, a fine, upstanding, muscular horse, he seemed small (though actually rather above medium height) and moulded on somewhat slender lines. Captious critics likened him to a polo pony, which was, of course, ridiculous. He has well-placed shoulders, long quarters, and unimpeachable hind legs. His forelegs are truly made, but he is light of bone below the knee. When racing, his action is free and graceful.

It was a cheerless, disagreeable day. A good deal of rain had fallen the previous night, and continued until sport commenced. Fortunately there was hardly any while racing was in progress, but the sky was leaden and visibility poor. Notwithstanding the soaking it had received, the track was in fairly good condition, though naturally on the 'dead' side, especially in Swinley Bottom. As luck would have it, the following day was very fine! Before he left the paddock Brantôme was sweating freely on his flanks, and during the parade in front of the stands began to lather between the thighs. These characteristics were always shown before his races in France. When turned loose to go to the starting post he made a big bound and then set off at a hard gallop, heedless of the efforts of his jockey, Bouillon, to restrain him. He had, however, sobered down when the race began.

According to plan, Bright Bird at once went to the front and set a good pace. Passing the stands the first time he was followed by Tiberius, behind whom, side by side, came Brantôme and Alcazar. Bright Bird ran wide when rounding the first turn, and presently led Tiberius by five or six lengths, with Brantôme and Alcazar, still together, in the wake. Coming out of Swinley Bottom, a mile or so from home, the favourite moved closer to Tiberius, who was being hand-ridden to induce him to get in touch with Bright Bird, still fulfilling his mission in fine style. Alcazar also quickened his pace, and so did Denver II.

When nearing the bend into the straight, Bright Bird began to falter, and retired. Tiberius now assumed the lead, and when headed for home was followed by Alcazar, Brantôme and Denver II. The onlookers had their gaze fixed on the favourite, expecting every moment to see him go forward to challenge Tiberius. What they did see, however, was his jockey, Bouillon, drawing and using his whip. Up went the cry, 'He's beaten!' Sure enough, Brantôme had shot his bolt. Tiberius was now forging further and further ahead to an accompaniment of loud cheers. His triumph was assured two furlongs from the goal, but his rider, Weston, kept him on the go right away to the winning post, which he reached eight lengths ahead of Alcazar. Two lengths further back Denver II finished third. Caymanas was fourth, and Brantôme fifth, Bright Bird being tailed off.

Tiberius was clocked to run the two miles and a half in 4 min 35$\frac{1}{5}$ sec. This comparatively slow time is, no doubt, explained by the state of the track. It surprised many of the experts who, while the race was being run, were under the impression that the pace was exceptionally fast. The record for the race is 4 min 17 secs, made by Golden Myth in 1922. The following year Happy Man won in 4 min 20 sec. Since then the best time is 4 min 22$\frac{2}{5}$ sec, credited to Foxhunter in 1933. The going was heavy when Solario took 4 min 45 sec to run the course in 1926, but good when Trimdon's time in 1931 was 4 min 40$\frac{3}{5}$ sec, and 4 min 44$\frac{1}{5}$ sec when he won again the next year. It will be seen, therefore, that the time test is very unreliable when applied to the Ascot Cup. The idea that in the pre-Sloan days the race was 'a dawdle and sprint' would seem to have little justification when we find that St Simon won it in 4 min 32 sec, and Foxhall in 4 min 36 sec. Ignoring Bosworth's 5 min 5 sec in 1930, the year of the great thunderstorm, when the course was waterlogged, the average of the Ascot Cup times in the last ten years is 4 min 33$\frac{2}{5}$ sec.

The astonishing failure of Brantôme at Ascot was, in France, attributed solely to that escapade of his at Chantilly – the four days' idleness and the anti-tetanus injection it entailed. There were many who stressed the probable debilitating effect of the injection. On the other hand there were critics in England who advanced the opinion that Brantôme's performance indicated that he could stay barely two miles in good-class company. This latter contention had, however, no foundation if there was real substance in the plea that the son of Blandford had produced nothing like his true form. French sportsmen averred that it was unnecessary to look beyond Denver II for justification of the view they held. They were supported by 'Faraway', the Englishman who sends from Paris to *Horse and Hound* those entertaining and instructive articles from which we often have occasion to quote. In his allusions to the Ascot Cup, 'Faraway' wrote:

'We only have to look at the position of Denver as third to prove that Brantôme ran stones below his true form. Mr Boussac's son of Banstar, on all form, is only just useful; in fact, his owner described him to me as a bad animal with only one pace. In eleven outings last year he won twice, and this in the company of handicappers over distances of 13 and 14 furlongs. He ran fourth behind Admiral Drake, Foulaubin and Easton in the Grand Prix, in which Brantôme did not take part, and the latter had shown on more than one occasion, last year and this, what he can do with Admiral Drake. As recently as the Prix du Cadran (2½ miles) he beat the son of Craig an Eran, it is no exaggeration to say, by twenty lengths, and Admiral Drake had already won previously on the same course this year in good style.'

With regard to Denver II, it need only be added that he finished last of five runners in the race for the Doncaster Cup, though the day before the Ascot Cup M. Boussac's horse won the Churchill Stakes, two miles, by a length and a half from Enfield (giving 4 lb).

It is possible, perhaps even probable, that Brantôme at the top of his form would have had to play second fiddle to Tiberius. The latter's trainer, Lawson, held a very high opinion of his charge, and greatly regretted the absence of Windsor Lad, Tai-Yang, and Felicitation. Tiberius would, he declared, have beaten them all; and, be it understood, he was talking like that before as well as after the race. This praise would, however, have had fuller value if Brantôme had finished a respectable second, instead of where he did. The real Brantôme was not there at all. When he returned to the paddock he was blowing hard and continued blowing for several minutes. Baron Edouard de Rothschild must have felt very sad, but he screened his disappointment when subjected to the inevitable interview, and said: 'I realise now, too late, that the mishap which prevented my horse undergoing his scheduled training and gallops has caused him not to be at his best. I suppose I should not have sent him over, but I knew that such a wide interest was taken in him and the Gold Cup that I wanted to keep faith with the English public.' There spoke a true sportsman.

Tiberius finished his race in a way that delighted the crowd, who, as we have stated, flouted the traditional Ascot decorum and gave way to unrestrained enthusiasm. 'He wanted to go round again,' said his jockey, Weston. 'He is not a big 'un, but such a workman. The strong gallop was just what he wanted.'

Bred by Mr J. A. Hirst at his Sezincote Stud in Gloucestershire, Tiberius is a dark bay colt by Foxlaw out of Glenabatrick, by Captain Cuttle from Jura, by Gainsborough, the next dam being Sceptre's daughter Maid of the Mist, by Cyllene. He was one of five yearlings Mr Hirst sent to the Newmarket Sales in 1932. One was Valerius (by Son-in-Law), for whom the late Mr Simon Harrison gave 2,000 guineas on behalf of Sir Abe Bailey. None of the others was sold while in the ring. Tiberius was passed out when the bidding for him reached 750 guineas, to be subsequently bought by Sir Abe for 500 guineas after Mr Alec Taylor had inspected and approved the colt at Sezincote. He was dirt cheap.

Jura and Glenabatrick were both bred by Lord Astor, who bought Maid of the Mist when Sir William Bass dispersed his stud. Glenabatrick raced only when a two-year-old, and then but once, unplaced. The following year, 1930, she was mated with Foxlaw and, at the ensuing December Sales, sold to Mr Hirst for 470 guineas. To Lord Astor, therefore, belongs the credit for the mating of Foxlaw and Glenabatrick which resulted in Tiberius. It may have been the interest he thus had in the colt that induced him to allow Bright Bird to do the 'donkey work' in the race for the Ascot Cup. Lord Astor will also be interested in Quintilius, the yearling half-brother to Tiberius which Sir Abe Bailey bought at Doncaster last September for 3,700 guineas, because the youngster is by his horse Buchan.

Son-in-Law was a three-year-old when the war began in 1914 (he won the Goodwood Cup that year), and for the next four years there was no racing at Ascot. If the opportunity had been afforded him in 1915 or 1916 the son of Dark Ronald would probably have won the Ascot Cup. However, his name will always be associated with the event. His sons Foxlaw, Bosworth and Trimdon won it – the latter twice; and now we have two of Foxlaw's sons – Foxhunter and Tiberius – on the roll of winners. It is a wonderful family record; six Ascot Cup winners in the past ten years.

After his disastrous expedition to Ascot, Brantôme did not race until September 22nd, when, at Longchamp, he won the Prix du Prince d'Orange from four opponents. The distance was twelve furlongs, and he won very easily. Two weeks later he appeared on the Turf for the last time, again at Longchamp, and again in a twelve-furlong race, the Prix de l'Arc de Triomphe, one of the events he won last year. To the dismay of his admirers he was beaten into fourth place. He finished two lengths behind the winner, Samos. Again he had Admiral Drake behind him. By way of explanation the critics could only offer the suggestion 'he is not the horse he was before Ascot.' This defeat brought the record of his career on the Turf still closer in parallel with that of Pretty Polly, whose last race was the Ascot Cup in which she was beaten by Bachelor's

Button. Both failed only twice, once abroad and once at home; both were beaten in the Ascot Cup; both suffered defeat in their final races. Both, it may be added, were most brilliant performers.

Bahram's Triple Crown

Bahram entered the St Leger unbeaten in eight races and came out of it unbeaten in nine, including the Triple Crown of the Two Thousand Guineas, Derby and St Leger. He was the first to have won this triple run at Newmarket, Epsom and Doncaster since Rock Sand in 1903. However, in the meantime, Pommern, Gay Crusader and Gainsborough had also triumphed in those classics but during the war years when all three races were presented at Newmarket. In looking over the purse money won by the unsullied Bahram, it is interesting to note that the St Leger was the richest of the three classics, followed by the Two Thousand Guineas and then the Derby. Considering that it was thirty-two years between Rock Sand and Bahram and another thirty-five years before Nijinsky II accomplished the feat in 1970, England had but three Triple Crown winners in a span of sixty-seven years. Nor has there been another one at the time of publication. With changing times and priorites in racing, it is quite possible that England has saluted the last of its Triple Crown winners.

THE JUDGE'S verdict of five lengths in favour of Bahram was questioned by some of the onlookers, who thought two or three lengths might properly have been added, but a photograph of the finish shows that it was correct. According to the same 'witness', Buckleigh may not, however, have been so much as three lengths behind Solar Ray. The marvel was that Buckleigh had managed to finish third, because half-way through the race he was last of all and looked like being tailed off. Plassy was fourth, four or five lengths behind Buckleigh.

This was the third time the Aga Khan's colours had been successful in the St Leger for they were placed first by Salmon-Trout in 1924, and by Firdaussi in 1932. His Highness could not get to Doncaster to see Bahram win; he was detained at Geneva as the representative of India at the meeting of the League of Nations dealing with the Italy-Abyssinia dispute. There he received a telegram bearing the laconically-worded message: 'Won easily by five lengths. Butters.'

By adding his St Leger victory to those he gained in the Two Thousand Guineas and Derby, Bahram gained what has long been called 'The Triple Crown'. It first became possible for a horse to earn the distinction in 1809, when the Guineas was instituted, but Bahram is only the eleventh to win all three events. The other ten were:

West Australian	1850	Isinglass	1893
Gladiateur	1865	Galtee More	1897
Lord Lyon	1866	Flying Fox	1899
Ormonde	1886	Diamond Jubilee	1900
Common	1891	Rock Sand	1903

It will be seen that those ten horses came within a period extending over fifty years. We have had to wait thirty-two years to be able to make an addition to the list. It can, however, almost be taken for granted that, but for the war, Pommern, Gay Crusader and Gainsborough would have been 'crowned'. They all won the regulation Guineas and the Newmarket substitutes for the Derby and St Leger. There is little reason for doubting they would have been equally successful if the two latter races had been run at Epsom and Doncaster. Bayardo was another horse who ought to have joined the elect, for he was unquestionably the best of his year, yet secured classic honours only in the St Leger. Bahram is one of the very few horses unbeaten when saddled for the St Leger. Others in the last fifty years were Ormonde, Isinglass, and Pretty Polly.

Bahram.

Disclaiming any desire to belittle Bahram, we are bound to point out that his progress to the eminence he reached was, in all probability, made much easier than it might have been if all had gone well with Bobsleigh. Ormonde is among the giants because of his superiority to Minting, while Isinglass accounted for a formidable opponent in Ravensbury. Bahram is, of course, shown in the records as having beaten Bobsleigh many lengths the only time they met, but we have Perryman's word for it that he found Bobsleigh, when he won the Newmarket Stakes, a vastly better colt than when he was beaten in the Guineas. Are we, however, justified in measuring Bahram's abilities by the character of the horses he defeated? He won the Derby and St Leger so easily that he may be the best horse we have seen for many years. We shall never know for certain whether he is or not because the St Leger was his last race. So far back as June the Aga Khan let it be known that Bahram would not race after this season. In the autumn there was some talk of his competing for the Champion Stakes, but if the idea was ever seriously entertained it was abandoned. The son of Blandford has gone to the stud with a splendid record of achievements on the Turf. So great is his reputation that, at a fee of 500 guineas, his book was full for three years immediately after, if not before, he won the St Leger.

Here is the list of the races won by Bahram:

TWO YEARS OLD, 1934

National Breeders' Produce Stakes, 5 f, Sandown Park; 20 to 1 laid against him.	£5,559
Rous Memorial Stakes, 6 f, Goodwood; 5 to 4 on	£1,140
Gimcrack Stakes, 6 f, York; 7 to 2 on	£1,412
Boscawen Stakes, 5 f, Newmarket; 10 to 1 on	£600
Middle Park Stakes, 6 f, Newmarket; 7 to 2 on	£3,047
Stake total, 2 years old	£11,758

THREE YEARS OLD

Two Thousand Guineas, 1 m, Newmarket; 7 to 2 against	£9,339¼
The Derby, 1½ m, Epsom; 5 to 4 against	£9,216
St James's Palace Stakes, 1 m, Ascot; 8 to 1 on	£3,230
St Leger, 1 m 6½ f, Doncaster; 11 to 4 on	£9,543¼
Grand total	£43,086½

By way of showing how much more money there is to be won on the Turf today than there was fifty years ago, we may recall the fact that unbeaten Ormonde, though he won sixteen races, could only claim a stake total of £28,465½. His successes in the classic events netted £13,150, whereas in those three races Bahram earned £28,098½.

BBR–1935

Tribute to Brown Jack

It was with a feeling of intense regret, indeed emotion would not be too strong a word, that the news that Brown Jack had been put down was received by the racing world. Since 1934 Sir Harold Wernher's great horse had been in retirement at his owner's Thorpe Lubenham Hall, near Market Harborough. It had been intended to move him to Sir Harold's new home near Luton, but the horse caught a chill and had to be destroyed.

Foaled in 1924, Brown Jack was entered in one of the Dublin sales, but no buyer was forthcoming. He was afterwards sold for £110 to Mr Marcus Thompson, of Kilmore, Co. Tipperary, who had him cut. Mr Charles Rogers, the well-known Irish trainer, then bought him for £275, and the horse was run loose in a paddock at Ratoath all through his two-year-old days.

Brown Jack ran twice in Ireland, carrying Mr Rogers' colours. Aubrey Hastings, acting for Sir Harold Wernher, was rather impressed with the gelding, and purchased him for £750, with a contingency of £50 if he won a race. An accomplished trainer of jumpers, Hastings soon had Brown Jack racing over hurdles with success. He ran in ten races under National Hunt Rules, winning seven of them and being placed twice, earning £1,504. On his last outing over hurdles he won the Champion Hurdle.

It was, we are told, Steve Donoghue's suggestion that Brown Jack should return to racing on the flat. Under the Rules of Racing, Brown Jack ran fifty-five times, winning eighteen races worth £21,646, and was placed twelve times. His fame in Turf annals is due to his marvellous record in the Queen Alexandra Stakes at Ascot of two and three-quarter miles, the longest flat race in this country. Partnered by Steve Donoghue, who died three years ago, Brown Jack won this event six years in succession, from 1929 to 1934.

It is hardly likely that we shall ever see the equal of this feat, or anything approaching it, in our lifetime. One has to go back almost a hundred years to find a parallel achievement, when Beeswing, the dam of Newminster, won the Newcastle Cup, then one of the main Cup races, six times between 1836 and 1842, finishing second to Lanercost in 1840. She won the Doncaster Gold Shield (Doncaster Cup) four times in 1837,

1840, 1841 and 1842, also winning the Ascot Gold Cup in the last year.

The record for successive victories in an important race in this country, however, must go to Dr Syntax, the sire of Beeswing. Dr Syntax, who was trained at Tupgill, Middleham, won the Preston Gold Cup seven times running in 1815 to 1821, and finished second the following year.

Brown Jack was bred by Mr G. S. Webb, and was a brown gelding by Jackdaw out of Querquidella, by Kroonstad out of Garganey, by Wildfowler out of Sapphire, by Buckingham, a son of Galopin. In his pedigree appear three crosses of Galopin, for Jackdaw's dam was by St Frusquin (by St Simon, son of Galopin) and Kroonstad's dam was by St Simon. It may be taken this concentration accounts for Brown Jack's outstanding stamina, for his sire, Jackdaw, was by Thrush, a sprinter pure and simple, and a sire of sprinters, with the exception of Jackdaw, who himself won the Alexandra Stakes (or Plate, as it was then known). This is yet another instance of the unaccountable mysteries met with in breeding, though it must be said that Jackdaw generally got staying stock, the average winning distance of his progeny being around ten furlongs.

Kroonstad, a son of the 1887 St Leger winner, Kilwarlin, was a hardy

Brown Jack.

racehorse. He was in training for seven years, and in the colours of Lord Ellesmere ran in ninety-one races, winning twenty-two of them. Wildfowler, sire of Garganey, won the St Leger in 1898, and her grandson, Criosphinx, was a daughter of The Sphynx, third dam of another great stayer, William the Third, and Amiable, winner of the One Thousand Guineas and Oaks in 1894. Criosphinx was out of The Sphynx, by Newminster, which introduced the blood of Beeswing and her sire, Dr Syntax.

Among the other good races in which Brown Jack was successful were the Ascot Stakes (2 m) and the Hwfa Williams Handicap (2 m) in 1929, the Goodwood Cup (2 m 5 f) and the Doncaster Cup ($2\frac{1}{4}$ m) in 1930, the Chester Cup ($2\frac{1}{4}$ m) and the Ebor Handicap ($1\frac{3}{4}$ m) in 1931, the Prince Edward Handicap ($2\frac{1}{4}$ m) in 1932, and the Rosebery Handicap ($2\frac{1}{4}$ m) at Epsom in 1933.

It was later in the year after his sixth and last triumph in the Queen Alexandra Stakes that his Majesty King George V approved a suggestion that Brown Jack's achievements should be commemorated by a tangible memorial at Ascot. A bronze statue of the horse now stands in the Royal Box there.

Brown Jack's trainer, Ivor Anthony, did not watch the race at Ascot in 1934. As was recorded in the edition of the *Review* for that year, he firmly believed the old fellow would win, but dreaded seeing him beaten, so sat under a tree in the paddock until he heard the cheering which assured him that gallant old Jack had really won. The King sent for Brown Jack's proud owner, Sir Harold Wernher, and congratulated him on being the possessor of so remarkable a horse.

We cannot do better now than quote from a tribute to this great favourite, paid by 'Rapier' in *Sport and Country*:

'The incident (just described) shows the affection which a great horse can arouse in the human breast – an affection in this case, incidentally, shared by a vast public and in particular by the great jockey who invariably rode him in nearly all his races, Steve Donoghue. Steve loved the old fellow. He even sent him a telegram on his twentieth birthday!

Horses like this contribute something very valuable to racing. They raise it above its material estate and enrich it with the tradition of courage and steadfastness which they weave into its history. Let no one jeer at a sport which can produce such splendid animals. There are not many Brown Jacks, nor can his kind be classified except for the measure of regard in which they are held and remembered.

He was a funny old horse, full of character. The late Robert Lyle, of *The Times*, who wrote a book about him, told how he spent every spare moment he had in – sleeping. He used to prop his great behind on his manger and fall happily to sleep in his own droll fashion. Long may he rest in our memories!'

Mahmoud's Derby Victory

*Prior to the victory of the Aga Khan's grey Blenheim colt Mahmoud in the 1936 Derby, it was almost universally accepted that he was a doubtful stayer over 1½ miles because of the speed presences in his pedigree, primarily his grandam, Mumtaz Mahal, and others in that family. 'Among the comparatively few people,' noted the **BBR**, 'who refused to adopt the general opinion regarding Mahmoud's prospects in the Derby was Mr Tom Walls, owner of the (1932) Derby winner April the Fifth. His belief that the colt would stay the twelve furlongs and readily adapt himself to the Epsom gradients was published in the sporting Press. This was, however, a voice raised in a wilderness of scepticism, and longish odds continued to be laid against Mahmoud. Let it not be supposed that we are assuming the scoffer's mantle to deride those who prematurely consigned Mahmoud to the ranks of sprinters or middle-distance runners. We were numbered with the multitude and meekly receive any castigation that may be deserved.'*

A partial recounting of Mahmoud's Derby victory is presented here, especially for the benefit of Americans, for it was Mahmoud, along with another tail-female son of Mumtaz Mahal, Nasrullah, who were most responsible for changing the shape and direction of breeding in that part of the world in the past fifty years.

Mahmoud's Turf Record

TWO YEARS OLD, 1935

Unpl. Spring Stakes (5 f), Newmarket; 25 to 1 against him   £——

3rd New Stakes (5 f), Ascot; beaten 1½ and 3 lengths by Wyndham (Bossover colt) and Allensford; 6th favourite at 10 to 1   £——

Won Exeter Stakes (6 f), Newmarket; favourite 11 to 10; won by 3 lengths   £830

Won Richmond Stakes (6 f), Goodwood; gave weight to all but one opponent; favourite 2 to 1, and won by a length   £1,562

Won Champagne Stakes (6 f), Doncaster; favourite 13 to 8; beat Abjer and Wyndham three-quarters and two lengths   £2,700

3rd Middle Park Stakes (6 f), Newmarket; favourite 11 to 8; beaten 2 lengths and a head by Abjer and Wyndham. Began slowly   £——

THREE YEARS OLD

Unpl. Greenham Plate (1 m), Newbury; carried biggest weight; favourite at 11 to 4
£——

2nd Two Thousand Guineas (1 m); fifth favourite 100 to 8; beaten short head by Pay Up
£——

Won the Derby (1½ m) at Epsom; fifth favourite at 100 to 8; beat Taj Akbar, Thankerton and Pay Up by 3 lengths, three-parts of length, and 3 lengths £9,934¼

2nd St James's Palace Stakes (1 m), Ascot; 11 to 8 on favourite; beaten 5 lengths by Rhodes Scholar (rec. 7 lb) £——

3rd St Leger (1 m 6½ f), Doncaster; 2nd favourite at 5 to 1; beaten three-parts of length and 3 lengths by Boswell and Fearless Fox £——

Ran 10, won 4, second 2, third 3   £15,026¼

MAHMOUD'S triumph was a 'facer' for those of us who had doubted his ability to stay the twelve furlongs. We should have been astonished if he had won by a narrow margin, but there he was, a very easy winner, and he had run the course in time which beat the best previously recorded by a fifth of a second – another feature of his victory which nonplussed the sceptics, who had supposed he had, perhaps, half a chance of winning if the race was run at a moderate pace. There would have been no smashing of the time record if Thankerton had not made that amazing spurt when he did. It maybe cost him the highest honour; it assuredly deprived Pay Up, Boswell and others of the horses that entered the straight in favourable positions of the chances they would normally have possessed. Mahmoud alone, aided by his quick-witted jockey, was able

Mahmoud.

to adapt himself to the situation which so unexpectedly developed. Smirke, as we have stated, planned to make a dash for the winning post at a late stage of the contest, but when, at the top of the straight, he saw Thankerton so far ahead he had to abandon his preconceived ideas and formulate new ones on the spur of the moment. He therefore set sail after the lone leader. When he found he was going to catch Thankerton a quarter of a mile from home he feared he had made a mistake, and that he would be blamed for not waiting a little longer. Would Mahmoud keep going to the end? He wondered and wondered, and when at last the goal was reached and the tension over he shouted 'Whoopee!'

Although Mahmoud had far fewer backers than Taj Akbar there was the usual cheering when the Aga Khan and his son, Prince Aly, went on to the course to escort the winner to the unsaddling enclosure. His Highness was very elated and waved his hat to the crowd. It may be recalled that when Blenheim won the Derby the Aga Khan also ran Rustom Pasha, who was believed to be much the better of the two, while in the St Leger of 1932 his winner, Firdaussi, had a much smaller following than his other two runners, Dastur and Udaipur, who finished second and fourth. Betting, however, does not interest the Aga Khan. 'I race,' he has said, 'to prove my breeding theories and principles.' His Highness is the fifth owner to have his colours placed first and second in the Derby. The others were the Duke of Bedford in 1789, Lord Grosvenor in 1790, Lord Jersey in 1827, and Colonel Peel in 1844. In the last-named year the Colonel's Orlando and Ionian finished second and third to Running Rein, who was disqualified.

Frank Butters, the trainer of the Aga Khan's horses, and also of Noble King, said he was not altogether surprised when he saw Mahmoud win, but he had had every reason for believing that Taj Akbar would outstay the grey colt.

Gordon Richards has for many years been our champion jockey, but he has still to ride a horse to victory in the Derby. Two years ago he finished second on Easton. This year, when Taj Akbar was allotted to him, it looked as though his ambition would at last be realised and, like most people, he did not expect to be thwarted by the supposed non-stayer Mahmoud. He was inclined to blame himself for having restrained Taj Akbar so long and allowed Mahmoud to get first run. When, however, he won the Chester Vase on the son of Fairway he had 'waited' until two furlongs from home and then found his horse able to show a fine burst of speed. He had hoped the same plan would succeed in the Derby, but when he asked Taj Akbar to catch Mahmoud the colt could not run quite so fast as he did at Chester. As, however, he was staying on at the finish Richards came to the conclusion that he should, perhaps, have placed more reliance on his mount's stamina and begun his final run earlier.

Wotan's Astonishing Victory in the Melbourne Cup

The first Melbourne Cup was run in 1861. It had known some memorable surprises prior to 1936, but then the mightiest of upsets took place when the New Zealand-owned Wotan, who could not find backers at 500 to 1 a few days before the race, came home in front. Every major classic in international racing has experienced the old truism that 'the unexpected always happens', but there have been few surprise victories, if any, bolts from the blue to match that of Wotan.

MANY amazing Melbourne Cups have been run, but Wotan's victory will for ever be regarded in Australian racing circles as the most astonishing since the Cup was inaugurated in 1861. He was the rank outsider of the field at 100 to 1, for he had shown no form to cause him to be considered even a likely runner.

Wotan did not arrive in Australia from New Zealand until a few weeks before the race, and as he had finished tenth in a field of eleven in the W. S. Cox Plate at Moonee Valley ten days before the Cup – his only start in Australia – and had shown no form in private, the appearance of his name in the acceptance list surprised most people. His owners, the three Smith Brothers, who are farmers living near the village of Mangaweka (New Zealand), were regarded as cheerful optimists. The horse had only won two races. The first was a two-year-old event of five furlongs at Wanganui, and the other a Hack Handicap at the same track, less than two months before the Melbourne Cup was run. The distance of his second race was nine furlongs, and it was the way he finished that induced his owners to send him to Australia. The trainer, J. Fryer, was already in Australia with several horses, and probably he was as surprised as most people when it was announced that Wotan was to join his team.

Wotan had promised well as a two-year-old, and it was believed that he would develop good form the following season, when he was brought to Australia. He did not thrive here, however. He was scratched from the classics and the Cups, and only ran in one race, a three-year-old event at Randwick, made no show, and was sent back to the Dominion to be 'spelled' at his owner's farm. On returning to Australia, Wotan

refused to look at his feed, and Fryer despaired of racing him; but his
owners insisted on his having a run in the Cox Plate. His showing in that
race gave no indication of success in the Melbourne Cup, and 500 to 1
was offered against him, with no takers. A few days before the race his
owners announced that if the ground was heavy Wotan would not run,
and he was withdrawn from the Hotham Handicap the first day of the
VRC Spring meeting because of the going. Then the weather improved.
Wotan was saddled for the Cup and won!

The success of the New Zealand horse staggered the huge crowd at
Flemington on Cup Day. Thousands did not know the name of the dark
brown horse that suddenly loomed up a furlong from home and,
finishing better than Silver Standard, beat him a neck. No Cup winner
has ever returned to scale in such silence. Records were searched to find
a parallel. It was discovered that The Pearl was the only other winner of
the Cup to start at 100 to 1, and he won in 1876. Only Wotan's owners
backed him. They won about £10,000 from the bookmakers, and
approximately £3,000 through the totalisator for an outlay of a little
more than £100.

The 1938 Grand National won by Battleship

As the Review *explained in its account of the 1938 Grand National
Steeplechase, 'There is no race with which so much "romance" is
associated and none which makes a better story.' The 1938 renewal
lived up to every expectation and added a few gratuities of its own. It
was won by the tiny American-bred Battleship, a son of America's most
revered champion, Man o' War, and he was ridden by Bruce Hobbs,
the youngest jockey, at seventeen, to handle a Grand National winner.
Although there may have been smaller Grand National heroes, Battleship, owned by Mrs Marion du Pont Scott, was the first American-
bred and -owned winner of the world's most famous jumping classic. In
addition, he was an entire horse and the first such to complete the trip in
front since 1901. It also provided one of the 'tightest fits' in the race's
long history before the 'pocket' Battleship was declared the winner over
the Irish favourite Royal Danieli. Previously the American-bred Rubio
had won the race in 1908, but he carried the silks of an Englishman.
So, of all the Grand National runnings, that of 1938 will always
remain among the most memorable.*

REGARDED from the breeding point of view the Grand National is an event of minor importance. About 90 per cent of the horses that win it are geldings, have their day, and become mere memories. Regarded from the sporting angle it is, however, the most colourful and popular event of its kind in the world. There is no race with which so much 'romance' is associated and none which makes a better story. Year after year our Grand National folder, fed as material comes to hand, contains more documents than any other in the file. The contest staged at Aintree, Liverpool, last March furnished, one way or another, a wealth of picturesque features which it now becomes our duty, privilege and pleasure to recount in these pages.

For the benefit of readers abroad we will begin by stating that the Grand National course measures 4 miles and 856 yards. The circuit is half that distance, so it has to be traversed twice. There are thirty stiff fences and a broad water jump to be negotiated. The last fence is nearly three furlongs from the winning post. Two-thirds of the course is in the 'country', that is to say outside the territory used for flat racing. When at the far end of the track the horses are nearly a mile from the stands and their progress there can, naturally, only be seen when visibility is good, as it happened to be this year. The prize money varies in accordance with the contributions obtained from nominators in the form of sub-scriptions and forfeits. The executive add £4,000. The second horse receives 10 per cent of the whole stake, the third 5 per cent and the fourth 2½ per cent. There are also allocations to the trainer and rider of the winner. The race is, of course, a handicap, the weights ranging from 12 st 7 lb down to 10 st.

Last year's victor, Royal Mail, a nine-year-old horse by My Prince, was the only previous winner of the race among this year's seventy-eight entries, and he was automatically placed at the head of the handicap with 12 st 7 lb. Next to him, at 12 st, was Airgead Sios, an eight-year-old gelding by Werwolf; he is a fine jumper with good speed. At Aintree last year he won the Champion and Becher Steeplechases over a portion of the Grand National course. Cooleen, the ten-year-old mare who ran a good second in the 'National' last year when receiving 9 lb from Royal Mail, was allotted 11 st 8 lb, and therefore now got 13 lb from him. Battleship, aged eleven, an American-bred and -owned son of Man o' War, measuring only 15.2, was weighted at 11 st 6 lb; Royal Danieli, an Irish horse, carried 11 st 3 lb, while Workman, also an Irish 'hope', had only 10 st 2 lb in the saddle.

When, towards the end of January (two months before it was run), betting on the race was first recorded, Royal Mail was one of the favourites. He seemed to outclass his rivals, and to have an excellent chance of copying Reynoldstown (likewise a son of My Prince) who carried 11 st 4 lb to victory in 1935, and scored again the next year with 12 st 2 lb in the saddle. Royal Mail's weight was now 8 lb more than last year's. Backers had assumed Royal Mail would again be ridden by Evan Williams, and were astonished by an announcement made early in February that the horse's owner, Mr Lloyd Thomas, attached to the British Embassy in Paris, had decided to ride the horse himself in the Grand National. Mr Thomas was in his fiftieth year and had done little or no race-riding for two seasons. In 1932 he won the Grand Sefton Steeplechase on his mare Destiny Bay and was her pilot in the Grand National of 1934, when she fell three fences from home. But that had been four years back, and many of Mr Thomas's friends thought his determination to ride Royal Mail in the Grand National a somewhat rash one, but he would not be dissuaded and proceeded to get what riding practice he could so as to be keyed-up on the day. On February 10th he rode his horse Periwinkle II in a steeplechase at Derby. His mount fell but Mr Thomas was unhurt. Twelve days later he again rode Periwinkle at Derby. His horse and another came to the last fence together, leading the field. Periwinkle crashed into the obstacle and Mr Thomas was fatally injured by being pitched on to his head. Thus came to a tragic end the life of a man who enjoyed popularity in many spheres, not least in that of sport.

A few days later we learned that Mr Thomas's executors and family had decided that, unless other arrangements were made, Royal Mail would still run in the Grand National and be ridden by Evan Williams. The odds against the horse had lengthened when Mr Thomas resolved to take the mount himself, but when the revised plan became known Royal Mail at once became the favourite again at 10 to 1; indeed, that day he was the only horse backed. As luck would have it, while doing a schooling gallop at Lingfield the very next day, with Williams in the saddle, Royal Mail fell and his rider damaged a collar bone he had fractured two months earlier. It was stated that the jockey would be ready for the Grand National, but the odds against Royal Mail went out to 16 to 1. Later they shortened again, and for two weeks before the day of the race (March 25th) the son of My Prince was the favourite at or about $12\frac{1}{2}$ to 1.

In the meantime Royal Mail had been sold. A day or two after the Thomas family had intimated that the horse would meet his engagement in the Grand National it was suddenly decided that an immediate sale was advisable. The horse therefore came under the hammer at a race meeting at Hurst Park on March 12th. The first bid for him was 4,000 guineas. Offers rose by 250 guineas a time and one of 6,250 guineas was made by Mr Robin McAlpine. Mrs Camille Evans (née Clifford) then went to 6,500 guineas and at that figure Royal Mail became her property. When the hammer fell she turned to Ivor Anthony, who had trained the horse for Mr Thomas, and said, 'Take him back to Wroughton and do what you like with him.' As Evan Williams was the stable's jockey, the arrangement that he should ride Royal Mail at Aintree remained undisturbed.

At this date the most-fancied of Royal Mail's rivals were Takvor Pacha, a six-year-old French horse owned by the Marquis de San-Miguel; Blue Shirt, a seven-year-old belonging to Mr Arthur Sainsbury; Mr J. B. Snow's Delachance, and Mr James V. Rank's mare Cooleen. The previous day (March 11th) Takvor Pacha had won by eight lengths a three-mile steeplechase at Hurst Park, and three weeks before that finished second in a race at Newbury, beating Cooleen three lengths. It was widely recognised that he was a very good 'chaser and he had the reputation of being a fine stayer. There remained, however, the question whether he would be stumped by the stiff Grand National fences. Many readers will remember Lutteur III, who won the Grand National in 1909. He was then five years old, and came from France in the late winter to be prepared for the Grand National by Harry Escott. He had one preliminary outing; it was in a race at Hurst Park corresponding to that Takvor Pacha won. Lutteur started the outsider of four in the betting, but won in a canter by six lengths from Leinster. We were in those days writing the racing article for a Sunday newspaper, and with the utmost confidence tipped Lutteur to win the Grand National; and win he did, very comfortably. It was said of him that he might not like the Aintree fences, but the people behind him declared he was so clever that they hoped he would slightly touch one early in the race, because if he did he would not touch another. We heard much the same about Takvor Pacha, but, as will be seen presently, the upshot was very different. It is understood that during the week or so preceeding the Grand National his owner received and refused more than one offer for the horse. Mr James V. Rank wanted him.

Blue Shirt is a gelding by the Son-in-Law horse Apron. In each of his last four outings before the Grand National he had run in four-mile steeplechases and won three. There were, however, experts who regarded the quality of these achievements with less respect than the public inclined to do. Blue Shirt was racing in the Grand National for the first time, but last year he ran fifth in the Grand Sefton Steeplechase, and so demonstrated that he could cope with the Aintree obstacles. Delachance was a fancied runner in last year's Grand National, but got rid of his jockey at the Canal fence the second time round. He won a race at Lingfield six weeks before this year's contest, but his later form amounted to little. Cooleen's chance had to be gauged mainly by her running in the Grand National last year, when she finished a good second to Royal Mail, whom she was now meeting on 4 lb better terms.

These five horses were still the leaders in the betting when the race was about to be run two weeks later, but their ranking had then changed, the odds finally offered being: 8 to 1 each Blue Shirt and Cooleen, 100 to 9 each Delachance, 100 to 8 Royal Mail, and 100 to 7 Takvor Pacha. The previous day Cooleen was for a time a doubtful runner because the ground was so firm, but Mr Rank allowed his consideration for the public, who had backed her so freely, to outweigh his scruples. Ivor Anthony was at the same time also a little anxious. While declaring his belief that Royal Mail was a better horse than when he won last year, there was, he said, one point about which he was doubtful; his charge had never raced on hard turf and might not like it. Fortunately, however, these misgivings were 'dissolved' in the course of the next eighteen hours. There was copious rain during the night and more fell on Friday morning. In fact, up to midday it looked as if the Grand National was going to be ruined as a spectacle, and that the spectators would have a most uncomfortable experience. But before the afternoon's proceedings began there came a very welcome change. The rain clouds vanished, the sun appeared, and the atmosphere became crystal clear. Better conditions for the great contest could not have been desired.

Thirty-six runners lined up at the starting post and were quickly despatched. The leaders at the first fence were Airgead Sios and Lough Cottate. Then came Royal Mail, Bachelor Prince, Dunhill Castle, and Royal Danieli. At the canal turn, where half the first circuit had been completed, Airgead Sios was showing the way well clear of Royal Danieli and Rockquilla, but at the plain fence after Valentine's he over-jumped and fell on landing. Before reaching the racecourse Delachance raced past Royal Danieli, and they were first and second over the water. Half the race had now been run and there were still twenty horses standing up, but immediately afterwards one of them, Rock Lad, dropped dead. At this stage the immediate followers of Delachance and Royal Danieli were Lough Cottage, Dunhill Castle, Red Knight II, Rockquilla, Battleship and Workman. Farther back were Royal Mail, Cooleen and Blue Shirt.

Away the nineteen survivors went into 'the country' again, and the outlook now rapidly changed. Little Battleship passed horse after horse (including Delachance, who had lost the lead), and he and Royal Danieli were leading the field when they jumped Becher's Brook together. Close behind them were Lough Cottage and Delachance, followed by Workman, who had gone forward in Battleship's wake. Before reaching Valentine's, two furlongs further on, Lough Cottage began to fail, and presently Delachance also weakened. Meanwhile Workman was making good progress, and, approaching the last fence but two, was third to Royal Danieli and Battleship. At that fence, Battleship made a mistake which cost him several lengths, so that when his jockey had him balanced again he was third, Workman having passed him. Now, therefore, we saw two Irish-trained horses racing first and second, and it looked a fairly sage bet that either Royal Danieli or Workman would win, with odds on the former. There were only two more fences to jump, but, lo and behold, at the first of them Workman blundered. Before he got going again, Battleship had once more become second, and was so full of running that Royal Danieli led by only two lengths when they reached the last fence.

Battleship.

The winning post was still three furlongs away and the situation became complicated because of the intrusion of a riderless horse. It was Takvor Pacha. He had got rid of his jockey at Becher's the first time round, but went on, jumping every fence until he came to the last. When close to this he suddenly dashed to the left, skirted round the fence, re-entered the course, and came along with Royal Danieli on his left and Battleship on his right. In order to avoid him, Hobbs, Battleship's jockey, went over towards the stands. A moving picture of this critical stage of the race shows that Takvor Pacha did not really incommode either of the two leaders; he seemed intent on getting to the winning post, and was, in fact, the first to reach it. In the meantime, Battleship had gradually made headway. Fifty yards from the goal it was obvious to the excited onlookers that there would be very little between him and Royal Danieli at the finish, but the horses were racing so far apart it was practically impossible for the spectators to tell which was in front. There was the usual big contingent from Ireland in the crowd, and it was vociferously shouting Royal Danieli home. Immediately after the two horses had crossed the line there was 'a silence that could be felt'. Then up went Battleship's number. He had, decreed the judge, beaten Royal Danieli a head.

The Irishmen were crestfallen, but there was a great noise. The book-makers were cheering lustily. Battleship had started at 40 to 1 chance, and in many a 'book' not a single bet about him had been recorded. The Tote dividend was at the rate of $62\frac{1}{2}$ to 1. In the Tote's 'Daily Double,' speculators had to find the winner of the Grand National and the Bickerstaffe Plate. The latter was won by a $12\frac{1}{2}$ to 1 chance. A sporting peer was the only punter who picked both winners, and his reward was £5,062 2s for ten shillings. When the race started odds of 18 to 1 were offered against Royal Danieli, and 28 to 1 against Workman, who finished third, many lengths behind the two leaders. Ten others completed the course to finish in the following order: Cooleen, Delachance, Red Knight II, Blue Shirt, Hopeful Hero, Under Bid, Bachelor Prince, Lough Cottage, Provocative and Drim.

Custom ordains that the winner of the Grand National should be met by its owner and led to the unsaddling enclosure at the back of the main stand. Battleship had no such escort. His American owner, Mrs Marion Scott, a member of the wealthy du Pont family, remained shyly in the background. She arrived in England earlier in the week to see her horse run and, having witnessed his triumph, quickly left the course, travelled to London and caught the first available boat to New York. Her unemotional attitude during the period of excitement after the race was a remarkable exhibition of self control. When approached by a journalist who wanted a word or two with her she turned to her trainer and said: 'Let's go and see the horse.' How would an American 'news hawk' have handled the situation?

To go back to the race, let us see what Battleship's rider had to say about his experience. Bruce Hobbs his name, seventeen years his age, he is the youngest jockey to pilot a horse to victory in the Grand National, a fact he can be proud of as long as he lives. Percy Woodland was eighteen when he won on Drumcree in 1903. Bruce's father, Reg Hobbs, of Lambourn, Berkshire, trained Battleship, and the day before the race lamented that the boy had not a better horse to ride! Young as he is, Bruce Hobbs is an experienced horseman. He was hunting with the Quorn when five, and before he became a professional jockey in December, 1936, had ridden ten winners under National Hunt rules as an amateur. Here we have regretfully to mention that early in this last November he had a bad fall when riding at Cheltenham and one of his spinal vertebræ was fractured. A week or two later he underwent an operation. Fortunately it is believed he will make a good recovery.

We have, of course, to quote 'Ajax', of the *Evening Standard,* in order to present the best story Bruce Hobbs related about the Grand National. It reads:

'They went off at a fast pace, and, thinking there might be a doubt about my little horse's stamina, I was not in any hurry. I was only about tenth or so when we settled down. In the first circuit he was jumping perfectly. As we went into the country the second time there were half a dozen in front of me. He was going to my liking, so I let him move up to take a place just behind the leaders as we went along to Becher's. Then, without having bustled him or asked him for a real effort, I had got on terms with Royal Danieli, who had been making the running. We took Becher's together. At the canal fence my horse made his first mistake. It was nothing serious, and there was no danger of falling. He did not lose any ground to speak of, and I was quickly up with Royal Danieli once more.

'Over Valentine's we went together and then came to the last fence in the country, which is the third from home. Battleship hit it rather hard, and though he gathered himself together in wonderful fashion, he gave a deep sigh, and I knew it had robbed him of some of his energy. His mistake also cost me valuable ground, and for a moment I thought my chance had gone. That enabled Workman to take second place, and I was only third, several lengths behind Royal Danieli and Workman, who were racing for the lead as we came on to the racecourse. I knew then I had to do something, so I set about him, and to my surprise he began to gallop strongly again. The first fence on the race-course he took all right, but I was still well in arrears.

'Between the last two fences Workman dropped out, and I became second again. Royal Danieli went over the last fence three lengths in front of me. That was a lot to make up on the flat, and once over the fence I sent Battleship along for all he was worth. The loose horse, Takvor Pacha, was with us, and I took Battleship across to the stand side to escape his attentions. Then once more I sat down to ride my hardest. Gradually I closed the gap, but half-way along the run in I wondered whether I would get up in time. My little horse stuck to his work with remarkable gameness, however, and seeming to sense where the winning post was, he just pushed his nose in front in the last stride.'

Royal Danieli's jockey, Moore, who had only recently become a professional, was naturally disappointed when 'robbed' on the post of the victory he had felt certain of gaining as he came over the last fence with a good lead. After stating that his horse only made two slight mistakes, Moore went on:

'After going into the country the second time I was never headed except momentarily. Naturally I thought I was going to win when Workman began to drop away, and though my horse hit the top of the last fence but one he did not lose any ground. Getting first over the last fence I thought the race was mine. The loose horse interfered with me but probably not to a greater extent than Battleship. I continued to ride and thought I had won but the judge is the one man who can express an opinion in a close finish. What I do think is that if there had been another fence after the last one I would certainly have won, for my horse was always going like a winner so long as there was any jumping to be done. It was the long run from the final fence which beat him, and it is bad luck to be robbed of victory in such a manner.'

Workman's jockey, Brogan, also a young man, said his horse jumped well most of the time but made mistakes at Becher's and Valentine's the second time round. He was tiring as he approached the last fence but one, and Brogan thought it would be correct to say that his horse could not stay the full course, because the mistakes he made did not impair his chance.

The race was run in 9 min 29⅕ sec. The time record is held by Golden Miller who, in 1934, ran the course in 9 min 20⅖ sec. The following year Reynoldstown won in 9 min 21 sec.

Battleship has an interesting history. Bred by Mr Walter J. Salmon at his Mereworth Stud, a few miles from Lexington, Kentucky, and foaled March 19th, 1927, he is an entire chestnut horse by Man o' War (regarded as the best horse seen in the US this century) out of the French-bred mare Quarantaine, by Sea Sick (son of Elf II) from Queenie, by War Dance (Galliard) out of Quilda, by the Hermit horse Gamin. Man o' War is by Fair Play, in whose pedigree there is one line regarded by the English Stud Book authorities as unorthodox, so in this country Battleship is branded as a *half-bred*. So far as the Grand National is concerned he is in this respect in good company. He was the last foal produced by Quarantaine, who was nine years old when the British

Bloodstock Agency bought her for Mr Salmon who imported her to the US. She was half sister to Quénouille, a winner of the French Oaks, and the third dam of En Fraude, who won the French Oaks last year.

Because he was so small, Battleship did little racing when two years old, but was second over six furlongs. The next year, 1930, he was out eight times for three wins, one in a seven-furlong handicap. He then damaged a foot and was out of training for several months. As a four-year-old he was successful in six of his twelve races, and by the end of that season his record read: 22 starts, 10 wins, 2 seconds and 3 thirds, his earnings amounting to $18,880 (£3,776).

He was now offered to Mrs Scott, then Mrs T. H. Somerville. She already owned a colt by Man o' War named Annapolis (bred by Mr Salmon), who was shaping well as a 'chaser, and agreed to take Battleship, paying $12,000 (£2,400). The horse did not race in 1932 but won four steeplechases when six years old, and had been successful in four more the following season before achieving fame by winning the American Grand National at Belmont Park. Nothing was seen of him in 1935, and in July, 1936, he came to England, the Grand National at Aintree being his main objective. He was entered for that event last year but did not meet the engagement.

From October to May of his first season in England he took part in thirteen steeplechases, most of them over three miles, and won five, but perhaps he produced the best form when he ran fourth in the National Hunt Handicap at Cheltenham with 11 st up. In the 1937-38 season he had been out nine times before the Grand National but was only once the winner. That solitary success was gained in the Lonsdale Handicap Steeplechase (3 m), at Hurst Park early in December; having run a good second in a similar event at Newbury nine days earlier he started favourite in a field of useful horses. In January he ran unplaced in a race at Newbury, trying to give 21 lb to Delachance, who finished second. Early in February, in a 'chase over 3 m 5 f at Sandown Park, Kellsboro' Jack, Battleship and Reynoldstown came in fifth, sixth and seventh. Two weeks later, at Newbury, Battleship again ran unplaced, but at Cheltenham, a fortnight before the Grand National, he carried top weight, 12 st 1 lb, in the National Hunt Handicap Steeplechase and was placed third, beaten three-quarters of a length and a head. That was a good performance, and if the Grand National had been run over the Cheltenham course Battleship would almost certainly not have started at a 40 to 1 chance. The few who seriously took his prospects at Aintree into consideration boggled at the big fences there, and no doubt kicked themselves in due season. In that race at Cheltenham Battleship wore blinkers. As they appeared to answer their purpose they were again used in the Grand National and may have been helpful.

Standing 15.2, Battleship is one of the smallest of Grand National winners. When seen alongside some of his opponents he looked a mere pony, but if he lacks height he is not wanting in substance, nor in courage and resolution. Many writers asserted that he was the smallest horse that had ever won the race. Our friend 'Mankato' corrected them. He cited the 1872 winner, Casse Tête, a mare who, he stated, 'was not more than 15.2 and a wretched weed at that'. Regal (1876), was another winner measuring about 15.2 while Father O'Flynn, the mount of Captain Roddy Owen when the son of Retreat defeated Cloister in 1892, 'was smaller in every way than Battleship, and would have weighed appreciably less'. In the early days of the Grand National, says 'Mankato', 15.2 was not small for a 'chaser, and the dual winner Abd-el-Kader (1850, 1851) was about that height.

Battleship is not only an exceptional Grand National winner because he is diminutive, but also because he is one of the few entire horses that have won the race. There had been none since 1901, when Grudon won. The others are Wanderer (1855), Freetrader (1856), Half-Caste (1859), Huntsman (1862), The Lamb (1868 and 1871), The Colonel (1869, 1870), Disturbance (1873), Reugny (1874), Austerlitz (1877) and Shifnal (1878).

Early in June Battleship returned to his native land, and is now located at his owner's estate at Montpelier in beautiful Virginia. At the time he won the Grand National there were writers who stated that he was the first American-bred horse to gain the distinction. Maybe they are not old enough to remember Rubio, who scored in 1908. He was one of eighty-five yearlings James B. Haggin shipped to the Newmarket July Sales in 1899 from his stud in California. A chestnut by Star Ruby, a half-brother to Sceptre, Rubio was one of them, and Major F. Douglas-Pennant bought him for 15 guineas. Before he won the Grand National he had a spell of work as a bus horse at Towcester to harden his legs!

Battleship is the fourth Grand National winner owned by an American. In 1923 Sergeant Murphy carried the colours of Mr Stephen Sanford; in 1926 Jack Horner those of Mr A. C. Schwartz; and in 1933 Kellsboro' Jack those of Mrs F. Ambrose Clark. The last-named went to America in May of this year. We may add that Mrs Scott had a runner in the Grand National of 1933 – Trouble Maker, a 100 to 1 chance. He finished fifteenth.

Nearco's 1938 Grand Prix de Paris Victory

Realising that Nearco, a tail-male grandson of Phalaris, by Pharos, foaled in 1935, sired Nearctic, the sire of Northern Dancer; Nasrullah, the sire of Bold Ruler, and Nasrullah's three-parts brother, Royal Charger, the sire of Turn-to, there is no question but that he has been the supreme influence in international racing and breeding in the latter part of the twentieth century. Entering the stud he was, with ample reason, considered 'the most likely to succeed'. His book was filled for three years as soon as it was opened. Nearco completed his racing career with fourteen victories in as many starts and was never really fully tried. But it was his final triumph in the Grand Prix de Paris at Longchamp in 1938 which elevated his reputation to a plane few thoroughbreds have ever achieved. In this French classic the son of champion sire Pharos from the champion filly and dual classic winner Nogara, by the frequent champion Italian sire, Havresac II, proved his eternal greatness. Not only did the field include both the Epsom Derby (Bois Roussel) and French Derby (Cillas) winners, but others also wearing the classic stamp. The account of that race along with some family notes and his unbeaten Turf record appeared in the 1938 Review.

THE GRAND PRIX de Paris was run at Longchamp on June 26th. This coveted race, run over fifteen furlongs, is for entire colts and fillies, three years old, of any country. The eighteen competitors this year were all colts, except Féerie and Ad Astra. The colts carried 9 st 2 lb and the fillies 8 st 13 lb. Intense interest was shown in the contest because of the calibre of several of the candidates. The unbeaten champion two- and three-year-old of Italy, Nearco, was one of the starters. Bois Roussel, winner of the Epsom Derby, was another. Legend of France, winner of his only start in France last year and unbeaten in his two races in England this year, crossed the Channel to take part. In addition, there were Castel Fusano, winner of the Prix Matchem and Prix Lupin; Féerie, successful in the French One Thousand Guineas and Oaks; and Cillas, who had carried off the French Derby a fortnight previously. The favourite, at 29 to 10 against, was Nearco; Cillas and Accius stood at 11 to 3; Legend of France, 6 to 1; Bois Roussel, 29 to 4; Féerie, 10 to 1; Castel Fusano, 13 to 1; and Canot, 15 to 1. The supporters of Nearco were justified in their choice, as the following formal return shows:

Signori Tesio-Incisa's br. c.
  NEARCO, by Pharos–Nogara
P. Gubellini   1
M. Robert Lazard's ch. c. CANOT,
  by Niño–Canalette
                    W. Johnstone   2
Mr Peter Beatty's br. c. BOIS
  ROUSSEL, by Vatout–Plucky
  Liège   G. Richards   3
Mr J. E. Widener's b. c. Castel
  Fusano   G. Bridgland   4
  Also ran: Cor de Chasse (fifth), Legend
of France, Cillas, Accius, Lied, Spaghetti,
Vaisseau Fantôme, Molitor, Pylos, Six
Avril, Il Ka Cha, Cavallino, Ad Astra,
Féerie.

Won by a length and a half; length second and third; two lengths third and fourth; half length fourth and fifth. Time: 3 min 12 22/25 sec (record is held by Take My Tip, who won in 1926 in 3 min 10 3/5 sec). Winner received 1,152,800 francs; second, 150,000 francs; third, 100,000 francs; fourth 50,000 francs; and breeder of the second 50,000 francs. Breeder of the winner would have received 100,000 francs if the horse had been bred in France.

Winner bred in Italy by his owners, Signori Tesio-Incisa, and trained by Signor Federico Tesio.

After an excellent start, Accius took the lead in front of Pylos, Ad Astra, and Cillas. Soon after the top of the hill had been reached, Cillas was close behind Accius, and these two stable-companions were close together when they approached the turn into the straight. About this point there was a closely packed group of horses in front and another bunch a few lengths behind, among which was Canot. Elliott made an effort on Cillas, and for a short space Legend of France and Cor de Chasse came into the picture. A feature of the finish was the dash Johnstone made on Canot. Nearly all the way this horse had been in the rear; towards the end he came along with fine speed, but could not maintain it. Gordon Richards had found an opening on the rails for Bois Roussel, and challenged Nearco, who had then taken the lead. Gubellini gave an exhibition of magnificent riding on the Italian champion, and, defeating the formidable challenges of Canot and Bois Roussel, passed the winning-post a length and a half in front of Canot. Bois Roussel was beaten a length for second place.

It was Nearco's fourteenth race: his fourteenth victory. Before he started at Longchamp, his owners refused to entertain his sale. After the race they would consider disposing of their invincible colt.

A good-boned, well-grown, handsome colt, with a perfect disposition, Nearco made a very deep impression upon all who witnessed his great triumph in the Grand Prix. Four days after the colt had won in Paris, he became the property of Mr Martin H. Benson, of Beech House Stud, Cheveley, Newmarket. The news of Nearco's purchase for a record price of £60,000 caused a sensation in breeding circles all over the world. Yet apart from the essential veterinary examination in France, two days later, this striking transaction did not occupy a quarter of an hour. Mr Benson made up his mind without hesitation, and the deal was concluded through the British Bloodstock Agency, Ltd. A few hours later another well-known English breeder was expressing his disappointment he had missed the horse. He was told that Mr Benson telephoned while he had telegraphed! The breeder consoled himself at once by taking subscriptions to Nearco. Indeed within a few hours the horse was booked full for three years.

Mr Benson crossed to Paris *en route* to Chantilly. When Professor Reynolds passed the colt sound, his new owner thereupon decided that Nearco should not race again, though an extremely sound horse. He arrived at the Beech House Stud, Newmarket, in the early days of July, and since then there has been an almost endless pilgrimage of breeders from many countries to inspect and admire the great Nearco, who in the Grand Prix readily defeated the winner of our Derby and the winner of the French Derby – a most exceptional achievement.

Here is the tabulated pedigree of the Italian champion:

NEARCO (Br, c. foaled Jan 24th, 1935)	Pharos (B, 1920)	Phalaris (Br. 1913)	Polymelus (B, 1902) — Cyllene, Maid Marian
			Bromus (B, 1905) — Sainfoin, Cheery
		Scapa Flow (Ch. 1914)	Chaucer (Br, 1900) — St Simon, Canterbury Pilgrim
			Anchora (Ch. 1905) — Love Wisely, Eryholme
	Nogara (Br, 1928)	Havresac II (Br, 1915)	Rabelais (B, 1900) — St Simon, Satirical
			Hors Concours (B, 1906) — Ajax, Simona
		Catnip (B, 1910)	Spearmint (B, 1903) — Carbine, Maid of the Mint
			Sibola (B, 1896) — The Sailor Prince, Saluda

Pharos, the sire of Nearco, is one of the leading sires in both France and England. In the latter country he headed the sires' list in 1931. He sired the classic winners, in England, Cameronian (Two Thousand Guineas

Nearco.

and Derby) and Firdaussi (St Leger), as well as winners of classic races in France and Italy. Nogara, the dam of Nearco, was the best two-year-old in Italy in 1930, and the following season won the Italian One Thousand and Two Thousand Guineas. Nogara is in foal to Solariom and is due on January 28th. She will be covered by Cameronian, as will Delleana (the dam of Donatello II), who is now in foal to Mahmoud, and due on February 4th. The sire of Nogara, Havresac II, headed the Italian sires' list on ten occasions. The grandam of Nearco, Catnip, won in England and bred winners of over 1,500,000 lire in Italy. Her dam, Sibola, was bred in the US and sent to England, where she won the One Thousand Guineas, and ran second in the Epsom Oaks. Her sire, The Sailor Prince, won the Cambridgeshire.

Rockfel's Oaks' Triumph

While comparative times may be deceiving in some instances, they were hardly that in the case of Rockfel, heroine of both the One Thousand Guineas and the Oaks of 1938, for she was also an emphatic winner of the 'open' Champion Stakes. Her times in the One Thousand Guineas and Oaks were faster than those of Pasch in the Two Thousand Guineas and of Bois Roussel in the Derby under similar conditions. So the daughter of the 1928 Derby winner Felstead from Rockcliffe, by Santorb, deserves her place in history along with such legends as Sceptre and Pretty Polly. The **BBR** *account of her Oaks success attests to that.*

THERE CAN have been few tamer races for the Oaks Stakes than the one we saw this year. Rockfel took the lead soon after the start, was in front all the way, and won by four lengths without being extended. She covered the course in 2 min 37 2/5 sec. Two days earlier Bois Roussel won the Derby in 2 min 39 1/5 sec. Rockfel's time was, therefore, the better by 1 4/5 sec, which, in terms of distance, means at least thirty yards. In the One Thousand Guineas she beat Pasch's time in the Two Thousand Guineas by four-fifths of a second. All four races were run under similar conditions. We are well aware that the time test can be deceptive, but, taking it for what it is worth, it made out Rockfel to be the best of this year's classic winners. That estimate was most emphatically confirmed in the race for the Champion Stakes at the end of October. Last year Sir Victor Sassoon's filly, Exhibitionist, won the One Thousand Guineas and the Oaks at a pace slightly faster than Le Ksar won the Two Thousand Guineas and Mid-day Sun the Derby, her time at Newmarket being 4/5 sec and at Epsom 3/5 sec faster. In the three-year-old Free Handicap published at the end of the season she was rated the best of her year. Mid-day Sun was at the top with 9 st 7 lb, and Exhibitionist allotted 9 st 5 lb, which meant that when credited with the 3 lb sex allowance, she was deemed 1 lb better than the Derby winner. Before Exhibitionist and Rockfel only six fillies had this century won both the One Thousand Guineas and the Oaks, namely Sceptre 1902, Pretty Polly 1904, Cherry Lass 1905, Jest 1913, Princess Dorrie 1914, and Saucy Sue 1925.

There were fourteen runners in this year's Oaks. Seven of them, including Rockfel, Solar Flower, Radiant and Stafaralla, had competed in the One Thousand Guineas. The four named had not raced in the meantime. Of the newcomers, the most prominent were Knole Star and Shrew II, who, together with Night Bird (seventh in the Guineas), were expected to be Rockfel's most troublesome opponents. The evidence on which that supposition was based seemed somewhat slender, to say the least. Knole Star, a daughter of the Swynford horse Schiavoni and trained at Epsom, was unplaced in her only race last year, but this year had easily won over a mile at the Epsom Spring meeting and scraped home by a short head in a ten-furlong race at Hurst Park at the end of

April, with very moderate horses behind her. Since the One Thousand, Night Bird had won the Oaks 'Trial' at Lingfield by half a length, but had nothing much to beat. Shrew II finished third in the French 'One Thousand Guineas', and really the best that could be said for her was that it had been thought worthwhile to send her from France to Epsom.

On the face of things, Rockfel seemed in no danger from this trio. Laughing Water, who gave her a good race at Newmarket, was missing from the Oaks field. As Rockfel had in the Guineas finished lengths in front of Solar Flower, Radiant and Stafaralla, it should have looked highly probable she would win the Oaks without difficulty. Was there a doubt whether Rockfel would be able to stay the twelve furlongs? Surely nobody with any knowledge of pedigrees, and who had seen the way she gained her victory in the Guineas, could reasonably entertain any such fear. The fact remains, however, that when the race started, odds of 3 to 1 were offered against her chance by the bookmakers, and the Tote, whose dividends strictly reflect the views of the public, returned the same 'price'. Against Solar Flower odds of 11 to 1 were offered, and both Radiant and Stafaralla were quoted at 14 to 1.

Solar Flower was slow off the mark and, together with Knole Star, was for a time at the tail end of the field. Harry Wragg, having had no desire to 'beg off' this time, was now riding Rockfel. In accordance with the instructions her owner had given, she was allowed to run the race as she pleased. Her pleasure was to show her heels to all opponents from beginning to end. Five furlongs from home the nearest to her were Rattoo, Stafaralla, Shrew II, Radiant and Sly Abbess. Croix de Feu, who had been second for about six furlongs, had retreated. Soon after rounding Tattenham Corner Sly Abbess became second, but the spurt which took her forward quickly expired. Meanwhile, Radiant and Solar Flower had made headway, and half-way down the straight were Rockfel's immediate followers, but the favourite's lead was then so substantial that her victory was well assured, and without having to exert herself she went on to win by four lengths. Radiant, obviously second best, had 'held' her stable companion Solar Flower without difficulty.

Wragg, who said he had never had an easier ride, commented on the fact that the pace while the field came down the slope to Tattenham Corner was exeptionally slow, and he seemed surprised that no attempt was made to pass him at that stage. He added that Rockfel was going better than ever when nearing the winning-post, and after passing it did not want to stop. Well might her owner and trainer express regret that she was not engaged in the St Leger. Very seldom has Wragg ridden a long-distance race as he did this one. He usually waits behind until the winning post is in sight, and then makes a dash for it, his mount consenting. In the jockey's room he is known as 'The Waiter'.

Djebel's Win in the New Two Thousand Guineas of 1940

Djebel, a foal of 1937 by Tourbillon-Loika, by Gay Crusader, came over to England in 1939 to secure the esteemed Middle Park Stakes and he returned in 1940, despite the war, to present his owner and breeder, M. Marcel Boussac with his first classic success in England by winning the New Two Thousand Guineas over the Bunbury Mile at Newmarket. Also winner of a Prix de l'Arc de Triomphe and other important French fixtures, his fame, almost certainly, would have been further enshrined but for the war. As it was, he asserted himself very significantly at stud, solidly reflecting his brilliant, although partially obscured, performances on the racetrack. It is because he deserved more attention than he received that some mention is made here of his superior effort in the Two Thousand Guineas of 1940.

Physically, it was noted in the paddock before the race, that he 'was hard and well. He is neither an imposing colt, nor is he essentially a class type; his neck spoils him. But – what a horse to train! He was all wire and whipcord – to use a hackneyed but well understood expression – and he walked around the ring, master of himself, and with the recognisable air of the perfectly trained thoroughbred.' And he ran as superbly as he looked.

An excerpt from the description of the running from the BBR *of 1940 states:*

ELLIOTT alone was riding easily on the French colt. They approached the Dip. Elliott gave Djebel his head. There was an immediate response. Djebel, now freed from all restraint, strode up the hill, increasing his lead with every stride. Racing at top speed, he danced along in front; that is not quite correct, for his action is true, and he rather skims the ground with long, easy strides, usually with an apparent lack of effort, but always seriously and on business bent. At any rate, he had won the race long before he came to the Silver Ring, and with such ease that the efforts of his opponents seemed almost pathetic.

Nasrullah at Three

Despite the reservations being held by some in respect to Nasrullah, no other colt his age had better credentials and thus his topweight was generally accepted. This tribute seemed even more justified the following season when his victory in the Chatteris Stakes over the Bunbury Mile established him a clear choice for the Two Thousand Guineas in which he could only manage fourth. Although he won the Chatteris Stakes 'stylishly', his antics prior to the contest earned him a reputation as being quite temperamental. Indeed, the BBR of 1943 wrote of 'The Vagaries of Nasrullah'.

THERE WERE very few races open to three-year-olds, and certainly none of any importance, prior to the Guineas. This was due, as in previous war years, to the institution of regional, or localised, racing. Classic candidates from the country stables could not run against the Newmarket candidates, and vice versa. Moreover, even where inter-regional competition was possible, few trainers took advantage of it. There were no valuable prizes to be won, and it suited them all better to choose comparatively easy races for their charges. An example was furnished by the Manton Stable, which had no difficulty in selecting three different (and easy) races for their three candidates – Merchant Navy, Way In, and Kingsway; these candidates passed their tests satisfactorily and, having benefited by them, were in due course sent to Newmarket. When

Nasrullah.

they lined up for the Guineas, nobody knew how they stood the one with the other, or in relation to the rest of the field. Much the same happened in respect of the horses trained at Newmarket and, in the end, the nineteen runners which started in the Two Thousand Guineas (with the exception of Umiddad) had all had races, mostly against little opposition, and hardly ever in competition with each other.

The public, in the circumstances, could hardly be blamed for esteeming highly the Aga Khan's much-publicised Nasrullah. They knew, at least, that he had been officially assessed at two years as being the best colt. They knew also that he had won his pre-Guineas test, the Chatteris Stakes at Newmarket, with ease. Finally, for the Two Thousand Guineas he started at 13 to 8 against. How far this was justified is best illustrated by the following return and description of his race before the Guineas. If judged, as these notes must be judged, in retrospect, the whole affair may appear unworthy of mention. Yet Nasrullah's case is only typical of those of many other famous horses before him. Here is a return of the race, on the strength of which he was made a 13 to 8 favourite for the first classic:

Chatteris Stakes (for three-year-olds). Value to winner, £306 2s. Run on the Bunbury Mile, Newmarket, May 5th, 1943.
1 – H.H. Aga Khan's b.c. NASRULLAH (9 st 2 lb), G. Richards; 2 – Response (8 st 6 lb); 3 – Herald (8 st 6 lb). Also ran; Lady Sybil, Veracity.
Won by half a length; six lengths between second and third.
Winner bred by Owner; trained by Frank Butters at Newmarket.

In dealing with the race for the Chatteris Stakes, it must be recorded, in fairness to Nasrullah's trainer, that he had the colt in splendid condition. Nasrullah was as handsome as could be, cool and free in his walking paces. Once he tried to kick, but otherwise he behaved well. He was led and ridden in the parading ring. Asked to leave it for the racecourse, he was adamant. Richards induced him to go through the paddock gate, but one look at the course was enough. He turned back. He was eventually persuaded to go out, and an obliging person on a hack endeavoured to give him a lead. But no! He just stood still. Finally, with evident reluctance and with a show of outraged dignity rather than temper, he consented to walk postwards. He was still being led when the rest of the field was at the post, waiting for him. Nasrullah delayed the start by eight minutes. There was considerable anxiety as to his probable behaviour when he finally lined up. To the general relief, he behaved perfectly. He wheeled in as the strands flew upward, and in a matter of seconds was racing easily and well. Response had been making the running, Richards having decided, evidently, to hold Nasrullah in check and to keep a watching eye on Lady Sybil. She, in her turn, challenged Response after going five furlongs or so, failed to make any impression on him, and dropped out. Richards then made the effort which he had planned. He took the lead on the descent to the Dip, and, allowing Nasrullah to run very much his own race, found that he climbed the rise smoothly and easily. Nasrullah, in the end, was a stylish winner and, thus, was hailed enthusiastically as the likely winner of the Guineas. As for Lady Sybil, her running was disappointing. She failed to exceed six furlongs. It was destined to be that filly's last race in 1943, as a little later, after a slight accident at exercise, she was declared out of all engagements.

Then came his third in the Derby behind Straight Deal and Umiddad. His rider, Gordon Richards, gave 'Ajax' of the *Evening Standard* the following account.

> 'When I started my run at the top of the hill the colt produced such a good turn of speed that I thought I might win. He rolled a bit to the right as we reached the Dip, but I gathered him together again and went about threequarters of a length past Umiddad. He could not carry through up the hill, and I fancy that was because he was tiring a little. Even so, we were only beaten half a length for second place. It is difficult to say whether Nasrullah would have won had he gone straight through with his run.'

After his sixth place finish behind the filly Herringbone in the St Leger, his rider, M. Beary, spoke well of him but felt the distance caused his downfall.

> 'He ran a very kind race and did nothing wrong. I took up a good position at the end of a mile and a half but he does not stay more than that distance.'

Finally, there was 'Nasrullah's true form' shown in the Champion Stakes in which he avenged his Guineas defeat by Kingsway and shunted Umiddad, who had been second to his third in the Derby, into third spot.

This was Nasrullah's apotheosis. The champion two-year-old of his year, he was to prove the 'problem horse' of the season. His three-year-old career may be traced in notes running through the descriptions of the three classic races in which he ran. Summarised, his own story was one of defeat, due to his own wayward tendencies – but reverses often condoned by his adherents.

The fact remained that he seemed to develop an aversion, not so much for racing as for going down to the post. It is all the more to the credit of his trainer, Frank Butters, that Nasrullah gradually rid himself of his idiosyncracies. On October 5th, the day of the Champion Stakes, he went to the post like a perfectly good racehorse. Indeed, it was his stable companion, Umiddad, who pretended to be temperamental on the way out from the paddock. Nasrullah was, by comparison, the model racehorse. He completely outclassed his field for individuality, not excepting the fine-looking Kingsway, who ousted him for favouritism.

Champion Stakes of £14 each, of £4 if declared, with £1,000 added, for three-year-olds and upwards, entire horses and mares. Value to winner, £999 4s. Run at Newmarket over the last 1¼ mile of the Suffolk Stakes Course, on October 5th, 1943.

HH Aga Khan's b. c. NASRULLAH, by Nearco – Mumtaz Begum, 3 yrs, 8 st 6 lb

	G. Richards	1
Mr A. E. Saunders' KINGSWAY, 3 yrs, 8 st 6 lb	H. Wragg	2
HH Aga Khan's UMIDDAD, 3yrs, 8 st 6 lb	*C. Elliott	3

Also ran: Reprisal (3 yrs, 8 st 6 lb); Pink Flower (3 yrs, 8 st 6 lb); Lady Electra (4 yrs, 8 st 11 lb).

* Wore distinguishing cap.

Winner trained by Frank Butters, Newmarket.
Nasrullah won by a length, three lengths between second and third.

Gordon Richards rode an unusually patient race on the winner. He allowed the stable companion, Umiddad, to make the running to the bottom of the hill, when Kingsway took command. Less than a furlong from home, Nasrullah was given his head, and, running on easily, scored most stylishly by a length. There was no doubt as to Nasrullah's merit, and he retired subsequently to the Great Barton Stud, Bury St Edmunds, with the reputation of a good colt, especially brilliant at middle-distances.

Death of Exterminator

Every major racing country has had its prolonged romances with its heroic geldings. England had its fabulous Brown Jack and before the US had its five-time Horse of the Year Kelso and its two-time honoree John Henry, the country also had Exterminator – or 'Old Bones' or 'Old Slim' or whatever affectionate name that came to mind – who died aged thirty in 1945. His passing was richly reported in Stud & Turf in the USA section of the BBR of that year.

EXTERMINATOR, one of the heroes of American racing, died on September 26th at the age of thirty. Affectionately called 'Old Bones' or 'Old Slim' because of his somewhat angular appearance, he had become a folk hero by the time he was retired, having started one hundred times in eight years of racing. His full record is 50 wins, 17 seconds, 17 thirds, and earnings of $252,996. The factual record means little in portraying Exterminator – it was his honesty, courage, and great class by which he will be remembered and revered as a great horse.

A chestnut gelding by *McGee (by White Knight) and out of Fair Knightess, by Jim Gore, by Hindoo, Exterminator was foaled May 30th, 1915. He was sold for $1,500 as a yearling by his breeder, F. D. Knight, to J. Cal Milam for whom he raced at two years. At three years, Exterminator was purchased by the late Willis Sharpe Kilmer as a running mate for his *Sun Briar in preparation for the 1918 Kentucky Derby. However *Sun Briar was unable to start. Exterminator, his 'stand-in', went to the post the extreme outsider in the betting, and won the forty-fourth Kentucky Derby by a length. It was the winner's first start of the season, his first taste of fame which was to grow year by year.

Thereafter Exterminator remained a top-class horse. Racing against successive 'crops' of noted horses, he carried on until he was nine years of age, reaching the peak of his career as a seven-year-old in 1922, when he won ten of his seventeen starts, carrying weights of less than 9 st 6 lb on only two occasions. In the 1½-mile Independence Handicap at Latonia, he carried 10 st, was made an odds-on favourite, but finished 'out of the money'.

Though Exterminator started one hundred times, winning fifty races, he only once later gained a purse as large as the $14,700 he earned in the Kentucky Derby. This was in the Independence Handicap of 1921 when he won $15,725. When the old gelding was finally retired on June 21st, 1924, he had passed Man o' War's record, and was then the world's second largest money winner, next to Zev.

Exterminator's fame was not the result of one race, or one season of racing, nor one department of racing, nor any one section of racing. His fame was great because he kept adding to it year by year, accepting the highest weights handicappers would put on him, until his reputation had grown into a legend well before he had been retired.

Among other outstanding races of his time which he won, were the Latonia Cup (2¼ miles), Brooklyn, Clark and Kentucky Handicaps. He won the first three runnings of the Pimlico Cup (2¼ miles), four successive renewals of the Saratoga Cup (1¾ miles). In Canada he won the Windsor Jockey Club Handicap, George Hendrie Memorial Handicap, Ontario Jockey Club Cup (2¼ miles), and for three successive years, won the 1¼-mile Toronto Autumn Cup.

Distance and weight-carrying naturally brought 'Old Bones' his highest weights. At distances above 1½ miles he was beaten only twice in thirteen starts. He won nineteen races under weights ranging from 9 st 4 lb up to 9 st 11 lb.

Exterminator was retired to Remlik Hall, in Virginia. He was later moved to the late Mr Kilmer's Court Manor. At his owner's death, Exterminator was moved again to another Kilmer place, Sun Briar Court, near Binghampton, New York, where he died.   BBR–1945

* Indicates exported from England to USA.

Caracalla

Any dossier containing the greatest horses in the history of French racing must include the unbeaten French champion Caracalla, a foal of 1942 by Tourbillon from the superb French racemare and matron, Astronomie, by Asterus. Caracalla, unraced at two, raced four times at three, and four times at four without a blemish. His triumphs at three included the Grand Prix de Paris and the Prix Royal Oak, while at four his biggest prizes were England's 2½-mile Ascot Gold Cup and France's premier 'open' fixture, the Prix de l'Arc de Triomphe in which his great final burst of speed caught the French Derby winner Prince Chevalier by a head.

Caracalla's dam, Astronomie, must also be included among the finest classic producers of all time. Astronomie's other foals included Marsyas, one of the most splendid stayers in Turf history, the Ascot Gold Cup and Prix du Cadran hero, Arbar, and the Oaks heroine, Asmena. She also bred a remarkable stakes-winning filly in Arbelle. Marsyas won an incredible four renewals of the Prix du Cadran, once France's most respected staying fixture, along with runnings of the Goodwood Cup and Doncaster Cup.

Outside of Marsyas, who was by Trimdon, a son of Son-in-Law, Astronomie's other superior performers suggested a strong 'nick' with Tourbillon, the sire of Caracalla. Arbar and Arbelle were by Djebel, a son of Tourbillon, while Asmena was by Goya, also a son of Tourbillon.

When Caracalla captured the Ascot Gold Cup in 1946, he became the first French horse to make a successful Channel crossing in this event since Massine in 1924. When the French broke the skein they did it properly, filling the second (Chanteur) and third (Basileus) places as well.

The 1946 BBR carried Caracalla's complete racing record:

At Two Years

Not Raced

At Three Years, 1945

Won Prix Bay Middleton, Le Tremblay   63,520 fr.
Won Prix Reiset – 1 mile, 6 furlongs, by 6 lengths; Le Tremblay, 1 mile,
  7 furlongs, by 2 lengths   306,200 fr.
Won Grand Prix de Paris, Longchamp, 1 mile, 7 furlongs by 1½ lengths
                                                           1,378,900 fr.
Won Prix Royal Oak, Longchamp, 1 mile, 7 furlongs, by 4 lengths
                                                             858,200 fr.

At Four Years, 1946

Won Prix Edgard Gillois (2 miles, 3 furlongs), Le Tremblay
                                                             250,000 fr.
Won Prix de Dangu (2½ miles), Longchamp   209,200 fr.
Won Gold Cup (2½ miles), Ascot   £7,200
Won Prix de l'Arc de Triomphe (1½ miles), Longchamp, (from Prince
  Chevalier by a head – Pirette 3rd, and Ardan 4th)   2,000,000 fr.

The Story of Star Kingdom (Star King)

*One of the more glorious stories in racing and breeding, particularly as
it affected Australasia, is that of Star Kingdom, a chestnut colt by
Stardust (Hyperion) from Impromptu, by Concerto, foaled in 1946,
who raced in England under the name of Star King. A clever little
thing, he won five of his six starts at two and was only beaten a very
questionable shortest of short heads at level weights, by Abernant in the
Sandown National Breeders' Produce Stakes at five furlongs.
Abernant, also a grandson of Hyperion, went on to be acclaimed the
champion of his age and Free Handicap topweight at 133 lb, two
higher than Star Kingdom.*

*While Star Kingdom's sire, Stardust, did moderately well at stud,
he was the first decent runner from his female family in three
generations. Although he won several stakes again at three, he was a
well-beaten seventh behind Nimbus and Abernant in their tight
struggle for the Two Thousand Guineas of 1949 and was also out of
the frame in the six-furlong July Cup in which Abernant convinced
most observers that he was the best sprinter of the year. One account
noted that Star King (Star Kingdom) was 'outclassed'.*

So these were the racing and breeding credentials of Star Kingdom when the Australian Stanley Wootton, hearing that the horse was about to be put to stud in England, managed to acquire him in partnership with Alwen O. Ellison for the latter's Baramul Stud near Sydney. A Reg Moses of another stud farm was also allowed to take a share of the stallion.

Perhaps Mr Wootton, whose father had been in racing and breeding before him, was aware that Star Kingdom carried three crosses of the Oaks winner and exceptional matron, Canterbury Pilgrim, in his family tree. Canterbury Pilgrim's influential brothers, Chaucer and Swynford, appeared in his fourth generation as did their half-sister, St Victorine, the direct tail-female ancestress of Star Kingdom. In-breeding to a superlative distaff family through different individuals!

Star Kingdom's success was immediate. His first runner was his first winner, his first stakes winner and his first champion. This was the two-year-old Kingster. It was only the use of home mares that presented Star Kingdom with his first few books of mares. One competitive stud master said, 'I don't want to breed ponies' and a newspaper complained that breeding to him would be 'a setback to racing . . . by furthering a breed of "speedy squibs"'.

When Star Kingdom died in 1967, aged twenty-one, he had been champion sire five times. A year later, he became the leading sire of two-year-olds for the seventh time in fourteen years and the champion brood-mare sire for the first time. This was the first such breeding 'double' since statistics were kept in Australia.

In 1969 he again became the leading broodmare sire and made it three in a row in 1970. In 1969 he also became the first Australian sire to sire the winners of over $2,000,000. He was the leading sire of two-year-olds with his very first crop and remained so for his first six seasons until toppled by his own son, the flying Todman.

The late Neville Sellwood, tragically killed in a racing accident in France in 1962, declared that: 'Todman is the only horse who has ever frightened me during a race. When I asked him for speed he accelerated so quickly and so eagerly that I felt it was impossible for him to keep on his feet at the turn.'

While Todman is Star Kingdom's most celebrated racing son, Todman's full brother, Noholme, out of the Colombo matron, Oceana, has made the most lasting imprint at stud. An Australian Horse of the Year at three in 1959, Noholme was brought to the US for racing. His efforts were modest but, at stud, he exceeded his opportunities and sired fifty-four stakes winners, including the two-time American champion, Nodouble. The latter became a champion sire and sired nearly eighty stakes winners. So the saga of Star Kingdom, at home and abroad, endures.

Coincidentally, another son of Stardust, Smokey Eyes, a Stewards' Cup winner, subsequently became the most prolific sire of winners in Australia.

In light of what he accomplished in Australia, when he died in 1967 the BBR *correspondent in that part of the world explained: 'Star Kingdom is probably the greatest stallion influence, on immediate impact, in Australian turf history.'*

Nineteen years earlier, in 1948, the BBR *correspondent in England at the time, gave the following quite flattering account of his brilliant two-year-old season. Considering what he did at stud, it now makes the reading all that more interesting.*

A LIGHT-FRAMED, little colt, it was not surprising that Star King (Star Kingdom) should have come early to hand. He just missed going through his first season without a reverse. The sole occasion on which he suffered defeat was in that much discussed race at Sandown. No rival other than Abernant was able to make a race of it with Star King. His record at the end of the season was five victories and a short head defeat. It may be as well if I deal with him in the order in which the races were run. I was unable to be present when he made a first appearance at Salisbury on April 8th, but it is not often a two-year-old wins by ten lengths. In view of what the opposition accomplished subsequently it was by no means surprising that Star King should have won by such a wide margin.

Next he went to Sandown, less than three weeks later, and I was anxious to have a look at him. I found him a smallish chestnut, neatly put together, but with no depth to speak of, and a little lacking in substance. There were better-looking colts in the field, but when it came to racing there was only one in it. Sam Wragg was content to keep in close touch for about half-way. Then he set Star King alight. The colt raced off on his own and kept up the gallop so well that the judge was by no means liberal in his estimate of a five lengths' victory. To the eye it had seemed a sparkling performance. I was even more impressed when I looked at my watch. He had covered the journey in nearly four seconds faster time than the winner of the previous race, which was the two-year-old seller. The time was also a long way ahead of that of the two-year-old winner of the previous day. Only the top-class ones do that sort of thing, and I was sorry to learn the colt held no engagements at Ascot. I was told his next race would also be at Sandown, but I did not know at the time that Abernant would be in the field. That race can be passed over, but perhaps I should add that even in defeat Star King gained in stature.

His first-season activities included two other races. The first was at Goodwood. This time he was tackling six furlongs in the Richmond Stakes. He was not quite so impressive as in earlier races. For five furlongs he raced on the bit in front. It then became necessary to keep him going. He did not really find anything, and was practically all out to beat Bobo, who was receiving 7 lb, by a length. That may have suggested to some that we had seen the best of Star King and that he was training off. It also suggested he might be better at five furlongs than six. His final race of the season was at York, in the Gimcrack Stakes. The previous week-end we were racing at Windsor. I happened to run across Sam Wragg, and asked him how Star King was. We got talking about the opposition, and I rather got the idea the jockey took the popular view that Star King had not given him the same feel as in earlier races. To buck him up I told him that even though that might have been the case, Star King's time at Goodwood was still better than that accomplished by any other two-year-old at the meeting over the six furlongs course. And so we went to York with the following result:

Star King, ch. c., by Stardust out of Impromptu.

GIMCRACK STAKES, for two-year-olds. Value to winner, £2,325. Run over six furlongs at York, August 26th, 1948. (Going good.)

Mr W. Harvey's ch. c. STAR KING, by Stardust–Impromptu, 9 st   S. Wragg   1

HH Maharaja of Boroda's ch. c. Makarpura, by Big Game - Cap d'Or, 9 st
                                                                C. Smirke   2

Lady Bullough's ch. c. Luminary, by Fair Trial - Luciebella, 9 st E. C. Elliott   3

Also ran: Golden Triumph, Round Dance, Willoughton, Transatlantic, Ballynash, - El Barq, El Agdal, Spy Legend, Goyuca. Twelve ran.

Star King won by three lengths; threequarters of a length between second and third.

As I was strolling across the paddock to have a look at the horses, Sam Wragg came along and I had a word with him before he got into the parade ring. Obviously he felt there might be a doubt about the colt getting the sixth furlong, and he said he hoped he would be able to get a lead. I remarked that if he wanted to ride a waiting race there should be no trouble, as drawn with him on the far side of the course was a fast colt like Golden Triumph. The best of the others were all drawn on the other side.

It was a beautiful day, with a perfect light, and when the tapes went up I expected to see Star King steadied and dropped in behind. But the colt had other views on the matter. He jumped into his stride so quickly that he was out with a clear lead in the twinkling of an eye. Those on his wing of the field were soon many lengths in arrears. Star King was racing on the far rails. Under the stand rails were Luminary, Makarpura, and Transatlantic. To my amazement that trio had all been preferred to Star King in the market. With the horses so widely separated I could not say how far Star King was in front when half the journey had been covered. What I did know was that he was well clear of anything else in the field.

After the race I asked Charles Smirke, the rider of Makarpura, how far Star King got in front. 'Goodness knows,' he said, 'the nearest we got to him was at the winning post.' So in all probability Star King had gone out with a six lengths' lead, and that was against rivals hitherto thought to be almost up to the top class. In fact, that was the only time Luminary was beaten, and Makarpura was an Ascot winner. Sam Wragg was not taking any chances. At the end of five furlongs he brought out the whip and kept swinging it in Gordon Richards' style. It was not necessary to hit Star King, because he gave no signs of stopping ot shortening his stride. He kept on to the end for a three lengths' victory after a one-horse race. The owner was not present. The trainer was delighted, and said the colt would not run again as a two-year-old. He would be put by for the winter and prepared for the Two Thousand Guineas.

So ended the two-year-old career of Star King in, it might be said, a blaze of triumph. The colt had proved there was no fluke about his close fight with Abernant at Sandown, and I was rather sorry to hear people say, as he walked round the unsaddling enclosure, that we had seen the best of him, and that he would not train on. I prefer to think of the high-class thoroughbred in his most sparkling moments. Here we had seen a dapper little colt prove that action is the thing that counts. He had thoroughly trounced rivals worthy of his mettle and, whatever the future might have in store, I had nothing but admiration for the manner in which Star King had accomplished his task at York that sunny afternoon.

I believe Mr Wilfred Harvey bought the colt entirely on his own judgment as a yearling. He was bred by Mr Richard Ball, whose yearlings were the first lot to be sold on the morning of September 11th, 1947. Five lots were catalogued, and the best of them was the Stardust colt from Impromptu, foaled on April 30th, 1946. Mr W. Harvey had to go to 3,100 guineas to secure possession. Impromptu never ran owing to the war. She was foaled in 1939, and was full-sister to Wrong Note, one of the best two-year-olds of his year in Ireland and half-sister to two other winners. Star King is her second foal. Mr Harvey also bought her third foal, a chestnut filly by Orestes, for 5,600 guineas. Thoughtless, the dam of Impromptu, bred a sound stayer in Saintly Thoughts, though she did not boast of much class. She had another winner in Think Again, who won in Ireland. The next dam, Virgin's Folly, won the Thames Plate at Hurst Park and bred Last Chance, a winner in the US, and Sky Born. Virgin's Folly is by Swynford out of Widow Bird, tracing back to famed Canterbury Pilgrim. Star King is by far the best racehorse produced by this family in three generations, and, whatever the future may have in store, he was a brilliant two-year-old.

Coronation V

Coronation V represented a unique example of a top-class racemare who was a product of inbreeding that could be described as 'incestuous'. She was foaled in 1946 by Djebel (by Tourbillon) out of Esmeralda by Tourbillon. She was bred and owned by M. Marcel Boussac and was trained by C. H. Semblat. As a two-year-old, she came to England to win the Queen Mary Stakes and later won the Prix Robert Papin. As a three-year-old she dead-heated with her stable companion Galgala in the French One Thousand Guineas.

She finished second in the Epsom Oaks and the Irish Oaks, her defeats on these occasions being due to the fact that she was a bad traveller and was feeling the effects of the journey. However she wound up her three-year-old season with a splendid victory in the Prix de l'Arc de Triomphe. At stud she was not a success. She was covered during fourteen consecutive seasons, being barren to each mating.

In 1949 the BBR gave the following account of Coronation V's victory in the Prix de l'Arc de Triomphe.

The decision to organise a sweepstakes on the Prix de l'Arc de Triomphe was taken rather late by the Government, and it was only on July 14th that the new conditions of the race and the programmes for October 8th and 9th were published. Stakes of all the races on the two-day meeting were increased: the Prix d'Arenberg, reserved for two-year-olds and run on Saturday, was raised to 2,000,000 francs; none of the Sunday races had a stake less than a million francs, and the programme comprised, in addition to the Prix de l'Arc de Triomphe (raised to 25,000,000 francs plus the entries, for the winner), a Grand Criterium for the two-year-olds, worth 4,000,000 francs.

Entries for the Prix de l'Arc de Triomphe reached a total of 86 in France and 34 abroad. Of the latter, 18 were made in London, one in Dublin, two in Brussels, nine in Rome, two in New York and two in Buenos Aires.

Training and transportation difficulties prevented the participation of the North and South American candidates. Participation of the European candidates seemed practically assured, but a series of regrettable events reduced the field to an unexpected extent.

The English runners seemed particularly dangerous at the time the entries were made. The four-year-old Solar Slipper and the three-year-olds, Nimbus, Musidora, Pambidian, Swallow Tail and Royal Forest, were the principal runners feared by the French. But at the last moment none of them was able to come – following disappointing performances in Britain, or training accidents. In this way the British offensive was made with four horses imported from France: Vic Day, Flush Royal, Tsaoko and Royal Empire.

From Italy, classic winners were also entered and ten days before the date of the race Antonio Canale, brilliant winner of the Gran Premio di Milano and the Italian St Leger, seemed to be a very strong threat. But, a week before the race, he was barely able to run a dead-heat with the veteran, Grifone, and his owner decided not to send him to Paris.

Only the Belgian filly, Frinette, already beaten in the Prix Vermeille, and the Irish classic four-year-old, Beau Sabreur, winner of the Coronation Cup, came to Longchamp as representatives of foreign breeding. Also, there were two runners trained in France, but bred abroad: Coast Guard and Norval.

Twenty-eight runners – a record figure for the race – went to the post. The Pre-race odds on the pari-mutuel were:

35–10 Bagheera	40 Good Luck
35–10 Amour Drake and Val Drake	50 Tanagrello
	60 Double Rose
37–10 Coronation, Djeddah and Norval	60 Vic Day
	70 Vela
10 Beau Sabreur	80 Flush Royal
10 Rigolo	90 Frinette
11 Oghio	90 Rigoletto II
30 Medium and Coast Guard	95 Astramgram
33 Royal Empire	135 Goody
35 Menetrier	140 Kerlan
37 Flocon	160 Quatrain
40 Rantzau	160 Tsaoko

Bagheera, winner of the Prix de Diane, the Grand Prix de Paris and the Prix Vermeille, justifiably shared public favour with Amour Drake, whose last race had been his victory in the Prix Jacques le Marois. Of the Boussac stable, Djeddah, the brilliant four-year-old winner of the Eclipse Stakes and unbeaten during the year, seemed at first glance to have the best chance. But Coronation, second in the Epsom and Irish Oaks, had made great progress in training and her final gallop on the Tuesday before the race had astonished all those who saw it, even her connections. As for Beau Sabreur, despite an indifferent performance in Ireland, he appeared to be in excellent condition and was highly thought of. The former champion of the 1945 generation, Rigolo, had just made a very satisfactory reappearance, and Oghio enjoyed the prestige of his victory in the Prix du Prince d'Orange. These were the runners which received most support.

The start was excellent. Only Flush Royal and Goody lost a little ground. The Boussac stable's pacesetter, Norval, jumped quickly into the lead in front of Astramgram, Royal Empire and Djeddah. Tanagrello, Good Luck, Oghio, Beau Sabreur, Coast Guard, Frinette, Tsaoko and Rigolo were together in the front rank of the pack. Going up the rise, Norval was followed by Coast Guard, Oghio, Royal Empire, Beau Sabreur, Good Luck, Medium, Rigolo and Coronation. Djeddah had been slowed by his jockey and was in the rear ranks, along with Bagheera, Double Rose, Rigoletto II, Frinette, Tsaoko, Flush Royal, Vela, Menetrier and Goody.

This order did not change until they were four furlongs from the

Coronation, b. f., by Djebel out of Esmeralda.

finish. There, Norval yielded the lead to Coast Guard, who was pressed by Beau Sabreur, Royal Empire and Amour Drake, who had come up from the middle of the pack. A furlong farther on, Coast Guard, Beau Sabreur, Royal Empire and Amour Drake were racing together; behind them was a second line comprising Oghio, Good Luck, Medium, Rantzau and Double Rose. Coronation, Bagheers and Vela, in a third line, were preparing an attack on the leaders.

It was then that Coast Guard, followed by Royal Empire, gave up the struggle and left the lead to Beau Sabreur and Amour Drake as they straightened out. They were immediately challenged on the outside by Double Rose and Coronation, who were followed by Rantzau.

While Beau Sabreur was faltering rapidly, and Amour Drake was struggling with Double Rose, Coronation surged forward and left her opponents in a few strides. She crossed the line four official lengths in front.

Double Rose had succeeded in getting rid of Amour Drake, who finished a length behind her in third place, threatened by Rantzau, fourth by a neck. The winner of the Grand Prix de Saint Cloud, Medium, finished two and a half lengths behind Rantzau. He was followed by the two four-year-olds, Tanagrello and Beau Sabreur, the five-year-old Menetrier and the other four-year-olds, Djeddah and Flush Royal.

This result, obtained in the most exact conditions, clearly confirmed the superiority of the 1946 generation over the preceding ones. It also proved the calibre of this generation's fillies, and especially the exceptional value of Coronation.

Coronation ran five times as a two-year-old. She won her debut, the Prix du Chateau at Chantilly, and then won a narrow but clear victory in the Queen Mary Stakes at Ascot. Then, at Maisons-Laffitte, she cantered home in front of a field of excellent colts which included Fontenay. Brought to Deauville for the Prix Morny, she was a complete disappointment when finishing third to Amour Drake and Musette. Two months of rest failed to bring back her form and in the Cheveley Park Stakes she was fourth to Pambidian, Avila and Massilia. The latter was a stable companion whom she had constantly beaten in training gallops.

The filly's extreme consanguinity was then blamed for rendering her nervous and reducing her ability. The fact of the matter was that Coronation had not yet reached top form. It was very difficult to bring her into condition for the Poule d'Essai des Pouliches, in which she was still green. In better condition for the Oaks, she wasted herself in a front-running race which her jockey could not prevent. Then, at the Curragh, her nervousness recurred. Covered in sweat while she was being saddled, she ran listlessly and was able to get second place only by dint of her calibre.

In the Prix de l'Arc de Triomphe, Coronation was a new filly. Perfectly calm in the paddock and during the race, she raced with a fluent and easy stride in the stretch, and finished with plenty in reserve.

There is no need to elaborate here on Coronation's sire, nor on her grandsires; both of them are foremost in the glories of French breeding.

Her dam, Esmeralda, was the best filly of her generation. However, her superiority, unquestioned as a two-year-old, was compromised when she was three. After winning the Poule d'Essai, a tactical error by her jockey caused her to lose the Prix de Diane. Coming too late, she was unable to head Vigilance. In addition, she ran in the Grand Prix de Paris while under the influence of her sex, and was a long time recovering from these two mishaps.

Beaten by Vigilance and Guirlande, at the end of their season as three-year-olds, she regained her top form by the middle of her fourth year and finished that season and the following one by running honourably against the best of the colts. She was second in the Prix de l'Arc de

Triomphe, as a four-year-old, behind Verso II, and fourth in the same race the following year, behind Ardan. Each time, she was sacrificed as pace-setter. Her final outing at five resulted in a fine second place behind her stable-mate, Caravelle, over the seven furlongs of the Prix de la Foret.

Esmeralda's dam, Sanaa, also bred Narses (Blue Peter) and Abis (Umidwar), as well as Tanis, Esmeralda's full-sister and the dam of Estoc, and Geranium, the dam of Geraphar.

Deasy, Sanaa's dam, was also the dam of Tifinar, winner of the 1942 Prix Royal Oak, and the great-grandam of Palencia, winner of the 1944 Poule d'Essai.

Deasy traces back to Merry Dance, a full-sister to Pretty Dance, the great-grandam of Ultimus, who was inbred to Domino in the same way as Coronation is inbred to Tourbillon.

India's Great Filly, Her Majesty

Every racing country has had its thoroughbred legends – horses, the memory of which becomes larger rather than diminishes with the passage of time. In England, 'the cradle of the thoroughbred', there have been many such between Eclipse and Mill Reef; the same is true of France – from Gladiateur, 'the Avenger of Waterloo', to Sea-Bird, and not forgetting the fabulous filly Allez France. Italy's Federico Tesio was responsible for breeding those enduring, unbeaten giants of racing and breeding, Nearco and Ribot. America has had its epochal Man o' War and the equally revered Secretariat. In the lesser racing countries, Belgium will never forget Prince Rose while India, whose racing was of international quality when a British colony, never had a hero or heroine, before or since, to compare with the remarkable filly Her Majesty, a foal of 1943 by Barra Sahib from Laughing Water, by Walter Gay.

After her brilliant classic career in India in 1946–47, Her Majesty's owner, Mr A. C. Ardeshir who had served India's racing with distinction for nearly a quarter-century, decided, because of 'the uncertain racing policy of Government' to send Her Majesty to England, appreciating 'an invaluable opportunity of making an international experiment which would be of great interest to breeders in both countries'.

Unfortunately, this intriguing international venture ended in tragedy as Her Majesty died of heat stroke aboard the steamship Durenda just thirteen days after it had left Bombay.

As her demise came near the end of the glamour days of racing in India, it is likely – unlike those supreme champions in other countries – that she would have become a dim, if not lost, memory, had it not been for the touching account of her career published in the BBR of 1947.

THE STORY of racing in Bombay during the season 1946–47 is dominated by the exceptional feats of that great filly, Her Majesty, bred in India by her owner, Mr A. C. Ardeshir, from two imported horses, Barra Sahib (a son of Blenheim) and Laughing Water, who finished second to Rockfel in the One Thousand Guineas in England in 1938. Laughing Water is by Walter Gay out of Duchess of Mars, by Son-in-Law out of Princess of Mars, by Orby.

In her first season Her Majesty was unbeaten in her three races at Poona and Bombay, earning a total of Rs. 29,215, amongst them the Champagne Stakes, after which she was definitely considered the best of her age in India. In her second season she ran eight times, winning the Indian One Thousand and Two Thousand Guineas, Oaks and St Leger, and Idar Gold Cup, all at Bombay, and the Fillies Trial and the Gimcrack Stakes (1946) at Poona. Her only defeat was in the Derby, when, starting favourite at 6 to 1 on, she finished two lengths behind Bucephalus, after a race full of incident.

Never in the history of Indian racing has any other horse captured the imagination of the public as did Her Majesty during the season under review. Indeed, she was regarded as the 'people's filly', and the scenes after her success in the St Leger, when she avenged her defeat in the Derby by Bucephalus, will not easily be forgotten by those present. She was an odds-on favourite for all her races in both seasons, and her total of prize-money won in 1946–47 surpassed by some Rs. 20,000 the previous record of Rs. 224,959 won by Chakori, also a filly, in 1945–46.

The Idar Gold Cup, usually considered a first-class test for classic candidates, was run on December 21st. Her Majesty won easily by six lengths from Bucephalus (rec. 1 lb), with Zam Zam (by Zuyder Zee out of Hi-Ho) third, beaten a neck. Bucephalus is by Will of the Wisp out of Ice Wheel, by Six Wheeler out of Icilma, by Polymelus out of Mira by St Frusquin. Ice Wheel won two races in England in 1936 and 1937 and was sent to India in 1939. Her Majesty was prepared by W. Buckley for all her races, in which she was ridden by W. T. Evans.

In view of her easy successes in the Fillies Trial and the Idar Gold Cup, Her Majesty started a 5 to 1 on favourite for the Indian One Thousand Guineas, which she won by eight lengths from Gipsy Gem (a daughter of Gipsy Jack and Safety First), who was two and a half lengths in front of the third, Dragon Seed, as she passed the post. Dragon Seed, a winner at Poona previously, is by Will of the Wisp out of Tarte Chez Soi.

The field for the second of the Indian classics, the Two Thousand Guineas, comprised only four runners, Her Majesty, Bucephalus, Zam Zam and National Velvet, the last-named a bay filly by Bouldnor, who won the Ascot Stakes in 1936, out of Spanish Fly. They finished in that order, the official distances reading eight lengths, one and a half lengths, and ten lengths. Her Majesty started favourite at 10 to 1 on, Bucephalus being quoted at 15 to 1.

Her Majesty duly started favourite, this time at odds of 9 to 1 on, for the Indian Oaks, run on February 1st, in which seven other fillies somewhat optimistically also made an appearance. Second to Her Majesty as the winning post was reached was Kirti, a very useful filly by Celebrator out of Moreen, two lengths separating her and Mr Ardeshir's champion. Third, another three lengths away, was Gipsy Gem, who had finished second in the One Thousand Guineas. Dragon Seed was fourth.

The result of the Indian Derby, to be run on February 8th, 1947, was generally considered to be cut and dried. How could Her Majesty fail to win, after such a magnificent succession of triumphs? Yet here she was to

The 'People's Filly' – Mr A. C. Ardeshir's Her Majesty, by Barra Sahib, out of Laughing Water.

suffer the only defeat of her career, a victim of as cruel misfortune as ever befell a racehorse.

There were ten runners for the supreme Indian classic, Her Majesty starting at 6 to 1 on, Bucephalus at 7 to 1 against, Zam Zam at 15 to 1, with others at odds ranging from 20 to 1 to 40 to 1. Four of the runners were trained by A. L. J. Talib, amongst them the ultimate winner, Bucephalus, and Mr Ardeshir also ran, as pacemaker, a stable-companion of Her Majesty, Equity, a son of Centoi and Maid of Orleans.

After four furlongs the tragedy occurred. Evans, on Her Majesty, was behind Equity as they came to the turn. Equity fell and Evans was unable to avoid hitting him. With superb horsemanship, however, Evans managed to extricate the filly immediately, otherwise the majority of the field would probably have crashed and formed what might have been the worst accident in Indian racing history. Her Majesty managed to get alongside Bucephalus half a mile from home, but, despite her superlative courage, was beaten by two lengths, with Gipsy Gem third, three and a half lengths away, and Zam Zam fourth. Her Majesty returned to scale with her legs cut in four places.

Evans' views of the race give a graphic description of the events leading up to Her Majesty's only defeat. Making no secret of the fact that he considered himself lucky to be alive, he said:

'As we came round the turn near the ten I saw Uttam Singh go ahead on Equity on the outside, but I wanted for him to steer for the fence before getting my position. At the mile post I was several horses away from the fence at the time, and I knew Bucephalus would want that position.

'High Hopes had just started moving on the outside when I saw Equity, who was directly ahead of me and not yet edging for the fence, go down and then wobble to his feet. I jerked the mare, but was unable to avoid crashing head-on into his hind-quarters. It all happened so fast that I'm sure I went down for a split-second, but I pulled the mare up hoping that none of the others would crash into me. Had they done so it would surely have resulted in several jockeys and horses being killed.

'When I got alongside Bucephalus near the four she appeared to have her heart in the race but couldn't produce anything more. She sort of stayed there under sufferance, and it seemed as though only instinct prompted her to keep going.

'The mare has a great heart. She can fight and would have done so yesterday, but it was only after the race, when I saw her condition, that I realised that in finishing second she had put up the greatest fight of her career so far.'

It was generally thought that because of her injuries sustained in the Derby, Mr Ardeshir would withdraw his filly from the last of the classics, the St Leger, due to be run three weeks later on March 1st. An

anti-tetanus injection was administered to the filly, and she had to be
rested for a week. Her owner, however, decided to let Her Majesty take
her chance with an obviously improving Bucephalus, who would have
to concede her 5 lb.

There were five runners in the field, Her Majesty, despite her obvious
loss of condition, being made favourite at 5 to 4 on, with Bucephalus at 5
to 4 against. Though most racegoers realised that the meeting of these
two champions would provide a race worth watching few could have
anticipated the nine-furlong struggle culminating in the short-head
defeat of Bucephalus.

Evans set a terrific pace on Her Majesty for the first four furlongs,
getting rid of the rest of the field except Bucephalus, ridden by T. Burn.
He eased the filly along the back stretch and gave her two quick bursts at
the seven and four furlongs posts. Bucephalus matched the filly stride for
stride and would not be shaken off, but those two bursts of speed no
doubt cost him the race, and both jockeys seemed more tired than their
mounts as they returned to the unsaddling enclosure. But for stumbling
twice in the last three furlongs Her Majesty would probably have won
by a length. All the same, she had wiped out the bitter memory of defeat,
and her reception by the crowd as the came back was unprecedented in
the history of the Indian Turf.

Part 3

OWNERS

James Robert Keene.

Memorative Biography of James Robert Keene

English-born James Robert Keene came as a young boy with his parents to Shasta, California. By 1875, when he was around the age of forty, he was a multimillionaire. He started making his fortune by serving the mines of Nevada with his horses and mules during the famous Bonanza days in the 1870s. Living in San Francisco he purchased a seat on the Stock Exchange and his knowledge of mining stocks quickly pushed his fortune upward. He became a famous force in American racing and, as William H. P. Robertson noted in his book The History of Thoroughbred Racing in America, *his was the name that rang out most frequently on the American Turf between the Civil War and World War One.*

J. R. Keene bred Kingston, a winner of 89 races from 138 starts while being unplaced but four times; and he was co-owner of Domino, one of the most revered and brilliant horses ever to look through a bridle in the US. He also owned Spendthrift, the accomplished performer who sired Kingston.

While Keene enjoyed almost constant success in racing, he had a *roller-coaster ride on Wall Street and is said to have lost over $40,000,000 while trying to corner the wheat market. But he recovered from this depressing setback to once again ride in his private railway car.*

As a man who also raced successfully in England and France, Mr Keene's reputation was international. American Turf literature has excellent coverage of Mr Keene's fantastic life, but in no place is to be found a more delightful account than that by Mr Edward Moorhouse in the BBR *of 1913.*

BY THE death of James Robert Keene, which occurred when the present year was only three days old, there passed away a very remarkable personality. In the world of finance for half a century, in the realm of sport for thirty years or more, he had been a dominating figure. Some time before the final summons reached him he had almost loosed his grip of the Turf. The Anti-betting legislation passed four or five years ago by the New York State lawmakers – legislation which ultimately brought racing to an end in that part of the world – so curtailed opportunities for a stable like that maintained by Mr Keene, that he felt compelled practically to abandon the sport from which he had derived so much satisfaction and enjoyment. Latterly he had only had a few horses in training in England.

When the obnoxious Betting Bill was being considered by the State Legislature at Albany, Mr Keene was asked what course he would adopt if the Bill was passed. 'I shall retire from racing,' he replied, 'meeting my loss like a man. I would take no part in it, because it inevitably would deteriorate so much that no man loving horses as I do could derive any satisfaction from the sport. For more than twenty years I have bred and raced thoroughbreds for my own amusement, and, collaterally, for the amusement of the public. Up to three or four years ago it cost me a great deal of money each year. Lately my horses have improved, and I have raced without loss. But regardless of profit or loss, I shall drop the sport the instant it falls into the hands it inevitably must do, if the Bill passes.' It must be explained that the Bill to which Mr Keene was referring did not make racing impossible; it was an amending Bill which finally killed the sport. In November, 1911, Mr Keene sold the Castleton Farm, near Lexington, where so many of his great winners were bred and reared. Some of the stallions and mares were also sold; the others remained on the farm until last December, to be then removed to a neighbouring property leased by Major Daingerfield, Mr Keene's brother-in-law, who had managed the Castleton Stud. By a remarkable and melancholy coincidence, Major Daingerfield himself died only two days after Mr Keene.

The son of a merchant, Mr Keene was born in London in 1838, he therefore passed away in his seventy-fifth year. After receiving an education at schools in Lincolnshire and in Dublin he went to America with his parents in 1852. The family settled in the northern part of California. Keene's speculative inclinations found plenty of scope in the Far West in those lively times, and after he had tried his hand as a publisher of a little country newspaper, he became interested in mining ventures in Nevada. Thence he migrated to San Francisco, where he dabbled in mining shares and quickly made, lost, and remade a comfortable fortune. Presently he was elected President of the San Francisco Stock Exchange, and during a panic was one of four men who each contributed £200,000 to a guarantee fund that saved the Bank of California from bankruptcy. While still in California he married Miss Sarah Daingerfield, daughter of Colonel Le Roy Daingerfield, of Virginia. The lady had gone west with her brother, the late Major Daingerfield, then a law student.

Keene was worth over £1,000,000 when, in 1876, he was ordered by his doctor to cease work and take a sea voyage. He decided to try a trip to Europe, and made for New York. There he was caught by the lure of Wall Street. From what he had seen during the journey across the Continent, he came to the conclusion that it would be a good thing to become a 'bear' of railway stocks. He had not been many hours in New York before he had sold short 10,000 New York Centrals, and he was later able to buy them for £4 a share less than the price at which he had sold. A few months later he became a 'bull', and within two years had cleared £2,000,000 by his deals.

Then Keene turned his attention to wheat. Against his better judgment, it is said, he was drawn into the scheme for 'cornering' the Chicago market in 1880. It cost him £1,500,000. Other reverses followed, and by 1884 he had not only lost his entire fortune, but was £300,000 in debt. An experience of this sort would have crushed the spirit of most men. James Keene was, however, made of stern stuff. Here is a pen picture of him in the hour of adversity, written by one who knew him well:

'There was a man who was used to the best in the land, fond of the good things of life, accustomed to the flattery of lesser speculators, loving above everything to back his views in the market with millions, to whom operating in stocks was as the breath of his nostrils, a man proud by instinct, a bundle of nerves, impatient of obstacles – now flat "broke". Once so powerful and courted and feared, now unnoticed, unsought, regarded by the Street as an exploded bubble about to join the ranks of the vast army of Wall Street failures. What did he do? I used to see him going to and from his little cottage in the country because he was, like myself, too poor to live in the city. I was poor, too, but I could still afford to have my wife's phaeton meet me at the station. Not so with Keene. He walked from the station to his house. I have seen him in the dead of winter struggling through the snow-drifts, with his head lowered and his body bent, walking against the wind, a dismal figure on the chill landscape. How many men would have survived the sudden descent from millions to pennies? Keene did. He bent his head, when the storm raged and pushed onward, and twenty years later he was the admired and envied and feared king of Wall Street.'

It took Mr Keene about ten years to recover all, and more than all, he had lost. His genius as a manipulator was, says one of his biographers, too rare not to attract the backing of capitalists and promoters. In the ordinary sense he was not a Stock Exchange gambler. He did not bet on fluctuations; he made them. He created markets for securities that had hitherto been unsaleable. He would buy up apparently worthless shares and put them up point by point until the crazy public came in and bought them. It was he, for instance, who raised the shares of the Southern Railway and of the Steel Trust to their present height of popularity.

To most men, continues the same writer, even to expert operators, the tape merely conveys an idea of how the market is going. To Mr Keene, in the days of his power and activity, it reported how his lieutenants were executing his commands. He had an extraordinary instinct for appraising general and Wall Street conditions. Though a man of highly nervous temperament, who would pace up and down his office on dull days like a caged tiger, he had the patience and the organising foresight of a Von Moltke. His bear raids for dash and boldness and sheer hammering power were like nothing that had ever been known in Wall Street. He fought several of the most powerful financiers and groups from Russell Sage and Jay Gould to Harriman, and though he repeatedly stood to lose a million pounds in five minutes he never lost a night's sleep. He was often defeated, but never for long. In the end he almost invariably triumphed, partly because he stuck to his last and never sought to become identified with the management or watering or consolidation of the companies whose shares he bought and sold by the hundreds of thousands. A man of the plainest speech and the most absolute candour, he was probably the greatest Stock Exchange strategist that the world has yet seen.

This, then, was the business side of the man whose racing stable established in 1907 a world's record by winning Stakes to the value of £79,468, and so beating the total of £73,857 with which the Duke of Portland was credited in 1889, which today ranks as the second largest sum won on the Turf in any one year by an owner of racehorses. In the six years 1905–1910 Mr Keene's horses captured Stakes to the value of £247,410. In four of these years, 1905–1908, he headed the list of winning owners in the United States, and in 1909 he was second in the list.

It was in 1879 that Keene first came into prominence as an owner of racehorses. He had acquired by purchase, at a cost of £3,000, the colt Spendthrift, by Australian out of Aerolite. During that season of 1879 there were many good three-year-olds, notably Mr Lorillard's Harold, but Spendthrift was master of them all. That same year Keene sent a couple of yearlings to England. One was Foxhall, the other Don Fulano. The latter was expected to turn out the better racehorse, but Foxhall, for whom only £130 had been paid, proved to be far and away superior to his companion. Though entered for the Grand Prix de Paris, which he won, Foxhall was, unfortunately, not nominated for the Epsom Derby, and so Mr Keene lost the best chance that ever came his way of winning that greatest of all classic races. The chagrin this oversight occasioned was, perhaps, all the greater because the Derby of Foxhall's year was won by another American horse, Mr Lorillard's Iroquois. In the autumn, however, Foxhall achieved great fame by winning both the Cesarewitch and the Cambridgeshire. In the former he carried 7 st 12 lb, and in the latter the record weight for a three-year-old, of 9 st. Don Fulano, it may be mentioned, finished third to Peregrine and Iroquois in the Two Thousand Guineas, but ran unplaced in the Derby.

Then came the period of ten years during which Mr Keene had to devote all his energies to the repairing of his finances. It was in 1892 that he once more turned his attention to the Turf. In June of that year the yearlings bred by Major Thomas at the Dixiana Stud were offered for sale in New York by Tattersall's. Keene sent for Mr Easton, the Manager of Tattersall's, and asked him to look over the youngsters and pick out one or two that he might buy. Mr Easton, having complied with this request, particularly recommended a brown colt by Himyar out of Mannie Grey, a brother to a filly named Correction, who had run half a mile in $46\frac{1}{2}$ seconds. Immediately prior to the sale Mr Keene and his son, Foxhall, carefully inspected the colt, who happened to be the first of the Dixiana lots to enter the ring. The opening bid for him was one of £400, made by Mr Pulsifer, the owner of Tenny, a horse who at that time almost dominated the American Turf. The second bid was one of £600.

It was made by Foxhall Keene, and, there being no other offer, the colt was knocked down to him and his father. The Keenes were rather taken aback by the lack of competition for the colt, and asked Major Thomas if there were any hidden defects. The Major proudly replied: 'I am not in the habit of selling yearlings without calling attention to their defects, if they have any. You need not take him. I will keep the colt if you do not want him.' 'No, no,' said Mr Keene, 'your word is quite sufficient.'

By this transaction Mr Keene became the owner of the horse Domino, the founder of his fortune as an owner of racers. As the writer who relates the story says: 'Without Domino there would have been no Disguise, no Cap and Bells, and no Commando; and without Commando there would have been no Colin, no Peter Pan, no Superman and no Celt.' Disguise won in England races worth over £10,000, and ran third in the Derby won by Diamond Jubilee; while Cap and Bells was victorious in the Oaks. Domino himself carried all before him as a two-year-old, when he captured Stakes worth £34,000, and it was a great misfortune for Mr Keene when the son of Himyar died after he had had only a few seasons at the stud. His son Commando (who also died young) won five of the six races for which he started. Colin, son of Commando, was never beaten. As a two- and three-year-old he won fifteen races worth £36,180, the biggest sum ever amassed by a horse on the American Turf, his grandsire's (Domino's) total of £36,010 ranking second, and that of Ballot (another of Mr Keene's horses), who won about £35,000 in America, third. Colin is now quartered at the Heath Stud Farm, Newmarket. Another great horse owned by Mr Keene was Sysonby, by Melton out of Optime, by Orme. The mare Optime was imported to the United States, when carrying Sysonby, by the late Marcus Daly, who died very shortly after the mare's arrival at his stud in Montana. At the sale of Daly's brood mares, Keene bought Optime. It will thus be gathered that his luck in buying bloodstock was phenomenal, though it was offset by the early deaths of many of the best of the horses that carried his colours. Sysonby died from blood poisoning when a four-year-old. This was a great blow to Mr Keene, for he had expected the son of Melton to achieve great fame as a sire.

Under the management of Major Daingerfield the Castleton Stud, in the bluegrass region of Kentucky, was founded in 1893. The estate extended over more than a thousand acres, about equally divided between grassland and woodland. Shortly after the stud had been started Mr Keene gave a commission for the purchase of high-class brood mares in England to the value of £20,000, his conviction being that the best way to breed racehorses was to mate American sires with English mares. One of the mares he bought at this time was Pastorella, a daughter of Springfield, and she became the dam of Colin, who shows a good deal of Springfield character. It need only be said that the Castleton Stud went from triumph to triumph, turning out a long succession of great winners. Asked on one occasion, 'Which, in your opinion, is the best horse you have ever owned?' Mr Keene replied: 'I fancy that Colin is the best I have ever had in my stable. What is more, the boys in charge of my horses are of the same opinion.' He, however, had a great partiality for Domino, 'a great and wonderful two-year-old, a loyal horse, and a brave one'.

The human side of Mr Keene's character as a sportsman was fully revealed in an interview with a representative of the *New York Herald*. 'What,' he was asked, 'is the enjoyment of owning a successful race-horse, a horse with the reputation of a Commando, a Peter Pan, a Sysonby or a Colin?'

'It is,' said Mr Keene, 'the gratification of possessing something that you know is a little better than that possessed by anybody else. Beyond that, it is a matter of intense personal pride. It is not the sum the horse may earn; it is not the possibility that he may be employed for speculation that makes him desirable, because racing for gaming is not sport; it is the fact that he is a wonderful work of nature, a fine, high-spirited, perhaps gentle and intelligent, animal that is a little superior to all others of his time, and whose courage is tested by races he runs and the results that follow.' The feelings of a true sportsman could not, surely, be expressed in language more fitting, more admirable, than that of which these few sentences are composed.

'And what,' inquired the interviewer, 'is the gratification that comes of winning races?'

'An exaltation of spirit that is healthy and stimulating,' was the reply. 'A man,' continued Mr Keene, 'who has looked upon his horses from the time they were foaled until they walk into the paddock after a hard race, victorious over everything that could run against them, glows with enjoyment. How can he help it? Here is a handsome, clean-coated, sure-footed animal whom you have seen from the days when he stumbled awkwardly after his dam, who has developed every quality it was hoped would be revealed when he was bred. It may be that the colt selected as a yearling to be the star of the stable has turned out a disappointment. Some uncertain-gaited youngster, who did not appear at first sight to be so well advanced as another foaled in the same year, suddenly manifests qualities which indicate grand possibilities. If he wins in some contest which is to become a part of Turf history your blood tingles and you are proud of your results.'

In a communication to the *Horse and Hound*, a personal friend of Mr Keene wrote of him:

'He was a really great sportsman, and, with his clear and intelligent mind concentrated on what became his only pastime and amusement, a most successful owner and breeder of thoroughbreds. No one ever loved his horses so well or knew them better. For years, when in good health, he spent every Sunday at his training stables in America, summer and winter, lunching at his trainer's cottage, spending hours looking his horses over and studying and examining each in turn. He had a great eye for a horse, and was a very fine judge of an animal's looks and condition. He was a severe critic of his horses performances, and would rarely admit the many excuses made for defeats, unless apparent to even a blind man, thinking that really good horses always overcome the many unforseen difficulties they get into, which, indeed, his good ones always did. . . . He was proud of his horses and his colours, and no animal of his was allowed to start unless he was as fit as he could be made, and to do his best. Nor would he ever sanction manipulations for handicaps. Those were his orders wherever he raced, and he generally saw they were carried out.'

The first English Derby seen by Mr Keene was that of 1900, in which his horse Disguise ran third to King Edward's (then the Prince of Wales) Diamond Jubilee, and Simon Dale. Travelling back to London with Mr Somerville Tattersall, he said: 'I think my horse was unlucky, but (referring to the joy of the crowd over the success of the Royal colours) I have seen something which I shall never forget and I should have been sorry if my horse had prevented that scene of enthusiasm and loyalty.'

In the course of a speech he made three years ago, Mr Keene said:

'My love of horses has been a great comfort to me all my life. I have always kept my horses in their place, though. I haven't allowed them to interfere with my business. Some men carry their love of horses altogether too far. Such a one was a young father who stood with his fair wife before the crib of their first-born. "Isn't he wonderful?" the young mother cried. "Did you ever see anything like him at twenty-six months." "Maternal love is all very well," the father retorted, impatiently, "but please don't try to compare it with a two-year-old thoroughbred."'

It is the memory of Mr Keene as breeder and owner of racehorses the readers of this *Review* will cherish and preserve. The foregoing sketch of his career and of his high and noble aims as a sportsman has grievous shortcomings if it does not present him in the light of one well worthy of the amazing success that attended his ventures on the Turf.   E.M.

January 3rd – Death of Mr James Robert Keene, the most successful breeder and owner of racehorses the American Turf has known. He had for some years been in a delicate state of health, and passed away, in his seventy-fifth year, in a New York Nursing Home, a few days after undergoing an operation for an abdominal malady. His remains were interred in the family grave at Woodlawn Cemetery. A full sketch of his career as a financier and sportsman will be found elsewhere in this number of the *Review*. It may here be added that he was largely instrumental in founding, in the early nineties, the New York Jockey Club, which controls racing in the Eastern States of the Union, and up to the time of his death he was Vice-Chairman of the Club. Previously racing was managed by a Board of Control whose methods became very lax. Mr Keene perceived that unless the sport was brought under severer discipline it would quickly cease to exist.   BBR–1913

The Death of Mr Sanford

Was there ever another horse owner like Mr Stephen Sanford, a wealthy American owner and breeder who died in 1913? Imagine giving thousands of employees an afternoon off to watch the private trials of one's two-year-olds just prior to the Saratoga race meeting where they were to make their debuts. But that is what Mr Sanford did.

February 13th – Death of Mr Stephen Sanford, who for a long period was a notable figure on the American Turf. Living at Amsterdam in the State of New York, he amassed a big fortune as a carpet manufacturer. The breeding and racing of thoroughbreds was his chief hobby. He was the owner of the Hurricana Stud, where all the horses that carried his colours were bred and reared. None of his two-year-olds was allowed to race in public prior to the Saratoga Meeting in August. Great preparations were always made for the Saratoga 'campaign' by the Sanford Stable. The thousands of workpeople employed at the carpet factory were one afternoon in the preceding week given a holiday, and for their entertainment a series of trials took place on a private race track on the Hurricana farm. Every horse in the 'barn' was pressed into service on these occasions. If a 'good thing' for one of the Saratoga races was revealed every man and woman in Amsterdam would be sure to have something 'on'. Perhaps the best of several good horses General Sanford (as he was usually called) bred was Chaughnawaga. Many of his animals were given Indian names. The deceased gentleman was born at Mayfield, NY, in 1826. The Hurricana Stud is to be carried on by his son, Mr John Sanford.   BBR–1913

Major Eustace Loder.

Obituary of Major Eustace Loder

Major Eustace Loder, a shy and diffident gentleman who died at the young age of forty-seven in 1914, had his hands on three very exceptional thoroughbreds. He bred and owned the incomparable Pretty Polly, only twice defeated in twenty-four starts and the founder of a most formidable and enduring distaff dynasty; he personally picked up Spearmint, the eventual Epsom Derby winner and tremendously successful sire, for 300 guineas as a yearling; and he also owned and raced Star Shoot, a quality racehorse who became a champion sire on five occasions in the US. His memorative biography in the Review *of 1914 was written with a warm, personal touch and leaves one with a feeling of fondness for this introverted personality who apparently had an appreciation for life but did not know how to live it, although the world was better off for his having been here.*

IN THE guise of a deliverer, death came to Major Eustace Loder at his residence, Eyrefield Lodge, the Curragh, Ireland, on July 27th. For many weeks the life of this splendid sportsman had hung by a slender thread. Afflicted with Bright's Disease, he had suffered terribly, and death brought a merciful release.

As a sportsman, Major Loder was known by name at least, to the world at large and was greatly honoured and respected. As a *man* he was known to very few. The few held it a privilege to regard him and to be regarded by him, as a friend. His every thought and action was inspired by kindness and charity. But this lovable trait in his character was, as a rule, screened by an unconquerable timidity, and a reserve of manner apt to be misunderstood. His heart was not worn on his sleeve. The friendships he formed were mostly of slow growth, but once they had matured a severance was to him unthinkable. At all times, his word was his bond.

Major Loder's shyness must often have been rather painful and embarrassing to him. It prevented him doing many things which inclination prompted. Those who moved within his immediate circle are aware that owing to this curious little idiosyncrasy he often refrained from inviting to stay with him people whom he would have been delighted to entertain. And yet, if by chance, these same people suggested that they should pay him a visit he at once, and gladly, agreed to the proposal, and was grateful for their society. Though not one who shone as a conversationalist or raconteur, he thoroughly enjoyed a good story. He was an excellent companion and a generous host.

His opinion was always worth having, because it was formed only after he had regarded the matter under consideration from every point of view. This habit accounted for the soundness of his judgment. To all appearance he was a somewhat unemotional man; there is, however, little doubt that he frequently suffered from suppressed excitement when a casual observer would suppose he was not in the least affected. He was, perhaps, a better judge of other people's horses and their capabilities than he was of his own – a not uncommon failing, be it said, for one is apt to think of one's own as one would like them to be. He was very fond of horses, whether racers or hunters, and was pardonably proud of the products of his studs. As one of his closest friends puts it, 'through and through, he was a white man, and his like are very few and far between'.

Born May 16th, 1867, Major Loder was a son of the late Sir Robert Loder, and a twin brother of Mr Sydney Loder. They were the youngest of Sir Robert's eight sons, the eldest son being Sir Edward Giles Loder. After Eton and 'Trinity', Cambridge, Eustace Loder entered the army, securing a commission in the 12th Lancers. With that regiment, for which he always had a warm corner in his heart, he remained for fifteen years, being adjutant from 1895 to 1899.

It was during this period that he began to play a part on the Turf. He registered his colours in 1891. They were 'yellow, dark blue sleeves and black cap' – colours that had belonged to his father, who, however, raced very little. In 1892 he appeared for the first time in the list of winning owners, with a total of £1,401 to his credit. He had bought from Tom Cannon, then training at Danebury, the four-year-old mare Billow, and with her won the Ascot Stakes. This success was the fore-runner of many notable triumphs on the Turf. Mr Loder – he was then only a subaltern – was then as keenly interested in steeple-chasing as in racing on the flat, and owned some useful jumpers. One of them was Field Marshal, with whom he won the Grand Military Gold Cup at Sandown Park. In 1903 he won this trophy again with Marpessa. The best of all his 'chasers was, however, Covert Hack, winner of the Conyngham Cup at Punchestown in 1899, 1900, 1901 and 1903.

From 1893 to 1899 inclusive the Loder colours were, on the flat, borne successfully in only four minor races – two in 1893 and two in 1896. But in 1900 they were brought into prominence by Star Shoot, a colt by Isinglass out of Astrology, who, trained for the now Captain Loder by Huggins, the American, won three valuable two-year-old races – the British Dominion Plate and the National Breeders' Stakes at Sandown Park, and the Hurst Park Foal Plate. Strictly speaking the number of races was $2\frac{1}{2}$, because in the National Stakes, Star Shoot (who became a successful sire in the United States) ran a dead heat for first place with Ian.

Thenceforward the name of Loder became more and more familiar to the racing public. It was a familiarity that carried with it respect and confidence. Happy is the owner who has the public with him. From Huggins's stable, Major Loder's horses passed to the care of Mr P. P. Gilpin who, moving from Dorsetshire, settled at Newmarket, where at the far end of the Bury Road, he built the fine establishment known as Clarehaven. There Pretty Polly, Spearmint, Hammerkop and a long list of other horses owned by Major Loder were prepared for their engage-ments.

Pretty Polly and Spearmint! These are the two animals with which Major Loder will always be chiefly associated. He himself bred Pretty Polly at Eyrefield Lodge. She was a grand-looking chestnut mare by Gallinule out of Admiration. The dam, bred by Robert Peck, was bought when a yearling by Major Loder in 1893, at the Newmarket July Sales, for 510 guineas. Of no great account on the racecourse, Admira-tion, though by no means the nonentity she has been sometimes repre-sented, developed into a brood mare of extraordinary excellence. Going to the stud in 1897, Pretty Polly, born in 1901, was her fourth foal. Her third was Veneration II, dam of Craganour and Glorvina; while after Pretty Polly came Adula, Admirable Crichton, Adora, Miranda, Cock-a-hoop, Coriander and Addenda, together with a colt by Gallinule and a filly by Desmond in 1907 and 1908. She died in 1910 after producing foals with clockwork regularity for thirteen years. But, of course, Pretty Polly far exceeded all the others.

This remarkable mare would want several of our columns to herself if we attempted to do justice to her career on the Turf. She will always be given a prominent place in the gallery of racing celebrities. It was somewhat strange that she should have appeared on the scene so soon after Sceptre, who is two years her senior, because mares of outstanding merit as racers have not been numerous. For our purpose it must suffice to state that Pretty Polly ran twenty-four times, and was beaten only twice – in the Prix du Conseil Municipal at Paris as a three-year-old, and in the Ascot Cup by Bachelor's Button when a five-year-old. The Paris race was run in very heavy going, and she succumbed to Presto II, a colt of her own age to whom she was giving 9 lb. Zinfandel was behind her that day. When beaten at Ascot, in the last race she ran, Pretty Polly was not quite at her best, though it is probable that the distance, two and a half miles, was beyond her compass. She won nine races as a two-year-old, seven as a three-year-old, four as a four-year-old, and two as a five-year-old. Her total of winnings amounted to £37,297. Among the prizes she captured were the National Breeders' Produce Stakes, the Champagne at Doncaster, the Middle Park Plate, the One Thousand Guineas, Oaks and St Leger (she was not engaged in the Two Thousand and Derby won by St Amant); the Coronation Cup at Epsom twice, the Champion Stakes and the Jockey Club Cup.

It was in 1906 that Pretty Polly finished her racing career, and it was in that same year that Major Loder realised the ambition of every owner by leading in the winner of the Derby – Spearmint. This son of Carbine was bought as a yearling by Major Loder out of the batch sent to Doncaster by Sir Tatton Sykes. Again and again the statement has been made that by securing so great a treasure as Spearmint for 300 guineas – for that was the sum paid for the colt – the Major was indebted to the extraordinarily good luck which seemed to attend his Turf ventures. It was undoubtedly a rare piece of good fortune to be called upon to pay so small a price for the colt, but judgment rather than luck impelled Major Loder to bid for him. Accompanied by his stud manager, Mr Noble Johnson, the Major had gone to Sledmere a week or two before the Doncaster Sales. They there saw nine yearlings that were to come under the hammer, and the colt by Carbine out of Maid of the Mint was the one that appealed to them most. Major Loder went to Doncaster determined to buy this youngster, and we imagine that no one was more surprised than he when he found his bid of 300 guineas accepted.

Spearmint ran his first race, the Great Foal Plate at Lingfield, in July of the following year. That he had shown good form on the training ground is proved by the fact that he started favourite in a field of ten. And he won, but only by a head from Succory. At Derby the following month Black Arrow gave him 3 lb and a three lengths' beating, and at Newmarket in October he was unplaced in a Nursery handicap. This record contained no suggestion that Spearmint was a potential Derby horse, and in the following Spring his name was never mentioned in connection with the great Epsom classic. One of his contemporaries and stable companions was Sir Daniel Cooper's filly Flair, who the previous season won the Middle Park Plate, beating Major Loder's Admirable Crichton. Flair won the One Thousand Guineas with the greatest ease, and as the colts that year seemed very moderate, she forthwith became a pronounced favourite for the Derby. There had been some talk of Admiral Crichton carrying Major Loder's colours at Epsom, but, if we remember rightly, he broke down. In the meantime the idea of starting Spearmint was not entertained. He was believed to have no chance of beating Flair, and so it was decided that he should be specially prepared for the Grand Prix de Paris. But when out at exercise on Newmarket Heath one morning about three weeks before the Derby, Flair met with an accident which resulted in a badly lacerated leg. Her racing days were over. The stable had now perforce to fall back on Spearmint, who was at once put into strong work. On this he thrived amazingly, and a few days before the Derby a gallop he had with Pretty Polly revealed him in the light of a formidable candidate for Derby honours. He started second favourite to Lally at 6 to 1, and won by a length and a half from Picton, with Troutbeck third and Radium fourth. Verily on this occasion Major Loder's proverbial luck had come to his aid! Shortly afterwards Spearmint, followed by hundreds of British sportsmen, went over to Paris, where he duly won the Grand Prix. But unfortunately that race proved his undoing. Leg trouble supervened, and he had to be turned out of training to start a career at the stud which has begun and promises to yield splendid results. Major Loder was many times pressed by foreigners to sell Spearmint. He received an offer of £50,000, but refused to part with his Derby winner.

Other good animals owned by Major Loder, in addition to those already named, were Baltinglass, Galvani, Game Chick and Lance Chest, the last-named a son of Spearmint and twice a winner of the

Princess of Wales's Stakes. The last time his colours were borne to victory was at Whitsuntide, when Glass and China won at Wolverhampton. The following is his record as an owner so far as flat racing is concerned:

	Races Won	Value £
1892	4	1,401
1893	3	372
1896	2	242
1900	3	4,430
1901	6	9,820
1902	7	5,138
1903	12	15,738
1904	11	19,899
1905	13	11,584
1906	12	17,849
1907	10	7,647
1908	2	1,775
1909	7	6,294
1910	6	5,378
1911	4	8,132
1912	9	6,806
1913	6	5,611
1914	2	274
	118	£128,390

In 1904 and again in 1906 Major Loder's name came second in the Winning Owner's List.

Major Loder had two breeding studs – one attached to his residence, Eyrefield Lodge, the other at Old Connell, three miles away. He gradually collected a wonderful group of Gallinule mares, headed, of course, by Pretty Polly. The Major took the keenest personal interest in these establishments, which he maintained practically regardless of cost. The foaling boxes at Old Connell are models of their kind.

As an administrator, Major Loder was associated with the Turf both in England and Ireland. It was in 1906 that he was elected a member of the Jockey Club, and in 1912 he was appointed Steward. In the Spring of this year, when he should, in the usual course, have assumed the duties attaching to the office of Senior Steward, he was compelled by his illness, which had then got a strong hold of his system, to tender his resignation. This the Jockey Club regretfully accepted. As one of the Stewards at Epsom in 1913, it fell to Major Loder's lot to shoulder a share of the responsibility for the disqualification of Craganour. There is no doubt that he experienced much distress of mind over that unfortunate affair. Very shortly afterwards he discussed the case with us very freely, and we were made to realise that it was his absolute conviction that the course which he and his co-stewards took in depriving Craganour of his honours was not only justified but the only possible one in the circumstances. He used particularly scornful language when he referred to the suggestion, made in certain quarters, that the Stewards might have refrained from taking action seeing that it was the Derby. 'If,' he said, 'I am entrusted with the difficult task of administering the Rules of Racing, I shall apply them without fear or favour, whether the race is the Derby or a paltry selling event.' This pronouncement was typical of the man.

It is understood that Major Loder bequeathed to his nephew, Mr Giles Harold Loder, the studs at Eyrefield Lodge and Old Connell. Mr Loder is the eldest son of the late Mr Wilfrid Hans Loder, second son of Sir Robert Loder, who died in 1888.

The remains of Major Loder were interred in a vault in Slaugham Churchyard, in which rests the body of his brother, Mr Wilfred H. Loder, who died in 1902.   BBR–1914

England's First Lady

November 2nd – Statistics relating to the past racing season in England show that the following are the

Twelve Leading Owners

	No. of Winners	Races won	Value £
Lady James Douglas	2	5	14,735
Mr S. B. Joel	9	21	9,768
Mr W. M. Cazalet	5	12	9,416
Lord Derby	7	11	7,460
Mr A. W. Cox ('Mr Fairie')	2	8	7,077
Major W. Astor	3	5	4,734
Lord Glanley (Sir Wm. Tatem)*	10	13	4,423
Messrs Robinson and Clark	2	3	3,781
Sir Geo. Noble	1	4	3,139
Capt. A. de Rothschild	3	4	2,789
Mr W. T. De Pledge	3	5	2,770
Duke of Portland	5	5	2,531

* Not including races won in Ireland.

This is the first time a lady has headed the list of owners, and Lady James Douglas is heartily to be congratulated on gaining this proud distinction. Her success is the more notable because her two winners – Gainsborough and Bayuda – are both home bred. Lady James is, of course, one of the patrons of the Manton stable; so are Mr Cazalet, Mr Cox and Major Astor, all of whom are in the 'first six'. Never before, we imagine, has any training establishment been able to boast of so remarkable a record.

BBR–1918

Training Horses in 3000 BC

ADDRESSING the Academy of Inscriptions and Belles-Lettres in Paris, M. Hronzy, a Professor at the University of Prague, said an inscription of 1360 BC left by the chief riding master of the Indo-Aryan State of Mitanni, in Mesopotamia, was a veritable manual on the subject of horse training and management. Horse-racing is specifically mentioned in the document, which describes how the animals were first given a special reducing diet, accompanied by baths and gallops to induce sweating, while periodical purges of salt-water and malt-water were also part of the treatment. Trotting and short gallops over two or three furlongs were part of the regular training, which usually lasted about six months. M. Hronzy declared that in view of the methodical nature of the system described, there could be no doubt that it had been evolved as the result of long experience, and might have originated as early as 3000 BC.

BBR–1930

The Death of Mr Leopold de Rothschild

When Mr Leopold de Rothschild died in 1917 at the age of seventy-two, the English Turf lost one of its most honoured patrons and the racing public one of its most endearing owners. Few owners, especially in those days when it was most important to win a bet to pay expenses, took the public into their confidence. However, 'Mr Leopold' was most generous in this respect and his 'blue and yellow' colours were always joyously applauded when successful. Mr de Rothschild's most famous performers were St Frusquin and the Two Thousand Guineas and Derby winner St Amant.

AFTER A long illness, caused by a stroke, Mr Leopold de Rothschild died at Ascott, Leighton Buzzard, on May 29th. His passing leaves a big

gap in many circles. That of the Turf is one. 'Mr Leopold', as he was
often called, had been actively associated with racing in England for
nearly forty years. No member of the Turf hierarchy was more
universally respected; no colours were more popular than the 'blue and
yellow' which his horses carried. What was the secret of the affectionate
regard in which he was held by all and sundry? Simply that he raced for
the pure love of the sport. Nobody rejoiced more than he did when he
knew that every Dick, Tom and Harry had backed one of his winners.
His stable at Newmarket was a private establishment in one sense, but it
was essentially a public one in another sense. Very few of our stables are
run on these lines; few owners can indeed, afford to take the public into
their confidence in so generous a fashion. For that very reason it is the
more necessary to lay stress on the policy Mr de Rothschild pursued. He
was rewarded again and again by the certain knowledge, conveyed to
him in various ways, that he stood well with his fellow men.

Born November 22nd, 1845, Mr de Rothschild was in his seventy-
second year when he died. He was the third and youngest son of Baron
Lionel Nathan de Rothschild. The eldest son was the late Lord
Rothschild. They were nephews of Baron Meyer de Rothschild who

Leopold de Rothschild.

played so great a part on the Turf in the 'sixties and early 'seventies of last century. It was left to Mr Leopold to uphold the racing fortunes of the family after the death of his uncle, and to him the family colours descended. The Crafton Stud at Mentmore had passed to Baron Rothschild's daughter, Hannah, through whom it came, by marriage, to Lord Rosebery. Mr Leopold had, therefore, to form a new stud. He established it at Southcourt, close to Leighton Buzzard railway station. There he bred practically all the horses he raced, including St Frusquin, Persimmon's great protagonist, and the Derby winner St Amant, a son of St Frusquin. From the year 1879, when his first success on the Turf was recorded, down to the day of his death, Mr de Rothschild won 851 races worth £367,434. His yearly average was therefore, twenty-one races and £9,421. Whether or not that result produced a balance on the right side of the ledger is neither here nor there. As a guerdon of the success of his stud and stable it was adequate enough, and that would be all the deceased gentleman would concern himself about. His most successful year was 1896, when the value of the fifty-four races won by his horses was £46,766. In 1898, the fifty-three races won were worth £30,267, and the 'third best' year was 1895, when his horses won forty-one races and £20,749. In no fewer than fourteen years his winnings ran into five figures.

The Southcourt Stud was conducted on a big scale. It is well, but not extravagantly, equipped. At the present time the stallions located there are St Amant, Radium, Day Comet, and Mr August Belmont's Tracery. The establishment is under the management of Mr R. T. Ashby and its uninterrupted success pays a direct tribute to the skill with which he discharges the various duties which devolve upon him. Mr de Rothschild was equally fortunate in having Mr J. T. Wood as the manager of the racing stable, Palace House, at Newmarket. For many years the horses were trained by Alfred Hayhoe and John Watson. Of late years Watson and Tom Cannon, Jr, have shared the responsibility.

We might, of course, fill many pages of the *Review* with a survey of the notable achievements of bearers of the 'blue and yellow' bred and owned by Mr de Rothschild. The career of St Frusquin was fully dealt with at the time of his death in 1914, and it is, perhaps, as the owner of that son of St Simon, that the deceased sportsman will chiefly be remembered. St Frusquin, of course, won the Two Thousand Guineas, and ran Persimmon to a neck in the Derby. Possibly he would have won the St Leger but for breaking down while undergoing his preparation for that race. Mr de Rothschild won his only St Leger with Doricles in 1901 after a great struggle with Volodyovski. There is no doubt Volodyovski was knocked about at the bend which then existed but a furlong and a half from home – the course has since been straightened – but it is almost equally certain that Doricles was in no way responsible.

Much has been written about St Amant's Derby in 1904. The race was run in a terrific thunderstorm. Through it all Mr de Rothschild stood in the space reserved for members of the Jockey Club immediately in front of the Press box. He was without an overcoat and must have been soaked to the skin. Apparently, however, he was oblivious of everything except the great contest. Immediately after St Amant had passed the post a winner by three lengths from the luckless John O'Gaunt, Mr Leopold pulled a piece of paper from his pocket, and, handing it to a pressman said 'Will you please send that off for me. It is to my sons at Eton.' It was a stamped telegraph form on which he had previously written the news that St Amant had won! Some superstitious people would no doubt say that he was courting disaster by anticipating matters in this way. And many people *did* say that St Amant was a lucky winner – that his triumph was due to his being scared out of his wits by the lightning and thunder. This was sheer nonsense. St Amant had better public form than any of his opponents. He was certainly the best colt of his year as a juvenile, and we had seen him win the Two Thousand Guineas with the greatest ease without a thunderstorm to speed him along. His Derby performance was a very fine one, for, although drawn on the outside, he at once took the lead, crossed over to the rails, and was in front from start to finish. If immediately after that victory some mishap had occurred which necessitated his being retired forthwith to the stud, St Amant would, we feel sure, have been a sire much sought after, and he would have had chances with high class mares that never came his way. For, unfortunately, his subsequent record, with the exception of an unlooked-for victory in the Jockey Club Stakes the following year, was a very disappointing one, and he consequently frittered away his 'classic' reputation. How far his encounters with Pretty Polly were responsible for his growing sick of racing one does not know. They probably accounted for it in some measure. Luckily for St Amant, Major Loder's mare was not engaged in the Two Thousand or the Derby.

Though the late Lord Rothschild, who died in 1915, did not himself breed or race thoroughbreds, he took a lively interest in his brother's horses. When the foals at Southcourt were weaned, a batch of five or six colts or fillies were, as a rule, sent over to Lord Rothschild's place at Tring, and there they remained until it was time for them to go to

Newmarket to be trained. We frequently saw him at Newmarket and Doncaster, showing a connoisseur's delight in the proceedings. In 1902, when Mr Leopold's horses were doing comparatively little on the Turf, Lord Rothschild thought the luck might take a favourable turn if a grey-coated animal were included in the Palace House string. Accordingly, there was bought for him at Doncaster that year a colt by Grey Leg out of Pindi, one of the Worksop Manor yearlings. The price paid was 500 guineas. The colt received the name of Bass Rock, and Lord Rothschild gave him to his brother. Great things followed the advent of this mascot. The following season Bass Rock himself won six races worth over £4,700; but, what was of more consequence, St Amant that year came out as a two-year-old, and the following year won the Two Thousand Guineas and the Derby. Whereas in 1902 Mr Leopold de Rothschild's total of winnings was only £3,659, in 1903 it jumped to £18,836. Curiously enough, Bass Rock could not win a race as a three-year-old so it appeared as though, having successfully played the rôle of a mascot which was thrust upon him, his career of usefulness was over. As a matter of fact, however, he won three more races – one as a four-year-old and two as a five-year-old.

It is understood that Southcourt is to be carried on. Mr de Rothschild's eldest son, Major Lionel de Rothschild, is not particularly interested in thoroughbreds, but his younger brothers Evelyn and Anthony are, and they will probably share the responsibility of maintaining the family traditions on the Turf. Mr Evelyn de Rothschild has already had his colours 'blooded'.   BBR–1917

Robert Peck's Recollections of Barcaldine

Barcaldine, a foal of 1878, by Solon, was unbeaten in twelve starts in Ireland and England. This is quite a heady record for a horse of which the famous English jockey, Fred Archer, is claimed to have said to Robert Peck, his eventual owner: 'I hope you won't buy that horse, for he cannot win a selling race.' Actually, Archer was correct in his assessment at that time, but Mr Peck could see the possibilities of the horse and he was proved right.

For a time it appeared that Barcaldine had a good chance of perpetuating his branch of the Matchem male line through his son Marco and his classic-winning grandson, Hurry-On, a champion sire in England, but unfortunately it has not survived.

The following undated letter, written by the late Robert Peck, probably in 1890, was published by 'Rapier' in the *Sporting and Dramatic News*. It throws a little further light on Barcaldine:

'So far as I remember, I bought the horse on the day after Hackness won the Cambridgeshire, for, I believe, 1,150 guineas.* Whilst I was looking at him before going into the ring, the late F. Archer came up to me and said, "I hope you won't buy that horse, for he cannot win a selling race. He has no action at all." He was then trained by Golding, and Archer had ridden him.† My reply was that he was totally out of condition, and that his big frame had neither flesh nor muscle – in fact, he reminded me very much of Kaleidoscope, when I bought him from the late Lord Dupplin, a beautiful frame, but with all the working machinery out of order. The following morning I gave Barcaldine a canter, and found that what Archer had told me was quite correct. He could not stride over a straw; so I ordered him to be put through a course of physic, have a good linseed mash every other night, and do easy walking exercise. The horse made little alteration until about Christmas, when he began to lay on some flesh, gradually furnished, and filled out into one of the most magnificent horses I ever saw. He stood in a very large box in Hopper's stables, and when you went in with some friends to look at him you felt that the whole box belonged to him, as there was hardly any room to move.

'When you looked over his back and quarters he gave you the idea of carrying any amount of weight without any difficulty. In my opinion, the only two horses that ever looked like him were Doncaster, when he won the Ascot Cup and the Alexandra Plate at five years old, and Verneuil, when he won at Ascot. These two horses were, to use a vulgar phrase, as big as bullocks and as hard as nails, with a beautiful bloom on their coats which shone like satin, worth going a thousand miles to see. No course was too long for them, and no weight too heavy for them to carry.

'Barcaldine was never tried during the time I had him. He was not a taking horse in his slow paces, but won all his races in a hack canter. Eight days before the Northumberland Plate he gave way in the pan of the heel, and was really broken down. Mr Barrow, the veterinary, attended him. We had his leg in ice as much as possible, and he walked for two hours in the morning and the afternoon. We issued a report daily of the horse's progress, which, I think, was not believed by the British public, as when I arrived at Newcastle to see the race I received two anonymous letters in the weighing-room. One of them said that after all the veterinary reports that had been circulating in the papers if the horse won I should be hissed and hooted. The other was to the effect that if Archer did not win the race on Barcaldine we should both come in for a warm reception; so it was very difficult to please the two. I showed the letters to Archer and also to Mr Ford, the Clerk of the Course, and I decided to let Barcaldine fight his own battle in the race and take my chance after it. Archer lay last for the greater part of the distance, then, when he got into the straight, went to the front and won in a common hack

---

* Barcaldine cost Peck 1,300 guineas. It is somewhat strange that he had forgotten the sum he paid for the horse.
† Archer had only ridden him at exercise on Newmarket Heath up to that time.

canter. Barcaldine was, in my opinion, one of the greatest horses we have ever known. He was cheered to the echo – in fact, I never remember anything like it. Lord Durham, who congratulated me after the race, can tell you. When the horse got back into the box he was very lame, and never stood a preparation again. I sold him to Lady Stamford for £8,000, and he was very successful for her ladyship up to the time of his death.'

BBR–1917

The Recollections of E. C. Clayton

When looking back on racing and breeding as it was about three-quarters of a century ago in England, one has to be startled by the changes which have taken place. When Mr E. C. Clayton, then in his early eighties, permitted some of his reminiscences to be published in the BBR *of 1919 of what racing and breeding was like fifty to sixty years before that, the shock waves of change are also to be realised. As the* BBR *points out: 'In many ways the decade from 1860 to 1870 is one of the most alluring to students of Turf history.' Mr Clayton, in 1919, was one of the very few men, left living, 'who can draw for us a word-picture of Newmarket as it was in the early Sixties. In some of the books of a reminiscent character to be found on the shelves of a good sporting library, we get glimpses of the men of those days; but none of them, so far as we are aware, draws anything like an adequate picture of that period. Contemporary literature is, of course, searched in vain. The writers of the time took everything they saw and heard to be matters of course. It may be that fifty or sixty years hence some curiosity will be evinced as to the Newmarket with which we are all familiar. What seems to us commonplace and not worth reporting may then, perchance, appeal as something peculiarly interesting, and if this* Review *is still making its appearance, some octogenarian will, perhaps, be asked to give its readers the benefit of his recollections.'*

So, Mr Clayton, through the BBR, *presented 'an adequate picture of that period' which is probably not to be found anywhere else. His intimate comments on such famous personalities as Admiral Rous, on the outstanding horses and jockeys, and on his own personal involvement in the sensational activities at 'the Headquarters of the English Turf' are treasures whose time has come to resurface and be appreciated once again.*

These are precious and enthralling recollections – worthy, indeed, of a book in themselves.

A TINY TOT of a girl who was asked 'How old are you?' replied, reproachfully, 'I'se not old; I'se nearly new.' If you were to make the suggestion to Mr E. C. Clayton that he is an old man, his retort would be very similar. There is a world of truth in the saying that a man is as old as he feels. Mr Clayton was born in October, 1837, a few months after Queen Victoria ascended the throne. A correct count shows him, therefore, to be in his eighty-third year. If, however, you shut your eyes to that cold fact, ignore the grey hairs, and give heed simply to the man of action, to the man of virile temperament, resolution, extraordinary willpower, light-hearted and sound-hearted, you may readily imagine you are confronted by one who was born in the 'sixties or 'seventies. There are not, indeed, many men dating back only to the 'sixties who could live at the high pressure Mr Clayton does today and every day. Regularly each week he is out with the Cottesmore Hounds, is still able to find his way about, to gallop and enjoy himself. He will ride ten miles to covert, and will think nothing of the same or more in the saddle home again after the day's sport is over. And this without ever feeling tired; on the contrary, the mere fact of being on a horse is such life and youth to him that he is always sorry when he has to get off. He walks at the rate of four miles an hour. He can, and often does run, and that without any discomfort or distress. Mr Clayton attributes his wonderful health and prolonged activity in a great measure to his abstinence from tobacco; though he realises that he misses a good deal, he is convinced he gains in heart power and exceptional eyesight far more than he loses.

There is nothing Mr Clayton dislikes more than publicity*, and he will probably squirm at that opening paragraph. But the reminiscences about to be placed on record will be robbed of much of their charm and attraction if readers are not allowed to visualise the central figure. We shall, doubtless, carry with us the legion who claim the friendship of Mr Clayton when we declare that he represents the super-excellent type of English country gentleman occasionally met with in the annals of sport. The reader will please understand, therefore, that he is indebted for the entertainment and instruction derived from the following pages to a very striking personality, endowed with physical and mental attributes of an unusual order.

More than once Mr Clayton gave the warning that we were not writing his history – an intimation that he was to be kept in the background as much as possible. Nevertheless, a few words about the family to which he belongs may be interposed. In lineal descent he is not a Clayton, but a Walters. The Walters family trace their line direct to the Plantagenets. His paternal grandmother was one of the Claytons, an old

*The compilers were, therefore, unable to find a photograph to accompany this piece. Sorry!

Northumbrian family seated at Chesters, a locality rich in Roman remains. She married Robert Walters, of Newcastle, in 1788. It was her son, William Clayton Walters, who, after succeeding to the property of his maternal uncle, Ralph Clayton, Sergeant-at-Law, in 1813 assumed the name of Clayton. Mr William Clayton Clayton married a Miss Chapman, of Whitby, and Mr E. C. Clayton is their elder son. Inasmuch as the Claytons were settled in Yorkshire up to the end of the seventeenth century, Mr Clayton can claim to be associated with that county through both father and mother. It is worthy of mention that his father lived to be ninety-three, and his mother ninety-four years of age. The property to which the father succeeded was that of Bradford Abbas, in Dorsetshire.

Mr Clayton makes no secret of the fact that he has never enjoyed those comforts and luxuries which a large income can confer. The morning we left Cottesmore Grange there was a sharp frost, and as our host wrapped himself up he remarked, 'It is only a fool or a pauper who is cold. I hope I am not the former, but fear I am almost the latter.' Nevertheless, from the days of long ago, first when he was a boy at Harrow and afterwards at Oxford, he has somehow possessed the means (or chanced their coming his way) whereby he could extract much of the joy and gladness that life can give to one who has the wit and daring to make his opportunities, and no one has had more for his money.

The keenness with which Mr Clayton has throughout his long life devoted himself to the thoroughbred must have been an acquired trait, for none of his ancestors, immediate or remote, seems to have been in any way associated with the Turf. He himself, however, had barely come of age when his colours were registered. He was not twenty-five when he graduated as a member of the inner circle of the habitués of Newmarket, and, taking the advice given to him by George Payne to 'live with old men when you are young and with young men when you are old', he had the good fortune to become associated with such pillars of the Turf as Admiral Rous, George Payne, the Duke of Bedford, Colonel Lowther (afterwards Lord Lonsdale), Stirling Crawford and others. That was the year 1862. Thenceforward until the late autumn of 1917 Mr Clayton rarely, if ever, missed attending a race meeting at Newmarket. So for fifty-five years he was a diligent, faithful and enthusiastic adherent and upholder of the traditions that encompass the headquarters of the British Turf. October 25th, 1917, was the eightieth anniversary of his birthday. In honour of the event the Stewards of the Jockey Club named one of the races in that day's programme the 'Clayton Handicap'. The wartime discomforts Mr Clayton experienced when travelling to and from Newmarket became so intolerable that, as he says, he got 'train shy', and during the following season missed some of the extra meetings.

Apart from Lord Coventry, Lord Chaplin and Mr Clayton, there are very few, if any, men living who can draw for us a word-picture of Newmarket as it was in the early 'sixties. In some of the books of a reminiscent character to be found on the shelves of a good sporting library, we get glimpses of the men of those days; but none of them, so far as we are aware, draws anything like an adequate picture of the period. Contemporary literature is, of course, searched in vain. The writers of the time took everything they saw and heard to be matters of course. It may be that fifty or sixty years hence some curiosity will be evinced as to the Newmarket with which we are all familiar. What seems to us commonplace and not worth recording may then, perchance, appeal as something peculiarly interesting, and if this *Review* is still making its appearance, some octogenarian will, perhaps, be asked to give its readers the benefit of his recollections. Rack our brains as we may, it is impossible at this moment to imagine upon what features the narrator will think it worth while to dilate. We can rest assured, however, that he will be able to unfold a story calculated to make his juniors gape with astonishment. The conditions under which we conduct racing nowadays may well seem as odd to our great-grand-children as the conditions that obtained in the 'sixties do to us.

When asked to state the most striking differences between 'then' and 'now', My Clayton began with the racecourse. By way of emphasising the primitive character of the arrangements, he recalled that although there were the several winning posts on the Rowley Mile that still exist, only one judge's box was available. This was on wheels, and in course of the afternoon it was drawn from post to post, as required, by a donkey. Its position varied with almost every race. Nowadays the majority of events finish at the Rowley Mile post opposite the Jockey Club Stand, but fifty years ago the various other posts down the course were more frequently used. There was no stand worthy of the name. The structure in use was a small, ramshackle wooden affair on a rotten brick foundation. The Stand we now know was built in 1876 under the superintendence of Sir John Astley, one of the Stewards at the time, though the prime mover in the matter had been Lord Falmouth, for he it was who had plans prepared in 1875, the third year of his Stewardship. When the members of the Jockey Club were asked to sanction the erection of the new Stand there was considerable opposition, partly because of the expense involved, and partly because of a rooted objection to so drastic an innovation. Sir John Astley throws some light on the matter. In his lively volume of reminiscences he writes:

> 'It really was high time some new building should be erected, for the old stand was not only too cramped and uncomfortable, but the structure had for some time been condemned as unsafe, no one being allowed to use the upper part of it, and that was the only place from which a decent view of the races could be obtained. Some of the old hands grumble at times and declare they wish the new stand had never been built. A finer investment was never heard of, for the money that passed through my hands for the buildings and paddocks was only some £20,000, and now (twenty years after) the income from the new stands and paddocks in gross is about £25,000 per annum.'

It may, perhaps, be permissible to remark here that the 'new Stand' is now getting, if it has not actually become, out of date. Within the last few years certain improvements have been effected with a view to affording further protection from bad weather, but on big days, such as the Cesarewitch and Cambridgeshire afternoons, the accommodation is utterly inadequate. The time cannot be far distant when the Jockey Club will have to consider the advantage, if not necessity, of rebuilding. When they have provided a really satisfactory substitute they may discover that once again they are possessed of a profitable investment.

In the days of which Mr Clayton is speaking a Stand was of much less consequence than it is today. The general public were not wanted at Newmarket. The Heath was regarded as a sort of 'preserve' for the well-to-do followers of racing, and any encroachment on that 'preserve' was resented. Habitués were for the most part mounted on hacks, and it mattered not to them where a race finished, or whether the Stand was good, bad ot indifferent. They had no use for a Stand. The wide stretch of heath was all they wanted, with liberty to canter as inclination dictated. There were no rails to impede their movements. For a distance of a hundred yards or so approaching each of the winning posts, the course was guarded by ropes, attached to stakes, and there was a custodian of the track in the person of one Martin Starling, who rode a white horse and wore a scarlet coat. Thus attired and mounted, Starling is depicted in some of the prints of the period. He also officiated in a similar capacity at Epsom. We have seen his counterpart at a few courses in recent years – a picturesque survival of the days when railed courses were unknown.

It will be understood then, that the attendance at a Newmarket meeting in the 'sixties was small and select. There is a story told of Admiral Rous which, whether true or apocryphal, illustrates the anxiety of the 'old stagers' to prevent the place becoming a popular resort. One year an enterprising official of the Great Eastern Railway conceived the idea of increasing the company's revenue by running cheap trains from London to Newmarket for the races. The trains were crammed, and the Heath, in consequence, presented an unwonted spectacle. The bluff Admiral and some of his friends were furious. 'Leave 'em to me,' the Director of the Turf is said to have exclaimed. 'I'll soon persuade 'em to give Newmarket a wide berth.' His remedy is alleged to have been the arrangement of the programme in such a way that the post at which each race finished was as far as possible from that at which the preceding event was decided. There was ample scope for the exploitation of this vindictive scheme, and we are asked to believe that the unwelcome strangers were so disgusted by the tactics employed that they were seen no more for a long period.

At that time ladies were rarely present at the races. Mr Clayton has, however, a vivid recollection of the Countess of Cardigan making an appearance one afternoon, attired in a blue habit, and riding a beautiful chestnut horse, with a white poodle in her lap! Meetings often began on the Monday and continued each day until the following Saturday. It was not uncommon for the day's card to consist of ten or twelve events, including Matches and private Sweepstakes, so that it was often necessary to start racing at noon.

That Mr Clayton's familiarity with Newmarket has not lessened his enthusiasm for the outstanding qualities and characteristics of its racecourses was made abundantly plain when he said:

> 'Of the racecourses I have seen or heard of in this and other countries, that at Newmarket far surpasses them all. In so saying I am regarding it from the racing and not the spectacular point of view. It stands alone as a test for horses. It also affords a supreme test of jockeyship. The best jockeys are seen to the best advantage on the Rowley Mile. Fordham, Tom Cannon, and in later days, Maher and Wootton, were shining examples. I really believe they were 10 lb better on the Rowley Mile than anywhere else; or perhaps I should say the jockeys they had to ride against were 10 lb worse there than on other courses. The latter seem unable to appreciate the effect of the gradients, particularly the descent from the Bushes to the Dip, which tempts jockeys to take undue liberties. They often come down it as though they are close "home". Yes, as the poetical eleventh Earl of Winchilsea wrote, "Rowley's cruel Mile" reveals riding talent more than any other course in the world.'

Mention of Fordham caused Mr Clayton to dwell for a few moments on the great abilities of that jockey. 'There never was a better,' he declared, 'good as many have been. And next to him, in my opinion, comes Tom Cannon, with John Watts *proxime accessit*. In singling out these men I wish to imply no disrespect to others; but they were three fine jockeys,

Fordham being the finest. He was great in every respect. He used his brains, he had beautiful hands, he exercised great patience, and then there was the lightning rush when he did "go".'

Mr Clayton expressed great admiration for Maher and Wootton. He thinks Maher was never quite so good after as he had been before he met with his terrible motoring accident near Lingfield. In his latter years he often displayed some nervousness except when riding at Newmarket. As for Frank Wootton, he was a jockey with pronounced native genius, possessed of a wonderful knowledge of horses, and even as a mere boy no one could give him an ounce.

Jockeys of the present day are a pampered race compared with their predecessors of fifty or sixty years ago. The latter, Mr Clayton recalls, used to ride up to the course with their racing saddles strapped to their backs, and they did not earn anything like as big money as present-day jockeys. Retainers, when given, were very small and much more was expected in return for them than owners now demand or obtain. Though there was plenty of racing all over the country, most of it was of a very trifling and unimportant character.

About seven years ago Mr Clayton was invited to state his opinions on jockeys and jockeyship in the columns of the *Daily Telegraph*. His letter excited much interest, not to say admiration, and we yield to the temptation to quote the greater part of it. Mr Clayton wrote:

'We have many jockeys nowadays but few horsemen; and when the former find themselves opposed to the latter the result is generally a foregone conclusion. In justice to modern jockeys one must not forget that those of former days were not demoralised, as ours are, by the terrors of the starting gate. Nor were their constitutions undermined and enfeebled by the everlasting cigarette. Here let me interpose a note of surprise. It takes something uncommon to surprise me at my age; but I *do* wonder that the Jockey Club have not prohibited promiscuous smoking in weighing rooms and jockey's dressing rooms. Such an injunction might do much to suppress the evil – fatal sooner or later alike to heart, lungs and nerve. It is pitiable to look into the dressing rooms and find little lads with their cigarettes in an atmosphere blue with smoke!

'We hear a good deal about the insecurity of the modern seat, but I do believe it has one advantage – only one; the weight is carried more easily on the shoulders and neck of a racehorse than on his back, and certainly the "crouch" seat cheats the pressure of an opposing wind. As against these advantages, it has destroyed real horsemanship, encouraged and increased the use of the whip, and is the cause of much of the swerving, bumping and crossing which has become so lamentable. For, seated, or rather lying, as the jockey now is on the neck and shoulders of his horse, his heels are harmless and a spur superfluous. A celebrated jockey, in referring to the use of the whip, once said to me: "You know how seldom I pull out my whip, and I never do so without wishing afterwards that I had not." Nowadays, thanks to the gate, a whip has become almost a necessity to keep the horse up to the tapes, from which they have to be driven helter skelter, without any chance of getting balanced and into their natural stride – the whole affair a scramble, excepting in the case of a few of our artists, who have the hands and confidence which enable them to get their horses balanced. These win all our races, whilst the rest are left lamenting, and, worse still, are often blamed for the crossing, bumping, etc., which has now become so frequent, but which, I am sure, is by no means intentional, as some petulant people (who cry out because they have lost their money) would have us believe. Such interference is involuntary and unavoidable.

'We have heard, and still hear, frequent reference to the advantage of a truly-run race from start to finish, jumping off and coming through, as introduced by Tod Sloan – a wonderful jockey – who made a speciality of such tactics; but we must not forget that in his case, though imperceptible, he never failed, more than once in a race, to take a pull and give his horse a chance to get his second wind, an art which I have never seen in any other jockey, always excepting the immortal George Fordham. The result to us nowadays is that the majority of our jockeys come away from the gate, and unless they are fortunate enough to get shut in or interfered with, their horses never get a pull or breather, and of course drop out when it comes to a final effort. I think it only fair to exonerate our present jockeys from any intentional rough riding, and also from any dishonesty. The latter I will put on the lowest ground – lack of temptation. Evil-doers nowadays are neither rash enough nor rich enough to make it worth a jockey's while either to risk his neck by foul riding or his career by dishonesty. In former times, when ante-post betting, and indeed all betting, was a hundred times more serious and heavy than it is in these latter days, there may have been, and no doubt were, substantial inducements to jockeys and stable lads to manipulate their charges.

'To compare our present jockeys with former riders, I consider that taking into account the modern drawbacks of the starting gate and "crouch" seat, such as Frank Wootton, Maher, O'Neill, James Clark, and perhaps one or two others, compare quite favourably with those of former times – always excepting George Fordham, who was, in my opinion, *facile princeps*; but then I never saw Sam Chifney, James Robinson or Frank Buckle. Maher on the Rowley Mile at Newmarket excels even his great self, and I cannot recall anything finer than his riding on that particular course, which he has almost made his own.

'The essence of jockeyship, I have always been taught, may be summed up in one word – "hands". I have had some little experience of all sorts of horsemanship, from riding heats at a terrible place called Redditch, to some pleasant experiences in recent years at aristocratic Croxton Park with one's hunting comrades as friendly opponents, and have noticed that "hands" are the result of an easy assured seat, which makes the rider independent of the bridle. It is, however, presumptuous to attempt to write about "hands", for have we not been taught that there are three things that defy alike definition or explanation – charm in woman, hands in a rider, and the scent of a hunted animal. The great test of a jockey is the effect on his horse after a race. Such artists as Fordham, the still living John Osborne, Tom Cannon, his son Mornington, Tom French, Webb, John Watts and J. Daley would bring back your winner without scratch or mark on body or temper, having got the last ounce out of him in a severe finish; whilst Sam Rogers, and to some extent Aldcroft, John Wells and Custance, were so strong and resolute that, without recourse to whip and spur, the pressure of their legs alone – quite involuntary – squeezed half the life out of their mounts, and, particularly in the case of two-year-olds, often left an indelible mark not easily rubbed out or forgotten. The smooth flag starts gave ample opportunity for acquiring and perfecting delicate hands and touch on the mouth which nowadays is not possible with the gate, where a certain amount of forcible pressure on the mouth is inevitable if a jockey is to keep his horse up to the tapes and drive him on to his legs (I will not say into his stride, for that is almost impossible) from a standstill at the critical moment. Taking his youth into consideration, I must confess to a feeling of pleasure and admiration when I watch Frank Wootton on a horse. Perfect hands, good temper and patience inspire the animal with the confidence of his rider, resulting in an exhibition as smooth as it is successful. In his case, as in that of those great artists Sloan and Maher, we forgive their seat, realising that they are "to the manner born" consummate horsemen as well as jockeys! In most cases this "trick riding" as it undoubtedly is – has been copied and acquired by imitation, and is not the *real* art, which is innate. Like everything else the world over, in every walk of life there are, and ever will and must be, shining lights compelling success. So it is with jockeys, and we are perhaps fortunate in these degenerate days to have some, if only a few, whom an owner may dare to back, and to whom a trainer can hand over his horse without a pang.'

Match-making was in the 'sixties a favourite amusement of the nightly frequenters of the Jockey Club Rooms, to which we will now let Mr Clayton guide us. He became a member of these Rooms very early in his career, when membership was far more exclusive than it is now. For the benefit of Colonial and foreign readers I ought perhaps to explain that membership of the Jockey Club Rooms is not the same thing as Membership of the Jockey Club, though the members of the Club are equally members of the Rooms. In the 'sixties they played a much larger part in the social life of Newmarket during race weeks than they have done during the last twenty-five or thirty years. When Mr Clayton was admitted to membership the leading patrons of the Turf did not own private houses in the town. If there were exceptions to this generalisation they numbered only one or two. All visitors were accommodated in lodgings. Consequently there were no house parties and no private dinners. Members of the Rooms lunched and dined thereat, so the Rooms were the great rallying point. Dinner was one of the chief events of the day. There was one long table, at the head of which sat a Steward or one of the members of the Jockey Club, or a senior member of the Rooms. If only there had been a 'chiel among them takin' notes' what a treasure-book of stories we might have had, and what a light would be thrown on many a mystery of the Turf!

It was during these dinners, and later, when the cloth had been drawn, that challenges to matches were made and accepted. Sir Joseph

Hawley was a great hand at this game. 'A fine judge of racing Sir Joseph was,' says Mr Clayton, 'and a past master at trying horses. He could probably sum up a handicap better than any man of his time.' One day someone happened to say that a certain jockey had been giving an opinion about one of his (Sir Joseph's) horses. Whereupon, having raised his hands and brought them down with a bang on his knees, Sir Joseph exclaimed: 'Good God! The Almighty hatched a nest of fools and called them jockeys!'

Sir G. Chetwynd, in his 'Racing Reminiscences', thus describes an after-dinner sitting at the Rooms:

'Many a time have I assisted at these match makings when the cloth has been cleared after dinner at the Rooms, the Admiral in the chair, supported by such men as General Peel, Mr Henry Savile, Lord Annesley, Lord Falmouth, Lord Vivian, Lord Wilton, Colonel Forester and a host of others, all good men and true. After the snuff-box, made out of Eclipse's foot and mounted in gold, had been duly handed about, it was the custom to write down on paper the names of horses with which owners were willing to make a match. The Admiral, after consulting two of the owners as to whether they were willing to run, after, also, due consideration – and sometimes a scrutiny of a well-thumbed handicap book – would stand up and say: "Gentlemen, put your hands in your pockets. You shall run the last five furlongs of the Abingdon Mile for 100 sovs., 50 forfeit, the Blank colt shall carry 8 st 10 lb, the other 8 st 2 lb." All eyes were turned on the two owners. If, on examination it was found that both of them held money in their hands, the match was made and the half-crowns went to the Admiral, who smiled benignly on them and pocketed the coins. If only one held money, the non-content paid him; if neither held money there was neither match nor exchange of coin.'

Of Admiral Rous, Mr Clayton saw a good deal, especially at the Jockey Club Rooms.

'The Admiral's devotion to the Turf war absolutely disinterested. His honour was unimpeachable. His bluff and autocratic determination seemed to carry everything and everybody with it. Absolute confidence was reposed in him. His sayings were accepted as gospel and his proposals were rarely questioned. He therefore became a self-appointed dictator with the approval and gratitude of the whole racing community. His critics and his enemies were very few. He always wore a velvet jacket and carried a dog whip in his hand. He was a good handicapper, and made very few mistakes, but he always had three or four people watching for him, including George Hodgman.'

The change to the social life of Newmarket known to the succeeding generation came very gradually. One of the first to set up a private establishment where he could entertain his friends was Prince Batthyany, at Warren House. Then Prince Soltykoff built the Kremlin. Lord Lonsdale was at Lowther House, and Baron Meyer de Rothschild at Primrose Cottage; they had, indeed, been 'private' for some time, for they were numbered among the exceptions to the dwellers in lodgings. Later, Lord Hartington (afterwards Duke of Devonshire) built Montagu House, in the High Street, and as year succeeded year the number of 'racing boxes' steadily increased. Mention must not be omitted of Palace House, where for so many years the late Mr Leopold de Rothschild extended profuse hospitality to his friends, of whom Mr Clayton was lucky enough to be one of the oldest and most welcome. House parties for the race weeks became the fashion, and ladies went to Newmarket in ever-growing numbers. Meanwhile, the 'communal' dinners at the Rooms were losing their old character, and as they did so the habit of making matches began to dwindle. For some reasons this was a pity. Matches had for decades been a distinctive feature of Newmarket programmes, and a well-made match always possesses a special attractiveness. Nowadays many seasons come and go without our seeing one.

An attempt to depict the Newmarket of the 'sixties would be incomplete if no reference were made to the gambling rooms. These resorts were losing their vogue when Mr Clayton came on the scene. His acquaintance with the last of them was that of an observer whose curiosity was aroused by the fascination the dice and cards had for so many men of note and eminence. The chief resort of the gamblers in his time was known as Atkinos, the proprietors of which were bookmakers. The place is now an auction room, nearly opposite the Jockey Club's premises. Mr Clayton tells of looking in one night for a few minutes after dinner. Seated at the tables, playing hazard or baccarat, were several well-known patrons of the Turf, including a noble duke, a baronet, a well-known financier, and others. He left them deeply engrossed in their 'affairs'. After breakfast the following morning, about half-past ten, he happened to be passing Atkinos, and peeped in. To his utter astonishment there were the self-same players casting the dice and betting on throws! They kept at it until there was barely time for them to change their clothes, get a meal and reach the course before the first race was run. There was also an Atkinos at Doncaster during the September race week. But, as already stated, the days of these undesirable establishments, which wrought much mischief, were already numbered, and, aided by the activities of the police, they eventually disappeared, to be lamented only by their most hardened patrons.

In many ways the decade from 1860 to 1870 is one of the most alluring to students of Turf history. It may be said to have seen the end of the craze for heavy betting. Huge sums were won and lost over paltry selling

races, as well as over Derbys and St Legers, and the big handicaps. As
Clayton remarks that the present generation scarcely understands what
betting is, he punctuates the statement with a gesture that implies that it
is just as well. There can, he thinks, be no doubt that the vastness of the
sums that were often at stake engendered sharp practices and roguery.

Early morning work on the Heath was a much livelier business in Mr
Clayton's young days than it is now. It was the correct thing for visitors
either to take hacks with them to Newmarket or to hire them, and a ride
on the Heath before breakfast was the first item in the day's programme.
And so it was that the racehorses at exercise were scrutinised by a
congregation of expert critics, eager to discover the merits and prospects
of the animals. Of late years there has been a marked disinclination on
the part of owners and their friends to take the early morning air.

Mr Clayton has always had a rooted aversion to the starting gate,
though he realises, of course, that the instrument has become a
permanency. If you plead that it has relieved us of interminable delays
associated with the old flag-start days, he admits time has been saved,
but strenuously maintains that the saving has been gained at the expense
of starts worthy of the name. And he will add, 'What does time matter!
An hour more or less is of no consequence so long as you get what you go
out to see, which is that every horse shall be given a reasonable chance of
winning.' You tell him of the plan adopted abroad of packing the horses
close together behind the barrier, and he agrees it is most sensible. Or
again, you suggest that a trial ought to be given to the walk-up start, and
he admits that some of the best starts he has seen by the gate have
accidentally been from a walk-up. But he goes on to say that all the
starters he has consulted declare that the walk-up would fail if generally
adopted.

Apropos of the starting gate, Mr Clayton had a curious experience
with a horse trained by Cole at Exton for the late Lord Penrhyn.
Whenever an endeavour was made to give this animal practice at the
gate on the training ground he refused to go near the tapes and seemed
frightened out of his wits. One day Lord Penrhyn was present and so
convinced that it was useless to persevere with a view to overcoming the
horse's obstinacy or fear, that he decided to have him turned out of
training. Mr Clayton, however, said there was still one thing to be tried.
What was it? inquired the owner. 'Put him in a race, and then see what
happens when he gets to the gate.' Lord Penrhyn thought the suggestion
very daring, but consented to the experiment being made. The result
was astonishing. Of all the horses that went to the post for the race in

question, the one from Exton was the best behaved! The real truth of the matter probably was that the animal was so interested by his novel surroundings that he forgot all about the gate and his capers on the training ground. This method of overcoming the difficulty is one it might not be wise to adopt in every like case, but we may gather that the least obvious solution of a problem is sometimes the most effective.

Mr Clayton declares:

'Than the gate, nothing is more calculated to ruin the temperament of horses. To many of them it is like a "red rag to a bull". When the machine was first introduced we were told it was merely to be given a temporary trial, but once installed it remained. You cannot start level with the gate; it is impossible. Delays have been minimised, but at the cost of owners and the tempers of horses. There are ten times more bad tempered horses now than there were in my early days. Unless a horse is absolutely left at the post, or left a long way, you do not hear about what happens at the start. There are many fiascos. They seem to get off pretty well, but in a big field, eight or ten of the horses really have no chance, though they are not absolutely left.'

Mr Clayton was asked if he thought our present-day horses better than those of fifty years ago, and replied:

'I think they are undoubtedly better – in size, in physique, in bone and in conformation. There are more good horses now than there were then. Perhaps they are bred on more scientific lines; and of course there are more horses bred than there used to be. Modern breeders have a greater selection of high-class sires than their fathers and grandfathers had. I should also say that the system of training now followed is less severe than the one practised even twenty or thirty years ago. The old trainers, like John Scott of Malton, and Tom Dawson of Middleham, subjected the constitutions of their horses to great strain by hard training and sweating. Their methods were probably harmful, more particularly to fillies and mares. A good deal can be said for our more lenient system of training. Certainly the stallions and mares, when they go to the stud, have a better chance of producing good stock. I attribute the great success of Lord Falmouth (the father of the peer who died last year) to the fact that he rarely raced his fillies after they were three years old. Moreover, he seldom ran any of his horses in handicaps.

'Remember, too, the ordeals to which yearlings were subjected in the old days. When I was dining with Sir Richard Sutton one night during the Doncaster Meeting of 1864, he told me he had been trying his yearlings and thought he had got the winner of the Derby of 1866. And he had, too, because the yearling to which he alluded was Lord Lyon! The trial was over three furlongs, and the trial horse the then two-year-old Gardevisure, who won the Cambridgeshire the following season. General Pearson's yearlings, including Achievement, were always broken in April and put straight away into training. It is perhaps significant that both Lord Lyon and Achievement became roarers. In the case of Lord Lyon the infirmity did not develop until late in his career, but Achievement was afflicted soon after she won the Oaks. The old General, however, stuck to his principle of early training and trying, and it paid him.

'I am inclined to think that the best horse of my time was Cremorne. The still living Charles Maidment, who rode both Cremorne and Kisber when they won the Derby, has a great opinion of Cremorne; but though he was devoted to Mr Savile, he has told me he honestly thinks Kisber the best horse he ever rode. No doubt Kisber was a very good horse. The most beautiful horse I ever saw – and, despite what I have said about Cremorne, perhaps the best also – was Rosicrucian. He could win at five and six furlongs, and the fact that, when six years old, in 1871, he won the Ascot Stakes on the Tuesday in a canter, carrying 9 st over that severe two and a half miles, and won the Alexandra Plate, over three miles, on the Friday (giving 7 lb and a liberal beating to Musket) speaks volumes for the super-excellence of the horse and the skill of his trainer, John Porter. Petrarch was another beautiful horse, but he was delicate and lacked power and substance. Cremorne's failure at the stud was, I believe, solely due to mismanagement. He got no exercise after he went to Rufford, and was pampered by his doting groom. A stallion ought to be kept as fit as if he were still in training for racing. Robert Peck always had his stallions at Howbury in that condition, and the consequence was they got a large proportion of their mares in foal.'

As to mares, Mr Clayton said that regarding the matter from every point of view, including looks, he thinks Pretty Polly the best he has ever seen. He regards her as a wonder. As, however, he also has a great admiration for Sceptre, he is rather disposed to bracket her equal with Pretty Polly. Achievement was another remarkable mare. She would not, however, have taken a prize for good looks. Standing 16.3, she was somewhat leggy and very much 'split up'.

Though an enthusiastic foxhunter all his life, Mr Clayton has had very little to do with steeplechasing. In 1868, however, he won the big steeple-chase at Aylesbury on one of his hunters, a grey thoroughbred horse called Whitenose, by Bonnyfield (brother to West Australian) out of Homespun, by St Nicholas. The race was run in a snowstorm over the old Aylesbury course, which took some 'doing', as the fences were big and most of them untrimmed. Mr Clayton recalls that he took up the running after the second fence and was never afterwards headed.

After the lapse of some years he was intimately associated with the Grand National winner Zoedone. A chestnut mare by New Oswestry out of Miss Honiton, Zoedone was bought by Mr Clayton from a farmer at Oswestry for £170 for his own riding with hounds. This was in April, 1881. After riding her himself all the summer, and then cub-hunting with the Cottesmore, he found, long before Christmas, that she was so far in front of all ordinary hunters that he decided to put her into the Grand National, and was lucky enough to get his old friend Captain Arthur Smith, the invincible 'Doggie' of those days, a superb horseman, to ride her. It was too much to expect a five-year-old to win outright over such a course and distance, but Mr Clayton and his friends backed her for a place, which, thanks to the judicious handling of Captain Smith, she secured, for she finished third behind Seaman and Cyrus. Going on to Warwick, Captain Smith won the Grand Annual on her there.

Having quite as much as he could attend to with a full stable of flat racehorses at Exton to manage, Mr Clayton decided to sell Zoedone, and eventually did so to Count Kinsky for £800, with a contingency of another £200 should she win the Grand National, in which it was understood that Captain Smith was again to ride her. To Mr Clayton's disappointment, and greatly to that of Captain Smith, the Count evaded this implied agreement and rode her himself. He won, much to his own delight and to the surprise of everyone, for, as far as steeplechase riding went, he was a complete novice. He was well coached by the late W. H. Jenkins, who trained the mare for him, and, carrying out the combined instructions of Mr Clayton and Mr Jenkins not to be in a hurry, but to ride for the first three miles as if he was out hunting and then creep up to the front, he steered clear of any interference or mishap and won quite easily. It must, however, be confessed that he was lucky in having to meet a moderate lot of opponents. Mr Clayton calls attention to the fact that in these two consecutive years the winners of the greatest steeplechase in the world – the dream and ambition of all steeplechase riders – were ridden by two amateurs, Lord Manners and Count Kinsky, with absolutely no previous experience of steeplechase riding!

While on the subject of Mr Clayton's hunting experiences the somewhat romantic story of Lord Ronald should be recorded. This horse, a dark chestnut, was by Stockwell out of Edith, by Newminster. After winning many races on the flat for the late Duke of Beaufort he was sent to Epsom to be schooled over hurdles and fences but proved obstinate and hopeless, for he would not *gallop* at his fences. At last he was sent to Tattersalls for sale, and Mr Clayton, by the advice of the Duke, gave 140 guineas for him in the hope of making him a hunter. When Lord Ronald found he was not bustled, but allowed to jump slow, he soon took to it, and for two seasons Mr Clayton rode him twice a week in the Vale of Aylesbury. 'He took great care of himself and me,' says Mr Clayton, 'never put a foot wrong, and would jump in and out of the strong doubles in the Vale like a cat. He was no "toy" hunter, nor taken out merely to qualify, but had to take the crust as well as the crumb, the rough with the smooth, and often came home from a day in the Claydon Woods plastered with the mud in which he had been struggling up to his knees and hocks for hours.'

After Lord Ronald's second season Mr Clayton sold him for 400 guineas to go as a hunter sire to Ireland, where, in Co. Limerick, he soon made his mark as a sire of countless steeplechasers and hunters of the highest class. In the meantime he got Master Kildare out of a mare called Silk, by Plum Pudding. A brilliant horse this, for he not only won the City and Suburban with 9 st 2 lb in 1880, but became the sire of Melton, winner of the Derby. After this the Duke of Beaufort bought him back, paying something like a thousand guineas, and, after getting useful winners, Lord Ronald ended his days at Badminton. He was barely 15.2 in height, had no girth to speak of, and only $7\frac{1}{2}$ inches of bone under the knee; but he had long shoulders, short back, great arms and quarters, and faultless action – hence his superiority in deep ground. Mr Clayton is, presumably, the only man who can claim to have ridden as a common utility hunter the grandsire of a Derby winner; certainly no one else now living can make such a claim.

If we were writing the biography of Mr Clayton there would be very much more to tell. Nothing has been said of the many good horses he has bred, raced, and ridden, such as St Helen, Simonburn, Patron Saint, All Moonshine, Sweet Memory and Nesta; nor of the many others with which he has been associated while trained by Cole, at Exton, for Lord Penrhyn, Lord Cadogan, Lord Downe, Mr Reid Walker, and other friends. Quæsitum, winner of the Chester Cup, Gold Vase at Ascot and other races; King's Messenger, who won the Great Metropolitan twice, and very nearly a third time, in successive years; and Elba, who also won the Great Metropolitan, were among them.

By no means all the notes jotted down while Mr Clayton was reeling off his entertaining reminiscences have been utilised. Even so, it is to be feared he will complain because so many of them have been reproduced. We do not, however, expect to receive censure from any other quarter, and on behalf of the readers of the *Review*, take this opportunity of thanking Mr Clayton for giving us all this opportunity of sharing with him these interesting memories of his strenuous and varied life, every day of which he has lived and enjoyed to the full. Now he consoles himself with the reflection that –

> When Time, who steals our hours away,
>   Shall steal out pleasures too,
> The memory of the past shall stay
>   And half our joys renew.

It is fitting that we should state that Mr Clayton's greatest pleasure and solace throughout his long life have been the works of the 'Druid' – the late Henry Hall Dixon. When Time, 'who beats us all', shall claim him, his earnest hope is that he may just drop off his saddle into oblivion. In his enthusiastic, and still boyish, love of horses he quotes the charming lines of the gifted Will Ogilvie –

> When you lay me to slumber, no spot you can choose
> But will ring to the rhythm of galloping shoes.
> And, under the daisies, no grave be so deep
> But the hoofs of the horses shall sound in my sleep!

BBR–1919

Memorative Biography of Chevalier Ginistrelli

The most oft-told story of equine love is that involving St Simon's wonderful daughter Signorina, unbeaten in nine starts at two in 1889, including the prestigious Middle Park Stakes, and the Cesarewitch winner Chaleureux, 'not deemed of much account as a sire'. This unlikely mating between a champion and a comparative nonentity took place because Signorina's owner and breeder, the Italian-born Chevalier Ginistrelli, had noticed that 'an acquaintanceship sprang up between them' when Chaleureux, out for his morning exercise, 'skirted Signorina's paddock' and they regularly greeted each other 'with a neigh'. Unable to get a nomination to Cyllene, Ginistrelli sent Signorina across the road to Chaleureux and the resultant foal of 1905 when Signorina was eighteen and, at one time, had gone eight years without a live foal, was Signorinetta who was to capture both the Derby and the Oaks three years later. Mr Ginistrelli felt this was 'the boundless laws of sympathy and love' at work.

CHEVALIER GINISTRELLI died in Italy towards the end of September, at the age of eighty-two. He came to England early in the 'eighties and, living at Newmarket, remained with us for about thirty years. When the day at last came when he could no longer endure the fatigue of training his horses he sold stud and stable and went back to the sunshine of his native land, leaving behind him the reputation of a good sportsman. All Newmarket knew him as 'Gini'. The diminutive implies a familiarity which did not exist. There was a strong note of dignified reserve in the Chevalier's character. If he made no enemies he did not cultivate friendship. Small of stature, he was otherwise built on generous lines. He affected clothing distinguished for its comfortable appearance rather

Chevalier Ginistrelli.

than its style. A stranger would naturally have assumed he was an easy-going gentleman, inclined, perhaps to be rather shy. But behind the veneer of shyness were determination, independence and self-reliance.

In the management of his horses the Chevalier was a law unto himself, guided, no doubt, mainly by instinct. If he made grievous and costly mistakes, the notable successes he achieved afforded him all the greater satisfaction and pleasure. His independence was apt to make him 'touchy'. This was illustrated by an incident that happened in 1905, shortly before the Derby in which his colt Signorino was to compete. A writer had the temerity to state that the colt had greatly improved as the result of being 'under the eye' of a well-known Newmarket trainer. In a letter to one of the sporting journals the indignant Chevalier wrote: 'I wish to denounce that statement as a gross misrepresentation of the truth ... I have trained my own horses since 1866, and I am happy to state that I require the advice of no one, and that the corn my horses eat is paid for by me.' That was a characteristic outburst.

When he came to England Ginistrelli brought with him a few racehorses and broodmares. One of the mares was Star of Portici. Her credentials were moderate in the extreme, but before many years had gone by she became famous as the dam of one of the most brilliant mares even seen on the British Turf, and later as the grandam of a mare who won the Derby and the Oaks. Star of Portici was the foundation on which rested the Chevalier's reputation as a breeder and trainer. Bred in Italy, she was by imported Heir-at-Law, who, by Newminster, was merely a selling plater. Her dam, Verbena, raced four seasons in England before she went to Italy in 1867; her solitary victory on the Turf was gained during her two-year-old days. Verbena's sire was De Ruyter. He was a brother of The Flying Dutchman, but never raced.

Star of Portici was twelve years old when she came to England. That Ginistrelli had great faith in her was shown when he sent her to St Simon at the earliest opportunity. The result of the alliance was the wonderful Signorina who, as a two-year-old, raced nine times and was never beaten. The following season Signorina was generally in poor health owing to a liver complaint, and won only one race out of five. In the Oaks she ran second to Memoir whom she had easily beaten the previous year. As a four-year-old, however, Signorina once more reproduced something like her old form when she won the Lancashire Plate and so added nearly £9,000 to her stake total. On that occasion she defeated Orme (then a two-year-old), Martagon, Alicante, Gouverneur, Broad Corrie and Llanthony.

Signorina went to the stud in 1892. Much was expected of her as a broodmare, but her proud owner, who regarded her as 'the apple of his eye', had to wait long and weary years before he was rewarded for his homage and stoical patience. In 1893 and 1894 she 'slipped' to Sheen, and then, after a year's rest, was in two succeeding seasons barren to Martagon. Given another rest she was next put to Janissary and was again barren. The following year there came a dead colt-foal by Curio. Eight seasons at the stud and not a live foal! The outlook seemed hopeless, but the Chevalier did not despair. The mare's next mate was Best Man, and there was great joy in the Ginistrelli household when this mating resulted in a colt-foal. The youngster was named Signorino, and was good enough to run third to Cicero and Jardy in the Derby of 1905. Eventually he was sold to go to Italy where he has been at the head of the Sires' List.

After this happy interlude the 'tale of woe' was resumed. In 1903 Signorina produced to Martagon a filly, but this foal died in infancy. The following year, 1904, the mare was once more barren. But the glorious hour was drawing near. At that time there was located at Sir James Miller's stud at Newmarket the stallion Chaleureux, a Cesarewitch winner. He was not deemed of much account as a sire, and commanded only the modest fee of nine guineas. Fame came to him in fortuitous fashion. When taken out for exercise of a morning he generally passed along a road that skirted Signorina's paddock. In course of time an acquaintanceship sprang up between them, and they regularly greeted each other with a neigh. The observant Chevalier duly noted the development of this friendship, and when he failed to obtain a nomination to Cyllene, decided that his mare should go to Chaleureux. Thus did Signorinetta come to be born in 1905, and when, three years later, she won the Derby and the Oaks the Chevalier ecstatically proclaimed her an illustration of the working of 'the boundless laws of sympathy and love'.

It would be incorrect to say that Signorinetta was a friendless 'outsider' when she went to the Derby starting post. The Chevalier himself firmly believed she had a good chance of winning. He had even persuaded a few other people that her prospects were brighter than her racing record indicated, and these few had obtained odds of 100 to 1 to the money they risked on the filly. The public at large, however, never gave a thought to Signorinetta. Why should they? As a two-year-old she ran six times. In five of the races she was beaten and unplaced; the sixth she won. It was the Criterion Nursery, at Newmarket – a seven-furlong handicap. Signorinetta carried 6 st 3 lb that day. Her first outing as a three-year-old was in the One Thousand Guineas. Rhodora won the race; Signorina's daughter finished 'nowhere'. A fortnight later she competed for the Newmarket Stakes, and came in fifth behind St Wolf, Mercutio, Primer and Vamose. Contemplating this form, a student of racing, unassisted by special powers of divination, could scarcely regard Signorinetta as a Derby candidate with a claim to serious attention. The competitors chiefly in the public eye were Norman III, winner of the Two Thousand Guineas, Mountain Apple, winner of the only two races in which he had taken part; Sea Sick II, who, the previous Sunday, had dead-heated with Quintette for the French Derby; Sir Archibald and White Eagle, second and third in the Two Thousand; Llangwm, a recent winner of the Victoria Cup; Vamose, brother to Flying Fox; Mercutio and Perrier.

The least-fancied of the horses in that numerous group would have been called upon to give weight to Signorinetta in a handicap and then have been expected to beat her. At the same time none of them inspired real confidence, because their trainers had been beset by difficulties of one sort or another, and there was an impression that the majority of the runners were short of a gallop or two. That, no doubt, was the secret of Signorinetta's success. After her defeat in the Newmarket Stakes she had done a lot of hard work over the Derby distance and thrived on it. Her absolute fitness more than compensated for her other deficiencies, and, taking the lead a quarter of a mile from the goal, she won the Derby by two lengths, Primer and Llangwm being second and third. Wearing a weather-stained Panama hat, a lounge coat and a glad smile 'Gini' led his filly back to scale, and the crowd, losers almost to a man, generously cheered the exulting owner, recognising that, as breeder and trainer, he had achieved a notable feat.

Two days later Signorinetta also won the Oaks. This race was supposed to be virtually a match between the Derby and One Thousand winners. The latter, Rhodora, was favourite at 6 to 4, while odds of 3 to 1 were obtainable about Signorinetta. After going half a mile French Partridge fell and Rhodora, who had been immediately behind, sprawled over the prostrate filly and came down too. Signorinetta now had 'nothing to beat', and scored a tremendously popular victory. The crowd were hugely delighted. After the winner had weighed in, King Edward sent for Chevalier Ginistrelli and, having personally congratulated him, took him to the front of the Royal Box and 'presented' him to the hurrahing multitude assembled on the course opposite the stands. It was a memorable scene.

The modest and retiring Italian gentleman was a mighty proud man that day. He had reached the crowning point of his career. Signorinetta also had attained the limit of her fame. Her descent to the humbler sphere from which she had sprung with such startling suddenness was painfully rapid. A month or so after the Oaks she was beaten over ten furlongs at Newbury by White Eagle, Quercus and Linacre; in the St Leger she was seventh only to Your Majesty, White Eagle and Santo Strato; and in her last race, the Jockey Club Stakes, she ran sixth behind Siberia, Primer and Royal Realm. It became fairly obvious, therefore, that she was in luck's way when she won her 'classic' laurels at Epsom in that she there had to meet a lot of unfit horses, to many of whom she was really inferior. After her success in the Oaks an offer of

£30,000 was made for her, but the Chevalier turned it down, just as he always did the many offers he received for Signorina. To one would-be buyer of the latter he said: 'You keep your money and I'll keep my mare.'

The break-up of the Chevalier's stud came three years later in 1911. Signorinetta was offered for sale at Newmarket, but failed to reach her reserve of 8,000 guineas. Shortly afterwards, however, she was bought privately by Lord Rosebery for £6,000. We cannot do better than conclude this memoir with a story that reveals the passionate interest Ginistrelli took in Signorina and her daughter. It was a great wrench to him to part with Signorinetta, and if there were tears to be shed over the separation strangers were not to see them. When, therefore, Lord Rosebery's stud groom, Latimer, arrived at the Chevalier's Newmarket home to take the mare away he was not allowed to go near her until the moment arrived when she must leave for the station. Latimer was given a glass of claret and some cigars wherewith to while away the time of waiting. The cigars had an aroma that was, shall we say, distinctive. During the journey from Newmarket, Signorinetta became very nervous and began to walk round and round her box. With soothing words Latimer, from his adjoining compartment, tried to comfort her, but without success. He was just about to climb into the mare's box when he remembered the Chevalier's cigars. Lighting one of them he blew the smoke towards Signorinetta, who at once became interested. The odour was evidently a familiar one, and the mare, thus reminded of 'home', calmed down and gave her guardian no further trouble.

BBR–1920

Obituary of Richard Croker

Americans, particularly latter-day Irish-Americans, will probably be especially interested in the memorative obituary of Mr Richard Croker who died in Ireland in April of 1922. Mr Croker was born in Ireland and went to the States with his parents when just a lad. Eventually he became 'Boss' Croker of New York's bastion of politics, Tammany Hall. Becoming interested in racing, he came to England to indulge in the sport but then was prohibited from training on Newmarket Heath by an adamant English Jockey Club. Therefore, Croker decided to return to Ireland to continue his avocation with no love lost for the English.

Three years after this 'insult', his colt, Orby, won the 1907 Derby; the next year his filly Rhodora, a half sister to Orby, secured the One

Thousand Guineas and later he bred the Derby winner Grand Parade whom he previously sold on the occasion of his returning to America for a long visit. If revenge is sweet, imagine the pleasant gratification Mr Croker experienced.

A REMARKABLE life came to a close when Richard Croker died at his beautiful home, Glencairn, Co. Dublin, on April 29th. As an American writer expressed it, he passed away 'full of years, honours and troubles'. The impress he made on the Turf in England and Ireland, and on the records of the British thoroughbred was so great that we fell compelled to review his career at some length in order that future generations may know how it was fashioned by the force of circumstances as well as by his own strong will.

Born at Clonakilty, Co. Cork, November, 1841, Croker was only seven years old when he went to the United States with his parents. He was still a young man when, like so many of America's Irish immigrants, he began to interest himself in politics. Attaching himself to that peculiar but powerful organisation, Tammany Hall, which for generations has sought to control the civic life of New York, he rose, step by step, until he became the 'Boss' of that institution and all its operations. Thereafter he was always known to the world at large as Boss Croker. He disliked the appellation in his later years, but he could not get away from it.

In a character sketch he wrote for the *Daily Telegraph*, Mr T. P. O'Connor tells us that it was Croker's fighting quality that made him the man he was.

'He radiated courage and aggressiveness. The leonine head, the mighty jaw, the penetrating eye, the deep chest and the commanding voice all bespoke the power. . . . Whatever his faults as the head of an organisation that never was angelic, Richard Croker will be remembered for his virtues too. He knew neither fear nor hypocrisy.'

In the flood of adverse criticism to be found in the memoirs published in America after Mr Croker's death words of appreciation were occasionally to be found. One writer said of him:

'According to his lights, Croker was thoroughly honest. He dealt in the political game at a time when almost the only object of the game was to win it and when public opinion, particularly in the large cities, rather generously supported that view. But it could fairly be said of Croker that he was a man of his word, that he fought in the open, and that he never dealt in hypocrisy.'

Mr Chauncey M. Depew, widely separated from Croker by party lines and social ties, said of him:

'He was a king, and New York was his kingdom. He was the absolute master of the city, such as I don't believe could ever exist again. The Mayor and the heads of the various city departments recognised him as the absolute controlling power. . . . His outstanding characteristics were his intense loyalty to those who were loyal to him, and his quick punishment of those who were unfaithful. And he was perfectly fair. When he thoroughly understood a subject and made up his mind about it, he did, or had the city do, what he thought was right.'

There was, however, another side to the picture. In a quotation from the New York *Evening Post* we read:

'Richard Croker could not have lasted as dictator for a day if the Croker spirit of "working for my own pocket all the time" had not animated numbers of citizens who passed as respectable. . . . We are driven for comfort to the consideration that, inexcusable as Croker's misrule was, it was not the orgy of corruption that flourished under Tweed (a former "Boss"), and that it is not being duplicated in this city, or in any other, today. Nobody accuses the present head of Tammany of making his money, as Croker is supposed to have made his, by the sale of offices and legislation, and participation in the swollen profits of public contracts. . . . Mayors may compel self-respecting men and women to blush for their city, but at least they do not give them the sickening sense of degradation that afflicts them under the reign of a Croker.'

The phrase 'working for my own pocket all the time' was one Mr Croker used when giving evidence before a Committee in 1894. He declined to answer questions designed to show how he acquired his money, but stoutly denied that he ever received money from his political work other than his official salaries, or that directly or indirectly he ever 'blackmailed, bribed, corrupted or suborned' anybody. He was believed to have made his money or most of it out of New York real estate and by dealings in railway stock. Croker always maintained that Tammany succeeded on its merits, and that it was the most democratic institution in the world, standing for the poor man, and especially the newly-landed immigrant.

About twenty years ago, Mr Croker, by that time a wealthy man, came to England and settled at Wantage in Berkshire. All his life he had been fond of sport, and during the latter part of his time in New York became specially interested in racing. On reaching England he set about making the Turf his main hobby. He had brought over with him three American thoroughbreds – Rhoda B., Americus and Dobbins. He raced Americus for a few seasons before sending him to the stud, and eventually sold him to go to Italy.

In 1904 Croker decided to race on a bigger scale than he had been doing, and at Doncaster paid 8,800 guineas for three yearling fillies, which he sent to Newmarket to be trained by J. Brewer, the Australian.

Shortly afterwards the racing world was startled by an announcement that the Stewards of the Jockey Club would not allow any horse owned by Mr Croker to be trained on Newmarket Heath. The man who had for seventeen years ruled New York City thus became aware that the Jockey Club rules at Newmarket. The decision of the Stewards was by no means universally approved. It was obviously intended to mark disapproval of the methods adopted by Croker in New York, and many people thought they were no concern of the Jockey Club. However, the expulsion order stood and had to be obeyed. The following year the three fillies that caused the bother were sold privately to Captain J. Orr-Ewing for about £3,000 less than they had cost. They were Glencairn Maid, by Gallinule – Moira; Dramatica, by St Simon – Tragedy; and Galilee, by Gallinule – Tierce.

Whether or not Croker would, but for this upset, have spent the remainder of his life in England one cannot say. Anyway, he resolved forthwith to retire to his native land. Adjoining Leopardstown race-course, between Dublin and Bray, he purchased the Glencairn estate, situated at the foot of the picturesque Dublin Mountains. He practically rebuilt the residence he found there, spending, it is said, £60,000 on the alterations. Even then it was not a big house, but the fittings and furnishings were of a sumptuous character. Henceforth, Croker was closely identified with Ireland and its affairs. In a quiet way, he exercised, it is understood, great influence in political circles.

Orby, by Orme out of Rhoda B., was one of the yearlings Mr Croker took with him from Wantage to Glencairn, where his horses were trained privately. It was the day of days for the 'Boss' when Orby won the Derby at Epsom. The insult cast upon him three years before had been avenged. He gloated over this good fortune. Who could blame him? His satisfaction was all the greater because the colt had been trained at his home. It tickled him when he read that the training ground was merely a cabbage patch. As a matter of fact there was at Glencairn and on the adjoining property a twelve-furlong gallop, the last mile of which was practically straight.

The year Orby won the Derby his half-sister Rhodora, by St Frusquin, won the Dewhurst Plate, and, the next season, the One Thousand Guineas. Then, in Grand Parade, Mr Croker bred a second Derby winner.

In the autumn of 1916 he left Ireland for a prolonged visit to America, and before setting sail sold off much of his bloodstock. Grand Parade, by Orby, was one of the foals then put under the hammer. Lord Glanely secured the youngster for 470 guineas.

At his stud adjoining Glencairn, Mr Croker had, in addition to Americus and Orby, the stallions Lesterlin and Clonmell. But, of course, Orby was the horse in which he took the most pride.

Mr Croker must have mellowed in a remarkable way after leaving Tammany and its worries behind him. At his home in Ireland he was affability itself. Aggressiveness and pugnacity seemed entirely foreign to his nature. He was mild-mannered and gentle to a degree, thoroughly enjoying congenial company, and chuckling at his own or other people's jokes. Those of us who knew him only during the latter part of his life will prefer to remember the man as we always found him. It is an agreeable memory.   BBR–1922

Mr Joel's 'Vigorous Rejoinder'

Criticism comes easy to those who have done little or nothing in life to be criticised for themselves. It is the achievers who attract criticism and the under-achievers who mete it out. Occasionally, the criticism becomes so onerous that the person being criticised, who normally would not stoop to recognising such faultfinders, is encouraged to answer his or her disparagers. In 1922, J. B. Joel, one of England's most successful owners and breeders, decided it was time to answer some people who thought they knew more about his business than he did. His 'rejoinder' first appeared in the Daily Telegraph *and then was reprinted in the* BBR *of 1922.*

IT HAS NOT, of course, been allowed to escape my notice that criticisms have been made in more than one quarter of late in regard to the policy I have chosen to adopt with my horse Sunstar at the stud. The plain suggestion is that I have been only considering my pocket and sacrificing all consideration for the breed of the thoroughbred as well as for the horse in question.

One particular critic maintains that a stallion should be limited to a certain number of mares. My contention is that the whole question must be governed by knowledge of a horse's ability at the stud and of his constitution generally. Sunstar would do far less work when covering a hundred mares than many stallions I have had would do in covering twenty-five. I sold Sundridge because he was a bad foal-getter. He was limited to forty mares, and one season he got eleven foals. I thought that I was overdoing him, and tried him in the following year with only thirty mares, and he produced nine foals. I then gave him sixty-five mares, and he got forty foals, among the good winners being Silver Tag.

It is always open to a breeder before taking a nomination to inquire the number of mares that is visiting the horse, and he can please himself about taking it. I may say that as Sunstar is rising fifteen years of age, though still as vigorous as ever, it is my intention to reduce his list of mares next season by 25 per cent, and further reduce it every year. That must be, because he is getting older, and utility and constitution cannot be what they were when a horse was in the prime of life.

I am strongly of the opinion that in the present depressed state of the bloodstock market stallion fees are far too high, and if other stallion owners would come into line I would willingly reduce the fees which have been charged in recent years at the Childwick Bury Stud.

You cannot expect breeders to work at a loss, especially when you see many 400-guinea foals hardly realising that fee when submitted for sale. That is apart from the risk taken by owners of mares in having their mares returned barren. I have some experience of that from more than one of the most fashionable stallions of the present day, but at least owners of mares which have been to Sunstar will give my horse credit that their disappointments have been few and far between.

No doubt I shall be told to mind my own business, but at any rate my experience has been gained by practice. I recall that I gave £40,000 for Prince Palatine because of his breeding and his record as a racehorse. He was a most vigorous horse in the performance of his stud duties, but I did not hesitate to sell him when he proved a tremendous disappointment as a foal-getter. I wonder how many foals he has left in France?

In the matter of foal-getting and winnings I would like to ask my critics how many stallions there are at the stud today that can show a better record than Sunstar. Old records tell us that Melbourne, when fifteen years of age, covered sixty-eight mares and got sixty-four foals, and among them was West Australian, the first winner of the Triple Crown, and Mentmore Lass, the winner of the One Thousand Guineas. Two years later he got the winner of the Oaks, and still two years later again Blink Bonny, winner of both the Derby and the Oaks.

My critics should have lived in those days, when there were far fewer mares and few first-class stallions in existence. They would then have had an outlet for their pious concern for the thoroughbred and their unctuous attitude towards those who have some claim to know their own business best. If some people think that I would harm the horse that has brought more pleasure into my life than I should have thought possible, then I suppose I must live and die much misunderstood.

BBR-1922

In the paddock before The Derby. From left to right: Sir Charles Cust, Lord Jersey, HRH the Prince of Wales, S. Donoghue (Humorist's jockey), C. Morton (trainer), Mr J. B. Joel (owner).

Memorative Biography of Mr J. B. Joel

THE DEATH occurred at his home, Childwick Bury, St Albans, on the 13th of November, of Mr Jack Barnato Joel. Born on September 29th, 1862, he was in his seventy-ninth year.

Financier and partner in the firm of Barnato Bros, later prominent owner and breeder of racehorses, Mr J. B. Joel went to South Africa as a comparatively young man. There he made a large fortune. He was a nephew of Mr Barney Barnato who speedily became a millionaire in South Africa. When his interests in that country became too varied for one man efficiently to control, he got out Jack and Solly Joel, who in their turn became millionaires.

Eventually, Mr J. B. Joel returned to England. Almost every day he was to be found in his City office in Austin Friars superintending the important details of his vast financial interests. Gold, diamonds, breeding and racing were the dominant interests in Mr J. B. Joel's life. He was permanent Chairman of the Johannesburg Consolidated Investments Company. He controlled mines, breweries, collieries, and other properties in South Africa. Mr Joel did not believe in luck; he believed in hard work and plenty of it.

It is, however, only with Mr J. B. Joel's racing and breeding activities this review may deal.

His famous colours, black jacket, scarlet cap, were registered in 1900. That season he won four races, value £2,554. For forty years there were only two seasons when his name did not appear in the winning owners' list. One was 1918; he had then sold all his racehorses to the United States. No horses ran in his name in 1938. He 'lent' them to a friend in the city. His wife had died the previous December. They had been married thirty-seven years, so he did not race that year.

From 1900 to 1940 Mr J. B. Joel, in England, won 504 flat races. The stakes amounted to £348,394.

Mr Joel as a breeder and owner of winners of classic races was exceptionally successful. Set out in datal form, his record is as follows:

Two Thousand Guineas

Sunstar	won in 1911
Black Jester	3rd in 1914
Humorist	3rd in 1921
Greenfire	3rd in 1924

One Thousand Guineas

Jest	won in 1913
Princess Dorrie	won in 1914
Radiancy	2nd in 1911
Bright	3rd in 1915

The Derby

Sunstar	won in 1911
Humorist	won in 1921

The Oaks

Our Lassie	won in 1903
Glass Doll	won in 1907
Jest	won in 1913
Princess Dorrie	won in 1914
Verne	3rd in 1909
Bright	2nd in 1915

St Leger

Your Majesty	won in 1908
Black Jester	won in 1914
Prince William	2nd in 1906
Lycaon	2nd in 1911
White Magic	2nd in 1913

In addition, Mr Joel won nearly every important race in the *Calendar*, with the notable exception of the Ascot Gold Cup, which persistently eluded him.

Probably his best-remembered performer, outside his classic horses, was old Dean Swift, who twice won the City and Suburban, and then the Coronation Cup in 1909.

Mr Joel turned to racing for relaxation and recreation. He brought to it his extremely sound judgment, with intense attention to detail. He set his mind on winning the Derby. He had been racing just eleven years when he achieved this ambition. Ten years later, he again won our great classic with the ill-fated Humorist.

Three times Mr J. B. Joel headed the list of winning owners. In 1908, 1913, and 1914, his horses won respectively £26,246, £25,115 and £30,986 in stake money.

His best year was 1911. Then his racehorses won £34,574. That season, however, Lord Derby was at the top of the list of winners with £42,700.

As a breeder of thoroughbreds, Mr J. B. Joel was phenomenally successful. The first winner he bred appeared on the Turf in 1912, and that season horses bred at his stud farm won £12,249.

In 1913, and again in 1914, Mr Joel was the leading successful breeder, when the horses he bred won £25,291 and £32,523.

From 1912 to 1940, Mr J. B. Joel is recorded as the breeder of 515 flat races and stakes (first monies only) amounting to £217,134. Statistics are not available for the years from 1900 to 1912. If the sums won by the horses bred by Mr Joel in those years could be added to the figures named, it is certain that he bred the winners of about £300,000.

There would also be races captured in the US by horses he bred, for in 1916 Mr Joel won the Middle Park Plate with North Star. A few weeks later, that colt was sold to Mr A. K. Macomber and sent to the US. Later, he was acquired by Colonel E. R. Bradley and became an exceptionally successful stallion in Kentucky.

Star Hawk was another good winner who went out at the same time.

During the winter of 1915-16, Mr Macomber bought three three-year-olds and thirteen two-year-olds from Mr Joel. Most of them were raced in the US. A good number of fillies became successful broodmares and exercised influence on American tracks, notably Sunbonnet and Marian Hood (half-sister to Polymelus).

Mr Joel's first winner, Kilcheran, captured the Lancashire Breeders' Produce Stakes (£1,612), at Liverpool in 1900. He bred that colt at Northaw House Stud, Potters Bar, Middlesex.

At first his horses were trained by W. Jarvis, senior, at Newmarket. At the end of the 1901 season Mr Joel engaged the late Charles Morton as his private trainer. It was an association of a classic character; unbroken for a happy twenty-five years. Morton lived through the memorable seasons when Mr Joel's colours were successfully carried in the classic races mentioned. All these animals were trained by Charles Morton, who enabled Mr Joel to realise his great desire of owning some of the best horses of his time.

Morton retired in 1925. He was succeeded by Charles Peck, who was formerly his assistant.

It was a strange coincidence that neither of Mr Joel's Derby winners was able to race again after his Epsom triumph. Sunstar practically finished the race on three legs, and was lame when he came back to the paddock. Humorist was found dead in his box at Wantage. He was rested at Epsom after the Derby, before returning home. A fortnight later, in the gallop over the Ascot course, he bled. The owner took his trainer's advice not to run the colt. The following Sunday afternoon Humorist was found dead in his box. An autopsy revealed the horse had been suffering from consumption and severe hæmorrhage of the lungs.

Sundridge, the sire of Sunstar, was purchased for 1,450 guineas in December. The horse was then a four-year-old. He was an extremely lucky purchase. When in training, a very angular horse, Sundridge was a real flyer.

He was retired to the stud first at Northaw, then at Childwick Bury, and proved an exceptionally successful stallion. He sired Jest, White Star, Absurd (five times at the head of the winning stallions' list in New Zealand), Sunder, Radiant, Sunspot, and many others.

At the time of his death in 1923, Sundridge had sired the winners of over £126,000. He was in France from 1911, but returned to England in January, 1920. He had spent two seasons at Cobham Stud before Mr Joel took his old horse back to Childwick Bury.

Sundridge went to the stud in 1905, and was at Northaw. A syndicate of French breeders purchased him for £16,000. The success of the offspring of Sundridge became so pronounced that Mr Joel tried to buy back the horse for £21,000, but was unsuccessful.

Sunstar went to the stud in 1912. Breeders will recall the controversy over the alleged excessive number of mares that especially virile horse was allowed to cover. Sunstar, however, was such a powerful horse that this had little effect on his constitution.

He sired endless great winners. A few that might be mentioned are Buchan, Galloper Light (Grand Prix), Alan Breck, Craig an Eran, Saltash, Somme Kiss, Blink, and Lammermuir.

When he died in 1926, at the age of eighteen years, Sunstar had then sired the winners of £209,200 in England. Daughters of Sunstar were greatly sought after by our breeders and their success as producers of winners of our great races is remarkable. Among their foals were Tiffin, Priscilla, Ellangowan, Coup de Lyon, Bright Knight, and so on. For example, in 1928, his daughters bred the winners of 77½ races, value £36,048, which placed Sunstar at the head of the list of successful sires of dams of winners.

By comparison, Black Jester failed entirely to make any reputation as a sire.

Your Majesty was, of course, bred by Mr Joel, who had the horse a few years at Childwick Bury Stud. He was then sold to Argentina in the summer of 1911 for £22,000. In that country he became one of the leading stallions. His purchase was regarded as one of the greatest acquisitions ever made by Argentine breeders. His name figures prominently in the pedigree of that great American winner, Kayak, whose dam is by the son of Persimmon.

Many romantic stories have been circulated describing how Mr J. B. Joel obtained Doris, the dam of Sunstar.

That mare was owned by his brother, Mr Solly Joel. When Doris broke down, the latter mentioned to his brother that as he had no stud, he intended to dispose of his filly. 'J. B.' suggested to Solly he should not do so, because the mare bore his daughter's name and had won him races. Solly then offered to give Doris to his brother. Mr Jack Joel gladly accepted her. She was sent to Northaw, and later to Childwick Bury, where she died, and where is the memorial her owner erected to her memory. It was, however, not until she produced Sunstar to Sundridge that she bred anything of much account.

If Mr Joel obtained the dam of a Derby winner as a gift, he himself made a gift of another mare destined to produce a classic winner. It was Rosaline. He donated her to the Children's Fresh Air Holiday Fund, and she was sold for £25. Later, mated with St Frusquin, she produced the Oaks winner, Rosedrop. She herself became the dam of that great horse, Gainsborough.

It was in 1929 that Mr Joel acquired the Foxhill property in Wiltshire, which came in the market owing to the tragic death of the former owner. Romance is endless concerning the great winners trained at Foxhill. It was in 1907 that Mr J. B. Joel bought Childwick Bury from the Executors of the late Sir J. Blundell Maple.

He carried on the traditions of that famous breeding establishment with infinitely greater success than his predecessor. He improved the property in every possible way, building boxes and yards which were replete with all modern conveniences.

A few of the other famous horses which carried Mr J. B. Joel's colours might be named, such as White Star, Blue Stone, Spanish Prince, His Lordship, Elmstead (Stewards' Cup winner who went to Uruguay), Golden Sun (so successful as a stallion), Royal Dream, Submit, Sunfire.

As mentioned, his most popular horse was Dean Swift, who became a public idol.

Another of Mr Joel's bargains was Priory Park, for whom he paid £3,000. Priory Park won the Lincolnshire in 1927, and also the Stewards' Cup at Goodwood, while the following season his victories included the City and Suburban and the Royal Hunt Cup. He was eventually sold to Japan as a stallion.

A great racing sensation was Mr Joel's purchase of Prince Palatine for £45,000. That was in 1913. He had never seen the horse when the offer was made and accepted. There was a contingency that if the horse were beaten in the Goodwood Cup, the price would be reduced to £40,000. Twenty to one was laid on Prince Palatine, who was beaten by Magic.

Although he was given a great chance at Childwick Bury, where his fee was 400 guineas, he was not a success, because he was not a particularly fertile horse. He was sold to the Duc Decaze for £25,000, but did no better in France. Eventually the horse was sent to the United States, where he died.

There is no question that throughout his life, Mr Joel's enduring interests were always the same – work, racing and racehorse breeding.

He was most approachable. His knowledge of bloodstock breeding was profound, and he was also a very great judge of a thoroughbred. He took a delight in answering letters on racing and breeding in his own hand-writing. Nothing gave him greater pleasure than to meet any old friend with whom he could chat about his horses, their performances, and their lineage, plus his hopes for their future.

A few years before he died Mr Joel made an offer to purchase Dona-tello. He was only just beaten in the negotiations to acquire that horse. The present owner had asked about the horse before running in the Grand Prix, while Mr Joel's agent did not enquire until immediately the horse had finished, unluckily, second to Clairvoyant.

He also made a very big offer for Le Ksar on the evening that colt had won the Two Thousand Guineas. The offer was not accepted.

It is a pity that since the days of Sunstar there has been no really outstanding stallion at Childwick Bury.

Mr Joel was an early riser. He would frequently leave his London home by six in the morning to visit and inspect the inmates of Childwick Bury Stud, to be back in his office in the City by ten o'clock, where he would put in a long day's work, often until seven in the evening.

The beneficent influence of the notable winners bred at Childwick Bury is worldwide. It always gave intense pleasure to Jack Joel to hear of successes from horses or mares he had bred and sold.

He was rarely more happy than when in the company of a particular friend who could appreciate and discuss with him the merits (even the lack of them) of the many noteworthy horses with which he was intimately concerned.

Any breeder of note, or otherwise, from abroad or the Colonies was a very welcome visitor at Childwick Bury, for Mr Joel took keen personal pleasure, as he so often put it, in making that visitor feel at home.

In his early racing days he took some interest in National Hunt sport.

Over thirty years ago Mr Joel, then at Northaw, one day asked his old friend, Captain Percy Whitaker, to go to the stud and select three horses which he thought might prove successful under National Hunt Rules.

Captain Whitaker took Black Plum (by Persimmon), Royal Birthday (by Queen's Birthday) and Mount Prospect II (by Wildfowler). He, of course, trained them. Moreover, Captain Whitaker himself won races on all of them. Royal Birthday at Manchester; Black Plum at Hurst Park; and three times on Mount Prospect II.

Altogether Black Plum won eight races. A day of great delight to Mr Joel was when Captain Whitaker trained Black Plum to win him the Imperial Cup, at Sandown Park, in 1910. Ridden by Mason, the horse won by four lengths, and for his owner landed a coup in the neighbourhood of £20,000. Mr Joel in his pleasure over this victory made a present of the stake to his trainer.

It is very pleasing to know that Mr Harry J. Joel has registered his father's famous colours and intends to maintain and extend, in good time, the already wide fame of the Childwick Bury Stud.

BBR–1940

The Aga Khan's First Venture as a Vendor

As the BBR *of 1929 noted: 'The irony of it!' The reference was to the fact that two years earlier the Aga Khan, for years 'the most liberal of buyers' of expensive yearlings, had, for the first time, himself sold twenty-one yearlings at Deauville. Incredibly, two of them became classic winners. Indeed 'the irony of it!'*

AT THE Deauville Sales in 1927 the Aga Khan, who had for several years been the most liberal of buyers, assumed for the first time the rôle of a vendor. He sent twenty-one yearlings into the auction ring. Two of the fillies were Ukrania (by Ksar out of Uganda) and Taj Mah, by Lemberg out of Taj Mahal. The late Comte de Rivaud gave him 970,000 francs for Ukrania, who this year won the French Oaks; M. Simon Guthmann paid 250,000 francs (about £2,000) for Taj Mah, who won the One Thousand Guineas at Newmarket. The irony of it! The Aga Khan has given far more for many a yearling than he received for these two fillies in the hope – destined all too often to be unrealised – that it would win a classic race for him. If he were not the philosopher and good sportsman he is, the achievements of Ukrania and Taj Mah would have annoyed him. There was really no occasion for annoyance. A vendor of yearlings may account himself fortunate if they give satisfaction; the buyers will come back for more. Putting aside this consideration, it was, however, remarkable that two such fillies should be obtained in this way from a man who has spent money so lavishly in the endeavour to win races like the One Thousand and the Prix de Diane. The Aga Khan did not breed Ukrania; she and her dam were among the bloodstock taken over when his Highness bought the Haras de St Crespin in 1926. Taj Mah, on the other hand, is a product of the Prince's stud in Co. Kildare, Ireland. Because she was not foaled in France, and therefore excluded from most of the French races, her value as a yearling at Deauville was less than it would have been otherwise.

BBR–1929

Memorative Biography of Mr James White

The 'Memorative Biographies' appearing in the Review *through the years were very unforgettable in their own right because they were so well done. For the most part they were concerned with people who had distinguished themselves in the classic ebb and flow of the Turf. However, the one of Mr James White, appearing in the* BBR *of 1927, was quite a different story. True, Mr White was involved in racing and, to some extent, breeding, but his contributions were not truly that significant. What probably earned Mr White his place was 'the romance and tragedy' of his life of extremes. The biographer did such a touching article, an account which reflects on what overheated ambition and greed and vanity can do to a person so pregnable to the many foibles and frailties to which the human race is exposed. Certainly not a man to be remembered for his admirable qualities, Jimmy White is to be remembered for his very expressive suicide note and for the fascinating manner in which his life was treated by the* BBR.

HERE WE HAVE to deal with a career that was at once a romance and a tragedy. The son of a bricklayer in Rochdale, a bricklayer himself in his 'teens, James White went forth into the world and, spurred on by an overpowering ambition and by a profound belief in himself, became the master of millions. Then his wealth disappeared as suddenly as it had accrued. To regain the lost fortune he indulged in a desperate gamble and was beaten. Faced with ruin, unable to bear the humiliation of the plight to which he was reduced, he committed suicide. That, in a nutshell, is the story of Jimmy White, for Jimmy he was not only to those who knew him, but to all and sundry throughout the land. It was in June, 1918, that White became directly connected with the Turf by purchasing from Mr R. B. Thorburn, for £10,000, the then three-year-old colt Irish Elegance, who, a week or two later, won for him the July Cup at Newmarket. During the next few years he owned a number of good-class handicap horses, and his name became familiar to everyone interested in racing.

The impression White left on the Turf as an owner was not deep, and so far as that aspect of his career is concerned, a brief survey will suffice. He has, however, to be placed in the considerable group of men associated with racing whose personality and abnormal gifts and frailties are so fascinating to students of psychology and human nature. It is no exaggeration to state that the death of James White, and the revelations that followed, stirred the emotions of the whole nation in an extraordinary way. Though we cannot give more than an outline of the life story of this man, it will serve to inform future generations of the amazing character of one who, as another writer has said, could not live without gambling, and finally gambled with Nemesis.

White was not yet fifty when he died, for he was born in 1878. The child of a poor home, he became a wage earner when only ten years old, and was allowed twopence per week pocket-money. Later he found employment as a telegraph messenger, and later still was an apprenticed bricklayer. During this period he was biding his time, gaining experience, keeping his eyes and ears open, awaiting an opportunity to strike out for himself, for he had already determined that he would 'make' money – a lot of it. When he had been laying bricks for a few months he knew all there was to be known about that particular work, and also a good deal about other branches of the building trade. His employer appointed him foreman of a job. The men placed under him refused to be bossed by a lad and struck. White scoured Rochdale, got together another gang of men, and carried on. He was still only nineteen when he became the proprietor of a circus at a cost of £100, which he managed to borrow, and during the two years he owned the circus he blossomed forth as a master builder, bought a theatre at Matlock, and interested himself in one or two other ventures. His speculative appetite was growing apace.

Seeking new worlds to conquer, White gravitated to London, there to receive his first set-back, for in 1900, when twenty-two years old, wishing to return to Rochdale, he had to walk the 180 miles because he had no money wherewith to pay the railway fare. Twenty years later he could casually engage a special train to take him from London to Manchester.

As the years went by he took note of the way other men were making fortunes by floating companies and juggling with figures. He made it his business to get to know some of these people, studied their methods, and before long he himself had become a company promoter. He waxed bolder and bolder, gathered around him men who commanded money, and was soon playing with millions. He was in his element. The more he made the more he wanted, in the sense that the accumulation of wealth gratified his vanity and gave him power in the world of finance.

During this era of prosperity White's fortunes fluctuated; there were occasions when, with all his money locked up in his various ventures, he was actually short of ready cash. From time to time rumours were afloat in financial circles that he was in difficulties. Nothing really serious happened, however, until the early months of 1927. Some of his intimate friends then knew that his affairs were approaching a crisis. He had recourse to moneylenders and paid very stiffly for the accommodation he received. Scores of bills with his name attached were being hawked about the City of London.

To extricate himself from his troubles, he decided to attempt to 'corner' the market in preferred shares of the British Controlled Oil-fields Company, a concern in which he had long been interested, and in whose shares he had twice gambled with some profit. There were 4,500,000 of the shares, and he planned that by the Stock Exchange settling day, June 29th, he and his friends should have bought more shares than there were in existence. He intended to put the money down on June 29th and call for immediate delivery of the shares. If all had gone well with the scheme the sellers would, of course, have found it impossible to meet the demand because the requisite number of shares did not exist. There would, consequently, have been a sensational rise in the price of the shares, and White and his friends would have won a fortune and, incidentally, ruined their opponents.

The 'cornerers' began their operations in April, and the market soon discovered their purpose. A powerful group of operators, believing the scheme was bound to fail, proceeded to sell shares they did not possess, confident they would be able to purchase at a lower price when required to make delivery. When White learned the identity of his opponents he rejoiced, exclaiming, 'They are playing into my hands.' Up to June 27th or 28th White thought he could obtain the big sum of money he would require on the 29th. At the last moment he realised he had been mistaken. He needed at least £750,000 cash, and could not put his hand on it. The fortune for which he and his friends had gambled slipped away. He was financially doomed. Unable to face the ignominy his failure involved, he committed suicide in the early hours of June 29th at his stud farm, King Edward's Place, near Swindon. That morning the price of the preferred shares fell from 13s to 9s in an hour. They have since fallen to a lower level.

In this final gamble White made a headlong plunge. He had by his rashness, and by his overbearing conduct, long since alienated most of the rich men who supported him in former ventures. Some of the few business friends he still possessed warned him of the grave risks he was running, and did their utmost to convince him that failure was almost inevitable. Their pleadings only angered him, so that when the crash came he chose to be alone in his agony. There was no one at hand to give him sympathy and encouragement. In truth, he sought neither. Instead, when the dread, stark truth was revealed, he shut himself up in his private room at Daly's Theatre (the purchase of which had been another of his speculations) and penned an apologia in which, commencing with the words, 'Whilst on the threshold of Eternity,' he unburdened his soul. This strange document was deliberately written for publication after his death; he addressed it to the Editor of the *Sunday Express*.

By way of explaining that he felt entitled to express an opinion of life as he saw it, he wrote:

'I have entertained royalty, called dukes and earls by their pet names, been on the inside of politics, owned a yacht, run a large racing stud, owned a theatre, had interests in newspapers, brought off some of the largest financial deals, raised over one hundred and fifty million pounds for various undertakings, promoted prize fights, subsidised boxers, given large sums of money to charity, made over £750,000 in one day, been feted by all and called Jimmy White by a world of people.

'Yes, I have had the thrills of life. I have known what it is to be hungry. I have also known what it is to have all you desire and to have thousands waiting to eat out of your hand. I have felt the injustice of life and I have had its lucky rewards. I have been guilty of folly but I have never refused a pal. I have won in a single bet on a racecourse £100,000, and I have played bridge for a shilling a hundred with more gusto and joy. I have known men who, but for me, their positions in life would be different. I have known men and women who, while you were useful in cash and kind, spoke kindly, and even affectionately, of you, and changed to aloofness when your bank balance dwindled. On the last day of my life, before my eyes, my brain unwinds the film of the past. In quick succession episode after episode unwinds, and I can now judge that life today is nothing but a human cauldron of greed, lust and power. . . Life is no longer charitable except to the lucky one half of the world seeking new pleasures and vices, and the other half

James White.

groaning at their lot. Judging from the above, it does not look as if one misses much by sleeping for evermore.'

Leaving that strange document behind him, Jimmy White was driven in his car from Daly's Theatre to King Edward's Place. When he bought it the house was comfortable but unpretentious. Regardless of expense, White had it transformed into a miniature palace. Four of the smaller bedrooms were converted into bathrooms at a cost of £2,000 each, the walls marble, the metal work solid silver. Surrounded by such luxuries as these amid the peace and solitude of the rolling Wiltshire Downs, James White ended his life. After his arrival at King Edward's Place he ordered all the servants to go and spend the evening in Swindon. During their absence he visited the stud buildings, and from the storeroom took some medicinal prussic acid and a bottle of chloroform. The following morning he was found dead in his bed. He had drunk some of the prussic acid, and then, as that did not kill him, soaked a sponge with the chloroform and placed it close to his face. The body was interred in the little churchyard at Wanborough, a mile or so from King Edward's Place. It was conveyed thither on a farm wagon, and was followed by another wagon filled with floral tributes which, together with the presence of many well-known people, bore witness to the fact that the poor fellow had not lost all his friends when adversity overwhelmed him.

Without going into the legal and financial complications that resulted from White's death, it may be said that it was officially announced that there were debts amounting to many hundreds of thousands of pounds and an enormous deficiency. At a sale of his office effects, one of the lots was four cheques in silver frames, which had been drawn by White in connection with some of his gigantic deals. One was for £3,160,000. Somebody thought them worth £7 17s 6d as curiosities.

Now as to Jimmy White's activities as a breeder and owner of race-horses. As an owner, he was attracted to the Turf mainly, if not entirely, because it provided further scope for the exercise of his gambling proclivities. Very rarely did he go to the trouble of seeing either his own or other people's horses run; he just sat in his office and made bets over the telephone. Presumably he went in for breeding because he thought it was the correct thing to do. The infrequency of his visits indicated that he took little interest in his stud. Nevertheless, his Wiltshire estate was equipped and conducted on model lines. In addition to King Edward's Place and Foxhill, he bought hundreds of acres of adjoining land, built houses, a club and recreation rooms for his employees, and throughout the neighbourhood was regarded as a sort of fairy prince, for it had never before known so generous a benefactor. The gloom his death cast over the locality can, therefore, readily be imagined.

As previously stated, it was with Irish Elegance that White began to court Fortune on the Turf. That was in 1918. The following year this good and handsome horse carried 9 st 11 lb to easy victory in the Royal Hunt Cup, had 10 st 2 lb on his back when beaten three-parts of a length by King Sol (7 st) in the Stewards' Cup at Goodwood, and the same weight when he readily defeated his opponents in the Portland Plate at Doncaster. Though the son of Sir Archibald always bore White's colours, Mr Alec Ormrod owned a half share of the horse. That same year White's Ivanhoe won the Cesarewitch, while in 1922 he won the Lincolnshire Handicap with Granley, and the Manchester Cup with North Waltham. Sir Berkeley and the smart filly Pharmacie also carried his colours, 'pale blue and khaki hoops, quartered cap'. White made one deep dip into the yearling 'bran tub' and pulled out Noblesse Oblige at a cost of 9,600 guineas. It proved a costly experience.

In the earlier years the horses were trained by H. Cottrill, but subsequently were trained privately at Foxhill, though before his death White leased Foxhill to Mr J. B. Joel. The bloodstock from King Edward's Place was sold at Newmarket in October, when twenty-five broodmares (covered by such stallions as Gay Crusader, Gainsborough, Warden of the Marches, Craig an Eran, Diophon and Salmon-Trout) realised 19,640 guineas, eighteen yearlings 3,640 guineas, and seven foals 1,365 guineas. One yearling by Son-in-Law made 1,300 guineas, and one by Gay Crusader 810 guineas. Eleven of the others fetched less than 100 guineas each.

A quotation, by way of conclusion, from a character sketch by Mr James Douglas, the Editor of the *Sunday Express*:

'James White was a man whose soul was consumed by one of those terrible passions which poison and destroy their victims. . . He was never educated. All his knowledge was gained by gambling in various forms. . . He was the Napoleonic type, with the piercing and penetrating glance of the concentrated egoist. He talked like a Napoleon, domineeringly, arrogantly, imperiously. He never really listened. His brain was deaf. His cold egoism was masked by his humour. Behind his torrent of jests it watched sleeplessly. You could detect its vehement energy under the suave and bland jocundity of his steely smile.'

A pitiless portrait, but a true one.   BBR-1927

Memorative Biography of Lord Rosebery

When Archibald Philip Primrose, the fifth Earl of Rosebery, died in 1929 at the age of eighty-three, England lost a distinguished statesman, historian and sportsman. Titles borne by the Earls of Rosebery began to accumulate in 1651. There is a story, which the Earl never did refute, that when at Oxford he made a wager that he would marry the richest woman in the world, become Prime Minister and win the Derby. He accomplished all three; marrying Hannah Rothschild, daughter of Baron Meyer Rothschild, he became Prime Minister and he won the Derby three times – first with Ladas, again with Sir Visto and once again with Cicero.

Lord Rosebery bought his first horse, the first Ladas, in 1868 at the age of twenty-one. He won his first race in 1869 and his last just a week before he died. In the meantime, particularly through his purchase of the noted foundation matron, Paraffin, second dam of the exemplary producer and One Thousand Guineas heroine, Chelandry, Lord Rosebery's name was associated with many of the most successful performers and influential producers in English racing at that time. He also owned and bred the Two Thousand Guineas winner Bona Vista (a half-brother by Bend Or to the Second Ladas) who secured Turf immortality as the sire of champion sire Cyllene, sire of five-times

champion sire Polymelus, sire of Phalaris, the pre-eminent sire of the twentieth century. He also sired Vahren, dam of another paramount influence, The Tetrarch.
at the dinner at York in 1897 was 'of special interest because of the revelation of his attitude towards the Turf'.

The BBR *'found the speech in a volume of the late Joseph Osborne's* Horse Breeders' Handbook, *and, after reading it, felt that it should someday find a fresh home in our* Review'. *Lord Rosebery's death was considered 'an appropriate occasion for bringing it along' and now it is felt it is time to bring it along again.*

THE MORNING of May 20th it was announced that the aged Lord Rosebery, who had for many years suffered physical weakness, was confined to his bed at The Durdans, Epsom, with a feverish cold. A few hours later came the news that the illness had become critical, and in the evening of the 21st the noble Earl – statesman, historian and sportsman – passed peacefully away. He was one of the outstanding figures of the Victorian era. As Secretary for Foreign Affairs, and as Prime Minister, he occupied positions which brought him in contact with the world at large. His abilities, his culture, his transparent honesty of purpose, and his independence, commanded universal respect.

Archibald Philip Primrose, fifth Earl of Rosebery, was born in London on May 7th, 1847. At the time of his death he had, consequently, just entered his eighty-third year. He was only a boy when his father died, leaving him heir to the Earldom, to which he succeeded on the death of his grandfather in 1868, when he was at Oxford. He was elected a member of the Jockey Club when he was twenty-three years of age.

Lord Rosebery bought a horse in 1868 'to win the Derby'. It was a colt named Ladas (by Lambton), who had run and won three races as a two-year-old. Sent to James Dover, at Ilsley, the horse not only failed in the Derby, but turned out a disappointment generally. The only time he won for Lord Rosebery was when he scored by a head in a Match for £200 at Newmarket. His owner would, however, seem to have had an affection for him. Waiting twenty-five years, he bred a colt that showed great promise, named him Ladas after his first horse, and with him won the Derby. For the first Ladas Lord Rosebery gave what was considered a very big sum. The purchase caused a lot of talk, and Lord Huntly tells us that for many years Lord Rosebery was called 'Ladas' by his intimate friends.

We are, however, anticipating, for there was much that happened before the second Ladas arrived. The chief events must be summarised:

1869 – April: Won first race on the flat – Plate at Newmarket. November: Sold all race-horses at Tattersall's because of criticism of the running of one of them at Stockton.

1873 – Won Gimcrack Stakes at York with Padoroshna, bought a day or two earlier for 410 guineas.

1874 – Couronne de Fer, bought in March for 2,500 guineas, ran second in Derby to George Frederick. Aldrich won City and Suburban Handicap.

1876 – Controversy won the Lincolnshire Handicap and a big sum in bets; also the Liverpool Summer Cup. This year Lord Rosebery started three horses in the Derby, and they were the last three to finish. Third in the list of winning owners with a total of £13,390.

1877 – Bellicent won the New Stakes and Rosbach the Wokingham Stakes at Ascot, and The Snail was successful in the Liverpool Summer Cup.

1878 – Bonnie Scotland, bought from Robert Peck for £6,000, started second favourite for the Derby, but ran badly. Afterwards won St. James's Palace Stakes at Ascot.

1879 – Touchet won the Lincolnshire Handicap. Visconti, a 66 to 1 chance, third in the Derby. Ascot Stakes won with Ridotto, the Cambridgeshire with La Merveille.

1880 – Cipollata second to Robert the Devil in the St Leger and the Cesarewitch.

1881 – Town Moor third in the Derby, in which Lord Rosebery also ran Voluptuary, who, three years later (then owned by Mr H. T. Boyd), won the Grand National. Myra third in the Oaks. With the two-year-old filly Kermesse (bought as a foal from Mr Chaplin) won New Stakes, July Stakes, Champagne Stakes and Middle Park Plate.

1882 – Early in the spring Kermesse split two of her pasterns, and could not race until the latter part of the year, when she won the Newmarket Oaks. But for the accident she would probably have been Lord Rosebery's first classic winner, because as a two-year-old she defeated St Marguerite, Shotover and Dutch Oven. His lordship's Prud-homme won the Chester Cup.

1883 – Vista (who became the dam of Bona Vista, Sir Visto and Velasquez) won the Great Metropolitan Handicap, and Roysterer the City and Suburban. Bonny Jean won the Oaks, Ettarre (also owned by Lord Rosebery) finishing third.

Three lean years followed. In 1886 his lordship's horses won three races worth only £693, and he thereupon decided to take a temporary rest from racing, the yearlings from his studs being sold. Four years later his name reappeared in the owners' list.

1890 – Corstophine won the Dewhurst Plate.

1891 – No race won. Corstophine second to Mimi in the Oaks.

1892 – Only race won, a Plate worth £195.

This barren period was, as it turned out, a 'calm before the storm' – the storm which brought with it success Lord Rosebery had not previously experienced. Before we carry the story forward it is, however, necessary to go back to pick up threads that have to be interwoven. In the years 1877 and 1878 Lord Rosebery became the possessor of two stud farms, the one at The Durdans, Epsom, and the other at Mentmore, near Leighton Buzzard, in Buckinghamshire. Two or three years before he died, old Ben Ellam, who owned The Warren, which adjoins Epsom racecourse and is the site of Charles II's hunting box, told us that one day in 1877 he met Lord Rosebery and told him that the Heathcote family wanted to sell The Durdans estate, were asking only a few thousands, and that he ought to buy the property. 'I should very much like to own it,' his lordship replied, 'but unfortunately, Ellam, I cannot afford to buy.' 'That's no obstacle,' said Ellam. 'You buy the place and I'll find the money.' We cannot vouch for the truth of that story, but the fact remains that Lord Rosebery did buy The Durdans from the Heathcotes, and it became, especially towards the end of his life, his favourite residence.

The following year, 1878, Lord Rosebery married Hannah, the daughter and heiress of the millionaire Baron Meyer Rothschild, who died in 1874. We are almost afraid to repeat the oft-told story that, when at Oxford, Lord Rosebery made a bet with a friend that he would marry the richest woman in England, be Prime Minister, and win the Derby. So far as we know, Lord Rosebery never denied having made the bet. In any case, the three contingencies became realities. By his marriage with Hannah Rothschild (who died in 1890), Lord Rosebery commanded riches, and added to his possessions the stately palace at Mentmore and the many acres surrounding it, including the land Baron Meyer had used so successfully as a stud farm. For fifty years Lord Rosebery maintained, and was ever improving, the studs both at The Durdans and Mentmore. The one was complementary to the other. At Mentmore the subsoil is solid clay to a depth of 180 feet. The foals were sometimes sent to The Durdans, where, with a thick layer of chalk beneath the sod, they were on drier and warmer ground.

In Volume V of the *Bloodstock Breeders' Review* will be found a long article, entitled 'Mentmore and its Associations: History of the Famous Paraffin Family.' For the most part it consists of stories told by Joseph Griffiths, who for over thirty years was Lord Rosebery's stud groom. As there are probably many present-day readers of the *Review* who do not possess the fifth volume, we will reproduce a portion of the article which deals with Paraffin. It reads:

'Paraffin, a bay foaled in 1870, was by the Derby winner, Blair Athol, out of Paradigm, by Paragone... Long before Paraffin was born, Paradigm had gained distinction as a broodmare. In 1862 she bred, to Vedette, the Cambridgeshire winner Gardevisure. That year, and the following season, she was mated with Stockwell, and threw Lord Lyon (winner of the Two Thousand Guineas, Derby and St Leger) and Achievement, who won the One Thousand Guineas and the St Leger. Put to Stockwell again, Paradigm gave birth, in 1868, to the filly

Chevisaunce, who became the dam of the Oaks and St Leger winner Jannette, the mother of Janissary. Having done so well with Stockwell, Paradigm was, in 1869, allied with his best son, Blair Athol, and Paraffin came into the world the following season. Students of breeding will not, of course, need reminding that Rouge Rose, the dam of Bend Or, was a half-sister to Paradigm.

'As a racing proposition, Paraffin could not be compared with Lord Lyon and Achievement, nor even with Gardevisure. Her form was moderate in the extreme. As a two-year-old she raced eight times. Carrying the colours of her breeder, General Pearson, she was unplaced in the Acorn Stakes at Epsom, and finished third in a £100 Plate at Newmarket in the autumn. Her third outing was a successful one, for at the Newmarket Second October meeting she won a little Nursery Handicap. That day she ran as "Mr Dover's". She was, however, actually the property of Lord Rosebery, for whom Dover trained. In the last weeks of the season she ran second in a Nursery and won another at Shrewsbury. But it was not until the following summer that she raced in Lord Rosebery's name... As "Lord Rosebery's" she won a £50 handicap at Abingdon, and finished second in a small race at Worcester. Then she went to the stud. In two season she raced fifteen times and won thrice, the total value of the stakes credited to her being only £210. Yet this is the mare to whom Lord Rosebery is indebted for his most conspicuous triumphs on the Turf.

'But for a misunderstanding Paraffin would in all probability never have found her way to the Mentmore paddocks. General Pearson, the owner of Paradigm, had his race-horses in the same stable as Lord Rosebery's (Dover's), and his lordship obtained a promise from the General that he should have an opportunity of buying Chevisaunce when she had completed her racing career. The General had, however, forgotten that he previously made Lord Falmouth a similar promise. When the difficulty thus created came to be solved, Lord Falmouth established his prior claim to Chevisaunce, and so Lord Rosebery, anxious to have a daughter of Paradigm for his stud, bought Paraffin.'

This story was read by Lord Rosebery when it first appeared in the *Review*, and he did not question its accuracy. The fact that he wanted to buy Chevisaunce is beyond dispute, and, having been disappointed, it was natural enough that he should 'console' himself by securing another of Paradigm's daughters. After all, however, the one thing that matters is that he did get possession of Paraffin.

In 1876 Paraffin produced a small filly by Cremorne. This was Footlight, who, in 1880, had a dead foal. Lord Rosebery took a dislike to her, sent her to a sale at Epsom, and there she was sold for fifty-five guineas. Two years later she was bought privately by Lord Rosslyn, who sold her in 1889 to Mr William Cooper for 350 guineas. She was then transferred to the latter's brother, Sir Daniel Cooper, for whom she produced Glare, the dam of Flair, and the grandam of Prince Palatine.

Paraffin's foal of 1877 was Illuminata. While at Mentmore the mare bred ten living foals. Eight of them ran, and six (including Illuminata) won races, but none was of much account on the Turf. Lord Rosebery sold Paraffin in 1886, and she had three more foals, but none of them raced. It might well have happened that Illuminata, as well as Footlight, was sent to that sale at Epsom in 1880 for his lordship was in a selling mood. Another of the lots he offered was the mare Casuistry, sister to Controversy. She, together with a foal by Kisber, was bought by the Grahams, of Yardley, for 130 guineas, and from her they bred the good horse Paradox, winner of the Two Thousand Guineas, and beaten a short head in the Derby by Melton.

We left our chronological record at the year 1892, when Lord Rosebery had to be content with one win of £195. The following year the second Ladas appeared as a two-year-old. He was a beautiful bay colt by Hampton out of Illuminata. His first race was the Woodcote Stakes. The favourite, at 3 to 1 on, was his first cousin, Glare, but Ladas, a 10 to 1 chance, won in a canter. The good impression that performance made was deepened when the colt afterwards won the Coventry Stakes at Ascot, the 'Champagne' at Doncaster, and the Middle Park Plate at Newmarket. The fame of Mentmore had been revived. The following year, when Lord Rosebery was Prime Minister, Ladas easily won the Two Thousand Guineas from the Kingsclere candidate Matchbox, next the Newmarket Stakes, and then the Derby, in which Matchbox again finished second. There was a great scene at Epsom that Derby day. When Lord Rosebery went on to the course to lead his colt back to the Weighing-room door he was greeted by round after round of enthusiastic cheers. Ladas was the second Derby winner to carry the colours of an owner of The Durdans. The first was Sir Gilbert Heathcote's 'pony' Amato, who won in 1838. There was still another feature which made the victory of Ladas distinctive, for, with odds of $4\frac{1}{2}$ to 1 laid on him, he was the hottest favourite for the race there has ever been.

The Derby was the crowning point of the career of Ladas. He did not win another race. Isinglass and Bullingdon beat him in the Princess of Wales's Stakes at Newmarket, and in the Eclipse Stakes at Sandown Park, Ladas was second to Isinglass, results which showed that while Ladas was a good horse his four-year-old rival was a better one. It was expected that in the St Leger, again opposed by horses of his own age, Ladas would be successful and join the limited circle of wearers of the 'Triple Crown'. Once more he met and defeated Matchbox, but both were beaten by the latter's despised stable companion, the filly Throstle. One more rebuff awaited Ladas. A month later (when not thoroughly fit owing to some training trouble) he was a competitor for the Jockey Club Stakes, and finished fourth only, to Laveno, None the Wiser and Benia.

Lord Rosebery.

He was then turned out of training and sent back to the Mentmore Stud. As a sire he was fairly successful, two of his offspring – Gorgos and Troutbeck – winning classic races. Shortly after leaving the Turf, Ladas became very queer-tempered and required careful handling. He was destroyed in 1914.

Then came Sir Visto, by Barcaldine out of the Macaroni mare Vista. Among the mares at Mentmore when Lord Rosebery married Miss Rothschild was Verdure, sister to the Cesarewitch winner Corisande. In 1879 Verdure produced Vista, who was one of the first group of Mentmore-bred foals registered in the name of Lord Rosebery, and for him she won four races, including the Great Metropolitan and the Great Yorkshire Handicap at Doncaster. Of the many fillies that came from Vista none could win a race, but her three colts all gained fame on the Turf. They were Bona Vista (1889), Sir Visto (1892), and Velasquez (1894). Bona Vista was sold as a yearling at Newmarket for 1,250 guineas to Mr (afterwards Sir) Charles D. Rose, for whom he won the Two Thousand Guineas. Velasquez was the best of the three, but he had the misfortune to be born the same year as Galtee More, to whom he ran second in the Middle Park Plate, Two Thousand Guineas and Derby. In the Eclipse Stakes he was second to Persimmon.

Sir Visto, as a two-year-old, raced twice. He ran unplaced in the Woodcote Stakes at Epsom, and in the autumn won the Imperial Produce Stakes at Kempton, his only other race that season. The following year he made his first appearance in the Two Thousand Guineas, to finish third to Kirkconnel and Laveno. Two weeks later he was third again in the Newmarket Stakes. It was already evident that the three-year-olds that season included no horses of outstanding merit, and that anything might happen in the Derby. Lord Rosebery had as good cause to be hopeful as any of the owners concerned, if only because Sir Visto was bred to stay. Coming round Tattenham Corner Sir Visto's prospects seemed almost hopeless, for there were seven horses in front of him, but his stamina then began to tell, and he got up close home to beat Tom Cannon's gelding Curzon by three-quarters of a length, with Kirkconnel third. The crowd, of course, cheered Lord Rosebery, but the demonstration lacked the spontaneity of the one given the year before when Ladas had won. After a failure in the Princess of Wales's Stakes a month later, Sir Visto waited for the St Leger, for which he started favourite, to win by three-quarters of a length from Mr Washington Singer's Telescope. He was then beaten in the Jockey Club Stakes, and, as a four-year-old, ran five times, always unsuccessfully. Sir Visto spent a few years at the Mentmore Stud, then went to Ireland for a time. Later he was at the Cobham Stud for a season, and then returned to The Durdans, where he was destroyed in 1914, a few months after Ladas had been 'put away'. He was a very moderate horse both on the Turf and at the stud.

In 1896 Lord Rosebery's name remained prominent in the owners' list by reason of the achievements of the two-year-olds Velasquez and Chelàndry. The former gained much fame by scoring easy victories in the New Stakes at Ascot, the July Stakes at Newmarket, the Prince of Wales's Stakes at Goodwood, and the Champagne Stakes at Doncaster, and nothing seemed more certain then that in this son of Donovan and Vista, Lord Rosebery had a colt as good as, if not better than, Ladas. The race for the Middle Park Plate brought a change of outlook, however. Odds of 3 to 1 were laid on Velasquez, but he was beaten six lengths by the Irish colt Galtee More. The ground was very heavy, and the plea was advanced that it had hampered Velasquez, who had small feet; but as we have shown, it was clearly demonstrated the following year that Galtee More was a horse quite out of the ordinary. This was unfortunate both for Velasquez and his owner. The colt, however, with Galtee More out of his way, won the then valuable Princess of Wales's Stakes, and also the Champion Stakes, while, as a four-year-old, he won the Eclipse Stakes. His stake-total was the handsome one of £25,365. Towards the end of his life he became blind, and was destroyed in 1906.

Chelàndry was a half-sister, by Ormonde's son Goldfinch, to Ladas. As a two-year-old she proved herself the best filly of her year by winning the Woodcote and Great Surrey Breeders' Foal Plate at Epsom, the National Breeders' Produce Stakes at Sandown Park, and the Imperial Produce Stakes at Kempton. She followed up these successes by winning in 1897, the One Thousand Guineas on Lord Rosebery's birthday. In the Oaks she was surprisingly beaten by Limasol, and in the St Leger was one of Galtee More's victims. The Guineas was, in fact, the last race she won. At the stud she was, as we shall see later, brilliantly successful.

In 1897 Lord Rosebery again won the Gimcrack Stakes at York, the prize being captured by the filly Mauchline. This gave his lordship an opportunity of making a characteristically interesting speech at the ensuing banquet of the Gimcrack Club, to which reference will be made later. After the retirement of Velasquez in 1898, there came a period of five years during which Lord Rosebery's Turf fortunes were at a low ebb. The first of the offspring of Ladas had appeared, and had not come up to expectations. Sailor Lad was believed capable of winning the Two Thousand Guineas in 1900, but ran unplaced to Diamond Jubilee, and that year Epsom Lad, a winner as a two-year-old, also failed. In July, 1900, the Mentmore yearlings were sold, and in December the horses in training also came under the hammer. Mr James Buchanan (now Lord Woolavington) gave 1,050 guineas for Epsom Lad, and a rare bargain he proved to be, for, among other races, he won the Eclipse Stakes in 1901. The yearlings were again sold in 1901, but those of 1902 were retained and raced the following season.

We will, however, pass on to 1904, when Cicero appeared as a two-year-old. This colt was by Cyllene out of Gas, by Ayrshire out of Illuminata. He was unbeaten as a two-year-old, winning five races, including the Coventry Stakes at Ascot (in which he defeated the more-fancied Vedas) and the National Breeders' Produce Stakes. He was not entered for the Two Thousand Guineas (which Vedas won easily), but reappeared as a three-year-old in the Newmarket Stakes and scored readily. Then he started favourite for the Derby, which M. Edmond Blanc hoped to win with Jardy. The latter had come from a stable in which there was an epidemic of coughing and fever. He was all right when he reached England, but then started coughing. As Vedas had met with an accident, and so could not run at Epsom, Cicero appeared to have a fairly easy task, odds of 11 to 4 being laid on him. He and Jardy were in front a quarter of a mile from home, and were presently joined by Signorino. Towards the finish Cicero began to creep ahead, and finally beat Jardy by three-quarters of a length. What would have happened if Jardy had been in perfect health can only be conjectured. Seven weeks later Cicero started an odds-on favourite for the Eclipse Stakes, but was, after a great race, beaten half a length by Val d'Or (receiving 3 lb), one of Jardy's stable companions. Just before the St Leger, which he was expected to win, Cicero went lame and had to be scratched, and no more was seen of him until the following year when, in the spring, he won a Biennial at Newmarket. His next and last outing was in the Ascot Cup. He had been difficult to train for this severe ordeal owing to leg trouble, and cut an indifferent figure. This was the race in which Bachelor's Button defeated 'peerless Pretty Polly'.

In 1906 Lord Rosebery had a good two-year-old in Traquair, but, after winning the Woodcote, Coventry and National Breeders' Produce Stakes, he became a roarer. The following year he was sold to go to Australia, where he did well at the stud. Another of the Mentmore-bred two-year-olds in 1906 was Bezonian, who, the next year, ran second to Slieve Gallion in the Two Thousand, and fourth in the Derby to Orby.

Passing on to 1909, we come to Neil Gow (by Marco out of Chelàndry) racing that season as a two-year-old. After two failures he won the National Breeders' Produce Stakes, the Prince of Wales's Stakes at Goodwood, the Champagne Stakes at Doncaster, and then the Imperial Produce Stakes at Kempton. His performance in the last-named race was one of the most extraordinary ever seen on a race-course. The going was dreadfully heavy – so bad, indeed, that Lemberg, who was to have opposed Neil Gow, was not allowed to run. Lord Rosebery's big and powerful colt had only two opponents – Sunningdale (who was bigger still) and Santa Fina. When the barrier was raised, Neil Gow whipped round and began to race in the wrong direction. By the time Maher had checked him and got his head turned for home, the other two were nearly a furlong away. To everybody's surprise, Maher decided to set off in pursuit of them. If the going had been sound Neil Gow would have had no chance whatever, but he gradually closed the gap, and the spectators, who could hardly believe their eyes, were thrilled with excitement when he got up on the post to beat the floundering Sunningdale by a head.

In the Two Thousand Guineas the following May, there was a memorable duel between Neil Gow and Lemberg. For two furlongs they raced side by side, with never more than a head between them. The judge's verdict was a short head in favour of Neil Gow. No one who saw that prolonged battle is ever likely to forget it. In the Derby, which

Lemberg won, Neil Gow finished fourth. After the Guineas there was trouble in one of his hocks, and he was unable to do himself justice at Epsom, the descent to Tattenham Corner being a considerable hindrance to him. He and Lemberg met again in the Eclipse Stakes seven weeks later. Neil Gow was then quite sound again, and we saw a repetition of the wonderful tussle they had in the Two Thousand, except that this time they ran a dead-heat, and really there could not have been a more satisfactory verdict. They were two first-class horses. A few weeks later Neil Gow (named after a Scottish violinist) broke down again. This time the mischief was irreparable, and he began his stud career the following season. He did not achieve greatness as a sire.

In 1912 Lord Rosebery had yet another winner of the National Breeders' Produce Stakes. This was Prue, who, the next year, was a close third to Jest and Taslett in the One Thousand Guineas. She made no show in the Derby or the Oaks, but won the Coronation Stakes at Ascot. In 1914 the Newbury Spring Cup was won by the medium-sized, sturdily built Wrack, whose dam, Samphire, was a daughter of Chelàndry. The following year Wrack again won the Spring Cup at Newbury. At the end of that season he went to the US, and at Mr A. B. Hancock's stud in Kentucky, has sired a host of winners, some of them very good. In 1915 Vaucluse won the One Thousand Guineas. She was by Dark Ronald out of Valve (half-sister to Cicero), by Velasquez out of Gas, daughter of Illuminata, and therefore the fifth classic winner Lord Rosebery obtained as a result of his purchase of Paraffin from General Pearson.

Lord Rosebery's achievements as an owner and breeder during the last fifteen years are so well known to most of our readers that there is no need to refer to them in detail. In 1920 Valescure, half-sister, by Swynford, to Vaucluse, ran third in the One Thousand; three years later Ellangowan won the Two Thousand and the Champion Stakes; and in 1924 Plack was successful in the One Thousand and second in the Oaks to Straitlace. Ellangowan (now owned by Mr J. Jarvis and doing well at the stud) is by Lemberg out of Lammermuir, a granddaughter of Kermesse; Plack (a very good stayer) is by Hurry On out of Groat, whose dam, Sixpenny, is half-sister to Lammermuir. Less than a week before Lord Rosebery died his colt Midlothian (by Son-in-Law out of Lammermuir) was beaten two short heads by Hunter's Moon and Mr Jinks in the Newmarket Stakes, and at once became a strongly fancied candidate for Derby honours; but owing to the void nomination rule, which will presently cease to operate, the colt could not run at Epsom. Ellangowan, Plack and Midlothian are all representatives of the family

Lord Rosebery established when he bought Kermesse as a foal from Mr (later Lord) Chaplin.

In the foregoing survey, emphasis has been laid on the great part played by Paraffin and her descendants in upholding the prestige of Lord Rosebery's stud. We must not, however, overlook the fact that Lord Astor also owes much of his success as a breeder and owner to this family. He had the great good fortune to be able to persuade Lord Rosebery to sell him the mare Popinjay, by St Frusquin out of Chelàndry, and as a result of that transaction has possessed the classic winners Pogrom, Saucy Sue and Book Law.

The last race in which Lord Rosebery's colours (primrose and rose hoops, rose cap) were borne to victory was the Norfolk Two-year-old Stakes, run at Newmarket on May 14th, just a week before he died. The winner was the filly Annis, by Lemberg out of Lake Leman, a daughter of Vaucluse – the Paraffin family again.

Long as the story we have written is, it does not profess to be anything like a complete record. We have had to exclude features to which many of our readers may attach importance. However, we are satisfied that the story as it stands is comprehensive enough to convey a fairly good idea of Lord Rosebery's successful endeavours as a breeder and patron of the Turf. In this, as in all other spheres, he had a keen sense of his responsibilities, and was ever animated by a determination to uphold the great traditions that are associated with the British thoroughbred. His enfeeblement had prevented him attending a race meeting for many years, but his interest in the sport did not wane in the slightest. Mr George Lambton says of Lord Rosebery:

> 'I have known no man who had retired from active participation in racing for so long and yet had kept his love of it, and all that belonged to it, as Lord Rosebery did. The last time I saw him I was astonished to find how keen was his interest, and how alive he was to everything that was going on. To me it has always been an interesting study when big races are being run to watch the faces and demeanour of owners of favourites. Outwardly cool and calm, I am sure Lord Rosebery's sphinx-like face hid a very considerable nerve strain, and that the defeat of one of his favourite horses went to his heart more than is the case with most people.'

Lord Rosebery employed many trainers in his time. He began with James Dover, and then followed Robert Peck (at Russley), Matt Dawson, Joe Cannon, Sam Darling (Beckhampton), R. C. Dawson (Whatcombe), Percy Peck, George Blackwell, W. Nightingall (Epsom), Fred Pratt, William Walters, Frank Hartigan (Weyhill), and, lastly, Jack Jarvis. He occasionally had horses trained to race under National Hunt Rules, but that was only a side line.

It is a curious fact that Lord Rosebery never headed the list of winning owners. The nearest he got to securing that distinction was when he gained second place in 1894 with a stake-total of £17,208. Three years later his total was £20,595, but that was beaten by two other owners. Another surprising fact is that none of his horses was able to win for him any of the Cups so coveted by owners.

We promised earlier to make a reference to the speech Lord Rosebery delivered at the Gimcrack Club's dinner at York in 1897. It is of special interest because of the revaluation of his attitude towards the Turf. 'I very seldom go to races,' he said, 'and if I go to see a particular race, I usually arrive not long before the race takes place and go very soon after it has been decided.' Remarking that it was the prerogative of a person who had nothing to say to give advice, he proceeded:

'If I am asked to give advice to those inclined to spend their time and money on the Turf, I should say as *Punch* did to those about to marry, "Don't". . . In the first place the apprenticeship is exceedingly expensive; in the next place, the pursuit is too engrossing for anyone who has anything else to do in life; and in the third place, the rewards, as compared to the disappointments, stand in the relation of, at the most, one per cent. I will give you my experience, and you shall judge whether I have not some foundation for the advice I give. A great many years ago, at an early age, I conceived the ambition to win the Derby. For a quarter of a century I struggled, sometimes ran second, sometimes third; very often I ran last. But the time arrived when I was about to realise the fruition of my hopes: I was, with the second Ladas, about to win the Derby, and I ought to have been the happiest of men.

'I won the Derby, and what was the result? I, at that time, held high office under the Crown. I was immediately attacked for owning racehorses at all – attacked with very little knowledge of the facts, and with much less of the charity that thinketh no evil. I made the discovery, too late in life, that what was venial and innocent in the other offices of the Government, in the Secretary of State and the President of the Council, was criminal in the First Lord of the Treasury. Although without guilt and offence I might run second and third, or even last, it became a matter of torture to many consciences if I won the Derby.

'But my troubles did not end there. Shortly afterwards we had a General Election, and I then found that, having received abundant buffets on one cheek from the smiter, I was now to receive them on the other. I was assailed – or rather, those associated with me were assailed – not because we were too sporting, but because we were not sporting enough. Leagues and Associations with high-sounding names and unerring principles were started to attack us on the ground that we were not supporters of the sport, I having already suffered so severely from having been too much of a sportsman. I then hoped my troubles were over. I withdrew into the sanctity of private life, and felt that I should be able to pursue what is facetiously called the "sport of kings" without any particular detriment.

'But again I was mistaken. Last year I thought I possessed the horse of the century (Velasquez), and I believe I did own a very good horse until he was overtaken by illness. I began, as foolish Turfites do, to build all sorts of castles in the air – to buy yachts and all sorts of things my means would permit. But from the very moment I began to form these projects, the curse fell upon me. From October 1st, 1896, to October 1st, 1897, I was second in every great race in which I ran except two, which I won. I think, when I advise those who are about to race not to do so I am justified by the experience I have laid before you in so harrowing a manner.

'Is there no compensation for those who pursue a sport carried on under such difficulties? There are friendships formed and a knowledge of the world gained on the Turf which are invaluable to any man who wishes to get on in life. There was a famous lady who lived in the middle of this century, Harriet Lady Ashburton, who summed up her views on the subject in a remark which has been preserved by the late Lord Houghton. She said: "If I were to begin life again I should go on the Turf merely to get friends. They seem to me to be the only people who really hold together. I do not know why. It may be that each man knows something that would hang the other, but the effect is delightful and peculiar." If that was the cause of Turf friendship the effect would be most peculiar, but I am perfectly certain that is not the real basis of Turf friendship. I know nothing that would hang any of those I have known on the Turf, but I am quite sure that if anybody had known anything that would hang me about three years ago I should not be in life at this moment.

'But there must be more than friendship, more than secrets which are too dangerous for people to carry about with them, which constitute a real bond of union on the Turf. Of course, many say that it is gain. I do not think anybody need pursue the Turf with the idea of gain. . . So far as I am concerned, the amusements of the Turf do not lie on the racecourse: they lie in the breeding of a horse, in that most delightful furniture of any part or enclosure, the broodmare and the foal, in watching the development of the foal, and the exercise of the horse at home.

'I don't believe, however, that even that would be sufficient if we had not some secret ambition to lure us on. . . After very careful analysis of all the facts that have come under my observation, I believe it to be an anxious desire of aspirants for fame connected with the Turf, to become the owner of what is called "the horse of the century". Whether they will ever do so or not is a matter of very great doubt in their minds, and how they are to set about it must be a matter of still more anxious inquisition. There is the method of purchase. I speak in the presence of some who, perhaps, breed horses for sale, and I therefore do not venture to speak of that method with disparagement; but I do not think the "horse of the century" will be acquired at auction.

'Then there is the method of abstract theory and historical law. There is an idea that by some connection with the Byerly Turk (which in itself has a horrible Eastern flavour about it) you may acquire the "horse of the century". Lastly, there is the method of numbers – that new and fashionable method. You do something on paper that looks like a rule-of-three sum, and in a moment you have the "horse of the century". I am sure we do not believe in any of these ways. I believe the Goddess of Fortune plays a great part in the production of the "horse of the century".'

At the end of this speech Lord Rosebery referred to the horse Gimcrack. 'He lived,' said his lordship, '130 years ago. How many poets, how many philosophers – aye, how many statesmen – are remembered 130 years after they have lived? May we not draw the conclusion that the sport we honour tonight was never better and purer than at this moment; never more honest in its followers, never pursued with greater interest. This sport will not perish in our land, whatever our enemies may do.'

We have reproduced the greater part of the speech, with some reluctance because it occupies so much precious space, but with a confident feeling that today, more than thirty years after its delivery, it will be read with great pleasure. It may almost be regarded as Lord Rosebery's apologia as a supporter of the Turf. The oration was charged with sound sense as well as with bright humour, and can be taken as an example of the happy way in which he always adapted himself to his surroundings. We found the speech recorded in a volume of the late Joseph Osborne's *Horse Breeders' Handbook*, and, after reading it, felt that it should some day find a fresh home in our *Review*. This has seemed to us an appropriate occasion for bringing it along.   BBR–1929

Tribute to the Turf

MR WILLIAM REGINALD HERBERT HUDDLESTON, who died at his home, Clytha Park, Monmouthshire, in October, aged eighty-eight, was in his younger days devoted to sport, and especially racing. He rode many of his own horses in steeplechases. His colours were 'rose and white diamonds', and when, later in life, he wrote his reminiscences, he called the book *When Diamonds Were Trumps*. The joy and satisfaction he derived from racing stand revealed in the following extract:

'Beginning with racing, I have moved in many a world – Artistic, Theatrical, Political, Doggy, and others – each thinking itself the hub round which the remainder of the universe revolved. Having hunted, on and off, all my life, seventeen years as Master of the Monmouthshire, I may be said to know something about it; but for all that I unhesitatingly affirm that, given good health and a fair supply of the needful, "there's nowt like racing". The more I think of it, indeed, the more I'm convinced that there's more pleasure to be got out of a racing career than any other. A life led mostly in the open air, constant change, excitement of the highest order, a broad-minded cosmopolitan company full of intelligence and up-to-date ideas, with, as a rule, the best of good fellowship overflowing with generosity.'   BBR–1929

Obituary of Mr Edgar Wallace

Of Mr Edgar Wallace, an Englishman who died in Hollywood, California, where he had gone to write screenplays, in 1932, the BBR *said, 'He is not the least notable of self-made men.' How true; he did not know his parents and joined the army to obtain an education, which later enabled him to become an outstanding novelist and writer of plays. He also loved the Turf and was responsible for getting the obtrusive 'void nominations' problem solved. Betting, or rather too much of it, 'became one of his foibles' and he was in debt, to the surprise of many, when he died. But he was a man to remember.*

IN THE late autumn of last year Edgar Wallace left England for Hollywood, California, to fulfil a contract to write some scenarios for cinematograph films. Early in February, he was down with pneumonia, and, to the dismay of his family, friends, and a host of admirers, he succumbed after a very brief illness. His body was brought to England for interment. Who his parents were he did not know. He

Edgar Wallace.

was born in 1875, somewhere in the East End of London, and when nine days old, was (for a 'consideration' no doubt) adopted by a Billingsgate porter, who lived at Deptford. How, as a boy, he lived surrounded by squalor and had to associate with people frequently in prison; earned a few coppers by selling newspapers in Ludgate Circus; resolved to get an education by entering the army; went with his corps to South Africa, where he eventually drifted into journalism; and how he returned to London to gain fame and fortune after experiencing many vicissitudes is all told in his remarkable autobiography.

Wallace was an extraordinary man in many ways. When he had got well into his stride as a writer of mystery novels, his fecundity was amazing. Book followed book in rapid succession. They sold by tens of thousands all over the world. Later on he turned his attention to plays, and they too came in a veritable spate. He revelled in his popularity, but success did not spoil him. In a quiet, unassuming way he was always affable and companionable. His geniality made him countless friends; that he had a single enemy is inconceivable.

It was to the Turf that Wallace turned for relaxation. Not the least astonishing feature of his career is the fact that he found time to write frequent racing articles. He took a particular pride in them, but if the truth must be told they carried little weight. This is hardly surprising. Racing journalism is a whole-time job, but Edgar Wallace regarded it as a mere hobby. His articles were, of course, readable, but as a rule made no lasting impression. When his purse began to wax fat he set sail on the perilous sea of ownership, and later joined the ranks of breeders. Betting became one of his foibles. These adventures proved ruinous. Two or three years ago Wallace was able to boast that he had earned over £50,000 in twelve months. That did not satisfy his ambition, however; he aimed at £100,000. Shortly after his death everybody was astounded by the news that an examination of his financial affairs had revealed a deficit amounting to no less than £60,000. His widow attributed this seemingly incredible state of things to losses due to his association with racing. In a memoir she tells a story that illustrates Wallace's happy-go-lucky disposition. One morning he received a cheque for £1,000. Turning to his wife he said: 'Let's go to Newmarket and make it £10,000.' They went, and at the end of the afternoon the bookmakers had garnered all but a few shillings of the £1,000.

There was one great and lasting service Edgar Wallace rendered to the Turf; he solved the age-old 'void nominations' problem. For generations the Jockey Club had discussed the question and, with legal guidance, always decided that the executors of a deceased owner could

not be compelled to pay forfeit that would become due in respect of the
unfulfilled engagements made for the owner's horses. A Rule of Racing,
therefore, stipulated that when an owner died his nominations became
void. This was regarded as a vexatious necessity. It occurred to Wallace
that it was ridiculous to act in this way on a mere supposition. He therefore approached the Stewards of the Jockey Club and suggested that the
validity of his belief that they were legally entitled to exact payment
of forfeits should be tested in the Courts. His offer to pose as defendant in
an action which would prove or disprove his contention was accepted.
He entered two of his horses for races at Newmarket, did not run them,
refused to pay the forfeits, and was formally sued. To his chagrin, the
High Court Judge ruled that he was not legally liable. When, however,
the case went to the Court of Appeal the verdict was in favour of the
Jockey Club, who thankfully paid all Wallace's costs, and promptly
annulled the obnoxious 'void nominations' Rule. It was a signal
triumph for the 'defeated' defendant.

Wallace was beyond doubt a genius. What he would have made of his
talents if, when he was a child and a youth, they had been well nurtured,
we can only conjecture. By sheer determination and willpower he
emerged from the humble sphere in which he found himself when able to
appreciate the disabilities he was enduring. He is not the least notable of
self-made men.   BBR–1932

Pre-Derby Luncheon at the
Press Club in 1935

*As tradition dictated, the customary pre-Derby luncheon was held at
London's Press Club in 1935. As usual, the speeches were 'more
amusing than illuminating' which prompted Lord Derby to suggest the
gathering was taking part in the 'Ananias Stakes' – a rather polite,
Biblical way of saying the guests were probably being deceived or lied
to. But it was fun and, on this particular occasion, Lord Derby
managed to make the Aga Khan the target of some gentle ribbing.*

THE SPEECHES made at the Press Club's luncheon two days before the
Derby were, as usual, more amusing than illuminating. Major J. J.
Astor, chief proprietor of *The Times*, who presided, informed the guests
about to address the company that the public wanted to know about the
chances and idiosyncracies of their runners in the Derby, and at the
same time warned his other hearers that they might not get the truth!

Whereupon Lord Derby suggested that they appeared to be taking part in the 'Ananias Stakes'. Apparently, if a man did speak the truth nobody would believe him. If, he went on to say, Bobsleigh had been running he should have told them the colt would win. As it was, he could only express the hope that his colt Fairhaven would run jolly well. If they could make anything of that statement they were at liberty to do so. Might he offer a suggestion? If, about the middle of next year, the Aga Khan had two or three horses entered for the Derby apart from those he intended to run, would he lease them to other people? If so, there might be an interesting race, and the outsider might turn up!

Lord Astor, owner of Field Trial, said his sentiments could be summarised by the words Faith, Hope and Charity: the faith which every owner must have when he started a horse; the hope that generally speaking the best horse would win; and a real feeling of charity towards the person who had three horses to race, because he himself was going to start two to show that he could also start more than one. (Lord Astor intended to run Plymouth Sound as well as Field Trial, so that the latter should have the services of a pacemaker, but the morning of Derby day Plymouth Sound rapped a joint and had to be withdrawn.) As for Field Trial, continued his lordship, he was a lazy horse at home and did not tell his trainer much, but he was quite well.

The next speaker, Sir Abe Bailey, said: 'For forty years I have been trying to win the Derby and I have failed. However, they say the world loves a good loser, and I think the bookmakers do too!' We may add that a few days earlier Sir Abe told a journalist that he believed his colt Robin Goodfellow would run much better in the Derby than most people appeared to expect.

BBR-1935

The Death of Walter Spencer Vosburgh

Walter Spencer Vosburgh, associated with the Jockey Club in New York from 1894 until his announced retirement in 1934, made such a reputation for himself that he was, unquestionably, the most revered and most respected man in the profession during his lifetime – and afterwards. This respect and reverence was felt almost as much in Europe as in the US. A frequent writer for the Review *as well as a regular contributor through articles reprinted from other publications, Mr Vosburgh's obituary, appearing in the* BBR *of 1939 expresses it all – briefly, beautifully, admirably.*

WALTER SPENCER VOSBURGH, an outstanding figure on the American Turf since 1866, died at his home in New Rochelle, New York, September 11th. He was in his eighty-fourth year, and had been in delicate health for the past four years. At the end of 1934 he announced his retirement as Chairman and Steward at the Metropolitan tracks, but attended racing every day until the Saratoga meeting in August. He is survived by his son, Harold O. Vosburgh, who assisted him in much of his work, and who succeeds him as Steward. During the 'eighties and early 'nineties Mr Vosburgh was the prince of the *Spirit of the Times* under the *nom de plume* 'Vigilant', and continued throughout his life to write occasional articles on racing. He was the author of *Racing in America, 1866–1921*, a book written at the request of the Jockey Club. In 1894 he was appointed by the Jockey Club Racing Secretary, Forfeit Clerk and Handicapper. Ten years later he relinquished the post of Racing Secretary and Forfeit Clerk, but retained that of Handicapper. He was appointed a Steward in 1929.

Mr Vosburgh had the reputation of being the most competent handicapper in Turf history. Over a period of sixty years he missed only three days' racing in New York State. His handicapping was based upon his personal observation. He invariably went to the paddock to see the horses saddled and noted every detail of a race. He was the silent man of racing. Though he enjoyed the respect of thousands, his intimates could be numbered on the fingers of one hand. He had decided opinions on all phases of racing and breeding, many of which were far from orthodox, but he never made the mistake of trying to force his opinions on anyone else. Supreme in his own field, he never sought advice, nor threw it elsewhere.

He was an heroic figure – one of the greatest the American Turf has produced. His like will never be seen again.   BBR–1938

Part 4
TRAINERS

Physiological Aspect of Training

Everyone realises that some trainers are better than other trainers. In the 1915 Review, an article by 'Mankato', which first appeared in the Sporting Chronicle, was republished. It dealt with the three cardinal points of the 'physiological aspect of training', resulting in the following conclusion: '. . . the worst sort of trainer is the one who is a slave to the orthodox preparation, and the best the one who treats the individual thoroughbred as a living entity capable of very fine adjustment'. What came through as the truth then, still comes through as the truth now. Every successful trainer has a sensitive knowledge of his charges. Hawthorne probably expressed it best: 'Sagacity and a nameless something more – let us call it intuition.'

SON-IN-LAW'S dual success in the Cesarewitch and Jockey Club Cup, after receiving what has been described as a light and insufficient preparation, raises anew, states 'Mankato', in an article in the *Sporting Chronicle*, the physiological aspect of the training of the racehorse. It is generally recognised that three cardinal points are involved:

(1) The education of the nervous system and the education of the voluntary muscles, and also the heart muscles;

(2) A change in the volume of the tissues;

(3) An alteration in the chemistry of muscle-fibre, and also the elimination of superfluous fat generally.

Dr Sherrington, in an illuminating paper which appeared in *Science Progress* in April, 1911, points out that in properly balanced muscular movements there is a period of rest between each successive contraction which is recuperative in nature and opposed to fatigue. The education of the muscles and the nerves which stimulate them to contract is of the most importance in bringing about this momentary rest following each contraction.

Further, in the well-trained racehorse antagonistic muscles offer little or no resistance to their opponents. For example, the muscles which extend and flex the limb and foot should do their work with perfect rhythm, whereas in the hackney the action never can be made rhythmical for the simple reason that the flexor muscles over-inhibit the muscles of extension, and therefore a hackney when galloping moves in discordant jerks.

This homely illustration brings into prominence the part played by heredity. The nervous and muscular systems of the hackney have no capacity for education in rhythmical contraction. In some thoroughbreds very little education is necessary. Son-in-Law is evidently one of these animals, since he seems to have acquired the faculty as a two-year-old. Put another way, the action of a stayer may be resultant upon very little practice.

Under the second clause it may be laid down as a great principle that no horse can be too big in muscle if the individual fibres are in that condition which permits them to work with a minimum of waste. Here the great art of the trainer comes in. The really clever man knows when he has his horse in this condition. He refuses to be influenced by public opinion, though, as old Professor Williams used to say in connection with the treatment of diseases in horses, it takes infinitely more courage to do little or nothing than to fill the patient with the contents of a pharmacy.

Even slightly attenuated muscle-fibres result in staleness, a fact which is easily demonstrated by experimenting with various sorts of muscle and the myograph. It has been proved over and over again that the recuperation and nurture of muscle-fibre varies very greatly in different thoroughbreds. Reginald Day seems to have recognised that Son-in-Law's muscular vigour would be impaired by much long and fast work, and the result shows that his diagnosis could not have been far wrong inasmuch as the horse's condition in both the Cesarewitch and Jockey Club Cup was just about the acme of fitness.

The third point is the one to which trainers, as a rule, pay the greatest attention, and from the time of Gervase Markham, who wrote in the reigns of Queen Elizabeth and James I, to about the beginning of the last century, the 'melting of the grease' was considered the all-important function in the trainer's art. Hence the everlasting sweats which were in vogue, even for two-year-olds, a hundred years ago and later. Even the 'melting of the grease', or, more correctly, the elimination of fat from the muscle-fibre, may be carried too far.

For some unexplained reason a very small quantity of carbohydrate, or fat, is essential to the proper nutriment of muscle-fibre. No horse thrives for long on a purely nitrogenous diet, but the nitrogenous equilibrium and increase in weight may be restored by the addition of carbohydrates to the food. Some horses, however, make fat very rapidly, and this type of animal requires almost constant work of one sort or another; otherwise a few days on the easy list throws him back very considerably in his preparation.

On the contrary, there are horses which when once fit remain so on very little work for lengthy periods. Old Melayr, a son of Ayrshire, for example, after being a whole season at the stud, regained his very best form after he had been less than a month in training, and what is more remarkable, stayed better than during his first Turf career. It will, therefore, be gathered that the worst sort of trainer is the one who is a slave to the orthodox preparation, and the best the one who treats the individual thoroughbred as a living entity capable of very fine adjustment.

BBR–1915

Middleham and its Memories – John Osborne at Home

For much of the nineteenth century, the Middleham area in Yorkshire, Northern England enjoyed its 'palmy days' as a great training centre. In 1917, Mr Arthur W. Coaten revisited Middleham and found the renowned jockey, trainer and breeder, John Osborne, born in 1833, 'at home'. Mr Osborne, still hale and hearty and clear of mind, at the age of eighty-four, was able to reminisce about 'the good old days' with authority, recalling horses and events that should never be covered with the dust of time. Mr Coaten, 'with a couple of days to spare', made this pilgrimage to Middleham with the thought of setting it down in conversational form for the edification of readers of the Review *who otherwise might have known little or nought of this glorious era in English racing and breeding.*

What Turf Titans are part of the region's history! The malevolent Lottery, a foal of 1820 who captured the Doncaster Cup and even covered mares while in training. His daughter Rebecca bred the immortal Alice Hawthorn, a racemare Mr Osborne had the highest regard for and who was also a Middleham inhabitant. There were also The Flying Dutchman (1846) and Voltigeur (1847) and the latter's son Vedette (1854).

Mr Coaten recounts The Flying Dutchman's 'struggles with Voltigeur which 'form one of the most fascinating chapters in racing history'. It is also fascinating to realise that it was Voltigeur's son, Vedette, who sired the epochal Galopin, and The Flying Dutchman's daughter, Flying Duchess, who produced the Derby winner Galopin, the sire of St Simon and the maternal grandsire of Flying Fox and Bayardo.

Middleham was also the home ground for the matron, Agnes (1844), founder of one of the most influential distaff families in the history of the Stud Book, as well as the magnificent racing filly

Apology (1871), heroine of the One Thousand Guineas, the Oaks, the
St Leger and the Ascot Gold Cup.
This is a delightful piece of journalism whose value is timeless.

NO RACING, and I am in Yorkshire with a couple of days to spare. So
how about that visit to the historic moor of Middleham that I had
promised myself for a long time? There is no time to fix up appointments
with the people I would like to see there; but, no matter, I will take my
chance of finding some of them at home. In any case, I shall enjoy the
ramble in a spot that has made so much racing history. A hurried glance
at the North Eastern time-table, a few things thrown into a handbag,
and I am on my way from one side of the far-spreading North Riding to
the other.

It is early autumn, and the purple of the Yorkshire moors is exquisite.
Through some lovely dales and then the first change – Picton. Hard by is
a steeplechase course where before the war a sporting little meeting was
usually held on Boxing Day and another in the early spring. Only a few
miles away is the home of Mr J. L. Dugdale, at Crathorne, where he has
had many winners to carry the familiar scarlet and yellow hoops.
Indeed, Picton is known by name to thousands of racegoers who have
never seen that tiny Yorkshire village, for it gave its name to a horse,
the best yet bred by Mr Dugdale, who would have won the Derby
in 1906 with Spearmint out of the way. His half-brother, Hector,
was also bred there. How good a horse Picton really was can only
be estimated, because he was not seen in public after the Derby. But
in that race he had behind him such smart animals as Troutbeck,
The White Knight, Radium, Beppo, Gorgos, Lally, and Malua. We
know, too, that Spearmint was an exceptional horse, judging him by
his gallops at home with Pretty Polly and his performance in the Grand
Prix.

Yes, Picton would assuredly have brought further fame to this border-
land of Yorkshire had he stood a longer period of training. Perhaps Mr
Dugdale will breed one by him to make up for his sire's abbreviated
career on the Turf. His son Light Brigade was not far removed from first
class, and they say that this young stallion is much liked in Kentucky.
But enough of Picton. Here is our connection to Northallerton, and
within twenty minutes we stand in that busy railway centre. It would be
strange if a racing man did not encounter someone he knew in such a
sporting quarter. Sure enough, just as I am comfortably seated in the
train for Leyburn, who should appear but the Special Commissioner of
Sporting Life. He is post haste from York on a visit to the Langton Hall

John Osborne.

Stud, and before we arrive at Ainderby he has scarcely time to tell of all
the good stock he has already seen during his Yorkshire tour.

On we go leisurely to Leeming Bar and Bedale, names which awaken
within me memories of a visit long ago to the Theakston Hall Stud. I saw
there that charming horse Best Man, who, as a sire, was destined to do
not much better in Yorkshire than he did at Newmarket. The best of his
stock in the south was probably Signorino, who had made a good name
at the stud in Italy, while in the north the smartest of Best Man's get was
Stolen Kiss, whose successes in the Portland Handicap and other good
short-distance races gladdened the hearts of sporting folk of Malton as
they had not been gladdened since Mintagon's Cesarewitch triumph.

Stolen Kiss now graces the Sledmere Stud and her two-year-old colt
Somme Kiss – rather a feminine name, is it not? – for whom Mr Charles
Garland gave 3,000 guineas at Newmarket last year, has shown useful
form. I recall Queen's Birthday, Tarporley, and Clwyd as standing at
Theakston Hall when I was last there, but they are long since gone. The
first-named, however, is well represented by Holiday House, so that

with Hector to keep him company, Mr John McIntyre's stud may be reckoned to be still up to its old strength.

The line from Northallerton to Hawes knows no flying expresses, and as we push slowly on through Jervalux, Constable Burton and Spennithorne we have ample time to reflect on the sporting associations of this district. We are here within touch of Hornby Castle, the home of the Duke of Leeds. The present Duke is more associated with fox hunting, coursing, and yachting than with the Turf, but his ancestors played no small part in racing and horse-breeding. In the early part of the nineteenth century the sixth Duke of Leeds's colours were regularly seen on the Town Moor and other racecourses in the north, and there was, no doubt, a great night in the Black Swan at Bedale, as well as in all that district, when Octavian won the St Leger of 1814. Of Octavian's owner, who for a time was Master of the Horse, it was written that 'he invariably sent his horses to the post win or lose, with a most generous and noble spirit'.

In early times a member of this family, Lord Godolphin, owned the Godolphin Arabian, who, it is said, stood at Bedale for some years, though this is rather a doubtful point. Anyhow, he died at Gog Magog in Cambridgeshire, where a plain flat stone, in a covered passage leading to his stable, marks the grave of one of the great progenitors of the British thoroughbred.

Looking due north from our carriage window imagination travels – it is not many miles – as far as Richmond and its famed moor, where such giants of their day as Voltigeur, Fandango, and Vedette were trained, and the 'Aske spots' of the second Earl of Zetland were among the most familiar colours at the chief meetings. Happily the same colours are still occasionally to be seen, but another Voltigeur is a very long time arriving.

Richmond and Middleham were great rivals in the old days, and excitement ran high at the local meetings. Then there were also the stables of John Scott – the 'Wizard of the North' – and of William I'Anson at Malton, as well as others at Hambledon to add to the great power which Yorkshire wielded on the Turf in those times. It would be wrong to suppose that these northern training centres are in any sense played out. The facilities for training are as suitable at Middleham and Richmond and Malton as they were in the old days, as is shown now and again when the trainers get hold of a good horse.

Within the last few years we have seen Rossendale sent from the north to beat the southern cracks in such races as the Craven Stakes and the Princess of Wales's Stakes, while in 1916 R. W. Colling, with no meeting nearer to Middleham than Newmarket, won fourteen races with eleven horses, value £4,658, placing himself seventh on the list of successful trainers. This noteworthy revival in the fortunes of Middleham is satisfactory, for we all like to see the honours go round.

We are now at Leyburn, and a handy conveyance to Middleham in the shape of the local 'bus' is waiting outside the station. No time, therefore, to visit various places of interest, such as The Shawl and Queen's Gap, named after Mary, Queen of Scots, who, according to local history, was recaptured here in her escape from Bolton Castle. The drive of a couple of miles to Middleham is pleasant enough, and we cross the river Yore by a suspension bridge which looks a good deal more substantial than the old bridge could have been, for that collapsed under the weight of a drove of bullocks! One catches a glimpse of charming river scenery, and there are deeps which promise good sport with pike, chub, perch, and barbel.

Entering the little town we pass Warwick Lodge, where Mr G. W. Smith has a number of horses in training, and Manor House, the home of Mr Dobson Peacock, who has long ranked as one of the foremost of north country trainers. Mr Peacock's establishment rests in the shadow of Middleham Castle, and though Crafty Lassie was the only winner from this quarter in 1916, many past triumphs for Manor House will be recalled. Middleham had a good time when this stable sent out Wardha to win such races as the Doncaster Handicap, the Cumberland Handicap, and the Manchester November Handicap in 1914. Sir Harry's successes in the Great Yorkshire Handicap and the Northumberland Plate are also pleasantly remembered at Middleham. Before the war it was not uncommon for Manor House to pick up something like forty races in a season. When you contrast this with the single success gained last year you will realise once more the crushing time some of these northern stables experienced through the absence of meetings north of the Trent.

It was a delightful afternoon when I set foot on Middleham Low Moor; the sun shone radiantly on as fair a scene as you can find in Yorkshire. The atmosphere was clear and the air invigorating. In the town I had inquired the way to Breckongill. 'You can go round by the road, but the moor's the quicker; you won't go wrong if you follow the track.' Very pleasant was that gentle climb over the fine old turf. About half a mile had been covered when conclusive evidence that there were racehorses about presented itself in the shape of a starting-gate. Close at hand was a gallop, locally known, I think, as 'The Nailer', which stretches its way across the moor for a couple of miles or more. This is

where The Flying Dutchman and many other celebrities did most of
their work, but I fancy that the gallop is not used so much by the
Middleham trainers in the summer nowadays as that on the High Moor,
which affords better going when the ground is hard. Looking at these
long gallops one can understand why so many good stayers have come
from Middleham. The turf is not, perhaps, comparable with the velvety
Wiltshire downs or the Limekilns, but for all that it is good training
ground.

Reaching the highest point of the Low Moor we pause to look round.
The scenic panorama is glorious. High green-coated hills rise in the east,
with thick belts of woodland in the near distance. To the west, many
miles of fair country shelves away in every verdant shade. This is the far-
famed Wensleydale, and in its centre rests the pretty grey-stoned village
of Wensley. Overshadowing all is the noble Penhill, standing 1,792 feet
above sea level, and here and there patches of purple betoken the home
of the grouse.

All around the moor cattle and sheep add to the picturesqueness of the
scene, while below us Middleham nestles cosily with its wealth of
historical associations behind it. Ruins of Middleham Castle rise to
remind us of the glories of the Earl of Warwick – 'The King Maker' – the
last of the feudal barons. 'The mightiest peers, the most renowned
knights, gathered to this Hall. Middleham, not Windsor, nor Sheen, nor
Westminster, nor the Tower, seemed the Court of England. As the last of
the Barons paced his terrace, as far as his eye could reach, broad
domains extended, studded with villages and towns and castles,
swarming with his retainers, and the name of Warwick was in all men's
mouths.'

Such is the glimpse of Middleham in early mediæval times which
Lord Lytton gave us.

But this is not the moment to go into the fascinating records of
Middleham Castle; we push on over the moor, and presently come to
Ashgill, now in the tenancy of Colling, who uses it as an adjunct to
Spigot Lodge, and I took this opportunity of looking round its old-
fashioned but comfortable boxes which have been tenanted in the past
by many good horses. It was at Ashgill that John Osborne, senior, the
father of the famous jockey, made his reputation as a trainer, to be
succeeded in due course by his sons. Even earlier than his time Ashgill
had become known to fame, it being there that Lottery and Longwaist
were trained by George Oates. It is quite probable that the former was
one of the best horses ever quartered at Ashgill. He originally belonged
to Mr Watt, who at the same time had Barefoot in his stable, both being

sons of Tramp. Both were allowed to run in the St Leger of 1823, but at home Lottery (then known as Tinker) could run clean away from Barefoot, so at the time of saddling the former was favourite at 7 to 4 and 2 to 1, whereas Barefoot stood at 13 to 1. The race is worth recalling because it was one of the most remarkable classic events on record. This note was appended to the result in the 'Racing Calendar':

'There was a field of twenty-seven horses mounted and ready at the time appointed for the race, when after two or three false starts, twenty-three of the number went away without the word having been given, and although the bugle was sounded to call them back, they persevered and ran the course through, the Rosanne colt coming in first, Barefoot second, and Comte d'Artois third.'

Lottery was one of the fifteen who were not brought out a second time, and his stable companion won comfortably. Mr Watt subsequently sold Lottery for 450 guineas, and he came to Ashgill as the property of Mr Whittaker, who at one time is said to have refused 3,000 guineas for him. Here is an interesting account of the horse:

'The temper of Lottery was very bad, but, though the spirit was nearly galloped out of him, he was never subdued. When he could not get his rider out of the saddle, he would lie down and roll. . . One morning, while at exercise, he rushed at a farm labourer, and struck him with his foreleg. . . Many of his races were splendid exhibitions of courage and speed. His finest race was for the Doncaster Cup, when he made his own running all the way, beating Longwaist by half-a-neck, and leaving the rest of the field half-a-mile behind. . . At one time he was miserably treated and mismanaged, serving mares and being only half-trained at the time that he was engaged to compete in long courses, and with some of the best horses of his time. At York on one occasion his condition was so bad as to excite the public indignation, which vented itself in exclamations of "Take him away; he isn't fit to run a yard".'

Lottery had been at the stud in France for a long time when John Osborne, senior, went to Ashgill in the spring of 1837. His neighbour at that time at Spigot Lodge was John Fobert, while at Breckongill, Thomas and John Dawson, brothers of the redoubtable Matthew, were also turning out good winners, subsequently continuing their successes at Tupgill and Thorngill. You will perceive, therefore, that they had some notable trainers at Middleham in those days, and as I walked round the unpretentious Ashgill establishment I could picture the stir which prevailed there when some of its good horses of the past returned from their triumphant visits to the racecourse. John Osborne, senior, was a successful breeder as well as trainer. Within the stone-walled enclosures which adjoin Ashgill lived Agnes, by Clarion, a mare destined to have an extremely important influence on the British

thoroughbred. She was a foal at the side of Annette (by Priam) when old
Osborne bought the pair for about twenty guineas. On the course she
was rather a failure, but at the stud she produced thirteen living foals,
her second being Miss Agnes, by Birdcatcher, from whom came Lily
Agnes, the dam of Ormonde. John Osborne, senior, had as many as sixty
brood mares at Ashgill in the "sixties', and must have found himself
hard pushed to provide accommodation for them, as well as for the
horses in training. He solved the difficulty by placing the mares out on
various farmsteads around Middleham.

The racehorses at Ashgill also numbered about sixty at that time, the
trainer having the assistance in the stable of his sons William, Robert
and John. The old man died in July, 1865, and his breeding and racing
studs, sold by Messrs Tattersall, made a grand total of 11,488 guineas.
The sons, as I have already noted, carried on the stable at Ashgill with
only a few horses to begin with, but the establishment soon regained
some of its old importance, especially when it won many good races in
the "seventies' with Mr R. N. Batt's Thorn, a handsome son of King of
Trumps and Lady Alice Hawthorn. There were also Lily Agnes and a
good two-year-old in Holy Friar. Best of all, Apology came to Ashgill as
a two-year-old in the spring of 1872. There is no need to remind you of
the brilliancy of that Oaks and St Leger heroine. Castlereagh,
Palmbearer (second in the Derby to Sir Bevys), Stone Clink (winner of
the Cesarewitch), and Gloriation (winner of the Cambridgeshire) were a
few of the good horses subsequently trained at Ashgill, which had to
mourn the loss of Robert Osborne in 1892. William retired soon afterwards, and John was left to 'carry on' at Breckongill.

From Ashgill one has to walk less than a quarter of a mile to John
Osborne's quarters. Fortunately the veteran is at home, and he gives us a
hearty welcome. Born on January 7th, 1833, he is more vigorous than
many men thirty years his junior. He thinks nothing of walking to
Danby and back, a journey of eight miles, and he regularly rides his own
horses at work. Seventeen years have elapsed since Mr J. B. Radcliffe
wrote *the Life and Times of John Osborne*. The subject of that excellent
book has outlived its author. What is more, he has accomplished enough
since it was written to provide material for more interesting chapters. He
has trained in recent times the winners of two Northumberland Plates
and one Chester Cup, and hopes to turn out some more good winners
yet. Can you wonder that such a man is the admiration of the racing
world?

After tea at Osborne's hospitable board the opportunity occurs of a
chat with the veteran trainer. His stock of reminiscences is inexhaustible.

Stories of races of fifty or sixty years ago come as fresh as though they were run yesterday, and his recollection of weights and names and other details is extraordinarily accurate. Young J. R. Colling's name was mentioned. The old jockey paid a high tribute to the riding ability of his neighbour's sons. He thinks, however, there are fewer good boys riding than in the old days. 'Young jockeys used to begin earlier than they do now,' he said, 'and trainers were more often the owners of horses themselves than is now the case, so they were able to give their own lads better chances of riding in races.'

Regarding modern handicaps Mr Osborne is decidedly of opinion that there is not sufficient margin between the top and the bottom.

'I once told Mr Richard Ord my views, and he replied, "Well, there is a limit." "Yes," I said, "a limit for the bottom but not for the top." Mr Ord then declared that owners would strike out their horses if the handicappers gave them too much weight. I am sure people under-estimate the weight-carrying powers of racehorses. Somebody has said I once wrote that 9 st 10 lb was not a fair racing weight. That is not my opinion, and I do not remember ever saying so. I recollect many instances where the winner has carried 10 st or more, giving as much as 5 st to some of the other animals in the race. I have always believed that Alice Hawthorn could have won the Cesarewitch under 10 st with the bottom weight at 4 st.'

Mr Osborne has worked out the weights to support his estimate of Alice Hawthorn's prowess, including her marvellous effort in the Chester Cup, in which she was second under 9 st 8 lb, giving 5 st 8 lb to Red Deer, while in the same season she won the Goodwood Cup under 9 st 5 lb. It is evident that the old trainer's respect for Alice Hawthorn's memory is profound. He remarked: 'Talking over the question of the greatest horses with an old friend, who knew the mare well, I said, "What about Alice Hawthorn on her form in Queen's Plates and other races?" He said, "Yes; you are not far wrong. She was a wonder."'

There chanced to be a photograph of The Tetrarch on Mr Osborne's table. I asked him what he thought of that brilliant animal.

'He was, of course, an extremely good colt, but I have seen horses win just as easily at Ascot – for instance, Galopin; he did not score by so many lengths, but drew away from his field in the same style as The Tetrarch did. Did you know that I trained Vahren, his dam? She was a useful filly, but not great, though she won us two races at Pontefract and another at Manchester. She belonged at that time to Mr Oscar Rayner, a Liverpool gentleman, who would, I think, have continued to race in the North of England if he could have found a suitable place, but he took Chieveley Manor, near Newbury, where he has now a good stable and stud farm. It is a pity that so many North of England gentlemen send their horses South.'

It is natural that the veteran should recall with a note of regret the palmy

days of Yorkshire as a training centre. He has many memories of John
Scott, who, long before Osborne was born, was at Middleham under
James Croft, learning the business of which he became so great a master.
His brother, the brilliant jockey William Scott, also served his
apprenticeship at Middleham. In those far-off days James Croft was the
leading trainer, and he made a remarkable record by sending out the
first four horses in the St Leger of 1822. This feat is recorded on a tablet
to be seen in the back garden of Glasgow House at Middleham, which is
thus inscribed:

> 'This stone was erected by R. Rodes Milnes, Esq, to commemorate the honesty
> and skill of James Croft, as the trainer of the Hon. E. Petre's Theodore, Mr
> Gascoigne's Wild Violet, the Duke of Leeds's grey colt, Mr Gascoigne's chestnut
> colt, beating nineteen others for the St Leger Stakes, 1822; 75 subscribers.'

While John Osborne was winning his spurs as a jockey, John Scott had
already built up a great fame as trainer. 'I used to go to Whitewall and
stay several days riding gallops and exercise,' says Osborne. 'In his later
days the old man was very well served by his head lads. He used merely
to drive out on the moors in his brougham and watch the work.'

Osborne had his first mount in public in 1846 – seventy-one years ago!
He rode a mare called Miss Castling at 4 st 10 lb. Eleven years later he
could still ride at 7 st 12 lb, though not without working hard. It goes
without saying that a jockey who rode regularly in public for forty-
six seasons without a break (except through accidents) cannot have
been so seriously troubled by the question of increasing weight as many
riders are. Still, John Osborne always had to be careful. 'Many of us
jockeys,' he says, 'had to go very steady all through the racing season,
but when the last meeting was over we used to meet together and cele-
brate the event with a really good dinner. At that feast we always had
roast goose.'

During the winter of 1862 Osborne experienced a bit of a shock. 'I had
been shooting with some friends and generally having a very easy time. I
wasn't bothering about weight. One day we entered a barn where some
scales were kept. I proceeded to weigh, and to my horror found I was
10 st 2 lb! But I rode at 8 st 2 lb in the same year, though it meant a good
deal of severe work.' Long sweating walks were the chief means for
getting down weight in those days, more irksome maybe, but more
healthful than the modern regimen of Turkish baths.

John Osborne took a pleasure in showing me some of his racing
trophies and pictures. A conspicuous object in his parlour is a fine
equestrian group, one of the best of its kind I have seen.

'That is the Warwick Cup of 1862. It represents Sir T. Leigh receiving Charles I at Stoneleigh Abbey, near Kenilworth. It was modelled by Elkingtons, and exhibited at the Great Exhibition. I have good reason for remembering the race. Rapparee, a fine staying Rataplan mare (on whom I had won the Ascot Stakes earlier in the year, beating George Fordham a head on the well-backed Knutsford), was entered for the Warwick Cup. She belonged to my father, and the ground was so hard at the time that she was not sent to the meeting. When I arrived at Warwick, however, a lot of rain fell, and I at once wired to Middleham to that effect, and he was able to send the mare just in time for her to run. Only one turned out against her, and my father gave me the trophy as a memento of our success.'

Another souvenir is the Potter's Plate of 1858, which led Osborne to recall that Alderman Copeland, of Stoke, used to present dinner services and jugs to the winners of certain races at the North Staffordshire meetings. A more modern trophy which adorns old John's sideboard is the cup presented by the York Race Committee on the occasion of the inauguration of the improvements in their course in 1897, when Laughing Girl, owned and trained by Mr Osborne, won the chief event of the spring meeting, the Great Northern Handicap.

Appropriately enough, the most prominent picture in the Breckongill dining room is a painting by Harry Hall of Pretender, on whom, in 1869, John Osborne won the Derby, his only success in thirty-eight rides in the great Epsom race. In the *Romance of the Derby* you may read all about the exciting struggle in which Pero Gomez, undoubtedly unlucky in being somewhat interfered with at Tattenham Corner, succumbed by a head to Pretender. The race was a genuine triumph for Middleham, as, besides being ridden by the local jockey, the winner was trained by Thomas Dawson at Tupgill. Many other good winners came from Tupgill at that time. Previously Bob Johnson trained Beeswing and Nutwith there, and in more modern times came Fred Bates. The stables are now tenanted by Captain N. H. Scott, who has trained some useful horses for Mr Bell-Irving and others, but he, like Colling, temporarily has his string at Newmarket.

Osborne rode Caller Ou once or twice and speaks highly of her prowess and endurance. 'I remember buying one of her yearlings by Adventurer for Sir Robert Jardine for 1,850 guineas, but he did no good. Sir Robert spent a great deal of money in buying bloodstock and on racing generally.'

I suggested that Caller Ou's comparative failure as a broodmare was due to the excessive way in which she was raced – she was brought out on 101 occasions, winning 51 races. Osborne, however, smiled at the suggestion, and expressed the opinion that there is no definite rule.

'Look what some of the mares used to do when races were run in heats. Their hard work did not prevent them from breeding good winners. If we run a horse twice in one week we are told we are overdoing him, but we thought nothing of it years ago. I remember a horse belonging to Mr Jaques who, having won a race at Lancaster, was at once vanned to Goodwood, ran there in the Stewards' Cup, and in the same week won a race of three and a half miles, and the animal was nothing the worse. Where is the owner who would sanction such a programme now?'

In view of the difficulty of comparing the horses of one generation with those of another, Mr Osborne does not care to decide which is the best horse he has seen during his unique career, but he told me Fisherman would have to take very high rank. He mentioned some of the weight-carrying performances of Mr Tom Parr's champion as among the finest things he has known in racing.

Looking round his little picture gallery Osborne pointed out a good portrait of Admiral Rous and another of Mr George Payne – 'both fine sportsmen'. 'There is the late Mr Scrope, of Danby – the Scropes are a very old family. This is Dr Syntax, who won five cups at Preston in successive years. Next to him is The Flying Dutchman, one of the best ever trained at Middleham; and here we have Filho-da-Puta, who ran some famous matches with Sir Joshua. We don't see many sporting matches nowadays. I expect owners are frightened of their horses being beaten and so losing value for stud purposes.'

A picture of the redoubtable Apology shows her to have been a mare of exceptional substance, though by no means a big one. Alongside is a portrait of Mr Launde, the sporting parson who owned her. A likeness of her contemporary Lily Agnes is also on the walls of Breckongill. 'She was a really good mare in training', says Osborne of the dam of Ormonde. 'True, she became a roarer, but that was not until the end of her four-year-old career. I was not certain of it at first, but it became so bad that one foggy morning on the Moor I heard her before I saw her. It was decided to wait until the following spring, when Mr Snarry came, and she then made an undoubted noise, but she won several good races that year.'

Seventy acres of land are attached to Breckongill, of which Osborne lets off about half. The house is prettily situated on the edge of the moor, and the stables are on either side. In taking me to look at his few horses Osborne reminded me of some good animals quartered in these stables in the past, including Charles XII, who won the St Leger after a dead-heat with Euclid, and won the Doncaster Cup on the following Friday.

Never in any sense a betting man, Osborne is still cautious in his modest tilts at the ring. 'I had,' said he, 'twenty-five shillings each way on The Guller when he won the Chester Cup. After the horse had run at Stockton a bookmaker from Thirsk asked me if he would run at Chester. I said "Yes, I think so." He offered me 20's and 5's, saying, "You won't do better." So I had five shillings each way with him, and Mr Crallon also put me on a sovereign each way. When Mynora won the Northumberland Plate I had ten shillings each way on her. A friend said "I can get you 20's, and you had better back her if you fancy the filly." I answered, "The class looks a bit too good for her, but she has some chance, so put me on five shillings each way." I did not see him again until the day of the race, and I then had another five shillings each way.' Breckongill cannot, therefore, be classed among the heavy gambling stables. You cannot be long with John Osborne without appreciating his fine simplicity of character.

I did not leave Middleham without paying a visit to Spigot Lodge. Here The Flying Dutchman was trained. His struggles with Voltigeur form one of the most fascinating chapters in racing history. It was interesting to stand in The Flying Dutchman's box, a roomy compartment which has apparently not been altered since the days when Lord Eglinton's champion stepped from it to do battle at Doncaster and York.

BBR-1917

The Hon. George Lambton

The Hon. George Lambton, who began training in the 'nineties, was probably the best known trainer of his time. Knowledgeable, successful and accessible, he was therefore quoted more often than any other person in his profession. He made history with his views on famous horses and famous people in racing and breeding. The news he made in 1933 was less happy than usual for that was the year he was relieved of his duties by Lord Derby. That he didn't take it 'lying down' is well recorded by the BBR of that year.

FOUR DAYS before the season ended there came from Mr George Lambton the astonishing, because utterly unexpected, news that his long association with the racing interests of Lord Derby was to terminate on December 31st. Two days later Lord Derby announced that next year his horses would be trained by Colledge Leader, and that he had made the change solely because he thought Mr Lambton (who is seventy-three) had reached an age when he ought to be relieved of the burden and anxiety of training so large a stable as that at Stanley House. Mr Lambton demurred to the suggestion that he was getting too old for

The Hon. George Lambton.

his job. He issued the statement: 'I wish to emphasise that I am not retiring and that I shall continue to train as a public trainer as soon as I can obtain a suitable establishment. I shall leave Stanley House, but I hope to remain at Newmarket. If I cannot obtain a suitable establishment at Newmarket, I shall take a place elsewhere.'

Mr Lambton began training in the 'nineties when a serious accident brought his career as a gentleman rider to an end. For fifteen years he had charge of the late Lord Derby's horses and since 1908, those of the present Earl, except during the four seasons 1927–30 when they were trained by Frank Butters under his management. His record as a trainer is a remarkable one. He has prepared winners of nearly every important event in the Calendar, except the Cesarewitch. His classic successes are:

Two Thousand Guineas: Colorado.
The Derby: Sansovino and Hyperion.
The St Leger: Swynford, Keysoe, Tranquil and Hyperion.
One Thousand Guineas: Canyon, Ferry and Tranquil.
The Oaks: Canterbury Pilgrim and Keystone II.

BBR–1933

Memorative Biography of The Hon. George Lambton

George Lambton died at Newmarket on July 23rd, after a longish illness. His brilliant gifts and personality, and even his individuality, were remarkable only inasmuch as he typified, in the twentieth century, a breed of Englishman which has made our country what it is from the day of racing's beginnings. He was eighty-five when he died, having been born in and lived through an age when the Turf was an institution not to be despoiled, but to be enjoyed and graced by those who loved it. If anyone ever loved the Turf it was George Lambton.

Born in 1860, the fifth son of the second Earl of Durham, the Hon. George Lambton was educated at Eton. At school he did not neglect to equip himself with that knowledge of the book of form which forms so important a part of the curriculum of the young Etonian. He rode in his holidays – he had been blooded at the age of seven – and visited Ascot races in his early teens. His studies at Trinity College, Cambridge, cut short by the death of his father, were followed by a spell with Mr Faithful, of Storrington. Apparently, cramming for an entrance to Sandhurst had fewer charms for him than riding with his tutor. He won 'the Storrington Derby' and, as he wrote in his brilliant book, *Men And Horses I have Known*, took nearly all the money in the place.

The young Lambton's early career, however, scarcely belongs to this short review. The winning of his first real race, on Pompeia at Nottingham (October, 1880), his further exploits as an amateur rider, the great company of men and women with whom he rode and raced are all described in his book. Barely may it be mentioned that he rode in five Grand Nationals, won a National Hunt 'Chase (at Sandown Park), the Grand Steeplechase de Paris. In February, 1892, he had a serious fall at Sandown Park. He recovered sufficiently from this accident to win a Bibury Stakes (flat) later in the year, but devoted himself shortly afterwards to the training career which he followed until his death. He took a small yard in St Mary's Square, Newmarket, in 1892, when he started as a trainer with twelve horses.

In 1893 he was invited to train for the 16th Earl of Derby. It was an important year in Mr Lambton's life, it was also a very important year in the history of the British Turf, for Lord Derby, his son (then Lord Stanley, aged twenty-eight) and Mr Lambton between them set deliberately about the task of restoring the fortunes of the Stanley colours and of laying anew the greater foundations of the Knowsley Stud. It happened in that year that Canterbury Pilgrim was born.

At the sale of the Duchess of Montrose's yearlings in 1894 the filly whose subsequent mating with St Simon and John o'Gaunt was to have such an important effect on the present Lord Derby's stud, was bought for 1,800 guineas. Her story is told in Mr Lambton's book, notably of her success in the Oaks (1896), and of her trainer's advice to the owner to send her to stud at the end of her second season. Mr Lambton went abroad for reasons of health in the autumn of 1896 and we need not pursue his history until the year 1903, when 'that beautiful little horse' Chaucer was a three-year-old.

It was then that Lord Derby decided to buy the Sefton Stud Farm and to build the Stanley House Stables – the now world-famous establishment in the Bury Road, Newmarket. A spell of ill luck followed, culminating in a fire in 1908. It was punctuated by the classic victory in 1906 of Keystone II, winner of the Oaks. Nineteen hundred and eight brought triumph and sadness to Stanley House. George Lambton ended the season as the leading trainer of the year, but he lost his best friend and patron in the course of it. Lord Derby died, suddenly, on the Sunday before Ascot week. The great Swynford had been foaled about two months earlier.

The new Earl, now forty-three years old, allowed no gap to occur in the continuity of his stud and stables, although there were temporary reductions in both establishments. Vacant boxes were filled with yearlings sent by Lord Wolverton, Lord D'Abernon (then Sir Edgar Vincent), and Mr Arthur James. It might be of interest here to recall the classic triumphs for which Mr Lambton was responsible during his career as a trainer, even if the period stretches beyond the point so far reached in this brief sketch:

Two Thousand Guineas – Colorado (1926).
One Thousand Guineas – Canyon (1916), Ferry (1918), Tranquil (1923). Also Lord D'Abernon's Diadem (1917).
Derby – Sansovino (1924), Hyperion (1933).
Oaks – Canterbury Pilgrim (1886), Keystone (1906).
St Leger – Swynford (1910), Keysoe (1919), Tranquil (1923), Hyperion (1933).

It need hardly be mentioned that, interspersed among these horses, Mr

Lambton trained the winners of nearly every important race in the *Calendar*. His record of successes in Liverpool alone is such that it may never again be approached. One has only to instance names like Stedfast, Bridge of Canny, Glasconbury, Spithead, Phalaris and his sons Pharos, Caerleon, and, finally, these great mares Diadem and Selene to recall the greatness of the brilliant trainer, to pay tribute to whom the present writer's pen is all too inadequate. Nor can there be many men who were so happy and privileged in their friendships and acquaintances, whether kings and princes or jockeys and stable lads. Among those he trained for alone, apart from the Stanleys, were his brothers – Lord Durham and Brigadier Charles Lambton – Lord Wolverton, Lord D'Abernon, Mr and Mrs Arthur James, Lord Queenborough, Mr Raphael and, at different times, Sir Abe Bailey, Major 'Buck' Barclay,. the Duke of Portland, Major McCalmont and, for a spell, M. Marcel Boussac.

As long ago as 1906 Mr Lambton was our leading trainer. He filled that honoured and arduous position again in 1911 and in 1912. It will be noted that he prepared no fewer than thirteen winners of classic races.

In Sansovino's year, 1924, the great trainer was second in the winning list among his confrères, with £48,156 won in stakes. In 1926 he was third, for although Colorado had won the Guineas, he had failed in the Derby and also at Ascot. Lord Derby then arranged for Mr Frank Butters to take over at Stanley House, with Mr Lambton remaining as manager. Nineteen thirty-one saw Mr Lambton once again in charge, with forty horses in the yard, among them Caerleon (4 yrs), Salmon Leap (4 yrs), the filly Fara and a useful, but not outstanding, set of juveniles. At the end of the year a chestnut yearling colt by Gainsborough out of Selene joined the stable. Lord Derby had named him Hyperion.

It follows that, at the end of the season 1933, Lord Derby, owner of Hyperion, once again occupied the proud position of the chief winning owner; his trainer was third in the list. Lambton had trained twenty-three winners of thirty-five races, including, incidentally, his own filly Dorigen, who had won the Lincolnshire Handicap.

George Lambton left Stanley House in 1933, but, far from retiring, emerged in the spring of 1934 with a string of eleven horses. In the following season he had forty-five including the aged Pricket and that wonderful mare Corrida, then a three-year-old. His subsequent successes, with all kinds of horses, were evidence of his versatility, as well as of his marvellous gift for training. The last winner saddled under his direction was the very fast, four-year-old Golden Cloud, who won the

Horningsea Handicap on the July Course at Newmarket on June 9th. It was appropriate that Michael Beary rode him in Mr Lambton's own colours – light blue, brown cap.

Mr Lambton was always interested in breeding. The records from 1920 to 1945 reveal that at his Moreton Stud, Newmarket (where Mr Jinks stood for a while), Mr Lambton bred the winners of 107 flat races and stakes value £36,513.

In 1943 he was joint breeder of a chestnut yearling filly by Hyperion out of Celestial Way by Fairway, which, coming from the Moreton Stud, was sold at Newmarket for 8,000 guineas.

Celestial Way was the daughter of a remarkable mare, owned all her life by Mr Lambton – Princess Sublime (1921) by King William. She produced ten winners. They won forty-two races. The best was Light o' Love (by Pharos), sixteen races in seven seasons. He became a successful sire on the Continent. The others were Peace Pact, Lantern, Sublime Prince, Immortal Hour (the very last foal sired by Phalaris), Celestial Way, Litlun, Fairchance, Prince Tetra and Exaltation. All these were bred by Mr Lambton.

From the mare Wandering Maid he bred Bunker and Joyce W., the winners of ten races and £5,627. From Wife of Bath he bred Mr Clever (won two races, £1,212, in 1925, and then went to India).

The latest winners from his stud were Golden Girl and Orsino in 1944 and in 1945 the smart two-year-old Vilmorin. Orsino won again this year and then was exported to the US.

It must be recorded that Mr G. Lambton was one of the most ardent partisans of the Thoroughbred Breeders Association. He became a Member of the Council of the Association in 1921.

The Thoroughbred Breeders' Association's first President was Lord D'Abernon, for whom Mr Lambton was then training. Mr Lambton was very prominent and enthusiastic in assisting to found the TBA.

Possessing a lively appreciation of his expert judgment of the possibilities of a thoroughbred, when the Aga Khan decided to race on an extensive scale in England it was Mr Lambton (in conjunction with Mr R. C. Dawson, who was to train them), who was commissioned to buy yearlings in the sales. Thus were laid solid foundations of the stable and studs which have produced such an amazing number of winners of classic races and all the most important Stakes in the *Calendar*.

A filly in the care of Mr Lambton in 1905 merits some attention. Her name was Gemma. She was a sister to Vedas, who won the Two Thousand Guineas.

Gemma, in Lord Derby's colours (though Lady Meux bred the filly), won the Sandown Park Stud Produce Stakes and later the Lavant Stakes at Goodwood. That was the race with which the tragedy of Black Arrow is always remembered.

Next year Gemma, whose disposition was far from placid, raced nine times without being placed.

In 1908 she was barren. Then Gemma, covered by Carbine, went to France that year. Her foal was no use. Then she was barren. However, in 1911 came her last foal. It was a bay colt by the bad-legged Prestige. That colt was Sardanapale, the best horse in Europe in 1914. Sardanapale became one of the greatest stallions ever known in France.

George Lambton's life would make a subject for many books were the historian sufficiently diligent to write of his many adventures, his feats of riding and training and of his experiences on the Turf. The present writer remembers him as a man of great charm, with his quizzical smile, the tilted hat and his elegant figure – he was a tremendous dandy. It is not so easy to think of him in his last days. Always the memory of him is of a man who seemed never to grow old. His friends and admirers were legion. Most of his stable hands at any time would willingly have died for him. He was a very wonderful man, a brilliant judge of horses and a great trainer.

Two days before the death of Mr Lambton, it was officially announced that he had relinquished his licence to train, to be succeeded by his son, Edward, who had not long since received his demobilisation papers after completing his service with the Royal Horse Guards. Edward Lambton forthwith assumed the mastership of the Kremlin House Stables, Newmarket. Edward Lambton – 'Teddy', of course, to his friends – and his mother, The Hon. Cecily Lambton, continue to keep the esteem and affection of the very wide circle of their friends, and, may it be hoped, will enjoy a very long spell of success and fortune on the Turf to which 'the Honourable George' was so great an ornament.

BBR-1945

Recollections of a Trainer – Felix Leach

One of the most commendable features of the BBR was its policy to reprint articles of especial merit from other publications. Because of the inherent quality of the material in the BBR, this was a manifest compliment to those publications and the authors so used. One such, 'Recollections of a Trainer', written originally by Willie Standring

('Warren Hill' of the Sporting Life*), appeared in the* BBR *of 1937.*

The 'Recollections' resulted from a conversation with trainer Felix Leach whose association with racing began the day he first set eyes on St Simon. It was Emerson who said: 'Only so much do I know as I have lived.' Well, that qualified Mr Leach as a man of great knowledge in racing. He was 'the right-hand man' for two of England's greatest trainers, Mathew Dawson, who gave Mr Leach his first job as a youngster, and Richard Marsh. His experiences with these gentlemen and such famous horses at St Simon, Ladas and Persimmon, among many others, make for the kind of reading that will for ever be treasured by those who appreciate the intimate episodes in the history of racing whenever and wherever they took place.

THE STORY begins with a Lancashire lad, not much advanced in his teens, who was about to return home, much to his regret, after a holiday spent at Newmarket with his elder brother, who had a number of years previously established a veterinary practice in a small way at the Turf headquarters. The bag had been packed ready for the mid-day train, but the boy could not resist the idea of having one more look at the Heath and the horses at work.

Walking along, he came across an old gentleman searching on the ground for something apparently lost, and asked if he could help. Presently some horses galloped past, and the boy's attention was attracted to one above the rest.

'Excuse me, sir,' he asked. 'Would you know what that is?'

'Oh!' was the reply. 'That horse is called St Simon.'

In a little while it was the old gentleman's turn to question, and a brief conversation ran on these lines:

'H'm! You seem to like horses?'

'I do that, sir.'

'Well, St Simon is in my stable. Would you like to come and live with me and my horses?'

'I would that, sir.'

'Where do you come from?'

'Wigan, sir.'

'Is that as nice a place as Newmarket?'

'No, sir.'

And so, having told all about himself and his relations, the boy was bidden to ask his brother to 'come round and see me tonight,' and the end of it all was that he did not go back to Wigan. Nor has Felix Leach, now one of Newmarket's bright lights, ever wanted to do so since. He was the young Heath wanderer on this morning, which was to prove such an eventful one for him. His brother was the late Mr E. H. Leach, who became one of the heads of his profession in the town. The 'old gentleman' was the late Mathew Dawson, leading trainer of his time.

And as the one wanderer from the north prospered, so did the other after many years of patient devotion to a labour of love, subsequently becoming 'old Matt's' right-hand man; then, for a spell, being associated in a like capacity with the late Richard Marsh; eventually returning to his former master as junior partner; and, after the great man's death, setting up as a trainer on his own account.

Even an incomplete narration of incidents in the colourful life which Felix Leach has spent amongst thoroughbreds would fill many pages of the *Review*. As might be imagined St Simon was the one object of his affectionate curiosity in early days in stables.

'His box was on the other side of the yard, but I often slipped over to peep in and see him being "dressed over" by the still living Charlie Fordham, who had a rare old handful with him, so full of life was the horse. "They talk about Job and patience," one day said Fordham, who was sweating as much as was his charge, "but Job never done St Simon".'

The subject of our sketch has one particularly vivid recollection of his first favourite winning the Ascot Cup. There were only five runners, but one of them was the older Tristan, also a celebrity of the period, although 'Matt's' confidence in St Simon was such that Wood, who rode him, was instructed to be easy and not win by more than two lengths. To the old man's consternation, St Simon galloped right away from the others at the distance. The explanation was that the jockey could not hold him. Tristan, according to Wood, was going so well at the distance that he gave his mount just one touch with the spurs, whereupon St Simon bounded away, and the two lengths' victory, as arranged, was extended to twenty lengths. And Tristan had been winner of, amongst other notable events, the Ascot Gold Cup and the Hardwicke Stakes at Ascot the previous year, by way of showing what a fine all-rounder he was. He was supposedly as good as ever when he met St Simon at Ascot, although he was twice the latter's age.

Old stagers will readily recall what influence for the good of the Turf was exercised by these two horses who were concerned with the Ascot Cup race of 1884. Younger enthusiasts will also be aware that St Simon, bought by Mathew Dawson for 1,600 guineas, made the racing and stud fortunes of the Duke of Portland. But it may be less generally known that the alliance of Tristan with Pilgrimage produced Canterbury Pilgrim, who, purchased for 1,800 guineas, was the founder of Lord Derby's Stud, and its grand array of winners.

At an interval of several years there came Ladas into Mathew Dawson's stable. Leach described him as 'just about as bonny a horse as you could wish to set eyes on, with action such that he never seemed to touch the ground'. But it was recognised also, in the Ladas camp, that the previous season's three-year-old crack, Isinglass, was the stouter. The older horse was sluggish, but more equably tempered. Ladas was somewhat of a hothouse product, brilliant, but highly strung and delicate by comparison.

It was through Ladas that Felix Leach was brought into close contact, on occasions, with the colt's owner, the late Lord Rosebery, who, after having taken only a passive part in racing for a lengthy period, persuaded 'old Matt,' who had been on the point of retiring, to train his horses, and the future Derby winner was one of them.

Ladas, too, was an especial favourite with his regular jockey, the late John Watts, and the latter, in turn, was immensely liked by the young man who was now the trainer's able lieutenant. According to Leach:

'Watts was a horseman as well as a jockey; quiet, unassuming, but a treat to listen to, although he never said much, and even at home, spoke little of the winners he might have ridden. But I had it from Mrs Watts, that after he had won on Ladas for the first time, when the colt was a two-year-old, he was talkative at the tea-table, and predicted the Derby triumph of the following season.

'And that reminds me of an occasion when the great horseman stood in awe of the great politician when the former was late to keep a riding appointment on the Heath. "John Watts," said his lordship sternly, "you're the only man who has ever kept the Prime Minister of England waiting."'

The veteran trainer was too ill to see Ladas run for the Two Thousand, but he anticipated the news which his trusty young henchman brought to the bedside by simply asking, as soon as the sickroom door was opened, 'How far did he win?' And Leach, by the way, holds no stronger opinion concerning the horses with which he has been connected than that Ladas would have followed suit with the greater Isinglass, and been a 'triple crowner,' could Watts, who was claimed under the Kingsclere retainer to ride Matchbox, have taken the mount in the St Leger.

Tommy Loates was chosen as the jockey for Ladas at Doncaster, and Loates, short in the leg, and riding only a few pounds above 7 st, had not fancied the engagement very much after morning work on the Moor. In the race Ladas again took charge and, although once more finishing in front of Matchbox, had run himself out before the judge was reached, and was caught and just beaten by the Kingsclere outsider, Throstle.

Ladas. J. Watts up, Felix Leach at head, and Matt Dawson.

That was the St Leger of which the late John Porter said that, after having backed his chief hope, Matchbox, in a mild way, and saved on Ladas, he 'nearly fell off the stand when he saw Throstle winning'.

Incidents immediately leading up to the Derby victory of Ladas, and his journey to Epsom on the day preceding the race, have probably been narrated before, but will bear re-telling, and so we call upon the stable's head man, or rather the trainer's confidential associate, as Leach was at the time, for some details:

'Ladas was a hot favourite, there appearing to be only Matchbox, whom he had beaten comfortably in the Two Thousand, as a danger. But for some time before the race Lord Rosebery had received anonymous letters hinting at "nobbling", and so we made travelling arrangements unknown to all outside the stable save the railway company. The usual horse-box train from Newmarket was due to leave somewhere about six o'clock, but Ladas and a travelling companion went by an "extra special" two hours before, and we were at Epsom well in advance of breakfast time. Yet, at the station there, some people had got to know of our arrival, and no sooner had we pulled up than one big chap, with a ferocious-looking face and moustachios to match, opened the carriage door, saying he would take charge. I didn't like things, however, and took charge of him, with a hand on one wing of his "tash", and asked what was doing; but it turned out that he was one of Lord Rosebery's specially engaged detectives, and there were mutual explanations and apologies. And so to his lordship's place, The Durdans, where Ladas was being stabled. In the grounds, there approached two persons on foot accompanied by a terrier, which left them and came on barking at us. The next thing was my brigand-faced detective friend bellowing out, "Pick that damned dog up!" And it was the owner of Ladas, who was one of the two pedestrians, who did so. That was the only time I saw the Prime Minister actually laugh.'

Having had much to do with one Derby winner, Felix Leach subsequently became closely associated with another, Persimmon, for our energetic and capable young friend of the period migrated to Egerton House when Mathew Dawson's health no longer permitted him to keep stables in the grand style, and Leach was with Richard Marsh until 'old Matt' desired him back to look after a few horses with which the veteran still interested himself just prior to his death in 1897.

'There was not much between Persimmon and Thais in the home gallops, and so we reckoned on scoring the "double" at Epsom, although recognising that St Frusquin would want some beating in the Derby. Persimmon nearly missed the special train the day before. Nearly all Dullingham villagers were at the station, where Egerton House had its own siding, to see him off, and it seemed as though every man jack flew at Richard Marsh's offer of a sovereign a head to help get the horse in his box, as Persimmon, for quite a time, was like a mule. Yet when he was inside after a shove mightier than the rest, he just looked at the crowd as much as to say, "Thank you for nothing."

'I had to stay at Egerton on Derby day, but got permission to go to the Oaks to see Thais, and found her nearly everything she shouldn't have been on the morning of the race – sweating, fretting, off her feed, and thoroughly dejected. And so we gave up hope until we heard that Canterbury Pilgrim, whom we most feared, was much in the same way. But she was too good for my favourite, though she pressed close to Thais and hampered her a little.'

It is appropriate, at this juncture, that we should mention that Richard Marsh wrote in his book, published in 1925, when referring to the history of Egerton House and its horses of the previous decade: 'I had the good fortune, at that time, to have as head man Felix Leach.' But Marsh's head man of the 'nineties was thinking of his future, and after having answered a call back from his old master, Mathew Dawson, who made him partner in the Exning stable, and actually persuaded the authorities to grant the young 'un a trainer's licence, 'F. L.' found himself with less than half-a-dozen horses at the veteran's death.

It was the kindly offices of Lord Marcus Beresford, with whom Leach had so frequently come in contact while at Egerton, that gave the eager aspirant the first real footing on the ladder. There came, by way of

'Marky', as the manager of the Royal racing stud was affectionately named, an introduction to Mr H. J. King, just back from South Africa, and the purchase for the mining magnate of a colt of the name of Wild Irishman, which was soon a winner, and so began the good work. There followed, as patrons of the newly established stable, the Americans, Messrs Keene, but it was Mr King who was the steadfast one, with Orchid that gentleman's first noteworthy money-spinner. And so, with other enthusiasts sending horses, Graham Place stable rose to one of importance in the town, its boxes always full, its winners regularly returning a high percentage. Even now, although its master is much more concerned with his stud and farm interests, he can find time to look after just a few racers, and Carnival Boy's record last season tells its own tale.

Orpheus was the best horse which was housed at Graham Place. He was no more of a stayer than was his Derby-winning sire, Orby, but the latter had the luck at Epsom, whereas Orpheus got in the wars, and was carried out very wide at Tattenham Corner. He could outpace Spion Kop over shorter cuts, but in after life his best course was round about ten furlongs, at which he beat all comers two years in succession, while as a handicap weight-carrier, probably only Wychwood Abbot's name has been mentioned during more recent times in the same breath.

A tremendous array of winners from Felix Leach's stable has included nearly every species of racer, hurdling platers not excepted. On three occasions he carried off the Goodwood Cup, a record favourably comparing with that of his former master, Richard Marsh, who, for a time, 'farmed' that particular race. And Leach saddled its most sensational winner, Magic, who, at a big difference in the weights, just held off the mighty Bayardo.

While 'F. L.' always trained on the lines which Mathew Dawson and Marsh laid down, he was one of the first to 'bow' to the style of jockeyship introduced from America in the shape of the forward seat. Let him tell how he was so early converted:

'My brother James at Bolton worked this thing out, with a view to obtaining a definite idea as to the advantage gained by the American style of riding, and I at once saw the "drift" of his reckoning.

'He took Sloan's method of guidance, and sent me a table of figures showing what poundage was saved by Sloan's horse if running at the rate of a mile in even only 1 m 50 sec. The figures showed that even with the wind hardly perceptible, there was a saving, so how much more when the horses were running into a head wind of varying strength?

'With a following breeze the English style, generally speaking, enabled the English jockeys to hold their own; but against the wind, those who persisted in the old style of riding were usually at a great disadvantage. And so, wherever possible, I engaged either Americans or "converts" amongst the home jockeys. Herbert Jones was the one who seemed to strike the happy medium, and he rode many winners for me.'

Later Mr Leach put his three sons through stables, each serving an apprenticeship, and being treated on all fours with the rest of the lads, and each being brought up in the American school of riding, with changed mounts from day to day, orders being to make the running one morning and to play a waiting game the next day. Very successful in the saddle until increasing weight became the trouble, each of the three – the late Felix, Jack, and Henry (better known as 'Chubb', and so christened, we believe, by the American trainer, Andrew Joyner, who used to watch them regularly and encourage them) – subsequently took to training as to the manner born, and again the results have spoken of a wonderful family. 'And,' says the founder, 'to the lad who loves horses, an apprentice's life is a joyous one.'

If there is in being such a body as the Society for the Preservation of Historic Landmarks, Mr Leach qualified for a Fellowship, for did he not save the Queen Anne's Betting Post from probable – nay, almost certain – vandalism? This wooden structure is in the 'aged' class indeed; a relic of the eighteenth century, which, when Newmarket racecourse and its environment were just open heath with no public stand and no Tattersall's, marked one of the spots that was the rendezvous of aristocrat and commoner, and occasionally that of Royalty, all attracted for the purpose of wagering? According to a painting by the caricaturist Thomas Rowlandson of the scene conjured up in the artist's mind of what happened nearly a hundred and fifty years ago, the proceedings had a resemblance to those at a foreign Bourse at 'High Chance', save that everyone was on horseback.

The Red Post under notice will be well remembered by many present-day visitors to the races at Newmarket, standing as a weather-beaten sentinel on that side of the Heath which offers the opportunity of a breezy walk to the Rowley Mile stands, and over part of which the Cambridgeshire was formerly run. Strangers to sport at the Turf head-quarters were taught to regard it with reverence. 'Regulars' either patted it or rubbed a banknote or coin against it for luck on the way to the meetings. When repairs were necessary they were effected with almost a watchmaker's deftness. One morning, however, something like thirty years ago, the structure – which was as much a signpost on the old Criterion course as is the railed-off clump known as 'The Bushes' on the Rowley Mile – was found smeared with vermilion paint, possibly the work of some Cambridge undergraduates who had found its supposed 'mascot' properties to be all rubbish. It was then that Mr Leach, probably thinking that the next change might be to a heap of firewood, obtained permission to secure it, and it is to be found, in good preservation, behind his residence at Graham Place, a stone's throw from where it originally stood.

When I cast back to the prodigious number of long-priced winners which the founder of Graham Place used to turn out, I get wishing that Felix Leach could have his day over again, in a whole-time training capacity. And that reminds me that he once set out to try to win a Lincolnshire Handicap with a horse whose trouble was that of having been given too little weight. This was Cerisier, who, ridden by an apprentice, Bott, at 6 st 1 lb, finished just behind the placed group. Cerisier then belonged to Lord Marcus Beresford, who soon afterwards accepted an offer of £1,000 from Lord Westbury for the horse. He tried again in the City and Suburban, and was third to Robert le Diable and Dean Swift, this 'ragged urchin' of a three-year-old, as he was at the time, finishing up 'from nowhere'. In the 'Jubilee', Cerisier improved to second, Ypsilanti, the previous year's winner, being in the way. His next effort was in a £1,000 race at Haydock. Trigg was engaged, a good-sized commission went out, and it looked like staying out! Cerisier, who was not an amiable sort at the post, took charge at the start and lost the best part of a dozen lengths, but hard riding achieved the desired result. At the fourth time of asking, then, during a very few weeks, Cerisier's luck changed, and Lord Westbury thus got the horse for nothing, plus a nice stake.

He marked his appreciation of Leach's handiwork by presenting him with oil paintings, formerly the property of the famous John Gully, of that celebrity's Pyrrhus the First and Mendicant, respectively winners of the Derby and the Oaks in 1846. The 10 per cent bonus to trainers was not the fashion in Cerisier's time.   BBR–1937

Fred Darling's Training Achievements in 1940 and 1941

When Fred Darling trained both the New Derby winner Owen Tudor and the New Oaks victress Commotion in 1941, it gave the BBR's correspondent justification for 'delving into the subsequent careers of some of the classic winners in the same season prepared by the same trainer'. There is some wonderful history here involving such

memorable trainers as John Porter (whose record seven Derbys was
then equalled by Fred Darling), Alec Taylor and Roger Peck.

FRED DARLING is again the leading trainer in 1941, as he was in 1940.
He previously headed the list of winning trainers in 1926 (when he
trained the winners of £63,095), and also in 1933, with the winners of
£44,279. He was second in the list of successful trainers six times between
1925 and 1938.

Taking his career in 1907 to 1909, and again from 1920 to 1941,
inclusive, Fred Darling's record as a trainer in England reads:

Flat Races Won	1,020
Stakes Won	£720,372

The third son of the late Mr Sam Darling, who trained Galtee More and
Ard Patrick, both winners of the Derby, Fred Darling commenced his
brilliant career in this country in 1907. That year he won eight races. His
first winner was at Sandown Park, on July 20th, 1907. This was Li
Hung, winner of the Warren Handicap. Darling proceeded to win the
very next race with Nancy Lee. In August he won a race with Geyser.
That colt, by Merman, won again at Lingfield. In between came
victories by Gold Sand, Nancy Lee (again), Shy Lad and French Doll.
Those were his six winners of £1,291. That year he bought, on behalf of
Mrs Langtry, the colt Yentoi. The next season Darling trained Yentoi to
win handicaps at Sandown, Windsor and Folkestone. Then he went to
Doncaster to take the Rufford Abbey, prior to winning the Cesarewitch.
The record for 1908 reads: twenty-six races won, value £5,735. In 1909
he prepared the winners of fifteen races, £3,044. From 1907 to 1909,
inclusive, he was training at Newmarket.

A year later Fred Darling was training for the eminently successful
and powerful Weinberg stable in Germany. That was from 1910 to
1912. By 1913 he had become private trainer to Prince Hohenlohe
Oehringen. There he remained until he returned to England.

Horses trained by Fred Darling in Germany won the equivalent of
about £40,000 each of two succeeding years. Among the best horses in
his charge were Fervor (who became a highly successful stallion), Letizia
(Oaks winner), for the Weinbergs, while for Prince Hohenlohe the big
winners were Landluft, Laudanum and Rafael.

He took over his father's place, Beckhampton, in 1914. That year he
purchased Hurry On for 500 guineas as a yearling at Newmarket. That
famous horse was trained by Fred Darling in 1916, when he was
unbeaten. Naturally, the outbreak of war caused great dislocation of

plans. Fred Darling joined HM Forces in 1916, when Hurry On had finished racing. When he obtained his Commission he was posted to the 9th Lancers, remaining with that Regiment for the duration of the war.

As a jockey, Fred Darling first rode in this country in 1901. He had twenty-five mounts, winning four races. As a record his first winner was Happy Bird, in a two-year-old Plate at Kempton Park, on May 9th. The

F. Darling.

next day he won an Apprentice Plate on Sinopi. A fortnight later, at Salisbury, for his brother, he rode Miss Pac, who won a Selling Race on the 24th. Twenty-four hours later he was successful again on Uncle Sol. The other three winners were trained by his father. Thus Fred Darling's riding triumphs in this country were crowned in a comparatively few days. Darling has also ridden winners in Jamaica, and visited many different countries to view their racing conditions.

It was in 1920 that Fred Darling's name again appeared in the list of successful trainers. From that time he has greatly added to the world-wide fame of Beckhampton, he having purchased the whole establishment after the death of his father on May 16th, 1921.

In addition to Galtee More and Ard Patrick, other classic winners trained at Beckhampton by Fred Darling's father were Wildfowler (St Leger), Slieve Gallion (Two Thousand Guineas), and Cap and Bells II (the Oaks).

Owen Tudor, when he won at Newmarket last June, enabled Fred Darling to equal John Porter's unique record, who trained seven winners of the Derby at Kingsclere. They were: 1868, Blye Gown; 1882, Shotover; 1883, St Blaise; 1886, Ormonde; 1890, Sainfoin; 1891, Common; 1899, Flying Fox.

Those from Beckhampton are: 1922, Captain Cuttle; 1925, Manna; 1926, Coronach; 1931, Cameronian; 1938, Bois Roussel; 1940, Pont l'Eveque; 1941, Owen Tudor.

When Fred Darling trained the Derby and the Oaks winners this season the word 'record' was again used loosely. It was a fine, but by no means an exceptional achievement. During the period of the last war Mr Alec Taylor, in 1918, trained Gainsborough and My Dear, having in 1917 prepared Gay Crusader and Sunny Jane. Those successes were also at Newmarket. Mr Taylor, however, in 1910 trained the Derby and the Oaks winners at Epsom in Lemberg and Rosedrop. Mr R. C. Dawson was the trainer of Fifinella, who won the New Derby and the New Oaks in 1916.

The late John Porter, in 1882, was responsible for the filly Shotover, the Derby winner; two days later he trained Geheimniss, the Oaks winner. Shotover, though entered in the Oaks, did not run because she was inferior to Geheimniss. To have secured both the great Epsom classics for colts and fillies, *with fillies*, is most probably unique, for at that time Shotover was only the third filly to win the Derby, though Eleanor in 1801, and Blink Bonny, 1857, had both won the Derby before capturing the Oaks.

In this connection a reference should be made to the late Robert Peck.

He trained Doncaster, the Derby winner of 1873, and from his stable came Marie Stuart to win the Oaks forty-eight hours later. The filly and colt ran in the St Leger, when Doncaster was beaten a head.

Curiously, some of these dual winners mentioned appear to have exerted profound and widespread influence upon bloodstock breeding, especially the colt and filly last named. Doncaster was the sire of Bend Or, in particular, and he was the grandsire of Cyllene, which means Polymelus, Phalaris, Pharos and Fairway. Another branch, through Kendal, led to Bachelor's Double. In passing it may be noted, Marie Stuart became the grandam of that high-class mare, Merry Gal. She produced White Eagle. He sired Blanche, the dam of that exceptionally successful stallion, Blandford.

It is worthy of mention that Blink Bonny produced a Derby winner in Blair Athol, though she had only three foals ere she died. Blair Athol was the leading stallion in 1872, 1873, 1875 and 1877. His half-sister, Borealis, is the fourth dam of Galicia, and she was the dam of Bayardo and Lemberg. The former, of course, is the sire of Gainsborough.

These facts, though somewhat apart from the subject of our notes, would appear amply to justify delving into the subsequent careers of some of the classic winners in the same season, prepared by the same trainer.

Apart from his seven Derby winners, Fred Darling has trained Hurry On, (St Leger, 1916), Coronach (St Leger, 1926), Manna, Cameronian, and Pasch, all winners of the Two Thousand Guineas, as well as Four Course, who won the One Thousand Guineas in 1931.

BBR–1941

Memorative Biography of Alec Taylor

The English Turf of the twentieth century knew no more successful trainer than Alexander (Young Alec) Taylor who died in 1943 at the age of eighty-one. He was the leading trainer on twelve occasions – seven years in a row from 1917 through 1923. Horses in his stable at one time or another included the legendary filly Sceptre, Triple Crown winner Gainsborough and such other classic winners as Bayardo, Lemberg, Gay Crusader, Craig an Eran and Book Law. Included in the Review's *Memorative Biography is a rundown of the more notable horses he trained along with their most important victories. It is hard to imagine one man having had his hands on so many superior performers, many of whom have left an enduring influence on the breed.*

ALEC TAYLOR, the celebrated Master of Manton, died at his home, The Grange, Thorpe, nr. Chertsey, Surrey, on January 28th, 1943; he was in his eighty-first year. His death marked a break in the Manton tradition established by his father and grandfather before him. It was a good, solid tradition, which others, contemporary with the Taylors, had built up. John Porter and Mathew Dawson belonged to it in common with other great figures of the second half of the last century.

Alexander Taylor, known in his early days as 'Young Alec', was the younger son of 'Old Alec'. Taylor, who, during a long and successful career as a trainer, trained Sefton to win the Derby of 1878 for W. S. Crawfurd. 'Old Alec' died in 1894 and left the already very considerable Manton property to Alec and his elder half-brother, Tom. The two brothers ran in harness until 1902, after which date 'Young Alec' assumed the entire charge of the property.

Alec Taylor seemed to assume all the virtues of the somewhat severe tradition into which he succeeded. His father was greatly respected but he appears to have been very hard on his horses. It was always said, for example, that the Manton yearlings were always galloped a couple of miles just before Christmas to see if they had any racing merit.

Alec Junior did not hold completely with his father's methods, although he respected his knowledge, judgment and especially his stable craft. The new Master of Manton took the view that horses were babies until they began to reach their third year. He never spoiled them – in fact he always found plenty for them to do – but neither did he force them. He was extraordinarily patient and, it has been said, refused to hasten the preparation of Bayardo for the Derby rather than prejudice his later career. His reward was the winning of the Eclipse Stakes, a little later, and the St Leger. This is only one example of the patience he always showed; the man who would not spoil a good colt on the off-chance of his running well in the Derby was not the sort of man to hurry any horse if he thought it would prejudice its future.

Taylor was fortunate in his patrons. Most of them were rich men and all of them seemed to be of the type most desired by trainers as owners. The majority of them bred their own horses and sent them to Manton to be trained according to their individual capacities. They did not expect sows' ears to be turned into silken purses, nor backward yearlings to be forced for two-year-old sprints. On the other hand, although Manton specialised in turning out winners of the classic type, it did not disdain the handicap race if the race and other conditions happened to fit the horse. Taylor won practically every important event in the calendar; the Cambridgeshire was one of the very few that evaded him.

Alec Taylor.

His owners included Lady James Douglas, Lord Astor, Sir William Bass, Mr Calmann, Mr W. M. Cazalet, Mr A. R. Cox, Mr W. M. G. Singer, Mr Somerville Tattersall and Mr Reid Walker. His association with Robert Sievier was confined to a very brief exchange of a letter and a telegram when Sceptre entered the stable in the spring of 1903. She was then, of course, the property of Sir William Bass, then Mr William Bass. Sievier once told the writer in his usual colourful style that, after Sceptre had arrived at Manton, Taylor wrote to him enquiring how she should be trained. 'Treat her like a selling plater' wired back the genial Robert.

The partnership with his elder brother was not particularly success-ful and when Tom Taylor retired in 1902 – he died two years later – 'Young Alec' assumed the full responsibility of the Manton establish-ment. From that time onwards Manton entered into a period of continued prosperity, as the following table sets out to show.

So many notable horses were trained by Taylor that it is only possible, in the space available, to give the records of the more important ones. They are, however, set out in detail inasmuch as they really constitute the history of Alec Taylor's great career as a trainer. The name of the redoubtable Sceptre is included, as she joined the stable in the Spring of 1903. Classic winners are shown in capitals.

1903 – SCEPTRE (Hardwicke Stakes, Jockey Club Stakes, Duke of York Stakes); Grey Tick (Cesarewitch).
1905 – CHALLACOMBE (St Leger).
1906 – Sancy (P. of Wales's Stakes); Gold Riach (Chesterfield Cup).
1907 – Sancy (Rous Memorial, Ascot, Jockey Club Stakes); Torpoint (Queen Alexandra Stakes).
1908 – Bayardo (New Stakes, Nat. Breeders' Stakes, Middle Park Stakes, Dewhurst Stakes, Richmond Stakes); Torpoint (Queen Alexandra Stakes).
1909 – BAYARDO (Prince of Wales's Stakes, Eclipse, Champion and St Leger Stakes); Lemberg (New Stakes, Chesterfield, Middle Park and Dewhurst Stakes).
1910 – LEMBERG (The Derby, Jockey Club Stakes); ROSEDROP (The Oaks, Gt Yorkshire Stakes); Elizabetta (Chester Cup, Northumberland Plate).
1911 – Lemberg (Coronation Cup, Doncaster Cup).
1912 – Aleppo (Jockey Club Cup).
1913 – Kennymore (Dewhurst Stakes); Aleppo (Jockey Club Cup).
1914 – KENNYMORE (Craven Stakes, Two Thousand Guineas); Aleppo (Chester Cup and Ascot Gold Cup).
1915 – St Eloi (Newmarket October Handicap).
1916 – Gay Crusader (Criterion Stakes); St Eloi (Newmarket October Handicap).
1917 – GAY CRUSADER (Two Thousand Guineas, Derby, Newmarket Gold Cup, St Leger and Champion Stakes); SUNNY JANE (The Oaks); My Dear (Dewhurst Stakes); Haki (Newmarket October Handicap).
1918 – GAINSBOROUGH (Two Thousand Guineas, Derby, Newmarket Gold Cup); Buchan (July Stakes, Chesterfield Stakes); MY DEAR (The Oaks and Champion Stakes); Air Raid (Cesarewitch).
1919 – Buchan (Craven Stakes, Princess of Wales's, Eclipse and Champion Stakes); Haki (Ascot Stakes, Goodwood Stakes, Doncaster Cup); BAYUDA (The Oaks); My Dear (Liverpool Autumn Cup); Flying Spear (Coronation Stakes).
1920 – Buchan (Eclipse Stakes and Doncaster Cup): Lemonora (Champagne Stakes); Pompadour (Imperial Produce Stakes); Manilardo (Coronation Cup); Kentish Cob (Ascot Gold Vase); Haki (Queen Alexandra Stakes); Braishfield (Gt Yorkshire Stakes).
1921 – CRAIG AN ERAN (Two Thousand Guineas and Eclipse Stakes); Lemonora (Newmarket Stakes and Grand Prix); LOVE IN IDLENESS (The Oaks).

1922 – Two Step (Portland Handicap); POGROM (The Oaks and Coronation Stakes); Flamboyant (Goodwood Cup); Leighon Tor (Gt Foal Stakes, Newmarket); Air Balloon (Queen Alexandra Stakes).

1923 – Saltash (Eclipse Stakes); Blue Lake (Criterion Stakes); Light Hand (Craven Stakes).

1924 – Picaroon (Imperial Produce Stakes and Middle Park Plate); St Germans (Craven Stakes); Hurstwood (Newmarket Stakes); Daimyo (Gt Yorkshire Handicap); Saucy Sue (Criterion Stakes).

1925 – Caravel (Rous Memorial Stakes); Picaroon (Craven Stakes, Gt Foal Stakes, Newmarket and Champion Stakes); Crossbow (Newmarket Stakes); St Germans (Coronation Cup, Doncaster Cup); SAUCY SUE (One Thousand Guineas, Oaks, Coronation Stakes).

1926 – Crossbow (Royal Hunt Cup); Tournesol (Princess of Wales's Stakes); Lancegaye (Hardwicke Stakes); Sparus (Liverpool Summer Cup); SHORT STORY (The Oaks).

1927 – BOOK LAW (Coronation Stakes, St Leger and Jockey Club Stakes); Duke of Buckingham (Ascot Stakes); Tournesol (Queen's Prize).

The hundred-odd races set out above do not, of course, include the many valuable events he won with so many of Lord Astor's horses – notably his fillies – in conditions events; these embraced mainly richly endowed races at Liverpool, Ascot, Goodwood and Newmarket, as well as innumerable races of value at the smaller meetings.

Altogether Taylor trained the winners in this country of 1,003 races, value £839,070, up to when he retired in 1927. This, however, excludes the value of Lemonora's Grand Prix. He headed the list of winning trainers on twelve occasions including the years 1917 to 1923, when he occupied the top place in the seven successive seasons. To speculate as to which were the best of all the horses he trained would be to raise a controversial point. At this distance of time, however, it may presumably be conceded that Bayardo, Lemberg, Gainsborough and Buchan stood out from the others as racehorses.

Yet, were the great trainer still alive, it is doubtful whether he would agree that the list was complete. He often stated that the best horse he ever trained was Picaroon, the cause of whose untimely death remains a mystery. His illness was never satisfactorily diagnosed.

It will be noted in passing that the list of Manton winners contains the names of very few two-year-olds. Manton had its very considerable share of the glittering prizes at the Ascot meetings but profited rather from those offered for three-year-olds and upwards than from those for juveniles. The results, analysed, provide their own solution. Because the two-year-olds were not hurried, the rewards came in the races for them as they matured. This was undoubtedly the keynote of Taylor's success as a trainer. He was patient beyond all things.

In 1919, that is to say when Buchan was a three-year-old, Taylor sold the Manton property to Mr Joseph Watson, who later became Lord Manton. The arrangement, however, was that the trainer stayed on and in due course Lord Manton became one of his best patrons. Lord Manton died in the hunting field in March, 1922 and, after a series of protracted negotiations, the property came into the possession of Messrs Tattersall (at that time Mr Somerville Tattersall and Mr Gerald H. Deane). The Manton property when sold in 1919 extended to about 5,500 acres, largely downland.

In his early days, Alec Taylor, although maintaining a watchful eye over the Manton fortunes, found more time in which to enjoy the society of his friends. He delighted in the company of two very old friends, particularly – Somerville Tattersall and Robert Sherwood. Bob Sherwood was a friend of his youth and Taylor always stayed with him for the Newmarket meetings. The two were strangely contrasting characters – Sherwood with his love of the good things of life, Taylor with his simplicity which bordered on, but did not extend to, austerity.

At least he had in common with both Tattersall and Sherwood the love of the racehorse and a fine appreciation of whatever was good. There was nothing cheap nor tawdry about him. He had a dignity born of self-restraint and inherent good taste. He was always beautifully dressed, unhurried in his manner, kind and polite in all his ways.

He died a very rich man, leaving an estate of £595,790, with net personalty of £593,098. He was unmarried, and left most of his pictures to his sister for her lifetime, after which they were to go to the Jockey Club. He made many generous bequests, including £20,000 each to the RAF Benevolent Fund, the Royal Veterinary College and the Royal Agricultural Benevolent Institution. In addition there were £1,000 each to the Bentinck and Rendlesham Funds and many legacies to various hospitals including the Rous Memorial Hospital at Newmarket. There can· be but few who, professionally connected with racing, have acquired and kept such fortunes. But it was always said of Alec Taylor that he never, or hardly ever, had a bet.   BBR–1943

The 'Curse' of Derby Preparation

'I wonder,' asks Mr George Lambton, 'how many good horses have been ruined in an endeavour to win the Derby? I have seen many that, figuratively speaking, have been either trained to death, fussed or coddled to death, shaken to death, and of late years sometimes ridden to death.

That great trainer, Mathew Dawson, once said to me that if only people would treat their Derby horses like their selling platers they would get on much better. He added that nothing was so likely to spoil a horse as making a fuss over him, and I have no doubt that there was much truth in what he said.'   BBR–1930

The Death of Andrew Jackson Joyner

The same year, 1943, in which England lost a great trainer, Alexander Taylor, so did the United States with the passing of Andrew Jackson Joyner. Both were men of impeccable character whose long careers were a credit to the sport. England was particularly fortunate as it enjoyed and appreciated Mr Joyner during the time the reform laws practically closed down racing in the US. In that country he trained for Harry Payne Whitney, including such notable performers as Borrow and Whisk Broom II. Borrow captured the leading English two-year-old fixture, the Middle Park Plate, before returning home to secure the Brooklyn Handicap. Whisk Broom II was also a good winner in England before he went back to win both the Brooklyn and Suburban Handicaps. Other memorable horses trained by this Hall of Fame conditioner included Hamburg Belle, Fair Play, St James, Jamestown, Evening, Your Chance and Eight Thirty. He trained mainly for George D. Widener, nephew of Joseph E. Widener. The latter also died in 1943 as did Sickle, the stallion Mr Widener bought in England to establish the male line which continues to be a growing influence through Native Dancer, Raise a Native and the latter's sons Mr Prospector and Alydar. 'The Gentleman from North Carolina' in 1904 entered 40 horses to win 60 races from 230 starts. His is a memory to be treasured.

ANDREW JACKSON JOYNER, dean of American trainers and one of the most honoured men ever associated professionally with the sport, died September 1st at Mr G. D. Widener's Erdenheim Farm, near Philadelphia. Ever since his 'teens he had been 'crazy over horses'. Through virtually all his adult life he was recognised as an accomplished trainer.

Born August 18th, 1861, by his own account (or on August 18th, 1860, by family evidence which seems reliable), he grew up in the village of Weldon, North Carolina, where, as soon as he could do so, he seems to have begun to participate in local racing. In 1879 he left Weldon, and soon after took employment with W. P. Burch, an excellent trainer and

Mr G. D. Widener
(left) and Mr A. J.
Joyner.

teacher. In a few years he became foreman for him. Joyner won his spurs
in his first job as trainer 'on his own' by scoring a success with a
supposedly broken down horse called Oriflamme.

About 1890 Mr Joyner opened a public stable, developed for himself a
high-class horse called Chesapeake, and handled a few horses for the
younger August Belmont with such success that Mr Belmont engaged
him as head trainer. He held that position until 1895, a year in which he
won about forty races. He then trained for David Gideon, W. Astor
Chandler, and Perry Belmont; for the last-named he developed Ethel-
bert, a horse of extreme class whose exploits gave substance to his
growing reputation as a trainer.

His later years brought a procession of successes for various owners.
He trained Waterboy, Hamburg Belle, Tradition, and, again in the
employ of August Belmont, handled Fair Play, a top-class colt whose
light was dimmed only by the brighter glory of the unbeaten Colin. In
1908 he was leading trainer, with a total of 171 winners and $170,775 in
earnings. In the autumn of 1908, as reform laws began to close in on
racing, he went to England to train for Harry Payne Whitney. He took
with him Fair Play, who failed to train well and was shipped back.
Among the Whitney horses he trained there were Borrow and Whisk
Broom II. The latter's class caused Mr Joyner to cable Mr Whitney the
advice to purchase Whisk Broom II's sire, Broomstick, at the Senorita
Stud dispersal. The purchase was made: Broomstick became one of the
most important foundation stones of the fabulously successful Whitney
Stud.

Not long after his return to the States in 1915 Mr Joyner became
trainer for George D. Widener, nephew of Joseph E. Widener. This
successful connection lasted until his death. Among the most noted

horses he trained for Mr Widener were the Futurity winners St James and his son Jamestown; the high-class mare Evening and her son Your Chance; and the handsome Eight Thirty, which is now among the most promising young stallions in Kentucky. Largely following Mr Joyner's advice, Mr Widener built up a stud on a farm adjoining his uncle's Elmendorf. Though he has never operated on an extensive scale his success has been almost continuous. Mr Widener had high esteem for his trainer. After the death of Mr Joyner he commissioned Neil Newman to write a biography. This full length 'portrait' of a famous horseman – which will be something new in American Turf literature – is now in preparation under the direction of *The Blood-Horse*, in which it ran serially. When conditions permit it will be published under Mr Widener's sponsorship.

Andrew Joyner made many solid friendships while in England. Any visitor to the United States had to reply at length as to the well being and welfare of his numerous English friends (especially at Newmarket) of whom he so eagerly and earnestly desired to learn all the news. His lasting regret was his health and interests at home prevented a visit to England in his later years.   BBR–1943

Our overbred racers; the nightmare of an anxious owner. Flash-in-the-Pan suddenly realises the enormous issues depending on him and faints in his trainer's arms.

Part 5

JOCKEYS

Regarding Jockey Fees

Owners and trainers today will go to extraordinary means and make extraordinary deals to acquire the jockey they consider best suited to their horse. Apparently, it wasn't always thus. The 1922 BBR *offers an account by the racing authority 'Audax' which appeared in* Horse and Hound *regarding a situation which took place as far back as 1826.*

'A well-known and true racing story is that concerning John Day, who, after having ridden Devise to victory in the Two Thousand Guineas of 1826, and two days later secured the One Thousand Guineas on Problem for the fourth Duke of Grafton, was sent for by His Grace, who, having intimated his intention to make him a present for the manner in which he had ridden his horses that week, gave him £20! Nowadays jockeys – in addition to absurd retainers – are given perfectly farcical presents for winning quite unimportant races, which in practice only spoils them, and does much harm. The Duke's gift, although in this instance a distinctly mean one, in my opinion was wiser on the whole than the present of £500 to a jockey for winning such a race as the Goodwood Cup, as I know was done not very long since. This amount was over half the value of the race, while I believe Maher was given all the specie for winning a certain Gold Cup at Ascot some years ago.'

Realising that most British owners in those days had to win an occasional bet to remain in business, it might be suggested that the riders weren't overpaid at all.

Better Late Than Never

October 22nd: There is a notification in the *Racing Calendar* to the effect that the Stewards of the Jockey Club have cancelled the order issued in October, 1901, warning Lester Reiff off Newmarket Heath. Curiously enough a precisely similar announcement was published in the official journal in April, 1904. We are not told why it has been deemed necessary to repeat it now. The 'warning off' sentence was passed because the Jockey Club Stewards in 1901 (Lord Falmouth, Mr L. Brassey, and the Hon. H. W. Fitzwilliam) were persuaded that Reiff had not tried to make a horse called De Lacy win a race at Manchester. His mount was beaten a head by Minnie Dee, a better favourite, ridden by John Reiff. De Lacy was a moody horse, and there were many people who thought Lester Reiff was unjustly punished. He retired to his home in Los Angeles, California. During the three seasons he was riding in England his record read:

	Mounts	1st	2nd	3rd	Percentage
1899	184	55	33	26	29.88
1900	553	143	117	82	25.85
1901	322	75	63	60	23.29

His percentage of wins to mounts proves clearly enough that he was a jockey of the very first class. In 1900 he was the leading jockey, Sam Loates and John Reiff coming second and third. In 1901, Lester Reiff rode Volodyovski to victory in the Derby. Very spare in build, he was unusually tall for a jockey. He was almost equally responsible with Sloan for bringing about the adoption in this country of the crouching seat.

BBR–1914

Buckle's Correct 'Seat'

FROM *The Times* of February 15th, 1832: The celebrated jockey, Buckle, died last week. Fifty years' experience proved him to be the best rider ever known. His last race was at the close of the Houghton Meeting, 1831, when he took his leave of the Turf.   BBR–1922

Review of the Book,
'The Life of Fred Archer'

The jockey, Fred Archer, who died in 1886, was such a dominant force in English racing that 'at the zenith of his fame, might with truth be described as a Dictator of the Turf quite to the same extent as either Lord George Bentinck or Admiral Rous before him'. This quote is lifted from the review of the book The Life of Fred Archer*, *written thirty-seven years after his death, in the* BBR *of 1923. While admitting the book 'fills a gap in the literature of the Turf', the reviewer suggests it would have been a better book if written some thirty years earlier. In any case, one is left to feel that much of the good in the book is quoted in the review. This is probably true and readers of the following will no doubt agree that 'the real Fred Archer' is to be found in these passages.*

IT IS thirty-seven years since Fred Archer died. We now have with us, therefore, a generation to whom the famous jockey is, so to say, merely a superstition. They hear their elders telling wonderful tales to the glory of the man who for a space was the most dominating figure on the English Turf. It is, therefore, rather curious that until now no serious attempt

---

* *The Life of Fred Archer*, by E. M. Humphris. Published by Hutchinson and Co., London. 18s net.

Fred Archer.

has been made to produce a biography of so remarkable and world-famous a character.

Mr Humphris, it seems, had the editorial assistance of Lord Arthur Grosvenor. A considerable number of the 300 pages of the book are filled with matter that might with advantage have been discarded, while others make rather tiresome reading. The work, in fact, needed sub-editing rather than editing. Mr Humphris evidently found himself hampered by a shortage of the material required to build up a really satisfactory biography. He, or somebody else, would probably have found the subject an easier one to deal with thirty years ago when so many more of the people intimately associated with Archer were alive. Custance, years ago, and Donoghue, just recently, have proved that the story of a jockey's career can be told better by himself than by anyone else, provided he has the power of narration.

Archer was all but illiterate. When he left home, eleven years old, to become an apprentice to Mathew Dawson at Newmarket, he could neither read nor write. He afterwards attended a night school, but in later life he rarely used a pen except for signing cheques, or letters written for him by others. The charm and value of most biographies is in the human documents they present. They are largely missing from the book under notice. Mr Humphris has done his best to get along without them, and, let it be said, we are glad to have the book. It gives us a vivid picture of many sides of Archer's character. The whole truth is not, of course, told. Archer was by no means a saint. When he had acquired his power he was apt to use it unscrupulously. We have heard stories of him that almost make one's hair stand on end, revealing, as they do, a shameless audacity. The risky things he did show that he believed his position so supreme that the Turf authorities dare not punish him, even if he were found out. He often treated owners as puppets, ordered them when to run or not to run their horses, and, generally arranged many a race to suit himself and his bets, for he was a big gambler.

Two pages of the book are filled with a letter Mr Humphris received from Lady Hastings, whose husband's horse, Melton, ridden by Archer, won the Derby in 1885. Here is a document which throws a considerable light on the jockey's character:

'I think he (Archer) was the gallantest creature that ever lived. He was simply afraid of nothing. . . When Melton won the Derby we were all nearly off our heads with excitement. We were very young, both my husband and I, and while Lord Hastings lived racing seemed part of my very life. . . I could not go to see the Derby because about a fortnight before it one of my sons was born. But afterwards they came up and told me that Archer was downstairs and would like to see me. I begged my husband to let him, and he came up. I was just up enough to be lying on a sofa, and he brought me the whip he had used in the race.

'Well, Archer told me all about it and then the baby was brought down, tied up in our racing colours – eau de nil and crimson. Of course, Archer was very pleased about it (the Derby), for many people think it was one of his greatest, if not his greatest, race.

'Archer's was a very complex character. Generous to a fault in many ways, I did not admire him at all in the same way I did Mathew Dawson – not as a man, I mean. Of course, he was a genius – never was such riding seen – and many people thought him an angel as well. But I never did. He had always the same simple, unassuming manners – never wishing to push himself forward. He never would even come to lunch with my husband and me – he didn't think it was his place – though I think Lord Falmouth sometimes got him to go to him. That was partly why people liked him so much; he never put himself forward.

'Lord Hastings was very fond indeed of Archer. I think he knew that Archer, like everyone else, had his faults and I should not be too careful to ignore them. Archer was great enough to have the truth told about him. He had not always a nice expression; indeed, I think at times it was almost diabolical. But I have always been a straight-spoken person.

'Nearly all Archer's acquaintances were, to put it vulgarly, titled people, and he practically spent his life among them. The way in which some women ran after Archer was amazing. They would not let him alone. People in society went simply mad about him and hunted after him. It was their fault more than his; they would not let him alone. It's just the way with some people.

'He was a marvellous man and a marvellous jockey. I should think there was never anybody a bit like him – one of the most extraordinary men that ever lived, and great enough to bear having the light thrown upon him. And through all the flattery and absurdity of all those ridiculous women, his manners remained quite unspoilt – just perfection.

'My husband used often to go about with Archer. Lord Falmouth – a shrewd, clever man – was always simply devoted to him. He would never hear a word against him, and though, as I say, I think Archer had his faults, my husband, if he saw them, ignored them and never spoke of them, and Lord Falmouth never would own he had any.'

If this 'Life' of Archer had been written thirty years ago it would, perhaps, have been possible to collect many character sketches similar to the graphic one Lady Hastings has supplied. There is another good one in the book, furnished in the form of a Preface by Mr Arthur B. Portman, who writes:

'Archer had a keen, intelligent brain and iron nerve. . . He showed the most wonderful courage when riding, although otherwise he was a very highly-strung man. This was probably brought about by excessive wasting, which naturally affected his nerves, and also by the terrible amount of strong medicine which he was constantly taking to get off a pound or half a pound in weight when there was really nothing to take off, for he was a mere bag of skin and bones.

'Archer was not an elegant rider, he crouched too much for that; but he gained an advantage by it, for Tom Cannon and his school sat upright, and even began to lean back and meet the resistance of the wind. Archer rode long, whereas modern jockeys ride short, as Sloan did, and are right forward on their mount's withers, and crouching as well.

'I am sure, however, that Archer would have held his own among modern jockeys. He was the best jockey I have ever seen, and I should say he was probably the best all-round jockey on every type of racecourse who has ever lived. . . The feats Archer accomplished and the number of races which he won that less skilful riders would have lost were enough to convince me that he was an absolute genius in the saddle. One rather amusing story told of Archer was that when quite a boy he was found crying because he could not ride both winners in a dead-heat. It was this temperament which made him work so hard and waste so much in later life.'

Mr Portman goes on to say that Archer, having great influence, and being permitted to do things by people above him socially that no other jockey had ever dreamed of doing, was very much inclined to bully other jockeys, and especially the smaller boys. He almost invariably weighed out first, or, if not doing that, got to the post first so as to take the most advantageous position on the course, there being then no draw for places at the start.

Mr Portman declares:

'In fact Archer, at the zenith of his fame, might with truth be described as a Dictator of the Turf quite to the same extent as either Lord George Bentinck or Admiral Rous before him. Very clever and a very close observer of all that was going on around him, Archer certainly had a sufficiently brilliant brain, had his education been profound enough, to have made him a better Prime Minister of England than some of the people who have held that exalted post since his days.'

For any shortcomings there may be in *The Life of Fred Archer* Mr Humphris is not blameworthy. He has obviously gone to infinite trouble to collect material where it was obtainable, and has succeeded in giving us a very good idea of the greatness of the hero. The book fills a gap in the literature of the Turf.   BBR–1923

The Death of Tom Cannon

When Tom Cannon passed away in his seventy-second year in July of 1917 it marked the end of one of the most composite careers spent in racing and breeding. Mr Cannon experienced it all. As a jockey he was grouped with George Fordham, John Osborne and Fred Archer, a quartet of the finest horsemen associated with the Turf in the latter half of the nineteenth century. 'All masters of their profession' who 'played their parts in stirring times.' During his thirty-two years in the saddle he captured thirteen English classics, including a triumph with Shotover in the Derby of 1882, and was also successful in five runnings of the Grand Prix de Paris along with two winning rides in the French Derby. He also fared extremely well as a trainer and as an owner. Mr Cannon had four sons follow him in the riding profession and two of them, Mornington and Kempton, also had winning Derby mounts. In the Eclipse Stakes of 1888, Tom Senior had the satisfaction of beating Tom Junior by a length. Unfortunately, Mr Cannon's varied and exciting lifetime was not translated into biographical form and 'recollections of notable people and horses which ought to have been preserved in permanent form for the benefit of future generations' were lost.

The Review *was not to blame, for it attempted to obtain his reminiscences, but was denied because of his failing health.*

AFTER A long, wearying illness Tom Cannon, one of the great jockeys of his day, died at the Grosvenor Hotel, Stockbridge, Hampshire, on July 13th. He was born April 23rd, 1846, so that he passed away in his seventy-second year. Some months ago dropsy supervened on serious heart trouble, and it had been obvious for a considerable time that the end could not be far off. Curiously enough, the morning of the day he died he seemed rather better than usual, but after breakfast he suddenly collapsed. For twenty years or so he had suffered from several illnesses, each of which seemed likely to cause his death, but again and again he displayed wonderful rallying power. At the time of the last December Sales news of his death was momentarily expected, but once more his vigorous constitution enabled him to ward off the final summons. It is one of our deepest regrets that we did not obtain Tom Cannon's reminiscences for the benefit of readers of the *Review*. Some two years ago we approached him but he did not at the time feel equal to the exertion an interview would have entailed. Subsequent inquiries revealed the futility of pursuing the quest, and so he has taken with him to the grave recollections of notable people and horses which ought to have been preserved in permanent form for the benefit of future generations. And all because we were too late with our importunities! That, if favoured with more luck, we should have been able to present a story, or series of stories, at once valuable and interesting there can be no doubt, for Tom Cannon was an excellent raconteur, and loved to talk of his experiences.

Cannon had been in retirement so long that he was known to the younger generation of sportsmen by reputation only. Happily, however, there are many still living who remember him as a man distinguished alike by the rectitude of his conduct, the skill he displayed as a jockey and, later, as a trainer, and the assiduity and enthusiasm with which he pursued his calling. He leaves behind him a name that will always be respected, and one that will ever figure prominently and honourably in the annals of the Turf. As a jockey he was a contemporary of George Fordham, John Osborne and Fred Archer. Since it became a great national institution, racing has never been associated with a more famous group of horsemen. They were all masters of their profession, and played their parts in stirring times. Fordham and Cannon were for many years attached to the Danebury Stable near Stockbridge. George was Tom's mentor, and the latter was ever ready to acknowledge with gratitude the assistance he received from 'The Demons'. It was Fordham who taught him the knack of getting well away at the start of a race, and who instilled into him the advantage to be got by steadying a horse preparatory to the final effort. Even the best of jockeys have their weaknesses, and Cannon had one which he shares with many another rider – that of trying to win by the narrowest possible margin. It was, of course, only occasionally that he thought it worth while to resort to this trick, but it was alleged against him that by playing it he lost races he should have won. For all that, Tom Cannon well earned the right to be called a great jockey. Throughout a riding career extending over a period of over thirty years, his reputation for honesty and straight-forwardness was never so much as singed by the flame of scandal. He lived a righteous and upright life. All his sons – Tom, Mornington, Kempton and Charles – followed on in the profession he had adorned. The father had not yet retired when Tom junior and 'Morny' were in the race saddle. Many readers will doubtless remember the contest for the Eclipse Stakes at Sandown Park in 1888 when Tom senior on Orbit beat Tom junior on Ossory by a length, both horses belonging to the late Duke of Westminster. 'Morny', too, was beginning to make a name for himself as a jockey at that date. He afterwards became the leader of his profession. To Kempton Cannon belonged the distinction of being one of the first of the English jockeys to appreciate the value of the crouching seat adopted by Tod Sloan. The success he achieved in consequence secured him a retainer from Mr Leopold de Rothschild, and gave him the mount on St Amant in the Derby of 1904. Curiously enough Tom Cannon and his sons 'Morny' and 'Kemmy' all won the Derby once only. Tom rode Shotover in 1882, and 'Morny' Flying Fox in 1899. The coincidence did not extend to the St Leger, for whereas the father and Kempton rode one winner each of the Doncaster 'classic', Morny was successful on both Throstle and Flying Fox.

Mention of these isolated incidents will serve to show that the sire transmitted some at least of his genius for race-riding. But the 'old man' was the artist of the family. In the handling of two-year-olds he has probably never had an equal. He seemed to have an intuitive knowledge of the youngsters he bestrode, and so was able to get out of them the most they had to give. An owner could entrust a highly-strung two-year-old to Tom Cannon with the confident assurance that nothing would be done calculated to ruin its future career. The jockey was patient though firm if necessary, and had an uncanny way of coaxing horses to do a little more than they wanted to do, or knew how to do.

Tom Cannon was born at Eton, where his father kept the George Hotel. When thirteen years old he was apprenticed to Mr Sextie, who enjoyed some fame as an animal painter, and who ran a small training stable in Wiltshire. The following year Sextie, who raced as 'Mr Williams', was running a mare named Mavourneen at Plymouth, and took his boy Cannon (who then weighed 3 st 12 lb) with him to ride her. While the race was being run Mavourneen struck into the heels of a horse in front of her and fell. None the worse for the mishap, Cannon finished second in a race later in the afternoon. One of the winners that day was a horse called My Uncle, who was promptly bought by Lord Portsmouth for 47 guineas. My Uncle was entered for a six-furlong 'heat' race the second day. Needing a boy to ride, Lord Portsmouth took Sextie's advice and put up Cannon. My Uncle won the first heat by a head, dead-heated in the second 'go', and won the third heat by half a length. And so it came to pass that the name of little Master Cannon was given a lowly place in the list of winning jockeys. In a letter to *Horse and Hound* detailing these particulars, Mr Gerard Wallop, a son of the late Lord Portsmouth, adds: 'My father remained a warm admirer of Tom Cannon's graceful seat and tender handling, which I always understood were in accordance with the traditions and teaching of John Day at Danebury.'

Tom Cannon gave up race-riding in 1891, so that his career as a jockey extended over a period of thirty-two seasons. In his last year he had eighty-two mounts and rode twenty-one winners, giving him the excellent percentage of 25.61. He scored his last win on Mr Houldsworth's Orvieto in the Sussex Stakes at Goodwood, and donned silk for the last time to ride Bendetto in the Hanworth Plate at Kempton Park in August. His mount was placed third to Colonel North's Sheldrake, ridden by Morny Cannon. Even at that date he suffered from indifferent health. From first to last he rode 1544 winners – an average of 48 per annum. The following is a list of the winners of classic races ridden by Tom Cannon:

Two Thousand Guineas
1878 – Lord Lonsdale's Pilgrimage
1882 – Duke of Westminster's Shotover
1887 – Mr D. Baird's Enterprise
1889 – Mr D. Baird's Enthusiast

One Thousand Guineas
1866 – Marquis of Hastings' Repulse
1878 – Lord Lonsdale's Pilgrimage
1884 – Mr Abington's Busybody

The Derby
1882 – Duke of Westminster's Shotover

The Oaks
1869 – Sir F. Johnstone's Brigantine
1873 – Mr J. Merry's Marie Stuart
1882 – Lord Stamford's Geheimniss
1884 – Mr Abington's Busybody

The St Leger
1880 – Mr C. Brewer's Robert the Devil

On five occasions Cannon rode the winner of the Grand Prix de Paris, viz:

1866 – Duke of Beaufort's Ceylon
1874 – Mr W. R. Marshall's Trent
1878 – Prince Soltykoff's Thurio
1883 – Duc de Castrie's Frontin
1884 – Duc de Castrie's Little Duck

He was twice successful in the French Derby. From 1866 to 1890, both years inclusive, there was never a Derby at Epsom in which he did not have a mount. This was, however, one of his unlucky events. As already stated, the only winner of it he rode was Shotover. Once only did he finish second. In 1887 he rode The Baron, on whom odds were laid, but the horse was easily beaten by the very moderate Merry Hampton. Four times Cannon was on the horse placed third in the Derby – Rustic in 1866, Julius Caesar in 1876, St Mirin in 1886 and El Dorado in 1889.

A curious combination of names arose out of the result of the race for the One Thousand Guineas in 1866. Repulse, who beat Bayonette a head, was out of Sortie and was ridden by Cannon.

But we must pass from Tom Cannon's career as a jockey to make a brief mention of his achievements as a breeder and owner of racehorses. In 1873 he registered his colours, 'red, yellow sleeves and cap', and the following year changed them to 'scarlet, white hoops', which were the colours of the ill-fated Marquis of Hastings. They were last seen on a racecourse in 1913. At one time Cannon had a long string of horses in training – many of them owned by him in partnership with Mr Tom Robinson, of High Wycombe. No doubt the best animal he possessed was the filly Geheimniss. He bought this daughter of Rosicrucian and

Tom Cannon.

Nameless as a yearling at Doncaster in 1880 for 300 guineas. Getting her
fit early the following season, Cannon won with her races at Sandown
Park and Bath, together worth £965. Then Lord Stamford, who had
recently become a patron of the Kingsclere Stable, came along as a
buyer, Cannon having intimated to John Porter that he was willing to
sell. A deal was quickly effected, the price paid being £2,000. For his 330
guineas outlay, Tom Cannon had thus received nearly £3,000, and he
had done well out of Geheimniss; but he would have done much better
had he stuck to her. She went through her two-year-old career
unbeaten, winning five more races for Lord Stamford, their value being
£3,414. The following season she made her first appearance in the Oaks,
which she won by beating St Marguerite, Nellie and two others. That
race was worth £3,375. Her five other efforts that season were
unsuccessful, and during the following winter Lord Stamford died.
Lady Stamford then leased Geheimniss to Lord Alington, for whom,
during the next two seasons, she won twelve races worth £4,307. After
Cannon had parted with her Geheimniss won, therefore, stakes
amounting to £11,096.

Among the animals Tom Cannon bred, owned and trained, the most
noteworthy were Reminder and Curzon. The former ran third in the
Derby of 1894 to Ladas and Matchbox; the latter was placed second in
the following year's Derby, beaten three quarters of a length by Sir
Visto. Until close home Curzon looked all over a winner, and the fact
that he was a half-bred gelding gave some of the purists a terrible shock.
Shortly afterwards geldings were barred from the Derby. In 1895
Reminder won the City and Suburban. He and Curzon were bought by
Baron Hirsch for, it was reported, £8,000.

Cannon trained jumpers as well as flat racers. Playfair, winner of the
Grand National in 1888, was prepared by him. He was part owner, with
Mr Brayley, of Casse-Tete, who won the Grand National in 1872.
Another good 'chaser he owned and trained was Horizon. Cannon was
also a good trainer of jockeys as well as horses. Mention has already been
made of the riding skill of his sons; others who served their apprentice-
ships with him were John Watts, Sam Loates and W. T. Robinson.

In 1865 Tom Cannon married Miss Kate Day, a daughter of John
Day, of Danebury. She died in 1892. Some years later the widower
married again. His second wife also predeceased him. Tom Cannon's
fourth daughter married E. Piggott, the steeplechase jockey.

In 1879 Cannon took over the lease of Danebury, but did not take
possession until the death of his father-in-law, three years later. Some
twenty years ago he bought the Garlogs estate, and then built the

Chattis Hill establishment near Stockbridge. This he disposed of a few years ago to Mr Persse, and went to live at Springfield House, Stockbridge. After the death of his second wife he removed to rooms at the Grosvenor Hotel, which he owned.

Visitors to Danebury who went on to the Downs of a morning to see the horses at work, were often allowed to ride a little hog-maned horse. Not until they returned to the house were they told that their mount was Duke of Parma, and Cannon would add drily, 'Now you can say you rode the winner of the Cesarewitch.' The 'Duke' won the long-distance handicap as a three-year-old in 1875.

There were times when Cannon had eighty horses of his own to provide for at Danebury. These would include about forty broodmares, together with yearlings and foals. He also had the stallion Melanion, whom he eventually sold at a big price to the Italian Government. Cannon had to leave Danebury owing to a death causing a portion of the training grounds to pass into the ownership of a lady who refused to allow racehorses to be trained on her land! The abandonment of Stockbridge Races was necessary for the same reason.

At Danebury and Garlogs Tom Cannon lived the life of a country squire, farming between 2,000 and 3,000 acres, mostly his own property.

BBR–1917

Gordon Richards

On the jockey standings for 1927, the **BBR** *noted that it was a case of 'Gordon Richards first, the rest nowhere'. This was just three years after he had 'emerged' from his apprenticeship and two years after he had headed the jockey list for the first time. It was also the first year after he had recovered from an illness which threatened to terminate his career. In any event, this remarkable young rider, who was to set all kinds of records and later become 'Sir Gordon', was asked by a* Sporting Life *reporter if he could give a reason for his success. He could and he did and what he said was reprinted in the 1927* **BBR***:*

'It just comes natural to me. I train hard, ride four or five horses a day, and always race from the moment the tape drops till the end. You see, I have had some wonderful horses to ride, and that makes all the difference. I don't suppose I should have ever become a jockey if it had not been for two girls in a warehouse office at Oakengates in Shropshire, where I worked. We used to have our threepences or sixpences on our fancies. Mine was always Steve Donoghue's mounts. Steve Donoghue was my boyhood idol, and it was a great moment when I met him. He was attached to the same stable and he watched me out for gallops

several times. Then, one day, he stopped me and told me I would be a good rider if
I trained hard. After that he used to come round two or three times a week and
give me hints how to improve my style. He would say: "Now watch me", and off
he would canter in that beautiful way of his. I tried my best to imitate him, and if I
have any particular style at all it is thanks to Steve. He gave me all the teaching
I've had.   BBR-1927

His Beautiful Feet

FRED WEBB, jockey and trainer, long a sufferer from diabetes, died at
Eastbourne on March 27th. Born at Derringstone, near Canterbury,
January 25th, 1853, he was in his sixty-fifth year. When aged ten he was
apprenticed to his uncle, Tom Brown, then a trainer at Stockbridge, but
who later moved to Newmarket. It was in 1865 that Webb first rode in a
race, and he had his first winning mount at Lewes the following year.
Not, however, till 1869 did he come into prominence. He then became
attached to Mathew Dawson's stable, and rode Cherie to victory in the
Cesarewitch. In 1873 he won the Derby on Mr Merry's Doncaster, and
was on Peregrine when that horse won the Two Thousand Guineas in
1881. He was twice 'placed' second in the Derby – on Highland Chief in
1883, and on Paradox two years later. The defeat of Paradox by Melton
was the outcome of one of the most exciting finishes ever seen at Epsom.
Archer had ridden Paradox when he won the Two Thousand Guineas
and discovered the colt's disinclination to be in front. In the Derby he
made the most of his knowledge, and the chances are that if any other
tactics than those he employed had been brought to bear on the situation
Melton would not have won on the post as he did. If Paradox had
finished first instead of second Webb and John Porter, the trainer of the
colt, would have divided the stake between them. Webb occasionally
rode under National Hunt Rules, and was in the saddle when Captain
Machell's horse, The Scot, finished fifth in the Grand National. During
the twenty-four years he was riding he won 669 races – a number that
would have been greatly exceeded but for the difficulty he experienced
in keeping his weight below 9 st.

If ever there was an 'all-round' man in the sporting line, it was Fred
Webb. He was an expert billiard player, won many races on the cinder
path, excelled at the high jump, was a skilled pigeon shot and a first-rate
boxer. 'Cocking' was another of his amusements. He had a good singing
voice, and could play two or three instruments.

He rode as a jockey for the last time in 1895, and then started as a
trainer. Lady de Bathe (then racing as 'Mr Jersey') entrusted her horses
to him, and he prepared Merman for the Cesarewitch of 1897. In 1905

Webb went to Alag, in Hungary, to train for Prince Taxis, Count Andrassy and others. He remained there for seven years.

'Audax,' in *Horse and Hound*, relates the following story:

> 'I have seen Webb beaten on horses through looking down and admiring his beautifully shaped feet, of which he was extremely proud, instead of getting home as quickly as possible, as far more inferior riders would have done. Regarding this habit, that droll character Tim Jefferson, whose fair and handsome daughter Webb married, once said of his son-in-law when he had thereby lost a race: "By gad, if Slinky had only got bunions he would be the best jockey in the world, as then there would be no looking at his feet." "Slinky" was the name by which his intimates always called this perfect horseman and at that time most powerful, beautifully made man of his size possible to find.'   BBR–1917

Jockey Quotes of Charlie Smirke

Jockey quotes are an inseparable part of any comprehensive story covering a major Turf event. That was not always the way it was. Back around 1900 the practice of giving the jockey's view of the race was started in England by a Mr Phipps. In 1934 Mr Phipps was given his due by the BBR *following the quotes of winning rider Charles Smirke who had been up on Windsor Lad:*

> 'From a good start I took up a position just behind Colombo, on whom I naturally keep an eye. Thereafter I was never out of the first five. I had a perfect run all the way. Not for a stride had I to check my mount, nor was I interfered with in any way; I was able to go along on the bit. When Colombo dropped back coming down the hill, I got the inside position, about a length and a half behind Tiberius and Fleetfoot. As soon as we reached the straight, Fleetfoot dropped away and I joined Tiberius. I had not asked my mount for an effort up to then, but when we got to the road which crosses the course I let my mount go. Tiberius was soon left behind, and I knew I had the race in my pocket. Gordon Richards, on Easton, was the first to tackle me, and then Johnstone came along on Colombo. They were unable to head me. I brought out my whip and just gave him one. He answered at once and shot ahead. I gained the day fairly comfortably.'

How interesting and informative these 'interviewettes' are. They were invented, if the term is permissible, some thirty years ago by a journalist named Phipps, who was connected with the racing news service conducted by the now defunct *Sportsman*. 'Phippo', as he was called by his friends, took upon himself the duty of looking after the welfare of young jockeys, many of whom owed a great deal to him. The boys grew up to regard Phipps almost as a father, and when he wanted the story of a race from any one of them they willingly obliged him. Phipps, one of the nicest and kindest of men, died many years ago, but to the end of his life he was almost the only racing journalist who specialised in interviews with jockeys after a big event. In these days of 'personal' journalism, every Turf reporter considers it his duty to get stories out of jockeys. Some do the job well, but 'Ajax' excels all. It was upon him that the mantle worn by Phipps descended.   BBR–1934

Between the Derby and St Leger of 1934, Windsor Lad was sold by HH the Maharajah of Rajpipla (popularly known as 'Mr Pip') to the well-known English bookmaker Mr Martin H. Benson with the stipulation the stallion should never leave England. Thus, Windsor Lad became the first runner since 1827 to have changed hands after winning the Derby and the only horse to win both events under different ownership. After the St Leger, as was the case after the Derby, Charles Smirke was lavish in his praise of Windsor Lad and the BBR *has saved those quotes for us.*

IT CAME as a surprise to most people when the watch holders made known the fact that Windsor Lad had run the course in time which equalled the record for the race set up by Coronach in 1926, because at the outset the pace had seemed rather slow. Some day we shall, perhaps, have these important races timed at two or three stages as well as at the finish. The information so obtained would be both interesting and valuable. If, as seems probable, the record was this year equalled because of the pace during the last mile, Windsor Lad's inability to win by a bigger margin than two lengths is accounted for. The crowd had expected him to give a spectacular performance. It was understood that Mr Benson had intimated that the more lengths his horse won by the better he would be pleased. Viewing the matter in a commonsense way it can, however, be said that Windsor Lad won in convincing style. He proved, beyond what the late President Wilson would have called a peradventure, that he is, *pace* Colombo, the best of his age, a fine stayer with a good turn of speed. Interviewed after the race, Smirke brushed aside all quibbles regarding the character of Windsor Lad's victory. Talking to our friend 'Ajax', the jockey said:

'He would have won with another stone on his back. I don't think I have ever ridden such a lazy horse. You see, it was rather a poor gallop, and he never got thoroughly roused up. I was hoping they would go along, but they did not do so. Naturally, I wanted to keep in close touch with the leaders, and from the time we fairly settled down I was never out of the first four.

'I went up into second place just behind Tiberius on the turn and was content to stay there until we got about a furlong in the straight. I then joined Bob Jones in the lead. He hung on very well, but I was going much better than he was. Even so my horse was reluctant to take a definite advantage, so I had to bring out the whip to make him realise this was a serious business. I did not hit him; I merely flourished the whip. This had the necessary effect and he speedily went clear of Tiberius. From that point there was never the slightest doubt about the result. I was not taking any risks, so I kept him going to the end.

'Take it from me, he is a good horse, and even now you have not seen the best of him. He will fill out a lot between now and next year, and I only hope he is given the opportunity to show what he really can do. If all goes well, he will prove himself one of the best horses of modern times.'

Mr Benson had to admit that he was unable to see the race because his hands were shaking so much he could not use his glasses. An attack of nerves is not infrequently experienced by owners expecting their horses to win important races. The winner of a Grand National many years ago belonged to a man whose nerves were so taut that he had to walk about behind the Grand Stand while the race was being run. Mr Benson went on to say that Windsor Lad would not begin his stud career next year, because he had been advised that, as the colt was not yet fully developed, the experience might harm him.   BBR–1934

Jockey Quotes by Bernard Carslake

After HH the Aga Khan's Salmon-Trout captured the 1924 St Leger by two lengths, B. Carslake, his rider, gave 'Kettledrum' of the Sporting Chronicle *'a detailed and most interesting description of the race as he saw it'. It was reprinted in the* BBR *and goes as follows:*

'I had my orders, of course, and I made up my mind to be with Polyphontes in the early stages. When we settled down, the last three were Sansovino, on the rails; Polyphontes, in the middle; while I was on the outside. The others were all streaming away ahead, but I had my policy mapped out, and I meant to stick to it. When we got to the top corner, Sansovino began to move up a bit, and I saw Polyphontes also go up to take his place. I let him go, and made no attempt to follow. There is a long run-in, I said to myself, and Polyphontes will want a lot of reserve if he is to last it out, so I stayed where I was. It was not until seven furlongs from home that I improved my position, and I was able to do this while still keeping a firm grip on my horse. I was moving up on the outside, but there was some bunching at the turn, and all of them swung wide. I pulled to the inside, and got a clear run in the straight. I must have been ten lengths behind at that time, and I could see Polyphontes and Santorb having a fight. For a time I let them get on with it, and not until a furlong and a half from home did I make a move. The horse answered at once, as I knew he would, and though I only got up in the last hundred yards I never had an uneasy moment in the last half-mile. The fact that I was a clear winner showed how the horse was travelling at the finish.'

Steve Donoghue.

The Death of Steve Donoghue

England's extremely talented jockey, Steve Donoghue, retired in 1937 at the age of fifty-two. However, he made a classic exit – twice – winning both the One Thousand Guineas and the Oaks with Exhibitionist. During his career, which spanned about twenty-five years, Donoghue was ten times England's champion jockey, sharing one of those titles, in 1923, with Charlie Eliot. His reign was in consecutive years, 1914 through 1923.

NOT ONLY the whole country, but sportsmen everywhere would have felt a sense of personal loss when it became known that Steve Donoghue, the most popular jockey of our time, passed away so suddenly in London early in the morning of March 23rd. The news, broadcast at 7 o'clock, caused wide consternation.

To many the loss of Steve came as stunning news so very difficult to believe. Some had spoken with Steve only a few hours before his passing, for he was in London on business when he became ill.

I had talked with him two days earlier. At the time he was troubled about someone whom he had not seen for years, about whom he had received news of a distressing character. As ever that great heart of sympathy and kindliness was asking 'What can we do to help in their distress?' Little did he then realise that his own trouble was much more grave.

Some time ago he was not well at Newmarket, but kept his secret closely. His recent hazardous journey to Portugal cannot have improved his health.

For sixty years the sporting world has not been so saddened as it was by the report of the death of this very famous jockey. He was known so well through his broadcasting talks, after his retirement from riding. No other jockey of great repute in the older days could ever have had so wide a public.

Memories of Steve crowd upon one. His racing record and his wonderful career as a jockey had the fullest references in all our newspapers and in every country where there is racing. His marvellous feats over the Epsom course are part of the history of racing.

What an appreciated gesture if the Epsom executive would rename one of their events in Steve's memory. We have races named after well-known journalists, famous horses and owners, why not one bearing the name of Donoghue?

Steve seemed to know everyone; everyone found the greatest pleasure in knowing Steve.

He was so kindly and courtly, with his seemingly perpetual and generous smile, plus the slightly husky voice. From his own wide, personal experience he was ever ready to assist others. No one in this connection paid a higher and more sincere tribute to Steve than Gordon Richards when Donoghue finally retired to become a trainer.

He was a far, far greater jockey than a trainer. It is to be admitted that his disposition did not allow him to be easily 'tied' in one place. He must be at the races. He was always full of plans. So rarely did he find the right people with sufficient time at their disposal to carry them out for him.

Steve always gave of his utmost; he naturally expected the best from others. Sometimes he was disappointed, especially in recent years.

These setbacks he felt deeply, for he did take matters to heart. To his intimates he would talk quietly over the happenings, rather seeking excuse for the others than consolation for himself. Through all vicissitudes of his changing career and circumstances his character never changed.

His fame and reputation gained Steve Donoghue a place not only in the hearts of the uncountable host who knew him, but a place in the hearts of his countrymen, so that he became a national figure.

His feats in our classic races have perhaps been excelled taken on the whole, but his record in the Derby and his unique and prolonged association with Brown Jack and their feats in the Alexandra Stakes at Ascot will be told and retold so long as there remains anyone interested in racing.

Pommern and Gay Crusader in the 1914–1918 Derbys at Newmarket. Humorist, Captain Cuttle, Papyrus and Manna, all Derby winners at Epsom from 1921 to 1925. I well recall congratulating the late Mr J. B. Joel, late in the afternoon of Humorist's Derby, the first time I could get near him. That great sportsman with his well recalled sweeping gesture of his right arm, briefly replied: 'No, not me. Steve won it for me; congratulate him.' What a marvellous tribute from an owner who had just won the Derby!

Later in his career Steve was not doing so well for reasons which many of his friends understood. About the time, Sir Victor Sassoon, who was in India, entertained high hopes of one of his colts and he sent his trainer a telegram reading: 'Engage for me this year the jockey who knows the best way round Epsom.' No need for names. Steve was sought. Late in his riding days he had the felicity of winning the One Thousand Guineas and the Oaks on Sir Victor's filly, Exhibitionist. Donoghue was then fifty-two years of age.

Remarkable as it may sound, Exhibitionist was Steve's first winner of the One Thousand Guineas, though he had been placed in that race on Silver Tag, My Dear and Golden Corn. He never won a St Leger over the historic course at Doncaster, his best being a second on Papyrus. He did win St Legers during the 1914–1918 war at Newmarket with Pommern and Gay Crusader. The Oaks he also won in war-time (1918), with My Dear. Then he had to wait for Exhibitionist (1937).

In addition to his English Derby winners Steve also rode four winners of the Irish Derby, the last when he was over fifty years old.

In France as long ago as 1922 he secured his first Grand Prix de Paris on Kefalin. Again he won the great race on Admiral Drake in 1934, his victory that year being one of the outstanding romances of the great French stake. Steve arrived in Paris that Sunday first 'to see the good horses'. A few hours later he was borrowing breeches and boots. He donned the second colours. At the distance Easton, the leader, was challenged by Admiral Drake. Steve at last found a narrow opening among his rivals. With magnificent judgment he brought Admiral Drake through on the rails to win the greatest of French races. It was only after the second event that afternoon arrangements were made for Steve to ride Admiral Drake in the Grand Prix. Steve won the French Oaks as long ago as 1925 on Aquatinte II.

It is impossible to mention the many notable winners he rode of outstanding stakes in other countries. He had done very well in several continental countries, as well as in India, South Africa, and even the West Indies.

One never forgets the unfortunate match race between Papyrus and Zev in the United States over twenty years ago. Also Steve's association with the unforgettable, unbeaten flyer, the Tetrarch. No other jockey but Steve could ever have won at Kempton Park on Colombo. As a rider of two-year-olds Steve excelled.

Steve rode his first winner at Hyeres (France) in 1904. His last mount was in the Final Plate, Manchester, November, 1937. That season he rode twenty-eight winners. Steve could aver that in his thirty-three years' career as a jockey he had never once been summoned before the Stewards for infringing a rule of racing. Another very striking tribute to his ability and fairness.

His uncanny skill with nervous two-year-olds was a unique feature of his brilliant career.

Who, however, will forget Steve's unbelievable escape on Abbot's Trace when that colt fell in the Derby (Spion Kop's year) near the winning-post and rolled over him? The rider was dazed for a while. Such a fall would have terminated the career of many riders, but Steve rested an hour, and although still feeling greatly the effects of the mishap, took the mount on Prince Herod.

This race provided a terrific finish, with Steve driving Prince Herod home a winner by a head from two dead-heaters for second place. Years later he told me 'I pulled myself together because I knew the colt's owner had backed this horse heavily, and I could not let him down.'

Still more marvellous, Steve was riding again half an hour later that day. In a field of fourteen he got his mount, Acushla, up in the last stride, due to his perseverance and indomitable will, to force a dead-heat with Star of Hope. Not content, Steve rode the first two winners at Epsom the next day!

Such an exhibition of courage and ability has rarely if ever been witnessed at Epsom, the scene of some of Steve's greatest triumphs.

Though his chances of success grew fewer in his later years, his skill and superb horsemanship never deserted him – that remains a beautiful memory. Steve Donoghue is an imperishable heritage of our racing world. His memory will not fade so long as the British Turf endures.

In his career Steve rode the winners of upwards of two thousand races on the Flat. In his final season he won the Irish Derby and Irish Two Thousand Guineas on Phideas. For the last time, at the end of 1937, we heard from the racing crowds that thrilling call of 'Come on, Steve', an encouragement which has been incorporated into the English language.

When Steve retired from riding he was guest of honour at a dinner in London attended by all the leading jockeys and not a few owners. In acknowledging a presentation of silver plate Steve said: 'I am not saying good-bye. I am merely stepping from the ranks.'

In his well-remembered book *Just My Story*, Steve tells how in 1899 on the Cup day he went to Chester, where he dared approach the great trainer, John Porter. The upshot was in a day or so Steve went to learn his first lessons in the stable at Kingsclere, Hants. A little later he was in the stables of the late M. D. Peacock at Middleham, Yorks.

As a trainer Steve did not meet with much success, rather the contrary. Perhaps his best horse was Rogerstone Castle. He cost 240 guineas as a yearling. Steve saddled the colt to win the National Breeders Produce Stakes of £5,000 at Sandown Park. During the years of the war Steve had charge of a number of the horses which were foaled in this country being the produce of mares which M. Boussac had sent from France early in 1940. Those charges and all the incidental difficulties due to war-time control caused Steve intense anxiety.

For a few years Steve owned a few mares, but for the past twenty-five years he had not been the breeder of any winners. However, it is on record that Steve Donoghue was the breeder of By Jingo!, winner of the Ascot Gold Cup in 1919. This big angular horse won five other races from 1916 to 1919.

Donoghue was a warm-hearted and over-generous Lancastrian. The idol of racegoers for two decades said his final good-bye and, in his own words, stepped from the ranks. His last resting place is in the cemetery at Warrington, Lancashire, in which rather grimy town Steve was born in October, 1884.   BBR–1945

Charles Elliott's Winning Derby Ride on Bois Roussel in 1938

In this day and age, jockeys are not quoted as extensively as they were in the past. Whether that is because turf writers are not as aggressive in their newsgathering or there is not the time nor the space nor the interest, it is not for this observer to say, but many of the old-time quotes were stories unto themselves and they have been responsible for some of the most fascinating material associated with great Turf events. For example, what Charles Elliott had to say to 'Ajax' following his winning ride aboard Bois Roussel in the 1938 Derby – 'a startling victory' which 'was all very bewildering and thrilling'.

CHARLES ELLIOTT had an interesting story to relate when he unburdened himself to our friend 'Ajax' (J. H. Park), of the *Evening Standard*, as jockeys are always willing to do. About sixteen years ago he was one of Jack Jarvis's apprentices, and after he had been race-riding only a short time his master entertained a high opinion of his skill and intelligence. He has for many years been one of the leading jockeys in England. Elliott rode Call Boy when he won the Derby eleven years ago. He won the Oaks on Brulette, 1931; the Two Thousand Guineas on Flamingo, 1928, also the One Thousand Guineas on Four Course (1931), and Kandy (1932). His record this year is exceptional, for a few days subsequently Elliott won the French Derby on Cillas, a very unusual, if not unique, 'double'. Cillas was Elliott's third success in the French Derby, as he rode Thor and Tourbillon, all three owned by M. Boussac. With Gordon Richards required for Pasch, Fred Darling had to look around for a jockey to ride Bois Roussel, and no doubt was well content when he secured the services of Elliott, who, in part, spoke to 'Ajax' in this wise:

'It may be that the failure of Bois Roussel to jump out of the gate and pick up his stride with the others had something to do with his victory, but it was a long time before I had any idea I would be concerned with the finish, let alone win the race. I did not want to stay behind too long, so as we went up the hill I niggled at him to see if he could take up a better position. He could not do so, and I was still last when he got to the top of the hill. Then I realised I had to do something if I was not to finish in the ruck; up to then he had not given me a "feel" at all. There was nothing about his galloping to suggest to me he was going to do anything. He was taking hold of his bit all right, but could not make any progress.

'When I put some pressure on him as we started the descent to Tattenham Corner, there was no noticeable improvement. I did pass a few horses on the downward slope, but they were already beaten and dropping back. I had a look at the leaders and found I had gained practically nothing on them. Half-way down the hill I had not the slightest hope of winning. It was about fifty yards before we got to the Corner that I gave him a hearty crack with the whip. It was more or less a last resource, and you can imagine my surprise when he bounded forward.

'Then I remembered that Fred Darling had said: "Now don't forget, when you really get at him he will find a bit." It was after I had "given him one" that I realised for the first time I was on a racehorse. But it was a long way from home, so I did not ask him to keep it up over too long a stretch. I steadied him until we got smoothly round the turn and into the straight. I was not then in the first dozen and I should estimate I was something like twelve lengths behind the leaders. But that touch with the whip had transformed him entirely. Off he went in a style which not only gave me some hope, but made me sure I would make a fight of it after all. Along the straight he tore at a much faster pace than anything else. One after another I passed them as if they were standing still. With a furlong to go, I got on terms with Pasch; then there was only Scottish Union to beat. I just sailed past him to win almost in a canter by four lengths. If there had been another furlong to do I should have won by half a furlong.'

It may never again happen that a rider of a Derby winner will have so extraordinary a story to tell, and all our readers will, we imagine, feel indebted to Mr Park for collecting it.

The Death of Frank Wootton

When the most famous jockeys of the English Turf are discussed, Frank Wootton, who died in Australia in 1940 aged forty-six, belongs with a select group which would include George Fordham, Fred Archer, Steve Donoghue, Gordon Richards and, of more recent times, Lester Piggott. Although he did not win as many championships as the others, Wootton, who only rode on the Flat for seven years, garnered four championships, which were two more than his great rival, Danny Maher, while riding at a 23 per cent winning pace. He also captured a riding championship in 1921 under National Hunt Rules. While the Derby escaped him, he did win an Oaks and a St Leger, the latter aboard the best horse he ever handled – Swynford. Upon the occasion of his death, the BBR *befittingly published the following:*

FRANK WOOTTON, idol of the great racing public twenty-five years ago, died in Sydney, Australia, on April 4th, at the age of forty-six. He was the eldest son of Richard Wootton, and brother of Stanley Wootton.

His father was, of course, a very distinguished and successful trainer in Australia, South Africa and England.

When only thirteen years of age Frank Wootton rode his first winner in England. This was at Folkestone on August 26th, 1906. Retrieve, owned by his father, was the forerunner of his sixteen successful mounts that season.

'Frank' captured the imagination of the public in a manner only equalled by Gordon Richards and Steve Donoghue since his day. Yet Wootton did not ride the winner of the Derby. He won the Oaks on Perola in 1909, and the St Leger on Swynford, perhaps the best horse he ever rode. In the Two Thousand Guineas he was second on Stedfast; third on Perola in the One Thousand Guineas; third on Hair Trigger II,

Frank Wootton.

and Bill and Coo in the Oaks; second on Valens and White Magic and
third on King William in the St Leger.

In his riding career on the Flat extending from 1906 to 1913, Frank
Wootton had 3,866 mounts. He rode 882 winners; was second in 705
races, and third in 452 races. Thus he had about 23 per cent of successful
rides which is truly exceptional, and is a high tribute to his skill and
ability. He was an uncannily brilliant horseman and seemed to know
what was the 'form' of most of the other horses against which he was
competing. His great rivalry with the late Danny Maher fascinated the
racing crowds, for there were some doughty struggles between them. In
1908 'Frank' was second to 'Danny', 129 wins against 139 victories. In
1909 and again in 1910, Wootton was the leading jockey and Maher was
second to him. In 1911 Frank was the leader, when C. Trigg was closest
to him. In 1912 it was again Wootton and Maher, Frank had best with
118 victories to 109, but Danny in 1913 was in pride of place with 115

wins against Wootton's 91. By this time increasing weight was causing Wootton much concern, and he was obliged to take fewer mounts. Really, in 1912, for the reason stated, Wootton's opportunities were much restricted.

He was but fourteen years old when he rode Demure to win the Cesarewitch and a great fortune for the Australian owner and his friends. The filly then carried 6 st 9 lb.

A few of Frank Wootton's brilliant riding achievements may be recalled. In 1907, Demure's year, he was third in the Cambridgeshire. In 1908, he rode seven winners at the Doncaster St Leger Meeting. Three of these were successive. In 1911, at Goodwood, he won ten races. On the third day he had six mounts, of which four were successful and in the others he was second and third.

He scored another remarkable record in 1912, when he rode no fewer than seven winners at the Ascot Meeting. The names of the many famous horses on which he was successful in the big races is too formidable a list to mention, but they included a Doncaster Cup (Lemberg), a Cesarewitch (Demure), a Chester Cup (Glacis), a Manchester Cup (Marajax) and the Eclipse on mighty Swynford.

Frank Wootton rarely rode on the Continent. He, however, did win the Grand Prix de Paris on Houli in 1912.

He joined the Army during the Great War and went to Mesopotamia. He naturally rode at a number of military meetings, winning the Bagdad Grand National.

When he returned to England, Frank Wootton rode with very striking success over hurdles. Claiming an 'allowance' in his first year he was up on eleven winners. In 1921 he headed the list of winning jockeys under National Hunt Rules, with sixty-one wins, and his record in the two following years was forty-two and fifty-two successful rides.

He then visited Australia, but returned to this country and for a time was training. He turned out over one hundred winners. He had only one mount in the Grand National. This was in 1921 – Shaun Spadah's year. Frank rode Any Time, who that season had won half a dozen events over fences. Yet he fell at Aintree.

About seven years ago, Frank Wootton returned to Australia, where his father had settled again, and is still living. His fame as a jockey is unforgettable, for without doubt he was one of the most intelligent riders ever known in the history of the British Turf. His greatest number of winning mounts in any season was 187 in 1911. By comparison the record is Gordon Richards' 259 in 1933, when he surpassed Fred Archer's 246 successes scored in 1885. Between those years came Tommy Loates, the 'next best' with 222 winning rides in 1893.

Frank Wootton, a most daring rider and resolute finisher, never forgot that the best position was nearest the rails. At the height of his career the racing public blindly followed the mounts of 'Frankie' as he was named by thousands who never had an opportunity of seeing Wootton ride in a race.   BBR–1940

Jockey Quotes After the Derby of 1942

Jockey quotes have held a very great attraction for most followers of the Turf. English riders have always been most adept at telling it like it was and Harry (The Waiter) Wragg was always one of the best. His trip aboard Watling Street in the 1942 Derby is an ideal example of how he earned his sobriquet. His post-race quotes were collected by Mr J. A. Park, 'a very old friend of the Review' *who wrote under the nom de plume of 'Ajax', as were those of E. L. Smith, who handled the runner-up Hyperides, and Gordon Richards, rider of the beaten favourite Big Game, whose stamina was found wanting in the only race of his nine-year career he was to lose.*

HARRY WRAGG (Watling Street):

'I thought it all out carefully many times before the race, and came to the conclusion that my own mount, Watling Street, and Hyperides were the best stayers in the field. I did not believe in the stamina of Big Game, and decided that if I had the choice I should follow Hyperides in preference to Big Game. I had complete faith in the ability of Watling Street to last every yard of the journey no matter how fast the pace might be. I was hoping Big Game and Hyperides would have a tussle for supremacy before I wanted to make my run; it so happened that they did so. I did not want to come on the scene too early, because, from the experience I gained in the home gallops, I thought my colt might want to pull up after hitting the front. So I let him go out of the gate at his own pace, and was one of the back-markers for the first half mile. As we made the turn into the straight I was last but two, but shortly afterwards went to the outside so that I could take up whatever position I wanted without meeting with interference. I moved up a little, and when they started to race in earnest about three furlongs from the finish I had the option of going over to the right to follow Big Game or staying on the outside and have Hyperides as a pace-maker. I decided to stay where I was, and though I was about four lengths behind with only a quarter of a mile to go, I felt fairly sure of winning. I could see Big Game was wavering and Hyperides was being ridden right out. At the top of the hill I gave my colt one tap with the whip just to liven him up. That was the only time I hit him and it had the desired effect. He closed in a bit, but I was still a couple of lengths in arrears as we started the climb to the winning post. Watling Street had lengthened his stride and was laying himself down to his work in the style which made me feel he had the necessary reserve. I collared Hyperides fifty yards from the winning post and won by a neck. I have no doubt I could have made it a bit more if I had hit him again, but I did not want to take any risk and just pushed him through with the hands. It was more or less what I had planned to do and it all came off as I had anticipated.'

E. SMITH (Hyperides):

'It was bad luck being caught close home. But I must say I had a perfect run all the way, and so far as that is concerned I have no excuse to make. I did feel that I was going to win when I went into the lead and started the rise to the winning post with an advantage. But when we struck the rise my colt hung a bit and that may have made all the difference.'

GORDON RICHARDS (Big Game):

'I was disappointed at the way the colt ran his race because he had been working so quietly at home. But instead of settling down smoothly as I had hoped, he ran all too freely from the start. For half a mile he fought for his head, but I then got him nicely settled, and for a bit I thought I had got him going to my liking. When we got to the seven furlongs post, one came on either side of me and away he went again. I was able to restrain him, but realised I would have to let him go and we went into the lead perhaps about a quarter of a mile from the finish. He did not last long after that as he had used up all his energy.'   BBR–1942

Harry Wragg Hangs up his Tack

There was a very appropriate ending to the great riding career of Harry Wragg when, late in the 1946 season, he rode Las Vegas to victory in the Manchester November Handicap, his last winning ride. He closed out this career for another, that of a successful trainer, when he was seventh of twelve aboard Viva in the last flat race of 1946. A more complete record appeared in the Review *of 1946.*

ALTHOUGH he had thirteen mounts in 1919 (when apprenticed with Mr R. W. Colling), Harry Wragg rode one winner and was placed five times – an augury for his future career. From 1919 until his retirement in 1946 – comprising twenty-eight seasons – Harry Wragg rode in 11,658 flat races in Great Britain and in Ireland. He had mounts in France and probably elsewhere.

The full record of Harry Wragg reveals he rode no fewer than 1,762 winners – just over 15 per cent of his mounts. He was placed second in 1,568 races and third in 1,500 races – a percentage of 27.

Therefore Harry either won or was placed in just over 42 per cent of his mounts – a remarkable tribute to his riding ability over so many years. His Derby winners were Blenheim and Felstead. He won the Oaks four times on Rockfel, Commotion, Sun Stream (1945) and Steady Aim

Blenheim (H. Wragg up) led in by HH Aga Khan after the 1930 Derby.

this year. His St Leger victories were on Sandwich and Herringbone. Garden Path was H. Wragg's only winning ride in the Two Thousand Guineas. Thrice he rode winners of the One Thousand Guineas, viz: Campanula, Herringbone and Sun Stream.

His name was generally associated in England with that very good horse, Finalist. Among his very many Cup winners is to be mentioned Foxhunter in the Ascot Gold Cup. Harry Wragg's record as a rider of five winners of the Eclipse Stakes, £10,000, at Sandown Park, is probably unexcelled. They are Polyphontes (1925), Rustom Pasha (1930), Miracle (1932), King Salmon (1934) and Gulf Stream, this year. In 1924 H. Wragg rode for the Royal Stable. He headed the Winning Jockeys' List in 1941 and finished in second position in 1931, 1932 and 1935. The record of Harry Wragg is especially consistent proving him one of the best jockeys of our times. Harry Wragg each season had over 100 winning mounts, best of all being 1931 with 110 winners; 1929 (103), 1931, 1932 (102), 1935 (102) and 1937 (102). Perhaps it should be remarked that fairly early in the 1941 Season Gordon Richards sustained a broken leg.   BBR–1946

Part 6

BETTING

Legalisation of the Tote in England

*In 1928 Mr Winston Churchill was Chancellor of the Exchequer.
That was two years after he had sought a duty on wagering. In those
two years he had finally succeeded in setting the pace in making pari-
mutuel betting legal. It marked a great victory for reformers of the
Turf. 'British Turf Freed From Shackles' was the sub-head in the lead
story by Mr Edward Moorhouse in the BBR of 1928. Portions of that
momentous story are presented here, including the conclusion of Mr
Churchill's 'interesting and characteristic speech' before the House.
The bookmakers are still 'big time' in England, Scotland and Wales,
but this is a part of British Turf history that belongs to the ages.*

IN THE last volume of the *Review* we had the pari-mutuel on the door-
step. After a vast amount of argument, and opposition of a somewhat
virulent character, it was, during the past summer, allowed to cross the
threshold. In other words, the law no longer condemns as illegal the use
of the pari-mutuel or totalisator for betting purposes on any approved
racecourse in England, Scotland and Wales. Nor is that all, for the
Betting Act of 1853 does not now apply in any way to racecourses when a
race meeting is in progress. The Turf authorities, therefore, have
acquired the right to control racecourse bookmakers, exact fees from
them, and compel them to conduct their business at specified places.

Three short years ago those of us who desired to see these reforms
instituted seemed to be toying with a chimera. The higher authorities of
the Turf were afraid to approach Parliament with a view to securing a
relaxation of the anomalous restrictions on betting lest a ventilation of
the question in the House of Commons should end in discomfiture and,
perchance, the imposition of additional hindrances. It may be conceded
that any such effort made then, or earlier, would have been abortive.
The situation, however, completely changed when, two years ago, Mr
Churchill persuaded Parliament to enact the duty on betting.

The Chancellor referred to the moral issue, to 'the doctrine of the
unclean things'. It was the doctrine that had become dominant in the
United States in regard to liquor legislation. There was, however, no
reason to suppose that prohibition had been more effective than our
policy, which was to tax and not prohibit – to take a profit to the State, if
in so doing we were able to diminish the evil.

Mr Churchill went on to say that he could not see any moral distinction between a gang of bookmakers shouting in a ring and the
totalisator, electrically worked, ticking off the odds from moment to

moment. They could have an eager discussion about capital punishment, but if they had decided in favour of capital punishment, it was a very minor question, though one of interest, whether they should chop a man's head off with an axe or use the machinery of the guillotine. In this case, as in others, added the Chancellor amid general laughter, he was in favour of the machine. If this were such a horrible method that was to be introduced, he was astonished that it should already be in operation in every important country in Europe, in all our Dominions, and in India.

Towards the end of his speech, the Chancellor said one reason why the Bill should receive a second reading was set forth in the following extract from a speech Lord D'Abernon made when last year he introduced a deputation to him (Mr Churchill). Lord D'Abernon said:

'England has been till now the fountain head of the thoroughbred horse and has hitherto supplied the world with the best stock. The prominent position of England is, however, threatened by other countries. France and the United States must be regarded as serious competitors. Thus the horse-breeding industry which, apart from considerations of international prestige, is of commercial value to this country, the volume of trade reaching considerable dimensions, requires careful guidance and intelligent support. The basic necessity is to retain in England the best mares and stallions. Fundamentally, this depends upon the prizes open to horses in this country compared with the prizes offered abroad. The best horses gravitate to those countries where the best rewards await them. This aspect of the question has hitherto received very inadequate attention here.'

Mr Churchill brought his speech to a conclusion by saying:

'One of the practical considerations which had led him to support the second reading was the undoubted improvement that would be effected on our racecourses. More betting was done in England than in any equal community of the world, and it was done under more disagreeable, rowdy and unsatisfactory conditions than anywhere else. The contrast between British racecourses and French racecourses was a contrast between eighteenth century barbarism and rowdyism and the new civilisation which they hoped the twentieth century would offer for very large numbers of people. Twenty years ago he spoke from that box as President of the Board of Trade, pleading for the Daylight Saving Measure. It was received with the same incredulity, doubts and misgivings as the present suggestion, and yet no one would dream of going back on such a decision at the present day. In the same way, when this particular piece of machinery was introduced into our sporting life, the convenience and the cleansing effect would be such that there would never be any question of altering again.'   BBR-1928

Pari-mutuel Method approved by 'The Times'

COMMENTING on the Jockey Club's decision in favour of the adoption of the pari-mutuel method of betting, *The Times*, in a leading article, declared:

'If betting is to be taxed, it is to the general advantage that it should be taxed in the most scientific manner, and there can be no question that this condition is best satisfied by the totalisator, which provides by far the easiest method of collecting the tax that has yet been devised by the wit of man. But that is by no means its only recommendation. . . It is fair, since the totalisator cannot cheat. It records the exact state of public opinion about the chances of the horses; declares the odds more accurately than is possible in any other way; will raise a sum of money which will not only be of real service to the interests of the sport, but is likely also to benefit the cause of charity; and will tend to mitigate the turmoil and discomfort inseparable from the betting rings.'

BBR-1927

What the Pari-mutuel has Done

THAT THE pari-mutuel form of betting has now obtained a firm footing in the United States and Canada, and that its advantages are being more and more realised, is made evident by the following statement by Mr Charles F. Grainger, a member of the Kentucky State Racing Commission, which we quote from the *Thoroughbred Record*:

'The salvation of racing in Kentucky and Canada is due to the revival of the pari-mutuel style of wagering on horses. With the exception of New York, where the sport has been curtailed by rigorous laws, the Turf is in sounder condition today than ever before in the history of running races in this country. There is fairer racing and a better satisfied public, all the result of the change from the bookmaking system of betting to the pari-mutuel style. Between the two there is no comparison.

'The law permitting the pari-mutuel form of betting has been on the statute books of Kentucky for years. I was familiar with the system as it prevailed at the Downs track in 1878–79–80 and other seasons. It was decided to return to this system, and it was the efforts in this direction of myself and Messrs Winn and Applegate that finally caused the Kentucky Racing Commission to permit this as the only style of betting allowed on Kentucky race tracks. Indirectly this has led to the system being adopted in other States in this country, as well as in the Dominion of Canada.

'So successful has been this form of betting that purses and stakes on the tracks in Kentucky have increased nearly 100 per cent since the installation, and as a result Eastern turfmen come to Kentucky to race the best horses of their establishments. It has also resulted in wealthy men establishing breeding farms on a big scale in this State.'

BBR-1915

Did Times Like These Ever Really Exist?

MUTUEL BETTING IN NEW YORK STATE: DISPARATE OPINIONS: Last March Mr Joseph E. Widener, who is vice-chairman of the New York Jockey Club and head of the Belmont Park Executive, was reported to have stated that, in conversation with Governor Frank D. Roosevelt, he had put forward reasons why he would welcome the legalisation of pari-mutuel betting in New York State. Mr Widener explained that he was merely expressing his personal views and that he had no desire to 'commercialise' racing, much preferring that it should be conducted, as at Saratoga and Belmont Park, on a non-dividend-earning basis. Revenue derived from betting would, however, enable them to meet on more equal terms the competition of tracks favoured with pari-mutuel profits.

When the attention of Mr William Woodward, Chairman of the Jockey Club, was drawn to Mr Widener's observations, he is reported by *Daily Racing Form* to have said:

> 'Mutuel betting is all right if you want that kind of racing, but we are racing for sport's sake, without profit and with no commercial angle. The wealthy men who are supporting New York racing with money and time are putting in an enormous amount of work. They love it, and I believe they will continue to do it.'

In answer to a question, Mr Woodward said further:

> 'I would be in favour of a perfect pari-mutuel law, but do not think one can be drawn. I have an open mind on the matter. We of the Jockey Club are always alert, but I believe an acute situation is several years in the future. We will be ready to meet it when it comes.'   BBR–1931

Part 7

BREEDERS

A Hazardous Form of Speculation

The following was excerpted from an article in the BBR *and, since it is so applicable to racing and breeding, regardless of time or place, it is being repeated here.*

THERE ARE, we suppose, few more hazardous forms of speculation than that of bloodstock breeding. The prizes forthcoming are fugitive, the disappointments appallingly frequent. The public hear little about the latter. Breeders themselves have no inclination to dwell on them.

'Ten Pour Cent' Commissions

It is 10 per cent here and 10 per cent there and 10 per cent everywhere in the horse business. According to this article by 'Faraway' which first appeared in Horse and Hound *and was reprinted in the* BBR *of 1926, it is 'a canker' which first took place in France shortly after World War II and 'was fostered by an American trainer'. Anyone reading it will probably think that the age of 'secret commissions' is still very much with us.*

IN ONE of the very interesting articles on French racing he has during the past season contributed weekly to *Horse and Hound*, 'Faraway' referred to a controversy which had arisen over the commissions many French breeders have habitually paid to trainers on the purchase price of yearlings at the Deauville Sales. It is known as the '10 pour cent'. Several breeders have always declined to pay this commission, among them some of the most powerful.

'The matter was brought before the Breeders' Association last back-end, but no tangible result has been arrived at up to the present (end of July), and now the sporting papers are talking about what they term "rémunérations occultes," or, in plain English, "secret commissions". This canker, which has entered into all public sales of thoroughbreds in this country, started since the war, and has now become a positive scandal, as some of the trainers – I will not say all of them – will hardly attend the sales of those breeders who do not pay the commission. The payment of this commission was fostered by an American trainer, since dead, and a well-known dealer, who also died recently, and it became worse when a certain well-known Indian prince, for whom they bought, started racing over here, and paid high prices for yearlings. It is difficult to see how the practice is to be stopped, because there is not the slightest doubt that if most of the breeders banded themselves together and declined to pay the commissions, there would always be some who would stand out and pay. It is known to everybody, but it had not been brought so prominently before the public eye until last week. The auctioneers themselves are perfectly cognisant of what is going on, and, in fact, when they themselves show yearlings before the sales to trainers or owners with a view to assisting the sale, they invariably ask the breeder beforehand whether he is prepared to pay the regular 10 per cent commission. . .

'The papers now propose that this commission should be transferred to the purchaser – that is to say, that instead of the breeder being saddled with the 10 per cent the owner who buys the horse should pay his trainer 10 per cent, and there is a long explanation how this should be done to become equitable according to the performances of the animal purchased, as the papers point out that the trainer is acting for the owner, and, therefore, it is to the owner he advises to whom he should look for his commission, and that to take it from the breeder becomes illicit. There is not the slightest doubt that this is true. The owners, however, are already saddled with considerable payments to their trainers and jockeys, as on every race won in this country it is a *sine qua non* that the jockey and the trainer each receive 10 per cent of the stake, and if a horse is sold either privately or at public auction, or even claimed out of a selling race, the owner pays the recognised 10 per cent to his trainer on the amount of the purchase price. Personally, I am convinced that nothing will come of the agitation to stop this very unpleasant arrangement. I should like to make it quite clear that I do not think any of the leading trainers would buy a bad animal for one of their owners for the sake of the commission. In fact, I have seen positive proof to the contrary on many occasions; but there is not the slightest doubt that several breeders do not sell as well as they ought to do because they decline to pay a commission to the trainers.'   BBR–1926

The Centenary of the Dispersal of the Royal Stud

In 1937 the BBR *made note of articles which had appeared a century earlier in the* Sunday Times *and* The Times *reporting the dispersal of the Royal Stud at Hampton Court, including the sale of The Colonel who had dead-heated for first in the Derby of 1828 with Cadland. The writing is most delightful and deserves preserving as much as the historical incident.*

FOLLOWING the accession of Queen Victoria, the Royal Stud at Hampton Court was dispersed October 25th, 1837. The *Sunday Times* recorded the event thus:

'Despite all that has been said and sung in monthly, hebdomadal, diurnal, and evening prints – despite the groaning, grumbling, aye, and threatening, of the Tories – the Royal Stud was most remorselessly sold on Wednesday last. The 80 lots fetched £15,782.'

The Times of the day following the sale made a feature of the appearance in the auction ring of the twelve-year-old stallion, The Colonel (by Whisker), who won the St Leger in 1828. Its report read:

'The sale of the Royal Stud, which has been so long announced, and so repeatedly a subject of controversy, took place yesterday, in accordance with the advertisements, at Hampton Court paddocks. . . The great feature in the sale was The Colonel. The excitement produced by his appearance was astonishing; scores of people were running to meet him as the grooms led him out. He was in beautiful condition. This noble horse was full of life and spirit: his gambols were a little too vivacious for his admirers to approach very close to him, and when brought into the circle, he very soon succeeded in enlarging the boundaries of it. . . (He) was bought of the Hon. E. Petre, after winning the St Leger, for 4,000 guineas. He broke down at Ascot in 1831, after running a dead-heat with Mouche, and it is a proof of the excellence of George IV's judgment that when he first saw him after his purchase he pointed out the leg on which he would fall. He fetched 400 or 500 guineas less than was expected (1,550 guineas), and goes from Hampton Court to labour in his vocation at Mr Tattersall's, Dawley, near Uxbridge.'

The Colonel started favourite for the Derby of 1828, and ran a dead-heat with Cadland, by whom he was beaten half a length in a 'decider'. George IV bought him from Mr Edward Petre, hoping the colt would win the Ascot Cup; but that race was won by Zinganee, trained by William Chiffney. Asked by Lord Darlington for his opinion about the runners, Chiffney, writing the Monday of Ascot week, stated his belief that Zinganee would win easily. Concerning The Colonel's chance he wrote:

'The Colonel is badly shaped: his ribs and quarters are much too large and heavily formed and will cause him to tire and to run a-jade. Independent of this defect the course, of all others, is especially ill-suited to him, and will cause him to fall an easy victim. Still, his party are so exceedingly fond of him as to think no horse can defeat him and they have backed him for an immense sum. In face of all this I entertain the most contemptible opinion of him *for the distance of ground*, and I fear nothing whatever from him.'

After Zinganee had won the Ascot Cup the King bought him for 2,000 guineas, but his reputation diminished, and after a few seasons at the stud he went to America.   BBR-1937

The Eaton Stud and its Memories

Eaton, one of the most enduring, renowned and successful studs in the great history of English racing and breeding, was founded near the ancient city of Chester around 1780 by Richard, the first Earl Grosvenor. One of his first purchases was Eclipse's legendary son, Pot-8-os, the tail-male ancestor of a majority of the world's thoroughbred population tracing to Eclipse, exclusively through Pot-8-os' son Waxy, the sire of Whalebone. Through the years, Eaton has been the home of such historic and revered animals as Touchstone, Doncaster, Bend Or, Ormonde, Orme, Sainfoin and Flying Fox, among many others of distinction.

In 1914, Edward Moorhouse, one of the directors of the Review *as well as being as superlative a writer as was ever concerned with the Turf, managed a lengthy interview with Richard Chapman who had been appointed Stud Groom at Eaton in 1880 and was privy to much of the romance and the intimate realities associated with the House of Grosvenor during the preceding century as well as his own very active years with the Stud.*

It is an engrossing narrative that Mr Moorhouse authored for the Review *in April of 1914. With so many more years having separated us from those times, the realisation that these fascinating stories of those famous horses and the people associated with them may be brought back, as in a time capsule, assures the history of the Turf a freshness and a perpetuity that few, if any, other sports can match. The glories which belonged to Eaton really belong to all of us who enjoy the glorious thoroughbred – past, present and future.*

ON THE LEFT bank of the river Dee, some two miles from the ancient City of Chester, lies Eaton, the ancestral home of the Grosvenors. There, round about the year 1780, Richard, first Earl Grosvenor, established a stud for breeding and rearing thoroughbreds. The Earl was then forty-nine years of age, and had long been regarded as one of the pillars of the Turf. Writing in March, 1761, Horace Walpole makes the following reference to him: 'Sir R. Grosvenor is made a lord, viscount or baron, I don't know which; nor does he, for yesterday, when he should have kissed hands, he was gone to Newmarket to see the trial of a racehorse.' In an article which appeared in a magazine nine years ago the statement is made that before he founded his stud at Eaton Lord Grosvenor must have bought his racing stock. That he was an occasional buyer is certain. For instance, in 1778 he purchased from Lord Abingdon Pot-8-os, who was then a five-year-old. The deal took place after Pot-8-os had beaten Lord Grosvenor's Grey Robin for a Sweepstake at Newmarket. The sum paid is said to have been 1,500 guineas, and the late Joseph Osborne is not far wrong when he states that at this price Pot-8-os was one of the greatest bargains ever made. The horse won thirty-five of the forty-six races in which he ran, and most of them for Lord Grosvenor. Pot-8-os was eleven years old when he began his career at the Eaton Stud, and there it was that he begat Waxy, the sire of Whalebone.

A reference to the first volume of the *General Stud Book* makes it quite clear, however, that Lord Grosvenor (who became an Earl in 1784) was breeding racehorses long before 1780. A broodmare by Hobgoblin was his property in 1750, and it is recorded that during the next six or seven years he was breeding from three daughters of Partner. Nevertheless it is undeniable that his activities as a breeder of bloodstock greatly increased after the formation of the paddocks at Eaton. I have gone through the first volume of the *Stud Book* and find that no fewer than 196 of the mares included therein belonged at one time or another to Lord Grosvenor. He retained the majority of them not more than two or three years. It would, indeed, seem that he was somewhat fickle in his likes and dislikes, because he frequently bought and sold a mare two or three times over. In very few instances did a mare remain in his possession during the whole of her stud life.

Lord Grosvenor died in 1802, at the age of seventy-one, and it was at the time estimated that his passion for the Turf had cost him a quarter of a million sterling. A great deal of this money was lost by betting, for he had the reputation of being one of the biggest gamblers of his day. He won the Derby three times – with Rhadamanthus in 1790, with John Bull in 1792, and with Dædalus in 1794. Rhadamanthus and Dædalus were own brothers, being by Justice out of Flyer, one of the seven mares that have produced two Derby winners. The others are the Highflyer mare, dam of Spread Eagle and Didelot, Horatia, dam of Archduke and Paris; Arethusa, dam of Ditto and Pan; Emma, dam of Mundig and Cotherstone; Perdita II, dam of Persimmon and Diamond Jubilee; and Morganette, dam of Galtee More and Ard Patrick. In 1782 Lord Grosvenor had an aggravating experience. His horse Sweet Robin ran second in the Derby to Lord Egremont's Assassin. Angelica (a mare by Snap), the dam of Assassin, was in Lord Grosvenor's stud from 1769 to 1771. She then became the property of Mr Shafto, who sold her to Lord Bolingbroke. From the latter Lord Grosvenor bought her back in 1777 but, after mating her with Sweetbriar in 1778, he transferred her to Lord Egremont, for whom in 1779, she bred the Derby winner Assassin.

The associations of the Grosvenors with the Turf were maintained by the son of the first ennobled member of the family. This son was, in 1831, created Marquis of Westminster, and he it was who bred Touchstone, winner of the St Leger in 1834. There is no need to dwell here on Touchstone's record as a progenitor of his species. Let it suffice to say that he was the sire of the classic winners Cotherstone, Orlando, Surplice, Blue Bonnet, Newminster, Mendicant, Flatcatcher, Nuny Kirk and Lord of the Isles. Touchstone died at Eaton when thirty years of age, and his skeleton is to be seen there today, set up in a small shed which adjoins the stallion boxes. Close to his fore-feet are some of the bones of Beeswax, who, to him, produced Newminster.

The first Marquis of Westminster also won the St Leger with Launcelot and Satirist in 1841 and 1842, and the Oaks with Ghuznee in 1841 – achievements which supply ample evidence of his vigorous endeavours to keep the Grosvenor colours, 'Yellow, black cap', to the fore.

It was in 1869 that the late Duke of Westminster became head of the House of Grosvenor. He received the Dukedom in 1874 on the recommendation of his friend and neighbour, Mr Gladstone, who was a frequent visitor at Eaton. When he succeeded to the estates the stud had been allowed to dwindle to insignificant proportions, but he set to work to place it once again on a sure foundation. To this end a high-class stallion was deemed requisite. The Duke, in the first instance, contemplated the acquirement of either Knight of the Garter or Gladiateur, but neither of them satisfied his ideas concerning the essential characteristics of a stallion. It chanced that at this particular juncture the merits of Doncaster were brought to his notice.

By Stockwell out of Marigold, Doncaster was bred at Sledmere by the late Sir Tatton Sykes. Bearing the awkward name of All Heart and No Peel, he was sent as a yearling to the Doncaster Sales, and there Mr James Merry, acting on the advice of his trainer, Robert Peck, bought him for 950 guineas. Two years later the colt, who had been re-named Doncaster, won the Derby. After he had won the Ascot Cup in 1875, Mr Merry sold the horse to his trainer for £10,000, and a few days later the Duke of Westminster acquired him for £14,000. Thus it came to pass that Doncaster was installed at Eaton, where he was destined to revive the glories of the days of Pot-8-os and Touchstone. Among his first crop of foals that came into the world in 1877 was a chestnut colt out of Rouge Rose. This youngster received the name of Bend Or, and in 1880 he won the Derby. He in his turn begat Ormonde, the sire of Orme, who was to become the sire of Flying Fox. It is with these giants of the Turf and Stud that the most brilliant chapters of the modern history of the Eaton paddocks are concerned.

In 1875, Colonel Barlow, of Woodbridge, Suffolk, was appointed Master of the Horse to the Duke. He took with him to Eaton, Richard Chapman, who had for some years been in his service. Chapman was born in 1848 near Cambridge. As a youth he obtained employment with the notorious Marquis of Hastings, in Leicestershire, and it was after the Marquis's death that he went to Woodbridge to look after Colonel

Barlow's hunters. For the first five years he was at Eaton the Duke's hunters were Chapman's chief concern, but in 1880 he was chosen to succeed Arnull as Stud Groom. This important step in his career was made in July. A month previously Bend Or had won the Derby and at that time Arnull was under notice to leave the Duke's service. He it was who started the rumour that Bend Or and Tadcaster, both sons of Doncaster, had been 'mixed up' when foals, and it was by means of his evidence that an endeavour was made to prove that it was really Tadcaster and not Bend Or who won the Derby. Chapman is still in charge at the Eaton Stud. It occurred to me that he must have

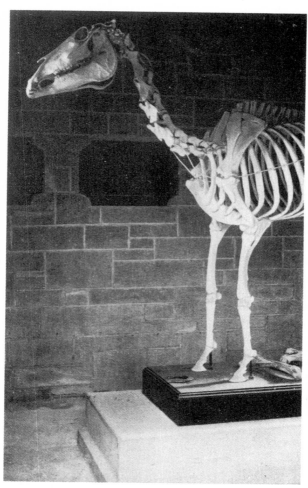

Touchstone's Skeleton with Beeswing's bones at his feet.

accumulated a rich store of recollections during the thirty-four years he has filled his highly responsible post; and so I asked, and obtained, the permission of Colonel Wilford Lloyd, the agent at Eaton, to visit the stud and interview Mr Chapman.

Chapman was waiting for me in the stud yard. We looked, as I had done more than once before, at the graves of five equine celebrities, inspected the skeleton of Touchstone, had a peep at the stallions, Troutbeck and Pipistrello, and went to the boxes in which there were mares with new-born foals at foot. It was all very interesting. 'But,' said I to my guide, 'this is not what I came for. I want to have a quiet talk with *you* about bygone days.' 'Very well,' he said, and, leading the way, he conducted me to his cottage, the little garden of which is lapped by the flowing waters of the Dee. For the next two hours or so we sat in Mr Chapman's office. The walls of this sanctum are almost covered with mounted horse-shoes, worn by Eaton-bred animals when winning some important race or other. The date and value of each race are duly inscribed on the yellow mount in black lettering. It is an imposing array. 'There are many more I could put up if I only had room for them,' says Chapman.

Having mentioned that he succeeded Arnull the year Bend Or won the Derby, Chapman was asked if he could make any contribution to the recently-revived discussion concerning the identity of Bend Or and Tadcaster.

> 'Everybody here knew that the colt running as Bend Or was in fact Bend Or and not the Clemence colt called Tadcaster. I was at the time given to understand that when, after the Derby, Arnull hinted that Bend Or was really Tadcaster, Mr Brewer, the owned of Robert the Devil, who finished second, promised him £1,000 if he could prove his allegation. There was a certain similarity between the two colts, though Bend Or's near hind heel was white and he had a faint streak down his face, whereas Tadcaster was a chestnut without any markings.'

Doncaster was, of course, 'in full go' when Chapman went over to the stud. The Duke at that time had about sixteen broodmares. Says Chapman:

> 'There was not a "worst" among them. Any mare that showed defects was at once weeded out and replaced by a better one. This strictness resulted in other studs securing many a bargain, but the Duke never expressed regret for having parted with a mare that afterwards turned out well. Indeed, he was always more pleased than sorry. Nothing vexed him more than to find he had sold to someone else an animal which had done the buyer a bad turn. That showed a good feeling, did it not?'

Bend Or was turned out of training in 1881, and retired to Eaton. Listen to Chapman singing aloud his praises:

'He was the sweetest-tempered horse in the world. A child could do anything with him. During the season he walked, on an average, a hundred miles a week. We used to send him a different route each morning. He was led by his attendant, Ben Jenner, who had looked after him when he was in training and who came with him to Eaton from Russley. Jenner was a real good fellow. He left here to enter the service of Lord Crewe, and when Lord Crewe dispersed his stud Jenner went as Stud Groom to Sir Waldie Griffith. I say again that Bend Or was as docile as a lamb, but he had the courage of a lion. I was always very fond of him.

'The Duke was dead against overdoing his stallions. As a rule he only allowed them to have about a dozen mares in their first season. In no year did Bend Or have more than forty. By thus drawing a hard and fast line a stallion's power is husbanded. What vitality Bend Or must have had to the very last, for he was twenty-five years old when he got Radium! When, in the latter part of his time he had finished the season we used to turn him out and let him down in condition by stopping his corn. That partly explained why he lasted to long. After all, a horse is very like a man; if he eats to excess and goes short of exercise it is sure to tell on him in the long run. In his very first year Bend Or gave us Ormonde and Kendal. A pretty good start, eh? He died of heart failure. The morning of the day he passed away he seemed to be as well as ever, and went out for his usual walk. But after he had gone half a mile through the Park, he just crouched down at his attendant's feet and died without a struggle. He was twenty-six years old.'

Then we came to the story of Ormonde – or that portion of it which is associated with the Eaton Stud. Said Chapman:

'His dam, Lily Agnes, when the property of Mr Snarry, of Malton, came here on a visit to Doncaster. I liked her so much that I urged the Duke to buy her. His Grace had not, however, made up his mind to adopt my suggestion by the time the mare was ready to go back home; but a few weeks later he sent me to Malton to examine and report upon her. Eventually the Duke decided to buy her, but he made the stipulation with Snarry that nobody, apart from themselves, should know how much he had paid. It was not until after Ormonde had won the St Leger that I learned that the Duke gave for Lily Agnes £2,500 and two free subscriptions to Bend Or, whose fee was then 200 guineas. The Duke afterwards bought Lizzie Agnes, sister to Lily Agnes, and dam of Orwell.'

When Lily Agnes went to Eaton she was carrying Rossington, a colt by Doncaster, who eventually went to America. She was again put to Doncaster and the produce was Farewell, who gained classic honours in the One Thousand Guineas. Lily Agnes's next alliance was with Bend Or, to whom she bred Ormonde.

Chapman relates:

'It was at half-past six on Sunday evening, March 18th, 1883, that Ormonde was born. I was getting ready to go to Eaton Church (the Duke expected us all to attend) when I was summoned to the box occupied by Lily Agnes. Ormonde was an extraordinary foal. When he came into the world his mane was already three inches long. His mother had carried him twelve months, although for two or three weeks she had shown the normal signs of approaching foaling. For several months Ormonde stood very much over at the knee. I had never before, and have never since, seen a foal with this characteristic so pronounced. It seemed impossible for him ever to grow straight. But he did, though the improvement was very gradual.

'Did the Duke at that time regard Ormonde as a wonder? No, I should say not. Like a good many others who came to the stud that year, the Duke preferred Kendal and Whitefriar, who were contemporaries of Ormonde. He was one of the slow-maturing sort, was Ormonde. In his early days he was a three-cornered beggar that might be anything or nothing. When he did begin to develop on the right lines he went ahead very quickly, and when he left here as a yearling to go to Kingsclere to be trained by John Porter, he looked a high class horse, and I quite expected him to do big things.

'The late Duke expected you to express your opinion, and to be prepared to give good reasons for holding that opinion. Nothing annoyed him more than to receive an answer that was intended merely to please him. If I suggested that a certain mare should be mated with a certain horse, the Duke would be sure to want to know the why and the wherefore. He was a great believer in the principle that "nothing succeeds like success," and it was his constant aim to breed "a good one or nothing". He always wanted to deal with facts, and believed there was a reason for everything. When you gave him your reason he would see clean through it in a moment. He believed in two sound and perfect animals being mated together, but he thought it far more important to have a sound mare with a sound pedigree than to insist on a stallion with the same qualities. He used to say that the secret of his success lay in the unswerving application of that theory. The Duke was a very keen observer and would often draw my attention to some point that had escaped my notice.'

Turning over the pages of his Stud Register, Chapman came to those relating to Ormonde's first season at the stud, and the only one he spent at Eaton. Sixteen mares were mated with him that season. Among them were Shotover, who produced Orville; Fair Alice, who bred Orbit; Thistle, the dam of Goldfinch, winner of the Two Thousand Guineas; and Angelica, whose alliance with Ormonde resulted in Orme.

One wonders whether the Duke was a believer in coincidences. Earlier on in this article I have shown how the mare named Angelica, by Snap, was twice in the possession of the first Earl Grosvenor; that on the second occasion he mated her with Sweetbriar; that he then sold her to Lord Egremont, who got from her Assassin, the first of his several Derby winners. The modern Angelica was bred in 1879 by Prince Batthyany. By Galopin out of St Angela, she was an own sister to St Simon. She went up for sale as a yearling and was bought by Mr Taylor Sharpe for 50 guineas. She never raced, and was put into the stud at Baumber, Lincolnshire, as a three-year-old. In 1883 she produced the filly Dingle, by Glendale, and the following year the filly Mezzotint, by Coeruleus, who was standing at Baumber. In 1886 Angelica, again in foal to

Coeruleus, was offered on approval to the Duke of Portland, who, however, decided not to buy her. She was then offered to the Duke of Westminster, and he agreed to give Mr Taylor Sharpe 1,000 guineas for her. The foal she was carrying was Blue Green, who ran third to Surefoot and Le Nord in the Two Thousand Guineas; second (beaten a short head) to the Duke of Portland's Memoir in the Newmarket Stakes; second to Morion in the Payne Stakes; second to Alloway in the Prince of Wales's Stakes at Ascot, where he won a Triennial; second again to Memoir in the St Leger and second once more to Morion in the Great Foal Stakes at Newmarket – a record which shows him to have been a good but unlucky horse. In 1887 Angelica was mated with Bend Or, and to him she produced Order, who went to the United States and became a successful stallion. In 1888 Angelica was allied with Ormonde and the result of the mating was Orme, who so brilliantly maintained the reputation of his family, both on the Turf and at stud.

And now we will let Chapman resume his story:

'Ormonde's first season at the stud progressed on perfectly normal lines. We had no fault to find with him, and there were no indications of the coming troubles. To put the matter in a nutshell, there was nothing whatever wrong with him. He got a good proportion of foals and several of them turned out high-class winners.

'In 1889 Ormonde was leased to Lord Gerard, and stood at the Moulton Paddocks, Newmarket. Why did we send him away from Eaton? Because we had Bend Or and other stallions here, and though we were using a relief farm a few miles away, we were hard pressed for paddock accommodation. While he was at Newmarket, Ormonde contracted a serious illness, caused by a chill. The consequence was he could not fulfil all the duties that had been allotted to him, though he served a few mares. He came back here in the summer. I went to Newmarket to bring him home. I found him in a very weak state. When the Duke saw him before he left Newmarket he told me that the horse looked incapable of walking the two miles to the station, and suggested that I should take him in a van. However, Ormonde managed to walk. He had not been at Eaton very long before he began to pick up, and he was soon improving rapidly.

'Now came the sale of Ormonde. He was bought by Captain England on behalf of Senor Boucau, an Argentine breeder. It was arranged that the horse was to leave England the following September unless in the meantime either party to the deal regretted the sale or the purchase, as the case might be. It is, of course, well known that Ormonde became a roarer while he was in training, and it has again and again been asserted that the Duke sold him to prevent English breeders using him and spreading the infirmity from which Ormonde suffered. This undoubtedly was a point that weighed with the Duke, but he was also thinking of the welfare of the "poor horse", as he called him. A change to a warmer and drier climate had been known to benefit, if not to cure, some horses similarly afflicted, and the Duke hoped that Ormonde would derive advantage from the Argentine climate. The Duke, I believe, actually received £12,000 for Ormonde. The price originally agreed upon was a higher one, but before payment was made the rate of exchange altered to his Grace's detriment. That, at any rate, was what I was given to understand.

'The Duke saw Ormonde leave Eaton without a pang, great horse though the son of Bend Or was. For many weeks before Ormonde left here we were giving him walking exercise for five or six hours every day in order to get him thoroughly fit for the voyage to Buenos Aires. He was thirty-one days on the water, but he stepped ashore perfectly fresh, and in a letter we received we were informed that directly he landed he neighed loudly, as much as to say, "Here I am".

'We had parted with Doncaster in 1884. The Austrian Government bought him. When hunting one season in Cheshire, the Empress of Austria saw Doncaster at Eaton, and she then said she would like to buy him if ever he was for sale. The idea of selling him never occurred to the Duke until after Bend Or's success at the stud was assured.

'In 1894 Orme was put out of training and, of course, came to Eaton. The Galopin mare, Vampire, bought from Mr Noel Fenwick, arrived about the same time. The Duke had paid £1,000 for her. The first time he went to look at her in her box after she had reached Eaton she backed towards him and tried to kick him. This caused his Grace to take a great dislike to her, and he seriously contemplated the idea of at once getting rid of her. Fortunately, however, he finally decided to let her remain. The first season we had her she was put to Gonsalvo. When carrying her foal we sent her to the Kremlin Stud, Newmarket, to be mated with Prince Soltykoff's Sheen. The foal was born in due course, but, Vampire, in a fit of temper, killed it and injured the man who was looking after her. After that we never sent her away again when she was in foal or had a foal at foot. Not until 1906 had we an opportunity of mating her with a stallion not our own. That year she was barren to Orme. We had a nomination to Persimmon and sent Vampire to Sandringham to fill it; but though we sent with her a man who was accustomed to her vagaries, the services of Persimmon were refused her. Vampire was brought back to Eaton and was here three weeks, while we were deciding what to do with her. We then withdrew a mare we had intended putting to William the Third, at Welbeck, and sent Vampire instead. She was at Welbeck only one night. To "William" Vampire produced Mangalmi, whose first foal is Aldford, by Mauvezin. During the spring of her three-year-old season Mangalmi, in training at Kingsclere, was constantly amiss from sexual causes, and it became necessary to put her to a horse. I was asked for a suggestion. As it was impossible to obtain a nomination to a fashionably-bred stallion at that time of the year I proposed that she should be walked across the Downs to Lord Carnarvon's stud at Highclere and be mated with Mauvezin. It was virtually a case of "needs must", but the result was eminently satisfactory, for, as you know, Aldford was unbeaten as a two-year-old.

'But I have got along too fast. To Sheen, Vampire produced Batt, who, you will remember, ran Jeddah to three-quarters of a length in the Derby. Strangely enough, Jeddah was born at Eaton. More strangely still, he and Batt were foaled in adjoining boxes, and almost at the same moment. Jeddah was born in the box in which both Sainfoin and Flying Fox were foaled, so we may well call that our "Derby box". Batt was a strong and robust foal, but Jeddah was so overgrown and weak that he had to be supported by two men at feeding time, and even then he did not get much, for his dam, Pilgrimage, was pretty old and had very little milk.

When the old Duke was going the rounds of the boxes one day and came to the one in which Jeddah was housed, he turned to me and said, "You will never rear that foal, Chapman." He really was a gigantic weakling, but he gradually gained strength. After Jeddah had beaten Batt at Epsom the Duke remarked to me in a jocular way, "It would have been as well if you had let Jeddah go. You struggled night and day to rear him and he has rewarded you by beating our horse in the Derby."

'Other Derby winners foaled at Eaton were Common and Sir Visto. It is recorded in the Stud Book that Sainfoin was bred by Queen Victoria. When he was born Sir George Maude, who was the Manager of the Hampton Court Paddocks, was staying at Eaton Hall for Chester races, for it was May 3rd. I sent word up to him that the foal was "a real good one". Common was a tremendously big and strong foal – one of the finest I ever saw. He never looked back. There was more bulk than quality about him. I may say that Vista, the dam of Sir Visto, came here to Bend Or with a view to repeating the cross which produced Ormonde, for, like Lily Agnes, she was a daughter of Macaroni; and also, of course, the mating which had, three years previously, produced Bona Vista.

'To return to Vampire. We were in a fix when we realised that she was in foal to Sheen, and that it would be unwise to send her away to another stud. The Duke was reluctant to mate her with Orme because the produce would have three close crosses of Galopin. However, he came to the conclusion that there was no other course open to him, so to Orme Vampire was put; and that is how Flying Fox came into being.

'Flying Fox was a remarkably fine foal, very deep through the heart and with beautiful shoulders. In July of the following year John Porter, who was attending the Liverpool race meeting, came over to have a look round the stud. When he saw Flying Fox he exclaimed, "Here is the winner of the Derby." He was immensely taken with him. We all were, in fact. He was a big, though somewhat lean, horse. The Duke always treated him as a great favourite. Flying Fox had a wonderful constitution. It is a noteworthy fact, as the Duke often remarked, that none of the great horses we bred here ever had a moment's sickness up to the time they went into training. Moreover, their dams, during the time they were carrying them, were also entirely free from illness.

'It may interest some to know that when Flying Fox won the Eclipse Stakes at Sandown Park in 1899, the Duke gave the whole of the Stake, amounting to £9,285, to the Royal Alexandra Hospital, Rhyl. That gift is commemorated by the presentment of a fox which acts as a weathervane. The foundation stone of the Home was laid by King Edward, when Prince of Wales. The institution was short of funds in 1899, and the Duke was appealed to for help. He promised the deputation that waited upon him that if Flying Fox won the Eclipse Stakes they should have the money. It so happened that the Duke's horse, Frontier, finished second. The Duke spent practically all the money his horses won – and it averaged about £25,000 a year – on church building, estate improvements and charity.

'Just a word about Orme. He was a topping good foal. He was born at Lord Gerard's stud at Newmarket, for Angelica had been sent there to be mated again with Ormonde. When Ormonde became incapacitated, Angelica was transferred to Macheath, who was standing at Newmarket.

'We made very few mistakes when appraising the value of our foals. This is proved by the fact that none of the many good horses bred here was left out of the big engagements.

'There was nothing haphazard about the Duke's method of mating his mares. He went about the business in a very systematic and practical way. Sometimes I would put my own ideas into writing and submit them to his Grace. He would go carefully through the list and probably cross-examine me on it. Frequently he would make sundry changes and then, having got the matings to his liking, he would append his signature and hand the list back to me. But I'll tell you what he often did. If one of our mares was in foal to a horse to whom we had a nomination, he would have the mare foal at home, in order that he might judge whether the sire was a suitable mate for her. If the foal was to his liking, then, and only then, the mare was again sent to the same stallion. The Duke had no patience with the Figure System and such-like fantastic notions.

'The Duke was a remarkably fine horseman, and one of the best judges of horses I ever came across. In his judgment of men he depended entirely on his own instinct and knowledge. He trusted every man until he found he was mistaken in so doing. To detrimental gossip he would give no heed whatever. He demanded evidence, and the evidence had to be conclusive before he would take action. Then again, I never came across anyone who could take a reverse more philosophically than the Duke, and he never showed much elation when he was successful. If a horse of his started a hot favourite for a big race and got beaten, his first thought would be one of regret that the public had lost their money over the defeated animal. He was charitable and sympathetic almost to a fault.'

I asked Chapman if he had any objection to urge against the practice of mating a mare year after year with the same stallion. He replied:

'I prefer to make a change after the second or third time. I'll tell you a plan in which we have always had great faith here. If a mare has given us a good animal, take an early opportunity of putting her to the best available son of the sire with whom she has succeeded. We made a hit with Lily Agnes in that way. She gave us Farewell first try to Doncaster. We thought we could go one better by mating her with Doncaster's son, Bend Or, and lo! she gave us Ormonde. In any case, as a mare gets older you must mate her with younger horses. That must be a true rule to work to. There is no comparison between the offspring of old and young parents. The year before Radium was born the Manager of Mr Rothschild's stud asked me to choose one of three mares they could send to Bend Or. I chose the Donovan mare Taia, because she was the youngest of the three (ten years old) and that put the thing right.

'After the Duke's death in 1899 the bloodstock was sold off – or the greater part of it. At any rate, our paddocks were sadly depleted, and we had to start almost afresh again. The sale of Sceptre turned out, of course, to be our greatest loss. When the yearlings came under the hammer the present Duke bought five of the colts. I was longing for him to buy Sceptre. We were the runners up, but lost her at 10,000 guineas. If only we had got her, what a difference it would have made to us here! Troutbeck, who won the St Leger in 1906, was bred by the Duke. He was a big colt and a good one. He shaped so well before he went into training that I was not in the least surprised when he turned out so well on the Turf. He did not come properly to hand until he was a three-year-old, but that season, apart from his

Mr Richard Chapman, Stud Groom at Eaton.

defeat in the Derby (he was third to Spearmint and Picton) he carried all before him, winning nine races. In view of what I have heard about Spearmint's trial for the Derby, I don't suppose Troutbeck could have beaten him under any circumstances, but the fact remains that he had bad luck at Epsom. For one thing he was handicapped at the start by being drawn on the outside of the twenty-two competitors. By finishing third he had Radium, The White Knight, Beppo, Black Arrow, Lally and other good horses behind him. Of course we have Troutbeck here at the stud now, together with Pipistrello, an own brother to Flying Fox. Given a reasonable chance, both horses should do well.'

Early on in this article I mentioned that while we were in the stud yard, Chapman took me to view the graves of five of the equine celebrities connected with the stud. Now that we have heard something about these animals let us go back and look again at their graves and head-stones. These stones are let into the wall which separates the yard from the road-way leading to the stud buildings. At the top of the row lie the remains of Bend Or. The inscription on his stone gives his dates, 1877–1903. While we are gazing at it Chapman tells me that after Bend Or had lain under the sod for a fortnight his body was exhumed and the head cut off. The authorities at South Kensington Natural History Museum wanted it for their collection. Next to Bend Or lies, appropriately enough, Lily Agnes, the dam of Ormonde. She is 'dated' 1871–1899. Then, in order, come the Derby winner, Shotover, 1879–1899; Ornament (the dam of Sceptre), 1887–1910 – Chapman forgot to tell me anything about her; and lastly Angelica, 1879–1899. It will be noticed that three of these worthies passed away in 1899, the year the late Duke himself was gathered to his fathers.

In the adjoining ground there is plenty of room left for Orme and Vampire when their day is done. They have both been placed on the retired list, to pass the remainder of their lives in ease and luxury. It so happens that both Orme and Vampire were born in 1889, so that they are now twenty-five years old.

With regard to Shotover, Chapman told me that Robert Peck bought her for the Duke for 1,400 guineas at the sale of Mr Chaplin's yearlings in 1880. When the Duke went to see her for the first time at Russley he said he did not care for her very much. 'Very well,' was Peck's rejoinder, 'I will take her myself at the same price.' After Peck had tried Shotover to be a good filly, the Duke expressed a desire to buy her back and Peck let his Grace have her.

In all there are twenty-two paddocks at Eaton. The oldest of them range from about $3\frac{1}{2}$ to 5 acres, and are surrounded by high stone walls, like those at Lord Derby's stud at Knowsley, near Liverpool. These stone-walled enclosures are, with one exception, allotted to the yearlings. The exception is the one set apart for Orme. Each yearling colt has a paddock to himself, but the fillies run in pairs.

Some six years ago the Duke of Westminster was advised to try the experiment of sending his weaned foals over to Ireland, and for that purpose purchased and, at great expense, laid out the Ballymany farm on the borders of the Curragh. For some reason or other the scheme did not come up to expectations, and two years ago it was abandoned. In the meantime the old paddocks at Eaton were ploughed up – a process they had not undergone within living memory, and probably not since they were formed by Earl Grosvenor towards the end of the eighteenth century. After the plough had done its work, oats were sown. The result was astonishing. So rich was the soil that the oats grew to a height of about seven feet, and became so top-heavy that they fell to the ground before the seed had ripened.

It seems that about the year 1875, shortly after the late Duke had re-established the stud, some busybodies warned the Duke that he could not reasonably expect to breed racehorses at Eaton because there was no limestone there; the soil is clay on sandstone. The Duke was not prepared to accept without question the advice of his critics. He bethought him to have the soil of his paddocks analysed, and at the same time he obtained samples of soil from three or four other important studs, two of them being Lord Ellesmere's at Worsley, and Lord Falmouth's at Mereworth. Chapman believes that Hampton Court was another. When the analysts had completed their work they reported that the soil at Eaton was out and away the best of the lot for rearing animals of all descriptions, for it would produce more bone. muscle and fat than any of the others. For many years Aberdeen-Angus cattle were grazed in the Eaton paddocks, and year after year they carried off the chief prizes at the Christmas Fat Stock Show at Chester.

A year or two after the analysis had been made, a colt foal, three months old, met with an accident and had to be destroyed. His cannon bone was submitted to the great veterinary authority, Professor Flemming, and he declared that he had never seen bone of such wonderful quality taken from a thoroughbred. Chapman handed me a section of the bone in question, and it has the texture of ivory.

At the present time there are eighteen mares attached to the Eaton Stud. Six of them will this season be mated with Troutbeck, viz.: Grey Lady (by Grey Leg-Vampire), Princess Mary (by Bend Or-St Mary), Beaker (by Bend Or-Kissing Cup), Mowsali (by Flying Fox-Miss Unicorn), Bally (by Just Cause-Rockhill), and Westaria (by Gallinule-Wetaria). Beck and Call (by Troutbeck-King's Favour) is to be put to Pipistrello, who had two or three good seasons in Ireland before he came to Eaton. The other eleven mares are going to stallions in other ownership – Crown Gem (by Persimmon-Ornament) to Swynford; Haurdina (by William the Third-Grey Lady) to Spearmint; Mangalmi (by William the Third-Vampire) to Sunstar; Blind Justice (by Just Clause-Vampire) to Llangwym; Mystery (by Troutbeck-Vampire) to Mauvezin; Favourite (by Troutbeck-King's Favour) to Marajax; Keadean (by Gallinule-Maisie) to William the Third; Ballymany (by Volodyovski-Grey Lady) to Sunder; Galore (by Fowling-piece-Nada) to Willonyx; Rydal Mount (by St Serf-Rydal) to

Cocksure II; and Eageress (by Eager–Last of the Queens) to Bayardo.

The Duke of Westminster's two-year-olds in training are: – *Manxman* (bay colt by Troutbeck–Mangalmi, and therefore half-brother to Aldford), *Luxford* (brown colt by Troutbeck–Galore), *Eager Eyes* (bay filly by Troutbeck–Eageress), *Blue Trout* (bay colt by Troutbeck–Dead Heat), *Ormesby* (chestnut colt by Orme–Bally), *Welsh Rarebit* (brown filly by Llangibby–Crown Gem), *Prince Amadeus* (bay colt by Amadis–Princess Mary), and *Wordsworth* (bay colt by Bayardo–Rydal Mount).

There are ten yearlings now to be seen at Eaton, viz.: – *Shadowland* (bay colt by Dark Ronald–Rydal Mount), *Mincra* (chestnut filly by Radium–Grey Lady), *Amanthe* (brown filly by Amadis–Beaker), *Ali Bey* (bay colt by Bayardo–Mowsali), *Mettlesome* (brown filly by Radium–Galore), *Abbot-a-Becket* (by Troutbeck–Keadean), *Balorma* (chestnut filly by Orme–Bally), *Polyandria* (chestnut filly by Polymelus–Mangalmi), *Hortense* (bay filly by Troutbeck–Haurdina), and *Humility* (chestnut filly by Orme–Beck and Call).

It will be observed that these two-year-olds and yearlings are all endowed with fine possibilities. There is the blood of great racers flowing in their veins, and in bringing this long, but, I hope, not uninteresting article to a close I cannot do so better than by expressing the fervent hope that one or more of them will be the means of placing the Grosvenor colours – 'yellow, black cap' – in the forefront once more.

BBR–1914

The Eaton Stud and its Memories: Some Corrections

One or two errors have been discovered in the article 'The Eaton Stud and its Memories', which appeared in the last number of the *Review*. The statement that Goldfinch was a winner of the Two Thousand Guineas was an obvious slip. In that race he ran unplaced to Bona Vista, St Angelo and Curio.

Goldfinch, by the way, died on April 27th last at Mr James B. Haggin's Elmendorf Stud. He was quite a successful sire. Many of his offspring were shipped to England and won races here. Among them were Convamore, Bronzewing, Celerina, Gold Coin, and Addra.

With regard to the earlier portion of the article the following communication has been received from Mr J. B. Robertson:

'I rather think you are in error in saying that Pot-8-os stood at Eaton when he sired Waxy (1790). In 1789 the horse stood at the Oxcroft Stud, Balsham, Cambridgeshire, in company with Fortitude; and Pot-8-os and Justice were located there in 1790. Lord Grosvenor seems to have kept a number of his mares at Oxcroft at that time. Probably Pot-8-os went to Eaton in 1791 or 1792.

'Lord Grosvenor (the first Earl) began racing as Mr Richard Grosvenor, his father, Sir Robert (who died in 1755) being then alive. When you say Lord Grosvenor owned many mares two or three times over, have you not overlooked the fact that up to the Sixth Volume of the Stud Book the name opposite a mare's offspring was that of the first nominator, and not necessarily the breeder? (That fact was, it must be confessed, overlooked.) For example, Lord Grosvenor never owned the Hobgoblin mare (p. 102, Vol. I.). As Mr Richard Grosvenor, he owned her daughter (1750) by the Godolphin Arabian, and ran her once at Chester, then called the West Cheshire meeting. The Hobgoblin mare and her sister were the property of Lord Godolphin, and died at the Gog Magog Stud, which is close to Balsham.

'It appears from the Stud Book that in his earlier racing days Sir Richard, afterwards Lord, Grosvenor, bought more racehorses than he bred. He never appears to have owned the mare Angelica by Snap, and I rather think all her offspring were bred by Mr Shafto. Certainly Medëa was not bred by Lord Grosvenor (see Vol. I, p. 322), nor Flora (p. 269). Perhaps Lord Egremont bought Angelica from Mr Shafto in foal to Sweerbriar, but I think you will find that Lord Grosvenor never owned her. In the first six volumes, acceptance of the name opposite the produce as the breeder is risky, and many errors have arisen in books of reference from this cause.

'I hope you don't mind my calling your attention to these academic details, but I know you are a believer in historical accuracy.'

In matters of this sort accuracy is most certainly essential, and I am grateful to Mr Robertson for drawing attention to the points raised in his letter. The Preface to the first edition of Vol. I of the *GSB* gives no indication that the names opposite the produce of the several mares are not those of the breeders. In the Fifth Edition, published in 1891, there is, however, the following notice.

'N.B. In these earlier volumes the name of the person attached to the produce is generally that in which the horse ran, as the indexes to the early Racing Calendars were arranged under the heads of the owners.'

It follows, therefore, that unless a filly went to the stud it is often impossible to ascertain definitely by whom she was bred; and a similar dubiety obtains in the case of nearly all the colts. If the mare was put to the stud, we find her recorded as 'Bred by So-and-So'. Thus, as Mr Robertson points out, although Lord Grosvenor's name appears opposite that of Medëa (by Sweetbriar out of Angelica, by Snap) in the return of the produce out of Angelica, Medëa herself is, on p. 322 of the fifth edition, definitely stated to have been bred by Mr Shafto, who was also the owner and breeder of Angelica. It necessarily follows that the statement made in the article on the Eaton Stud that no fewer than 196 of the mares included in Vol. I belonged at one time or another to Lord Grosvenor, requires considerable modification.

Mr Robertson has chapter and verse in his favour when he states that Pot-8-os was standing at the Oxcroft Stud, Balsham, when he begat Waxy.

BBR–1914

The Death of James Ben Ali Haggin

When, in September of 1914, James Ben Ali Haggin died at the age of ninety-three, it closed a remarkable chapter on American racing and breeding as Mr Haggin, at one time, was the world's largest breeder of thoroughbreds at his Rancho del Paso, a spread of 44,000 fertile acres near Sacramento, California. In one year, 1901, he sold no fewer than 241 yearlings bred on that vast estate. At the dispersal of the stud in 1905, there were 464 mares catalogued. Mr Haggin raced as well as bred and two of his finest were Salvator – one of the best horses bred in the US in the latter part of the nineteenth century, and Firenze – a splendid racemare who also excelled as a producer. The James Haggin story has been well told many times because of the vast numbers involved, but this observer believes that the memoir of Mr Haggin, appearing in the 1914 Review *is one that especially deserves preserving because it presents the character of the man in such a full-flavoured and admirable manner.*

MR JAMES B. HAGGIN was ninety-three years of age when he died at the Villa Rosa, Newport, Rhode Island, on September 12th last, for he was born in Mercer County, Kentucky, in 1821. A lawyer by profession, he came to be known to the world at large as the biggest breeder of thoroughbreds in either hemisphere. That he was indeed the biggest is substantiated by the fact that in 1901 he sold no fewer than 241 yearlings which he had bred on his Californian farm, Rancho del Paso. The career of the man who organised a stud of such gigantic dimensions cannot fail to be of interest to our readers, and we offer no apology for dwelling at some length on its more salient features.

There was a mixture of English, Irish, Turkish and Greek blood flowing in the veins of Mr Haggin. His father was a son of Captain John Haggin and Nancy Haggin, who emigrated to Virginia from Ireland in 1775. Mr Haggin's father married a daughter of Ibrahim Ben Ali, a Turk and a Christian, and whose mother was a Greek. Owing to persecution, Ibrahim, a practising physician, left Turkey, and, after spending some years in England, proceeded to the United States and there married a lady of English parentage.

James Haggin, the subject of this memoir, was in his younger days

Mr James B. Haggin.

something of a puzzle to his contemporaries. The Eastern strain in his pedigree was denoted by his intensely dark hair and eyes, and by his swarthy skin. All sorts of conjectures were hazarded regarding his ancestry. When he gave the name Ben Ali to his son he was at once pronounced to be a Turk! We may assume, therefore, that he had not taken the trouble to enlighten his neighbours concerning his lineage.

After leaving school, James Haggin studied law, and by the time he was thirty-four years old had migrated to California by way of New Orleans. Settling down at Sacramento, he there entered into a law partnership with Lloyd Tevis. The firm prospered, and acquired a big reputation as land and company attorneys. They acted as legal advisers to several of the larger landowners and mining companies, and the information they acquired in this capacity enabled them to make many profitable deals on their own account. The two partners thus became wealthy men, and in course of time they bought the Rancho del Paso, an estate near Sacramento extending to 44,000 acres of fertile land.

Mr Haggin had reached California just in time to participate in the great mining boom which produced a batch of millionaires. He himself became a bold speculator in mining properties, and transferred his office to San Francisco so that he could be nearer to the heart of the movement. One who knew him at the time writes as follows:

> 'Haggin had nothing in common with good fellowship. He was always silent, sober and cold. But he must have had a head. He was the only one I ever knew who remembered the men who helped him to acquire wealth. Every man, without exception, who rendered Haggin faithful and efficient service he made rich. And he was very loyal to his friends. At a crisis of his fortunes, George Hearst was saved from ruin by Haggin, at a sacrifice to himself. In these days, and other days, when men of power exhaust the energies of their subordinates and then toss them without compunction on the scrap pile like so many sucked-out oranges, and treat their business associates just a shade better, an example like that Haggin gave ought not to be overlooked.'

At the outset the Rancho del Paso was used chiefly, if not entirely, for pasturing sheep. After a while, Haggin assumed complete control of this estate (his partner, Tevis, commanding another property the firm had acquired) and, acting on the advice of his friend John Mackey, began to breed trotting horses. Presently, 'as there was plenty of room for them', he decided to experiment with thoroughbreds, and, with Mackey's help, several thoroughbred mares and a stallion or two were bought from breeders in California. He tried to purchase Norfolk (the grandsire of Americus) and Joe Hooker from Theodore Winters, but their owner refused to sell. Haggin was, however, able to buy a number of fillies from Winters when the latter removed from California to Nevada.

The products of his thoroughbred mares were put into training by Mr Haggin, and the successes they gained on the Californian tracks afforded him much gratification. He was, indeed, so pleased that he straightaway set to work to enlarge his stock of mares. His next important move came in 1885, for that year he sent a number of horses he had bred to race in the Eastern States. Among them were Tyrant and Hidalgo, both of whom won good stakes. Within five years his colours had been brought into prominence by the performances of Salvator, Ben Ali, Firenze and King Fox. In 1890, however, Mr Haggin began to reduce his racing stud and to apply himself more thoroughly to the rearing of thoroughbreds for the market. To this end he sent John Mackey to England, Ireland,

and the European Continent to buy broodmares and stallions. He had already brought Sir Modred from Australia, and Darebin and Maxim from New Zealand. In England he secured Star Ruby, Watercress, Greenan, St Gatien, Goldfinch, Dieudonne, Toddington, Gerolstein, and Royal Flush.

At one time he had no fewer than 600 broodmares at Rancho del Paso. He sold his yearlings in California and New York. In order to facilitate his business, he bought the Elmendorf Farm, near Lexington, and stocked it with stallions and mares. The Elmendorf estate covered about 10,000 acres, and he built himself a residence there at a cost of £60,000.

In 1905 there was a great dispersal of the thoroughbreds at Rancho del Paso. The catalogue (a remarkable volume) comprised 20 stallions, 464 mares, 13 yearlings, and 27 two- and three-year-old fillies. The sale was held for the purpose of ending the partnership between Haggin and the Tevis family, and it meant the abandonment of Rancho del Paso as a nursery for thoroughbreds. The following 'announcement' appeared in the catalogue:

'Not in the Turf history of the world is there record of a breeding establishment of thoroughbreds of the magnitude of Rancho del Paso. Established in the 'eighties, its first sale of yearlings, 64 in number, was held in 1888, when all were disposed of, and these won during the following season about $62,000 (£12,400), while the two- and three-year-olds of the next season earned nearly $200,000 (£40,000). From thence on, the success of Rancho del Paso-bred stock has increased with the years. In 1892 it turned out 117 winners of 500 races, and in 1893 no fewer than 180 winners. . . The Rancho del Paso yearlings of 1901 (there were 241 catalogued) sold for a total of $234,025 (£46,800). A dozen of these alone won in 1902 and 1903 the sum of $259,325 (£51,860). Each one of these twelve won upward of $10,000 (£2,000), Africander as much as $81,680 (£16,300), and Hurstbourne $35,655 (£7,100).'

Then follows a list of the most successful racehorses bred at Rancho del Paso. Those which won £5,000 and over were:

	£		£
Sir Walter	25,700	Waltzer	8,600
Tournament	21,750	Dr Hasbrouck	8,600
Africander	21,200	Hurstbourne	7,500
Montana	11,800	Sir Excess	7,400
Tradition	11,600	Proper	6,900
Savable	11,200	Sir Matthew	6,750
Waterboy	10,900	Kildeer	6,550
Cairngorm	9,550	Connoisseur	6,450
Watercolour	8,700	Sir John	6,300

	£		£
Eclipse	6,300	Sombrero	5,100
Old England	6,100	Lavator	5,100
Ormonde's Right	6,100	Gloaming	5,000
Kenilworth	5,400	Fitz James	5,000
Dainty	5,300	Song-and-Wine	5,000
St Bellane	5,200		

When, five or six years ago, the faddists got the upper hand in New York State, and racing became an impossibility, Mr Haggin began to dispose of his thoroughbreds. They were sent to all parts of the world to be sold, many of them to England, France, Germany, and the Argentine. He retained only a few mares and one or two stallions. More recently, however, his interest in the thoroughbred had again quickened, evidence of the revival being forthcoming when, for £8,000, he bought Ballot from the executors of the late Mr J. R. Keene. Elizabeth M, who won many races in England, and is now at the Sledmere Stud, was bred by Mr Haggin.

In 1849, Mr Haggin married a daughter of Colonel Louis Sanders, a lawyer. She died in 1894, and three years later he was married to Miss Voorhies, whose mother was a sister of his first wife. He left a son (Louis) and a daughter (Mrs Loundsberry), both by his first wife. Mr Haggin was supposed to be worth anything from £10,000,000 to £20,000,000; but when his will (dated January 13th, 1913) was filed for probate, the estate was valued at £3,000,000.   BBR–1914

The Death of Count George Lehndorff

Count George Lehndorff, 'the maker of the Prussian Army Horse' and the greatest authority on horse-breeding in Germany during his lifetime, died in April of 1914 just months before the outbreak of World War I in which the Prussian horse played such a valiant and noble role, although in a losing cause. Count Lehndorff, who joined the army at seventeen, became infatuated with racing at that tender age when racing was practically unknown in Germany. At the time of his death at the age of eighty-one, due largely to the Count, the German Turf was prospering.

BY THE AID of his book, *Horse Breeding Recollections*, published in English in 1883, Count Lehndorff's influence spread all over the world. Here are a few epigrammatic sayings culled from his work:

'The principal requisite in a good racehorse is soundness, again soundness, and nothing but soundness.'

'The grand ideal principle which places the racecourse test so incomparably higher than any other is the absolute and blind justice personified in the inflexible winning post . . . the irrefutable certainty that neither fashion nor fancy, neither favour nor hatred, neither personal prejudice nor time-serving – frequently observable in the awards at horse shows – have biased the decision of hotly-contested struggles, as recorded in the Racing Calendar for the space of one hundred and seventy years.'

'The straighter the running track the more infallible the result.'

'In principle I do not disapprove of running two-year-olds; on the contrary, I take it, if done in moderation, to be an unerring means of ascertaining the soundness of the constitution.'

'I consider the test by hurdle racing, and especially by steeplechasing, rather one of acquired cleverness than of consequence of breeding.'

'Jumping is more a question of agility than of power.'

'The thoroughbred stands to the half-bred in the same position as the plantation tree to the wild tree of the forest. The former thrives in any locality where trees grow; the latter feels at home only where it first struck root.'

'The only practical test of soundness of limbs, digestive organs, nerves and temper, remains the public trial on the racecourse.'

'With young mares, be careful that habitually they be neither too gross nor too poor; either extreme is inimical to a healthy progeny.'

'A rat-tail is a great eyesore; but how rare is a bad horse with a rat-tail?'

'The more quality the mare possesses, the more marked must be the expression of her sex.'

'Let the breeder of thoroughbreds never adopt the principle that quantity better than quality will succeed.'

'I require in the sire intended for the production of thoroughbreds, for every per cent less performance three per cent more exterior.'

It is a matter for regret that Count Lehndorff did not in recent years give us another book embodying the teaching of the great experience he gained during the long years he was in supreme control of the Prussian studs. Such a work would have possessed an inestimable value. His *Horse Breeding Recollections* will, however, keep the name of Lehndorff prominent long after those of most of his contemporaries are forgotten.

Most of the leading English and Irish breeders knew Count Lehndorff personally, for he frequently visited their studs and was a regular attender at the Newmarket Sales, where he was often a big buyer. The Count was, indeed, one of the most popular men in Turf circles throughout Europe and an honorary member of many Jockey Clubs, that of England included.   BBR–1914

Signor Tesio and Mr Madden

*In the 1923 Review, Italy's Federico Tesio and the United States'
John E. Madden, two of the Turf's leading breeders, then and forever*

more, were given some space; Tesio and his Dormello stud because of an incredible classic season and Madden because of his quotes on the enjoyment a person may gain from the breeding of thoroughbreds.

Curiously, perhaps, both of these super successful breeders did not consider keeping a stallion the wisest choice. Tesio wanted to be 'untrammelled by a horse of his own' so that he could make his own selection of stallions wherever they might be, and Madden, of the same mind, said: 'Without a stallion, the breeder is free to patronise the best stallions available, according to the blood lines of his mares.'

In 1923 when Mr Federico Tesio's Dormello-bred colt Cima da Conegliano gave the Italian owner and breeder his tenth Derby victory in thirteen years, as well as winning all the other Italian classics, excepting the Two Thousand Guineas, with the Italian Grand Prize at Milan thrown in, a correspondent for the BBR gave graphic recognition of this ascendent force in international breeding.

WHAT A LOVELY place this Dormello is! There can be few studs so picturesquely situated, better equipped, or more carefully managed. It is situated not far from the southern end of Lake Maggiore. The land is fertile and the climate ideal. The paddocks are arranged in three groups, each group being used at the most suitable period of the year. One is on the lake side. That is used during the winter months. In the spring and autumn the mares and their produce are in paddocks another 150 feet above sea-level. During the summer months the bloodstock is accommodated in paddocks still higher up. This is, of course, an ideal plan and most breeders will envy the opportunity Captain Tesio has of adopting it.

This good fortune does not, however, entirely account for the great success that has attended the Dormello Stud. With the constant aid of his charming and accomplished wife, Captain Tesio has made a deep study of blood lines and has spent money in securing from England mares belonging to the best thoroughbred families. Moreover, he personally manages both his breeding stud and his racing stable. The prosperity of the stable, which is remarkable, is due to the way the stud has been organised and conducted, and the whole enterprise serves as a monument to the skill and judgment of the proprietor . . . Captain Tesio has always placed quality above quantity.

The class of mares to be seen in the Dormello paddocks is equal to that found at any stud in the world, for there are daughters of Flying Fox, St Frusquin, Persimmon, Spearmint, Thrush, Cicero, Cylgad, Bayardo and Tracery. There is no stallion located at the stud. Captain Tesio prefers to be untrammelled by a horse of his own, so that he may mate his mares in the way that seems best. Every year he sends some of them to the best sires in England and France, while the others go to good stallions available in Italy. . . Incidentally, it may be mentioned that Captain Tesio thinks it advisable to leave the mare and her foal together for six months, his experience having led him to the conclusion that this plan favours the foal better than an earlier weaning.   BBR-1923

To John E. Madden, Breeding was a Pleasure

AN ENGLISHMAN was recently heard to remark that, yielding to persuasion, he took up breeding as a hobby and had found the pastime a veritable nightmare. Mr John E. Madden, of Lexington, Kentucky, who has these many years headed the list of breeders in the United States declares there is no greater relaxation for a businessman than the breeding of horses on a modest scale. He proceeds:

'The study of mating mares and the consideration of their blood lines is a fascinating occupation to which any desired amount of time and thought may be given, and when it comes to thrills there is none greater than seeing a youngster of your own breeding flash past the post a winner in the Futurity or other classic race. Half a dozen mares and no stallion form the best equipment for the beginner. The mares should be the best procurable, and the selection should not be influenced too much by racing ability.

'Without a stallion, the breeder is free to patronise the best stallions available, according to the blood line of his mares. These mares should be well enough bred to make any colt from them acceptable as a stallion for stud services, and in purchasing his mares let the breeder have this end in view. I am convinced that this is the most satisfactory method to follow. Pleasure is assured and a profit on the venture is possible. After a reputation has been gained, the rest is comparatively easy. Like a man making his first ten thousand, the struggle is at the start.

'The man who breeds a racehorse never loses him. Though the horse may run in another man's colours, the glory in part always goes to the breeder. Whenever a horse wins that was bred at Hamburg Place it gives me the keenest pleasure, no matter who owns him.

'The expectation and exhilaration created by breeding and racing of thoroughbreds furnish the best remedy for all kinds of depression. No lottery ticket was ever found in the pocket of a suicide. If the wealthy, idle and the tired businessmen will take up the breeding of thoroughbreds as a pastime, they will at least enjoy life, even though they die poor.'   BBR-1923

Memorative Biography of Lord Wavertree

Of the twenty-seven distinguished breeders covered in his excellent book, The Great Breeders and Their Methods, *Abram S. Hewitt, late doyen of American Turf writers and a most gracious gentleman with an international reputation, appeared to be most impressed with England's Lord Wavertree (Col William Hall Walker) if this reader sensed it correctly. Lord Wavertree's stud farm was in Ireland. It was called Tully and the products of this stud captured every one of England's classics. Lord Wavertree's name was not known importantly in flat racing in England until around 1900. By 1905 he was the country's leading owner and he repeated that achievement in 1907. How he managed to do this is most intriguing. Quoting Mr Hewitt:*

'A much more interesting thing about Hall Walker was his ability to select mares with apparently the poorest of credentials, or very nearly so, both in terms of racing performance and pedigree, and from these mares "breed up" so that as second dams with such credentials they became the ancestresses of the following very remarkable group of stallions: Blandford (1919), by Swynford; Challenger (1927), by Swynford; Sickle (1924), by Phalaris; Hyperion (1930), by Gainsborough; Big Game (1939), by Bahram, and Princequillo (1940), by Prince Rose.

'Consider the odds against such an achievement. Lord Derby did not breed the second dams of Chaucer, Swynford, Phalaris, Pharos and Fairway and was only technically the breeder (Hall Walker made the mating) of the second dam of Sickle and Hyperion (and Pharamond). Tesio did not breed the second dams of Nearco or Ribot. Calumet Farm did not breed the second dam of Bull Lea. Wheatley Stable did not breed the second dam of Bold Ruler. Nor did the Aga Khan breed the second dam of Nasrullah, Mahmoud, or Blenheim. Boussac did not breed the second dam of Tourbillon. Belmont did not breed the second dams of Fair Play or Man o' War. James R. Keene did not breed the second dam of Domino, Commando, Sweep, Broomstick or Ben Brush. Nor did A. B. Hancock, Jr breed the second dam of Round Table. So far as the author knows, Hall Walker's achievement in breeding the second dams of the "blue ribbon" list of sires set out above was unique, and it is all the more remarkable when we consider the background of the mares in question.

'This was what I have called the "Hall Walker" type of pedigree, accumulating superior genes in the BACK PEDIGREE through inbreeding, and then following this accumulation with an outcross to the "Top Class" sire.'

Lord Wavertree was a fascinating personality. He appeared eccentric to many people and seldom did anything to dissuade that impression. His addiction to astrology was well known and the role it played in the dramatic victory of Minoru in the Derby of 1909 is a classic story in the true classic sense.

In any event, Lord Wavertree's Memorative Biography which appeared in the BBR of 1933 and is presented here in full is truly justified when one considers the enduring and felitious impact he has had on thoroughbred breeding.

Lord Wavertree.

A PROMINENT OWNER and breeder during the first fifteen years of the
century, Lord Wavertree died from the effects of a chill on February
2nd, at his London residence, Sussex Lodge, Regent's Park. He was
born on Christmas Day, 1856, the third son of the late Sir Andrew
Barclay Walker, Bart, of Gateacre, Liverpool, so was in his seventy-
seventh year when he passed away. His christian names were William
Hall. From Harrow, where he acquired considerable proficiency in field
games, he went straight away into the family's big brewing business at
Warrington, known as Peter Walker & Sons, of which he eventually
became the managing director. At one time he interested himself in
Liverpool's municipal affairs, and was a member of the City Council.
From 1900 to 1919, when he was raised to the peerage, he represented
the Widnes division of Lancashire in the House of Commons, while
earlier he joined the Volunteer Force and rose to be Colonel of the 55th
(West Lancashire) Divisional Engineers. In 1896 he married the
younger daughter of Mr Algernon Brinsley Sheridan, of Frampton
Court, Dorchester. There was no heir, so the peerage is extinct.

It was in 1895 that Lord Wavertree (then known as Major Hall

Walker, but later as Colonel) registered his colours under the Rules of
Racing. They were 'blue and white check, cerise cap'. Before that,
however, he had for twenty years been associated with the racing of
ponies and Galloways, and during that period owned many good
animals, some of which he trained and rode. He won over forty races on
his Galloway Dorothy in three years, and in Mulberry possessed a very
fast pony that was sold for £2,000 to go to India, where he twice won the
Civil Service Cup. In 1896 his horse The Soarer won the Grand
National Steeplechase, being one of several winners of that event owned
by Liverpool businessmen.

So far as flat racing is concerned, it was in 1900 that Colonel Walker
first came into prominence, for that season his horses won stakes
amounting to nearly £9,000. A year or two later he founded a breeding
stud at Tully, on the outskirts of Kildare and bordering on The
Curragh. He installed the stallion Count Schomberg there. The stud
quickly began to make history. In 1905 Cherry Lass won the One
Thousand Guineas and the Oaks, and ran third to Challacombe and
Polymelus in the St Leger, while her half-brother Black Arrow, by
Count Schomberg, was one of the best of the season's two-year-olds.
That year Colonel Hall Walker headed the list of owners with a total of
£23,687. The next season his winnings amounted to £14,355, towards
which Polar Star, two years old, and an unbeaten winner of twelve races
that year, contributed £5,937. This colt was one of four bearers of the
Colonel's colours that won the Gimcrack Stakes at York within a period
of five years. The others were Colonia (1905), Royal Realm (1907), and
Lily Rose (1909). There would have been an unbroken sequence if
Queen Mother had not been narrowly beaten by Blankney II in 1908.

Colonel Walker again topped the list of owners in 1907 with £17,910
to his credit. Witch Elm won the One Thousand Guineas and Polar Star
(who had no classic engagements) performed the notable feat of carrying
7 st 12 lb to victory in the 'Jubilee' Handicap at Kempton Park. No
other three-year-old has won the race bearing so heavy a burden, but
Polar Star's merits were such that he started favourite and beat by half a
length the four-year-old Marcovil, who was receiving 7 lb. Polar Star's
next race was the Coronation Cup at Epsom, wherein he suffered his first
defeat, finishing fourth to The White Knight, Troutbeck and
Polymelus. He then finished second in two races before winning one
worth £100 at Warwick. In the contest for the Coronation Cup, Polar
Star and Polymelus ran themselves to a standstill in the first mile, with
the result that the former's shoulder muscles were affected, and it was
not until the following year that he fully recovered. He then easily won

the Manchester Cup (carrying 8 st 7 lb) with odds of 16 to 1 laid against him, and, a few days later, took the Rous Memorial Stakes at Ascot. His total of winnings was £12,172. Immediately after Ascot he was sold for 18,000 guineas to go to the Ojo de Agua Stud, in the Argentine, where he sired winners, but none of his own class.

Colonel Hall Walker never made it a practice to buy fashionably-bred, and therefore high-priced, mares. On the contrary, his inclination was to pay very little for those he acquired. He bought Gondolette from Lord Westbury for 360 guineas, and, after breeding Let Fly and Great Sport from her sold her, when ten years old, to Lord Derby for 1,550 guineas. For the latter she produced the classic winners Ferry and Sansovino; and Serenissima, dam of Tranquil and Bosworth, and of Selene, the dam of Hyperion.

Go On, the dam of Polar Star, was another mare bought cheaply. After winning selling races in Ireland and England, she went to Belgium, to return when six years old in 1901. Sent to Tattersalls, the late Mr E. H. Leach bought her for 90 guineas, and presently she was to be found at the Tully Stud. After Go On had produced two foals by Count Schomberg, it was suggested to Colonel Walker that she should be mated with Gallinule, who was standing only a mile or two away. He said: 'No, Gallinule is too soft,' but he let her go to Gallinule's half-brother, Pioneer, and Polar Star was the result. Sir Bold, brother to Polar Star, followed, and Go On was then sold at a high figure to Mr Prentice who, however, got little for his money.

There has been a tendency to assume that Polar Star was not entered for any of the classic races because his horoscope was unfavourable. The actual reason was set forth in a communication from Colonel Hall Walker published in *Baily's Magazine*. He wrote: 'The simple history of the horse not being entered is that he was a very plain and timid youngster that never had been seen to go out of a trot until just before he left for England, in the autumn of his yearling days. He was under-sized and ewe-necked and was condemned by every good judge who visited the stud.'

In 1908 Colonel Walker's horses won £10,446, but after that earnings were on a smaller scale. Among the winners not already named there were Night Hawk (St Leger), Great Sport (third in the Derby), Let Fly, White Eagle and Merry Gal. Others he bred but sold were Charles O'Malley and Prince Palatine. The latter was the best of the products of his stud. Mr J. H. H. Peard bought him privately as a yearling on behalf of Mr Thomas Pilkington. He won the St Leger, two Ascot Cups, the Coronation and Doncaster Cups, and the Eclipse and Jockey Club

Stakes. The day before the Goodwood meeting of 1913 began, Mr J. B. Joel bought Prince Palatine for £45,000, with the proviso that £5,000 should be returned if the horse failed to win the Goodwood Cup that week. To the utter astonishment of everyone, he ran unplaced. After he had had four years at Mr Joel's stud he was sold to the Duc Decazes for £18,000, and went to France. There he remained till 1920, when he was shipped to the United States, having been sold to Mr Simms, a breeder in Kentucky. Four years later Prince Palatine was burned to death in his stable.

Then there was Minoru, bred at Tully in 1906. There was a scarcity of yearling colts at the Sandringham Stud in 1907, so King Edward leased six from Colonel Hall Walker. Minoru, by Cyllene, was one of them, and in 1909 he won the Two Thousand Guineas and Derby for His Majesty. After King Edward's death in 1910, Minoru reverted to his breeder, and was sold for £20,000 to go to Russia.

It is just possible that if Prince Palatine and Minoru had gained their fame on the Turf bearing Colonel Walker's colours he would have retained his interest in racing and breeding longer than he did. The reason why he practically retired at the end of 1915 he explained in a conversation the writer had with him in 1918 in the dining-room at the House of Commons. He mentioned that he had seen his colours success-ful in four classic races, and expressed his belief that he should have had that satisfaction on at least one other occasion. He was convinced that if Cherry Lass had been ridden with better judgment she would have won the St Leger instead of finishing third to Challacombe and Polymelus. His interlocutor suggested there was still time for him to breed another classic winner. 'No,' he replied, 'I've finished. I shall not start again. My experience with Let Fly settled me.' He went on to complain that Let Fly was allowed to run in the Guineas without shoes, 'though I had the night before selected the plates he was to wear'. A further complaint was that in the 'New' Derby, in which Pommern and Let Fly finished first and second, his instruction that Let Fly was to keep with Pommern and try to beat him for speed at the finish was ignored. It was obvious that those incidents rankled in his mind, but the probable explanation of Let Fly's failure to realise his expectations was that the colt was still feeling the deleterious effects of the series of gruelling races he had with Redfern the previous season. The latter suffered the same way.

In the course of that talk Colonel Hall Walker also referred to Night Hawk. He said that if his trainer, 'Jack' Robinson of Foxhill, had had his way, the horse would not have won the St Leger.

'I had told him that I wanted Night Hawk specially trained for the Cesarewitch, but when the Doncaster meeting came round I informed him that, as I should be there, I wished my horse to run in the St Leger. Robinson raised the objection that Night Hawk was not fit enough, but I knew the colt required very little work and expected him to win. In order to have the laugh over Robinson I put £50 on for him without telling him. To my utter surprise I got 50 to 1 to the money.'

In November, 1915, Colonel Walker startled us all by offering his blood-stock to the Government, provided they would purchase his stud farm at Tully and his racing stables at Russley, a few miles from Lambourn, in Berkshire, for £75,000 or any less sum at which the properties might be valued. The offer was referred to the Army Council and the Board of Agriculture. The avowed purpose of the proposed gift was to enable the Government to breed stallions that could be used to increase the supply of horses suitable for the Army.

The war had been in progress fifteen months, and the nation's finances were being severely strained; moreover, it was open to doubt whether the stud could be conducted in a way calculated to achieve the aim suggested. It was understood at the time that the Army Council favoured acceptance of the offer, but that the Board of Agriculture took a contrary view. Anyway, the proffered gift was politely declined. Thereupon Colonel Walker entered all his bloodstock in the catalogue of the approaching December Sales at Newmarket. Although thorough-breds were then fetching comparatively poor prices, it was realised that the breeding stock at Tully would be eagerly sought after. Agents in England were, indeed, commissioned by stud masters in distant parts of the world to bid for many of the lots. Meanwhile, Lord Lonsdale and one or two others were busy behind the scenes striving to persuade the Board of Agriculture to reverse their decision. These efforts were success-ful, and the day before the mares and other thoroughbreds from Tully were to have come under the hammer, Colonel Walker received from the President of the Board of Agriculture a telegram reading: 'Gladly accept your generous offer, and buy your properties at Tully and Russley.'

And so it came about that the big establishment at Tully was converted into the National Stud. The result of a valuation of the land and buildings there and at Russley was the payment to the vendor of £65,625. Captain Greer (now Sir Henry) valued the bloodstock presented to the nation at £74,000. It consisted of the stallions White Eagle and Royal Realm, thirty mares, ten yearling fillies, twenty foals and eight horses in training, including Night Hawk, Great Sport, and the fillies Dolabella, White Lie, Flash of Steel and Tillywhim.

It cannot be claimed that the National Stud has achieved more than a private stud of similar standing would have done, but, despite unavoidable losses the last two or three years, it has been a great financial success, thanks largely to the able management of Sir Henry Greer. Owing to the political and fiscal troubles in which the British and Free State Governments are now involved, and perhaps also to the fact that it is obvious the stud does not, and never will, serve a national purpose, the existence of the establishment in its present form is likely to come to an end when a favourable opportunity for disbanding it comes along. The Russley branch was sold many years ago.

The generosity of Colonel Walker's gift to the nation has always been freely and widely acknowledged. If it had not been accepted, the bloodstock would have realised a big sum under the hammer. Why was the Colonel so determined to rid himself of his responsibilties at Tully? He had spent money lavishly on making the place not only a high-class stud but also one possessing many attractive and picturesque features, especially the beautiful garden made by Japanese experts, who took three years to complete their work. The stud had furnished him with a succession of colts and fillies that conferred lustre on his racing colours, and in many ways it seemed a desirable possession. Mention has been made of the annoyance he experienced over Let Fly, but there is reason for believing that his resolve to close down was to a large extent reached because of apprehensions concerning the political outlook in Ireland. One may, indeed, suppose that when he heard of the Easter rebellion in 1916 he thanked his stars that Tully was off his hands. In his latter years Lord Wavertree maintained only a slight connection with racing and breeding. The five broodmares he owned at the time of his death were disposed of at the Newmarket Second July Sales. The highest price obtained was 50 guineas, and the whole batch yielded only 185 guineas.

There were features of Lord Wavertree's character and individuality which puzzled many people who came in contact with him. It surprised them to find that a man who had in several ways made a conspicuous success of his life should be so much of a mystic and adventurer. His faith in astrology was unbounded. He required his stud employees to make a note of the time at which his mares foaled – not the approximate time, but the exact minute. The time-table was sent to an astrologer (a lady), who prepared an elaborate horoscope of every foal so that the owner might know the propitious and unpropitious periods of its life and act accordingly. His friends frequently twitted him about his belief in these signs and portents, but he went serenely on his way, oblivious of scoffers and sceptics. In the conduct of his stud there was, however, a thoroughly practical side, and those who knew him well realised that his judgment was usually very sound. He took a delight in evolving and testing theories, and the results he obtained from his experiments served him as a guide. His great success as a breeder during the fifteen years he owned the Tully Stud testified to the skill with which he applied the knowledge he possessed, no matter how it might have been acquired. There were occasions when it amused him to pose as an eccentric person and invent weird answers to questions people asked about his breeding theories.

It may interest many readers to learn that he bought Gondolette, a flat-footed round-actioned mare, solely because Doncaster, the sire of her dam, was so close up in her pedigree. She was a conspicuous example of Lord Wavertree's dictum (embodied in a letter we received in 1916): 'The mare's the thing. The merit of a good mare cannot be destroyed; and not only that, it can, by breeding into it, be built up again.'

As a businessman Lord Wavertree well knew the importance of securing the services of highly-qualified assistants, and in the conduct of his stud he had the good fortune to be aided by two able men, Mr William Chismon and Mr Harry Sharpe. The former has a deep understanding of breeding lore and the characteristics of blood lines: he can 'read' in a pedigree far more than meets the eye of the ordinary scrutineer. As for Harry Sharpe, his ability as a stud groom and manager is unexcelled. It is only just, therefore, that in a record of the successes achieved at Tully the parts played by these two experts should be acknowledged. Lord Wavertree would have been the first to admit his indebtedness to them. That he was by no means an easy man to work for may be inferred from the frequency with which he changed his trainers. He was imbued with the idea that no professional trainer knew more about the preparation and management of racehorses than he did himself. As he paid the piper, he claimed the right to call the tune, and that way friction was apt to arise.

No one has more respect for Lord Wavertree's judgment as a breeder of thoroughbreds than the Aga Khan. In a letter to 'Hotspur', of the *Daily Telegraph*, the Prince wrote:

'It was entirely due to Lord Wavertree and to my personal friendship for him that I started to race on the English Turf. I would probably never have been known as an owner west of Suez had he not, during and after my visit to Tully in 1904, urged me to take up racing in England. He undoubtedly gave me much good advice, and up to the last I never took an important decision without asking his opinion. Great as have been my successes on the Turf – for during the ten years I have been racing I have four times headed the list of winning owners, almost a record in its way – had I absolutely listened to the advice he gave me those successes would have been infinitely greater. Bygones are bygones, but it just shows that those who pooh-pooh science, knowledge and study in connection with racing do not know what they are talking about. Lord Wavertree's own successes as a breeder were enormous, and he spent very little money. He always told me that had the amount I invested in horses been spent according to his views there would have been no limit to the success I would have had. Looking back now, I see that this was not mere optimism on his part; it would have proved true in practice year by year.'

In another paragraph of that letter the Aga Khan stated that in October before the King's grave illness, Lord Wavertree 'most distinctly and clearly foretold that His Majesty would soon be very ill, and then recover and resume his normal life and duties. Of course, Lord Wavertree went by the King's horoscope, which he had worked out.'

Lord Wavertree left estate the gross value of which was £838,290, with net personalty amounting to £749,408. He left his racing cups and trophies, together with pictures of horses, to the Corporation of Liverpool. In 1920 he was, somewhat belatedly, elected a member of the Jockey Club.   BBR–1933

Memorative Biography of Sir Henry Greer

If Sir Henry Greer, who died in 1934 at the age of seventy-nine, had listened to anyone but himself, there would, almost certainly, never have been a Pretty Polly nor that incredibly prolific family tracing to Lady Josephine, as well as a multitude of other significant racehorses and influential producers in the sphere of racing and breeding. Sir Henry Greer, who had a 'long, honourable and useful career', however, will always be best remembered as the owner of Gallinule – beyond question one of the most important sires, particularly as a broodmare sire, in the expansive history of the Turf.

Sir Henry obtained Gallinule in 1889 when the five-year-old son of Isonomy-Moorhen, by Hermit, was known as a 'bleeder' to almost everyone and as a 'roarer' to not as many.

Put to stud in Ireland by Sir Henry, Gallinule's first crops, as might be expected, were rather small and the mares he covered were hardly fashionable. Nonetheless, Gallinule got precocious stock and there is nothing like a steady stream of two-year-old winners to attract breeders, especially if they show quality as well. Within a very few years, Gallinule had his pick of mares and in 1904 and 1905, thanks primarily to his daughter Pretty Polly, he headed the stallion list. He was also second twice and third twice. Gallinule also sired Palotta, she

Sir Henry Greer.

the dam of Americus Girl, the dam of Lady Josephine, she the dam of Lady Juror and Mumtaz Mahal!

Mr Charles Morton, Gallinule's trainer for a time, is quoted in the BBR's 1934 tribute to Sir Henry Greer (and Gallinule): 'But it just goes to prove the irony of this fascinating business when Gallinule, who, by all the canons of breeding, should have turned out a complete failure at stud, instead became one of the most successful sires of his time.'

THIS FINE SPORTSMAN, whose name will, in racing and breeding annals, be associated with Gallinule and the National Stud, died August 24th, at his home, Curragh Grange, Kildare, aged seventy-nine. He was christened Joseph Henry, but nobody ever spoke or thought of him otherwise than as Harry Greer. The eldest son of Lieutenant-General H. H. Greer, he was born at Moy, Co. Tyrone, February 9th, 1855. After schooling at Wellington, he went to the Royal Military College, and in 1874 joined the 74th Highlanders. He retired from the Army a captain in 1890, having done most of his service in India, where polo, cricket, rackets and golf were his chief recreations.

Greer's active association with the Turf began in 1889, when he registered his colours, 'white, tartan sleeves, red cap', and thereafter he was a familiar and much respected figure in English and Irish racing circles. He became a member of the Jockey Club and of the Irish Turf Club, and to both bodies rendered great service as a legislator and administrator.

It was in 1889 that Greer became the owner of Gallinule, a big and handsome chestnut horse with a lot of white about him. By Isonomy, he was out of Moorhen, a daughter of Hermit, the line going back in tail-female to Cast Steel, by Whisker. Greer always declared that Gallinule appealed to him for two reasons; he had a great admiration for Isonomy, and an abiding faith in the Cast Steel family. Why he thought so highly of the Cast Steel tribe is not by any means obvious, for up to the time of Gallinule its leading members had been Gamester (a St Leger winner), Vespasian, Sabinus, Upas (a winner of the French Derby), and Cambuslang.

Moorhen was bred by Lord Hartington (afterwards Duke of Devonshire), and had an unusual career on the Turf. From first to last she ran in seventy-eight races on the flat, and over fences and hurdles, and won twenty-six of them. When three years old she was sold for 200 guineas, and the following year was carrying a foal by Vulcan when, at the Doncaster Sales, she was bought for 150 guineas by Mr J. C. Hill, a Lincolnshire sportsman. The foal of 1878 never ran. In 1879 she 'slipped', was put back into training, and proceeded to win most of the successes to her credit. Returning to the stud, she produced a foal by Gladiateur that was of little account, and then, two years later (1884), bred Gallinule, sold when a yearling at Newmarket for 720 guineas to a Mr Wood, who died the following year. Lord Savernake, who was presently to become Earl of Ailesbury, then bought Gallinule for 800 guineas, and for him the colt won the National Breeders Produce Stakes at Sandown Park and other good races. The next year Lord Ailesbury was 'warned off' the Turf because of orders he gave to a jockey riding one of his horses in a race at York, and his horses came up for sale. Mr Abington Baird secured Gallinule with a bid of 5,100 guineas. The purchase occasioned him a succession of disappointments. In 1889 Gallinule started favourite for the Lincolnshire Handicap, but half-way through the race began to bleed and finished 'nowhere'. When he was running in a race at Newmarket the following July the same thing occurred. Captain Greer then came along, and bought Gallinule for £900 or £1,000, for accounts of the transaction vary to that extent.

In his memoir of Sir Henry Greer which appeared in *Horse and Hound*,

'Audax' relates the following as the 'true story' of what happened:

'The son of Isonomy was on offer to him (Greer) for £1,000, and he agreed to decide whether he would buy on the morning of July 10th, 1889. The previous day Gallinule had broken a small blood-vessel when contesting the Visitors' Handicap at Newmarket. Few people were aware of Gallinule's mishap, and Charles Morton, his trainer, fearing that Greer would find this out, when he (Greer) hummed and ha'ed about giving this figure, said: "Well, as I know Mr Baird wishes to sell, I will risk it and take £900." To this Greer agreed.'

In his book, *My Sixty Years of the Turf*, Charles Morton tells the tale very differently. Here is his version:

'Could anything illustrate the chanceable nature of horse-breeding more aptly than the story of Gallinule? This horse originally belonged to the Marquis of Ailesbury, and Abington Baird bought him at auction for 5,100 guineas. Evidently there must have been a good reason for selling the horse, a fact I did not discover until I began to train him for the Lincoln Handicap. Then, to my dismay, I found that he was in the habit of breaking blood-vessels. He certainly ought to have won the Lincoln that year, but, as I feared, he broke a blood-vessel in the race. I had tried him with a horse named Acme, who just got beaten in the Lincoln, and in the trial Gallinule had beaten Acme six lengths.

'I gave him another run at the July Meeting at Newmarket; but in the meantime he had turned roarer. It was touch and go whether I ran him, but I told Sam Loates, if he could not win, not to knock the horse about. However, Gallinule himself decided the matter by breaking another blood-vessel. Back in the paddock, Captain Greer came up to me and observed what a pity it was that such a nice horse should be so unlucky.

'"Yes," I replied, "it is, because he is a very good-looking horse and beautifully bred. What I shall do with him now, I don't know."

'"Well," said the Captain, "he is just the horse I should like for a stallion. I'm about to start a stud. Is he for sale?"

'I knew, of course, that "The Squire" (Baird) wanted to get rid of the horse, so I told Captain Greer we would take £1,500 for him.

'"I would not mind giving you £1,000; fifteen hundred is a little too much for me."

'"All right," I said, "you can have him for a thousand." Baird had given me authority to do as I liked with the horse, and I don't mind saying (I felt) that the sooner I got rid of him the better I would like it. Captain Greer agreed, and wanted to know if I would mind his sending Barrow, the principal veterinary surgeon in Newmarket in those days, to see the horse. "Not at all," I said.

'The next morning Barrow came round, carefully went over Gallinule, and found him perfectly sound. "Now," he said (he was a kindly old man, one of the best in the world), "I would like you to put a saddle and bridle on him and try his wind." But time was flying on, and I had a horse running in the first race. "I'll tell my head man," I said. "You'll have to excuse me now. I must get away." "Oh," said the old chap, "I don't suppose it matters much, Mr Morton. I'm sure the horse is all right."

'I knew that Captain Greer did not mind about Gallinule breaking blood-vessels; he understood all about that, but possibly he would not have bought the horse if he had known him to be a roarer. However, he took the horse away and duly paid for him. When I informed Baird that I had got rid of him, he remarked that he was sorry for the fellow who had bought him. But it just goes to prove the irony of this fascinating business when Gallinule, who, by all the canons of breeding, should have turned out a complete failure at the stud, instead became one of the most successful sires of his time.'

That, it may be conceded, is an entertaining narrative, but it furnishes evidence that Morton's memory cannot implicitly be relied upon, so perhaps he allowed his imagination to run away with him. For example, there is his statement that he did not discover why Lord Ailesbury had parted with Gallinule until he began to train the horse and found he was a 'bleeder'. He must have known at the time of the sale, and should not have forgotten, that the Marquis had been 'warned off', and so had no further use for his racehorses.

The only fact that really matters is that Greer became the owner of Gallinule in 1889, and sent him to the Brownstown Stud, on the edge of The Curragh, which he had recently bought. His judgment, so far as Gallinule was concerned, did not meet with general endorsement. That the horse was, according to Morton, a roarer was evidently a stable secret, but that he was a 'bleeder' – a weakness inherited from his maternal grandsire, Hermit – was common knowledge, and there would, in consequence, be a prejudice against him in breeding circles. But Greer never made it a practice to act on other people's opinions; he preferred to rely on his own, and before many years had gone by his purchase of Gallinule was widely acclaimed a wonderful bargain. It provided him with a fortune, and placed him in the front rank of breeders.

It was at Brownstown that Birdcatcher gained his fame as a sire: Gallinule added another vivid chapter to its history. From first to last he sired winners of 663 races worth £316,963. After his stock had been racing five seasons no such figures as these seemed likely to accrue, for the winnings had then averaged little more than £5,000 per season. That was partly accounted for by the comparative fewness of his runners, for during his early seasons at the stud he had an unsatisfactory record as a stock-getter. As a result, however, of changes at Brownstown there was a remarkable development; from being unfruitful Gallinule became notably the reverse while the calibre of his offspring reached a high standard, culminating with the advent of Pretty Polly. He headed the list of stallions in 1904 and 1905, was second in 1903 and 1907, and third in 1900 and 1909. As a sire of winner-producing mares he was a marvel, and headed the list five seasons.

It was probably fortunate for Sir Henry Greer that Gallinule stood in

Ireland, for Irish breeders are far more inclined than their English confrères to give a well-bred stallion with otherwise indifferent credentials a chance. In his first season he got eight foals. Seven won as two-year-olds, and six of the seven raced in Ireland. All through his career Gallinule was conspicuously successful as a sire of two-year-old winners. No fewer than eleven of the foals he got when twenty-five years of age were successful on the Turf as juveniles. He died in January, 1912, aged twenty-eight.

Needless to say, so soon as it became evident that Gallinule was a sire far removed from the common rut, the leading breeders were after him to a man. His list would probably have been filled easily at a fee of 300 or 400 guineas, but Greer, after raising it to 200 guineas, kept it at that figure – a singularly altruistic ordinance. There is a conflict of evidence regarding the financial arrangements for Gallinule's first season. It has frequently been stated that no fee was that year charged for his services, but we have also been told that there was a fee of 25 guineas. Likely enough there was a fixed fee, which was not charged for certain approved mares. This was, we remember, the plan adopted when Desmond began his stud career.

Among the winners sired by Gallinule were Pretty Polly (stake total £37,297), White Eagle (£15,822), Slieve Gallion (£11,995), Hammerkop (£10,793), Phaleron (£10,376), Game Chick (£9,789), Sirenia, Admiral Hawke, Princesse de Galles, and Wildfowler. The list could be greatly extended. As we are here interested in Gallinule only so far as his success at the stud concerned Sir Henry Greer's personal affairs, it is merely necessary to single out Wildfowler and Slieve Gallion for special attention. Before securing Gallinule, Greer had bought a filly by Ben Battle, named Tragedy, from her breeder, and with her, just before the Gallinule deal, won the Irish Derby. She had been sent to Beckhampton to be trained by Sam Darling. Presently Greer suggested to Darling that they should 'go partners' in some mares and their produce. The proposal was agreed to. Darling put two into the 'pool', Hirondelle and Bonnie Morn, which he bought from Lord Rodney; Captain Greer contributed three, one being Tragedy. Bonnie Morn was in foal to Kilwarlin, and in due course produced the colt Kilcock. From Tragedy came Wildfowler, while some years later Slieve Gallion (out of Reclusion) added lustre to the partnership. All three horses were, of course, trained by Darling, and there are allusions to them in his *Reminiscences*, published twenty years ago.

Wildfowler was backward when he finished fourth in the Guineas, and could not be trained for the Derby; but he won the St Leger 'with his head in his chest', beating the Derby winner Jeddah, who was a hot favourite. Captain Greer then bought Darling's share of the colt and sent him to the stud. Wildfowler had sired the Eclipse Stakes winner Llangibby, and Silver Fowl (dam of Fifinella, winner of the New Derby and Oaks, and of Silver Tag, who won the Cambridgeshire) before he was sold, in 1908, to a French syndicate. In 1916, when twenty-one years old, Wildfowler was disposed of in Paris for about £15.

Slieve Gallion, Greer's own property, was a brilliant performer as a two-year-old, winning the New Stakes at Ascot, the Champagne Stakes at Doncaster, and other events. The following spring he was victorious in the Guineas, but failed in the Derby, finishing third to Orby. Darling states that when he first saw Slieve Gallion he told Captain Greer that his neck was set on wrong, and that he would be difficult to ride. In his book the trainer gives it as his opinion that the horse's awkward mouth prevented him winning the Derby. Most people, however, attribute his failure to lack of stamina; his speed was terrific. Two weeks later he was a winner at Ascot, and was then sold to go to the Kisber Stud in Hungary, where he proved disappointing.

Both Captain Greer and Darling lost heavily by backing Kilcock to win the Kempton 'Jubilee' in 1896. His weight was only 6 st 12 lb, and the trainer thought he would have been worth betting on if he had had to carry 8 st 7 lb. Victor Wild, with 9 st 7 lb in the saddle, beat Kilcock three-parts of a length. The latter was ridden by the veteran Wall, who, lacking strength, 'was absolutely useless'. Kilcock subsequently won good races, and was eventually sold to go to Hungary.

When, in 1908, Captain Greer was elected a Steward of the Jockey Club, the partnership between him and Sam Darling was dissolved. Later, when Darling went into retirement, he received a letter from Greer reading, in part:

'We have worked together on the Turf for many years, and they have been marked by unremitting care and attention to my interests on your part. . . I can look back on every incident connected with my racing career not only with pleasure, but with the knowledge that I owe most of that pleasure to you.'

After the severance of the partnership Captain Greer gave most of his attention to his stud and to his duties as a Steward until he was appointed Director of the National Stud, which came into being in December, 1915. Colonel Hall Walker (afterwards Lord Wavertree) had offered to present to the nation all his bloodstock if the Government would purchase, at a valuation, his stud farm at Tully, Kildare, and his racing stable at Russley, in Berkshire. It was only after considerable hesitation that the offer was accepted; indeed, in the first instance it was declined.

Immediately after his appointment as Director, Captain Greer was invited to write a short article about the National Stud for our *Review*. His request to be excused was not unexpected. He explained that as he had become a Government official 'it would not be correct' to contribute the suggested article. He, however, proceeded to explain that Colonel Hall Walker's gift had been accepted principally because of urgent representations made by the Army Council, who considered it 'essential to the efficiency of the Army that the quality and number of horses available in the United Kingdom for military purposes should be improved and strengthened.' He went on to state that the Government fully recognised that the foundation stock of horses for the Army was the thoroughbred, and their intention therefore was to utilise the National Stud for breeding thoroughbreds only. In conclusion he wrote:

'With regard to the disposal of the stock bred at Tully, it is probable that a few colts and fillies will be leased for racing purposes and the remainder sold as yearlings. I am, however, sure you will realise that these are matters requiring much consideration and experience of the circumstances and requirements of the Stud on the part of the Director, who has only very recently been appointed to the charge of eighty-four head of blood-stock, which he will have to segregate and docket in his mind before committing himself to the declaration of a fixed policy.'

It was universally recognised that Captain Greer was the man above all others worthy to be entrusted with the difficult task assigned to him. His qualifications were such that he could both speak and act with authority. He made a great success of his job in so far as success was possible. He had at the outset hoped to convert the Russley property into a depot for stallions that would travel the country districts serving farmers' mares as the King's Premium horses were doing, but that aim was thwarted when the Government sold Russley; or perhaps he had abandoned it as unworkable. It therefore only remained for him to conduct the National Stud more or less on the lines of a first-class private stud, and make as much profit as possible. For many years there were substantial surpluses, and a total exceeding £100,000 had accumulated, or been absorbed by the Treasury, when, about five years ago, there came a set-back, and losses began to whittle down the former gains. Last year there was a good recovery, and this year the products of the Stud sold at Newmarket in July yielded a fine total and average. This return to prosperity must have been very pleasing to Greer, though he had resigned his post as Director last January because of his failing health. He controlled the establishment for nineteen years, and it stands today a monument to his skill, wisdom, and business aptitude.

About two years after his appointment as Director of the National

Stud, he sold Brownstown to Mr W. Parrish, but when he had everything working smoothly at Tully permitted himself to assume the
management of the Aga Khan's neighbouring Sheshoon Stud. This
establishment, which comprises six farms, is now the property of Prince
Aly Khan. In this memoir we have, of necessity, dealt only with the
outstanding features of Harry Greer's long, honourable and useful
career, but we have surely written enough to reveal him a man
conspicuous in his day and generation. He received a knighthood in
1925, and was a Senator of the Irish Free State. In 1886 he married a
daughter of Major-General George de la Poer Beresford, who survives
him. They had two sons, who, during the war, served in the Irish
Guards. Both were killed in 1917.   BBR–1934

The Remarkable Story of Eugene Leigh

*It is one of the idiosyncracies of racing and breeding history that the
American, Eugene Leigh, is best remembered through the mists of time
as the trainer of the famous French horse Epinard, second in all three of
the much-publicised International races in the United States in 1924.
Few people realise that Mr Leigh, who trained with considerable
success in France, had also at one time stables in England and that he
dabbled in breeding as well.*

*As the unfathomable forces of history were taking shape it turned out
that Mr Leigh in 1902 purchased two mares by the names of Merry
Token and Ulla for £400, £200 more than Mr E. J. Keylock, from
whom he bought them, had paid for them.*

*Both mares wound up in the US. Merry Token became the property
of Major August Belmont and among the foals she presented him was
Mahubah, the dam of Man o' War, still hailed as perhaps the greatest
performer ever bred in that country. Ulla had a filly foal named Korea
who became the property of Senator J. N. Camden. When anti-racing
legislation stopped racing in New York in 1910, Korea was sent to
Argentina. There, when bred to Old Man, she produced Botafogo, still
regarded as one of the all-time 'greats' in Argentine racing.*

*Nor was that all of the story. Years earlier Mr Leigh had a peculiar
affection for a horse named Bramble who had few other admirers even
when free services were offered. So he arranged a mating between
Bramble and his mare, Roseville. The result of that union was Ben
Brush, winner of the 1896 Kentucky Derby and subsequently champion
sire in the US in 1909. Ben Brush's sons included Broomstick and*

*Sweep. Broomstick won three sire championships and Sweep topped the
list twice. Roseville, the dam of Ben Brush, was, incidentally, by
Reform from Albia, the daughter of Alarm who also bred Roseville's
own brother Azra, hero of the 1892 Kentucky Derby.*

The **BBR** *of 1937 expressed an appreciation of Mr Leigh's
'profound' influence and his involvement with Man o' War, Botafogo
and Ben Brush is a story which needs resurrection.*

EUGENE LEIGH had a limited contact with bloodstock breeding.
However, his influence was profound. In 1902, when his stables were
close to Foxhill, near Swindon, he purchased two mares and their filly-
foals from the late Mr E. J. Keylock, of Broome Manor. One was Merry
Token, by Merry Hampton, covered by Missel Thrush and with a filly
by Avington. The other was a Barcaldine mare named Ulla. She was
nursing a filly-foal by Raeburn. They had cost Mr Keylock less than
£200. He sold them for £400. Both went to the United States. Merry
Token was passed on to Major Belmont. For him she bred Merry Task,
Sandmole, and his sister Mahubah, dam of Man o' War, possibly the
greatest horse ever raced in the US. How different would have been the
present-day history of racing and breeding in the United States if
Eugene Leigh had not made his venture.

The Raeburn filly out of Ulla was known as Korea. Senator J. N.
Camden became the owner. Korea won four races. When in 1910
legislation stopped racing in New York State, she was sent to Argentina.
In that country, to Old Man, Korea produced Botafogo, without doubt
the best of all horses to race in South America. He ran nineteen times,
winning eighteen races and over £32,270. When he was beaten it was a
'fluke'. A fortnight later he met his conqueror at the same weights, and
beat him by 'the length of a street'. Botafogo, who was sold to Messrs B.
Villaneuva and M. A. Martinez de Hoz for £45,000, unfortunately died
after only two seasons at the stud. It will be seen that rather momentous
consequences followed the purchases of two mares and their filly-foals
for an insignificant price.

Eugene Leigh always had a great affection for the descendants of Bonnie
Scotland, the son of Iago and Queen Mary. His eyes always sparkled as
he recalled he gave $8,000 for Bramble, a price, he used to say, about 800
times as much as anyone else would have ventured. Bramble suffered
greatly from lack of opportunity. Leigh acquired the mare Roseville,
covered her by Bramble, and passed her on. The produce was Ben
Brush. Previously no one would use Bramble; free services were spurned.

When Ben Brush came along it was too late. Bramble had met with an accident. It was difficult to get him to serve a mare after his second stud season.

Ben Brush was later bought by Mr J. R. Keene, and afterwards owned by Mr J. N. Camden, at whose farm he died in 1918. Ben Brush was the leading stallion in the US in 1909. He sired those very successful stallions, Broomstick and Sweep. Broomstick was the 'champion' sire in the States the three successive years 1913, 1914 and 1915. Sweep was premier stallion in 1918, and again in 1925.

Eugene Leigh once mentioned that imp. Bonnie Scotland ended his life in Illinois, where in his day there were not ten thoroughbred mares. Perhaps Leigh's fondness for Bramble was due to his purchase of that sire's son Clifford, one of the greatest horses of his time. In 1894 he sold him for £5,000, when Leigh's stable of twenty-three head realised over £16,000 – big money in those days.   BBR–1937

Memorative Biography of Joseph E. Widener

Mr J. E. Widener.

When Philadelphia Joseph E. Widener died in 1943 at the age
of seventy-one, the Review *in its Memorative Biography said:*
'Joseph E. Widener was unquestionably one of the most famous,
wise, well informed, forceful personalities ever known in International
racing.' Donator, prior to his death, to the US Government of an
art collection estimated to have cost Mr Widener's father, Peter A. B.
Widener $50,000,000; Mr Widener, a Jockey Club member since
1909, continued the beautification of Belmont Park after the death
of Major August Belmont in 1924, became president of the West-
chester Racing Association the following year and then was instrumen-
tal in creating Hialeah Park, still one of the loveliest racetracks in
the world. Although his name honours one of America's most presti-
gious handicap races, the Widener, run at Hialeah Park, few
Americans today probably realise the numerous contributions Mr
Widener made to racing and breeding, including his importation
of Sickle. That these contributions and his memory be not forgotten, one
could hardly find a better documentation than that presented by the
Review.

JOSEPH EARLY WIDENER, who died at the age of seventy-one years on
the morning of October 26th, at his home, Lynnewood Hall, in the
Philadelphia suburb, Elkins Park, was well known to the Turf in
England and France, especially in the latter country, where his horses
had raced prominently for years and where he kept many mares at the
Haras du Mesnil not so far from Le Mans. But in the United States he
was a pre-eminent figure and one of the most influential sportsmen of his
time.

Born in Philadelphia on August 19th, 1872, Mr Widener inherited
part of a vast fortune accumulated by his father, the traction magnate
and financier Peter A. B. Widener. He extended the great art collection
begun by his father, until it was one of the most valuable privately
owned galleries in the world. Before his death he presented it to the
United States Government to be housed in Washington. It had been
collected at an estimated cost of $50,000,000. This Art collection, 'rarely
if ever equalled in any period of collecting in Europe or America,'
contained more than three hundred paintings – among them sixteen
Rembrandts. One was 'The Mill' bought for £100,000 so it was said at
the time. There were many examples of the work of Titian, Raphael,
Gainsborough, Van Dyck and Holbein. Curiously his collection of
sporting pictures was not at all notable. Through the latter years of his

life his leading interest was in the breeding and racing of thoroughbreds and in the improvement of the sport of the Turf.

Mr Widener was a director of many of the chief financial, industrial and commercial undertakings of the city of Philadelphia.

Mr Widener showed his first interest in racing as long ago as 1890. Then he bought two horses whose performances gave him no encouragement to proceed further. A few years later he tried again with a group of yearlings bred in New Jersey by Lucien Appleby, once more to meet failure. About 1900 he turned enthusiastically to steeplechasing. J. Howard Lewis was his trainer. Mr Lewis, one of the 'wizards' in this field, was very successful. Numerous good horses represented the stable. By the time the reform group in New York had succeeded in closing racing in that State, at the end of the 1910 season, Mr Widener found himself one of that considerable group of American sportsmen who preferred sending their horses to Europe rather than giving them up entirely. Thus he established in France not only a jumping stable but also one of flat racers. For the remainder of his active life, except for the interruption of wars, he continued to race both in Europe and in the United States.

After the great war of 1914–1918, the Turf remained a major interest with him. Mr Widener had been elected to the Jockey Club of New York in 1909. In 1920 he became one of its Stewards, and later its vice chairman. Major August Belmont, who had made Belmont Park America's greatest racecourse, died in 1924. Next year Mr Widener succeeded him as President of the Westchester Racing Association. Though revenues were not large, because the tracks in New York were obliged to operate under a bookmaking system of wagering, without benefit of the revenues from pari-mutuels, Mr Widener added further to the beauty and magnificence of the great track.

He was also chiefly responsible for the creation in Florida of the present beautiful Hialeah Park course, in which he proposed to set a new standard in the outward attractiveness of American racing – and succeeded. When he had finished it he pronounced it the finest racecourse in the world.

Shortly after the First World War he turned his attention to the breeding of thoroughbreds. He purchased a part of the old Elmendorf Farm just outside of Lexington. As a thoroughbred nursery Elmendorf had been famous for half a century. Mr Widener added further improvements, including thousands of trees – which, next to horses and art, seemed to hold a fascination for him. On a hilltop he established an equine cemetery which was presided over by a heroic statue of the great stallion Fair Play, sire of Man o' War. Elmendorf became a sort of privately owned park which – in keeping with the local tradition – was open for the enjoyment of the public.

One of the first mares bought by Mr Widener when Elmendorf Farm was to his satisfaction, was Ormonda, a daughter of Superman and Princess Ormonde, by Ormonde's son Ormondale. A good-class winner, she was bought in 1920, when she was a four-year-old, for $5,500. She outlived Mr Widener, and when she was finally destroyed early in 1944 she was famous as the dam of two top-class horses, Osmand (winner of $157,975), and Brevity, both of which were narrowly beaten for the Kentucky Derby, and also as the grandam of Reaping Reward, King Cole, and Whirlaway, the world's largest money-winner.

After the death of Mr Belmont, whose Nursery Stud had produced Man o' War and dozens of other noted horses, Mr Widener purchased first the yearlings and later the entire lot of thoroughbreds. The breeding stock was offered for sale in May 1925. The prices secured represented a high point in the history of American bloodstock. Mr Widener himself participated in the bidding. He took Fair Play for $100,000. He also outbid others for a number of the mares, among them Quelle Chance, the dam of Chance Play and Chance Shot, two first-class horses by Fair Play. Though Quelle Chance was in France at the time, and only a picture could be presented for the scrutiny of the bidders, she brought $45,000. Fair Play got no great horses at Elmendorf as he had done at the Nursery, but much of Mr Widener's later success as a breeder came from his purchases from the Belmont estate.

Racing in three countries, Mr Widener sent numerous horses across the ocean in both directions. He brought Stefan the Great to Kentucky, but later returned him to England. The most successful of his importations was Sickle (son of Phalaris and the great mare Selene) which horse he first leased and later purchased from his good friend the Earl of Derby. Sickle, whose undulant fortunes were, when at their best, phenomenal, was twice leading sire in the US. When he died late in 1932 it was a great loss for Kentucky breeders.

The most successful horse Mr Widener bred in America was Stagehand, a bay colt, foaled in 1935, by Sickle out of the stakes-winning Fair Play mare Stagecraft; sold at the end of his two-year-old season while he was only a promising maiden, he went on to win $200,110. Mr Widener led the list of American breeders in 1940 and was usually prominent on the list of leading owners. He won the Futurity with Chance Sun and he won the Belmont Stakes on three occasions, with Chance Shot, Hurryoff, and Peace Chance. In general, however, his greatest successes were with steeplechasers; among his stars in this field were Duettiste, Lizard, Arc Light, Fairmount, Best Play, and Bushranger. The first two were imported.

Mr Widener was for many years a valued and consistent patron of the yearling sales in France. He however, bred some of his greatest winners like Victrix, Gossip and Confidence. His first trainer for many years was Jerry Welsh. Later the horses were with that great trainer Frank Carter until the latter's death: then to Geoff Watson. The mares were with M. Jean Couturié at Savigne l'Eveque near Le Mans. Many of their produce won big races since 1939. The best was Dogat (by Rodosto) who won the French Two Thousand Guineas. Victrix was at the stud in Normandy.

All the years Mr Widener raced in England his horses were trained by Captain Boyd-Rochfort at Newmarket. He was a valiant purchaser of yearlings, most of the fillies going to his stud in Kentucky. Mr Widener won the Cesarewitch with Seminole (1933) and the Victoria Cup, Hurst Park, with Unbreakable (1939). Joseph E. Widener was unquestionably one of the most famous, wise, well informed, forceful personalities ever known in International racing.

On the night before Mr Widener's death his son, Peter A. B. Widener II, had suffered a broken hip in an accident at Elmendorf Farm, so was not informed of his father's death until he had recovered from the shock and subsequent complications. Some weeks later he announced a new policy for the operation of Elmendorf. The farm had been purchased by him and would be operated under his personal ownership and direction.

The racing stable would be greatly reduced, and horses would be raced by him, by his wife, and by his son and daughter, but only on a small scale. The bulk of the yearlings bred at Elmendorf would be sold; the best of them would be consigned to the auction sales set up at the Lexington course, Keeneland, by the newly formed Breeders' Sales Company. Mr Widener proposed to spend most of his time at Elmendorf. Asked about his intentions as to racing and breeding in France after the war, he said that he hoped to carry on to some extent but indicated that he did not think it likely he would be able to resume operations on as large a scale as his father.   BBR-1943

The Death of Mr E. E. Coussell

IT IS WITH DEEP regret that we announce the death of Mr Ernest Edward Coussell which took place at Hove, Sussex, on Sunday, December 28th, 1947. He was working practically to the end and was deeply engrossed with this, the 35th volume of *The Bloodstock Breeders' Review* at the time of his death.

In August, 1911, Mr Coussell joined with the late Mr Edward Moorhouse in the formation of The British Bloodstock Agency, Ltd. A few months after the inauguration of the Company the idea of *The Bloodstock Breeders' Review* was conceived and the first number appeared in April, 1912. It was then published quarterly and continued so until 1920, when it became an annual.

For twenty-seven years Mr Moorhouse was Chief Contributor and Editor of the *Review*. On his death, in February, 1939, most of this work fell upon Mr Coussell, who had the arduous task of producing the book during the difficulties of the war years. There is no doubt that his labours in this connection, together with the heavy burden entailed by his business activities as a Director and Secretary of The British Bloodstock Agency, particularly during the absence of his co-directors on war service, took their toll.

Mr Coussell's profound knowledge of pedigrees, his devotion to the cause and enhancement of the British thoroughbred, his work as Hon. Secretary, and later as a member of the Council of The Thoroughbred Breeders' Association, and his ready assistance and advice to friends and clients, can be left for detailed mention in the memorative biography to be included in volume XXXVI (1947) of the *Review*. Suffice it to say here how much we regret the passing of an outstanding personality, who will be sadly missed by all who knew him, whether personally or through his devotion to the thoroughbred.

THE ANNOUNCEMENT of the death of Ernest Coussell on Sunday, December 28th, came as a great shock to his many friends throughout the world. He had been confined to his home near Lewes, Sussex, for some days with heart trouble. At three o'clock in the afternoon of December 28th he suffered a relapse and, taken to a nursing home, died there four hours later.

The story of Coussell himself is as romantic as any of the stories he loved to tell of the many and famous personalities with whom his great experience brought him in contact. It is the story of the rise from comparative obscurity as a young man to a position unique in the history of the development of the thoroughbred. The considerable part played by Coussell in this field through his connection with the British Bloodstock Agency, the Thoroughbred Breeders' Association and the *Bloodstock Breeders' Review*, apart from his numerous contributions to sporting papers, are a matter of worldwide knowledge.

Born in Stockport, Coussell came to London at an early age. Attracted to the breed, but unable to indulge his love of the thoroughbred by practical means, and with no inclination towards betting, he took the only path offered him, that of journalism. In 1902 he joined the editorial staff of *The Sporting Life*. It was about that time that he met William Allison, the foremost figure in racing journalism of the period, and principal of the International Horse Agency in Pall Mall. Allison was for some time 'Special Commissioner' of *The Sporting Life*, and a great advocate of the Bruce Lowe Figure System.

It was in 1909 that William Allison published a book, compiled for him by Coussell, giving the Bruce Lowe Numbers of the Mares in Vol. XXI of the *General Stud Book*. This work was similar to one printed privately by Lord Wavertree (previously Colonel Hall Walker) in 1898, which gave the family numbers of the mares in Vol. XVII of the *General Stud Book*. Coussell, however, went further, for he indicated the family number of the sire of each mare. In addition, he listed the records of the Bruce Lowe families in all flat races from 1900 to 1908. The enormous amount of detailed work involved in such a publication cannot easily be appreciated, but his successful accomplishment of such a task was to stand him in good stead in future years.

Whilst on *The Sporting Life* he met the late Edward Moorhouse, then 'Special Commissioner'. Moorhouse was a great racing journalist, and he, Coussell and another, Robert Bunsow, founded in 1911 the British Bloodstock Agency.

The story of the British Bloodstock Agency cannot adequately be told within these pages. It was in 1915 that Wrack was bought for Mr A. B. Hancock, for his Claiborne Stud in Kentucky, US. There he soon established a great reputation as a sire. A short time afterwards, Light Brigade was bought by the British Bloodstock Agency for Senator Johnson N. Camden, and thereafter the British Bloodstock Agency were concerned with most of the important sales to America, including Sir Gallahad III, Blenheim, Mahmoud and Bahram.

In 1912, Moorhouse and Coussell decided to found a magazine devoted to the British thoroughbred. This they called *The Bloodstock Breeders' Review*, and it was first published quarterly. The first number was circulated in April, 1912. Six months previously they had created a

E. E. Coussell. This photograph was taken at the Newmarket December Sales, 1944, the day after Mr Coussell had announced his retirement as Hon. Secretary to the Thorough-bred Breeders' Association.

'Breeders' Bureau', its purpose and aim to supply members with information collected from all over the world.

One of the members, in sending his subscription of two guineas, sent an accompanying letter, heartily approving the scheme, but adding: 'I think it would be better if you increased the subscription to five guineas and gave us a periodical dealing with matters pertaining to the thoroughbred. If you will adopt this suggestion you will, believe me, be doing breeders a great service.'

'There' wrote the principals in the Foreword to the first edition, 'is the germ of the idea which has resulted in the publication of the first number of *The Blood-stock Breeders' Review*. It has not been deemed necessary to increase the Bureau subscription, but the suggestion that, by means of a magazine, the work can be considerably extended was so happy we decided to act upon it.

'Such, then, is the genesis of the *Review*' continued Moorhouse and Coussell. 'This, the first quarterly number, cannot be allowed to go forth without a word or two of explanation of its scope. There might be the less to say if its wanderings were to be confined to the British Isles, the home of the thoroughbred. The *Review* has, however, an international mission. Copies of this and every succeeding issue will cross the wide seas, and find student readers in far-off lands. It is to be a cosmopolitan magazine in every sense of the word. Where the thoroughbred is to be found, thither will it travel, conveying information calculated to be of interest and value to breeders.

'We have set our hand to an ambitious undertaking. . .'

As the *Review* grew, so did the Agency. It was, however, on the outbreak of war that the original partnership was disturbed. Bunsow, of German origin, had failed to obtain his naturalisation in 1915, and was interned. After the war he divided his time between England and the Continent, and died in 1931.

Moorhouse and Coussell continued their work together during the war and until 1924, when Moorhouse decided to retire and yielded his share in the Agency to his friend 'Jock' Crawford. Moorhouse had played a great part in the formation in 1917 of the Thoroughbred Breeders' Association, of which he was secretary from its inception until his retirement in 1924.

Crawford was one of the most popular figures of recent years on the thoroughbred breeding scene. He proved a great asset, and contributed greatly to the development of the Agency by numerous travels abroad. He was tragically killed in a car accident in South Africa in 1938. Moorhouse died nearly twelve months later. Crawford's shares in the Agency had been taken up by Gerald McElligott, who was an old friend of Crawford's in India.

Thus, in 1940, soon after the outbreak of the Second World War, the directors of the British Bloodstock Agency were Coussell, McElligott and Brigadier E. S. Scott, CIE, who had joined the Agency in 1938. Brigadier Scott had spent many years in India, where, as Director of Remounts, he played a leading part in the foundation and organising of the principal stud farms which were being established at the time.

Both Scott and McElligott were recalled for service, and the main work of the firm fell on Coussell, who, in addition, was also Honorary Secretary of the Thoroughbred Breeders' Association, a position he had held since the retirement in 1924 of Edward Moorhouse. He had also taken over the major part of Moorhouse's duties on the *Review*, in addition to his contributions to *The Sporting Life*, under the pen-name of 'Ithuriel'. When *Horse and Hound* was bought by Odham's Press after the death of Arthur Portman in an air raid, Coussell wrote the 'Audax' notes on breeding and racing which were such a feature of that publication.

It is impossible to recount the details of the tasks undertaken by Coussell during and after the war until the return of his co-directors. *The Blood-Horse* (of Lexington, Kentucky) sagely wrote: 'The cablegram brought no details of his death, but his many friends in America would assume at once that "E.E.C." had postponed too long the day when he would slow up.'

Coussell's friend for many years, Mr A. B. Clements, Editor of *The Sporting Life*, paid this tribute at his passing:

'Those who knew Coussell intimately will feel most keenly the loss of a lovable friend. He was a charming companion in town or countryside, and an afternoon's racing or a visit to a stud farm in his company was a delight.

'He knew more about pedigrees, about stallions and mares, living and dead, more about owners and breeders, stud and stable secrets than any man in the country. He never betrayed a confidence, was always courteous and kindly, and established for himself and his Agency a reputation for integrity that is honoured in every country in the world where the British thoroughbred is known.

'He was as much at home in Normandy as in Newmarket, and he was known and respected by every breeder of note in the Dominions and the United States.

'Few people can comprehend the complicated detail of a business such as the British Bloodstock Agency, and war-time and post-war regulations have made the maze still more difficult, particularly with regard to the export and import of horses.

'It is probably no exaggeration to say that Coussell understood every detail better than anyone, and it was no infrequent occurrence for experts from the various Ministries concerned to seek his help in unravelling problems that arose in administering the regulations.

'Coussell still found time to indulge his flair for journalism. He was with the late Edward Moorhouse, then the Special Commissioner, on *The Sporting Life* staff in the early 1900s, and in 1911 they decided to start the British Bloodstock Agency.

'Some few months after the launching of the Agency they produced the first volume of the *Bloodstock Breeders' Review*, which was to develop into the foremost work of its kind.

'Since Moorhouse died, some ten years ago, Coussell took over the major part of the work entailed in producing the *Review*, a task which he found increasingly arduous as a consequence of present printing difficulties.

'During the war, after the death of Arthur Portman and the taking over of *Horse and Hound* by Odhams Press, Coussell came to our aid and wrote "Audax" notes on racing and breeding for two or three years.

'No one, since the days of Allison and Robertson, has been so well qualified as Coussell to write on the breeding side of racing. Although he may have lacked Allison's literary graces and Robertson's scientific precision, he could beat both in relating in interesting and intimate fashion the story that can be told of every thoroughbred foaled and in linking that story to the animal's racecourse achievements.

'Occasionally, and all too rarely in recent years, Coussell contributed to *The Sporting Life*, under the *nom de plume* of "Ithuriel", articles of interest and value to breeders.

'It will not be possible for any individual to fill the place that Coussell leaves. There is no one with his knowledge of the ramifications of the vast bloodstock breeding industry. The thoroughbred has lost a great advocate and British breeders their best ambassador.'

In 1944 Coussell resigned his Hon. Secretaryship of the Thoroughbred Breeders' Association, a position he had held for twenty years. At the Annual General Meeting of the Association, held at Newmarket in December 1946, the President (Lord Rosebery) presented him, on behalf of the members, with a memento of his long period in office.

Coussell was elected a Member of the Council and, in his speech, said that 'it had meant much to him to know what the Association had done to enhance the prestige of the British thoroughbred'.

Coussell was a well-known and popular figure in the US, which he visited regularly. He was frequently at the Saratoga Sales, where, in the years preceding the Second World War, he purchased a number of yearlings for clients in this country.

It was perhaps in France that he spent his happiest days of recent years. Intimately acquainted with all the breeders and owners in that country, he had acquired a fluent knowledge of the language, and was equally welcome on the racecourses of Paris and the studs of the Normandy countryside.

Coussell had been Secretary of the Agency since its foundation. He is succeeded as Secretary by Brigadier Scott. The other directors are Gerald McElligott, MRCVS, and Lord Manton, who joined the firm in 1945.   BBR–1947

Presentation to Mr Coussell by the Thoroughbred Breeders' Association

THE PRESIDENT of the Thoroughbred Breeders' Association said he now had a very pleasant function to perform. Mr Coussell had resigned from being Hon. Secretary after many years of hard work for this Association, and the members thought it would be proper for them to give Mr Coussell some memento of his long period with us. They started subscriptions with Mr Deane as secretary. The president then handed Mr Coussell a cheque, on behalf of the members, and wished him every success and long life, and thanked him for all he had done in the past years and hoped he would continue to do in the future what he had done for the Association in the past.

Mr Coussell expressed his appreciation and gratitude to the members of the Association for the remarkable token of goodwill and esteem, and said that when he entered the hall he had no idea what was in store for him. Therefore he did not find it easy to express himself. In reality, the very fact of being closely associated with the Association since its foundation in 1917 had, in itself, been adequate reward for any services he had rendered. He had personal gratification in witnessing the growth of the Association. He thought it had become the premier Association in the world. The Stud Book had been copied and was the foundation of the registration of thoroughbred stock in all other countries. This Association may also claim a little credit for the principles on which Thoroughbred Associations had been founded in other countries. He regarded it as a personal tribute that when at Saratoga the American breeders decided to form an Association he was invited to attend the first meeting, and asked to explain the principles upon which the Thoroughbred Breeders' Association had been established in this country. Those principles were adopted. He still remembered that in 1939, at Mr Whitney's home in Saratoga, the Annual Meeting of the American Thoroughbred Breeders' Association was held. Routine business was quickly achieved. Mr Whitney said: 'We have a visitor from England. Perhaps it would be of interest for Mr Coussell to tell us some of the principles on which his Association has worked with great success.' He accepted that opportunity and thanked the American Breeders' Association for a chance to explain our work. The Australian Breeders' Association had communicated with Lord Rosebery more than once and if we could bring other Associations in league with ours we could do something for the breeders in all countries. It had been much to him to know what his Association had done to enhance the prestige of the British thoroughbred.

Lord Rosebery's Comments on 'The Problems of Breeding'

Lord Rosebery, president of The Thoroughbred Breeders' Association, in his speech before that organisation in 1947, suggested that he might not be 'a good person to speak to you on breeding, having sold the dam (Indiscretion) of this year's Oaks winner, Imprudence. I can only say that she refused to start three times out of four as a two-year-old, and was no good when she did. That is all part of the mystery and interest in horse breeding; but to judge from the mass of advice that we breeders have received from every side, including some who, I think, can never have bred anything at all of any kind, one would think that breeding Derby winners was a simple matter of ABC or arithmetic.'

In response to the 'flood of abuse' he had received from across the Atlantic for apparently having given the impression that he thought American blood did not stay, Lord Rosebery injected a disclaimer and added: 'I also recollect Sibola (an American-bred winner of the One Thousand Guineas), an ancestress of Nearco. She would have won the Oaks in a trot if her jockey had not thrown the race away; and in more recent times Mr Woodward has sent over great stayers like Omaha. I have, however, never yet found anybody who did not admit that the line of Americus was a short-running line.'

On the 'problems of breeding' he had this to say:

THERE IS, of course, nothing more difficult than breeding what you want. If you want to breed stayers you find that your staying lines get slower and slower; then if you try to breed from speed you find that your speedy lines get shorter and shorter. The difficulty is to maintain speed and stamina. That is why you see studs going up and down, increasing or diminishing in excellence; but I must admit that I was perturbed at the Yearling Sales at Doncaster when I saw that the big prices were almost entirely for animals who had no pretence to stay more than a mile, if so far. I cannot help thinking that it is the state of the times in which we live that is largely responsible for this. Nobody knows what is going to happen, and people are desirous of cashing in quickly with speedy two-year-olds, as they feel that if they buy animals that require time to mature, as most stayers do, something may happen in the meantime. If ever conditions become more settled I think you will see a difference. It is not more long-distance races – praiseworthy and welcome though they may be – that are required, but a greater feeling of security among the buyers of the thoroughbred. Remember that it is the buyer who is the customer, and the breeder who supplies the goods; and it is only human nature for the breeder to produce the goods which are most in demand and which will fetch the highest prices.   BBR–1947

Memorative Biography of the 17th Earl of Derby

UNIVERSAL REGRET was felt and expressed at the death of Lord Derby, which occurred on February 4th. With his passing the whole country mourned the loss of one of its most outstanding and popular personalities, whose activities in many spheres had secured for him a hold on the affection of the public, and a prestige worthy of his famous name. He was truly an outstanding figure in the British scene, and his reputation was world-wide.

The Right Honourable Sir Edward George Villiers Stanley, Bt, KG, PC, GCB, GCVO, seventeenth Earl of Derby, was born on April 4th, 1865. His mother was the eldest daughter of the Earl of Clarendon. After leaving Wellington College, he served for ten years in the Grenadier Guards, and spent two years in Canada as ADC to his father, who was Governor-General. Returning to England in 1891, he was the following year elected for the West Loughton Division of Lancashire, which constituency he represented until 1906. During the South African War he was first Chief Press Censor, and later Private Secretary to Field-Marshal Lord Roberts, his services being twice mentioned in despatches. In 1903 he was appointed Postmaster-General, with a seat in the Cabinet, which office he held for two years. On his father's death in 1908 he succeeded to the Earldom, and concentrated his life more than ever in the North, becoming Lord Mayor of Liverpool in 1912.

In May, 1915, Lord Derby was appointed Director-General of Recruiting, and brought out a scheme designed to obviate the necessity for compulsory conscription. It was found necessary, however, to introduce conscription the following year. After Lord Kitchener's death, Lord Derby served as Under-Secretary to Mr Lloyd George at the War Office, becoming Secretary of State for War when Mr Lloyd George assumed the Premiership. Later, in 1918, he was appointed Ambassador in Paris, where he achieved immense popularity, and where his name is still well remembered as an Englishman of outstanding personality and charm. Invited to succeed Mr Edwin Montague in 1922 at the India Office, he declined the offer, but a few months later returned to the Cabinet as Secretary of State for War under Mr Bonar Law, and remained at the War Office until the election of the Labour Government. After his retirement from active politics in 1924, Lord Derby's activities in many spheres of public life were by no means lessened, but continued almost until the end of his life. The British Legion, the Lancashire Territorial Association, Liverpool University, the British Cotton Growing Association, the Liverpool Chamber of Commerce, and King George's Jubilee Trust were some of the many bodies which derived benefit from his control and support.

It will be seen by this brief account that the late Earl played a leading part in the political life of his country, but it is with his turf activities that we are chiefly concerned.

Lord Derby inherited to the full that devotion to the Turf which had been so conspicuous in his ancestors. The Stanley family have been connected with the British Turf since the earliest days of racing, for in the seventeenth century their name had already appeared in connection with the sport. Edward Stanley, the twelfth Earl (1752–1834), was one of the first 'pillars of the Turf', and was in fact the founder in 1779 and 1780 of our two great classic races, the Oaks, named after his residence at Banstead, Surrey, and the Derby. In the course of his long connection with English racing, the twelfth Earl won the Oaks on two occasions, with Bridget in the first renewal and in 1794 with Heroine. In 1787 Sir Peter Teazle carried his colours to victory in the Derby. It proved to be the Earl's only success in this race, and it was, in fact, not until 1924 when Sansovino was victorious, that the famous colours were again to the fore in this great race.

Since the twelfth Earl of Derby's death only two members of the family have raced horses on a large scale. The fourteenth Earl, who was twice Prime Minister during Queen Victoria's reign, had numerous successes when his horses were trained by John Scott, the 'Wizard of the North'. His best-known horses were Canezou and Ithuriel. Canezou won the One Thousand Guineas of 1848 and was twice successful in the Goodwood Cup. She was a daughter of Melbourne, and as a brood mare was equally successful, for her son Fazzoletto won the Two Thousand Guineas, while her daughter La Bossue produced the great French horse, Boïard. The descendants of Canezou include Chicle, leading sire in the US in 1929, and his half-brother Dis-Donc, sire of the great American two-year-old filly, Top Flight. Ithuriel was not a distinguished racehorse, but is remembered today as the great-grandsire of Musket. Ithuriel was a roarer, and was sent out of the country to Russia shortly after begetting Musket's grandsire, Longbow.

The fifteenth Lord Derby took no active part in Turf history, but the family tradition was renewed by the sixteenth Earl and his son, Lord Stanley, the subject of this memoir.

Lord Derby's father, who was the younger brother of the fifteenth Earl, entered actively into racing late in life. It was in the summer of 1893, when the future seventeenth Earl was twenty-eight, that the foundation of the great racing and breeding establishment was laid.

The Hon. George Lambton in his book, *Men and Horses I Have Known*, had this to say of the beginning of a great career on the Turf:

'Early in the summer of 1893, I had a great surprise and a very pleasant one. I was staying at Ascot with Mr Leopold de Rothschild, and Lord Stanley, who had just come back from Canada, was also there. He told me that his father intended to start racing the following year, and hoped to revive the old prestige of the Derby Stable. Greatly to my surprise, he asked me if I would train for him. On thinking it over, I did not feel that with my little experience I was equal to taking on a job of this sort, and I suggested that he should let Joe Cannon train the horses, and that I should manage them; but this he would not have, and stuck to his original proposition. So then began my association with the Stanley family, and for thirty years I have trained for father and son.

'At that time I did not know the late Lord Derby. If I had, I do not think I should have been so diffident in accepting the offer of training his horses. I have had many good friends in my life, and known many delightful men, but the most perfect gentleman of all was Lord Derby. . .

'He took a great interest in his horses, and the breeding of them, and there was nothing he enjoyed more than coming to Newmarket when there was no racing, and when he could see his horses peacefully without any fuss or bother. . .

'I thought at first he did not know much about racing, but I soon found out that little escaped his notice. As a young man he had been very fond of it, and had seen a great deal of John Scott, of Whitewall, who trained for his father. What he had learned there he had not forgotten.'

Lord Stanley shared the love of racing and breeding which animated his father. He was elected to the Jockey Club as early as 1895, and served as a Steward, notably at his home meeting, Liverpool, and Manchester, where he was most popular and his horses had many successes.

This is Mr Lambton's account of Lord Stanley's début as an owner:

'Before the Liverpool Summer Meeting of that year, Lord Stanley asked me to find him a horse to win some little race there. I bought him old Greywell, a horse belonging to Charles Kinsky, for there happened to be a race with conditions which I thought would suit him well. Greywell, by Marden out of Seakale, was a dear old horse and had done us, in his time, some good turns, although he had on occasions let us down badly. But this time, when carrying the Derby colours, which had not been seen on a racecourse for many years, he did his part nobly. In a great finish, for the first and last time, he ran as game as a fighting cock and won,

setting an example which has been followed by many another bearer of the Black
and White Cap. . .'

After Greywell, Mr Lambton persuaded the seventeenth Lord Derby to
purchase Hettie Sorrel, a rather plain daughter of Peter and the
Speculum mare, Venus' Looking Glass. For her new owner Hettie
Sorrel won two races, and, although she did not herself produce a good
racehorse, she can now be regarded as one of the foundation mares of the
Stanley Stud, for her family has come into great prominence in recent
years through the deeds of her descendants, the half-brothers Borealis
and Alycidon, and Sayani and My Babu.

It was in 1894 that it was decided to restart the stud at the family seat,
Knowsley. Perhaps the greatest contributing factor to the phenomenal
success which was to be gained both on the racecourse and in the
paddocks, was the ability of both Earls in selecting the best available
talent. Just as they had selected an able trainer in Mr Lambton, they
now secured the services of a great stud-groom in John Griffiths, who
was at that time in the employ of the Duchess of Montrose. In Volume
IV of the *Bloodstock Breeders' Review* was published an interview with
Griffiths. We can do no better than reproduce the part appertaining to
the early days of the great stud. To quote Griffiths' words:

'I stopped with the Duchess till 1894. That year I heard that she had, at her dinner
table, announced her intention to sell off, adding that she would take this step
without regret were it not for "poor Griffiths", who had been a real good servant.
Somebody told the present Lord Derby, then Lord Stanley, that I should be at
liberty shortly, and within a few days I received a letter from him saying that his
father contemplated restarting the stud farm at Knowsley, and that he would like
me to take charge of it. I gladly accepted the offer.

'When I told the Duchess what I had done, she was in a terrible way. It seemed
she intended retaining some of the younger mares, hoping that her son, the Duke
of Montrose, would carry on the stud and that I should remain in charge. She did
leave the stud and young mares to the Duke, but as he was not a great racing man,
he quickly sold both mares and property. The latter was bought by a building
syndicate, who, finding they could not deal with the land as profitably as they had
hoped to do, sold the greater part of it to Lord Derby, who built Stanley House
and stables, and reformed the stud, which has since been greatly extended. There
are now three farms, two of which are the Plantation Farm and the Woodlands.
The Newmarket studs, and also that at Knowsley, are managed by Mr Alston.

'The paddocks at Knowsley, when I went there, had been derelict for about
twenty years – since the days of the Lord Derby who was known as "The Rupert of
the Debate" and who raced on a big scale (the fourteenth Lord Derby). The stud
dates back, I believe, to the time of the twelfth Earl of Derby. The old paddocks
have high stone walls, like those at Eaton and Wentworth. I found them in a very
dilapidated state. The famous old grass had become sour and full of weeds, but by

treatment with liberal dressings of salt, lime, bone meal and basic slag, the paddocks soon recovered their tone and are now in fine condition.'

In 1894, on Griffiths' advice, Lord Stanley purchased a broodmare and a yearling from the Duchess of Montrose. The yearling was named Canterbury Pilgrim and the mare was Broad Corrie. At the same time he also purchased Bridget from Lord Hastings. Therefore within a year of taking up breeding, Lord Derby had the great fortune to purchase four of the great foundation mares of the Stanley Stud, for, as previously mentioned, Hettie Sorrel was also capable of transmitting great ability to her descendants.

Canterbury Pilgrim, a daughter of St Simon's rival, Tristan, was out of the dual Guineas winner, Pilgrimage. As a youngster, she was not an outstanding individual for she was rather small but was possessed of a good back and loins, although short of her neck, and low-withered.

During her two-year-old days it appeared that she was of very little worth, for she did not grow and was excitable in her work. She ran five times that year and was unplaced on every occasion except one. She was, however, a different proposition as a three-year-old, and after easily defeating the One Thousand Guineas winner, Thais, in the Oaks, she completed the season with but one defeat, in the Coronation Stakes at Ascot, a traditional pitfall for many Oaks winners. Her victories included the Liverpool Cup, Park Hill Stakes, and the Jockey Club Cup at Newmarket. After this race she was retired to stud, where she produced ten foals, of which seven were winners. Her place in Turf history is secure, through her splendid sons Chaucer and Swynford, and her name appears in practically every Stanley House pedigree to this day, chiefly through Chaucer, perhaps the greatest sire of broodmares foaled this century. The tail-female line from Canterbury Pilgrim is not now strong but she is represented in direct line through Nun's Veiling, and the latter's daughter, Disguise.

Broad Corrie, a daughter of Hampton and the Cesarewitch winner, Corrie Roy, passed on her line through her first-born, Glasalt, by Isinglass. Glasalt, who won the Liverpool Cup and the Ham Stakes, in turn produced the One Thousand Guineas winner, Canyon, a great broodmare and dam of seven winners of £51,694, including Colorado and Caerleon. Another daughter of Glasalt was Glacier, by St Simon. A winner of only one small race, she produced Toboggan, winner of the Oaks and grandam of the great American colt, Citation.

Bridget, the other purchase of 1894, was a full-sister to the Derby and St Leger winner, Melton. She had raced five times, without success, but her produce included a good winner and an excellent broodmare in Santa Brigida, by St Simon. She won £4,762, including the Princess of Wales's Stakes at Goodwood. Santa Brigida's first foal was Bridge of Canny, a first-class winner of fifteen races worth £14,499, who after a few years at stud in England, during which time he sired Cantilever, was sold to the Argentine, where he gained great renown as the sire of Picacero, one of the foremost stallions of his day in that country. Santa Brigida's last foal was Santa Cruz, a daughter of Neil Gow. Santa Cruz produced seven winners including Drift, dam of Tide-way, winner of the One Thousand Guineas in 1936, and Sun Stream, who won the war-time One Thousand Guineas and Oaks in 1945. In addition to these two classic winners, Drift produced Fairhaven and Heliopolis, who is now one of the leading stallions in the US. Other notable descendants of Santa Brigida are the classic winners Mid-day Sun, and Brown Betty, and an excellent stallion in Light Brigade who was exported to America during the First World War.

Another notable purchase during the lifetime of Lord Derby's father was Lock and Key, by Janissary out of Seclusion. To Persimmon, she bred Keystone II, winner of the Oaks in 1906 and the sixteenth Earl's second and last classic winner. In 1908, on the death of his father, Lord Derby succeeded to the title, and the bloodstock, which he had owned in

The late Earl of Derby, leading in Keystone II after winning the Oaks, 1906.

all but name. Lord Derby's first classic winner was Canterbury Pilgrim's splendid son, Swynford.

By John o' Gaunt, Swynford's early career ran on similar lines to that of his dam and although he won the St Leger of 1910, beating Bronzino a head in record time, he was in fact far and away a better horse at four years, and but for breaking a fetlock joint in September of 1911, he would in all probability have been invincible as a five-year-old. His four-year-old victories included the Eclipse Stakes and the Princess of Wales's Stakes in which races he defeated his great rival, Lemberg. His only defeat in 1911 was in the Coronation Cup at Epsom when Lemberg defeated him by three-quarters of a length. It is thanks to the skill and patience of the veterinarian, the late Mr Livock, that Swynford was saved for stud duties.

Stedfast was another good horse which carried the Derby colours at that time. One of the first crop of Swynford's half-brother, Chaucer, Stedfast won twenty races and £26,479½. His victories included the Jockey Club Stakes, the Coronation Cup and the Hardwicke Stakes, and he was placed second to Sunstar in the Two Thousand Guineas and Derby of 1911. He was only fairly successful at stud, his best winners being Brownhylda (winner of the Oaks and dam of Firdaussi, winner of the St Leger), and The Night Patrol, a very successful racehorse, winner of ten races in England, and ten more races worth over £8,000 in Australia.

In 1912, Lord Derby bought Gondolette and Anchora. At the time, no one could have visualised the great influence these two mares were to wield in the Stanley Stud. Gondolette, a bay mare by Loved One out of Dongola by Doncaster, was in a batch of mares consigned to the December Sales by Lord Wavertree. Foaled in 1902, she was bought as a yearling for 75 guineas for George Edwardes. During her racing career she won two selling races and was eventually sold to Lord Wavertree for 360 guineas. For Lord Wavertree she bred Great Sport and Let Fly, but at the time of the sale Great Sport was a two-year-old and had won two unimportant races only, whilst Let Fly was still a foal.

Apart from her individuality, Gondolette's prospective value as a broodmare lay in her ancestry rather than her deeds on a racecourse or at stud. Her fourth dam, La Favorite, had produced the great French stayer, Flageolet and her dam, Dongola, was a three-parts sister to Quetta, the dam of Grey Leg, a very good-looking grey horse which had won good races for the late Duke of Westminster. Covered by Minoru, Gondolette was bought for 1,550 guineas.

Her foal of 1913 was Serenissima, the dam of Selene, Tranquil,

Bosworth, and Composure. Tranquil won the One Thousand Guineas and St leger of 1923, and Bosworth won the Ascot Gold Cup, and sired Plassy and the St Leger winner, Boswell. Selene raced in none of the classics, but was probably the best filly of her generation, winning $15\frac{1}{2}$ races value £14,386, whilst at stud she has gained immortal fame as the dam of Hyperion, Sickle, Pharamond and Hunter's Moon. Composure in her turn bred Fair Copy, who has done very well as a sire in France, Sayani being his best son.

Gondolette herself bred, for Lord Derby, two classic winners, Ferry and Sansovino, both by Swynford. Ferry won the One Thousand Guineas in 1918, but was a rather jady mare and produced nothing of note at stud. Sansovino, foaled when his dam was nineteen years of age, won for his owner his first Epsom Derby. Although not an outstanding success as a sire of winners, his mares are producing well, one of them, Sansonnet, being the dam of Tudor Minstrel. Gondolette's fame does not rest here, for her foal of 1911 was Dolabella, a foundation mare of the National Stud and the grandam of Big Game. Between them, Gondolette and Anchora are the direct forebears of six classic winners owned and bred by Lord Derby.

Lord Derby did not confine his racing and breeding activities to England. During the time he was Ambassador to France his name figured on the winning list of owners in that country. The black and white cap were carried to victory in the Poule d'Essai des Pouliches in 1922 and 1935 by Frisky and The Nile respectively.

In France, Lord Derby also raced in partnership with Mr Ogden Mills, and, after that gentleman's death, with his daughter, Lady Granard. The most notable successes gained by the partnerships were the Grand Prix de Paris in 1928 and 1933 with Cri de Guerre and Cappiello, and the Prix de Diane of 1937 with En Fraude. However, the best horse to carry the colours was Kantar, who won the Prix de l'Arc de Triomphe in 1928. During the German occupation, to avoid confiscation all Lord Derby's French bloodstock passed into the hands of his manager, the Marquis de Saint Sauveur, and it was in his colours that Nepenthe, Arcot and Laborde raced during that time.

Three of the principal classic winners of recent years stem from French mares. Ranai was bought by Lord Derby's daughter, Lady Victoria Bullock, for 95,000 frs. at the Deauville Sales of 1926. By the great stallion Rabelais, she was a small, quality mare whose racecourse performances hardly indicated her subsequent fame at stud. In fact for the first eight years of her stud career, she was not considered a suitable mate for Fairway or Hyperion. However to such diverse stallions as

Diophon, Schiavoni and Coronach, she consistently produced winners and at the age of fourteen, to her first mating with Fairway, she produced Watling Street, winner of the 1942 Derby and two years later, to the same stallion, the Two Thousand Guineas winner, Garden Path.

Another French-bred mare which has contributed greatly towards Lord Derby's successes in recent years was Aileen. Purchased in 1928 from the Duc Decazes, she was then a ten-year-old mare by Nimbus out of Yveline, a daughter of Gardefeu. She had won ten flat races and four hurdle races during her turf career and was a half-sister to a good racehorse, named Ivanoe. However, her breeding career after Lord Derby purchased her was very disappointing, for in 1930 she produced a filly by Phalaris which died, and in 1931 her foal by Sansovino was born dead. She was not covered in 1931 and was barren in 1933 and 1934. then in 1935 she produced a filly by Schiavoni which was named Schiaparelli, and in 1936 her last foal, a filly by Caerleon, named Caerwys. Schiaparelli won five small races, and has produced the One Thousand Guineas and St Leger winner, Herringbone.

Space, unfortunately, does not permit the mention of many of the other famous horses bred at the Stanley Studs.

In the records of winning owners Lord Derby was seldom far from leading the list, and in fact occupied the premier position on six occasions between 1908 and 1947, a remarkable record in view of the fact that at no time did the number of his brood mares exceed thirty-five at stud, and that he rarely raced any horses not of his own breeding. In all Lord Derby won twenty classic races as follows:

One Thousand Guineas – Canyon (1916); Ferry (1918); Tranquil (1923); Fair Isle (1930); Tide-way (1936); Herringbone (1943); Sun Stream (1945).

Oaks – Toboggan (1928); Sun Stream (1945).

Two Thousand Guineas – Colorado (1926); Garden Path (1944).

Derby – Sansovino (1924); Hyperion (1933); Watling Street (1942).

St Leger – Swynford (1910); Keysoe (1919); Tranquil (1923); Fairway (1928); Hyperion (1933); Herringbone (1943).

In addition to the many classic victories recorded above practically all the important races in the *Calendar* have been won by Lord Derby's horses. The Ascot Gold Cup by Bosworth and the Eclipse Stakes by Colorado, Fairway and Caerleon, were only a few of his successes in the other great races.

The better to estimate Lord Derby's influence on English breeding, a glance at the list of sires which have gained the premier position during the last twenty-five years will show that, since 1923, on thirteen occasions one or another of his stallions has headed the list. In addition,

Blandford (a son of Swynford), and Nearco (a son of Pharos), have between them attained that position in five of the other years.

Since 1912, Lord Derby has headed the list of winning breeders in nine seasons – 1919, 1920, 1923, 1927, 1928, 1929, 1930, 1938 and 1945, and in every other year has been close up to the leaders, being second on eleven occasions and third five times. It would be impossible to estimate his influence on breeding all over the world. In America alone the stallions Sickle and Pharamond have had the distinction of heading the sires' list, and Light Brigade and, more recently, Heliopolis have also had great success. In the Argentine, Silurian, Bridge of Canny, and Hunter's Moon have been notable sires.

Since 1912 the stallions which have stood at Lord Derby's Studs include the following:

Chaucer (**1900-1926**) brown horse, by St Simon out of Canterbury Pilgrim by Tristan. Winner of eight races value £5,663, including the Gimcrack Stakes, York, and Liverpool Cup (twice). Retired to stud in 1907, his progeny won 341 races value £171,754, the principal winners being Stedfast (20 races, value £26,362½), Selene (15½ races, value £14,386), Pillion (One Thousand Guineas), Canyon (One Thousand Guineas), Prince Chimay (four races, value £6,673, sire of Vatout). He was leading brood mare sire in 1927 and 1933. His daughters have produced the winners of 556 races, value £376,432¾, including Hyperion, Colorado, Pharos, Fairway, Caerleon, Colombo, Sickle and Pharamond.

Swynford (**1907-1928**) brown horse by John o' Gaunt out of Canterbury Pilgrim by Tristan. Winner of eight races value £25,508, including St Leger, Eclipse Stakes, Princess of Wales's Stakes, Hardwicke Stakes (twice). Retired to stud in 1913 he was the leading sire in 1923. His progeny won 350½ races, value £233,125, the principal winners being Sansovino (six races, value £17,732, including Derby), Tranquil (eight races, value £21,909, including One Thousand Guineas and St Leger), Saucy Sue (eight races, value £25,284, including One Thousand Guineas and Oaks), Ferry (One Thousand Guineas), Keysoe (St Leger), Bettina (One Thousand Guineas), Blandford (three races, value £3,661, leading sire 1934, 1935, 1938), St Germans (eight races, value £7,963, leading sire in the US). He was leading sire of broodmares in 1932. His daughters have produced the winners of 484 races value £261,040¼, including Tide-way, Sun Stream, Orpen, Salmon Leap, Caissot, Truculent, Miracle, Sunstone, etc.

Phalaris (**1913–1931**) brown horse by Polymelus out of Bromus by Sainfoin. Winner of fifteen races value £5,478, including Challenge Stakes, Newmarket (twice). Retired to stud in 1919, he was the leading sire in 1925 and 1928, and his progeny won 403½ races value £334,975¼. The principal winners were Manna (four races, value £23,534 including Two Thousand Guineas and Derby), Colorado (nine races, value £30,358, including Two Thousand Guineas and Eclipse Stakes), Fairway (twelve races, value £42,722, including St Leger and Eclipse Stakes, leading sire 1936, 1939, 1943, 1944), Pharos (fourteen races, value £15,694; leading sire 1931 and in France in 1939), Fair Isle (One Thousand Guineas), Sickle (leading sire US in 1936 and 1938), Pharamond (a leading sire in US), Caerleon (Eclipse Stakes). He was leading sire of broodmares in 1937, 1940 and 1942. His daughters have produced (to 1948) the winners of 564½ races, value £255,328¾, including Midday Sun, Windsor Slipper, Enfield, Plassy, Hyperides, Godiva, Picture Play, etc.

Colorado (**1923–1929**) brown horse by Phalaris out of Canyon by Chaucer. Winner of nine races, value £30,358, including Two Thousand Guineas, Coventry Stakes, Eclipse Stakes. Retired to stud in 1928, he died the following year and was second leading sire in 1932 and 1933. His progeny won 112½ races value £86,349, and include Felicitation, Loaningdale, Colorado Kid, Coroado, Riot (the dam of Commotion), etc.

Fairway (**1925–1948**) brown horse by Phalaris out of Scapa Flow by Chaucer. Winner of twelve races value £42,722, including St Leger, Coventry Stakes, Champagne Stakes, Eclipse Stakes. Retired to stud in 1931, he was the leading sire in 1936, 1939, 1943 and 1944. His progeny have won (to 1948) 399 races value £298,023¼, the principal winners being Blue Peter (Two Thousand Guineas and Derby, and £31,964½), Watling Street (New Derby), Pay Up (Two Thousand Guineas), Kingsway (New Two Thousand Guineas), Garden Path (New Two Thousand Guineas), Tide-way (One Thousand Guineas), Fair Trial, Portmarnock, Fair Copy and Honeyway. Leading sire of broodmares in 1946 and 1947.

At the time of Lord Derby's death the stallions in service at his studs were Hyperion, Watling Street and Borealis. Hyperion, the Derby and St Leger winner of 1933 has been one of the most successful sires within living memory. On five occasions (1940, 1941, 1942, 1945 and 1946) he was champion stallion and to 1948 he has sired eleven classic winners in

England. He may well equal, if not eclipse, Chaucer as a sire of brood-mares, for in 1948, when his oldest daughters were twelve years old, he attained the premier position in this sphere for the first time.

Other stallions which Lord Derby owned during the last twenty-five years include Stedfast, Sansovino, Bosworth and Caerleon.

Sansovino, who won the Derby of 1924, sired the winners of £113, 425¾, but the highest position he reached on the winning sires' list was fifth in 1931, when his son Sandwich won the St Leger.

Bosworth also sired a St Leger winner in Boswell and, for Lord Derby, he got Plassy, a good racehorse who won the Coronation Cup, and has sired good winners in France, including Nepenthe and Arcot.

Caerleon, a full brother to Colorado, died at the comparatively early age of twelve years. He sired some useful horses and his daughters are producing well.

Mention must also be made of Lord Derby's stallions in France. The most successful was Pharos, who was sent to France in 1928 after standing for three seasons in England. His English crops of foals included Cameronian, winner of the Derby and Two Thousand Guineas of 1931, in which year Pharos headed the English sires' list, and Firdaussi, winner of the St Leger in the following year. In France, Pharos headed the sires' list in 1939, when his fine son, Pharis, won the Prix du Jockey Club and the Grand Prix de Paris.

Truly a great stallion, Pharos died in 1938 at the height of his career. That year his unbeaten son, Nearco, won the Grand Prix de Paris. His influence on present-day breeding is increasing year by year in England through Nearco, who was champion sire in 1947 and 1948, and Nearco's son, Nasrullah, who has made an excellent start to his stud career, and, in France, through Pharis and Fastnet.

Lord Derby also had Fairway's son, Fair Copy, at stud in France. Fair Copy, who won the Middle Park Stakes and finished second in the 1937 St Leger, was third on the French sires' list in 1946 when his great son, Sayani, was a three-year-old.

It is probably true to say that throughout the long history of the British thoroughbred, no single breeder has exercised more influence on the breed than the late Earl. Luck has played a certain part in the success of this great enterprise, but the greater part of Lord Derby's success was due to his sound judgment in selecting the very best talent available to manage the various branches of the organisation. The Hon. George Lambton was intimately connected with the racing establishment up to 1933, when C. Leader became private trainer. Leader died in 1938, and

W. Earl has been in charge at Stanley House since that year. From 1926 to 1931 Lord Derby's horses were trained by Frank Butters under the management of Mr Lambton.

John Griffiths was Stud-groom until his death in 1918, and was succeeded by his son Walter. Mr Alston, who died in 1933, managed Lord Derby's breeding studs for many years, and to him must go much of the credit for the great success obtained. A man of decided opinions, he followed the policy of avoiding the speedy lines in favour of stamina despite the great success of the Orby blood in other studs. In recent years the management of the Stanley Stud has been under the able direction of Mr Adrian Scrope.

T. Weston rode the winners of eight of the twenty classic races won by Lord Derby. Others to ride classic winners for him were F. Wootton, B. Carslake, E. Gardiner, F. Rickaby, R. Perryman and H. Wragg, who rode Lord Derby's six war-time classic winners. D. Smith also won many races wearing the Stanley livery.

Lord Derby married, in 1889, Lady Alice Montagu, youngest daughter of the Duke of Manchester, by whom he is survived. His eldest son, Lord Stanley, who became Secretary of State for Dominion Affairs in 1938, died in October of that year. His only daughter, Lady Victoria Bullock, was killed by an accident in the hunting field in 1927, which tragic bereavement saddened Lord Derby's latter years.

He is succeeded by his grandson, Edward John, Lord Stanley, who was born in 1918.

Some measure of the esteem in which Lord Derby was held by the Royal Family can be obtained from the fact that when King Edward VII died the Royal horses were leased to him for the period of Court mourning. A similar arrangement was made on the death of King George V in 1936.

Lord Derby's sympathetic character and record of service to his country, combined with his great services to the Turf and to horse breeding, will ensure for him a lasting name in the history and affections of the British people. BBR–1948

Obituary of Colonel Edward Riley Bradley

When Colonel Edward Riley Bradley died in the early morning of August 15th, 1946, aged eighty-six, in a hospital-like bedroom at his beloved Idle Hour Farm near Lexington, Kentucky, US, his demise, although expected, was mourned and felt intimately by friends from every walk of life throughout the world. Father D. J. Boland of St Francis of Rome Church in Louisville, said: 'Only those who knew him intimately are able to estimate his great warmth as a benefactor to humanity. His outstanding virtues were kindness to the poor, love of truth and strict adherence to the principles of justice.'

The Thoroughbred Record *concluded its account of his death thus: 'And so, in his time, passed one of the American Turf's most colourful and most beloved figures. The niche he earned through his generosity, honesty and sportsmanship, in the hearts of horsemen will never be filled.'*

The kind things said about Colonel Bradley were never forced; they were spontaneous. He was internationally respected and universally loved. He established a permanent influence on the American Turf. Several breeders, including the Phipps family, are still enjoying some of their most notable successes through Bradley-bred matrons.

Most prominent of these, of course, was the storied La Troienne, a foal of 1926 by Teddy from Helene de Troie, by Helicon. Five years older than her three-parts sister Adargatis, a French Oaks victress and classic producer herself, La Troienne bred such champions as Black Helen and Bimelech as well as a bevy of daughters who, as producers, were responsible for the family going from strength to strength. Indeed, in La Troienne's own lifetime, she was described 'as the most influential brood-mare imported into this country (US) in this century'. She died in 1954 at the grand old age of twenty-eight full of honours and of promises which were to be kept by her descendants.

It is most fitting that The Bloodstock Breeders' Review *should extol Colonel Bradley as it did in the following obituary – its publisher, The British Bloodstock Agency, had a number of amenable and successful bloodstock transactions with the Colonel. These transactions included La Troienne, whose foals included the classic-winning Bimelech, generally considered the best horse Colonel Bradley bred, as well as the matrons Padula and Vaila, members of the same female family and both of whom appear in the pedigree of Blue Larkspur, generally accepted as the second best horse Colonel Bradley bred and certainly the most important breeding influence he ever produced. As it turned out, both his bloodstock and that of the American Turf improved dramatically because of Colonel Bradley's association with the BBA.*

COLONEL EDWARD RILEY BRADLEY, who earned the affection of the people more completely than any other man of the American Turf of his time, died on August 15th, at his Idle Hour Farm home near Lexington, Kentucky. He was a self-admitted gambler, a philanthropist, a thorough horseman, and the only owner to win the Kentucky Derby four times. His death, at the age of eighty-six, was indeed a heavy blow to the American Turf.

Facts concerning his early life are still rather vague, for it was not of himself that he talked – he talked about horses. He was born December 12th, 1859, in Johnstown, Philadelphia, of Irish immigrant parents. After working in the steel mills in Pennsylvania, he is reputed to have gone west in his teens. According to legend he was a cowboy, a scout in Indian campaigns, gold prospector and miner. He learned during those days that if one was to make a business of gambling one had to be on the side the percentage was.

He returned to the midwest as a bookmaker, and in the middle 'nineties he became a partner with brother John Bradley, in a gambling club at El Paso, Texas. In 1898 he opened the Beach Club, at Palm Beach, Florida, America's most successful and long-lasting casino. A block away from the Beach Club he built a handsome church which the congregation calls St Edward's.

It was in this same year that Colonel Bradley was advised by his physician that unless he got out into the open air he had only a year to live. He turned to racing and purchased from the American and French trainer, Eugene Leigh, a selling plater named Friar John. On July 27th, 1898, the Bradley colours first appeared at the Harlem track near Chicago and won. Since then his horses have won nearly 1,400 races and $3,300,000.

In 1906 he purchased a 336-acre farm near Lexington and his wife named it Idle Hour. It was to become one of America's great nurseries, and to grow in size to 1,292 acres. He decided that he would breed good horses and own a Kentucky Derby winner. Consulting with Dr M. M. Leach, an English veterinarian and America's leading authority on thoroughbred pedigrees, Colonel Bradley was told that if he studied hard, accumulated good stock, and was persistent in weeding out the less successful, he would with luck breed a Derby winner in fifteen years.

Fifteen years later Behave Yourself won the 1921 Kentucky Derby, the first of four such wins for Colonel Bradley. He also had the second horse in Black Servant. Behave Yourself was a failure at the stud, but Black Servant was later to play an important part in the Colonel's fortunes by siring Blue Larkspur 'one of the two best horses I ever owned'. Bimelech was the other.

In 1926 Colonel Bradley scored another one-two in the Kentucky Derby when Bubbling Over (by North Star III) and Baggenbaggage ran in that order. Burgoo King (by Bubbling Over) won in 1932, and Broker's Tip (by Black Toney) in 1933. His two best horses – Blue Larkspur and Bimelech – were defeated in the Kentucky classic; Blue Larkspur losing in 1929 in the mud, and Bimelech, the last colt sired by Black Toney in 1940, to the 35 to 1 outsider, Gallahadion.

Even without these Kentucky Derby victories, Idle Hour Farm would have been one of America's outstanding farms. The foundation sire was Black Toney (by Peter Pan–Belgravia, by Ben Brush) which the Colonel purchased as a yearling for $1,600 in 1912 from a draught bred by James R. Keene at Castleton Stud. In 1915 Colonel Bradley sent his trainer to England and France to buy broodmares, and he came back with *Vaila, *Padula, *Macaroon and *Mailbird, among others. Fifteen years later he sent Dick Thompson off to Europe and he returned with a few which included *Silver Hue (dam of the top-class stakes winner Bazaar), and *La Troienne, one of the greatest producers in modern times.

*La Troienne produced, among others, Bimelech and Black Helen, and is the grandam of a very high class group of horses, including the world's leading money-winning filly Busher, and Bridal Flower, one of 1946's leading three-year-old fillies. Bridal Flower was the last top-class horse to race in Colonel Bradley's 'white with green hoops' colours.

His interests in racing were not confined to breeding and racing. He once tried to make New Orleans America's winter racing capital; but sold out after a big loss. He also invested heavily in Hialeah Park, and then disposed of his stock after the track was a success. The Colonel was a great experimenter. He introduced the fibre skull-cap which jockeys now wear. He tried walk-up starts, spectacles for horses, streamlined blinkers, and a solarium at Idle Hour.

His charities were many, only a few were known. He gave $10,000 each year for Thanksgiving and Christmas dinners for the under-privileged children of Kentucky. This was an outcome of a special race meeting which he held at Idle Hour Farm, the profits of which went for this purpose.

On November 6th his Idle Hour Farm (of 1,292 acres and eighty-five horses) was sold to a syndicate composed of Greentree Farm, Ogden Phipps, and King Ranch. The main portion of the farm was re-sold to Edward S. Moore and forty-three of the horses were also re-sold. Ten days later the furnishings of Idle Hour Farm were sold at auction, and the famous Bradley Thoroughbred holdings were liquidated. Forty-eight years had elapsed since Colonel Bradley was advised to get out in the open by his physician.

Part 8

STALLIONS

The Most Beautiful of God's Creatures

THERE IS LITTLE DOUBT that a thoroughbred stallion is the most beautiful of God's creatures. The lion is called 'The King of Beasts', but he is not, to the artist's eye, symmetrical, his power lying too much in the fore-hand, unlike the exquisitely balanced speed machine, the thoroughbred horse, whose head, neck, sloping shoulders, muscular limbs and springing ribs are in glorious proportion, from his lovely pointed ears to the tip of the last tiny vertebra of his tail.

Eclipse

It would seem that Eclipse is the most honoured name in the lengthening history of racing and breeding. Roughly 90 per cent of the world's stakes winners trace to Eclipse in tail-male. This great, great grandson of the founding progenitor, the Darley Arabian, completely overwhelms the Byerly Turk line through Herod, and the Godolphin Barb line through Matchem. England's Eclipse Stakes, first run in 1886, honours this mighty patriarch and the champions of racing in the US gain Eclipse Awards.

Just who was Eclipse to the people who knew him 'then'?

Eclipse (1764), by Marske, by Squirt (1732), by Barlett's Childers, by Darley Arabian. His dam, Spiletta, by Regulus, by Godolphin Barb. Eclipse was foaled on April 1st, 1764 – a day on which a remarkable eclipse of the sun occurred. He was bred by the Duke of Cumberland, after whose death he was sold to Mr Wildman, and subsequently to Mr D. O'Kelly. Eclipse was a chestnut horse with a white blaze down his face. Between May, 1769 and October, 1770, he ran or walked over for eighteen races and was never beaten.

Dr H. E. Platt, who wrote a most absorbing article in the 1916 Review on fourteen 'Unbeaten Horses', made the following comments about Eclipse, which certainly bear repeating.

PERHAPS the most remarkable thing about Eclipse's career was that he did not run in public until he was five years old. After his sale as a two-year-old to Mr John Wildman for 75 guineas, it was found that he possessed a violent temper, so he was turned over to a rough-rider, who hacked him daily – and even nightly, sometimes keeping the horse out all night while he was poaching. At one time it was thought he would have to be made a gelding. What an irreparable loss to the Turf this would have been! He was quieted sufficiently to race him when he was five and six years old, but no jockey who rode him ever touched him with whip or spur, and he won all his races without being extended.

His first race was at Epsom on May 3rd, 1769, a fifty-guinea plate, four-mile heats for horses that had never won £30, matches excepted. The celebrated adventurer, Dennis O'Kelly, was well acquainted with the horse's merits and backed him for every shilling he could get on, and, it is said, he also betted even money that he would place the whole field, giving the celebrated declaration, 'Eclipse first, and the rest nowhere.' It must be remembered that in those days the judge frequently 'placed' only the winner if he won very easily. Several times, even in the classic events, we find only two horses officially 'placed', although the Press naturally gave their views as to the horses occupying the third, fourth, fifth, and remaining places. Sir Theodore Cook explains that when, in bygone days, a horse was 'distanced' – that is, beaten by over two hundred yards – he was not placed by the judge. O'Kelly's bet therefore resolved itself into this: he wagered that Eclipse would win by more than 200 yards. He won his bet.

After Eclipse had won his first heat O'Kelly bought a half-share in the horse from Wildman for £450; and before he started for his second race at Winchester, had bought the remaining half for £1,000. Eclipse won over £25,000 on the Turf for O'Kelly, as well as earning fees for his stud services; the winnings of his stock were estimated at three times this amount.

BBR–1916

The Most Perfectly Made Horse

The BBR *of 1915 published the following interesting communication from Mr G. A. Wilson, of the Sheffield Lane Paddocks:*

'In his letter which appeared in the last number of the *Bloodstock Breeders' Review*, Mr Simons Harrison described Hermit as "the most perfectly-made thoroughbred of the last half century". I won't dispute this, but should like to cite the opinion of an old friend of mine, the late W. H. Hopkins, who was a painter of racehorses, and a man of considerable repute in his profession. Among his patrons were the late Duke of Beaufort (for whom he painted Reve d'Or and Petronel), the late Lord Bradford (Retreat, Sir Hugo and many other horses), the late Lord Falmouth (Dutch Oven, Galliard, etc.), the Duke of Portland (St Simon, Ayrshire, Donovan, Semolina, and Memoir), the late Mr James Lowther (King Monmouth, Workington and Houndsditch), the late Sir Robert Jardine, the late Lord Hastings (Melton), and the late Captain Machell.

'Mr Hopkins used to send me a photograph of all his pictures taken before they left his studio. I have two albums filled with them. It is a collection no one else has, not even his own family. When he paid me a visit on one occasion, I showed him what I had done with the photographs and he told me with regret that he had failed to keep a collection for himself.

'When delineating his "subjects", Mr Hopkins adopted the plan of carefully measuring them, and making his drawing exactly to scale. He kept a record of all these measurements, and from them made a table denoting the most perfect sizes of head, limbs, girth, etc, according to the height of the horse, and I remember his telling me that, according to his system, Melton was the most truly made horse he ever painted, though by no means the biggest. So far as I know, he did not paint Hermit; at any rate, if he did I have no photograph of the picture.

'Mr Hopkins was also very skilful as a painter of hounds. One of his best efforts in this line was his picture of Lord and Lady Lonsdale with horses and hounds, painted at the time his lordship hunted the Woodland Pytchley. Through my introduction he was commissioned to paint a similar picture of the late Earl Fitzwilliam with two of his daughters, huntsman, horses and hounds, which was presented to the Earl by the members of the Hunt. Towards the cost of that painting £1,400 passed through my hands as hon. secretary and treasurer.'

BBR-1915

The Domino Family

As far as American Turf legends go, that of Domino (1891–1897) appears destined to never let go. A living legend in his own brief life span, he accentuated his Homeric deeds as a racehorse by becoming a most remarkable sire despite having but twenty living foals from a first crop of six and a second crop of fourteen. Incredibly, from these twenty foals he had fifteen winners, including seven stakes winners. Among his stakes winners were the Epsom Oaks victress of 1901, Cap and Bells, and the Belmont Stakes winner Commando whose breeding career was almost as short as that of Domino and, at the same time, quite as fabulous. His sire line, although threatened throughout this century, has managed to survive through the unlikely auspices of his unbeaten grandson, the mighty Colin whose stud career suffered severe roadblocks, first standing in England where he was barely patronised and then returning to the US when the sport was in a deep depression. Nearly a century after Domino's birth, this branch seems to have some assurance of continuing through the very successful stallion Ack Ack, a foal of 1966, who has a number of quality sons at stud. And, in the deeper recesses of the pedigrees of a multitude of splendid stakes winners one will find a repetition of the names of several of Domino's most influential daughters, including Pink Domino, the dam of the classic winner and two-time leading sire, Sweep.

Of the charismatic charmers of the American Turf, Domino belongs right there with Man o' War and the latter-day hero, Secretariat.

Given the sobriquet the 'Black Whirlwind', Domino who was

officially a brown whose coat appeared black when he perspired, which he did often and profusely, won nineteen of twenty-five starts. An avid Kentuckian, seeking the best of both worlds, insisted that Domino's coat colour was identical to that of a well-ripened Kentucky coffee bean – 'a peculiar shade of black shading down to a sort of dark olive'.

However, his official record is hardly the true story of his talent. He was practically invincible running short, winning eighteen of nineteen starts at a mile or less and being second in his only loss. In three starts at 1$\frac{1}{8}$ miles, he was first, second and third and the only three times he was unplaced throughout his career were when he was asked to race beyond nine furlongs. The only sprint he lost was at age four when he failed to concede 24 lb to the three-year-old filly The Butterflies, heroine of the Futurity Stakes the previous year.

When Domino retired with earnings of $193,550 he was the world's leading money winner, having made the quickest rise to the top of the American earnings list, a feat he accomplished in his first year.

What especially endeared Domino to racegoers was his bold, dashing and aggressive style. He disdained restraint and as he was probably the fastest horse the American Turf had produced up to that time, it was a sight to see other horses try and live with him over shorter distances. That, along with his fine size and the glistening black hue of his perspiring body, made him an enduring delight to watch, a picture which never left one's mind's eye.

All this is merely to preface and to bring a bit more timeliness to the wondrous article on the enthralling story of Domino contributed to the **BBR** *of 1934 by the distinguished American turf writer and historian, John (Salvator) Hervey.*

This editor believes this to be one of the finest contributions ever made concerning the history of American racing and breeding.

ON FRIDAY, July 30th, 1897, a strangely impressive scene was enacted near Lexington, Kentucky. At Hira Villa, not far back from the Huffman Mill Pike, which now leads to the gate of Faraway Farm, the home of Man o' War, a group of men and women stood with bared heads about the grave into which the body of a stallion, shrouded in a white winding sheet, was being lowered by reverent hands. At the head of the grave stood the horse's breeder, Major Barak G. Thomas; at its foot was Major Foxhall A. Daingerfield, his manager. Gathered around were fifty or more men and women, members of the families, close friends or trusted employees of the two gentlemen. As the clods of earth fell upon the sheeted form of the animal, until gradually it was lost to sight, tears might have been seen running down the cheeks of some of the mourners. No word broke the silence. When at length the interment had been completed, Major Thomas laid upon the centre of the mound a large wreath of flowers, and the company slowly dispersed.

During the century and a half that Kentucky has been America's breeding centre, many great and famous horses have been interred there. Within a radius of, let us say, twenty miles from Lexington it is probable that the remains of more of them mingle with the soil than in any other area of similar extent in either America or the world. Their return to the earth that bore them has so long been a familiar incident in that region that such an event as a rule causes little stir and no ceremony. It is a part of nature's processes and of the routine of breeding operations, and is so generally accepted. So marked the exception as the scene just described could therefore betoken only one thing – a loss so far out of the ordinary as to have evoked extraordinary emotions. And such was the fact. It was felt by the mourners gathered at the burial that a terrible blow had been sustained, not only by themselves but by the whole thoroughbred interest, one so grave and so sudden that no common expression of grief would suffice. Nor in this were they mistaken. Nearly forty years have

Domino.

elapsed and they have demonstrated that the death of Domino was a far greater loss than at the time it was believed to be. We are still unable correctly to estimate it; but we do know that had all the citizens of Kentucky interested in the racehorse gathered about his grave that day to witness his burial, they would not have paid him too much honour. It may truly be said that no other progenitor that has died so young has done so much for the breed.

The morning of the previous day Domino, then six years old a month after finishing his second season at the stud, had been turned out in his paddock at Castleton in apparently perfect health and condition. Not long afterwards he was found lying on the ground, unable to rise and almost completely paralysed. Major Daingerfield immediately summoned all available veterinary assistance and within a short time six of the best practitioners of Lexington were working over the horse in the effort to get him on his feet. But everything was fruitless. In a few hours the horse was dead. The cause officially assigned was spinal meningitis. There is little doubt, however, that the real cause was an accident. Domino, one of the sweetest-tempered of stallions, was also of exuberant spirits. When turned out he had a habit of rearing on his hind legs, flinging his forefeet high in the air, and doing so repeatedly before he quieted down. It was, and is, the belief of those most familiar with the son of Himyar and Mannie Gray that while doing this that morning he made a misstep, tripped, crossed his legs or in some way was thrown so heavily as to cause paralysis and death.

When informed of what had occurred, his owner, Mr James R. Keene, of New York, telegraphed the request that Domino be buried at the farm of Major Thomas, his breeder, and that a suitable monument of granite be erected to mark the spot, adding the epitaph he wished carved upon it: 'Here lies the fleetest runner the American Turf has ever known and one of the gamest and most generous of horses.' Major Thomas decided that Domino should lie beside the famous old mare Dixie, in whose honour he had originally named his stud Dixiana. The tract of land chosen is now part of the Mount Brilliant Farm. The monument was formerly plainly visible to all passing by, but is not so any longer.

The progenitor of the Domino line (as it is now familiarly known) in America was the bay horse Eclipse, foaled 1855, a son of Orlando and Gaze (sister to Gaper), by Bay Middleton, and running directly back at the fifth remove to Web, and thence to Penelope and old Prunella. Eclipse was bred by Mr C. C. Fulke Greville, the owner of his sire, and passed to 'Mr Howard' (Henry Padwick), for whom he raced with distinction as a two- and three-year-old. At two he won the Clearwell Stakes, at Newmarket; at three the third Hampton Court Sales Stakes at Newmarket and a Biennial at Ascot; ran a dead-heat with Beadsman (winner of that year's Derby) in the Newmarket Stakes and received forfeit in a match from the same horse at the Newmarket Houghton meeting. Eclipse was second choice for the Derby but ran unplaced in it, as also in the St Leger, both races seeming too far for him. Like many of Orlando's offspring, speed and something not beyond ten furlongs suited him best. In the late autumn of his three-year-old career he was bought privately by Richard Ten Broeck, of New York, then engaged upon his first 'English invasion', in whose colours he raced twice. That was in 1858. Evidently he did not stand training in 1859; evidently also Ten Broeck, whose judgment of horses was uncommonly keen, considered him the right kind for a stud horse, for in the late summer of that year he sent him home to the US to be used for breeding purposes. In 1860 he stood on Long Island, but in 1861 was sent to Kentucky to stand under the management of Major Thomas at Lexington. The Civil War broke out that spring, and after two seasons, during which he covered a few mares, he returned north. Shortly after that he became the property of Francis Morris of New York, and, following a season or two in New Jersey, went to that gentleman's stud at Throg's Neck, not far from New York City, where he passed the rest of his life, dying in 1878, aged twenty-three.

Eclipse's stud opportunities were slight. For a horse living so long he got very few foals, and among them fillies preponderated. The success of his get on the Turf, allowing for these facts, was remarkable. He twice stood second in the list of winning sires, and was twice third during the long hegemony of Lexington. His sons and daughters won forty-seven stake events and matches, including many of the most important of that era. The special gift of the tribe was extreme speed, in which they excelled all others then extant in America. Some of them stayed well, but this was exceptional.

Alarm was the outstanding son of Eclipse, alike upon the Turf and at the stud. He was a bay, foaled 1869 and bred by John Hunter, whose Annieswood Stud was near to that of Francis Morris in Westchester County, New York. His dam, Maud, was one of the few daughters of Stockwell ever brought to America. She had but six foals, of which almost all attained distinction. Her dam, Countess of Albermarle, was by Lanercost, and the family was the Miss Cranfield branch of that stemming from the Large Hartley Mare and tracing back to Flying

Whig and a Royal Mare, Bruce Lowe's No. 15. As a two-year-old he ran four times and won a match for $5,000 at Saratoga against Inverary. At three he ran five races without defeat and among his feats was the lowering of the American mile record to 1.42$\frac{3}{4}$. He ran but once at any longer distance, this being at one mile and a quarter. Alarm was considered by far the fastest horse that had been seen in America up to his time, his speed being such that in his three-year-old days nothing he met could live with him. In imitation of Prince Charlie, then the meteor of the English Turf, he was dubbed 'Prince of the TYC'. He went to the stud in Kentucky when four years old and was an immediate success.

Later he succeeded imported Leamington at the head of the Erdenheim Stud. The winners from his loins were plentiful and kept him high on the sires' list for many seasons. But, like many other progenitors, his ultimate fame rests upon one son, Himyar, got when he was a five-year-old and foaled in 1875, his breeder being Major B. G. Thomas, already frequently mentioned, and his dam Hira, by Lexington.

Major Thomas, who died in 1905, aged eighty, was said to have been the last surviving American turfman who witnessed the historic races between Wagner and Grey Eagle, run at Louisville in 1839 over the old Oakland Course, the predecessor of Churchill Downs, where the Kentucky Derby is now run. He began training and racing horses when a mere boy in conjunction with his brother, later Judge Charles B. Thomas. Among others they got hold of Flight, a daughter of imported Leviathan (son of Muley and, in America, a most successful sire) and Charlotte Hamilton, by Sir Charles (son of Sir Archy), the next two dams being by imported Sir Harry and imported Diomed, both winners of the Epsom Derby. Flight had been a good race mare and her first foal, Oliver, by Wagner, was a 'crack'. From Flight and imported Ambassador (son of Emilius), C. B. Thomas bred Hegira in 1846 and, later, several other famous foals. Hegira, trained by B. G. Thomas, made herself famous by running two miles in 1850 at New Orleans in 3.34$\frac{1}{4}$ – the fastest time recorded up to that date. When put to breeding she proved an excellent producer but an unlucky one, many of her foals dying young. When the Civil War broke out in 1861 B. G. Thomas espoused secession and joined the Confederate army, serving with it until peace was declared in 1865. C. B. Thomas remained loyal to the Union, but as soon as the war was over the brothers resumed their old relations. During the interim Hegira, in 1864, had produced a filly by Lexington that was a yearling when Major Thomas returned to Kentucky once more. She became his property and in his hands won a stake for three-year-old fillies at Louisville which did much to put him on his feet financially, the war having left him almost penniless.

After her Turf career Hira became a matron in Major Thomas' Dixiana Stud, where she produced a long list of notable foals, of which Himyar was the fourth. It has already been related that when Eclipse was sent to Kentucky to stand in 1861 he was under the management of Major Thomas, and the American Stud Book shows that that season he bred old Hegira to him, but her foal died. At this time the Major must have formed a high opinion of Eclipse, for when that sire's son, Alarm, was making his second stud season, in 1847, he sent Hira, the daughter of Lexington and Hegira, to him and Himyar was the result.

Like his sire, Himyar was a 'speed marvel', but – perhaps because of his Lexington and other staying maternal strains – he could also stay. As a two-year-old he started in five stake events, winning three and being third in the other two. At three he again started in five stakes, to win three and finish second in the other two. One of the latter was the Kentucky Derby, in which he was defeated (after being considered a certain winner in advance) by Day Star in the fastest contest for the event made up to that time. That the result was wholly a false one was generally believed at the time and has ever since so remained, Himyar's chance being thrown away by the incompetent riding of his jockey. As a four-year-old Himyar won all four of his races. At five, he ran thirteen times, won four, was four times second and twice third. When six he ran but once, unplaced, and was then sent to the stud. All told he won fourteen of the twenty-eight starts, was second in six and third in four. He won at all distances up to two miles, could race well in all kinds of footing, and could 'repeat' in heat races. That speed was really his forte was, however, beyond doubt, and it was largely because of his great superiority in this regard that he was able to win at a mile-and-a-half and two miles. He repeatedly ran in sensational time and his defeats were most of them due to some cause other than his own inferiority, if the testimony of the witnesses is correct.

Himyar began serving at Dixiana in 1883, but at first very few mares were put to him. Major Thomas had two other stallions, imported King Ban and Fellowcraft, and the former, in especial, was just at that period very popular. In consequence Himyar for a number of seasons did little service, and up to 1890, when he was fifteen years old, only six of his get had been seen in public, of which three were winners. His real start as a sire was, therefore, long delayed, but he might have said in the words of a famous wit: 'I come late to the banquet but I shall dine well.' King Ban having died and Fellowcraft being sold as a disappointment, Himyar was finally given an adequate opportunity, to which he rose at once. He ascended the sires' list by leaps and bounds until, with the advent of Domino in 1893, he 'topped the tree', his get that season winning 138 races and $249,502. The previous American record had been $189,334 won by the get of Longfellow in 1891. Thus Himyar was the first sire to reach and pass the $200,000 mark in the US. The record he established stood for fourteen years, and was then excelled by his own grandson, Commando.

Himyar lived on to the extreme age of thirty, when he died in the Avondale Stud of E. S. Gardner, in Tennessee. The list of stake and other winners by him is long and imposing. Domino was, of course, his trump card, but he also begat another eminent son in Plaudit, winner of the Kentucky Derby of 1898 and other notable events, and subsequently one of the sires at Hamburg Place that for so many years kept John E. Madden at the head of American breeders. From Plaudit has stemmed the second direct male line to Himyar, Alarm and Eclipse that we now have in America. Plaudit got King James, the winner of twenty-four races and $107,546, and he in turn begat Spur, My Own, My Dear, King Nadi, Prince James and many other racers of class. Spur was the sire of Sting, a brilliant performer, and Sting has given us Questionnaire, the rival of Gallant Fox and winner of nineteen races and $89,611, now just beginning his stud career.

Let us now turn from the male to the female line of Domino. We have already learned that from Orlando, down through Eclipse, Alarm and Himyar, he came of a series of sires distinguished for their speed, which at times was prodigious and became the hallmark of the tribe, its members, as a rule, preferring short rather than long courses. There was also a certain individual uniformity about them. All were bays, and, saving Eclipse, who stood 16.1, were horses of moderate size, conspicuous for their great muscular development in the hind quarters and their rather light bone. They were remarkably quick off their feet and could get off 'flying'. They were also game as far as they could go, standing severe drives at the finish with rare courage. Good dispositions ran in the family, and they were free-running horses, generous in giving all they had.

The tap-root of Domino, in the US, was the grey mare Galopade, bred in 1828 by Colonel King. She was by Catton out of Camillina, by Camillus, back of which came a mare by Smolensko out of Miss Cannon, by Orville from a Weathercock mare, whose dam, Cora, was by Matchem, and so on finally to the foundress, old Piping Peg. It is the

No. 23 family of the Lowe hagiography, which in its earlier generations enjoyed high favour, especially when it produced the paragon
of greys, Gimcrack, but then began to lose ground and, while never
falling wholly into the background, did not regain its ancient splendour
until modern times, when Barcaldine in England and Domino,
Hamburg and others in the US lifted it to a higher plane than ever
before.

Camillina, says *GSB*, Vol. IV, p. 63, was foaled in 1822, had but three
thoroughbred foals, of which Galopade was the first, was put to a half-
bred horse in 1835, and then disappeared from the record. She had two
sons, half-brother and own brother to Galopade, Pilot and Schemer, of
which the former raced for many seasons, principally at country
meetings, where he occasionally won. The latter started twice and was
unplaced. Catton, the sire of Galopade, apart from his great contribution to England's bloodstock, was the sire of Trustee, who was ex-
patriated to America at nearly the same time as Galopade, and did
wonders for the improvement of its breed of racehorses; the most memorable of his offspring being the immortal Fashion, conqueror of Boston,
Lexington's sire, in the epic match race, 'North v. South', run on Long
Island in 1842 in four-mile heats. Who brought Galopade to the New
World, or when she arrived, history neglects to mention. The *GSB*
remains wholly uncommunicative on that interesting detail. Colonel
Bruce is less reticent but little more helpful, as in Vol. I, page 89, *ASB*, he
vaguely tells us that she was 'imported into Canada, 1833'. In 1836 she
produced her first foal, Fandango, by Leviathan, and that progenitor
had crossed the Atlantic as far back as 1830. The Racing Calendars
show that Galopade was raced by Colonel King in England as a two-
year-old, when she won her only start, a sweepstakes at Lincoln; and
again at three, when she failed to win in five essays, but was able to come
in second when there were only two starters. That was in 1831. From
that date until 1835 is a 'veiled chapter' in her history; how she got to
Canada we know not; nor how she got from Canada to the Far South of
the US and into the stud of James Jackson, of Alabama, the man who
had imported Leviathan in 1830, and in 1836 imported Glencoe, who
arrived at his new home when Galopade was nursing her first-born in
one of its pastures. If the hollow-backed son of Sultan, with the exquisite
head and swan-like neck, who had left behind him in his native land the
unborn daughter that was to become Pocahontas, as he looked abroad
from his paddock over the pleasant landscape of the strange new world
that he had come to live in, caught sight of a grey form in the distance,

with her foal gambolling beside her, and neighed his greeting, was it a salutation to a compatriot that destiny had also drifted thither, or an anticipation of mutual loves to come?

Galopade, between 1836 and 1846, produced two fillies by Leviathan, and then six foals, evenly divided as to sex, by Glencoe. She was one of the first mares bred to the latter in his first season at the stud in Alabama, and she was never again bred to any other horse. Today the descendants of Galopade are familiarly known as 'the Dance Family', owing to the large number of them that have carried names suggestive of Terpsichore. In Mr Robert L. Gerry's *Matriarchy of the American Turf*, compiled by Miss Margaret Bayliss and published in 1931, the list of them that won important stakes, tracing directly back to her, covers fifteen pages. It comprises seventy animals that won 114 such events. As this compilation includes nothing previous to the Civil War, nor numerous valuable stakes contested since then but now discontinued, it will be seen that the family has indeed been a fertile one. Many students of American bloodlines consider Galopade the ranking progenitress imported during the past hundred years, and it is difficult to name another capable of contesting the palm with her.

We cannot in this article allot her and her family more than a passing glance and must confine ourselves to her one daughter Reel, the double ancestress of Domino. Her dam's first foal by Glencoe, she was a grey, foaled 1838. Her portrait, which hangs in the rooms of the Jockey Club, in New York, is one of the finest efforts of Troye, and shows her to have been an exquisitely lovely thing at every point. As a race mare she was probably the best of the Glencoes, not even excepting Peytona who defeated Fashion. Defeat was never her portion until her last race, in which she broke down, and she shone in the long-distance heat contests of the 'forties. She carried the colours of General Wells, of Louisiana, and retired to his stud, Wellswood, but was domiciled for much of her life in Kentucky on visits to its stallions. All told she produced thirteen foals between 1844 and 1860. At least ten of them were of high class, while the best of them were nonpareils. To Boston she threw Lecomte, the only horse that ever beat Lexington; to imported Sovereign (son of Emilius and Fleur-de-Lis) she foaled Prioress; and to Wagner she brought Starke. Lecomte, Prioress and Starke were all taken to England by Richard Ten Broeck in 1856–58, where Lecomte died after running but once, when unfit. Prioress won the Cesarewitch, after a deadheat, and other notable events, and Starke the Goodwood Cup. Reel's last foal (1860) was War Dance, her only produce by Lexington.

And here the strange interweavings that mark equine as well as human events again enter into our tale. We have already seen how adversely the career of imported Eclipse in America was affected by the Civil War of 1861–65, he having arrived here in 1859, the year before War Dance was foaled. And now once more that historic and disastrous conflict becomes a factor in the pre-history of Domino. Reel was twenty-two when she foaled War Dance, the last of her brood. It is seldom that a mare so old, after producing, as she had, a dozen other foals, mostly of rare merit, brings anything worth while. However, her final effort at maternity was in a sense her crowning one, for by War Dance her blood has been more widely diffused through the American breeding fabric than by any other channel. Being by Lexington, so highly valued was War Dance at his birth that A. Keene Richards, of Kentucky, agreed to give $5,000 in gold for him – then an unheard-of price – when a year old if safe and sound. Mr Richards, incidentally, had been one of the financial backers of Ten Broeck's English adventures, and it is possible that his money paid for Eclipse when Ten Broeck bought him in the autumn of 1858.

Richards was one of the Kentuckians that espoused secession when the Civil War broke out in 1861. Not long afterwards he fled to New Orleans, where, and in Europe, he remained during the struggle. His chief business interests were in the 'Crescent City', and General Wells, the owner of Reel and breeder of War Dance, was its leading citizen. Friends and sympathisers of Keene Richards also smuggled many of his best thoroughbreds to Louisiana after him, and they were sent to Wellswood for safety, it being supposed that there they would be out of the reach of the hostile armies. However, in May, 1862, the Federals captured New Orleans and overran Louisiana. As General Wells was most obnoxious to the invading forces his property was promptly confiscated, but before Wellswood could be sequestered, his nephew and namesake, 'Jeff' Wells, had run off all his most valuable thoroughbreds, together with those of Keene Richards, into the neighbouring state of Texas, where General Wells had a large ranch. There the equine refugees remained in hiding until the war ended in 1865 and a general amnesty was proclaimed. Meanwhile General Wells had died, and when his horses were brought back to Wellswood they were sold and most of them disappeared. Keene Richards had returned from Europe, however, and reclaimed War Dance, taking him to Kentucky, where, at his Blue Grass Park, near Georgetown, he became one of Lexington's most successful sons and an especially valuable sire of broodmares.

Before Richard Ten Broeck took Lecomte to England late in 1856 the son of Boston and Reel, then but six years old, had covered a few mares at Wellswood. Among them was one named Edith, by imported Sovereign out of Judith, by Glencoe, and she from Fandango, the daughter of Galopade and Leviathan. The produce, a bay filly foaled in 1857, and never named, was among the horses that found refuge in Texas during 1862–65, and while there she was mated with the colt War Dance, the produce being a filly that became known as Lizzy G. The *American Stud Book* says that Lizzy G. was foaled in 1867 and bred by Colonel George Garner, of Louisiana, but that statement was based upon uncertain data and is manifestly incorrect, for, according to the most credible traditions, she was brought back to New Orleans with the other Wells horses after the war and sold when they were dispersed, being then bought by Colonel Garner, who sent her to Kentucky and kept her there breeding to various stallions until her death in 1881.

Lizzy G. was bred repeatedly to Enquirer (one of the most distinguished sons of imported Leamington, his dam being Lida, by Lexington) and produced three foals by him that attained celebrity. Goodnight (1876) was one of the fastest horses of his day; Faustus (1877) became a sire of many precocious colts and fillies, together with older horses of great speed over short courses; while Mannie Gray (1874) became the dam of Domino, Correction, Ten Strike, Bandala, Lady Reel, and others, and the ancestress of many of the most prominent performers, sires and dams of America in recent times.

As the dam of Domino represented a remarkable concentration maternally of the blood of one ancestress, it will be well by a brief diagram to show in just what manner this obtained.

	Enquirer		Lexington–Boston
MANNIE GRAY (1874)		War Dance	
			Reel–GALOPADE
	Lizzy G.		Lecomte — Boston / Reel–GALOPADE
		Mare	Edith–Judith–Fandango –GALOPADE

The triple descent from Galopade is accompanied by triple descent from Glencoe, the sire of both Reel and Judith, as well as by a double cross to Boston, the sire of both Lexington and Lecomte. Moreover, Enquirer, the sire of Mannie Gray, was from a Lexington mare, bringing in a third Boston cross. The in-and-in breeding of Boston-on-Glencoe-on-

Galopade that resulted in Mannie Gray is an interesting study in blood-lines and their combination.

Mannie Gray raced only as a three-year-old, when, in the colours of that Blue Grass celebrity, General A. Buford (once a partner with R. Ten Broeck in the ownership of Lexington), she ran eight times over courses in Kentucky, Ohio and Tennessee. Like her ancestress, Galopade, she was not a brilliant race mare. She won one six-furlong dash, was once second and twice third, and her stake essays were fruitless. This was in 1877. In 1880 she joined the broodmares of Major Thomas at Dixiana, where she died in 1896, aged twenty-two, having produced in the period 1881–94 eleven foals that lived and one that died as a yearling.

To present in detail an account of the produce of Mannie Gray is here impossible owing to spatial exigencies. Suffice it to say that her first foal, *Ten Strike* (1881), by Ten Broeck, was gelded and won the Tennessee Derby, Seaside Stakes and twenty-five other races; her second, *Sir Knight* (1882), by Fellowcraft, never raced; her third, *Bandala* (1883), by King Ban, won the Ladies' and Mermaid Stakes and three other races, produced four winners, is the third dam of the noted stake horse Audacious (twenty-eight races and $78,175) and the fifth dam of Zev, winner of the Belmont, Withers, Kentucky Derby, Realization and many other events to the value of $313,639, he being the first horse in history to pass the $300,000 mark; her fourth, *Bannerol* (1884), by King Ban, never ran; her fifth, *Lady Reel* (1886), by Fellowcraft, won the Beacon Stakes and five other races and produced Hamburg, the best son of Hanover (sixteen races and $62,378) and premier sire of America in 1905; her sixth *Madame Reel* (1887), by Fellowcraft, never started but produced winners; her seventh, *Correction* (1888), by Himyar, won thirty-eight stakes and purses, was considered the fastest mare of her day at six furlongs, and produced Yankee, winner of the Futurity, while her daughter, Miss Malaprop, produced Haste (five races and $73,325), the sire of Hurryoff, winner in 1933 of the Belmont Stakes; her eighth, *Freemason* (1890), by Fellowcraft, won two races, one of them the Bartow Stakes; her ninth (1891), was **Domino**; her tenth (1892). a bay filly by Himyar, died when a yearling; her eleventh (1893), *Swiftfoot*, by Himyar, ran once and did not win; her twelfth and last (1894), *Mannie Himyar*, by Himyar, never raced but produced several winners, most notably Blackstock (by Hanover) sire of Mentor, who sired Wise Counsellor (ten races and $115,470), winner of one of the International Specials from Epinard in 1924 and now the chief representative of the Hanover line in America.

The diagram previously given brings out the striking features of Domino's maternal ancestry as related to the three animals of whose blood it was so largely composed. The following tabulation shows his bloodlines on both sides:

		*Eclipse (B, 1855)	Orlando Gaze
	Alarm (B, 1869)		
		*Maud (B, 1859)	Stockwell Countess of Albermarle
Himyar (B, 1875)			
		Lexington (B, 1850)	Boston Alice Carneal
	Hira (Ch, 1864)		
		Hegira (Ch, 1846)	*Ambassador Flight
DOMINO (Br, 1891)			
		*Leamington (Br, 1853)	Faugh-a-Ballagh Pantaloon mare
	Enquirer (B, 1867)		
		Lida (B, 1858)	Lexington Lize
Mannie Gray (Bl, 1874)			
		War Dance (Ch, 1860)	Lexington Reel
	Lizzy G. (B, 1867)		
		Lecomte mare (B, 1857)	Lecomte Edith

* Imported.

Domino was bred Eclipse-to-Eclipse, with a very strong collateral Herod background, due to his close triple cross to Lexington, plus the triple Glencoe cross illustrated by the maternal chart. His top line was one of intense speed and short courses; maternally, while his dam, Mannie Gray, was from staying sources, her foals were non-stayers, a trait conspicuous in her descendants to the present day.

Miss Elizabeth Daingerfield is authority for the statement that Domino, though bred at Dixiana, was not foaled on that estate. Major Thomas's paddocks and pastures were so crowded with home and visiting matrons in the spring of 1891 that he was obliged to send some of his own away to rented land. Mannie Gray was one of them, and so it came about that her colt was foaled on May 4th in a field just across the road from

Dixiana. The son of a bay sire and a black mare, Domino was a deep, rich brown, so dark in hue that he was generally described as black, which he appeared to be on the racecourse when wet with sweat. On that account he was dubbed 'The Black Whirlwind' by a Turf scribe, a sobriquet thereafter widely applied to him. A very small star and a fleck of white on his muzzle, and white hind legs halfway to the hock, comprised his marks. He was not a big colt and at maturity barely measured 15.3 hands.

Major Thomas, who had long retired from racing, in 1892 sold his yearlings on June 6th at what was then known as 'Tattersalls of New York', the American branch of the famous English organisation. It was under the management of the late William Easton, so often referred to as the ablest thoroughbred auctioneer that ever wielded the gavel in America. Domino was one of thirty-four yearlings sent up from Dixiana and No. 1 in the catalogue – a position accorded him because his own sister, Correction, was then the champion sprinter of the Metropolitan courses and much in the public eye. Easton was 'taken' with the colt when he arrived in New York, and the day before the sale attracted the attention of James R. Keene to him, advising him to buy him. Mr Keene, however, was not greatly impressed by the son of Himyar and next day at the sale showed no aggressiveness in bidding. His son, Mr Foxhall Keene, had accompanied him to the ringside, being then actively associated with his father; their horses were raced and registered in the names of J. R. and F. P. Keene. Foxhall Keene was so much smitten with Domino – upon whom he later conferred that name – that he decided to buy him and accordingly bid up to $3,000, at which price the colt was knocked down to him. The sale report gives the buyer as Foxhall Keene. That was the top price of the consignment, whose thirty-four members averaged but $875 – a figure then considered not at all bad.

William Lakeland was at that time training for Messrs Keene. Of English birth (as was J. R. Keene also), he had been brought to America when ten years old, in 1863. Beginning as an exercise boy, then becoming a successful jockey, he was training and racing horses on his own account in 1876 and by ability and integrity worked his way up the ladder until he reached the top. In addition to his skill as handler of a racing stable, he was a student of blood lines and in his knowledge of them far superior to the average man of his calling. Owing to his intelligence and authority, the following reminiscences of Domino, which he gave not long after that horse's death, are of uncommon interest and value:

> 'I took Domino the spring he was two years old. He had wintered very poorly and was so delicate that I had to nurse him like a sick child. I built him up and he developed into a great racer. His legs, however, always troubled him. He was not one of the horses that you could give a severe preparation or run too frequently. He had speed enough to go the distance if properly rated, but if you started him when his tendons felt sore he would not extend himself and thus the impression grew that he would stop. He could run over almost any kind of track. As a three-year-old one of his feet troubled him. I have often seen the blood run from the heel where it is divided by the frog. If Domino had belonged to me he would never have been beaten, because I never would have started him when I thought he was not in condition to do justice to himself. He was a natural racehorse and required comparatively little work to keep him in condition for races, especially the kind of races in which he was engaged. Domino was as sound a horse when I returned him to Mr Keene to go into the stud as when I received him.'

The characteristics described by Lakeland explain why, though he received the colt in such poor physical form in the spring when he was two, Domino came so fast that he was soon the talk of the track at Sheepshead Bay, and was sent to the post for his debut on May 22nd, when, in a field of thirteen, he was favourite at 5 to 4 on. He started nine times that season, never being beaten. The races he won during it were:

	Runners	Distance	Weight		Value
			st	lb	$
A Purse	13	5 f	8	0	895
Great American Stakes	8	5 f	8	6	18,675
Great Eclipse Stakes	6	6 f	8	6	16,750
Great Trial Stakes	9	6 f	8	13	23,100
Hyde Park Stakes	9	6 f	8	11	16,900
Produce Stakes	11	6 f	9	2	19,875
Futurity Stakes	20	6 f	9	4	48,875
Match v. Dobbins	2	6 f	8	6	dead-heat
Matron Stakes	11	6 f	9	2	24,560
					$169,630

In his first race he stumbled at the start but quickly recovered and smothered the others with speed, winning pulling up by six lengths. His next five efforts were all easy victories by such margins as were elected. This brought him to the Futurity, in which for the first time he had a hard race. His stable companion Hyder Abad fell and impeded him and he was in the ruck until the last quarter-mile. The field of twenty made it necessary to pull out and come around the leaders. He got up to win by a head from Galilee, with Dobbins a head away third. This led Richard

Croker, owner of Dobbins, to challenge for a match, which was made at $10,000 a side and run two days later, when, after a thrilling struggle, a dead heat resulted and the match was declared null. Domino had appeared beaten near home but came again with rare gameness. These two extreme efforts, made within three days, one under 130 lb (9 st 4 lb) left him much exhausted and he was rested for four weeks. Then he won the rich Matron Stakes, running six furlongs under 128 lb (9 st 2 lb) in 1.09, a new American record for the distance. He then retired for the season. His winnings far surpassed those of any other two-year-old to that date, and were also a record amount for an American horse of any age.

When three years old Domino took part in eight races, of which he won five, ran a dead-heat with Henry of Navarre in another, was once third and once unplaced. His wins were in the Withers, Flying and Culver Stakes, the Ocean Handicap, and a special match against Clifford. He was ninth and last in the American Derby, won by Rey el Santa Anita, and third to Henry of Navarre and Clifford in his farewell effort of the season, the 'three-cornered' special given for the trio of rivals at Morris Park. As a four-year-old he also ran eight times, winning four – two Purses and the Coney Island and Sheepshead Bay Handicaps; was beaten a head by Henry of Navarre in the special given for the pair and Rey el Santa Anita at Sheepshead; beaten a head by The Butterflies in the Fall Handicap when carrying 133 lb (9 st 7 lb) and trying to give that brilliant filly 24 lb for the year between them; was fourth in the Suburban Handicap, won by Lazzarone; and fifth and last in the First Special at Gravesend won by Henry of Navarre.

All told, Domino ran twenty-five times, won seventeen, made two dead heats, was twice second, once third and thrice unplaced, earning $193,650. He never won at any distance beyond a mile, but made a dead-heat with Henry of Navarre as a three-year-old at nine furlongs. That day he gave a superb exhibition, being apparently beaten at the end of the mile, but coming again and almost nosing 'Navarre' out. In the Suburban, at a mile and a quarter, he was done at the end of a mile. In the American Derby, a mile and a half, any chance he might have had was ruined by the way in which he was ridden. Fred Taral, who rode him in every one of his twenty-five races, was instructed to stay well back until the first mile had been run and then give him free rein, these being Mr Keene's orders. Domino, accustomed to racing in an entirely different manner and unable to understand, began fighting for his head almost from the moment the flag fell and never stopped doing so, his desperate efforts to overcome Taral's restraint being plainly evident. The consequence was that when finally given free rein he was completely pulled out and had nothing left to come on with. The present writer has a vivid recollection of that occasion, and of his sympathy with the colt, who finished in a white lather of foam, utterly exhausted. Domino had not been in the race for an instant during the entire contest. He was also limping, having a foot wound, from which the blood was flowing.

The series of races between Domino, Henry of Navarre and Clifford, three truly remarkable horses, contested in 1894–95, provided a succession of the most brilliant and exciting affairs ever seen, and aroused the interest and enthusiasm of the American public to a pitch never since equalled. 'Navarre' proved himself the master of the other pair because he could go farther, but Domino was almost invariably the favourite of the crowd because of his dazzling speed, eagerness to race and splendid courage when overmatched. There has perhaps never been seen in America a horse able to get off at such a whirlwind clip. Nature obviously did not intend him for long routes; but at the same time, remembering the disabilities described by Lakeland, we cannot but concede that he deserves the homage of the lover of a good horse for the manner in which he acquitted himself. Taral, a great rider, but also a very rough one, again and again subjected Domino to terrific drives in which he never failed to give up everything he had until, at the very last, he began to rebel, never sulking or swerving but displaying temper in the saddling paddock and at the post, together with an unconcealed aversion for the jockey who had punished him so unmercifully.

Mr Keene had been breeding for several years at Castleton when, after his farewell to the Turf, Domino was sent there to begin stud service as a five-year-old, in the spring of 1896. He had several other stallions, including Kingston, Tournament, and St Leonards, and his stud was under the management of his brother-in-law, Major Daingerfield, whose success in that capacity again and again provided the material for making the 'white, blue spots' dominant on American courses. Mr Keene had begun as a breeder nearly twenty years before with Spendthrift, and from the first had shown a marked preference for English mares. His first stud had been dispersed after some years, but when he assembled another, with Major Daingerfield to preside over it, he again recruited its matrons largely from the sales at Newmarket and Doncaster, the late William Allison usually acting as his representative and adviser in making his purchases. It followed, therefore, that native-bred mares were in the minority at Castleton; and this was shown very markedly when the sixteen apportioned to Domino for his first season were selected, thirteen being English-bred.

The internal evidence would go to show that the young horse was either a shy foal-getter that season or else, for some obscure reason, the mares at the farm failed to get with foal. At any rate, of the thirteen English mares, the *American Stud Book* shows only four to have produced the next spring while two of the three native-bred ones proved fertile. Previous to his death in July, 1897, Domino had covered eighteen mares, of which fourteen were English and four American. From these came fourteen posthumous foals of 1898, ten from the fourteen English mares and four from the four Americans.

The total number of foals got by Domino, as recorded in the *Stud Book* was, therefore, twenty-six born in 1897, four being colts, and fourteen in 1898, five being colts. As to colour, there were nine chestnuts, eight bays and three browns. The preponderance of chestnuts, interesting to those who attach importance to coat-colour, is partly explained by the fact that the dams of four of the nine were chestnut mares, and partly, perhaps, because Domino himself was what many men call a 'black chestnut' rather than a brown. Here is the complete list of Domino's twenty foals, with the breeding of their dams:

1897

*Belle Rose, b. m., by Beaudesert–Monte Rosa, by Craig Millar. B. f *Pink Domino*.
*Bonnie Gal, br. m., by Galopin–Bonnie Doon, by Rapid Rhone. B. c. *Disguise*.
Ella T., b. m., by War Dance–Bonnie Kate, by *Knight of St George. B. c.
*Fair Vision, ch. m., by Touchet–Enchantress, by Scottish Chief. Ch. f. *Runaway Girl*.
*Mere Hill, br. m., by Macgregor–Miss Penhill, by Newminster. Br. c. *Unmasked*.
Lucy Wallace, ch. m., by Ballinkeel or War Dance–Blanche Rousseau, by *Mickey Free. Ch. c. *Doublet*.

1898

Belle of Maywood, b. m., by Hunter's Lexington–Julia Mattingly, by John Morgan. Ch. c. *Olympian*.
*Ben-My-Chree, b. m., by Galopin–Ulster Queen, by Uncas. Br. f. *Cap and Bells*.
*Calico, b. m., by Hampton–*Dimity, by Galopin. Ch. f. *Gingham*.
*Dancing Water, br. m., by Isonomy–Pretty Dance, by Doncaster. Ch. f. *Running Stream*.
*Dart Maiden, b. m., by St Gatien–Maid of the Isles, by Scottish Chief. B. f. *Spry*.
*Editha, ch. m., by Master Kildare–Violet Melrose, by Scottish Chief. Ch. f. *Dominoes*.
*Elsie, br. m., by See-Saw–Danish Rose, by Surplice. Ch. c. *Kimberly*.
Emma C., br. m., by *Darebin–Guenn, by Flood. B. c. *Commando*.
Gloaming, b. m., by *Sir Modred–Twilight, by Norfolk. B. f. *Double Six*.
*Miss Milly, b. m., by The Miser–Lady Milly, by Vanderdecken. B. f. *Costume*.
*Orchis, b. m., by Bend Or–Lizzie Agnes, by Macaroni. Br. f. *Climax*.
Paradox, ch. m., by *Rayon d'Or–Lizzie Cox, by *Glenelg. Ch. c. *Mardi Gras*.
*Royal Gem, b. m., by Napsbury–Royal Duchess, by Bourbaki. B. c. *The Regent*.
*Sundown, b. m., by Springfield–Sunshine, by Thormanby. Ch. f. *Noonday*.

* Imported.

For purposes of reference, the following tabulation has been prepared. The intention has been to give an 'abstract and brief chronicle' of the careers of Domino's twenty sons and daughters in tabloid form, only the salient facts about them being included. We may term it

The Doings of The Dominoes

CAP AND BELLS, br. f. (1898); dam, *Ben-My-Chree, by Galopin. Raced in America at two, winning the Criterion and Spinster Stakes. Was then sent to England, where she won the Oaks of 1901 by six lengths from eighteen others, being the only American-bred winner of that event. As a brood mare at Castleton she produced six winners, including two winners of stakes, a sire (Boots and Saddle) and several producing daughters.

CLIMAX, br. f. (1898); dam, *Orchis, by Bend Or. Never ran. As a brood mare at Castleton produced three winners, including Theo. Cook, winner of twenty-one races and the sire of the winners of over 900 races and over $800,000 in stakes and purses. During three successive seasons (1925–27) the get of Theo. Cook won annually over 100 races and $100,000.

COMMANDO, b. c. (1898); dam, Emma C., by *Darebin. As a two-year-old Commando won the Zephyr, Great Trial, Montauk, Brighton Jr, and Junior Champion Stakes, losing only the Matron Stakes owing to his jockey's misjudgment. As a three-year-old he won the Belmont and Carlton Stakes and finished second in the Realization, in which he broke down. Nine starts, seven wins and $58,196. Of Commando as a sire, see further on.

COSTUME, b. f. (1898); dam, *Miss Milly, by The Miser. Was bred as a three-year-old and produced seven winners, including Harcourt and Turncoat, two brilliant milers, and Fancy Dress, a winner for five seasons.

DISGUISE, b. c. (1897); dam, *Bonnie Gal, by Galopin. Raced only in England, where as a three-year-old he won the Jockey Club Stakes (1¼ miles; $35,950), with Diamond Jubilee, winner of that year's Derby, unplaced – in the Derby Disguise had run third to Diamond Jubilee and Simondale, beaten a length and a half. The next season he ran third to Epsom Lad and Ian in the Eclipse Stakes. Of Disguise as a sire, see further on.

DOMINOES, ch. f. (1898); dam, *Editha, by Master Kildare. Never ran. Bred at three and produced eight winners and two stake winners, one of the latter being Dominant (Hopeful, Saratoga Special and U.S. Hotel Stakes), also the sire of winners of over 300 races worth over $300,000.

DOUBLE SIX, b. f. (1898); dam, Gloaming, by *Sir Modred. Ran four seasons, and was a winner. She produced but two living foals, both of which were winners, and was then exported.

DOUBLET, ch. c. (1897); dam, Lucy Wallace, by Ballinkeel or War Dance. As a two-year-old won the Juvenile and ran second in the Eclipse Stakes. Did not run at three, was gelded and won for four seasons thereafter.

GINGHAM, ch. f. (1898); dam, *Calico, by Hampton. Produced six winners, including Outram (won in England the Lincolnshire, Brighton, Newmarket, Great Cheshire, Holiday and Royal Handicaps), Kashmir (Melrose Stakes), Swing Clear (Eglinton and Hamsey Handicaps in England) and Madras Gingham (dam of four winners).

KIMBERLEY, ch. c. (1898); dam, *Elsie, by See-Saw. Gelded. A useful plater for a number of seasons.

MARDI GRAS, ch. c. (1898); dam, Paradox, by *Rayon d'Or. Sent to England as a yearling; later gelded and a winner there for two seasons.

NOONDAY, ch. f. (1898); dam, *Sundown, by Springfield. Won the Belles Stakes at two and other races at three and four. Dam of eight winners, including five stake winners. Her son High Time won the Hudson Stakes and was America's premier sire in 1928. Another son, High Noon, twice won the Toboggan Handicap, America's principal fixture for sprinters (6 furlongs), a feat unequalled, and is the sire of many winners. Her daughter Suffragette won the Junior Champion and Surf Stakes, and Willow Handicap and was then sent to England, where she won for several seasons. Her gelded son Besom won twenty-nine stakes and purses. Her son Vandergrift won seven races and has sired numerous winners.

OLYMPIAN, ch. c. (1898); dam, Belle of Maywood, by Hunter's Lexington. Raced as a two-year-old in America, when he ran second to his stable companion, Commando, in the Brighton Junior Stakes and second to Ballyhoo Bey in the Futurity. Then sent to England, where at three he started in the Derby, leading the field until Tattenham Corner. Later a winner there, then was returned to America, where he covered a few mares and was re-exported in 1909.

PINK DOMINO, b. f. (1897); dam, *Belle Rose, by Beaudesert. Won several purses at three and produced six winners, including Sweep, winner of nine out of thirteen races, among them the Futurity, National Stallion, Belmont, Carlton and Realization Stakes and twice (1918–1925) America's premier sire. Two others were Selectman and Cabaret, winners in both America and England. Her daughter Curiosity produced Novelty, winner of the Futurity, Hopeful, Saratoga Special and other stakes and the Rensselaer Handicap with 135 lb; Wonder, daughter of Curiosity, produced John P. Grier, the rival of Man o' War, one of the fastest horses of modern times and now the sire of the winners of 640 races and over $900,000 to January 1st, 1934. Another daughter of Pink Domino, Swan Song, is the dam of Apprehension, sire of Larranaga, winner of the Cuban Grand National Handicap ($50,000) in 1933.

RUNAWAY GIRL, ch. f. (1897); dam, *Fair Vision, by Touchet. Won the Albemarle Stakes at two. Dam of nine winners, of which Meggs Hill, Gretna Green, Fleeing Sheik, Wedding Bells and Subahdar all won stakes, her produce having won in America, England and France. Among her producing daughters is Pankhurst, dam of Upset, the only horse that ever beat Man o' War. Upset won the Sanford Memorial at two and Latonia Derby at three and was beaten a head in the Kentucky Derby; to 1934 he has gotten the winners of 550 races and about $760,000.

RUNNING STREAM, ch. f. (1898); dam, *Dancing Water, by Isonomy. Sent to England as a yearling, she there won the July Stakes, at Newmarket, and the Temple Handicap at three. Dam of Runnymede, winner of five stakes and purses in England and sire of Morvich, winner of the Futurity, Kentucky Derby, etc., and $172,909 and a successful sire. Two other sons, Cataract and Pebbles, were both stake winners and are successful sires. A fourth son, Ultimus, ranks as one of the most potent sons of Commando, but never raced. Her gelded son Miramichi won many races. These, with Stepping Stone, her only daughter, a dam and grand-dam of winners, were her entire produce.

SPRY, b. f. (1898); dam, *Dart Maiden, by St Gatien. Won three races. Had produced but two living foals in nine seasons so was exported to the Argentine in 1910.

THE REGENT, b. c. (1898); dam, *Royal Gem, by Napsbury. Gelded. Winner of numerous races on Metropolitan courses.

UNMASKED, br. c. (1897); dam, *Mere Hill, by Macgregor. Gelded. Winner of
   twenty-three races, many in fast time at sprinting distances.
UNNAMED, b. c. (1897); dam, Ella T., by War Dance. This colt evidently died young
   as there is no trace of him.

* Imported.

From the foregoing summary it will be seen that of Domino's twenty
foals, fifteen were winners, seven being stake winners, while several
others were contenders for and placed in important stakes. Of his eleven
daughters, ten were the dams of sixty winners, an average of six each,
while twenty of these sixty horses were winners of stakes. Their wins
included classic and semi-classic events on both sides of the Atlantic. It
seems likely Domino might have won the position of premier winning
sire of America had not Mr Keene selected what were considered by him
the best and most promising of his get to race in England. They were
thus divided between the two countries, making it impossible for him to
gain that position.

Of the nine male foals by Domino, only two had careers at the stud,
Commando and Disguise. One other, Olympian, covered a few mares
during the short period he spent in the States between his return from
England, where he had gone to race, and re-exportation to France,
where, a few seasons later, he disappeared in the vortex of the First
World War. The other six were all gelded. The continuation of the
direct male line depended, therefore, upon Commando and Disguise,
and it was the former who proved the vital factor, becoming thereby, in
effect, an epochal figure in American breeding history.

'Life's little ironies' were never more pungently illustrated than in the
origin of Commando. As we have seen, James R. Keene did not at first
care for Domino; it was his son, Foxhall Keene, who stepped forward
and bought him as a yearling, when he himself declined to do so. But, in
addition to that piquant fact, it was also against the father's will that
Domino covered Emma C., from which mating Commando came. She
was a large coarse mare by the Antipodean stallion Darebin, himself a
rugged, unrefined stallion, though a grand racehorse and good sire. He
had been imported by James Ben-Ali Haggin, for his Rancho del Paso,
in California. By The Peer, son of Melbourne, and from Lurline, a great
Cup mare, by Traducer, of the Herod line, Darebin was a tremendous
stayer under high weights, winning the Sydney Cup with 134 lb (9 st
8 lb). Curiously enough, his get in America were mostly noted for speed
over short courses, few of them caring to go much over a mile. Emma C.
was one of the few, for she could go two miles, winning twice at that
distance, once as a three-year-old under 124 lb (8 st 12 lb) and again at

four, when, carrying only 92 lb (6 st 8 lb) she ran the distance in 3 min 29 sec, the American record at the time being 3 min 27½ sec. Mr Keene had bought her at auction as a yearling, but she was so 'growthy' that she could not race when two years old, and though she won four races at three, including the Dolphin Stakes at Sheepshead Bay, and was nearly always 'placed' when beaten, her fastidious owner conceived an aversion to her. Finally, it is said, he gave her to William Lakeland, his trainer. By the way, it is interesting to know that Lakeland one day in 1895 won races at Sheepshead Bay with both Domino and Emma C., whose alliance two years later was to produce Commando.

BBR–1934

'The Great Sire Lines' by Mr Wanklyn

Mr W. H. E. Wanklyn, editor of the New Zealand Stud Book, contributed an article to the Review *on 'The Great Sire Lines'. It was a monumental work and there was much about it to praise. However, the* Review, *after considerable research, concluded 'that consequently the soundness of Mr Wanklyn's hypothesis was questionable'. This brought a polite reply from Mr Wanklyn, who had been encouraged by the* Review *to do so, but once again the* Review *found itself unable to go along with some of Mr Wanklyn's theories and so this reply to a reply which follows from the 1913* Review.

ON PAGES 36–38 of this volume of the *Review* there appears a criticism of 'The Great Sire Lines', a publication which comprises a series of tables showing the way in which thoroughbred stallions of the present day are descended in tail-male from the Darley Arabian, the Godolphin Arabian and the Byerly Turk. These charts are very useful and interesting, and beyond that statement called for no comment. We, however, ventured to dissent from some of the pronouncements made by Mr Wanklyn in his prefatory essay. Invited by us to reply to our observations if he thought fit to do so, Mr Wanklyn, who is the Editor of the New Zealand Stud Book, has favoured us with a communication which we have much pleasure in reproducing.

May we here assure our readers that contributions from them bearing upon matters which come within the scope of this magazine will always be heartily welcomed. We have been just a little disappointed by the backwardness of breeders in sending us their views on questions pertaining to the development of the thoroughbred horse. *The Blood-stock Breeders' Review*, although only in its second year, has, we are proud to say, thoroughly established itself as a magazine with a world-wide circulation and reputation. There is not a civilised country on the face of the globe to which the blue-covered quarterly numbers are not sent. Large and increasing parcels go to each and all our Colonies. We are quite sure we voice the wishes of our home readers when we say that pertinent communications from Colonial and foreign readers will be very acceptable. May we, therefore, appeal to them occasionally to devote some of their leisure hours to the writing of letters or essays for publication in these columns. And let not the home breeder think that he is absolved from a similar responsibility. We want these pages to pulsate with life and vigour. Only those who have had any-thing to do with the conduct of a magazine can really know how easy it is to drift into a set groove leading to monotony. It shall always be our earnest endeavour to avoid that groove. Cannot some of you give a little help occasionally? We are acquainted with several breeders who wield a facile pen. Stand not upon the order of your writing, but write!

After that unpremeditated excursus we return to Mr Wanklyn's letter. For the benefit of those who did not see the April number of the *Review*, we may as well requote the extract from the introduction to 'The Great Sire Lines' which provoked our criticism. It is as follows:

'... The fundamental cause of the failure of any sire line, however promising at the outset, is universally attributable to a particular form of inbreeding. There is no instance of the male line surviving where its founder and his dam's sire descend within three generations from the same horse. The male line also fails when there are continuous repetitions in its female alliances of stallions belonging to its own line, as instanced in those of Catton and Emilius, which practically disappeared as male lines in their second generation of descendants. In both these lines the dam of the sire, grandsire and great-grandsire on the male side were near descendants of Tartar and Herod. It cannot be gainsaid that many closely inbred horses have proved champions on the Turf and as a consequence have had the best of opportunities at the stud, but they have all failed to maintain their male line.'

With reference to the statement that 'there is no instance of the male line surviving when its founder and his dam's sire descend within three generations from the same horse', we pointed out that a very large percentage of the founders of male lines that have become extinct were *not* inbred in the manner condemned as fatal to the longevity of the family, and that consequently the soundness of Mr Wanklyn's hypothesis was questionable. After a two hours' search we failed to find an example supporting that of Petrarch. Here is Mr Wanklyn's reply:

The Editors,

Bloodstock Breeders' Review

Sirs, First please let me thank you for your tribute to my work, 'The Great Sire Lines', and also for the criticisms. Your concluding paragraph, hoping that I will not take your observations amiss, was really unnecessary. I did not think for one moment that the opinions gained from my researches would be acceptable to other students and breeders without criticism, and I felt that in the interests of a great pastime, what I had learnt would probably induce others far more competent than I am to still further prosecute their studies, and, whether I am right or wrong, the result must be the same in the end. If it does not improve the breeding of horses it cannot do any harm.

I will only allude to two of your comments; the first is when you state that you can find no note explaining that the name of the horse in small type is that of the sire of the dam. You have probably overlooked the explanatory notes and tabular index in the sheets just prior to the main index, and I confess at once that its position, without special reference, is easily overlooked.

On the question of Petrarch being instanced as a failure (this word is your own) in the male line on account of his descent both in male and female tail from Touchstone, I have, as you surmised, numerous examples which I hope some day to tabulate. There are a great number of horses bred on similar lines who were good performers on the Turf, but who do not appear in the list of sires because nothing descended from them.

The successful male lines require no tables to inform students and breeders what they are, and the reason that the hundreds of others are in the tables is because they are part of the process required to show the successful ones. Every sire whose name appears has the corresponding sire of his dam included in the tables.

You mention twenty-four founders of families whose male lines are dead, but who are not inbred to their male line. As a matter of fact most of them could not be termed founders, as their male line was more or less dead before it came to them. I think Orville himself was the cause of the line becoming extinct. He was very closely inbred to Herod and had a very severe Turf career. His best sons were Emilius and Muley, who both continued the inbreeding to Herod. Emilius, with good opportunities, sired some good horses, Priam and Plenipotentiary being the best. There were other sons of Emilius that did not do badly on the Turf, but they are only in the list on account of pedigrees through their females.

I attach Plenipotentiary's extended pedigree, *(see page 452)*, which is a good example of what may be termed excess of inbreeding.

You will see that the dams of Beningbrough, Orville, Emilius and Plenipotentiary, and the latter's grandam, were all descended from Herod; that Evander's sire and dam were also grand-children of Herod. The only male line of Plenipotentiary and his immediate male ancestors that survives is that of Selim, whose pedigree is not unlike that of Galopin, his great-grand-sire's name coming both at the top and bottom of his pedigree in the third generation.

I will only give you one more instance of inbreeding which I have found is generally fatal to the male line, and that is Blue Gown. Blue Gown died early, but he lived long enough and had sufficient opportunities to prove his fitness, but he failed. His own grandam and the dam of his sire were daughters of Touchstone.

PLENIPO-TENTIARY

Emilius	Orville	Beningbrough	King Fergus	Eclipse M. by Black & All Black
			Daughter of	HEROD M. by Matchem
		Daughter of	Highflyer	HEROD M. by Blank
			Daughter of	Tantrum M. by Sampson
	Daughter of	Stamford	Sir Peter	Highflyer (HEROD) M. by Snap
			Daughter of	Eclipse M. by Blank
		Daughter of	Whiskey	Saltram M. by HEROD
			Daughter of	Dorimant M. by Blank
Daughter of	Pericles	Evander	Delpini	Highflyer (HEROD) M. by Blank
			Daughter of	Phoenomenon M. by Pacolet
		Daughter of	Precipitate	Mercury M. by HEROD
			Daughter of	Highflyer (HEROD) M. by Snap
	Daughter of	Selim	Buzzard	Woodpecker (HEROD) M. by Dux
			Daughter of	Alexander M. by Highflyer (HEROD)
		Daughter of	Sir Peter	Highflyer (HEROD) M. by Snap
			Daughter of	Trumpator M. by Florizel (HEROD)

BLUE GOWN

Beadsman	Weatherbit	Sheet Anchor	Lottery by Tramp *M. by Muley
		Daughter of	*Priam *M. by Orville
	Daughter of	TOUCHSTONE	Camel *M. by Master Henry
		Daughter of	Tramp M. by Bustard
Daughter of	Stockwell	The Baron	Birdcatcher M. by Economist
		Daughter of	Glencoe *M. by Muley
	Daughter of	TOUCHSTONE	Camel *M. by Master Henry
		Daughter of	Langar M. by Waxy

* Orville blood.

I have found as many sire failures from this form of inbreeding as from the male and female descent direct to the individual like Petrarch; but Blue Gown had in addition $\frac{6}{16}$ strains of Orville blood. You will also observe that Beadsman, the only surviving line of Tramp, had, like Galopin and Selim, the same male at the top and bottom of his pedigree, only a little further removed.

These two examples will, I hope, enlighten you generally upon the grounds I based my statement of the bad effects of inbreeding so far as the male line is concerned – Yours, etc.,

W. H. E. WANKLYN.

Christchurch, New Zealand,
14th May, 1913.

After perusing and re-perusing the foregoing rejoinder we are bound to say that we still think Mr Wanklyn has not succeeded in furnishing convincing proof in support of his ingenious thesis. In fairness to him we should, perhaps, await the 'numerous examples' of deleterious inbreeding which he proposes to tabulate. The case of Blue Gown, as he admits, is not strictly analogous to that of Petrarch. Blue Gown is inbred with what Herr v. Oettingen calls two free generations between the sire and dam and the common sire, Touchstone – one free generation on the sire's side and one on the dam's. Now nothing can be more certain than that inbreeding of this intensity is not necessarily fatal to a horse's prospects as a sire. Among stallions that were, or are, inbred with only two free generations there are the following:

Stallion	Inbred to
Amphion	Newminster
Boston	Diomed
Galopin	Vedette
Hanover	Hindoo
Partisan	Highflyer
Wisdom	The Baron
Bayardo	Galopin
Lemberg	Isonomy
Marcovil	Hermit
Orvieto	Thormanby

It is, of course, not possible at the present time to say whether or not the five last-named stallions are to be recognised as 'founders' of virile lines. Boston, too, may fairly be claimed by Mr Wanklyn in support of his theory. Both his sire and dam were grand-daughters in tail-male of Diomed, and though his 'blood' is treasured by breeders in America, it is now to be found chiefly in the descendants of the daughters of Lexington, the brilliant son of Boston, Americus (by Emperor of Norfolk, a grandson of Lexington) was the only modern sire of any consequence descended in tail-male from Boston. There have been a few successful stallions, notably Barcaldine and Flying Fox, with pedigrees showing only one free generation to a common ancestor of sire and dam. White Eagle is a living example of this exceptionally close inbreeding. But, as we maintained in our review of Mr Wanklyn's book, inbreeding on paper and inbreeding in fact are not necessarily co-relative. And we would again lay stress on the contention that, from the biological standpoint, it does not matter in the least in which portions of the pedigree the name of the common ancestor is duplicated. The segregation of heritable characters, which is the fundamental principle of Mendelian law, renders untenable all such theories as those advanced by Mr Wanklyn.

Mr Wanklyn does not effectively dispose of the point we raised by citing twenty-four founders of 'families' whose male lines are 'dead', although they were *not* inbred to their own male line. He suggests that their male line 'was more or less dead before it came to them'. That contention cannot possibly be applied to Warlock and Chanticleer by Birdcatcher; Velocipede and Brutandorf by Blacklock; Mountain Deer, Cotherstone, Flatcatcher and Surplice by Touchstone; Cathedral and Adventurer by Newminster; and Young Melbourne by Melbourne. There, at any rate, are eleven stallions who were not hampered by the inbreeding which is said to be fatal to the perpetuation of the line, and who yet failed as 'founders' of families, though they seemed to be shaping well for a time. A rule to which there are so many exceptions cannot be seriously accepted as gospel.

Just another word and we have done. Mr Wanklyn apparently puts Beadsman forward to support his contention that there is hope of a sure family foundation when a horse is inbred on the same lines as Galopin. So far as this country is concerned the Tramp line is virtually extinct in tail-male. Rosicrucian was its last representative of any note. But, of course, the blood – in other words the essential characters which Tramp transmitted to his offspring – is not extinct. It is to be found in many of our mares. Hereditary characters cannot be transferred in groups from generation to generation. They split up and go their several ways, and often remain dormant for a long period. Hence the utter futility of attaching undue importance to direct descent in tail-male or tail-female.

BBR-1913

A correspondent to the Review *also took exception to some of Mr Wanklyn's conclusions and offered the following reply:*

MR WANKLYN'S indictment of inbreeding must cause some of us to wonder what our forefathers were thinking about when they raised so many good horses in the past, and very many of them closely inbred. To these latter several of our best performers, our best sires, and our best mares, claim descent. For this reason, and also on account of the fact that in our own time good horses have been bred on this now decried system, it is well that the 'other side' should rebut the statements and statistics of the much-respected New Zealander.

I will take at random a few pedigrees, which I think have not been before cited in support of the contention that inbreeding is not so injurious as its opponents would make it out to be.

Voltaire, by Blacklock

LOLLYPOP (1836)

Belinda, by Blacklock

Lollypop may be remembered as the dam of Sweetmeat, to whom we owe Macaroni, Kendal, Ormonde, etc.

Commodore, by Tom Tug, by Herod

IRISH ESCAPE
(1802)

Buffer's dam by Highflyer, by Herod

This horse cannot be reckoned a failure, being the sire of Guiccioli's dam Flight, which in itself will be enough to keep his memory green.

Chanticleer, by Woodpecker, by Herod

BOB BOOTY (1804)

Ierne, by Bagot, by Herod

As the sire of Guiccioli, and consequently grand-sire of Birdcatcher, Bob Booty must escape inclusion in the list of failures.

Mercury, by Eclipse from dau. of Tartar

GOHANNA (1790)

dau. of Herod, by Tartar

Gohanna was grand-sire of Peri, the dam of Sir Hercules. The pedigrees of Barcaldine and Isonomy are two others showing close inbreeding. The former's is a peculiar case, for in it we find son and grand-daughter of a common ancestor mated, and this added to the fact that a common ancestor (Birdcatcher) existed in the third and fourth removes of the parents' pedigrees; and another (Hetman Platoff) in the fourth and fifth removes. Who will deny that both these horses are forces to be reckoned with?

Of course inbreeding to a bad or weak strain must give bad or worse results; but where a breeder has the opportunity of mating two representatives of a strain of proven excellence, and, as it were, massing his forces for a given purpose, then I think it is unwise and unprofitable to turn aside from the opportunity of adding good to good. If we were supplied with tables giving the failures who were not inbred set against these undesirables who are inbred I venture to think that the balance would be against the former.

We hear much nowadays from separate sources about male ancestry, and female ancestry, with one served up to the exclusion of the other. Should we not attend equally to both? How often do we hear of mares who will practically breed winners to any stallion? Are they not factors in building up successful families? Mares such as these will be forces in any pedigree, and are likely to transmit their excellence to their children's children.

Modern methods of breeding may try to achieve more than has been done by men who laid the foundations of British stud success; but without being pessimistic, it is not too much to anticipate that if these methods are applied generally we shall lower our standard of horses and undo all the good of past generations. Why attribute our present-day failures to inbreeding and kindred causes? Are causes not more easily found in the paddock, and the food-house? A hundred (and less) years ago breeders bred horses for themselves under natural conditions. Nowadays, quite 75 per cent are bred for sale at Doncaster, Newmarket, or Dublin. The result is that these 'sale' yearlings in a number of cases are unnaturally 'forced' so that when they come to bear the strain of training they break up and form food for selling races, the van, and the knacker. I know I have gone wide of the title of my notes and for my delinquency I claim the reader's pardon; but I wish to plead for more natural treatment of our young bloodstock. In this connection I am glad to observe that the leading breeder-owners have taken the van, and that they are being rewarded.   BBR–1913

The End of Birdcatcher

Writing in Sport, *Mr Pat Connolly, a nephew of the jockey who won the Derby on Coronation and the St Leger on Birmingham, gives the following account of the famous stallion Birdcatcher in 1860:*

AMONG THE MARES sent to the son of Sir Hercules that year was Mr Michael Dunne's Queen Bee. She was a mare of good size, and when Birdcatcher attempted to serve her he failed to do so. Mr Disney, who owned the stallion, thereupon decided that he should no longer survive. At once a messenger was despatched to the local police station with orders to bring back with him a constable with a loaded gun, as a horse was required to be destroyed. The policeman – his name was Preston – reported himself to Mr Disney, who gave the necessary directions for the destruction of Birdcatcher. The horse was placed on the brink of a sandpit situated on the flat opposite Conyngham Lodge, Curragh; without any ceremony he was shot and his carcase tumbled into the pit. Thus ended the career of a good racehorse and a mighty sultan at the age of twenty-seven years. His head was afterwards presented to the Royal College of Veterinary Surgeons, Dublin.   BBR–1913

Stallion Fees of Earlier Eras

As recently as the middle 1980s, stallion fees, particularly in the US, reached intemperate heights as validated by the precipitous decline which ultimately set in. Although it is not documented, it was rumoured that a season to Northern Dancer cost one million dollars without a guaranteed live foal. True or not, it indicates the engorgement going on at that time in some sections of the breeding industry. It also makes for an interesting comparison with some of the top fees being charged in England in 1914, in 1864 and in 1814 which were published in the Review of 1914.

THE FOLLOWING is a list of stallions whose registered fee for the season 1914 is £98 or over. In the majority of cases another sovereign or guinea is claimed on behalf of the groom:

	Fee		*Fee*
Prince Palatine	400gs	Chaucer	200gs
Tracery	400gs	Henry the First	£200
William the Third	400gs	Polymelus	200gs
Bayardo	300gs	Radium	200gs
Cicero	300gs	Sunder	200gs
St Frusquin	300gs	Tredennis	200gs
Sunstar	300gs	White Eagle	200gs
Swynford	300gs	William Rufus	£200
Willonyx	300gs	Marcovil	150gs
Lemberg	250gs	Santoi	£150
Spearmint	250gs	Neil Gow	£149

	Fee		*Fee*
The White Knight	£149	Littleton	£98
Earla Mor	£148	Orby	£99
Flotsam	100gs	Picton	£98
Bachelor's Double	£99	Roi Herode	£98
Cylgad	£98	Royal Realm	£98
Fowling-piece	95gs	St Amant	£98
Collar	94gs	Santry	£98
Greenback	£98	Symington	£98
John o' Gaunt	£98	Thrush	£98

It is interesting to compare the above fees with those which were being charged for the services of the best stallions fifty years ago and one hundred years ago. Turning to the *Racing Calendar* of 1864 we find announcements concerning seven Derby winners. One of them was Voltigeur who, standing at Mr Smallwood's paddocks at Middlethorpe, close to York, commanded a fee of £50. No other stallion was at that time at a higher fee than 40 guineas. The other Derby winners then claiming patronage were Caractacus, 20 guineas, at Highfield Paddocks, Tittenhanger, St Albans; Kettledrum, 30 guineas, at Root Stud Farm, Whitewell, near Clitheroe; Musjid, 15 guineas, at Benham Park, Newbury; Thormanby, 30 guineas, at the Croft Stud, Darlington; Wild Dayrell, 30 guineas, at Chilton Cottage, Hungerford; and Ellington, 15 guineas, at Willesden Paddocks, Kilburn, London. The advertisement of Ellington states that he gained the 100 guineas prize at the Royal Agricultural Show at Battersea, 'a proof of his perfect soundness and superiority of shape and action'.

Among the other stallions advertised in the *Calendar* of 1864 were Buccaneer, 12 guineas, at Neasham Hall, Darlington; Gemma di Vergy, 30 guineas, at Mamhead, Exeter; Gunboat and Lifeboat, 20 guineas each, at Bushbury Paddocks, Northampton; Oxford, 12 guineas, at Stanton, Shifnal; The Marquis, 20 guineas, at Dringhouses, York; Leamington (who afterwards went to the United States), 15 guineas, at Rawcliffe Paddocks, York; Rataplan, 40 guineas, at Tickhill, Bawtry; Skirmisher, 12 guineas, and Parmesan, 10 guineas, at Rufford Abbey; St Albans, 25 guineas, at Hampton Court; and Warlock, 20 guineas, at Sheffield Lane. It would seem that in those days 20 guineas was charged for stallions of the class that now command £98.

Going back another fifty years to 1814, we find that during the intervening period stallion fees did not advance so much as they have done during the last half century. Sorcerer, at Great Barton, Bury St Edmunds, where Diomed was at one time located, commanded 30 guineas. Waxy, at Newmarket, was advertised at 25 guineas; and this was the fee demanded for the services of Dick Andrews, who was also at Newmarket. At 20 guineas were Smolensko, at Oatlands, Surrey; Sooth-sayer, at Newmarket; Gohanna, at Petworth; and Orville, at the Luxborough Farm, Essex. Rubens (15 guineas) was at Barton Court, Newbury; and Thunderbolt (also 15 guineas) at Mr Kirby's stables, York. At a ten-guinea fee were Walton, at the Grantham Arms, Boroughbridge; Williamson's Ditto, at Snitterfield, Stratford-on-Avon; Election and Phantom, at the Royal Stud, Hampton Court; Golumpus,. at Low Catton, 'seven miles from York on the Hull road'; Haphazard, at Oxcroft, nine miles from Newmarket; and Scud, at Riddlesworth, near Thetford. BBR–1914

The Bend Or Controversy

There have been instances of questionable breedings throughout the history of the Turf, but none caused more notoriety than that of Bend Or, winner of the 1880 Derby and, subsequently, one of the most influential patriarchs in the Stud Book. A disgruntled stud groom had insisted that the real winner was Tadcaster, another Eaton Stud product and a Bend Or look-a-like. As the Review *of 1914 explained, 'The echoes of the controversy that raged round Bend Or after he had won the Derby in 1880 have lately been re-awakened.' Continuing, the* Review *said: 'There may be many among the younger generation of sportsmen who have but an indefinite idea of what the rumpus was all about. For their benefit we will briefly state the facts.'*

Now, these many years later, and for the same reason, only more so, the facts as presented then are presented once again.

BEND OR, who was by Doncaster out of Rouge Rose, was born at Eaton in 1877. Another of the Eaton products that year was Tadcaster, by Doncaster out of Clemence. Both Bend Or and Tadcaster were chestnuts. Shortly after they were weaned they, together with two filly foals, were taken to Newmarket, because there was sickness at the Eaton Stud. Immediately after Bend Or had won the Derby, a man named Arnull (who had been stud groom at Eaton, but who had just been discharged because of the unsatisfactory way in which he performed his duties) informed Mr Brewer, owner of Robert the Devil, who had run Bend Or to a head, that the winner of the Derby was Tadcaster and not Bend Or.

In his entertaining book *Racing Reminiscences*, Sir George Chetwynd makes the following allusion to the affair:

'Just before the (Newmarket) July Week Mr Charles Brewer asked to see me on urgent business in my then capacity of Senior Steward of the Jockey Club. He informed me that he was going to object to Bend Or, the winner of the Derby, believing him to be Tadcaster, his conviction being that the two colts had been mistaken when they were sent as yearlings to the training stable (at Russley). He told me that he had received a communication to that effect from the Duke of Westminster's stud groom, had gone to Chester and met the man there. The result of the interview had persuaded him that there could be little doubt about the correctness of his suspicions. I blamed him for not having gone to the Duke first, and he rather amused me by saying with an astonished air, "*Me* go up to the Duke of Westminster's front door, ring the bell, and ask to see him!" I told him the proper thing now was to lodge a formal objection, and this he did at Newmarket July Meeting. The Stewards at once went into the evidence and adjourned to meet in London afterwards, when, however, at my request, Lord Calthorpe consented to act for me, I having only just remembered I had backed Bend Or for a place in the Derby, and therefore was interested. On July 24th the following decision was given:

"We, as Stewards of Epsom, unanimously decide that the chestnut colt Bend Or, which came in first for the Derby of 1880, is by Doncaster out of Rouge Rose and therefore the objection lodged by Messrs Brewer and Blanton (trainer of Robert the Devil) is overruled.

(Signed) W. G. CRAVEN,
          JAMES LOWTHER,
          CALTHORPE (for Sir G. Chetwynd)."

'I do not see how it is possible that these gentlemen could have arrived at a different decision, looking at the fact that the whole of the evidence given to prove that Bend Or was Tadcaster was supplied by a stud groom under notice to quit, and by people connected with him; still, that man died a few years afterwards, and on his death-bed solemnly averred that he had spoken the truth. Furthermore, many good judges today will say that from the appearance of the subsequent progeny of Rouge Rose and of Clemence, combined with the remembrance of the looks of the two horses, Bend Or and Tadcaster, they firmly believe the colts were changed – accidentally, of course, as it need scarcely be added. After all, it would not be very wonderful if this had been the case, considering that only last year (1889) there was a similar occurrence in Captain Mitchell's stable, and here it was proved that a horse called Mortaigne was D'Orsay and *vice versa*.'

Mr E. Somerville Tattersall made an interesting contribution to the recent discussion in the form of two letters to *Horse and Hound*. In the first he wrote:

'I think it may interest your readers to know why I have been strongly of opinion for many years that the pedigree of Bend Or as it appears in the "Stud Book" is correct. The late Count Mokronoski, who had studied the "Stud Book" as thoroughly as anyone I have ever met, and knew the characteristics of every important horse, told me so many things in advance which turned out to be true years afterwards that I valued his opinion more than that of any man on matters connected with the "Stud Book". I remember being rather annoyed with him, for instance, when he told me that Throstle was an unsound brute, and would breed unsound stock. However, it is not easy to find one of her descendants with good legs. He disliked Wild Dayrell in her pedigree. He also told me that Bendigo would be a bad stallion, and that Bend Or would be a success at the Stud and Robert the Devil would not be worth a hair in his tail as a sire.

'He said that he attached great importance to the shape of the hoof in this particular case, for all the family of Paradigm have very round hoofs, low at the heel, absolutely different from the Newminster foot. He asked permission to look at Bend Or's foot at Eaton – the first time he saw him after his retirement from the Turf – and was convinced that he was related to Lord Lyon as soon as he had looked at it, and this round, flat foot is to be seen in Polymelus, Lemberg, and other horses descended from Bend Or.

'Allusions have been made as to the likeness between Bend Or and Sandiway. There was no resemblance, as far as I could see, in their appearance, though they both had good action; but there was, of course, a distinct likeness between Sandiway (by Doncaster) and Lenity (by Bend Or), both out of Clemence. Lenity, it may be noted, with less chance bred more winners than Sandiway, though Calveley, of course, was far better than any of the stock of Lenity. There was, however, a sister to Bend Or, Martlet by Doncaster out of Rouge Rose, sold by the Duke of Westminster and sent to South America. She was brought back to this country at the age of eighteen and sold at Newmarket. She was on a small scale, but was turned like Bend Or. She had more width than Sandiway and Lenity, and had the same white hind heel, and was a richer colour than they were. I bought her for 75 guineas for General Brocklehurst, and he and the late Major Fife-Cookson, and others who attended this small October sale, were struck by the resemblance between her and Bend Or. Bend Or was extraordinarily handsome and powerful. Sandiways was more like Pearmain, the dam of Corcyra – lightly built, and not remarkable in appearance.

'The fact, however, that a very large proportion of Bend Or mares were crib-biters puzzled me till I mentioned it to Huby, the Duke of Portland's stud groom at Welbeck, one day, and he said there was nothing very remarkable in that, for Rouge Rose came to Speculum when he was standing at the Moorlands Stud Farm, Huby being then with Mr Thompson, and she was one of the worst crib-biters he had ever seen. This last fact seems of evidence in favour of Bend Or being the son of Rouge Rose.

'It is an interesting fact, too, and rather a startling one, that only one Newminster mare ever produced a "classic" winner, and that winner was Lady Augusta (One Thousand Guineas). Yours faithfully,

E. SOMERVILLE TATTERSALL

Feb. 24, 1914.

'P.S. – The Duke of Westminster was such a good judge of horses, and had been connected with them all his life (having been a MFH, though he did not begin racing till 1875), that it is highly improbable that he could confuse three colts of such entirely different shades of chestnut. Bend Or was a golden chestnut, with grey hairs and black spots and a big black spot on his fetlock; Tadcaster was a red chestnut and had lop-ears; and Muncaster was extremely dark in colour.'

In the second letter, Mr Tattersall furnished additional testimony in support of his contention that there was no mistake made over Bend Or and Tadcaster. Indeed, it may almost be said to dispose once and for all of the suggestion that the 1880 Derby winner was by Doncaster out of Clemence. Here is Mr Tattersall's supplementary communication:

'Since writing to you last week, I have received some very interesting information with regard to Bend Or and Tadcaster from Mr M. Gurry. Mr Gurry, as your readers probably know, was under Mr Robert Peck at Russley for many years, and subsequently trained The Bard for him. No shrewder trainer than Mr Robert Peck could be named.

'Well, it appears that when Bend Or and Tadcaster went to Newmarket from Eaton they were sent to Mr Barrow's paddocks. Mr Barrow at once took their markings, and Colonel Barlow made frequent visits to his paddocks to see them, and reported on them to the Duke of Westminster. The latter, however, came to see the colts himself two or three times while they were at Newmarket. I do not know in what month they came to Newmarket, but I saw them there myself in the Craven week of 1878, and Mr Gurry tells me they went to Russley in June.

'On their arrival at Russley their markings were again noted, just as those of any other fresh arrivals in the stable. This was Mr Peck's rule. Therefore Mr Gurry scouts the idea of any mistake being made, and says he is tired of reading so much that strikes him as ludicrous on the subject.

'He tells me that Tadcaster had only one black spot, on his off quarter. I know myself that he was a red chestnut, with lop ears. Bend Or had black spots on the shoulder, neck, and quarters, and a large one on one of his fore fetlocks, so noticeable that the late Lord Falmouth, to the Duke's amusement, took it for traces of blistering. His colour was absolutely different from that of Tadcaster. Bend Or and the produce of Rouge Rose never gave the blacksmith at Newmarket (Deeks, who is still alive) any trouble to shoe, whereas Tadcaster would not have his hind feet touched, and the Russley blacksmith found the same difficulty with the others of Clemence's stock which came to be trained there. Mr Gurry describes them as bad-tempered brutes.

'Now, it always seemed to me that the Duke of Westminster has been rather ignored by correspondents on this question, so it is particularly important to state that the Duke saw his yearlings after their arrival at Russley probably more often than any owner who can be quoted, unless, perhaps, the late Sir Daniel Cooper, who lived within sight of his trainer's stables at Newmarket. Mr Gurry tells me that the Duke made a practice of going to Russley once a fortnight in any case, but that he also took Ashdown, Lord Craven's place, 1¼ miles from Russley, that year (1878), and would then come over nearly every day to see the yearlings, sometimes twice even, and had them occasionally taken over to Ashdown. Colonel Barlow often went to Russley, and Mr Peek also went to see the foals and yearlings when they were at Mr Barrow's place. Mr Barrow also, on his first visit to Russley after they had left Newmarket, recognised the colts at once.

'When Arnull, the stud groom, was for a very good reason given notice to leave, he hinted to Mr Gurry at Chester races in 1880 that there might be a mistake; but his son-in-law, Saxby, who "did" Doncaster at Eaton, never made any such suggestion. Some capital, I believe, has been made out of the fact that the markings of the colts had not been taken by Colonel Barlow; but these colts, Bend Or, Tadcaster, and Muncaster, were particularly easy to distinguish. There was only one other colt by Doncaster at Eaton – Prefect – and he was a bay. Mr Gurry says "No one could have mistaken Bend Or and Tadcaster, unless he did it wilfully." This "I most powerfully and potently believe," especially as I had many opportunities, I am glad to say, of looking at horses with the late Duke of Westminster, and could see how observant he was. I know, too, that he went round his stud every day possible when at Eaton, sometimes twice.'

It has been stated that Mr James Lowther, some years after the 1880 'inquest', confessed that, in the light of additional facts which had come to his knowledge, he and the other Stewards probably arrived at a wrong decision. In a letter which was recently published in the *Sportsman*, the writer declares that Arnull did not wait until Bend Or had won the Derby before making known his suspicion that the colt winning under that name was really Tadcaster. Of course, if that really was the case the suggestion that his evidence was tainted loses some of its force.

There is little likelihood of any further light being thrown on the dispute. For all practical purposes, the decision of the Epsom Stewards was final. We have cause to be thankful that it must stand, right or wrong.   BBR–1914

Obituary of Rock Sand

Rock Sand, who died prematurely in France at the age of fourteen, in 1914, was the tenth winner of the English Triple Crown, accomplishing this feat in 1903. While clearly the best of his own generation he cannot be considered 'one of the ones' in English Turf history as Ard Patrick, winner of the Derby a year earlier, and Persimmon's amazing daughter, Sceptre, also a year his senior, soundly defeated him in the Eclipse Stakes of 1903 and the filly twice more asserted her superiority over the son of Sainfoin. In all, Rock Sand had won sixteen of his twenty starts. After serving one full season in 1906 in England, his owner died and he was sold to American August Belmont and stood in Kentucky until 1912 when a French syndicate purchased him. His contributions at stud were significant despite his early death. His classic-winning son Tracery was a success at stud and, of course, his daughter, Mahubah bred none other than America's all-time most honoured thoroughbred Man o' War. The 1914 Review's account of his career follows.

ROCK SAND was in a class much superior to that to which Sir Visto belonged. Indeed, after he had won the Two Thousand Guineas and the

Derby there were many shrewd people who regarded him as a colt worthy to rank with horses of established renown. But before he was much older, Rock Sand, as we shall presently show, was relegated to a somewhat lower level than that. Still, it may be allowed he was well up to the average of Derby winners; and it is satisfactory to know that he has left behind him in Tracery a son worthy to uphold the credit of the thoroughbred family to which they belong.

Born in 1900, Rock Sand, a dark bay, was bred at the Hamilton Stud, Newmarket, by the late Sir James Miller. He was by Sainfoin out of Roquebrune, by St Simon out of St Marguerite. Sir James had bought Sainfoin in 1890, a few weeks before the colt won the Derby; Roquebrune he acquired when she was a yearling at the disposal of the Duchess of Montrose's stud in 1894, the price paid being 4,100 guineas. Rock Sand was the first produce of Roquebrune, and the only animal of any consequence sired by Sainfoin.

As a two-year-old, Rock Sand made a big name for himself. That season he won six races, and his only defeat was the one he suffered when competing for the Middle Park Plate. He opened his score by winning the Bedford Stakes at Newmarket in the spring. Presumably he was at that time deemed unready; at any rate, he was not 'fancied'. Nevertheless, he defeated his opponents in a canter. Then, in succession, came victories in the Woodcote, Coventry, Chesterfield and Champagne Stakes. He won all these races comfortably except the Coventry Stakes at Ascot; on that occasion he had to struggle hard to beat Baroness La Flèche by a head. His downfall in the Middle Park Plate was the next incident in the story of his career. He finished third, a head and two lengths behind Flotsam and Greatorex. Flotsam and Rock Sand were both trained by George Blackwell. If Rock Sand's lapse that day is capable of being explained away, the explanation has still to be made public. It was a mystery at the time and still remains one. Certain it is that the form was all wrong. Sir Daniel Cooper, who owned Flotsam, could, however, never be brought to that way of thinking, although strong proof of the falsity of the running was forthcoming a fortnight later when Rock Sand won the Dewhurst Plate with the greatest ease. In this race Greatorex, who finished third (King Edward's Mead being second), was receiving 3 lb from Rock Sand, whereas in the Middle Park Plate the pair carried equal weights.

Naturally enough, then, Rock Sand was, during the ensuing winter, favourite for the Derby. His first outing as a three-year-old was in the Bennington Stakes in the Newmarket Craven Week. In that race he had nothing much to do and did it very well. By this time he had a strong rival in Sir Ernest Cassel's colt Sermon, who had won the Newmarket Biennial in facile style and in remarkably good time. On this form Sermon was thought to have a great chance of winning the Two Thousand Guineas; indeed, if Newmarket opinion had controlled the betting Sermon would probably have started favourite. The general public, however, were loyal to Rock Sand, and when the flag fell the betting was 6 to 4 against Rock Sand, 3 to 1 Sermon, 7 to 1 Flotsam, and 8 to 1 Rabelais. As for the part Sermon played in the contest, it need only be said that he made no show at all, although the time was slower than that recorded for the Biennial. Rock Sand had no difficulty in winning by a length and a half from Flotsam, with Rabelais third another two lengths away.

The Derby was Rock Sand's next race. Here he again met Flotsam, but the French horse, Vinicius, was deemed, and proved to be, a more formidable opponent. Little danger was, however, apprehended from this Gallic candidate. Odds of 6 to 4 were freely laid on Rock Sand, who won readily by two lengths from Vinicius. Flotsam finished third, four lengths behind Rock Sand. These two stable companions were both admittedly in the best of trim that day, so we may take it that this form represents their actual merits.

At Ascot a fortnight later Rock Sand won the St James's Palace Stakes from some moderate opponents. Up to this point, therefore, the only blot on his record was the inexplicable defeat in the Middle Park Plate, and that had long since ceased to be weighed against him. His host of admirers had for some time persuaded themselves that he was a colt far and away above the average, and they welcomed the opportunity which was afforded him in the Eclipse Stakes at Sandown Park of meeting Ard Patrick and Sceptre. This contest has taken its place in Turf history as one of the most memorable of races. It occasioned enormous excitement. A very big attendance had been anticipated, but the crowd so greatly exceeded expectations that the arrangements made by the management proved utterly inadequate, and hundreds of impatient people clambered over the railings into the principal public enclosure without going through the usual formality of paying for admission.

So deep-rooted was the faith in Rock Sand that day that he started favourite at 5 to 4. Against Sceptre odds of 7 to 4 were laid, and Ard Patrick's backers got 5 to 1 to their money. The race revealed Rock Sand in the light of a colt whose merits had been overrated. The distance to be traversed was ten furlongs. Three furlongs from home, Sceptre and Ard Patrick began to leave him in the lurch, and the further he went the worse he fared. After a most exciting struggle, Ard Patrick defeated

Sceptre by a neck; Rock Sand finished third three lengths behind. The thousands of onlookers wore a very chastened look when the thrill which momentarily possessed them had spent its force. Nine-tenths of them had championed the claims of either Rock Sand or Sceptre. Those who had pinned their faith to the son of Sainfoin had good cause to feel depressed because his failure was of too emphatic a character to admit of extenuating circumstances being put forward on his behalf. He returned to Newmarket a dethroned idol.

Of course, Rock Sand still held the certificate proclaiming him the best of his contemporaries, and his right to the title was emphasised afresh when he won the St Leger just as he pleased. Then, in the autumn, in the contest for the Jockey Club Stakes at Newmarket over one mile and three quarters, he again measured his powers against those of Sceptre. It had been intended that Ard Patrick should take part in this race, but a few weeks earlier leg trouble necessitated his being taken out of training. He had, indeed, gone to the Graditz Stud, the Prussian Government having bought him for £21,000 about the time he won the Eclipse Stakes. At Sandown Park Sceptre and Rock Sand met on strict weight-for-age terms; but in the Jockey Club Stakes, the mare had to concede the colt an additional 6 lb. Owing to this Rock Sand again started favourite, odds of 11 to 10 being laid on him, while backers of Sceptre obtained 5 to 4. Sceptre beat the favourite pointless by four lengths. It was an astonishing performance, one which gave rise to an almost hysterical outburst of enthusiasm. Lucky it was for the reputation of Ard Patrick that he did not meet Sceptre that afternoon, for it is as certain as anything well can be that the daughter of Persimmon and Ornament would have taken ample revenge for the Eclipse beating.

The following year Rock Sand piled up a big score, for in successive outings he won the Hardwick Stakes, Princess of Wales's Stakes, the Lingfield Park Plate, the First Foal Stakes and the Jockey Club Stakes. But this fine series of victories was preceded by a defeat in the race for the Coronation Cup at Epsom over the Derby course. He finished third to Zinfandel and Sceptre. This was the first and only occasion on which he encountered Zinfandel. The result went a long way towards proving that the enforced withdrawal of the son of Persimmon from the classic races of 1903, owing to the death of his nominator, Colonel Harry McCalmont, removed a formidable obstacle from the path of Rock Sand.

During the winter of 1904–5, Rock Sand was kept in training with a view to his winning the Ascot Cup as a five-year-old. But in the following spring other counsels prevailed. In April he was sent to the stud, and was mated with a few mares during the latter part of that season. He had a full season in 1906, but unhappily, in the meantime, Sir James Miller died. The executors sold Rock Sand to Mr August Belmont, of New York, for £25,000, and in the early summer of 1906, Rock Sand was shipped across the Atlantic. He remained in America until 1912 when he was bought by a French syndicate for about £25,000. He died in France from heart disease on July 20th last. Appended is a summary of Rock Sand's racing record.

Two Year Old (1902)

	£
Won Bedford TYO Stakes, Newmarket	596
Won Woodcote Stakes, Epsom	930
Won Coventry Stakes, Ascot	1741
Won Chesterfield Stakes, Newmarket	780
Won Champagne Stakes, Doncaster	1780
3rd in Middle Park Plate, Newmarket	—
Won Dewhurst Plate, Newmarket	1647

Three Years Old

Won Bennington Stakes, Newmarket (one mile)	300
Won Two Thousand Guineas, Newmarket (one mile)	4500
Won the Derby, Epsom (1½ miles)	6450
Won St James's Palace Stakes, Ascot (one mile)	2400
3rd Eclipse Stakes, Sandown Park (1¼ miles)	—
Won the St Leger, Doncaster (1¾ miles)	4775
2nd to Sceptre, Jockey Club Stakes, Newmarket (1¾ miles)	—

Four Years Old

3rd Coronation Cup, Epsom (1½ miles)	—
Won Hardwicke Stakes, Ascot (1½ miles)	2404
Won Princess of Wales's Stakes, Newmarket (1½ miles)	7185
Won Lingfield Park Plate (1¼ miles)	2420
Won First Foal Stakes, Newmarket (1 mile)	275
Won Jockey Club Stakes, Newmarket (1¾ miles)	7435
Value of 16 races won	£45,618

BBR–1914

The Story of Stockwell

When Edward Moorhouse's interview with John Griffiths, then Stud Groom for Lord Derby at Knowsley, was published in the Bloodstock Breeders' Review *of 1915, it involved the story of Stockwell as well as recollections of other great stallions.*

Stockwell, foaled in 1849 by The Baron out of Pocahontas by Glencoe, was a magnificent chestnut with tremendous depth and power as well as wonderful bone. As a two-year-old, the colt was too big to be seriously trained but in 1852 he won the Two Thousand Guineas and the St Leger. He failed in the Derby, but apart from meeting with a lot of interference in that race he had just had a septic gumboil lanced.

At stud he earned the title of 'Emperor of Stallions'. He was champion sire on seven occasions and got three Derby winners – Blair Athol, Lord Lyon and Doncaster, the second of these three being a winner of the Triple Crown. In 1866 he was responsible for the first three to finish in the Derby. He is the ancestor of the Phalaris male line, the most powerful in English racing today.

Near the beginning of this really precious article, Mr Moorhouse, already attuned to the role of the Review *was destined to play in the abiding literature of the Turf, wrote as follows:*

'It has been my fate to write countless thousands of words that lie – fortunately perhaps – buried away in the musty files of newspapers. Much of that work was a joy to the writer, if not to the unoffending reader; but if I may be permitted to make a confession, there is infinitely more satisfaction derivable from the preparation of articles that are to find their way into the pages of a journal like the *Bloodstock Breeders' Review* which promises to have a permanent value.'

And that is the way those of us involved in rediscovering the 'Treasures of the Bloodstock Breeders' Review' *feel about it and why we feel that Mr Moorhouse's interview with Mr Griffiths, like so many other selections found in this book, should always be 'handy' on the desk of the true devotee of racing and breeding.*

IT WAS in 1862 that Stockwell arrived at Hooton, and what Griffiths has to say about that remarkable horse merely concerns the eight years he spent at Mr Naylor's stud. I propose, however, to take advantage of the opportunity that now presents itself to set down some of the salient facts which emerge from an analysis of Stockwell's stud career as a whole. There is no need to dwell on his racing performances. Suffice it to say that his victories in the Two Thousand Guineas and the St Leger ensured his receiving liberal patronage when, in 1855, he began his life as a stallion at his owner's, Lord Exeter's, place at Burghley, near Stamford. Lord Exeter had bought him as a yearling from his breeder (Mr Theobald, of Stockwell) for £180, with a contingency of £500 if he won the Derby. Stockwell was advertised in the *Racing Calendar* to serve in 1855 '30 mares at 30 guineas each, besides a few of his owner's'. How many mares he actually had is not recorded, but he was credited in 1856 with twenty foals – sixteen living and four dead. According to a writer in

Bell's Life, Stockwell was, while at Burghley, on offer to some foreigners at £2,000. They, however, rejected him because they thought there was something wrong with his back. At the close of the season of 1855 he was sent to Tattersall's to be sold, with a reserve of 3,000 guineas on him. Lord Londesborough's stud groom, Scott, secured him with a bid of 3,100 guineas, and Stockwell went to his new owner's stud farm at Grimston, near Tadcaster. The Kirkby Farm it was called; it is now the Stockwell Stud. West Australian was already located there, and 'filling' easily at 30 guineas. So long as the two horses remained at Grimston, West Australian was the more esteemed; at any rate, his name always appeared in front of Stockwell's in the stud's advertisement. And the preference was perhaps, quite natural, for West Australian was the first horse who had won what is called the 'Triple Crown', by gaining victories in the Two Thousand Guineas, Derby and St Leger. Stockwell, it may be observed, might perhaps have performed the same feat a year earlier but for the knocking about to which he was subjected in the Derby.

Lord Londesborough in 1856 definitely limited Stockwell to forty mares, including ten of his own, the fee charged remaining 30 guineas; but in 1857 the complement was enlarged to fifty mares. In 1860 Lord

Stockwell.

Londesborough died. His stud was dispersed at the Kirkby Farm, and it was then that Mr R. C. Naylor became Stockwell's owner, the successful bid being one of 4,500 guineas. His most persistent opponent was the representative of the Duc de Morny. Imagine, if you can, how differently the history of the English Turf during the last fifty years would have read if Stockwell had gone to France! West Australian did go there, for he was bought for the Duc de Morny at 3,000 guineas. Eventually he became the property of Napoleon II, and, curiously enough, he and Stockwell died within a few days of each other.

Mr Naylor did not take Stockwell right away to Hooton; in 1861, and again in 1862, the horse was quartered at the Rawcliffe Stud, near York. It had been stated that the Rawcliffe Stud Company had a share in Stockwell, and that Mr Naylor eventually bought them out. I can, however, find no confirmation of the alleged partnership. The son of The Baron and Pocahontas did not leap into fame as a sire. He was, in fact, at the outset a disappointment. When at the end of 1858 he was credited with only two winners of £270 all told, Lord Exeter may have harboured the consolation that he did well to sell him at 3,100 guineas. There was an improvement the following year, but, even so, an aggregate of £4,645 was nothing to boast about, for Stockwell had that year forty-two possible runners, that being the total of foals by him in 1856 and 1857. But the outlook underwent a complete change in 1860, the year Mr Naylor bought the horse, for that season Stockwell headed the list of winning sires with a total of £18,201, and his son St Albans gained classic honours by winning the St Leger. On the strength of his record, the Rawcliffe Company raised his fee to 40 guineas and allowed him fifty mares at that figure. In 1862 the fee was again 40 guineas, and the advertisement adds 'the subscription to this horse is full'. 'Everyone is trying to get a nomination to Stockwell,' wrote a contemporary chronicler. And no wonder, for in 1861 Stockwell's daughter, Caller Ou, won the St Leger, and another daughter, Lady Ripon, ran second in the Oaks. Moreover, he again headed the stallions' list with a total of £24,029.

At the close of the season 1862, Stockwell was transferred to Hooton. It may be mentioned here that in the two years he was at the Rawcliffe Stud he begat, in 1861, Regalia, who won the Oaks and ran second in the St Leger; and in 1862, Lord Lyon, winner of the Two Thousand, Derby and St Leger; Repulse, winner of the One Thousand; Monarch of the Glen, second in the Two Thousand; and Savernake and Rustic, second and third in the Derby. Savernake was also second in the St Leger. In no other years have the three 'placed' horses in the Derby been by the same sire.

The stud farm at Hooton was by no means an idle establishment. Says Griffiths:

'It was badly adapted to its purpose. The land was sandy and overrun with rabbits. It was never treated properly. The Squire was rather "close", and would not spend money unless absolutely forced to do so. In addition to the old farm buildings we found there, we erected some wooden sheds for the yearlings, and about forty boxes for mares, but they did not cost much. Stockwell was accommodated in a huge barn, big enough for him to run about in. It was certainly very airy. No attempt was ever made to give him a polished appearance. His coat always looked rough.

'Stockwell was looked after by a big, burly, good-hearted Yorkshireman named Mat Veal. Mat was a great walker, and when the weather was fine he used to take Stockwell a fifteen-mile tour along the by-roads in the district, leaving the stud at five o'clock in the morning. He followed a regular route, along which were four or five public houses. The landlords of these houses knew to a minute when Mat would be passing, and always had a pint of beer ready for him. He quaffed the lot without blinking. Stockwell must have seen a good many barrels full of ale go down the old fellow's throat!

'To the best of my recollection, Stockwell never had more than forty mares in any of the eight seasons he spent at Hooton. The majority of Mr Naylor's own mares were put to him every year, and a reference to the Foal Lists, published in the Racing Calendars in those days, shows that he bred ninety-nine foals by Stockwell.'

In 1863 Stockwell was advertised as standing at Hooton, but there was no mention of the fee; we are merely told that his 'subscription is full'. According to *Bell's Life*, however, the fee demanded for Stockwell's services was 100 guineas. His name is missing from the advertisements from 1864 to 1869 inclusive. Griffiths says that during the latter part of that period Mr Naylor exacted a fee of 200 guineas, an unheard-of figure in those days. All went well with Stockwell until the year 1869; he then suddenly dropped from the second place he had occupied in the Sires list in 1868 to the ninth place. Mr Naylor apparently came to the conclusion that he could no longer afford to 'ride the high horse' he had been doing, for in 1870 Stockwell was advertised at £75, or three mares the property of one owner at £200. Unfortunately the season of 1870 had not run its full course when Stockwell met with an accident which caused his death.

'I witnessed the accident' Griffiths told me. 'Stockwell had a habit of rearing when brought into the covering yard, and as he did so on this occasion he overbalanced and fell on to his tail. His spine was broken about four joints from the crupper and the rectum was pierced. It will hardly be believed, but when he got up he proceeded to serve the mare waiting for him – old Alec Taylor's Hetty – and the following year she produced a chestnut colt, who died when a few days old. We got Stockwell back to his box and tried to communicate with Mr Naylor, who was away yachting at the time. Day after day went by without our hearing anything.

Stockwell died about the ninth day, May 5th. It was the gamest death I ever saw. He had walked continually round his box, and at the end gave a loud neigh and dropped to the ground dead. I never saw a man so cut up as old Mat Veal. He cried for nearly a week. I heard him say in a sobbing voice: "I'd as soon 'ave lost our 'Ria," which was not exactly complimentary to his wife, Maria. Mat afterwards went to Lord Ellesmere's stud at Worsley.

'I have never seen, and never expect to see, so grand a horse as Stockwell. Both his hind legs were white up to his hocks, and he had a big blaze on his face. His coat was a beautiful golden chestnut, which deepened in tone as he got older. Here and there were dark spots, which were said to come from Eclipse, to whom he traced in several of his lines. He had great size (measuring over 16 hands), splendid bone and rare quality. I am bound to say, however, that he was not blessed with the best of tempers; indeed, he was a bit of a savage. So commanding was he in stature that he would hardly have looked out of place had one seen him between the shafts of one of the big drays they use in Liverpool. Mr Naylor was greatly distressed when he heard of Stockwell's untimely death. And well he might be, because the horse was only twenty-one years old, and as fresh and vigorous as ever. When Mr Naylor got home he had Stockwell's body exhumed and sent the skeleton to one of the Museums in London.'

I drew the attention of Griffiths to a description of Stockwell which I found in *Bell's Life*. The writer stated that Stockwell had 'a fine, large, expressive head, with a soft eye. His neck was extraordinary, and resembled very closely in height of crest the old pictures of the Godolphin Arabian. His shoulder was thick and loaded at the point, but his neck and hindquarters were perfect.' 'Quite right,' remarked Griffiths, 'except that I should say he had a fine bold eye. Some of Stockwell's offspring were too big to be of much use for racing and many had large, fiddle-shaped heads. A notable example was Glenlyon, who went to America in 1879. He was a great coarse fellow, with a head like a bass fiddle.'

Be that as it may Stockwell's sons and daughters were phenomenally successful on the Turf. From first to last he was credited, as the result of sixteen seasons at the stud, with 412 living foals, giving that extraordinary average of twenty-seven per season. We may assume that a certain proportion of those foals never raced; nevertheless, Stockwell could claim to be the sire of 208 individual winners, so that more than 50 per cent of his offspring were 'money spinners'. Those 208 individuals won on the flat in Great Britain and Ireland, 1,150 races worth £358,989. The value of the stakes won, was, of course, easily eclipsed by St Simon's total of £552,391; but it must be remembered that the average value of races was infinitely lower in Stockwell's day than in St Simon's. The difference will be made plain by the statement of fact that 415 of the races won by Stockwell's offspring were of less value than

£100; some even went below £20. It is, therefore, the more amazing that
in 1866 Stockwell headed the sires' list with an aggregate of £61,391.
That total still stands as a record. St Simon approached it very nearly in
1896 with £59,731. Hermit's best total was £47,311 in 1882, and
Galopin's best was £45,516 in 1889. The following is Stockwell's record
as a sire of winners:

	Races won	Value in £	Position in Sires List
1858	2	270	—
1859	29	4,645	13
1860	51	18,201	1
1861	89	24,029	1
1862	89	33,336	1
1863	77	20,978	2
1864	86	28,708	1
1865	88	33,502	1
1866	132	61,391	1
1867	113	42,521	1
1868	96	28,596	2
1869	47	8,349	9
1870	62	9,186	7
1871	60	10,174	4
1872	53	12,233	2
1873	21	13,650	2
1874	38	5,679	10
1875	12	2,871	—
1876	5	670	—
	1150	358,989	

The following is a list of the sons and daughters of Stockwell who were
'placed' in the classic races:

1860

St Albans – Won the St Leger

1861

Lady Ripon – Second in the Oaks.
Caller Ou – Won the St Leger.

1862

The Marquis – Won the Two Thousand Guineas.
Caterer – Second in the Two Thousand Guineas.
Knowsley – Dead-heated for third place in the Two Thousand Guineas.
Bertha – Second in the One Thousand Guineas.

The Marquis – Second in the Derby.
The Marquis – Won the St Leger.

1863

Lady Augusta – Won the One Thousand Guineas.

1864

Historian – Third in the Two Thousand Guineas.
Tooi Tooi – Third in the One Thousand Guineas.
Blair Athol – Won the Derby.
Blair Athol – Won the St Leger.

1865

Regalia – Won the Oaks.
Regalia – Second in the St Leger.

1866

Lord Lyon – Won the Two Thousand Guineas.
Monarch of the Glen – Second in the Two Thousand Guineas.
Repulse – Won the One Thousand Guineas.
Lord Lyon – Won the Derby.
Savernake – Second in the Derby.
Rustic – Third in the Derby.
Lord Lyon – Won the St Leger.
Savernake – Second in the St Leger.

1867

Achievement – Won the One Thousand Guineas.
Achievement – Dead-heated for second place in the Oaks.
Achievement – Won the St Leger.

1868

Athena – Second in the One Thousand Guineas.
Athena – Third in the Oaks.

1869

Belladrum – Second in the Two Thousand Guineas.

1871

Bothwell – Won the Two Thousand Guineas.
Noblesse – Third in the One Thousand Guineas.
Noblesse – Second in the Oaks.

1873

Gang Forward – Won the Two Thousand Guineas.
Doncaster – Won the Derby.

Gang Forward – Dead-heated for second place in the Derby.
Wild Myrtle – Second in the Oaks.
Doncaster – Second in the St Leger.

1874

La Coureuse – Second in the One Thousand Guineas.

Stockwell, all told, had eighty-two horses to represent him in the five classic races, and they started 128 times, as the following details show: Derby runners, 30; St Leger runners, 27; Oaks runners, 28; Two Thousand Guineas runners, 20; One Thousand Guineas runners, 23.

In 1862 Stockwell actually had what must be the record number of fifteen three-year-olds considered by their owners good enough to compete in the classics, and seven of them ran in the Derby. It will be seen that by him there were three winners of the Derby, six of the St Leger, four of the Two Thousand, three of the One Thousand, and one of the Oaks. Here is a list of Stockwell's offspring that were the most successful on the Turf:

	Races won	Value £
Lord Lyon	17	26,325
Achievement	16	22,442
Blair Athol	5	13,283
Athena	18	11,660
The Marquis	7	11,050
Caller Ou	49	11,014
St Albans	5	8,518
Gang Forward	10	7,591
Doncaster	4	7,510
Belladrum	10	7,390

With reference to Lord Lyon and Monarch of the Glen, Griffiths says: 'I helped to foal these two horses. Their dams were in adjoining boxes at Hooton. Lord Lyon was born two minutes before the "Monarch", so it was very curious they should finish first and second in the Guineas, with Lord Lyon just in front of the other.'

'Stockwell' wrote a contributor to *Baily* in 1866 'like Aaron's rod threatens almost to swallow up every other strain of blood. This cannot but be deplorable; its consequences will, I am sure, be most seriously felt before many more years have passed over our heads. Breeders, like the impulsive and hysterical public, fond of excitement, run after any popular idol. I by no means wish to disparage Stockwell, and willingly admit his sireship of many good performers; but considering that he has had the cream of the "Belgravian mothers" for some years past he has got an unprecedented number of bad horses; and were it not that scurry stakes and half-mile spins were so much in vogue, his name would not, I am confident, occupy so prominent a position in the financial ledger as it does. Staying and struggling endurance in good company are not as a rule the chief characteristics of Stockwell's progeny.'

One's first inclination is to assume that that paragraph was inspired by prejudice. It has already been shown that more than half of Stockwell's offspring were winners, so the accusation that he sired an unprecedented number of bad horses had no foundation. What is the extraordinary suggestion that his progeny were for the most part mere sprinters, and many of them unable to stay more than half a mile? I have analysed the performances of his winners in 1862 (this year was a random selection), and find that the average distance of the races they won that season was almost exactly twelve furlongs. Of course, I did not bring into reckoning races won by the two-year-olds; but had I done so the average would have been but slightly reduced, for there were only six of them. The individual winners that season numbered thirty (excluding two-year-olds), yet only seven took part in races over 4 to 6 furlongs, and but two of the races were half-mile affairs. How false, then, would be the impression of Stockwell's character as a sire by anyone who accepted the estimate put forth in *Baily*.

That the offspring of Stockwell matured quickly is more or less proved by the fact that 116 of his 208 individual winners were successful as two-year-olds. In five seasons he was represented by ten or more juvenile winners; in 1867 by no fewer than fifteen. From the time he went to Hooton, Stockwell sired 202 foals, of which 99 were out of mares owned by Mr Naylor. It was in 1869, when twenty years old, that Stockwell begat Doncaster, the son who has been chiefly instrumental in carrying on the line. When Doncaster was foaled, his dam, Marigold, was ten years of age.

In 1866, Mr Naylor, departing from his usual practice, sold his yearlings, or most of them. The Marquis of Hastings took a batch of six, paying, Griffiths thinks, £1,000 each. They were all by Stockwell. One was Mameluke who won a £2,000 race at Stockbridge; another, Belfast, winner of a £300 race, and there was also Housemaid, who received £250 forfeit in a Match. But the pick of the bunch was the chestnut filly Athena, who, as a two-year-old, won for the Marquis ten races worth £5,860. She then became Mr Padwick's property, and for him won, as a three-year-old, six races worth £5,665, in addition to running second in the One Thousand Guineas and third in the Oaks. Athena was then acquired by Lord Rosebery, and won for him two little races in 1869. After that there is no further trace of her, either in Racing Calendar or

Stud Book. Isola Bella, the dam of Isonomy and Fernandez, was by
Stockwell and bred at Hooton.   BBR–1915

The Death of Hamburg

*The death of Hamburg, a foal of 1895 by Hanover–Lady Reel, by
Fellowcraft, was reported in the* Review *of 1915. One of the
American Turf's finest achievers, winning sixteen of his twenty-one
starts, everything that could be said about a top-class horse was said
about him – he had speed, stamina, courage and the ability to carry
heavyweights against the best. His dam, Lady Reel, was no less than a
half-sister to the mighty Domino, a peerless racehorse whose influence
continues to permeate illustrious pedigrees. Hamburg was by Hanover,
a Belmont Stakes winner and leading sire in the US four times, 1895
through 1898. Hamburg, who started his stud career at Marcus
Daly's Bitter Root Stud in Montana before becoming the property of
the Whitney family, headed the US sire list in 1905. That was the last
time a male-line descendant of Herod was to gain this distinction.
Indeed, the Hanover branch through Hamburg almost immediately
began its disappearing act. This, despite the fact that Hamburg sired
Belmont winners in Burgomaster and Prince Eugene and a Preakness
winner in Buskin. Things might have been different had Burgomaster
remained in the US as he sired several quality performers in Chile.*

*Although his male line dissolved, Hamburg's name lives on through
several daughters, including the storied Frizette, dam of the French One
Thousand Guineas victress, Banshee, third dam of the renowned classic
winner and sire Tourbillon; and responsible for one of the most productive families in French racing. Frizette was also second dam of Myrtle-
wood, one of the most important American-bred matriarchs in breeding
in the twentieth century. Other daughters of Hamburg included
Hamburg Belle and Artful, both triumphant in the Futurity Stakes, as
well as Jersey Lightning, dam of the superior racing filly, Regret, the
first filly to capture the Kentucky Derby.*

September 11th – The well-known and highly successful American
thoroughbred stallion, Hamburg, died at Brookdale Farm, near Red
Bank, New Jersey. By Hanover out of Lady Reel, by Fellowcraft, son of
imported Australian, he was bred in 1895 by the late Mr James E.
Kittson. In this instance the term 'bred' means that Mr Kittson was
responsible for the mating of sire and dam, because Lady Reel had

passed into the possession of Mr C. J. Enright before Hamburg was foaled at the Elmendorf Farm, Kentucky. Mr Enright afterwards sold the mare to Captain Sam Brown, of Christianburg, Kentucky, who, in turn, passed her on to Mr Marcus Daly.

When still a foal, Hamburg was sold for £160 to Mr John E. Madden. As a two-year-old the colt displayed brilliant form. He ran that season in sixteen races, won twelve, finished second three times and third once. The value of the Stakes he won was £8,400. It was in December of that year that Mr W. L. Powers, acting for Mr Marcus Daly, gave Mr Madden £8,000 for Hamburg. Carrying his new owner's colours, the colt won four of his five races as a three-year-old, and so getting back £4,600 of the money he had cost. He retired from the Turf in August of his three-year-old days, and was sent to Mr Daly's big Stud, the Bitter Root, in Montana. There he had his first season as a stallion in 1899. Mr Daly died in 1900, and on January 30th, 1901, Hamburg came up for sale in New York. The late Mr James B. Haggin, and the late Mr William C. Whitney, were the chief contenders for the son of Hanover. Mr Whitney prevailed with a bid of £12,000. Sir Ernest Cassel had cabled from England an offer of £10,000. From that time until Mr

Hamberg.

Whitney's death in 1904, Hamburg was at La Belle Stud in Kentucky. He then came under the hammer once more in New York, to be bought for £14,000 by the deceased owner's son, Mr H. P. Whitney, and in his possession Hamburg remained until the end.

Summing up the career of Hamburg, in the course of a letter to the *Thoroughbred Record*, Mr W. L. Powers writes: 'It is a matter of record that he could carry weight and run at any distance. It is sufficient to say that he had few equals and no superiors, and, as he was a horse of great constitution and fine temper, it is probable that his fame will survive so long as the *American Stud Book* is published.'

In *The American Thoroughbred*, by Charles E. Trevathan, there appears the following tribute:

'Hamburg's place as a racing animal is among the real cracks of the Turf. He was, during his racing days, a commanding individual, who always enlisted the admiration of the crowd when he paraded for a race, on account of his exceedingly fine appearance. He had for dam that noted mare Lady Reel, and he was quite as good a one as ever came out of that brood-mare family, which traced back to the famous imported Galopade, the founder of another great broodmare line in America, which is frequently spoken of as the Dance Family.

'Hamburg did everything that could be asked of a first-class racehorse. He showed speed, stamina, courage, and weight-carrying ability of the highest order. No distance was too long or too short for him, and, moreover, his soundness of wind and limb, together with his robust constitution, perfect disposition, and excellent blood lines, are combinations which should bring about great results at the stud.'

In 1905, the year after the foregoing was written, Hamburg headed the list of winning stallions in the United States with thirty winners of sixty races worth £31,630. Good as many of his sons have been, they are surpassed by his daughters, one of whom, Artful, is regarded as probably the greatest race mare ever seen in the States. Hamburg mares have, moreover, been very successful at the stud. Thunderer, the winner of this year's Futurity, is out of one of them – Jersey Lightning, and so is Regret, winner of this year's Kentucky Derby. Hamburg's name is likely to remain prominent in the winning sires' list for several more years, because in 1913, 1914, and again this year, Mr H. P. Whitney put all his best English-bred mares to him. Here is Hamburg's pedigree:

		Hindoo	Virgil
			Florence
	Hanover		
		Bourbon Belle	*Bonnie Scotland
			Ella D.
HAMBURG			
(Br. h. 1895)		Fellowcraft	*Australian
			Aerolite
	Lady Reel		
		Mannie Gray	Enquirer
* Imported.			Lizzie G.

The fact that Lady Reel was mated with Hanover in 1894 was partly due to a mischance. In January of that year, Mr Kittson gave Colonel Milton Young £8,200 for Lady Reel, thirteen other mares, and three yearlings. It was a part of the bargain that if any of the mares proved barren or produced a dead foal, Mr Kittson had the right to send such mare or mares to one of Colonel Young's stallions. It so happened that Lady Reel's foal was stillborn, and Mr Kittson thereupon sent her to Hanover, the result being Hamburg.

Hamburg's stock appeared on the English Turf for the first time in 1909. Here they have won sixty-eight races worth £18,420. The best of them was the gelding Borrow, who won the Middle Park Plate. Other good performers were New York, Top o' the Morning, Major Jinks, American Beauty, Lady Frivoles filly, Hillside III, and Kiel.

BBR–1915

Cyllene

When Cyllene, a chestnut foal of 1895 by Bona Vista from Arcadia by Isonomy, died in 1925, 'thirty years had passed over his head', wrote the correspondent for the **BBR**. *The letter also noted that he was 'a fine, handsome horse, with exquisite quality and an angelic temperament'. It was also 'known that he had first-rate racing abilities before he carried silk for the first time'.*

Unfortunately, Cyllene, a very late May foal, was undersized for a long time and he did not have any classic engagements while a stablemate, who never reached the races, did. It was left to Cyllene to prove himself a horse of classic stature by winning nine of eleven starts, including an Ascot Gold Cup, against very formidable company.

His stud record underscored the classic talent he did not have an opportunity to expose. Cyllene began his stud career in 1900 and remained in England until 1908. He had been sold to the famous Ojo de Agua Stud in Argentina previously, but was committed to meet his 1908 contracts. Although he started off rather slowly at stud, by the time he left England he had sired four Derby winners, although only one was known at the time. This was Cicero, first home in 1905. Then there was Minoru (1909), Lemberg (1910) and the filly Tagalie (1912), conceived the same year he left for Argentina. Tagalie also secured the One Thousand Guineas.

Cyllene also sired three winners of the Argentine Derby, giving him seven Derby winners in two major racing countries.

Cyllene's daughters also excelled as producers. Bellavista foaled the

Derby winner Captain Cuttle; Maid of the Mist bred Oaks winner Sunny Jane and Two Thousand Guineas and Eclipse winner Craig an Eran; Mistrella produced the Oaks winner Beam, and Belle Vue foaled the French Oaks winner Doniazade. Cyllene's daughters also bred several Argentine classic winners.

The year after leaving England, Cyllene was Britain's champion sire and he repeated that success in 1910.

However, Cyllene's most enduring contribution to breeding was as the sire of Polymelus, a talented but less than classic performer who was to become a champion sire five times and also sired this century's most dominant influence, Phalaris.

Had Cyllene remained in England his illustrious record as a sire would have become only more so as his record in Argentina attests. However, the legacy that he did leave the world of breeding has been handed down from generation to generation with ever-increasing influence.

St Simon

Granted that the unbeaten Eclipse was the most influential sire of the eighteenth century, it is also granted that the unbeaten St Simon, 'the prototype' of the modern-day thoroughbred, was the most influential sire of the nineteenth century. Bred by Prince Batthyany in 1881 he was a bay son of Galopin from St Angela, by King Tom. Never really tested, he defeated Hermit's mighty performer, the older Tristan, by twenty lengths in the Ascot Gold Cup and was considered at least 21 lb superior to Harvester, the Derby dead-heater of that year – 1884. His trainer, Mathew Dawson, rated him 14 lb better than Minting, another classic performer of that era and thus, by comparison, superior to another unbeaten wonder horse, Ormonde.

If St Simon was unrivalled as a racehorse, such also held true of his stud career. The magnificent fillies Signorina, Memoir and Semolina were all in his first crop. Almost immediately it became almost impossible to secure a subscription to him. His fillies, which also included the peerless La Fleche, were generally considered to have been marginally superior to his colts, but it was through his sons, the Gimcrack winner Chaucer; The Derby, St Leger, Ascot Gold Cup and Eclipse winner Persimmon; and the Goodwood Cup hero, Rabelais, that the St Simon male line, surviving a threat earlier in this century, is still flourishing, although the Chaucer branch is being menaced once again.

St Simon, who died at the age of twenty-seven in 1908, was champion sire nine times, seven in succession. The records he set as a sire had never been approached previously.

Mr Huby, in the Review *of 1916, described his conformation as follows:*

'In conformation St Simon was almost perfect. His shoulder was a study. So obliquely was it placed that it appeared to extend far into his back, making the latter look shorter – and as a matter of fact it was shorter – than any horse's back I have ever known. With a shoulder so placed there is little wonder that he showed such marvellous liberty of action. His forelegs, too, were beautifully set on, and his bone was hard and good. In colour he was a rich brown, with a small star on the forehead. Except that he had a few grey hairs about his hind heels and fetlocks, he possessed no other white marks.'

Probably nothing much can be added to what has already been written about St Simon, who at the sale after his breeder's (Prince Batthyany) death, was bought by the Duke of Portland as a two-year-old for 1,600 guineas – 'the best bargain ever secured in the history of the Turf', writes Mr Sydenham Dixon. On both Turf and Stud career he was the best horse of the last century and probably the greatest horse of all time. There are still some people alive who believe that St Simon was prevented from running for the Derby by reason of the death of his nominator, Prince Batthyany. Even Sir George Chetwynd, in his Racing Reminiscences, *falls into this error.*

St Simon was entered for the Two Thousand but was not entered for the Derby or the St Leger, Prince Batthyany's only entry for the 1884 Derby being Arbaaces, a colt by Galopin–Penitent, who never ran at all.

There is no doubt whatever that St Simon could have won 'the Triple Crown' with the greatest of ease. Before the St Leger, in a gallop, he gave 20 lb and a hollow beating to The Lambkin, who won the St Leger, with Scot Free, the Two Thousand winner, and Harvester beaten off. Harvester, third to Scott Free in the Two Thousand, dead-heated with St Gatien for the Derby, but the latter on Derby Day was in nothing like the form that he showed later in the year when he won the Cesarewitch in a canter under 8 st 10 lb.

It is a pity that the two 'Saints' never met, but great a horse as St Gatien undoubtedly was when at his best, I think there can be no question that St Simon was the better of the pair over any distance. As Mr Sydenham Dixon has written; 'All courses were alike to St Simon; not only was he never beaten, but he was never even made to gallop, and

I do not suppose that Mathew Dawson himself had any idea how good he really was.'

If both Turf and Stud career be taken into account, the only horse I can find to compare with St Simon is Eclipse, who, like St Simon, won every race without being asked to do his best, and the stud careers of both may be said to have been of equal brilliance.

FAREWELL to Moorlands and enter Welbeck! When I went to Welbeck in 1895 the stallions holding court there were St Simon, Carbine, Donovan and Raeburn. What a splendid quartet! So much has been said and written concerning the great champion St Simon that it seems almost like attempting to gild refined gold for me to try and add anything to what has already been said and written. However, as I was so intimately connected with him for quite a number of years I may perhaps be able to give a few particulars worth recording.

Quite a score of years ago there lived in the neighbourhood of Welbeck a Doctor O'Connor, who owned a few thoroughbreds, and who was a very enthusiastic lover of horses. Whenever he looked over a yearling and expressed the opinion that it was 'sure to race' he would add, 'But it is the innate vitality that is everything.' And surely there is sense in this remark, which he delivered in the true Irish brogue. If ever a horse possessed 'innate vitality' it was St Simon.

Taking a casual look at him, as he stood leisurely in his box, nobody would have credited him with standing more than 15.3, but the moment he was led outside there was quite a transformation. There he looked, and in reality was, 16 hands, with a carriage that a king might have envied. I always thought there was something superior, both in his action and contour, to anything I had ever noticed in any other horse. He used to move along just as if made of elastic, and although he has transmitted many of his good qualities and good looks to his offspring, I doubt whether we shall ever again gaze upon such a perfect model as he was.

There was a time when St Simon had the reputation of being an evil-tempered horse, but he was nothing of the kind. Indeed, he might almost have been described as a good-tempered horse. His high-strung temperament (which he possessed to a degree) necessitated the most gentle and patient treatment. It was no use trying to compel him to do this, that or the other. Had brute force been used in his management war would have been declared at once, and either one side or the other would have had to 'go down'. It would not have been St Simon while there was a breath of life left in him.

St Simon lived to the good old age (for a horse) of twenty-seven years, and his death took place on the 2nd of April, 1908. He was returning from exercise just as sprightly and handsome as ever that morning, and so far as appearances went, might have lived for years. When, within twenty yards of his stable door, as he was passing over a soft sandy patch of ground, he suddenly dropped, and in less than twenty seconds his heart ceased to beat.   BBR–1916

A Prophecy re Phalaris

In the Review *item which follows, it is noted that Phalaris, then aged four, had picked up 131 lb in the St Ives Handicap at five furlongs, conceding from 15 to 47 lb (!) to his fifteen rivals while winning in a 'fine display'. The items also vouchsafed the opinion that 'Phalaris inspires one with the belief that he is destined to make a great name for himself when he goes to the stud.' How prescient! The item also mentions a winning race by Lord Derby's three-year-old filly Nun's Veiling. By Roquelaure, she was a half-sister to Chaucer and Swynford. She did not breed anything too important herself, but did become the distaff ancestress of some classic winners in Italy.*

September 11th–14th – Newmarket 'Fourth Extra' Meeting, and Yearling Sales. . . We were now back on the Rowley Mile. The first day Phalaris gave another fine display by winning the St Ives Handicap (5 f), carrying 9 st 5 lb, and giving from 15 lb to 47 lb to his fifteen opponents. His task was made all the harder by reason of a very long and irritating delay at the starting post. The fourth day Phalaris picked up the St Edmunds Plate, beating Bosket and Fifinella. This was a mile race, and the fifth placed to the credit of the son of Polymelus and Bromus this season. When he made his first essay as a four-year-old last April he finished second to Verdun, who was receiving 22 lb, but he has not been beaten since. From whatever point of view we may regard him, Phalaris inspires one with the belief that he is destined to make a great name for himself when he goes to the stud, and we imagine there will be a rare scramble to secure nominations. Lord Derby had another winner the first day in the three-year-old filly Nun's Veiling, by Roquelaure out of Canterbury Pilgrim. Lord Anglesey's smart filly Wilton, with 8 st 10 lb up, easily beat a big field in the Redmere Nursery.

                                                          BBR–1917

The Death of Bayardo

When that exceptional racehorse Bayardo, a son of Bay Ronald from Galicia, by Galopin, died prematurely in 1917 at the age of eleven, the Review preceded an account of his career with the following:

'The duty of writing the memoir of a famous horse is never a congenial one. A sense of the loss which his death means, not merely to the owner but to all interested in the welfare of the thoroughbred family, inevitably lessens the satisfaction which the endeavour to do full justice to an equine celebrity may engender. That feeling prevails even when the horse has passed the normal span of years; and it is, of course, intensified when he died while still in his prime.'

When Bayardo died in 1917, his son, Gay Crusader, a member of his third crop, had won only the first of his three Triple Crown victories. Another son, Gainsborough, who was to capture the Triple Crown of 1918, had yet to make his appearance as a two-year-old, and his Oaks winning daughter of 1919, Bayuda, was still a yearling. So Bayardo's loss was even more of a tragedy than it appeared at the time. As the Review noted: 'He has died full soon.'

BAYARDO died very suddenly on June 4th at the Manton Stud, near Marlborough. The cause of death was thrombosis, a disease which causes an artery to become clogged by clots of blood. It usually develops without the slightest signs of the coming trouble being shown, and it is always fatal. Curiously enough, it was thrombosis that carried off Comus in Uruguay two or three years ago – curiously because he, like Bayardo, was bred and raced by Mr 'Fairie'. Comus was examined a little while before his death for insurance purposes, and was declared to be in perfect health. Those who saw Bayardo two or three weeks before he died were impressed by the fact that he had never looked better or in more vigorous condition. In his case the disease caused paralysis of his hindquarters, but was all over in a day or two.

A handsome bay horse, Bayardo was by Bay Ronald out of Galicia, by Galopin out of Isoletta. Mr 'Fairie' did himself a wonderfully good turn when he bought the third dam, Lady Muncaster, after she had won eight races and over £3,500 in stakes. Isoletta, her first living foal, was not raced, but did not go to the stud until five years old. She produced three winners right away – Matoppo in 1896, Mahdi in 1897, and Galicia in 1898. When mated with Isoletta in 1897 Galopin was twenty-five years old. He died in 1899. Galicia was, as a two-year-old, tried to be pretty smart, and won a Biennial that season at Ascot. Unfortunately, when competing for the Exeter Stakes a few weeks later she split a

pastern. This mishap seems to have prejudiced her subsequent racing
career; anyway, she never again showed form worth mentioning,
though she ran several times as a three-year-old. She went to the stud in
1902. Mated with Eager, she was barren that season, but the following
year was again put to Eager, and bred, in 1904, the colt Eastern, who
won two races worth £1,696½, and was sent to Belgium in 1908, being
bought at the December Sales that year by Mr Dufour for 400 guineas.
In 1905 Galicia produced Carpathian, by Isinglass. This colt met with
an accident as a yearling and never ran. Then, in 1906 and 1907, came
Bayardo and Lemberg, the one by Bay Ronald and the other by
Cyllene.

Mention has been made of the fact that Isoletta was mated with
Galopin 'just in time'. Her daughter, Galicia, went to Bay Ronald the
very year, 1905, Mr Leonard Brassey sold him for £5,000 to go to
France. Darkie had been to Bay Ronald in 1904, and produced Dark
Ronald as the result of the alliance. That Mr Brassey entertained no
illusions about the son of Hampton and Black Duchess is plain, for he
wrote:

> 'Though Bay Ronald achieved a fair amount of success on the racecourse one
> cannot describe him as having been quite a first-class racehorse. His form was
> certainly somewhat variable, this being accounted for, I think, by the fact that his
> constitution as a young horse was not of a very robust character, and strong
> preparations for long-distance races may have rather taken the steel out of him
> later on.'

Bayardo made his first public appearance as a two-year-old at Ascot in
1908. As recorded by Mr Watson in his book *Galicia, her Forbears and her
Offspring*, he had won a trial at Manton the previous week in splendid
style. Nevertheless, odds of 7 to 1 were laid against him for the New
Stakes at Ascot, Perola (giving him 4 lb, and who won the Oaks the
following year), Perdicaas and Sunflower II all being better favourites.
Bayardo won easily. This was the first of seven races he won that season,
in which he was unbeaten. The only race that year in which his display
was not all that could be desired, was the Middle Park Plate, in which he
seemed to have to make a big effort to beat the late Sir Daniel Cooper's
smart filly Vivid (sister to Flair and Lesbia) at weight-for-sex. We have a
lively recollection of the performance, because immediately the contest
was over we wagered our friend Sydney Pardon a silk hat that Bayardo
would not finish in the first three in the Derby! On our part the bet was
made in a spirit of bravado. We miraculously won the hat, and, in
normal times, it is worn once a year – at Ascot – just for the sake of
hearing Mr Pardon's sarcastic observations. As our readers know, he is a

Bayardo.

worshipper at the shrine of Galopin, and his admiration for Bayardo was intensified by the fact that the dam was a daughter of his idol. He tried to lure us into making another bet of the same sort over Lemberg when that horse was a two-year-old, but we sternly declined the invitation. The Bayardo 'topper' looks none the glossier in his eyes because of the prudence we then exercised.

Bayardo was not quite himself the day he won the Middle Park Plate. His trainer, Alec Taylor, had noticed in the morning that he was very listless, though there was nothing definitely wrong with him. The lassitude had passed off by the evening, and a fortnight later the colt gave a sparkling performance in the contest for the Dewhurst Plate.

Bayardo was, of course, the winter favourite for the Derby, and when he went forth to compete for the Two Thousand Guineas odds of 13 to 8 were laid on him. To the amazement of the public he finished fourth only to Minoru, Phaleron and Louviers. Obviously there was something amiss, but no explanation was forthcoming. 'Audax' now tells us that he had been seriously troubled in his feet and also in his digestive organs. He was much better on Derby Day, but even then not quite himself. At Epsom Sir Martin started favourite at 3 to 1; Minoru was backed at 7 to 2, and Bayardo at 9 to 2. Minoru won by a short head from Louviers, with William the Fourth third, Valens fourth, and Bayardo a poor fifth.

There is a well-known and very successful picture of the finish of this memorable Derby showing Maher, who rode Bayardo, *standing* up in the stirrups. And that, in fact, was his attitude, for he had ceased to persevere a long way from home. Sir Martin stumbled on to his nose when making the descent to Tattenham Corner, and, on returning to the Weighing Room, Maher said he could not estimate the number of lengths Bayardo lost in the confusion which momentarily resulted from the mishap. It was the general opinion that, but for the accident, Sir Martin would have won, but Maher rather led one to believe that, with a clear course, Bayardo would have been successful. If we bring into focus the complete racing careers of all the competitors in the Derby of 1909 there is no gainsaying that Bayardo was easily the best. Fortunately he subsequently had abundant opportunities of demonstrating afresh the great qualities with which he was endowed, so that when the time came for him to go to the stud his failures in the Guineas and Derby had almost been forgotten, and were certainly not weighed in the balance against him.

From Derby Day until August of the following year Bayardo carried everything before him. As a three-year-old he won eleven races, including the Eclipse Stakes and the St Leger. The following season he won the Ascot Cup and three other races. His victory at Ascot was a brilliant one. There were no fewer than thirteen runners for the Cup that season – the biggest 'field' the event had ever produced, although it dates back to 1807. Sir Martin, and the French horse Seasick II, were among the competitors. Maher was content to wait with Bayardo until about six furlongs from home. Then the colt was given his head, and in a few moments was completely master of the situation. He went on to win in a canter by four lengths from Seasick II. Bachelor's Button alone of all the Ascot Cup winners had covered the two and a half miles in faster time by just one-fifth of a second. Had he been pressed towards the finish as Bachelor's Button was by Pretty Polly, Bayardo would assuredly have set up a time record. No supplementary evidence of that sort was, however, required to convince the onlookers that they had witnessed a wonderfully fine performance by an exceptionally fine horse. It had been no commonplace display. Bayardo's superiority over many fancied rivals had been proved in a manner that left not the slightest loophole for quibbling. Mr 'Fairie' had recently refused an offer of £56,000 for his horse. What was the colt worth after his triumph at Ascot? Be the valuation what it might, there was never the slightest chance of the horse being sold so long as Mr 'Fairie' had any say in the matter.

And now we come to Bayardo's defeat in the Goodwood Cup of that year. He was beaten a neck by the three-year-old Magic (now in America) to whom he was giving 20 lb more than weight-for-age. Many have been the reasons advanced for this totally unexpected result – how unexpected may be gauged from the fact that 20 to 1 was laid on Bayardo. The long grass on the course has been blamed, and so have the waiting tactics employed by his jockey, Maher. The truth probably is that the son of Bay Ronald was set a task just a little beyond his powers. Felix Leach had given Magic a long and strong preparation for the Goodwood Cup, and he was so thoroughly fit that those immediately associated with him did not hesitate to help themselves liberally to the long odds the bookmakers were very willing to lay them. The defeat of Bayardo was, naturally enough, greatly regretted by his admirers – the more so because this was his last appearance on a racecourse. The following year, 1911, he began his career at the stud. Here is a summary of his racing performances:

Two Years Old (1908)

	£
Won New Stakes, Ascot, 5 f	1,817½
Won National Produce Stakes, Sandown, 5 f	4,359
Won Richmond Stakes, Goodwood, 6 f	652
Won Buckenham Stakes, Newmarket, 5½ f	1,500
Won Rous Memorial, Newmarket, 5 f	730
Won Middle Park Plate, Newmarket, 6 f	2,505
Won Dewhurst Plate, Newmarket, 7 f	1,477

Three Years Old

4th Two Thousand Guineas, Newmarket, 1 m	—
5th Derby, Epsom, 1½ m	—
Won Prince of Wales's Stakes, Ascot, 1 m 5 f	2,150
Won Sandringham Foal Stakes, Sandown, 1¼ m	1,724
Won Eclipse Stakes, Sandown, 1¼ m	8,870
Won Duchess of York Plate, Hurst Park, 1¼ m	979
Won St Leger, Doncaster, 1¾ m	6,450
Won Doncaster Stakes, 1½ m	475
Won Champion Stakes, Newmarket, 1¼ m	900
Won Lowther Stakes, Newmarket, 1¾ m	470
Won Sandown Foal Stakes, 1¼ m	1,724
Won Limekiln Stakes, Newmarket, 1¼ m	425
Won Liverpool St Leger, 1½ m	630

Four Years Old

	£
Won Newmarket Biennial, $1\frac{1}{2}$ m	$573\frac{1}{2}$
Won Chester Vase, $1\frac{1}{2}$ m	1,595
Won Ascot Gold Cup, $2\frac{1}{2}$ m	3,700
Won Dullingham Plate, Newmarket, $1\frac{1}{2}$ m	830
2nd Goodwood Cup, $2\frac{1}{2}$ m	—

Total (22 races won) £44,534

Summary

	Races won	Value £
Two Years Old	7	$13,038\frac{1}{2}$
Three Years Old	11	24,797
Four Years Old	4	$6,698\frac{1}{2}$
	22	£44,534

Lemberg, it may be mentioned, won twelve races worth £41,694, while Eastern, as we have stated, won £1,696½. The three sons of Galicia accounted, therefore, for stakes amounting to £88,124½. This total exceeds that credited to Mowerina by over £5,000. The Germans reckon that Festa's produce won £84,500 on the Turf, but they include 'place' money in the total. Anyway Galicia is an easy first.

'Audax' informs us that Mr 'Fairie' had a great affection for Bayardo 'owing to his funny little ways'. His ways were both funny and stupid. Towards the end of his three-year-old career he manifested, at Newmarket, a strong aversion to the rule that he should pass the front of the stands on his way to the starting post. After turning the corner of the paddock he no sooner saw the straight ten furlongs in front of him than he stuck his toes in the ground and refused to budge. Eventually the difficulty was solved by taking him round the back of the stands. To the best of our recollection this performance had to be gone through every subsequent time Bayardo was called upon to race over the Rowley Mile. As to his 'funny ways', Bayardo had a curious eccentricity in that he would never allow any covering on his ears. His half-brother, Eastern, displayed the same objection. In the case of Bayardo it was probably accounted for by the fact that when walking he constantly moved his ears backwards and forwards in unison with his stride.

Bayardo's fee the first few years he was at the Manton Stud, under the management of Alec Taylor, was 300 guineas. When breeders were hard hit by the war, Mr 'Fairie' very properly reduced the fee to 200 guineas. Nominations were eagerly sought after. Bayardo did not, however, start any too well. True, he got a good filly in his first season in Major Astor's Good and Gay, but she was his only winner in 1914. The next year he was represented in the Winning Sires' list by a couple of two-year-olds only – Ali Bey and Bay d'Or. Ali Bey was decidedly useful, but a few more like him had been expected. Some allowance must, of course, be made for the curtailment of the racing programme that season. Last year Bayardo cut a much better figure, for he could claim ten winners of eleven races worth £4,082½ – a total which sufficed to place him eleventh in the Sires' List. Three of the winners were two-year-olds, one being Gay Crusader, who this year won the Two Thousand Guineas. Many of his two-year-olds have yet to come out, and behind them are two actual 'crops', and another to follow next year. Who shall say what his record as a stallion may be when, a few years hence, we are able to review it as a whole? He has died full soon. We commiserate with Mr 'Fairie' on the loss he has sustained; and with Mr Alec Taylor too. The latter probably feels the passing of Bayardo more than anyone.

BBR–1917

What Might Have Been – the Loss of Maiden Erlegh

One may only speculate, but 'what if' the young stallion Maiden Erlegh had not been lost at sea in 1917? Kentucky's Claiborne Farm through several generations of the Hancock family has been a vital influence in improving the breed in the United States. One such effort was being made when Mr A. B. Hancock purchased the Polymelus horse Maiden Erlegh. The latter, a foal of 1909, had accounted for the mile Rous Memorial when in training and, as a young stallion, had proven sure with his mares; his first crop showed him siring promising young stock. Additionally, he belonged to the distaff family responsible for The Tetrarch as well as the Belmont winner Peter Pan and other important performers. Would he have written another glorious chapter for Claiborne? Of course, one will never know, but the potential was there and for that reason alone he should be remembered.

THE IMMUNITY which had attended the shipment of thoroughbreds from England to America ever since the war started was unhappily broken early in September. A large and popular vessel, which was carrying a specially valuable consignment of bloodstock to New York, was torpedoed off the south coast of Ireland and sank. Regrettable as the loss of the horses was, the disaster was made infinitely worse by the loss of about thirty members of the crew.

The most notable of the animals on board was the stallion Maiden Erlegh, by Polymelus out of Plum Tart, by Persimmon. Representing Mr A. B. Hancock, of Paris, Kentucky, the British Bloodstock Agency bought him for 3,300 guineas at the dispersal sale of Mr Musker's stud at Newmarket in July. A week or two before he was shipped the Agency were approached by a breeder in England who wanted to know whether Mr Hancock would resell Maiden Erlegh at a profit. A cabled inquiry brought back the answer that the son of Polymelus was not for sale. If only the fate that was to overtake him could have been foreseen! And so there vanished a stallion whose arrival in America was eagerly awaited. Bred as he was, and under the skilful management of Mr Hancock, Maiden Erlegh could scarcely have failed to make a success at the stud in Kentucky. Among all the stallions in England there were few surer foal-getters, and the youngsters by him born this year, as the result of his first season, showed great promise. A man who had known Maiden Erlegh from his foalhood days exclaimed, when he heard that the Atlantic had swallowed him, 'I would have given all I can see rather than this should have happened. Never in my life have I been so fond of a horse.'

BBR-1917

A First Lady – Several Times

GAINSBOROUGH, thirteenth winner of the English Triple Crown in 1918, was the first Derby winner to RUN in the name and colours of a lady – Lady James Douglas. The 1901 Derby hero, Volodyovski, was bred and owned by Lady Meux, but she had leased him, first to Lord Beresford and then to Mr William C. Whitney; and it was in the latter's name that he gained classic honours at Epsom. Lady James, who also bred Gainsborough, actually became the first lady to breed, own and run an English classic winner when Gainsborough earlier accounted for the Two Thousand Guineas. Gainsborough's magnificent season also resulted in Lady James becoming the first lady to head the English owner's list. This is all the more remarkable when it is realised that Gainsborough failed to make his reserve when Lady James offered him as a yearling.   BBR-1918

Edward Moorhouse's Comments on Gainsborough

The noun 'apotheosis' is unlikely to crop up very often in writings on racing and breeding in this day. But it was a word used quite appropriately by Edward Moorhouse, one of two directors of The Bloodstock Breeders' Review, *in discussing the classic season of Gainsborough in 1918.*

Moorhouse considered Gainsborough an exalted and glorified example of the finest virtues to be found in the thoroughbred and he put this down on paper after seeing the colt as a two-year-old in 1917. Therefore, after Gainsborough had secured the Two Thousand Guineas and Derby, and before he completed the Triple Crown, seventeen years before Bahram was to emulate him in 1935 and fifty-two years before Nijinsky II was to win those three races again in 1970, Moorhouse wrote of 'the Apotheosis of Gainsborough'.

Like all of Moorhouse's warm and eloquent writing, it should not be hidden away and forgotten in some collector's item volume of a **BBR***, but exposed to posterity once again.*

Gainsborough, of course, reflected his own racing quality at stud. If he was worthy of deification as a racehorse, he was worthy of whatever is the next step up as a progenitor. Himself the son of Bayardo, a classic winner and superior sire, out of the Oaks winner Rosedrop, by the classic winner and splendid sire, St Frusquin, he sired another thoroughbred deity in Hyperion, along with other influential sons such as Solario and his numerous classic-producing daughters.

GAINSBOROUGH has fulfilled the promise of his youth. In a Diary note last year we declared that we had seldom seen a better-looking two-year-old; and that we might hazard the guess that Gainsborough would win the 'New Derby'. He was at that time officially rated 4 lb below Scatwell, and the equal only of Violinist. There was, however, that 'something' about the son of Bayardo and Rosedrop that induced one to give him the preference over his contemporaries. His name has now been added to the lists of winners of the Two Thousand Guineas and the 'New Derby'.

When the spring came round one's faith in Gainsborough was, let it be confessed, a little shaken. He had not risen in stature like some of his rivals. Today he measures barely 15.3. We are not, however, among those who crave for big thoroughbreds. It is always long odds on a colt standing 15.3 proving a better racehorse than one a hand higher. There are, of course, exceptions that prove this rule. All this notwithstanding, Gainsborough would, perhaps, have pleased the more if he had grown, say, another inch.

But there was more than lack of size to occasion disquietude when Gainsborough was seen for the first time this season at the Craven Meeting, a fortnight before the Two Thousand week. As a rule a prominent candidate for the Guineas is given a 'trial run' in the Column Produce Stakes or the Craven Stakes, both of which races are decided over the Rowley Mile. It was in the former that Gay Crusader last year heartened his admirers by giving 11 lb to Coq d'Or and running him to three-parts of a length by way of preliminary to his victory in the Two Thousand. Gainsborough, however, was not engaged in these or other mile races at the Craven Meeting. The one he was entered for was the Severals Stakes, a five furlong sprint. Under the best of circumstances this could not afford a conclusive test of his abilities as a competitor for classic honours. It so happened that the race was run on a miserably wet, cold day, with the going very heavy. There was little opportunity of inspecting Gainsborough in the paddock, but what we did see of him made an unfavourable impression. 'Nothing like ready', was the verdict of the majority of critics. That estimate was borne out by the betting and by the race. Though carrying no more weight than many of his opponents, to whom he would have been called upon to give lumps in a handicap last autumn, he had very few backers at 10 to 1, and ran unplaced to Syndrian (Sunder–Polkerris), Soap Bubble and Happy Iola.

A wonderful change came over Gainsborough during the ensuing fortnight. He was probably just ripe for the improvement that manifested itself. A change for the better in the weather, with an accompaniment of welcome sunshine, helped materially, no doubt. And then there were his further gallops, and a formal trial in which he readily defeated Blink, Thermogene and other stable companions. Mr Gilpin estimated that by freely sweating during her railway journey from Newmarket to Sandown Park the day before she ran her first race, Pretty Polly improved many pounds. It may, then, safely be concluded that the work Gainsborough did during the fortnight before the Two Thousand brought him on very appreciably. Certain it is that when he was seen stripped for the fray just before he left the paddock to go to the Rowley Mile starting post he excited the admiration of those who had decried him at the previous meeting. Judged by looks alone Gainsborough excelled all his opponents. In the race his success was scarcely for an instant in doubt after the first six furlongs had been covered. For a little more than another furlong the big and somewhat leggy Somme Kiss pressed him tenaciously, though even at that stage Gainsborough always seemed to have a little the better of the struggle. Towards the finish this advantage became more and more decided, until finally Gainsborough was a length and a half in front.

The result of the contest was popular for several reasons, but perhaps the one that weighed most was the fact that Gainsborough is owned, and was bred by Lady James Douglas. Never before has one of our classic races been won by a horse bearing a lady's colours. This alone made the occasion a notable one. During the last few years Lady James Douglas has been carefully establishing her stud at Harwood Lodge, near Newbury. It is about a couple of miles away from Lord Carnarvon's stud at Highclere, where Valens, Volta and Rivoli are quartered. Mr William Clark's stud is also in the immediate vicinity. Lady James has steadfastly aimed at breeding bloodstock of a quality second to none. Her policy has from the first been shaped to that end. She resolved, however, to breed for sale, and has, I believe, made it a practice to send

Gainsborough.

all her yearlings into the auction ring. Gainsborough was no exception to this rule.

Along with other of the Harwood Lodge yearlings, the son of Bayardo and Rosedrop went to the Newmarket Sales in 1916. We related what happened in our Diary, when commenting on Gainsborough's victory in the Autumn Stakes at headquarters last September. In one particular the story then told needs revision. We stated that a reserve of 2,500 guineas was placed on him when he went into the ring. The actual figure was 2,000 guineas. Bayardo had not then made the big name as a sire that he subsequently acquired. Had Gainsborough been offered a year later three or four wealthy owners would have wanted him, and the bidding might easily have gone to 4,000 or 5,000 guineas.

Gainsborough, however, passed out of the ring unsold. But he was still for sale. His owner was really rather glad that he had not 'gone' for 2,000 guineas, and by way of emphasising her satisfaction promptly raised the reserve price to 2,500 guineas. Someone came along and offered 2,300 guineas. But Lady James refused to accept that sum, and the end of it all was that the colt went to College Leader, of Newmarket, to be trained. When, shortly afterwards, Leader had to go into the Army, Gainsborough was transferred to Manton – to the stable, that is, where his sire and dam had been under the care of Alec Taylor. Further offers were then made. They were, however, below the reserve (which had again been raised), and Lady James refused to abate a penny from her price. 'I would not,' she writes to us, 'take 4,000 guineas for him then, and would take nothing for him now.' After Gainsborough had won his race last autumn Lady James was so pestered by people who wanted her to put a price on the colt that she was strongly tempted to ask permission to display a notice in the paddock reading: 'Gainsborough is not for sale at any price!'

The future career of Gainsborough is already planned. When he quits the racecourse he will spend the stud seasons at Manton, and the remainder of his time at Harwood Lodge. It is perhaps just as well that he does not know of the halcyon days awaiting him, or he might be in a hurry to 'quit'.

Many readers have no doubt wondered how Gainsborough came by the name he bears. Is he called after the famous portrait painter? The answer is in the negative. Lady James Douglas tried hard to find for him a name appropriate, euphonius and suggesting his breeding. Even Dr Platt will, no doubt, admit that the quest was an extremely difficult one. At last Lady James abandoned the search, took up a railway guide, and turned over page after page until she came to Gainsborough. 'That will do,' she thought; 'it sounds well and has a good masculine ring about it.'

Gainsborough's Win for Lady James Douglas

Two Thousand day – May Day – was dull, and there was a searching wind blowing from a northerly quarter. The going was, however, in perfect condition for racing, the turf being dry but springy.

For several days it had been expected that either Polyscope or Scatwell would start favourite. Last September, after winning the Autumn Stakes at Newmarket, Gainsborough was regarded as a highly promising candidate for classic honours, and if he had made his first public appearance as a three-year-old in the Two Thousand he would probably have had a bigger following than he actually secured; but the indifferent display he gave when competing for the Severals Stakes at the Craven Meeting frightened many who had inclined to him. He then looked unready; indeed, so much stress was laid on this point that those not self-reliant enough to form their own judgment, assumed he could not have come on sufficiently in a fortnight to be able to compete successfully with his Guineas rivals.

It would, perhaps, have been more to the point to stress the fact that the 'Severals' was only a five-furlong affair, and to recall the rapid improvement Gay Crusader, from the same stable, made after his defeat in the Column Produce Stakes at the 'Craven' last year. The week before the Two Thousand Gainsborough, in a trial, beat Blink half a length, with Thermogene and others behind; and when finally stripped for the race showed himself the pick of the 'field' on looks.

Polyscope seemed very 'fine drawn'. Scatwell was all right until one came to his fore feet. They were bandaged, for he was suffering from split hoofs. In the circumstances it was wonderful how he maintained his prominent position in the market. Somme Kiss, a big Sledmere-bred colt, carried the full confidence of his trainer, Sam Pickering, who had frankly declared that whatever beat him would win. He was quite right. After six of the eight furlongs had been traversed the race became a two-horse affair, and during this concluding stage Gainsborough always looked a winner, resolutely though Somme Kiss struggled on. By finishing third Blink more or less realised the Manton expectations. Had he not lost ground at the start he would assuredly have been much nearer the winner, even if he had not completely reproduced the home trial form.

This is the first time that an English classic race has been won by an animal bred, owned *and raced* by a lady. Gainsborough, a product of the splendidly-appointed Harwood Stud, near Newbury, Berkshire, was foaled on January 24th. Allusion is made on another page to the fact that when Lady James Douglas offered him for sale as a yearling he failed to make his reserve.

TWO THOUSAND GUINEAS, of £100 each, half forfeit, for entire colts and fillies foaled in 1915; colts 9 st, fillies 8 st 9 lb. The winner received £5,100, the second £400 and the third £200. Rowley Mile. Run May 1st.

Lady James Douglas's b. c. GAINSBOROUGH by Bayardo–Rosedrop, 9 st	J. Childs	1
Mr C. T. Garland's ch. c. SOMME KISS, by Sunstar–Stolen Kiss, 9 st	J. H. Martin	2
Major W. Astor's br. c. BLINK, by Sunstar–Winkipop, 9 st	R. Colling	3
Sir W. Cooke's Rocksavage, 9 st	F. Fox	4
Major D. McCalmont's Roideur, 9 st	B. Carslake	5
Sir A. Black's Jack Point, 9 st	W. Earl	6
Mr J. B. Thorneycroft's Thermogene, 9 st	O. Madden	7
Sir W. J. Tatem's Scatwell, 9 st	W. Langford	8
Sir W. J. Tatem's Sky-rocket, 9 st	A. Wheatley	9
M. M. Calmann's Bapaume, 9 st	A. Whalley	10
Mr S. B. Joel's Polyscope, 9 st	S. Donoghue	11
Mr W. Raphael's Shenley Boy, 9 st	J. Evans	12
Mr H. W. Rudd's Arwin	G. Hulme	13

Winner bred by his owner; trained by Mr Alec Taylor at Manton.

Betting: 7 to 4 agst. Polyscope, 3 to 1 Scatwell, 4 to 1 Gainsborough, 8 to 1 Somme Kiss, 100 to 7 Bapaume, 100 to 6 Blink, 20 to 1 Rocksavage, 33 to 1 each Thermogene, Roideur and Shenley Boy, 50 to 1 Sky-rocket, 100 to 1 each Arwin and Jack Point. Place Betting: 5 to 4 on Gainsborough; others one fourth the winning prices. Won by a length and a half, six lengths between second and third. Time: 1 min 44 3-5 secs.

When the tapes went up Bapaume swerved and cannoned into Shenley Boy, while Blink started slowly. For about six furlongs Somme Kiss, in the centre, led; Gainsborough on his right, and Polyscope on the extreme left, were well up. Nearing the Bushes Polyscope began to lose ground; a small blood vessel in his nose had burst. A quarter of a mile from home Gainsborough deprived Somme Kiss of the lead. Descending the slope to the Dip these two drew right away from the others, but the farther they went the more pronounced Gainsborough's superiority became, and he finally scored quite easily.

GAINSBOROUGH
(B. c., foaled Jan 24th, 1915)

Bayardo (B, 1893)	Bay Ronald (B, 1893)	Hampton (B, 1872)	Lord Clifden (B, 1860)	Newminster / The Slave
			Lady Langden (Br, 1868)	Kettledrum / Haricot
		Black Duchess (Br, 1886)	Galliard (Br, 1880)	Galopin / Mavis
			Black Corrie (Bl, 1879)	Sterling / Wild Dayrell m.
	Galicia (B, 1898)	Galopin (B, 1872)	Vedette (Br, 1854)	Voltigeur / Mrs Ridgway
			Flying Duchess (B, 1853)	Flying Dutchman / Merope
		Isoletta (B, 1891)	Isonomy (B, 1875)	Sterling / Isola Bella
			Lady Muncaster (Ch, 1884)	Muncaster / Blue Light
Rosedrop (Ch, 1907)	St Frusquin (Br, 1893)	St Simon (Br, 1881)	Galopin (B, 1872)	Vedette / Flying Dutchman
			St Angela (B, 1865)	King Tom / Adeline
		Isabel (Ch. 1879)	Plebeian (B, 1872)	Joskin / Queen Elizabeth
			Parma (Bl, 1864)	Parmesan / Archeress
	Rosaline (B or Br, 1901)	Trenton (Br, 1881)	Musket (B, 1867)	Toxophilite / West Australian m.
			Frailty (Br, 1877)	Goldsbrough / Flora McIvor
		Rosalys (Br, 1894)	Bend Or (Ch, 1877)	Doncaster / Rouge Rose
			Rosa May (Br or Bl, 1887)	Rosicrucian / May Queen

BBR–1918

The Death of Old Man

'GREATEST and most popular of Argentine racehorses, a champion of champions, and a veritable wonder at stud.' These are terms of praise bestowed by an admirer on the stallion Old Man who, after a brief illness, died at El Moro Stud early in August (1918). They are not undeserved. He was a remarkable horse, and has left an enduring impression on the Argentine thoroughbred.

Old Man was foaled at the Haras Viejo in 1901. He was one of four Argentine Derby winners sired by Orbit, a son of Bend Or, and his dam, a French-bred mare, Moissonneuse, was by Dollar. As a two-year-old she raced without success. At three, she ran nineteen times and won three selling events from 7 to 11 furlongs. 'As a four-year-old she again worked hard for her corn' taking part in twenty-one races, most of them over hurdles. She won six of these and the same number again at age five years old before being shipped to South America.

Many breeders have a prejudice against mares whose chief recommendation is that they were successful jumpers. If there is justification for that attitude, Moissonneuse can always be cited as an exception to the rule. Old Man was her seventh foal.   BBR–1918

The Bonnie Scotland 'line'

As the following article, appearing in the BBR *of 1918 will show, a Mr Eugene Leigh, acquainted with racing and breeding both in Europe and the US, believed that if the male line of Bonnie Scotland, imported into the US in 1857, had received the opportunities it deserved, it would have 'eclipsed the records of Domino and Commando'. Bonnie Scotland, a winner and classic-placed in England, was a year-younger half-brother to Blink Bonny, heroine of both the Derby and the Oaks and dam of, among others, Blair Athol, a Derby and St Leger winner and superior sire. Bonnie Scotland, by Iago, was out of Queen Mary, a family founder, by Gladiator. Bonnie Scotland's foals included the Belmont winner and champion George Kinney; Bourbon Belle, dam of the Belmont winner and superb sire, Hanover; and of the Saratoga Cup winner, Bramble.*

When Leigh also expressed the opinion that the Bonnie Scotland blood was equal in America in influence to that of St Simon in England and that of Musket in Australia, it was not entirely parochial pride.

Bonnie Scotland was twice the leading sire in America, in 1880 and 1882, two years after his death. As noted, his daughter Bourbon Belle produced Hanover, champion sire in four consecutive years – 1895–1898. His son, Bramble, was not a premier sire, but his foals included the 1896 Kentucky Derby winner Ben Brush, the champion sire of 1909. Ben Brush's foals included the Travers winner Broomstick, champion sire of 1913, 1914 and 1915, and the Belmont Stakes winner Sweep, champion sire of 1918 and again in 1925. Broomstick still has the highest percentage – 25 – of stakes winners from name foals of any stallion ever to stand in the US since such records were kept.

Yet, as secure and as flourishing as this Bonnie Scotland influence appeared early in the century, it had all but disappeared by mid-century. But now, more of Mr Leigh and his story.

IT WILL probably be news to many readers of the *Review* that Eugene Leigh, who was so successful as a trainer in England and France, and is now again following that calling in America, was years ago a breeder of bloodstock in the States. In the course of a recent interview he recalled some of his experiences as a breeder. For the descendants of imp. Bonnie Scotland, who was by Iago out of Queen Mary, he has a tremendous admiration. Indeed, he goes so far as to express the belief that that horse, his son Bramble, and his grandson Ben Brush, 'founded a family in the United States that stands out by itself, and equals the St Simon blood of England, and that of Musket in Australia'. Bramble, he avers, suffered from lack of opportunities as a sire. If given the chance Domino and Commando obtained, Mr Leigh thinks he would have eclipsed their records. The late General W. H. Jackson, who had Bramble at the Belle Meade Stud, was, we are told, a breeder for revenue only. 'He would throw away a stallion who did not get grand-looking sellers, but was never known to shoot a bad brood mare.'

One of the best sons of Bramble (whom Mr Leigh owned) was the horse Clifford, and he was bred 'in spite of' General Jackson, who had decided to send the dam, Dutchess, to the English Derby winner, Iroquois. 'Fortunately,' says Mr Leigh, 'I was at Belle Meade the day she had to be covered, and after a long argument, assisted by the old negro stud groom (the only friend Bramble had on the place) the General was reluctantly persuaded to allow Dutchess to be mated with Bramble.'

Mr Leigh bought Roseville, the dam of Ben Brush, at Guttenburg, and sold her, when carrying Ben Brush, to Colonel E. Clay.

'When Ben Brush was sold as a yearling, Dick Brown asked me not to bid against him. I compromised by agreeing to buy the colt in partnership. After he had been broken and tried an offer of £1,000 for him was reported to me. I telegraphed, "Don't sell. Will give you $3,000 for your half." Brown stuck to him. He was named Ben Brush after the superintendent of the Brooklyn race track. Old man Brush disliked dogs on the track. One day a bunch of trainers to whom Brush was always complaining about their dogs, asked him why my dogs enjoyed the privilege of the course, and even of the lawn. The old man looked at them and said "Not a damn one of you fellows ever named a Ben Brush."'

Mr Leigh bought Bramble for $8,000, and declares that that sum was just $7,992 more than any breeder in Kentucky would have given for him. He sent him to the Belle Meade Stud. The horse was duly advertised, but his owner never collected a single fee. In fact, he found it difficult to get owners to send mares free of charge! Bob Baker accepted one and got Beula, a good race mare and the grandam of one of Mr W.

K. Vanderbilt's best horses in France. Colonel W. S. Barnes offered to send a mare and pay the fee, but by that time Mr Leigh was anxious not to break a 'record' and so gave the Colonel a service on condition that he (Leigh) should choose the mare. The one selected was Maid of Balgowan, and she bred Prince of Melbourne. Bramble met with an accident the second season he was at stud and thereafter it was difficult to get him to serve a mare. 'In the short time I was a breeder," added Mr Leigh, 'I bred Ben Brush, Irish Lad (son of a Bramble mare), Ballyhoo Bey and Admiration; Ildrim and Vulcain, both out of Bramble mares; and many other winners.' Ben Brush went into the late Mr J. R. Keene's stud near Lexington, where, under the management of Major Daingerfield, he was given excellent chances, and made very good use of them. Later he became the property of Mr J. N. Camden, and as we go to press the news comes that he died early in June at that gentleman's stud at Versailles, Kentucky.

Horses of this family have, says Mr Leigh, always trained like good soldiers, done their work well, put their noses in the feed box, and kept them there as long as there was an oat left. There was no 'yellow dog' in their blood. If they were small it did not stop them from racing successfully.

With regard to Bonnie Scotland, Mr Leigh states that he was taken to Illinois when there were not ten thoroughbred mares in that State. Everything he sired could run. He was eventually bought by General Harding, then owner of the Belle Meade Stud. There were a few good, stout American mares there, and the horse got a fair chance. His yearlings never brought high prices, but they won good money on the Turf.

Towards the close of the interview, Mr Leigh strongly condemned the practice adopted by many American breeders of keeping their stallions 'private'. He considers it 'a crime' and the greatest drawback the breeder of thoroughbreds in the States has to contend against. Breeders were willing to pay stallion fees but not to accept favours. Owners of stallions should remember that they might possess fifty mares not one of which would nick with their 'private' horses. They should not, he maintains, act like selfish boys with a toy. Not only do they ruin their stallions; they disgust breeders.   BBR–1918

Recollections of Lexington

Lexington is unique in the annals of the Turf in America. He was the champion sire for a record fourteen years in a row and sixteen years over all. No other sire has come remotely close to the 'Blind Hero of Woodburn'. He was also a superior racehorse in the 1850s and his match races, especially with Lecomte, were the things that the history of the American Turf is made of. Unfortunately, his sire line ceased to exist about a hundred years after the son of Boston was foaled in 1850. Many believe that intense inbreeding caused the genetic mischief when breeders thought one couldn't have too much of a good thing.

Jacob Pincus, an American-born trainer who enjoyed considerable respect and success at his profession both in England and the United States, gave his recollections of this remarkable horse to the **BBR** *shortly before his death in 1918. Pincus, who conditioned the American-bred Iroquois (Leamington) to capture the Derby and St Leger of 1881, had enormous admiration for Lexington and the words of 'Old Pincus', appearing in the* **BBR***, offers an intimacy with that grand stallion that beautifully illuminates his historic feats both at stud and on the racecourse.*

'Lexington was always a free-running horse, but not at all crazy. He was a bright bay, with a large star and a snip on his nose of considerable size, and four white feet, the white not amounting to "stockings", but coming above the ankles all around. He stood a little short of $15\frac{3}{4}$ hands, had a clean and bloodlike neck, finely arched throttle; fine head tapering to the muzzle, ears which were thin, beautifully shaped and well carried, but not especially short; a deep, full chest, oblique shoulders and grandly muscled arm and stifle.

'His loin was splendid, and so were his quarters; but one peculiarity struck me especially the moment I had a chance to look him over, and that was he had the longest and most elastic pasterns I had ever seen under a horse. His style of running was also peculiarly impressive. He ran with his head extended, and he carried his tail rather high, so that he presented a top outline which was straight and level from his nose to the tip of his tail.

'Like all fast horses I remember to have seen, Lexington had straight hind legs, although they were not so straight as those of The Ill-Used, Kingfisher and Henry of Navarre. He was a quick beginner, but, as there were practically no races at less than a mile in those days, we made no effort to make quick beginners of our horses. We were more concerned in what they would do when making a finish in the stretch, and that was where Lexington never failed to make good. Then, too, many of our great races were matches, big stakes or sweepstakes, in which there were seldom more than four starters at the most, and, of course, there was no struggle to get out in the lead to escape interference.

'I look upon Lexington as one of the greatest thoroughbreds ever foaled, great on the turf and great in the stud. The weights carried in those days were not heavy, and the time would not compare with that made nowadays, but Lexington always did whatever was asked of him, and he was meeting great ones.'   BBR–1918

Remarkable Instances of Longevity

A LETTER from Kenya Colony to a reader of *Horse and Hound* mentioned that 'we have just shot our Arab stallion, aged thirty-five, and we were showing a yearling colt by him last week out of a mare that must be over twenty-four. . . The old Arab was the finest specimen of his breed I have ever seen.'

On reading the foregoing particulars, Mr J. Fairfax-Blakeborough wrote to *Horse and Hound*, stating that he had a record of a grey polo pony, Old Peter, who went from England to the Argentine, died there in 1915, aged forty-seven, and was reported to have sired seventeen foals the year he died. All his teeth had gone, so he had to be fed on mashes.

So far as longevity is concerned, Old Peter was easily beaten by Old Bill, the property of the late Mr Petrie, of Edinburgh. This horse lived to be sixty, his age being vouched for by Professor Owen Williams, whose father attended the horse.

Mr Fairfax-Blakeborough also states that until recently there was on a wall at Norton Conyers, near Ripon, a painting of a coach horse named Jolly, beneath which was the inscription, 'Born 1760, died 1822'. A century ago the Mersey & Irwell Navigation Company presented to the Manchester Natural History Society the head of 'Old Billy', who lived for sixty-two years. At Richmond (Yorkshire) in 1836 there was a trotting match between two horses aged thirty-six and twenty-six. The Tartar mare (by Tartar, dam by Mogul) is stated by Pick to have gone on breeding till she was thirty-four years old.   BBR–1927

Obituary of Dark Ronald

In the closing paragraph of its obituary on Dark Ronald, who died in 1928, the BBR *said: 'Five years after his arrival in Germany, Dark Ronald was at the head of the sires in that country, and at the head he remained for several seasons. It can, indeed, be said that he was a greater force than any stallion imported into Germany before or after him, and his influence will be apparent for many years to come.' Over fifty years after that was written, it is still true. His influence in Germany is, of course, legendary. It is also significant throughout the thoroughbred world. Consider that in his few seasons at stud in England he sired the line-founding Son-in-Law; the capable sire Dark*

Legend; Magpie, an enormously successful sire in Australasia; as well as the One Thousand Guineas winner Vaucluse, dam of the Doncaster Cup winner Bongrace, herself a notable producer; and, of course, the family-founding Popingaol, dam of five major stakes winners, including the Oaks heroine Pogrom and the superior racing filly Book Law, successful in the St Leger and numerous other fixtures.

Indeed, of all the sires England has sold, with subsequent regret, Dark Ronald belongs with the most missed. Surely, he would have left an even more profound and enduring legacy.

For that very reason, Dark Ronald is not as well known, probably, as he should be, among English-speaking people, and that is why the BBR's account of his career is presented here.

TWENTY-THREE years old, Dark Ronald was, at the end of March, or early in April, destroyed at the Titerfeld Stud in Germany. He was a handsome brown horse by Hampton's son, Bay Ronald, out of Darkie, by Thurio from Insignia, by Blair Athol. The late Mr Edward Kennedy bred him in Ireland, and sold him as a yearling at Doncaster to Sir (then Mr) Abe Bailey and Mr Donald Fraser for 1,300 guineas. The colt was handed over to Mr Francis Cobb to be trained. In his first race as a two-year-old he appears, according to the betting, to have been but little fancied. It was the Hurst Park Foal Plate of £1,135, for which Quelpart, then an unbeaten winner of four races, started favourite. Dark Ronald won, but in a similar race at Lingfield shortly afterwards he finished second, beaten three lengths by Little Flutter, to whom he was conceding 15 lb.

No more was seen of him that season: he was, indeed, a four-year-old when he re-appeared on the Turf. His long absence was due to training troubles of one sort or another. In the spring of his three-year-old days he seemed to be sound, but broke down while undergoing a preparation for the Derby, for which he was considerably fancied. Early the following season he came out again, cured of his ills, but made no show in the race for the Newbury Spring Cup. Evidently little was expected that day, for odds of 25 to 1 were offered against him. A few days later he won a £100 Plate at Leicester over ten furlongs, and was then put by until the summer. During the interval he developed form so good that those associated with him believed that, with only 7 st 2 lb to carry, he was certain to win the Royal Hunt Cup at Ascot. He was, accordingly, backed to win a big sum, and, starting favourite, duly did what was required of him.

Dark Ronald.

His next race was the Princess of Wales's Stakes at Newmarket. This also he won, and his success had a special interest and importance. Four of his opponents had run in the previous year's Derby – Primer (who finished second, beaten two lengths by Signorinetta), Royal Realm, White Eagle and Perrier. Apart from the fact that the stable companions White Eagle and Royal Realm changed places, these four exactly reproduced in the race for the Princess of Wales's Stakes the form they had shown in the Derby, and the distance was the same. Primer again finished second, and that he was in ripe condition could be inferred from the fact that two weeks earlier he had won the Hardwicke Stakes at Ascot. Dark Ronald beat him much more easily than Signorinetta had done at Epsom.

Dark Ronald's only other race was the Doncaster Cup, for which he started favourite to be beaten half a length and three-quarters of a length by Amadis and Roi Hérode; but as he practically broke down towards the end of the contest, no attention need be paid to the failure. It was generally believed at the time that he would have won readily but for the misfortune that overtook him. For a while there was some hope that he could be got sound again, but by the middle of October the idea of keeping him in training for another season was abandoned, and he was packed off to Mr Donald Fraser's stud at Tickford Park. His fee was fixed at £98. The value of the four races he won was £8,239.

Barely had the first of his stock appeared on the Turf than his sale to the Prussian Government was announced. English breeders received the news with regret. His loss was felt still more keenly when that other good son of Bay Ronald, Bayardo, died prematurely in 1917. There can be little doubt that the trend of subsequent events, as regards both racing and breeding, would have been appreciably different if Dark Ronald had remained in England. He did well enough during the four seasons he spent at Tickford Park to have ensured his being mated with some of the best mares in the country in the years that followed.

During those four seasons he sired winners of $81\frac{1}{2}$ races, worth £32,440. Among the winners were the brothers Ambassador and Brown Prince (both now in the US), Son-in-Law, Vaucluse (winner of the One Thousand Guineas), Magpie (beaten a head in the Two Thousand by Gay Crusader), Dark Legend and other good ones. Dark Ronald's sons here named have all done well at the stud. Magpie went to Australia, where he quickly became one of the leading sires. After a trip to India, Dark Legend came back to France, where he has gained a satisfactory reputation at the stud, siring the winners of the French Two Thousand Guineas and the Oaks in 1928 and the winner of the One Thousand Guineas and the Oaks in 1927.

Dark Ronald's fame as a sire of winner-producing mares stands high in England and Ireland. The daughters he left behind when he went to Germany in 1913 have so far bred winners of 191 races worth £106,171. The most notable are Popingaol, dam of the classic winners Pogrom and Book Law; Vaucluse, dam of Bongrace; Excelita, dam of Lex and Ceylonese; Cissy Brown, dam of Cistercian; Dark Flight, dam of The Night Patrol; and Pretty Dark, dam of Southern and grandam of Tiffin.

Five years after his arrival in Germany Dark Ronald was at the head of the sires in that country, and at the head he remained for several seasons. It can, indeed, be said that he was a greater force than any stallion imported into Germany before or after him, and his influence will be apparent for many years to come.   BBR–1928

Obituary of Polymelus

As the twentieth century is about to run out the clock, less and less is known about many of the shapers of the breed whose influence has persevered manifestly throughout this century. Take Polymelus, for instance. Foaled in 1902, this son of Cyllene from Maid Marian, by Hampton, was a sometimes accomplished and other times a less accomplished racehorse. He won eleven of thirty-one starts, including the Champion Stakes, but was never considered of true classic quality. Nevertheless, he was England's champion sire five times, was second twice and third on another occasion. And, of course, he sired the century's quintessential sire – Phalaris.

Of Polymelus, his life and his times, there is need of a refresher course. That was brought to life in the BBR of 1924 on the occasion of Polymelus's death. It bears repeating, so it is presented here.

AFTER BEING a martyr to rheumatism for five years, and gradually losing condition all the time, Polymelus was mercifully 'put away' at the Maiden Erlegh Stud on March 24th. A very good racehorse, he became a great sire. In five seasons he was at the head of the list of stallions; in two other years he was second.

Bred in 1902 by the Earl of Crewe, Polymelus was a big, leggy bay horse by Cyllene out of Maid Marian, by Hampton out of Quiver. Maid Marian was half-sister to Memoir, winner of the Oaks and St Leger, and to La Flèche, winner of the One Thousand, the Oaks and St Leger. One of a batch of yearlings sold at the Hampton Court Stud in 1886, Maid Marian was bought by Mr F. Lawson for 400 guineas. She was born the year before Memoir, and three years before La Flèche. Had she come after instead of preceding those famous sisters we may be sure that her history would not have been quite what it was. Maid Marian was, in fact, regarded as a very ordinary individual until the exploits of Memoir changed the position and caused her to be treated with considerable respect. Mr Lawson raced her seven times as a two-year-old, chiefly in selling plates. She won none of them, though more than once starting favourite, but was twice placed second. Her last race – for she ran as a two-year-old only – was one at Manchester in the autumn, the winner of which had to be sold at the upset price of £50. She was unplaced. Her owner, Mr Lawson, afterwards claimed one of the seven runners, and Mr Lawrance, owner of the winner, claimed Maid Marian on behalf of Dick Marsh, who thus got her for £150.

A few days later Mr Francis Luscombe bought Maid Marian from

Marsh for £300. The mare produced her first foal in 1890, and, in the autumn of that year, after her half-sister Memoir had won the St Leger, Mr Luscombe sold her to Major J. E. Platt for £3,000. There is an amusing sequel to that transaction. Some twenty years ago Mr Luscombe gave a dinner at the Windham Club to several of his racing friends. The company fell to talking of horses that had been bought cheaply and later sold at big prices. Nobody had recalled any startling case when Mr Luscombe joined in by stating he thought he had himself done some which beat anything they had just heard. He then told of his purchase and sale of Maid Marian, but merely called her 'a mare'. 'What mare?' somebody asked. Curiously enough, Mr Luscombe could not at the moment remember her name. Lord Carnarvon, however, came to the rescue, and said it was Maid Marian. Instantly Lord Marcus Beresford chimed in with 'Maid Marian, be damned; made Luscombe you mean.'

Major Platt had Maid Marian at Bruntwood, Cheshire, for seven years. One of her foals produced during that period was Grafton, by Galopin. Baron Hirsch gave 3,800 guineas for Grafton as a yearling, but within a few months the colt had become a bad roarer and he had not been on a racecourse when, the following year, the Hon. Agar Wynne gave 500 guineas for him and took him to Australia. In that warm climate Grafton thrived well and developed into a phenomenally successful stallion. He sired winners of over two thousand races worth £248,771. In four seasons he headed the list of stallions in Australia, and was four times second. He died at Woodlawn, NSW, in 1915. It was in 1897 that Major Platt, having had enough of Maid Marian, sent her to the Newmarket July Sales, covered by Ravensbury. Lord Crewe bought her for 620 guineas. There was no foal from her the following year. In 1896 Maid Marian produced a colt by Kendal, for which the late Sam Darling gave 370 guineas as a yearling, and passed him on to Mr W. C. Wilson. This was Ercildoune, who won three races worth £3,093, including the Duke of York Stakes at Kempton, and then went to Uruguay. As a sire he was a comparative failure.

It has more than once been asserted in print that Maid Marian was a roarer. In the course of a letter written because of a public reiteration of that allegation, Major Platt stated: 'When I bought her as a four-year-old from Francis Luscombe, I stipulated that she was to pass the vet, which she did. She was passed perfectly sound. I never had cause to suspect that she made the slightest noise. It is true her first two colts by Galopin 'went' in their wind, but none of her other stock to my knowledge.'

Polymelus:

Coming now to Polymelus himself, we find him one of the yearlings sent in 1903 to Kingsclere to be trained by John Porter. The colt's first race was the Triennial at Ascot the following year. He had, the previous week, been tried 'useful', and was expected to win, starting favourite at 'evens', but finished second only. His next outing was in the National Breeders' Produce Stakes at Sandown Park. Cicero won that valuable prize; Polymelus was unplaced. At Goodwood, however, Lord Crewe's colt won the Richmond Stakes, and in the autumn was successful at Newmarket in the Rous Memorial and Criterion Stakes. He was unplaced in the Middle Park Plate and the Imperial Plate at Kempton, but ran second in the 'Convivial' at York.

Polymelus reappeared as a three-year-old in the Newmarket Stakes. So little was thought of his chance in that contest that odds of 50 to 1 were laid against him. He finished fifth to Cicero, Llangibby and Signorino. He was engaged in the Derby, but his owner and trainer came to the conclusion that it was not worth while starting him in that event. The reasons for this decision were that there seemed no possibility of his beating Cicero or Jardy, and that twelve furlongs was then too long a course for him. When his racing career as a whole is surveyed it is found that Polymelus produced his best form in the autumn. Those who should know estimate that he was always 10 lb better in the latter part of the season than in the spring.

There may have been a third reason for not running Polymelus in the Derby. He had two engagements at Ascot two weeks later, and it was probably deemed wiser to keep him fresh for those races. The first was the St James's Palace Stakes. In this he ran second to Cherry Lass, on whom odds of 16 to 1 were laid; she had won the Oaks in a canter. The following day Polymelus won the Triennial, beating, by half a length at level weights, Llangibby, an odds-on favourite. In the Eclipse Stakes, five weeks later, Polymelus finished fourth to Val d'Or, Cicero and Llangibby. Cicero gave him 6 lb, the other two 3 lb each. Then, in the Stewards' Cup at Goodwood, he ran a good third, carrying 7 st 1 lb, to Xeny and Thrush. In the Durham Produce Plate at Stockton, over ten furlongs, he gained a meritorious victory, conceding from 10 lb to 28 lb to his four opponents. Another success in the Duke of York Stakes at York was followed by a failure in the Peveril of the Peak handicap at Derby. The following week he finished second to Challacombe in the St Leger, a performance that was the more creditable because he had Cherry Lass and Llangibby behind him. While, therefore, his best distance was a mile or ten furlongs, Polymelus could at times produce a fair amount of staying power. In the Jockey Club Stakes, run over the St Leger distance, he had the misfortune to be opposed by St Amant on the one occasion Mr de Rothschild's horse revealed his real form subsequent to the previous year's Derby, with the consequence that he was beaten three-parts of a length by the son of St Frusquin, but had the odds-on favourite, Gouvernant, behind him.

With a very easy win in the then valuable Gatwick Stakes, Polymelus satisfactorily rounded off his three-year-old career. He was the last winner John Porter saddled, for the old man retired at the close of that season.

Owing to the changes that then took place at Kingsclere, Lord Crewe decided to sell Polymelus. The colt was bought privately by Mr David Faber, for, it was said, £3,000, and went to Baker to be trained. The record of his first six races the following season reads: Unplaced in the City and Suburban handicap, carrying 8 st 2 lb, and starting favourite at 5 to 1; second, beaten a neck, in the Triennial, and unplaced in the Rous Memorial at Ascot; fourth to Dinneford, Llangibby and St

Amant in the Princess of Wales's Stakes, Newmarket; unplaced to Llangibby, Beppo and Wombwell in the Eclipse Stakes; and second, beaten half a length by Aurina (received 30 lb), in the Prince Edward Handicap at Manchester.

About this time Mr Faber decided to transfer his horses to the care of Frank Hartigan at Weyhill. The removal itinerary included, for some reason or other, the sending of Polymelus to the Newmarket First October Sales. Hartigan was instructed to attend the Sale and bid up to 4,000 guineas for the horse – a procedure, be it said, not quite orthodox.

The sale was held on a Thursday morning; the Jockey Club Stakes, in which Polymelus was engaged, was to be run in the afternoon. There happened to be a very small catalogue to dispose of, so there was no need to rush the proceedings. In due course Polymelus entered the ring. To the best of our recollection there were only two bidders, Mr Sol Joel, standing in the doorway on Mr Tattersall's left, and Frank Hartigan, who was on the other side of the rostrum. Eventually the latter got in a bid of 3,800 guineas. Instead of raising it a hundred with a nod, Mr Joel offered 4,000 guineas, and by so doing placed Mr Hartigan in a quandary. His limit had been reached, and as he then knew Mr Faber only slightly, he rather feared what the consequences might be if he exceeded the instructions he had received. Those of us who have had limits 'jumped' in the same way can readily understand Hartigan's perplexity. If Mr Tattersall, who was selling, had known – and perhaps he did know – how awkwardly the young trainer was placed, he could not have been more considerate in the way of deliberation. After a long pause Hartigan bid another hundred. Then Mr Tattersall, moved round to face Mr Joel, who, however, shook his head to indicate that he had retired from the contest.

Mr Tattersall now resorted to argument, a thing we have never known him to do, before or since, when in the rostrum. He began by pointing out to Mr Joel that Polymelus was in the Jockey Club Stakes, and that, if he did not win, there were substantial sums allotted to the second and third horses. 'And then,' continued Mr Tattersall, 'he is in the Duke of York Stakes at Kempton, which, on his running in the Prince Edward Handicap, he looks like winning.' 'Yes,' retorted Mr Joel, 'but they (the bookmakers) won't let you bet on him.' 'Very well,' said Mr Tattersall, 'but Polymelus is also in the Cambridgeshire, which he may win, and you can bet as much as you like on that race.' Thus challenged Mr Joel offered 4,200 guineas. The moment he did so Hartigan turned on his heels and walked away. The hammer fell and

Mr Joel became the owner of a horse who was to yield him what would be regarded by most of us as a handsome fortune.

Conceding more than weight-for-age to his four opponents in the Jockey Club Stakes, Polymelus finished fourth, but he fulfilled Mr Tattersall's bold prediction that he would probably win both the Duke of York Stakes and the Cambridgeshire. In each race his victory was an emphatic one. He had to carry a 10 lb penalty in the Cambridgeshire, which raised his weight to 8 st 10 lb, but he had the prize absolutely at his mercy two furlongs from home. At 11 to 10 he had started the hottest favourite there has ever been in this big handicap. What Mr Joel won on him that day we do not know, but his last bet, £6,000 to £5,000 taken from the late Mr Joseph Pickersgill, was made while the horses were on their way to the starting post. Three days after his success at Kempton, Polymelus won the Champion Stakes. That year he was most certainly 'an autumn horse'. He had never previously shown such great form, and it would have taken a mighty good one to beat him. The following year he was not quite up to the mark when third to The White Knight and Troutbeck in the Coronation Cup at Epsom, but a few weeks later he won the Princess of Wales's Stakes in a canter. That was his last race. His racing record is as follows:

	Races	1st	2nd	3rd	Value
					£
1904	8	3	2	—	2,353
1905	11	4	3	1	5,685
1906	10	3	2	—	3,925
1907	2	1	—	1	4,840
	31	11	7	2	16,803

It can be said of Polymelus that he was a good-tempered horse, though he was apt, especially in his younger days, to give trouble by rearing when at the starting post. Maher, who frequently rode him, declared that he had the longest stride of any horse he had known. Because of that characteristic he easily became unbalanced, which partly explains why he either won his races in a canter or gave a disappointing show.

Polymelus began his career at the stud at Maiden Erlegh, near Reading, in 1908 at a fee of £98. By 1915 he commanded 300 guineas, and in 1922 his fee went up to 400 guineas. Here is his record as a sire of winners:

	Winners	Races won	Value £
1911	4	8	1,437
1912	7	12	7,302
1913	9	17	9,809
1914	17	34	29,607
1915*	10	16	17,738
1916*	9	15	16,031
1917*	12	20	7,369
1918*	13	23	12,198
1919	30	30	22,654
1920	24	42½	40,447
1921	32	47	34,307
1922	20	26½	10,043
1923	16	24½	12,268½
1924	11	19½	21,928
		357	243,138½

* In these years racing was restricted owing to the war.

Polymelus was head of the Winning Sires List in 1914, 1915, 1916, 1920, and 1921, second in 1917 and 1918; and third in 1919.

The figures speak for themselves, and make it unnecessary to conjure up high sounding superlatives with a view to extolling his achievements as a sire. A few further facts may, however, be added. To date he has had 128 individual winners – ninety-five colts and geldings and thirty-three fillies. His sons have won 292 races and £203,141; his daughters sixty-five races and £39,997. The average value of the races won by the males is £695, that of the races won by the fillies £620. The successful colts and geldings have won an average of £2,138; the fillies an average of £1,212. Exactly half of the winners of Polymelus won as two-year-olds. The average distance of the races won by his stock (excluding two-year-old races) is a fraction under 8½ furlongs, so that his offspring have conformed to his own record in this respect. There are probably those who will tell us that one reason why Polymelus was so successful at the stud was the fact that there is not a trace of Galopin blood in his pedigree.

Though not a 'classic' winner himself, Polymelus sired several notable performers in our big three-year-old events. Here is an impressive list:

1912 – Maiden Erlegh, second in St Leger.

1914 – Black Jester, won St Leger and was third in the Two Thousand Guineas. Corcyra, second in the Two Thousand Guineas.

1915 – Pommern, won Two Thousand Guineas, Derby (at Newmarket), and September Stakes (substitute for St Leger run at Newmarket).

1916 – Fifinella, second in One Thousand Guineas, and won the Derby and the Oaks run at Newmarket.

1919 – Dominion, third in the Two Thousand Guineas and second in the St Leger. Glaciale, third in the One Thousand Guineas.

1920 – Cinna, won the One Thousand Guineas, second in the Oaks. Archaic, second in the Derby. Silvern (sister to Fifinella), second in the St Leger.

1921 – Humorist, third in the Two Thousand Guineas and won the Derby.

1922 – Craigangower, third in the Derby.

1923 – Parth, third in the Derby.

1924 – Polyphontes, third in the St Leger.

Winners of over £1,000 sired by Polymelus

COLTS

	Races won	Value £		Races won	Value £
Black Jester	9	15,680	Clarion	4	2,156
Pommern	7	15,616	Gask	3	2,078
Polyphontes	3	14,623	Polycrates	4	2,009
Corcyra	8	10,107	Pandion	3	1,707
Humorist	4	9,571	Pillory	6	1,512
Pomme-de-Terre*	8	8,150	Blue Cloud	3	1,297
Cannobie	3	7,829	Polemberg	3	1,258
Parth*	6	6,283	Polyphonic	3	1,249
Silvern	9	6,277	Golden Guinea	2	1,240
Maiden Erlegh	9	6,265	Polumetis	1	1,108
Phalaris	15	5,478	West Countryman	5	1,058
Evander	5½	5,475	* Also good winner in France.		
Polyhistor	3	4,955			
Dominion	4	4,573			
Polygnotus	6	4,277			
Soranus	6	4,241	**FILLIES**		
Polydipsia	5	3,817		Races won	Value £
Honeywood	6	3,652			
Archaic	2	3,519	Cinna	3	8,811
Tippler	3	3,120	Fifinella	4	5,397
Craigangower	3	3,061	Polkerris	1	3,300
Colossus	3	3,048	Benevente	5	3,212
Pelops	6	2,658	Polly Flinders	1	2,670
Napolyon	4	2,533	Glaciale	4½	2,479
Polyram	8	2,432	Confey	2	1,496
Poltava	4	2,336	Pittendynie	2	1,432
Polyorama	3	2,300	Plymstock	3	1,346
Polymestor	1	2,275	Roman Empress	1	1,100

It is yet too soon to make an assessment of the capacity of Polymelus as a sire of successful broodmares. So far Polemarch (winner of the St Leger), Sicyon, Syndrian, Lacrosse, Oojah and Loddington are the most prominent products of his daughters. The number and value of races won to date by colts and fillies whose dams are by Polymelus are shown in the appended table:

	Races won	Value £
1916	1	197
1917	4	1,023
1918	6½	2,457½
1919	13	4,070
1920	11½	5,957½
1921	26	19,618
1922	24½	8,571½
1923	24½	9,764½
1924	34	14,396½
	145	66,055½

Many of the offspring of Polymelus have gone abroad to race. In various parts of the world they have been successful in nearly two hundred races worth about £67,000. Parth and Pomme-de-Terre both won good races in France; Polycrates and Chantemerle did well in Australia; War Cloud in the US; and Polystome and Polychromy in South Africa.

From the day he arrived at the Maiden Erlegh Stud, Polymelus was always a 'shelly' delicate horse, and required a lot of attention. During his first season he fell over and injured his pelvis or his round bones. For three weeks he was out of action, and the only mare he 'dealt with' that season after the mishap was Winnie K. The result of that mating was Polywin. For the remainder of his career he could never balance himself on a mare without assistance.   BBR–1924

The Sale of Sir Gallahad to the US

A special mystery among the many mysteries in breeding concerns those superior sires who sire dynamic performers of both sexes only to have their enduring influence manifest itself through either their sons or daughters but not both – Sir Gallahad (111), for example. This son of Teddy from Plucky Liege, by Spearmint, exported to the US early in his career, enjoyed incredible success in North America. Four times did he pace the US sire roster. But he did three times better than that as a broodmare sire, accounting for twelve championships, including ten in a row.

With the possible exception of his own brother, Bull Dog, no sire of more importance has ever been brought into the US from France. But while Sir Gallahad's daughters and their daughters and their daughters have waxed eloquently as producers through the generations, the male line of Teddy through Sir Gallahad has all but evaporated.

(Coincidentally, this has also been true of Bull Dog, who became a champion sire and three times a champion broodmare sire and whose son, Bull Lea, topped the sire roster five times before becoming a champion broodmare sire four times.)

Roman, one of the least successful good racing sons of Sir Gallahad, also headed the American broodmare sire list.

The preceding information is offered as a preface to the **BBR** *account of the sale of Sir Gallahad to the US in 1925, including the very prescient forecast of his soon-to-be-realised success.*

IN DECEMBER Sir Gallahad was sent from France to the US. His sale by Mr J. D. Cohn to Mr A. B. Hancock was negotiated by the British Bloodstock Agency. Sir Gallahad, foaled in 1920, is a big and handsome horse by Teddy (son of Ajax and a grandson of Flying Fox) out of Plucky Liege, by Spearmint from Concertina, by St Simon. Concertina's grandam, Frivolity, was half-sister to Polly Agnes, the grandam of Ormonde. As a two-year-old Sir Gallahad won the last three of his five races, and the following season won his first three races, the third being the French 'Two Thousand'. In the French Derby he found the twelve furlongs rather beyond his compass, but even so was beaten two necks only after holding a substantial lead at the end of a mile. His runaway victory in last year's Lincolnshire Handicap is fresh in one's memory, and it will be recalled that two months later Epinard failed by a head to concede him 12 lb over $6\frac{1}{2}$ furlongs. At the end of his four-year-old career Sir Gallahad retired from the Turf, and was at stud last season, readily commanding a fee of 20,000 francs. Bred as he is, and endowed with great racing abilities when running over a mile or less, he appears to be an ideal stallion from the point of view of the American breeder. It will be surprising if, under the able management of Mr Hancock, he does not take high rank as a sire.   BBR–1925

Phalaris Winning Champion Sire Honours in 1925

Upon the occasion of Phalaris winning in 1925 the first of his two sire championships, the BBR *was thorough enough to include his complete racing record in its 'survey' of his career. Considering the inestimable and ramifying impact Phalaris has had on the breed, coupling his complete racetrack accomplishments along with information on his first premiership as a sire would seem to be appropriate.*

WITH MANNA contributing £21,335 to his total, Phalaris this year heads the list of successful stallions. As was the case last year, Swynford occupied the second place. Lord Derby bred, raced, and still owns these two sires. Here are the figures relating to the six leading stallions:

	No. of Winners	Races won	Value £
Phalaris, by Polymelus	20	34	41,471½
Swynford, by John o' Gaunt	14	25	31,976
Sunstar, by Sundridge	34	54	28,316
Gainsborough, by Bayardo	16	30	27,809
Pommern, by Polymelus	26	48½	23,004½
Son-in-Law, by Dark Ronald	22	40	19,627½

Phalaris had from the day Manna won the Derby always looked like gaining the championship. In the middle of July his total was £5,000 bigger than Swynford's. At that time Sunstar, with about £8,000 less than Swynford, was third, followed by Polymelus, Gay Crusader, Son-in-Law (last year's champion), Gainsborough and Pommern. With Polyphontes no longer helping, Polymelus practically stood still during the latter half of the season, while Gay Crusader also made little further progress. When Solario won the St Leger, worth £9,555, Gainsborough, however, leapt into third place, but Sunstar, who had more winners than any other stallion, regained the third place towards the end of the season.

Phalaris has secured the premiership within four years of the first appearance of his stock on the Turf. He had been progressing towards this eminence from the very outset. When he retired to the stud in 1919 there can have been few competent judges who entertained any doubt about his prospects. The confidence he inspired was materially reinforced when, in 1922, Phalaris could claim ten two-year-old winners of £11,820. One of those winners was Lord Derby's colt Pharos, who ran second to Papyrus in the Derby, and subsequently added great lustre to his fame. He also has now gone to the stud, and it may boldly be predicted that he, likewise, will achieve great success as a stallion. The record of Phalaris to date reads:

	Winners	Races	Value
			£
1922	10	18½	11,820
1923	12	20½	12,265
1924	19	36½	22,195
1925	20	34	41,471½
		109½	87,751½

There have so far been forty-two individual winners by Phalaris – twenty-two colts, nineteen fillies, and one gelding. The colts and gelding have won eighty-four races and £77,434½; the fillies twenty-five and a half races and £10,137. Nineteen of the colts and thirteen fillies have won as two-year-olds, an exceptionally large proportion, and one proving conclusively that Phalaris imparts great speed to his offspring. That the son of Polymelus will ever rank as a sire of stayers is in the highest degree improbable, but that he can get horses endowed with stamina, provided

Phalaris.

the mare contributes to that end, has been proved in the cases of Manna and Warden of the Marches.

Though capable of winning ten-furlong races, Phalaris was seen at his best over shorter distances, as the following summary of his performances on the Turf shows:

Two Years Old (1915)

	£
Unplaced in First Spring Stakes, 5 furlongs	—
Won Stud Produce Stakes, 5 furlongs	644
Won Redmere Nursery, 5 furlongs	262

Three Years Old

Third in Craven Stakes, 8 furlongs	—
Unplaced in Two Thousand Guineas, 8 furlongs	—
Unplaced in Handicap, 6 furlongs	—
Won Beaufort Stakes, 7 furlongs	295
Won St George Handicap, Windsor, 6 furlongs	877
Won Royal Stakes, 10 furlongs	200
Second in Limekiln Stakes, 10 furlongs	—

Four Years Old

Second in Crawfurd Handicap, 6 furlongs	—
Won Bretby Handicap, 6 furlongs	342
Walked Over for The Whip	—
Won Chesterfield Course Stakes, 5 furlongs	295
Won St Ives Handicap, 5 furlongs	435
Won Bury St Edmunds Plate, 8 furlongs	294
Won Snailwell Stakes, 5 furlongs	190
Won Challenge Stakes, 6 furlongs	310
Unplaced in Cambridgeshire	—

Five Years Old

Won Abingdon Plate, 5 furlongs	177
Unplaced in Beaufort Handicap, Manchester, 5 furlongs	—
Won June Stakes, 8 furlongs	580
Won Lanwades Plate, 7 furlongs	177
Walked Over for Challenge Stakes, 6 furlongs	300
	£5,478

Phalaris ran in twenty-four races, won sixteen, was second in two and third in one. It has to be borne in mind that he did all his racing during the war period, when the opportunities that, in normal times, come the way of a horse of his class, were denied him, and when stakes values were very low. Here is a list of his principal winners:

COLTS

	Races won	Value £		Races won	Value £
Manna	4	23,534	Phanarite (two-year-old)	2	2,040
Pharos	14	15,694			
Moabite	10	8,155	Colorado (two-year-old)	2	2,023
Legionnaire (two-year-old)	4	3,725	L'Aiglon	3½	1,636
Warden of the Marches	5	3,439	Field Argent	3½	1,633
Burnt Sienna (gelding)	6½	3,263	**FILLIES**		
Phalaros	5	2,811	Silver Grass	3½	2,892
Torlonia	5	2,510	Blanchisseuse	2½	1,865
Shambles	4	2,076	Halcyon	2	1,464

Up to the present, therefore, the daughters of Phalaris have been greatly inferior to the best of his sons. This is so with the majority of stallions, but the disparity is in this instance unusually marked.

Breeding Oddities

IN 1814 MR HENRY PEIRSE, of Bedale, who was one of the leading Yorkshire breeders of his day, put four of his mares to Comus (son of Sorcerer), who, at a fee of 10 guineas, was located in the neighbourhood. They were Rosette, Sister to Rosette, Albuera and Agatha's dam. All produced colt-foals the following year. Those out of Rosette and her sister were Reveller and Ranter, who remained the property of Mr Peirse. Albuera's colt, The Marshall, was sold to Mr J. Powlett, and Mr E. Petre bought Masker, out of Agatha's dam. Finishing in the order in which they are named, the colts filled the first four places in the St Leger of 1818.

BBR–1929

Sickle

In the late 1980s there was a remarkable changing of the guard in breeding in North America. The branch of the Phalaris male line through Pharos, Nearco, Nearctic and Northern Dancer and the latter's accomplished sons, was not only challenged but headed by the branch of the Phalaris male line through Sickle, Unbreakable, Polynesian, Native Dancer and Raise a Native, the latter sire of champion sire Mr Prospector, of the exceptional sire Alydar, along with Mr Prospector's sensational son Fappiano.

Sickle, the patriarch of this branch, was a foal of 1926, by Phalaris from the superb racemare Selene, by Chaucer. He was tied for third on the 1928 Free Handicap and, although highly considered at three, he could only finish a close third in the Two Thousand Guineas and fifth in the Derby. His most notable successes came while sprinting.

In 1929, Sickle came to Kentucky to stand at Joseph E. Widener's Elmendorf Farm; first on lease and then by outright purchase.

An immediate success with his first crop, Sickle, who sired stakes winners at a 14 per cent pace, won his first sire championship in 1936 and repeated this in 1938.

Selene, dam of Sickle, was truly a conveyer of 'sire blood'. She also bred Hyperion (Gainsborough), five times a champion sire in England and a champion broodmare sire who was also second in this respect four times; Hunter's Moon (Hurry On), a notable classic sire in South America; and Pharamond II, an own brother to Sickle who also established an enduring male line in North America.

Here is what the **BBR** *of 1926 had to say of Sickle after his two-year-old career.*

THIS COLT, bred and owned by Lord Derby, is the first foal of the handsome Chaucer mare, Selene, whose splendid racing record will be fresh in the minds of all. Dark brown in colour, he is very truly made; indeed, so far as appearances go, the only thing against him is his lack of inches, for he stands on short legs. Being by Phalaris, he is bred on the same lines as Pharos, Colorado and Warden of the Marches, who are all from daughters of Chaucer.

Selene, a smallish mare, is half-sister to Tranquil, who three years ago won the One Thousand Guineas and the St Leger. Her dam, Serenissima, is by the Derby winner Minoru out of Gondolette (dam of the Derby winner, Sansovino), by Loved One.

The capacity of this family in the way of producing first-class stayers has, it will be seen, been well proved. When to this stamina we have added, in the case of Sickle, the brilliant speed which Phalaris imparts to most of his stock, there is good reason for supposing that Lord Derby has more than an outside chance of seeing his colours successful in one or more of the classic races next season. It may well be the Two Thousand Guineas again, because Sickle is sure to come to hand early, like Colorado.

Though Sickle won but three of his seven races this year, he was a very consistent performer. He began by running second to Damon in the

New Stakes at Ascot, and next time out was second, in the July Stakes, beaten three-parts of a length by The Satrap. Then came two wins, the first in the Mersey Stakes at Liverpool, and the second in the Prince of Wales's Stakes at Goodwood. His close third to Damon and Call Boy in the Champagne Stakes at Doncaster followed. Subsequently he was an easy winner of the Boscawen Stakes at Newmarket, a race in which Treat, who had recently carried off the International Stakes at Kempton Park, finished a poor third. Finally came his brave effort to win the Middle Park Stakes. There were twelve runners for this race. Most of them, Sickle included, carried the full penalty. One of the exceptions was Call Boy, who received 3 lb from Sickle, Birthright, Applecross and others. The filly Cresta Run, who the previous week had easily won the Imperial Stakes at Kempton, started favourite at 3 to 1. Call Boy, a winner since Doncaster of the Linton Stakes, was heavily backed at 7 to 2. Sickle and Bold Archer – the latter winner of the Gimcrack Stakes at York and of a race at Doncaster – were quoted at 6 to 1 each, Birthright at 10 to 1, Treat and Prestissimo at 100 to 8, and Applecross at 100 to 7. It will be observed that Call Boy was allowed good credit by speculators for the half-length by which he beat Sickle in the Champagne Stakes.

As at Doncaster, Call Boy lost a little ground at the start. Early in the contest Birthright took the lead, closely followed by Bold Archer and Sickle. Two furlongs from home the three named were joined by Call Boy, and a strenuous tussle for the mastery was now witnessed. Bold Archer was the first to give way. As he did so Applecross came into the foreground. At the foot of the final ascending furlong Birthright held a slight lead, but presently Call Boy and Sickle were practically level with him. The upshot was that Call Boy won by a head from Sickle, Birthright was third, a short head away, and Applecross, close up, fourth. Truly it was a thrilling finish. Because of the 3 lb they were conceding, Sickle and Birthright may be said to have shown themselves slightly superior to Call Boy, though, of course, it could be urged on the winner's behalf that the 3 lb was more than counter-balanced by the length or two he lost at the start. Perhaps it is worth while to draw attention to the fact that the first four finished in the same order as in the Champagne Stakes at Doncaster.

Sickle's performance fully confirmed the high opinion the public had previously formed of his abilities. He displayed admirable courage and grit, attributes which are likely to carry him well up the ladder of fame next year. If to the qualities he possesses there were added an inch or two to his stature, he would today probably be standing well ahead of his

contemporaries. As it is, he must be assessed just about the equal of the
best of them.   BBR–1926

The Unique Story of the Stallion
Lucullus

*Certainly one of the more novel stories in breeding involves the stallion
Lucullus, a German-bred foal of 1908 by Epsom Derby winner Ard
Patrick out of Lucca, a German Oaks victress, by Cazabat. He was not
put into training in Germany before being sent to Calcutta where his
impeccable pedigree attracted considerable attention. However, as a
runner his pedigree didn't help him and he was totally useless. Shunted
off to England in the hope he would become a country stallion he again
disappointed when unable to attract more than a couple of mares.
Finally, a New Zealand breeder took a chance on him and took him
home with him. There he became the champion sire for the 1927–28
season.*

The article 'The Romance of Lucullus' appeared in the BBR *of
1929; it was originally published in* Horse and Hound *and was
contributed by Mr P. Leo Faulkner of The Curragh, Co. Kildare. It is
worth repeating here because of its uniqueness.*

LOOKING DOWN the passage of the years there are several incidents of a
classic nature which are cited invariably when the romantic side of
racing and horse-breeding is under discussion. To them must surely be
added the case of Lucullus, who is at present the leading stallion in New
Zealand. To clear the ground, so to speak, I begin with the following
extract from Vol. 23 of the *General Stud Book*: 'Lucullus, a brown horse,
foaled in Germany in 1908, and imported in 1914, got by imp. Ard
Patrick, his dam, Lucca, by Cazabat out of Lucerna, by Sir Bevys, out of
imp. Illuminata, by Kisber (sent to New Zealand).' It is well to bear in
mind that this Illuminata, a daughter of Kisber, was a different
individual from Illuminata, a daughter of Rosicrucian, who bred Ladas
and Gas, the dam of Cicero.

Lucullus was imported from Germany to Calcutta by Mr Max
Gutschke, the manager of the Deutsche Bank, at a cost of about £500.
That gentleman then proceeded to sell shares in the horse to Mr Roland
Pugh, of Calcutta, and to Mr Heath, a Ceylon tea-planter and racing
enthusiast. Mr Gutschke was very fond of a good horse, and, at the
period in question (*circa* 1911), his colours were often carried to victory
by Wise Hawk, a gelded son of Love Wisely.

Lucullus was a huge, upstanding horse, light brown in colour, with a capped hock due to some injury. I can well remember the mild sensation caused in Bengal riding circles by his arrival in Calcutta. In those days few highly-bred horses made the journey to the East, and was not Lucullus by Ard Patrick out of Lucca, a winner of the German Oaks, and reputed to be the best mare in the land of the Kaiser?

He had not been put into training in Germany, and in India it was quite out of the question to take the 'beef' off him. He was as placid as a cow and was never unready to eat. One thing he would not learn to do, and that was to gallop. In fact, he was so slow that it was not even feasible to exploit him in the amateur class. Now, an 'amateur race' was one for horses which had never won a flat race, hurdle race, or steeplechase value Rs. 500 (£33) or over. Welter weights were imposed, and only gentlemen riders were allowed. For the most part these races fell to the better type of Australian hack-hunter.

Eventually it was realised that Lucullus was so utterly devoid of galloping ability that he could not even be expected to win a charger race at the Tollygunge gymkhana meeting, where the first prizes were always little silver cups of the value of £3 3s. His trainer was afraid to let him travel more than two furlongs at his fastest rate of progression, as it was supposed that he would break down. In these circumstances the syndicate had to be wound up, and this policy was pursued on the basis that the horse was worth Rs. 500 (£33).

Mr Max Gutschke gave up his interest in the failure, and, at the suggestion of Mr L. P. Pugh, Messrs Heath and Roland Pugh sent Lucullus to England. Being so well bred, and of a big, lusty type, it was thought that the horse would, at least, pay his way as a country stallion. For one season he stood at the Cobham Stud, where he was not visited by more than a couple of mares. Indeed, Messrs Roland Pugh and Heath did not even send their own mares to their own horse. Moreover, about this time, the late William Allison was more concerned with Cornstalk.

As the end of the season the joint-owners of the son of Ard Patrick were so disgusted with the lack of success that they determined to be rid of him at any price. In the end they exchanged him for a two-year-old gelding owned by Jack Anthony's father in Pembrokeshire. This juvenile was by Whyte Melville out of Sappho Park, and he was christened White Sapphire. In due course he was despatched to Bengal, where he won many races. Away in the west of Wales no one wanted Lucullus. Mr Anthony found that he could not compete with the King's Premium stallion, whose service fee was only 25s. Thus, the horse made his way to Newmarket for the Second July Sales of 1914, where he became the property of Mr J. O. Andrews, a New Zealand breeder, for the mere bagatelle of 25 guineas.

From recent volumes of the *Bloodstock Breeders' Review* I cull the following statistics: in 1925 Lucullus sired the winners of £11,971; in 1926 of £9,966; in 1927 of £13,532; and in 1928, when he was the champion stallion, of £17,489. He stands at a fee of 50 guineas, and, at long last, has attained to glory.   BBR–1929

The Near Sale of Gainsborough to the US

Of all the 'might have beens' recounted in the course of racing and breeding history, that of England's marvellous classic winner and classic sire, Gainsborough, ranks either right at the top or very near it. The story of how close he came to being sold to Mr John Sanford, a prominent owner and breeder of Amsterdam, New York, was retold in the BBR *of 1930 following the victory of Gainsborough's son, Singapore, in that year's St Leger Stakes. But for the strong will of Lady James Douglas, owner and breeder of the son of Bayardo and the sire of Hyperion, who refused to sell the colt as a yearling once he failed to meet his reserve, these twice-told tales would not have been told the first time. At least in England. And would Gainsborough have been the influence in America that he was to become in Europe? Speculation will get one nowhere.*

SINGAPORE who, in the matter of looks, shared honours with Parenthesis, is a bay colt by Gainsborough out of Tetrabbazia, by The Tetrarch from Abbazia, by Isinglass out of Mrs Butterwick, by St Simon. Gainsborough, bred and owned by Lady James Douglas, won the Two Thousand Guineas and the substitutes for the Derby and St Leger run at Newmarket. He has sired many good horses and fine stayers, notably Solario, winner of the St Leger in 1925, and of the Ascot Cup the following year. It may not be generally known that when a yearling Gainsborough should have gone to the United States. Mr John Sanford, of Amsterdam, New York, commissioned the late Mr W. F. Smith, one of the leading 'vets' at Newmarket, to bid up to 2,000 guineas for the colt when he was offered for sale. After inspecting the youngster Mr Smith came to the conclusion that his frame was too heavy for his legs, and that he would probably not stand training. He therefore refrained from bidding, and in a cabled message told Mr Sanford why, adding that the colt had passed out of the auction ring unsold at 1,800 guineas. Mr Sanford was very vexed with his agent, and cabled instructions that an offer of 2,000 guineas (the reserve) should be made. The offer was submitted and refused. Mr Sanford then ordered an offer of 2,500 guineas to be put forward. When Lady James Douglas was asked to accept that sum she said: 'No, the colt is no longer for sale. I gave everyone a chance of buying, but nobody would have him at my price. I am going to keep him.' Fortune favoured her, and robbed Mr Sanford of a horse far and away better than anything he has owned. Poor Mr Smith, who had acted, as he thought, for the best, was never forgiven. If Gainsborough had gone to America many pages in the volumes of the *Review* would have read very differently. BBR–1930

Pharos – Champion Sire of 1931

When Pharos became England's leading sire in 1931, thanks mostly to classic victories in the Two Thousand Guineas and the Derby by his son, Cameronian, the BBR *of that year presented his complete racing record. As it shows, he probably had one of the more moderate racing careers of any great sire. As the sire of Nearco and Pharis and such producing daughters as Lavendula II and Mary Tudor II, he will live in perpetuity.*

PHAROS, who this year heads the list of sires of winners, had his first season at the stud in 1926. It was, therefore, but two years ago that his stock appeared on the Turf for the first time. That season he was represented by two winners of three races worth £550, so, like many a famous stallion, he made a very modest beginning. Last year his record was a little better, for he could claim five winners of nine races worth £2,952. One of the winners, successful in a race worth £333, was the two-year-old colt Cameronian. Little did any of us imagine that this seemingly unpretentious youngster was to develop into a winner of the Two Thousand Guineas, the Derby and St James's Palace Stakes, and thereby earn £29,484, and place Pharos in the position he occupies. Pharos has been represented by fourteen other winners this season, the best being the two-year-olds Firdaussi and Pollux. His record for 1931 reads: fifteen winners, twenty-seven races won, value £43,922. He left Lord Derby's stud at Newmarket for France in July, 1928, and there he is to remain for the present at a fee of 45,000 francs or £360 at par of exchange. It has been arranged that ten nominations each season will be reserved for British breeders who want to send mares to Pharos. Among those for

1932 are His Majesty, Lord Derby, Lord Astor, Sir Alec Black, Mr A. de
Rothschild, and Mr J. A. Dawson.

Bred by Lord Derby in 1920, Pharos is a dark bay or brown horse by
Phalaris out of Scapa Flow, by Chaucer from Anchora, by Love Wisely.
He is the second foal of his dam, and is brother to Fairway (winner of the
St Leger, Eclipse Stakes and Champion Stakes), and to Fair Isle, winner
of the One Thousand Guineas. Spithead, who won the Chester Cup, is a
half-brother. The record of his performances on the Turf is as follows:

Two Years Old (1922)

	£
Won Maiden Stakes, Newmarket, 5 f	281
Won Bedford Stakes, Newmarket, 5 f	708
Won Chesham Stakes, Ascot, 5 f	1,150
2nd, Chesterfield Stakes, Newmarket, 5 f	—
Won Mersey Stakes, Liverpool, 5 f	885
Won Lambton Stakes, Stockton, 5 f	337
Unplaced (dwelt at start), Nunthorpe Stakes, York, 5 f	—
2nd, Houghton Stakes, Newmarket, 1 m	—
Won Hurst Park Great T.Y.O. Stakes, 6 f	1,600

Three Years Old

3rd, Pontefract Plate, 1 m	—
Won Hastings Plate, Newmarket, 1¼ m	495
Won March Stakes, Newmarket, 1¼ m	660
2nd in the Derby to Papyrus, beaten a length, 1½ m	—
Won Royal Stakes, Newbury, 1¼ m	2,018
3rd, Prince of Wales's Stakes, Ascot, 1 m 5 f	—
2nd, Select Stakes, Newmarket, 1 m	—
4th, Cambridgeshire Stakes (Handicap), 1 m 1 f	—
3rd, Liverpool Autumn Cup, 1 m 2½ f	—

Four Years Old

Unplaced, City and Suburban Handicap, Epsom, 1¼ m	—
Unplaced, Kempton 'Jubilee' Handicap, 1¼ m	—
Unplaced, Rous Memorial, Ascot, 1 m	—
Won Liverpool Summer Cup (Handicap), 1 m 2½ f	1,820
Won North Sea Stakes, Redcar, 1 m	620
Won Duke of York Handicap, Kempton, 1¼ m	1,665
Won Champion Stakes, Newmarket, 1¼ m	1,790

Five Years Old

3rd, March Stakes, Newmarket, 1¼ m	—
3rd, Liverpool Summer Cup, 1 m 2½ f	—
3rd, Nunthorpe Stakes, York, 5 f	—
Won Duke of York Handicap, Kempton, 1¼ m	1,665
2nd (to Picaroon), Champion Stakes, Newmarket, 1¼ m	—

Races run, 30; won 14, 2nd 5, 3rd 6.   Total   £15,694

It will be seen that he was essentially a middle-distance runner. Only twice was he asked to race over more than 10½ furlongs – in the Derby and the Prince of Wales's Stakes at Ascot, to finish second in the one and third in the other. His running in the Derby very clearly showed that twelve furlongs was beyond his tether. At the end of the tenth furlong he took the lead from Papyrus, but, failing to stay the next two furlongs, he was caught by Papyrus, and beaten a length. Had he possessed a little more stamina he would have won that day.

Pharos since he went to France has been located at the well-appointed Haras d'Ouilly, about twelve miles from Falaise, in Normandy. He is in charge of Mr François Dupré. English-owned mares going to France to be bred to Pharos enter the country under bond to return in six months and thus avoid the import and surtaxes.

Pharos.

Lord Derby and Hyperion

In 1940 the BBR, *almost certainly reacting to the sales of Bahram and Mahmoud to the US, exalted Lord Derby for 'his inflexible resolution in retaining, in spite of world-wide offers, our most outstanding young*

*stallion since St Simon, nearly fifty years ago – Hyperion. With such
an example before us, we may surely face the future of the industry with
hope and confidence. So long as we have men and horses of such a type,
we may surely afford to look forward patiently to better days.'*

*Which recalls a story, probably mostly true, regarding Lord Derby
and Hyperion. It says that the famous Hollywood movie mogul, Louis
B. Mayer, then assembling a powerful racing and breeding
establishment in California, had offered Lord Derby a blank cheque to
write in the amount he would take for Hyperion. Lord Derby is
supposed to have thanked him with this answer: 'Even though England
be reduced to ashes, Hyperion shall never leave these shores.'*

*And he didn't. In 1940 he became England's champion sire for the
first time and duplicated that feat five more times.*

*Although the outside world didn't get Hyperion himself, five of his
sons were exported in 1940. They included Heliopolis, who was a
champion sire twice in the US; Quick Ray, who became a classic sire in
Argentina; and Helios, who became an exemplary sire of classic
winners in Australia.*

*Hyperion had but thirteen foals in his first crop, but twelve of them
were winners.*

The Sale of Bahram and Mahmoud to the US

*Unquestionably, the most sensational pieces of breeding news in 1940
were the sales of English Triple Crown winner Bahram and Derby
winner Mahmoud by the Aga Khan to the United States. There was
much indignation expressed in England over this and had it not been for
the war, there would, undoubtedly, have been a great deal more. The
Aga Khan, who had also won the Derby of 1930 with Blenheim, had
sold that enormously successful sire to the US in 1936 amid great
consternation. It was especially hard to accept inasmuch as Bahram
was the country's first Triple Crown winner in forty years. Not only
that, he was sired by Blandford, also the sire of Blenheim, while the
latter sired Mahmoud. Thus, the male line of Swynford through
Blandford was deprived of its three biggest guns. Three Derby
winners, three Derby winners sold!*

*In retrospect, England's resentment was well warranted. Blenheim
and Mahmoud both became premier sires in the US and while neither
carried on the male line with the anticipated strength and pre-potency, it
has survived. On the other hand, daughters of Blenheim and Mahmoud*

became matchless producers whose names will reside in the pedigrees of superior racehorses and producers for endless years.

Although Bahram sold for twice as much as Mahmoud, his record as a sire in the States was comparatively pallid. Nothing like his English-conceived offspring such as Big Game, Persian Gulf, Turkhan or Queen of Shiraz, materialised until he was sold to South America where his contributions were just as moderate.

Here is given E. E. Coussell's account of the sales, which appeared in the **BBR** *of 1940 and which aroused such pique in England.*

CONSIDERABLE astonishment was generally expressed last July when it was reported the Aga Khan had sold his great horse, Bahram, to a syndicate in the United States.

The announcement created vivid interest among breeders everywhere. At first, in this country, the news was hardly believed. Some people seemed to recall it had been stated that the horse would never be sold!

Yet the unbeaten winner of the Two Thousand Guineas, the Derby and the St Leger – the first colt to achieve that great distinction in nearly forty years – actually had been sold for export to the United States.

Negotiations were protracted and difficult, due to complications caused by war-time conditions. The official announcement could only be made that the business was completed when Bahram was actually *in* the ship at a North of Ireland port on the 8th of August.

The purchase price was £40,000. The purchasers comprise a group of courageous, young and keen breeders of thoroughbreds.

Negotiations for the sale of Bahram were conducted and completed by The British Bloodstock Agency, Ltd. The most important condition was that the horse must be certified by two veterinary surgeons that he was in good health and condition when he was actually *in* the steamer, because war risks could be placed only from 'port to port'.

Bahram completed the 1940 stud season at the Egerton Stud, Newmarket. He was sent to Ireland on the 2nd of July. Until he left that country to cross the Atlantic, the Derby winner was located at Old Connell, Newbridge, in Co. Kildare.

It may be interesting to mention that the members of the syndicate now owning Bahram are Mr Alfred G. Vanderbilt; Mr Sylvester W. Labrot, Mr Walter J. Chrysler, Jr; and Mr James Cox Brady. The last-named has a 1/16th interest in the son of Blandford. The other three members of the syndicate each contributed $50,000 of the purchase price. Of course, they can, if they wish, send a *pro rata* number of their mares to their stallion.

Bahram will make his first stud season in the US at Mr A. G. Vanderbilt's well-appointed and expertly managed Sagamore Stud Farm, at Glyndon, which is no long distance from Baltimore, in Maryland. He is by far the greatest horse ever to stand in Maryland. The terms of service will be $2,500. That sum will be refunded if a mare proves barren and the fact is notified by November 1st, 1941. Naturally, no services will be available for mares outside the ownership of the members of the syndicate unless they desire to make any transfers.

The first offspring of Bahram raced in 1939. They included Great Truth, £1,400; The Druid; Turkhan, £2,500. The Druid was, of course, the colt out of Trustful, sold as a yearling at Doncaster for 13,000 guineas. The only other yearling by Bahram submitted for sale in 1938 was 'bought in' at 3,000 guineas.

The story of the performances of the offspring of Bahram would doubtless have been vastly different had there been a normal season's racing in England and Ireland in 1940. As it was he finished second to Hyperion in the winning sires' list.

Turkhan, after running second to Pont l'Eveque in the New Derby at Newmarket, crossed to Ireland to win very easily the Irish Derby. On the last day of the season the son of Bahram won the Yorkshire St Leger (substitute for the Doncaster classic) over 1 mile 7 furlongs. Like his sire, Turkhan was retired to stud at the close of his second season on the Turf. Among Bahram's first fillies was Queen of Shiraz. She ran in and won the Irish Oaks by four lengths. The Druid revealed himself as about the fastest colt of his age.

The Turf career of Bahram is so recent there is no necessity to make lengthy reference. Never defeated, he ran in five races as a two-year-old. His victories included the Gimcrack Stakes and the Middle Park Stakes. His very impressive record for 1936 reads: won the Two Thousand Guineas; won the Derby; won the St James's Palace Stakes, Ascot; won the St Leger (by five lengths). Total of stakes won £43,086.

So great was then his reputation, that at the record fee (for recent years) of 500 guineas, Bahram's 'book' had filled for three years immediately after, if not before, he won the St Leger.

When he won the Derby, Bahram stood 16.2 hands high. He is the seventh foal of his dam, who had previously produced Dastur, winner of over £11,600, including the Coronation Cup and the Irish Derby. In addition, Dastur ran second in the Two Thousand Guineas, the Derby, and the St Leger when beaten a neck only.

Bahram's dam was by Friar Marcus. His grandam is a half-sister to Plucky Liège, dam of those tremendously successful stallions in the US – Sir Gallahad and Bull Dog. Thus Bahram represents a family which has already achieved great fame in America.

There are no fewer than seven lines of Galopin (four through St Simon) and five crosses of Isonomy in Bahram's pedigree. He won the Derby and St Leger so very easily that he was most probably the best horse we have seen for many years. It is certain that but for war-time conditions he would not have left this country. His sale and shipment was greatly regretted by breeders, for it was sincerely felt that a horse with his exceptional record of brilliant achievements would, in his turn, have sired exceedingly worthy sons and daughters. Bahram was the fourth son of Blandford to win the Derby. Trigo and Windsor Lad remain here. Blenheim and now Bahram are in the US.

Early in September last negotiations were commenced with a view to the sale of the 1936 Derby winner to the United States. Mr Cornelius Vanderbilt Whitney (cousin of Mr A. G. Vanderbilt, one of the owners of Bahram) was especially interested in Mahmoud, whom Mr Whitney's manager, Mr Ivor Balding, was also desirous should be acquired, believing that the blood of Mahmoud would prove most successful when crossed with American-bred mares of proved credentials.

Mahmoud, like Bahram, completed the 1940 stud season at the Egerton Stud, Newmarket. He was sent to Ireland on the 4th of July. Until he left for shipment, the horse was at the Aga Khan's Stud, Tully, Co. Kildare.

Once again the difficulties of transport became acute. Further, business was only possible provided the owner of Mahmoud was ready to accept war risks on Mahmoud until such time as he could deliver the Derby winner *in* the ship. The period of waiting was tedious and lengthy.

Negotiations were not easy. It was troublesome to communicate with the Aga Khan, who had been in Switzerland for some months. Ultimately it was confirmed that Mahmoud would be delivered as desired. The business was satisfactorily completed. The negotiations and the sale of Mahmoud were effected by The British Bloodstock Agency, Ltd.

It is now known that the price paid for Mahmoud was £20,000. The horse passed triumphantly every test. Finally on the 22nd of October he was safely shipped aboard a steamer in a North of Ireland port. Thus, many anxieties were ended. The voyage was not of short duration.

Eventually Mahmoud arrived safely in New York. His condition was regarded as satisfactory in every way; his new owner was particularly pleased with his horse. One well-known American trainer, who happened to be at the docks when the horse was disembarked, wrote to London saying, 'Mahmoud is one of the finest looking stallions I have ever seen.'

It is Mr C. V. Whitney's intention that Mahmoud shall stand for service at his stud farm, near Lexington, Kentucky. His 'book' is full with forty mares, of which thirty-five are dams of good winners or themselves were big winners.

Mahmoud was successful thrice as a two-year-old. His victories comprised the Exeter Stakes, the Richmond Stakes and the Champagne Stakes, Doncaster – a record which placed him 1 lb below top weight in the Free Handicap that season.

He ran in the Two Thousand Guineas, being beaten a short head by Pay Up, after losing about one length at the start, as his rider thought he ought to ride a 'waiting race', being just a little fearful about the colt's ability to stay the distance. Those fears were quite unfounded as Mahmoud finished very strongly.

Mahmoud created a new time record when he won the Derby. He finished three lengths in front of the second horse, with Pay Up no closer than fourth. The time was 2 min 33$\frac{1}{5}$ sec. The previous best was 2 min 34 sec, made by Hyperion and Windsor Lad.

Later on Mahmoud ran once more. The St Leger distance, 1 mile 7 furlongs 132 yards, was clearly beyond his ability. He finished third behind Boswell and Fearless Fox.

A few days after the Derby it was announced that Mahmoud would be retired to the stud at the end of the season. Thus he commenced stud duties at four years, like Bahram, Blair Athol, Desmond, Galopin, St Frusquin and The Tetrarch.

There is every justification for the claim that Mahmoud was the best three-year-old of his season to 1$\frac{1}{2}$ miles. His achievements in any event brought him the distinction of being given top weight in the Free Handicap for horses of that age.

His Turf record reads: raced ten times; won four races; placed second, twice; placed third, three times. Total stake winnings, £15,026. He was retired to the Egerton Stud at a fee of 300 guineas.

Mahmoud from the day he arrived at Egerton made great progress in development, and became a greatly admired horse, who, as was seen the next year, sired offspring with much more substance than was antici-pated. He got a high percentage of his mares in foal. Indeed,

Mahmoud's figures for 1940 season, result of mares covered in 1939, is 90.62 per cent – an exceptionally high figure.

It is difficult to assess the ability of his first runners, recalling the curtailed season of 1940. Among his winners are Boudoir, Mabama, Mabrouka. Mention could be made of Silver Scuttle, five times second in six starts. Altogether about ten of the first offspring of Mahmoud raced in 1940. Nearly all of them were placed, if not winners.

There is a strong suggestion of the Arab about Mahmoud. When he won the Derby he stood a shade under 15.3 h.h., but was very powerfully made, especially behind the saddle. He could certainly 'fly' when the going was firm. He is the first foal of Mah Mahal, by Gainsborough, from the 'flying' Mumtaz Mahal, who cost the Aga Khan 9,100 guineas, and won for him £13,933. Her sire was The Tetrarch. Her dam is Lady Josephine, the grandam of Fair Trial, whose first runners in 1940 were so successful that he is the leading sire of winners at that age. She won the Coventry Stakes at Ascot. Her dam was Americus Girl, a winner of twelve races, including the Portland Plate, at Doncaster.

There are many lines of blood in the pedigree of Mahmoud which will be thoroughly appreciated by breeders in the US. There can be no doubt that he is likely to prove an exceptionally successful stallion in that country.

Another feature of interest is that the Aga Khan won the Derby three times. All his three Derby winners were sold to the United States through The British Bloodstock Agency, Ltd. Bahram and Blenheim, both sired by Blandford; Mahmoud, sired by Blenheim. BBR–1940

Nearco's First Crop

Nearco foreshadowed his dynastic success at stud with his very first crop which made him the leading sire of two-year-olds. That was in 1942 and it was the first time in thirty years, with the exception of Fair Trial, that a first-crop sire had earned this crown. Appropriately, Nasrullah, Nearco's most influential breeding son, was a member of that first crop as was Lady Sybil who headed the Free Handicap, regardless of sex, while Nasrullah was the top-weighted colt. Thus, with his first crop, Nearco had the champions of both sexes. Oddly, Nearco's most notable breeding sons – Nasrullah, Royal Charger, Nearctic and Amerigo – did not win a classic among them.

THE LEADING SIRE of juvenile winners in 1932 was Nearco, whose six winning offspring won seventeen races and £6,637½. This was about 20 per cent of the amount credited to the other fifteen sires of the leading winning two-year-olds in 1942.

As may be expected, a son and daughter of Nearco, namely, Lady Sybil and Nasrullah, are at the head of the two-year-old Free Handicap.

Fairway, who usually occupies a high position in these statistics, and at times has headed them, is now second, the amount won being a little more than half that credited to the offspring of Nearco. These are the first runners sired by Nearco. The result of his first stud season (1939), when Nearco covered eighteen mares, show one mare (Foliation) exported to Italy, two mares slipped foals, three mares were barren. Thus there were twelve living foals. All have raced in 1942. There are six winners: Lady Sybil, Nasrullah, Liquid Amber, Nearly, Nearctic, and Shining Light. In addition, the following were 'placed': Hawaiian Lady, Lady Emma, Scandinavia, and Society Lady. The other two runners were Careless Talk and Cimbrone. The record of Nearco in his first season of very restricted racing is noteworthy.

Two years ago Fair Trial was the leading sire of two-year-old winners, with his first 'crop' of foals. Then Fair Trial sired eight winners of twenty-four races and £5,606.

In the past thirty years Nearco and Fair Trial are the only two stallions to be the leading sires of two-year-old winners with their first runners.

St Simon, with his first two-year-olds, probably excelled all records. In 1889 that famous stallion sired nine two-year-old winners of sixteen races and £24,280. That, no doubt, is a record result of a horse's first season at the stud. It is, of course, impossible to make any real comparisons between 1942 or 1940 and 1889. St Simon's figures are merely recorded. Among his first foals were the winners of four classic races in 1890.   BBR–1942

Part 9
Mares

Admiral Rous on Broodmares

ADMIRAL ROUS wrote as follows in 1869:

'*The Times* is of opinion that it would not injure the Turf to get rid of the speedy jady mares; these are the animals that have bred nine-tenths of the best racehorses – Plenipotentiary, Orlando, Venison, and a hundred others I could name, not excepting the dam of Pero Gomez. And the most extraordinary mares – Plover, Violante, Camarine, Virago – never bred a horse worth £300. Breeding racehorses is a lottery; every mare of pure blood may produce a first-class horse, although she may not be able to gallop. The slowest three-year-old colt I ever tried was a magnificent animal 16 hands 1 inch high, by The Flying Dutchman out of Virago.'

There is, of course, a germ of truth in the Admiral's sweeping assertions, but a little investigation would show that in his endeavour to emphasise the point he was making, he went much too far. Round about the date when Admiral Rous wrote his letter, another authority on breeding advanced similar opinions. He was answered by the following:

'An investigation of the Stud Book scarcely justifies the assertion that untrained mares have been most successful in the stud. . . Two very hard-worked mares, Beeswing and Alice Hawthorn, bred, besides some other average runners, the one Nunnykirk and Newminster, the other Oulston and Thormanby. Again, Celia and Pocahontas ran on and often, and each has had many good winners. Crucifix worked harder than any two-year-old, and yet she bred Surplice, Coral and Chalice, all very superior runners. There is much to be said on both sides, and probably an equal number of examples may be produced. Still, in buying for the stud, I should infinitely prefer a stock of proved good runners than those who might have been good, but were never proved.'

BBR–1917

Mrs Cradock's Treatise on 'Approved Mares'

'Approved Mares' in stallion advertisements can be a most ambiguous term. In some cases the stallion owner would probably approve of any mare he could get to come to his not-too-popular stallion, while the owner of the highly popular stallion would be as choosy as he wanted to be. However, even in the latter instance, it would be wise to have some guidelines. Those mentioned by Mrs Cradock, an honoured breeder in England, in the Review *of 1918, would still appear to be applicable in this day and age.*

The BBR *preceded Mrs Cradock's article thus:*

The writer of this article is not only a keen student of all matters pertaining to the thoroughbred; she is a practical breeder. It has been our privilege to pay many visits to her compact and well-ordered stud at Lound Hall, which is on the Duke of Newcastle's estate in Nottinghamshire. At such times we have listened with admiration to an outpouring of the knowledge and wisdom of our hostess, and entertained the hope that she would embody some of her well-reasoned views in an article to be published in these pages. We at length prevailed on Mrs Cradock to satisfy that hope, and here is her first, though we trust not her last, essay. The extraordinary amount of research which the article reveals will surely shame to silence those who profess to believe that the breeding of good horses is a mere matter of chance and luck.

LOOKING over the advertisements of fashionable stallions one often finds the expression 'approved mares only'. What does this really mean? Does the condition refer to make and shape, age, constitution, success either of themselves or their offspring on the Turf; or does it refer to their having such lines of blood in their pedigrees that the stallion owner considers suitable for his horse? The ideal answer would be the affirmative to all these points, but such perfection of mating would make breeding a far more difficult matter than it now is. The best-laid plans of mice and men too often 'gang agley', as so many of us know only too well. Also there is the financial side of the question – no small one, especially to small studs in these days.

It is quite likely, however, that in the best horses most of these ideals have been attained, together with those of environment – a never-to-be-forgotten factor. A story is told of a father and son who spent sixty years trying to breed a St Leger winner – capable men too – without success, but their neighbour accomplished the feat (in Challacombe) at almost the first attempt! So there is a certain amount of luck needed too, for, as an Irishman told me once, 'Horses make liars of us all.' This remark had reference to yearlings in the paddock. One such could neither run, walk, trot, nor gallop, only fall down; yet the first time out on the racecourse it spreadeagled the field! Granting, however, good common sense prevails as to make and shape and health of both parents, the next point must be the careful consideration of both pedigrees, especially that of the sire, in the following ways:

1. Does *he* or *his dam* plant impression on the stock?
2. With what lines of blood have he and his sire done best?
3. From what tap root does he spring? This is very important. Some high-class winners come from a very feminine line such as No. 4 family. Few stallions of this family have proved a success at the stud (the chief

exceptions being Rock Sand, Bona Vista and Tredennis) whilst the failures are many.

4. What preponderance of Eclipse, Matchem and Herod blood (which it is a cardinal rule to balance well) does he possess?

These questions also apply to the mare. But in her case notice should be taken of any marked resemblance she may bear to any well-known type (or individual) such as Melbourne, Gallinule and St Simon. I feel very strongly that the right idea for either sex is (after that above has been ascertained) to find what strains are lacking, and obtain them if possible in the *dam of the sire*, or the *sire of the dam* of the future foal. It cannot always be done in this way in the upper and lower sections of the pedigree; indeed, many breeders, including, I believe, the Dowager Lady Londonderry, prefer a good centre combination. This is what I venture to call complementary breeding. Fashion is, after all, only another word for success, and should I ever be the happy possessor of a good horse that is what 'approved mares' would mean to me.

That a sire should have a good dam is, everyone acknowledges, a most vital point. She need not necessarily have been a good winner (very often, indeed, we notice the reverse) but should come from such good stock that her son can transmit its merits given a mare that has another good line from her sire. Doubtless many high-class stallions have suffered at the stud in reputation by having many valuable but totally unsuitable mares sent him, much to their detriment and his. Several seasons may come and go before the right one comes along, as we have seen in Bayardo's case. BBR–1918

The Death of Chelandry

March 8th – Chelandry died at the Mentmore Stud after foaling a big colt by Junior. The foal also is dead. Thus ended the career of a mare who did more than her share to uphold the prestige of the very successful thoroughbred family to which she belonged – that of Paraffin. Last season she was barren for the first time in seventeen years. When a few months ago it was found she was in foal again the hope was entertained that all would go well so that she might leave one more treasure behind her. Unfortunately, however, old age – she was born in 1894 – and the size of her foal proved too much for her; she succumbed to exhaustion.

Chelandry was the winner of five races worth £13,183, including the Woodcote Stakes, the National Breeders' Produce Stakes, the Imperial Produce Stakes, and the One Thousand Guineas, and her sons and daughters have won races to the value of £38,290. These winners are

Skyscraper, Chelys, Traquair, Popinjay, Perdicaas and Neil Gow. The last-named won the Two Thousand Guineas. Luckily there are several mares and fillies out of Chelandry. Lord Rosebery has Chelys, by Sir Visto; Samphire, by Isinglass; Dark Flight, by Dark Ronald; Pennula, by Sunstar; Martial Note, by Carbine; and Cheronese, by Cylgad. Yippingale, her foal of 1909, by William the Third, and Bobolink, her foal of 1913, by Willonyx, were both bought by the British Bloodstock Agency – the former for an Australian client, Mr Norman Falkiner, and the latter for Mr A. B. Hancock, of Kentucky. Chelandry is sure of an abiding place in the affections of all associated with the Mentmore Stud. These many years she had been the pride of its paddocks.   BBR–1917

The Family of Lady Josephine

Lady Josephine, a foal of 1912 was a very fast filly whose successes included the Coventry Stakes at Royal Ascot. She was by Sundridge out of spectacular Americus Girl, whose versatility is illustrated by the fact that she won a 5-furlong dash at Epsom in record time under 136 lb and ran second in the Irish Oaks conceding 26 lb to the winner. 'Unquestionably one of the finest sprinters of modern times', Americus Girl was a daughter of the California-based Americus.

Lady Josephine was to become the dam of the outstanding racing filly Lady Juror and the 'flying filly' Mumtaz Mahal, two fillies who were to make Lady Josephine one of the most profound influences on quality in the history of the General Stud Book.

E. E. Coussell contributed an outstanding account of 'The Family of Lady Josephine' to the BBR *of 1946 and that author's knowledge and literary ability make it worthy of reproduction here.*

ABOUT THE END of the last century that remarkably successful judge, Mr J. H. H. Peard, on behalf of one of his friends, living at Cork (the home of Peard), in a Dublin Sale paid £200 for a young mare. The mare had raced four seasons and won a couple of races in twenty starts. The value of those races was £435 and £132. The distances five and seven furlongs.

She was the first mare ever owned by Mr A. H. Ledlie of Cork. Her name was Palotta. It is to be doubted if on many occasions £200 was invested to better advantage in bloodstock, though one recalls the stallions Beau Pere and Limond, each of whom cost half that meagre sum. Their offspring must have won about £500,000 in various parts of the world. Still Palotta was a true treasure.

Mr Ledlie had no stud farm. Later he acquired a very small property near Cork, where he kept two or three mares in what Peard humorously used to describe as 'a back yard with a small paddock adjoining'.

Therefore originally Palotta went to the Greenfields Stud near Tipperary. The first three seasons Palotta was mated with Galopin's son, Buckingham. The produce were all fillies. Only one was a winner; she raced a dozen times to win three races, value £46, £54 and £40, all flat races in Ireland.

Palotta now visited Islington before he went to the US. He was a much inferior brother to Isinglass. Again the result was of little value for racing. The mare was then barren to Hackler. Next year Mr Ledlie in 1905, sent Palotta to Americus, who was standing at Mr Croker's stud near The Curragh, Ireland. A miracle happened. The produce was the great mare Americus Girl (1906). That season Americus was standing at what Peard called the 'crushing fee' of twelve sovereigns!

The mating could not be continued for a year or so, because late in 1905 Americus went to Italy, having been leased to that country for breeding seasons 1906 and 1907. However, the fine achievements of Americus Girl led to her sire returning to Ireland. Palotta was again mated with Americus in 1908. The produce next year was Lady Americus, who not so good as her sister, did win the Coventry Stakes at Ascot. That was, of course, in 1911. However, in 1909 an offer for

Lady Josephine.

Americus had come from Germany. It was accepted. Americus went to Germany in 1909. His subsequent career and final fate are unknown.

Perhaps it would be well to mention that Americus was bred in the United States and foaled in 1892. This bay horse, after winning many important races in the land of his birth, came to England and continued his successful Turf career. In the United States, then known as Rey del Carreras, and winner of good races, he had cost Mr R. Croker the equivalent of about 8,000 guineas. Unfortunately, soon after he was brought to England and re-named Americus, he became unsound in his wind. That, however, made no difference to his owner who raced Americus almost without mercy.

The racing career of Americus is lengthy. He was running many times in 1901 when nine years of age, and already had offspring racing in the same season. Some of the weights he carried were crushing. At four years he ran twice. After taking part in the Jubilee Handicap, won by Clorane with 10 st from Victor Wild, the American-bred colt took on the fastest horses in England in the Portland Plate, Doncaster. His weight was 8 st 9 lb. Grig, with 8 st 12 lb, won the race by less than a length.

At five years old Americus took part in thirteen races. Second at Epsom with 9 st 6 lb, he was then unplaced, afterwards beating three others, by four lengths, for the Riddlesdown Plate at the Epsom Summer Meeting. Two days later, over the same course, Americus was second under 9 st 10 lb. Only three others had a higher weight than Americus in the Stewards' Cup, Goodwood. Forty-eight hours afterwards Americus took on the great sprinter, Ugly. He had 8 st 9 lb. Americus with 10 st was beaten by half a length.

Next week the horse was racing at Brighton, defeated with 9 st 5 lb, but the following day winning the Southdown Plate, six furlongs, carrying 9 st 12 lb. At the weekend he went on to Lewes. There, with top weight, he was beaten a short head in the De Warrenne Handicap. Then followed four unsuccessful essays with 9 st 13 lb, 10 st 3 lb and 8 st 12 lb, and perhaps some tiredness, for he was last of three at Newmarket, beyond his distance at one mile. Americus was then retired to the stud. He returned to the Turf at eight years old when he made four starts. He beat a big field over five furlongs at Gatwick, with top weight 8 st 10 lb and starting favourite. In the Goodwood Stewards' Cup Americus put up 8 st 2 lb, and ran fourth in a close finish.

Next season Americus was still raced, and started seven times. Twice in handicaps he carried 9 st 6 lb, once at Lingfield running third, giving the first 42 lb and the second 4 lb. Under 9 st 4 lb he finished third to Lord Bobs in the July Cup at Newmarket.

The Turf career of Americus has been related at some length because in his intermittent stud careers he naturally had little offspring and never more than a dozen mares named in the *Stud Book*. Outstanding were Americus Girl and Lady Americus.

Americus was sired by Emperor of Norfolk, who was by Norfolk, a son of Lexington. His dam was Marion, by Malcolm, by Bonnie Scotland. Both on his sire's and dam's side, Norfolk could not be traced to a source in early volumes of the *General Stud Book*.

The dam of Americus was a mare named Clara D. She was sired by Glenelg, a son of Citadel, who was a son of Stockwell. Clara D, was out of The Nun, by Lexington out of Novice, by Glencoe, sire of Pocahontas, the dam of Stockwell, Rataplan and King Tom. Thus again there are lines of blood now inadmissible to the *General Stud Book*.

The full breeding of Americus is given in volume 19 of the *Stud Book*, page 969, which records that he was foaled in 1892, and imported in 1895.

It reads: Americus, a bay horse bred in the US in 1892 and imported in 1895. Got by Emperor of Norfolk (son of Norfolk, by Lexington), his dam Clara D., by imp. Glenelg out of The Nun, by Lexington out of Novice by imp. Glencoe out of Chloe Anderson, by Rodolph (son of Sir

Americus Girl.

Archy Montorio, by Sir Archy) out of Belle Anderson, by William of Transport (own brother to Sir Archy Montorio) out of Butterfly, by Sumpter (son of Sir Archy) – imp. Buzzard – Dandridge's Fearnought (son of imp. Fearnought) – imp. Janus.

The position then ruling as regards qualification for entry in the *General Stud Book* may be explained by an extract from 'Advertisement' to Vol. 19 of the *General Stud Book*, dated May, 1901.

> 'The increased importation of horses and mares bred in the US and Australia, which, as stated in the last Volume, though accepted in the Stud Books of their own country, cannot be traced back in all cases to the thoroughbred stock exported from England, from which more or less, they all claim to be descended, induced the Publishers to refer the question of the admission of such animals into the *Stud Book* to the Stewards of the Jockey Club as the highest authority on all matters connected with the Turf. The Stewards after kindly consulting most of the principal breeders, came to the conclusion that any animal claiming admission should be able to prove satisfactorily some eight or nine crosses of pure blood, to trace back for at least a century, and to show such performances of its immediate family on the Turf as to warrant the belief in the purity of its blood. Therefore, all the imported horses and mares which are included in this Volume, have been submitted to this test.
>
> 'In the Appendix to this Volume 19 (p. 1060), will be found the *particulars of the case of Newhaven II*, whose claim for admission showed the necessity for some authoritative decision.'

It will be clearly noticed there was no differentiation against any particular country judged by the note concerning Newhaven II. A good handicap winner in England (1899) and of course, then entered in the Australian *Stud Book*.

There were some amendments later. For example in Vol. 21 of the *General Stud Book* (September 1909), appeared the following notification:

> 'The Editors beg to inform subscribers that since the last Volume (20) of the *Stud Book* was published, they have had cause to consider the advisability of admitting into the *Stud Book* horses and mares which cannot be traced to a thoroughbred root, but which have fulfilled the requirements given in the preface to Volume XIX (GSB). They have decided that in the interests of the English *Stud Book*, no horse or mare can be admitted unless it can be traced to a strain already accepted in the earlier volumes of the Book.'

Eventually in Volume XXII of the *General Stud Book*, dated November 1913, appeared the final condition of entry which our friends in the US erroneously term 'the Jersey Act'.

> 'The Editors beg to inform Subscribers, that to meet a suggestion made at a Meeting of the Jockey Club in May last and approved by the Members then present, they have, with a view to making the matter more explicit, slightly

altered the wording of the qualification for admission to the *General Stud Book*, which was contained in the preface to Volume XXI.

'The qualification will now read as follows: No horse or mare can, after this date, be considered as eligible for admission unless it can be traced without flaw on both sire's and dam's side of its pedigree to horses and mares themselves already accepted in the earlier volumes of the Book.

'The Editors reserve to themselves the sole right to decide what horses or mares can, under the above qualification, be admitted or excluded from the Book.'

We are able to return to Americus' daughter Americus Girl (1905), an especially robust and very good looking filly. She raced six times at two years, winning five races including the Phoenix Plate £1,179. Next year she ran eight times. After winning at Phoenix Park she came to Epsom to take the Royal Stakes. Then on to Ascot to secure the Fern Hill Stakes. Six times the filly was raced at four years winning at Epsom, then at The Curragh, and later the Portland Handicap, Doncaster, with highest weight 8 st 13 lb. She started favourite. The third carried only 5 st 12 lb, and was beaten two lengths. This fine mare was not yet to be retired, for at five years she competed in nine races. She won her first – Great Surrey Handicap, Epsom, with 9 st 10 lb leading from end to end, and winning in 59 secs, an outstanding performance. Then came a melancholy series of defeats, lightened once when Americus Girl under 10 st 3 lb, finished second to Spanish Prince (9 st 2 lb) in the King's Stand Stakes, Ascot, beaten a head in a desperate finish. That was her final great effort. Americus Girl had run in twenty-nine races in four seasons. She had won twelve of them, and earned £8,372 in Stakes. She once covered the five furlongs (downhill) at Epsom in 56 4/5 secs.

After this strenuous Turf career, Americus Girl was left in England to be bred to Sundridge in 1911. Once again chance intervened and a happy chance indeed. Sundridge that year was at Childwick Bury Stud, St Albans. After that stud season he was sold to France, where a few years later he had to be destroyed.

This mating resulted in a chestnut filly in 1912. She became known as Lady Josephine. Mr Ledlie was the breeder. To demonstrate the sound and solid constitution of Americus Girl it may be mentioned the first six years at the stud she failed only once to have produce – to Spearmint.

To Doncaster in 1913 Mr Ledlie sent two yearlings. One was Lady Josephine, already named. Mr W. M. Savill bought the filly for 1,700 guineas. The other was Lady Catherine, by Desmond out of Palotta. She brought 2,600 guineas. The previous December Mr Ledlie had reduced his stud by selling to Sir Ernest Cassell for 2,500 guineas the three-year-old maiden filly Lady Americus, who as hinted, had won at Kempton

Park and at Ascot, earning £2,568. In 1907 Palotta had another brilliant filly, in Trepida, by Grebe, a half brother to Eager, a horse standing at a small fee in Ireland. Trepida won the Duke of York Stakes, Kempton Park, the Liverpool Autumn Cup, and five other races totalling £4,895. Together with another 'flying filly', Wether's Well, Trepida also found her way to Sir E. Cassell's Moulton Paddocks Stud near Newmarket, at a cost of 7,500 guineas. As a broodmare Trepida was a dismal failure producing two winners of very small races. Lady Americus did better, but only a little better. Chicago, a colt by Cylgad, was her best winner. Possibly there are some of her descendants to be found but they rest in obscurity, while those of her older sisters have been so brilliant as to establish one of the most successful families of our times.

Lady Josephine showed herself a very smart filly. First time out at two years she won the Tattenham Plate, Epsom, and at the next meeting took the Acorn Stakes. At Ascot there were only seven runners for the Coventry Stakes. Mr Savill's filly made all the running and won easily by a couple of lengths. She went on to take the Bibury Club Champagne Stakes from weak opposition. In all these races the filly had been trained by 'Jack' Fallon. Then came a defeat by Silver Tag in a race worth £177 at Brighton, 5 furlongs 66 yards, Lady Josephine being favourite at evens.

By this time Lady Josephine had gone to Beckhampton. She raced once at three years, in June, when she was sixth of fourteen behind Volta. Friar Marcus ran fourth in that race. It was thought that she would not stand training so Lady Josephine was retired. Remarkable how many of her female descendants have had a similar two and three year old career, Sansonnet and her daughters for example. A month afterwards Lady Josephine was seen in the sale ring at Newmarket when a bid of 1,200 guineas secured this filly. The bloodstock market had not then yet recovered from the depths of depression caused by the war, 1914–1918, or Lady Josephine herself could have been expected to bring a far higher price than 1,200 guineas. The bid was made by that wonderfully good judge, Mr Henry Cholmondeley, who was then manager of the famed Sledmere Stud, and to Yorkshire away went Lady Josephine. It was then regarded as a very sound purchase. How astute the records of the past thirty years' racing reveal.

Lady Josephine made a disappointing start at the stud for in 1917, and again in 1918, she was barren to Roi Hérode and to Bachelor's Double. However, her first foal made great amends. It was Lady Juror. In the Doncaster Sales, 1920, Mr Joseph Watson, later the first Baron Manton, gave 3,000 guineas for the daughter of Son-in-Law.

Lady Juror did not win at two years old. After her owner's sudden death she was leased to Mr Somerville Tattersall, in whose colours she ran and won at Manchester, at Newbury, and finally the Jockey Club Stakes, 1 mile 6 furlongs, at Newmarket. In the race was Silurian, second in the St Leger. He was giving the filly 6 lb. The pace was fast for the distance. Lady Juror, held in reserve, cantered up the ascent to win by four lengths. She had, during the season, shown notable speed and fine stamina over varied distances from five to fourteen furlongs. She ended a winner of £8,057 in stakes.

The next episode in the career of Lady Juror was her appearance in the sale ring at Newmarket, as one of the lots which eventually made up the 'great Manton Sale'. In the keenest competition Lady Juror was run up to 8,600 guineas – the bid being that of the late Mr R. A. Brice, a close friend of the late Lord Dewar whose instructions were 'buy Lady Juror'.

It was foresight of an exceptional character. Away went Lady Juror to become an inmate of the Homestall Stud Farm near East Grinstead in Sussex. In regular succession came notable winners commencing with Jurisdiction, The Black Abbot (sire of Wychwood Abbot), The Recorder, Riot, Sansonnet and above all the very successful sire of classic winners, Fair Trial.

Riot in her turn became the dam of the war-time Oaks winner, Commotion, dam of Combat, unbeaten this year. Sansonnet was the best two-year-old filly of her season, but failed the next season. She is the dam of Neola, Neolight (sisters, sired by Nearco) and then this year's champion two-year-old Tudor Minstrel, by Owen Tudor.

It is a wonderful story of continuous and remarkable successes.

At the Sledmere Stud, however, Lady Josephine was to achieve, if possible, still greater fame as the dam of that extraordinary public favourite, Mumtaz Mahal, by The Tetrarch, foaled just two years after Lady Juror.

When Lady Josephine was sent to be bred to The Tetrarch in Ireland, the idea in mind was to mate two of the most speedy animals of the day, and perhaps two of the speediest animals of any time. The next step was to try and imagine the result which exceeded all hopes. This idea of breeding was quite contrary to views generally held at the time, namely that a speedy mare should be mated with a horse possessing great staying powers owing to the fact that the offspring of such breeding at least nine times out of ten must take after one or other parent. Lady Josephine was a fine lengthy mare, very much resembling Plaisanterie, for long years a valued and successful brood mare at Sledmere.

It is a very old story how this flying daughter of The Tetrarch was sold as a yearling at Doncaster, and bought for 9,100 guineas on behalf of the Aga Khan. Her remarkable fame and speed as a two-year-old placed her easily at the head of the Free Handicap, with 9 st, Diophon next on the list having 2 lb less. The achievements of Mumtaz Mahal would require many pages of this *Review*. At two years old the filly won five races worth £11,763. It was the thrilling fashion of her victories which caught and held the imagination of the racing public. Before she ended her racing career, 'Mumty' was a winner of £13,933. She set up a new time record for five furlongs at Newmarket.

At the stud the fame of Mumtaz Mahal is inextinguishable. Her first foal was of little service. Then she slipped twins to Gainsborough, to whom, however, the next year she produced a grey filly, named Mah Mahal. Of little racing merit, that filly in her turn became the dam of Mahmoud, the fastest winner of the Derby on record. Mahmoud went to the United States late in 1940, and was the leading stallion in that country this year with the winners of 101 races and $683,025 which at the present rate of exchange is £170,750, including 'place' money.

Others of her produce to be named, but not so very well noted, are Khan Bahadur, a chestnut brother to Mahmoud, as well as Pherozshah, who is now in New Zealand, but has sired a big number of useful winners here.

Mumtaz Mahal had produced but four foals in this country when the Aga Khan sent the great mare to his Marly-la-Ville Stud Farm about twenty miles from Paris. There 'Mumty' was to end her days. She was at Marly-la-Ville when the property was overrun by hordes of invading Germans. They had the decency to respect this wonderful mare and not take her, as they took all the others of the Aga Khan's bloodstock, to Germany. Two or three years ago Mumtaz Mahal died. In France she produced to Blenheim that outstanding colt, Mirza II, whose impelling action and brilliance of his victories at Newmarket roused the enthusiasm of racegoers as few horses have done in modern times. There was also her son, Furrokh Siyar, who has sired very numerous speedy winners. She was also dam of Badruddin, another useful racehorse, but better known to fame as sire of the dam of that very good horse, Sayani, winner of a record Cambridgeshire this year.

This story would be far from complete without a reference to Mumtaz Begum, a sister to Mirza II. That mare became the dam of Nasrullah, the best colt of his year and now at the stud in Ireland. There was another daughter named Sun Princess. Her son Royal Charger had revealed such great racing form that the Government of the Irish Free

State was content to pay 50,000 guineas for Royal Charger as a stallion for the National Stud of Ireland.

Much more might be written but then it also might be wearisome.

A record of Turf successes in classic and great weight-for-age races has been recounted which has rarely, if ever, been excelled in the annals of British racing.

Glancing back through these notes I find that I have not indicated the lineage of the first mare whose name I mentioned. Palotta, foaled in 1893, was by Gallinule out of Maid of Kilcreene, by Arbitrator, son of Solon, the sire of Barcaldine. Maid of Kilcreene died in 1903 when nineteen years old. She was out of Querida, by King John. Querida was a 70 guineas' yearling at the Middle Park Stud Sales, Eltham, Kent. Her sixth foal was Maid of Kilcreene. That mare never raced and was put to stud at three years. Eight of her eleven foals were winners. Palotta was her fifth. Palotta had ten winners under both rules and they captured $43\frac{1}{2}$ races and over £18,500. Lady Catherine, to whom reference was made earlier on, was exported to Russia where she was a winner, but whether she has left any outstanding produce in that far country, is beyond the power of the writer to state.

It may be of interest to refer to the fact that Maid of Kilcreene was a daughter of Arbitrator. He was not much of a racehorse. However he did sire Kilwarlin, who after 'stopping to kick at the post' went on to win a sensational St Leger in 1887. The dam of Kilwarlin was Hasty Girl, who also bred Bendigo – Eclipse, Jubilee and Champion Stakes winner, second in the Cesarewitch and third three times for the Cambridgeshire.

Kilwarlin sired a colt which early went to the US, and there made a fine reputation winning among other races, the Futurity Stakes at Belmont Park, New York. That colt was named Ogden. For many years he enjoyed much fame as a sire. Might it be beyond any possibility to suggest that the dams of big winners in the US sired by Ogden, would have carried the blood of Lexington, Citadel, Bonnie Scotland and Glencoe, which could account for those successes, and perhaps tend to explain why the crossing of Americus on a grand-daughter of Arbitrator might have started the foundation of this illustrious family? We know it rarely happens that lines of blood which on the face of it appear to denote success in one direction, also achieve anything like similar brilliance in the other direction, for example St Simon on mares carrying Musket blood – La Flèche, etc. Musket blood (through Carbine) on mares by St Simon with practically no successful results.

With many very good female representatives of this virile female line now having the finest opportunities at the Stud, it is certain that further great Turf honours will be gained by the descendants of Lady Josephine.

BBR–1946

The Day Mumtaz Mahal Ran for the One Thousand Guineas

Universally acknowledged as the best two-year-old of 1923, Mumtaz Mahal, despite the scepticism among the breeding intelligentsia as to her ability of 'getting' a mile in classic company, started at odds of 6 to 5 against her in the One Thousand Guineas.

As the **BBR** *reported in 1924:*

IF THE RACE had been run over six furlongs instead of over a mile, Mumtaz Mahal would have won by many lengths. She held a commanding lead at the Bushes, two furlongs from home, and appeared to be travelling so smoothly that nothing appeared more certain than that she would retain her advantage until the winning post was reached. But before another half-furlong had been covered it became fairly obvious that Mumtaz Mahal was in trouble. Plack and Straitlace, who had been lying second and third, began to reduce her lead. When called upon to resist these challengers, the favourite changed her legs and became momentarily unbalanced. This happened at the foot of the rise to the winning post, a furlong from the goal. Before the favourite had recovered her equilibrium Plack had raced up and passed her. Mumtaz Mahal struggled on gamely, but never looked like regaining the lost ground. If the winning post had been a little further away she would have been third instead of second, for Straitlace, running on the far side, all alone, was fast overhauling her.

Mumtaz Mahal had, so to say, failed gloriously. The defeat she suffered in no wise tarnished her reputation. On the other hand, the race had shown that she was still the speed marvel she revealed herself to be as a two-year-old. It had also been noted that she was looking a grander mare than she had ever done before. The previous season she always presented a somewhat unfurnished appearance, but she was now much heavier in muscle and looked extremely handsome.

Subsequently, Mumtaz Mahal was given another chance at a mile in the Coronation Stakes when in receipt of 7 lb from Straitlace who had, in the meantime, carried off the Oaks. Straitlace won easily with Mumtaz Mahal fifth of seven. Obviously, Straitlace had improved sharply, so the fact that Mumtaz Mahal had beaten her narrowly at level weight in the One Thousand Guineas and now was receiving 7 lb in no wise disputed the theory that 'a reduction of weight does not convert a non-stayer into a stayer'.

Mumtaz Mahal raced twice more, winning stakes at six and five furlongs, respectively.

'Those last two victories,' noted the BBR, *'had demonstrated that she was supreme in her own particular line. It may be doubted whether a faster filly – or colt either – has been seen on our Turf.'*

Sir Edward Hulton's Straitlace also avenged her loss to Plack in the One Thousand Guineas by proving a most 'meritorious' winner of the Oaks. This daughter of Son-in-Law–Stolen Kiss, by Best Man, proved to have genuine stamina in company with her miler speed. Like Mumtaz Begum, although not as dramatically, she became a foundation matron.

There is no question as from whom Straitlace inherited her staying power. Her sire, Son-in-Law, champion sire of 1924, won eight races. The average winning distance was two miles and he never won at less than a mile and a half.

All in the Family

The Tetrarch's sensational grey daughter, Mumtaz Mahal, is generally accepted as being the fastest filly or colt ever conceived in England. However, there have been dissenters. Mumtaz Mahal's own daughter, Rustom Mahal, by Rustom Pasha, never raced, but Gordon Richards described her as the fastest filly he ever rode. Although Rustom Mahal, a foal of 1934, never had the opportunity to prove she was faster in competition than her dam, she produced Brilliant chef-de-race Abernant, the best two-year-old in England in 1948.

Then there was Mumtaz Mahal's own son, Mirza II, by Blenheim. He was a brilliant stakes winner at two and his trainer, Frank Butters, stated he was the fastest horse he ever trained, although he could not be carried a full six furlongs.

So, if Mumtaz Mahal was not the quickest thoroughbred ever bred in England, perhaps either her daughter Rustom Mahal or her son, Mirza II, was.

Incidentally, Mirza II was a full brother to Mumtaz Begum, dam of Brilliant chef-de-race and imperishable sire influence, Nasrullah, as well as Sun Princess, dam of Nasrullah's three-parts brother, Brilliant chef-de-race and enduring sire influence, Royal Charger.

Mumtaz Mahal

As one of the most romantic and enduring forces in the history of the thoroughbred breed in the twentieth century, the equivalent of many books has been written about the grey filly Mumtaz Mahal, the daughter of The Tetrarch and Lady Josephine who was a super luminary both on the track and at stud. Therefore, it is a delight to realise how much she was appreciated even as a yearling when, in 1922, she elicited a bid of 9,100 guineas, the highest price paid for a yearling since another immortal, Sceptre, cost 10,000 guineas at that age in 1900.

The BBR, *writing of her sale in 1922 to George Lambton on behalf of the Aga Khan, said: 'As an individual, she is wonderful, as near perfection as imagination can conceive. Her conformation is ideal and she has both size and quality. This does not necessarily mean she is bound to be a racing paragon. The characters most essential for racing purposes are hidden until they can be subjected to a practical test.'*

Mumtaz Mahal exposed her 'hidden' character sublimely at the first 'practical test' and racing and breeding history was in the making.

The BBR *of 1923 recounts:*

Mumtaz Mahal.

IN THE early months of this year, Mumtaz Mahal showed her trainer (R. C. Dawson) that she was no ordinary filly. It was at the Newmarket Second Spring Meeting that she first revealed to the public what she could do. A week or two before, Mr Dawson had formally tested her capabilities. On April 7th he saddled the two-year-old Friar's Daughter to win the Enfield Plate at Alexandra Park from thirteen opponents. Second to her, beaten two lengths, was Golden Knight, who had previously won easily at Nottingham. Friar's Daughter was, therefore, a useful animal for trial purposes. Mumtaz Mahal was asked to give her 28 lb, and in the doing beat her half a furlong.

'I was so astounded and excited that I nearly fell off my hack,' said Mr Dawson when he told the story to this writer. 'Though I knew the grey to be an exceptionally good filly, I had no idea she was such a wonder.'

When Mumtaz Mahal made her debut at Newmarket in the Spring Stakes, Straitlace, coming off an impressive score in the Stud Produce Stakes, was one of her opponents. But 'tidings of the Whitcome trial had leaked out and Mumtaz Mahal was held at even money with Straitlace 5 to 2. As on subsequent occasions, Mumtaz Mahal played with her opponents that day and won in a trot by three lengths.'

Addenda:
Friar's Daughter, as a matron, produced the Triple Crown winner Bahram as well as the Coronation Cup and Irish Derby winner Dastur.

Straitlace proceeded to capture the Oaks the following season and became a quality stakes producer in France.

Maid Marian's Place in History

It is doubtful if there have ever been two more accomplished classic-winning full sisters than Memoir (1887) and La Flèche (1889), daughters of St Simon–Quiver, by Toxophilite. Memoir secured the Oaks and the St Leger while La Flèche, unquestionably the better of the two, captured the One Thousand Guineas, Oaks, St Leger and Ascot Gold Cup. In recounting her turf career, the BBR of 1916, noted: 'La Flèche never knew defeat until she ran in the Derby. The 11 to 10 choice, she was beaten by the 40 to 1 Sir Hugo when her jockey allowed Sir Hugo and Bucentaure to steal a march upon him at Tattenham Corner, and when it came to the descent of the hill he was not within ten lengths of the two leaders. They had slipped him. Later in the St Leger, La Flèche, 'a gallant little mare', beat Sir Hugo in a canter.

Both Memoir and La Flèche established quality families, but, oddly enough, it was their half-sister, Maid Marian (1886), by Hampton, who ran seven times without winning, but then produced five-time champion sire, Polymelus, sire of the epochal Phalaris. Maid Marian is also the distaff ancestress of richly influential French stallion Wild Risk.

Beauty is as Beauty Does

Beauty is as beauty does. Bonnie Agnes, a foal of 1875, by the classic-winning Blair Athol from the stakes-winning and family-founding Little Agnes, by The Cure, produced Bonnie Jean, heroine of the Oaks in 1883. This is also the family of the famous French Derby winner and superior sire Herbager. In a mention of Bonnie Agnes in the BBR *of 1916, she is described thus: 'A common-looking sort of mare, with long hair on her legs like a carthorse, straight pasterns, knuckle knees, and no size – altogether a most unlikely breeding proposition, apart from her pedigree. Family over the individual?*

Inbreeding to Superior Female Families

Inbreeding to superior female families through different individuals has resulted in numerous quality performers and producers through the years. Among the prominent producers in the history of the Stud Book, none is more legendary than Glencoe's daughter Pocahontas, a foal of 1837 and the dam of, among others, the incredibly successful stallion Stockwell, winner of the Two Thousand Guineas and the St Leger. Colonel Vuillier's original list of the most important names to be found in pedigrees counted up to sixteen. Of these, fifteen were sires and the only mare was Pocahontas.

In 1869, a horse was foaled by the name of Wellingtonia. Sent to France, Wellingtonia became a classic sire. One son, Clover, captured the French Derby and Prix du Cadran and a daughter, Clarisse, secured Italy's Gran Premio di Milano. Another daughter, Plaisanterie, an important stakes winner both in Germany and England, was a splendid producer; still another, Bluette, bred the French Derby and Prix du Cadran winner Omnium II, and yet another, Cromatella, foaled Cheri, best in both the French Two Thousand Guineas and the Grand Prix de Paris.

Wellingtonia's sire, Chattanooga, and his dam, Araucaria, were both produced by daughters of Pocahontas!

The Death of Festa

When the English-bred matron Festa, a daughter of St Simon from the Oaks victress L'Abbesse de Jouarre, by Trappist, died in Germany in 1914, the Germans claimed that her produce had earned more money than any producer other than Galicia, the dam of Bayardo and Lemberg. As the Review *explained, this was only because the Germans included 'place' money and the honour of runner-up to Galicia truly belonged to Mowerina, dam of Donovan among others. In any case, the* Review *was prompted to publish the producing records of Galicia and Mowerina and that information was gladly accepted.*

As for Festa, a moderate racing filly, she was an inordinately successful broodmare. She bred four German classic winners as well as one other outstanding performer. Festa was a full sister to the excellent racehorse and noteworthy sire, Desmond, whose offspring included both winners of the 1913 Epsom Derby – Craganour, who lost it on a disqualification, and Aboyeur, who inherited it but may have been best in any case. Desmond also sired Ayn Hali, a talented stakes winner who became dam of Sir Cosmo, and he also sired Pretty Polly's daughter Molly Desmond, dam of the Irish classic winners Spike Island and Zodiac and precursor of her own tremendously influential distaff family.

FESTA died recently in Germany. Little did anyone imagine when she went to that country in 1901 that she was destined to achieve the fame she did. Her produce have won stakes to the value of £84,500. This is a record which only Galicia, the dam of Bayardo and Lemberg, excels – according to the contention of the Germans. Their reckoning is, however, a 'slim' one. They credit Festa with all the 'place' money won by her produce, and it must have amounted to several thousands of pounds. In England, of course, the practice is to take account only of the values of races won outright. If the same test was applied to Festa, she would come third to Galicia and Mowerina. We do not make this statement with any idea of depreciating the achievements of Festa; but facts are facts, and in justice to Mowerina they should be set down fairly and plainly. Many of our readers will no doubt like to have the records of Galicia and Mowerina placed before them. Here they are:

Galicia

Bay or brown mare, bred in 1898 by Mr A. W. Cox. By Galopin–Isoletta, by Isonomy–Lady Muncaster, by Muncaster.

Winning Produce

	Races	Value £	s
Eastern (1904), br. c. by Eager	2	1,696	10
Bayardo (1906), b. c. by Bay Ronald	22	44,734	0
Lemberg (1907), b. c. by Cyllene	12	41,694	0
Totals	36	88,124	10

Mowerina

Chestnut mare, bred in Denmark in 1876. By Scottish Chief out of Stockings, by Stock-well–Go-Ahead, by Melbourne.

Winning Produce

	Races	Value £	s
Modwena (1883), b. f. by Galopin	10	6,267	16
Amoena (1884), ch. f. by Hampton	1	250	0
Donovan (1886), b. c. by Galopin	18	55,153	15
Semolina (1887), b. f. by St Simon	14	12,685	8
Raeburn (1890), b. c. by St Simon	5	8,374	0
Elizabeth Hardwicke (1895), ch. f. by Orme	1	100	0
Sir Joshua (1900), b. c. by St Simon	2	237	0
Totals	51	83,067	19

Festa was bred by Lord Dunraven in 1893. She was the first foal of her dam, L'Abbesse de Jouarre, who was, we believe, at that time partly owned by Lord Randolph Churchill, in whose name she had won the Oaks of 1889. L'Abbesse de Jouarre was by Trappist–Festive by Carnival. Festa was by St Simon. She was not of much account on the Turf. As a two-year-old she ran five times, without winning, but managed to get placed third in the Brocklesby at Lincoln, and second in the Fitzwilliam Plate at Newmarket. The following season she ran no fewer than fourteen times. At Brighton she won the Bevendean Handicap (6 f); and at Doncaster dead-heated for first place in the Melton Stakes, but was easily beaten in the 'run off'. In six other races she finished second and third. As a four-year-old she won a five-furlong handicap at Manchester, was once third and once unplaced.

In 1897 Festa went to the Stud, but was barren in 1898. Her produce in 1899 was a colt (who was cut) by Winkfield. Salute (also cut) by Carbine, came in 1900, and he won many races in England for Lord Dunraven. In 1901 Festa's foal was the filly Festal Air, by Ayrshire. On going to the Stud Festal Air was barren to Wildfowler in 1905, and, to

Laveno, produced the colt Rhinefall in 1906, but died the same year.

Reverting to L'Abbesse de Jouarre, she was barren to Saraband in 1894; in 1895 she produced Cowl by Galopin, and in 1896, Desmond, brother to Festa. She was covered that year by Isinglass, but died foaling the following year.

After reaching Germany Festa's produce was Festino, Fels, Fabula, Faust and Fervor – all colts with the exception of Fabula. The achievements of these animals brought their owners, Messrs Weinberg, of Frankfort into great prominence. For some years they carried almost everything before them.   BBR–1914

The Death of Sceptre

When she died in 1926 at the advanced age of twenty-seven, Sceptre, a bay daughter of Persimmon–Ornament, by Bend Or, was, arguably, as great a racemare as the Turf had ever seen. Her triumphs included four classics – both the Guineas, the Oaks and the St Leger. During most of her career she was owned and sometimes trained by Mr Robert S. Sievier, described by the **BBR***'s Mr Edward Moorhouse 'as the most picturesque figure we have seen on the Turf during the last thirty years'. Then there is Mr Moorhouse! In the opinion of many observers and students of the racing and breeding scene throughout the sport's history, he was, unarguably, unique in being able to present his vast knowledge of the game in the most absorbing, informative and fascinating style. He was the Eclipse of his profession when he was alive and, to most of us, like that great equine, he still owns that most lofty position some fifty years after his death in 1939.*

With the evaporation of the years since then, the writings of Mr Moorhouse have, to a large extent, become unknown to modern-day racing journalists and all other devotees of the sport. The pace is so much quicker and the proliferation of racing and breeding publications throughout the world in this day and age requires so much time just to stay up to date, that prose such as Mr Moorhouse turned out is a forgotten treasure.

Fortunately, many of the treasures he put down on paper are to be found in the early issues of the **BBR***. Hopefully, once he and other* **BBR** *contributors have been exposed again, which is the purpose of this book, there will be a slackening of the pace by some and they will take the time 'to smell some of the roses' along this rich and lovely highway of Turf literature.*

When Sceptre died, Mr Moorhouse said: 'The time has therefore come when the complete life-story of this famous mare can, and should be written.' He was equal to the task, and the posterity of the Turf will forever be the richer for that. So this triumvirate of Sceptre, her 'picturesque' owner, 'Bob' Sievier, and the abundantly talented Mr Moorhouse are brought together in their entirety in this wonderful essay on Sceptre which appeared in the BBR *of 1926. It is a treasure which should never be sunken by the passage of time.*

SCEPTRE died early in February. She was twenty-seven years old, so the news of her passing caused no surprise. Her days of usefulness ended so long ago as 1917, when she produced the last of her eight foals. Until 1922 persistent efforts were made to induce her to breed another foal. After that she lapsed into the state of an honoured pensioner. The time has therefore come when the complete life-story of this famous mare can, and should, be written. It is always hazardous to compare the thorough-bred giants of our own day with those of former periods, but it is hardly conceivable that there was ever a greater racing mare than Sceptre. As a broodmare she occupies a lowlier position, though even in this sphere her influence has been, and still is, considerable.

In assuming the duty of reviewing the remarkable career of Sceptre, I am beset by difficulties. These would not obtrude themselves if I were going to write a book about her, but inasmuch as I am compelled to compress the story into a few pages many features one would like to dwell upon, the avenues one would like to explore, must also be ignored. Sceptre merits tender and loving treatment. To those of us who were ardent and enthusiastic devotees of the Turf during the years she was in her prime, and who revelled in her queenly supremacy, she is a precious and an abiding memory. It would appear, however, that a generation has come along to whom her wonderful qualities and attributes make but a slight appeal. This indifference was rather painfully manifested at the time of her death. There were even journals of sport that referred to the event in the scantiest way. No advantage was taken of the oppor-tunity to instruct their younger readers, and make them realise the greatness of Sceptre, and what that greatness represented. The selling platers of the day were deemed much more important. It is not in this wise that the splendid traditions of the Turf are to be preserved.

When, early in the 'sixties of last century, the late Sir Tatton Sykes succeeded his father at Sledmere he sold off the large batch of mares he had inherited, and then began to stock the stud afresh. One of the first mares he bought was Miss Agnes, the second produce of the famous mare Agnes, though it was not until later that her fame became established. He mated Miss Agnes with The Cure. The resulting foal was Polly Agnes, who was so small and delicate that Sir Tatton, who hated the sight of her, gave her to his stud groom, Snarry, on condition that she left Sledmere forthwith. Snarry sent the foal to his son at Malton, a few miles away. Trained for two seasons, Polly Agnes won three races and was then mated with Macaroni. The produce of this alliance was Lily Agnes, who, though described as a 'light-fleshed, ragged hipped, lop-eared filly', had great merit as a racehorse, winning twenty-one times over long distances.

In 1880 Lily Agnes was sent to the Duke of Westminster's stud at Eaton, near Chester, to be covered by Doncaster. The Duke's stud groom, Richard Chapman, took a great fancy to the mare, and urged the Duke to buy her. This suggestion was not adopted at the time, but later in the year Lily Agnes was bought for the Eaton Stud, the price paid being £2,500, and two free subscriptions to Bend Or, who had just gone to the Eaton Stud at a fee of £200. In 1882 Lily Agnes produced the filly Farewell (by Doncaster), winner of the One Thousand Guineas; in 1883, the mighty Ormonde (by Bend Or), and in 1887 the filly Ornament, sister to Ormonde. Lily Agnes also bred other good horses for the Duke, but our attention can be concentrated on Ornament, because she it was who became the dam of Sceptre. Coming into the world as she did, at the time when Ormonde had established his tremendous reputation, Ornament must, in her early days, have caused the Duke much disappointment. Her racing abilities were of a very limited kind – indeed, she appears to have had none. She carried silk only once – as a two-year-old – and was then easily beaten by a very moderate horse, who was her solitary opponent.

Ornament began her career at the stud as a three-year-old. Her first foal, born in 1891, died in infancy. Her foal of 1892 was Star Ruby, who went to the United States, where he became a very successful stallion. Another of Ornament's foals was Collar, who, after winning good races, went to South Africa, to be brought back to England by the late Mr Allison in 1902. It was in 1899 that the mare produced Sceptre as the result of an alliance with King Edward's Derby winner, Persimmon. In the autumn of that year the old Duke of Westminster died. His death had important consequences, for it necessitated the dispersal by public sale of the whole of his bloodstock. Flying Fox, it will be remembered, was purchased by the late M. Edmond Blanc for 37,500 guineas, and went to France. How differently modern Turf history would have been fashioned if Flying Fox had spent his stud life in England!

It was in the summer of 1900 that the dead Duke's yearlings came under the auctioneer's hammer at Newmarket. The occasion was a remarkable one. There were twelve youngsters offered, and they made a total of 43,300 guineas. The young Duke of Westminster, a grandson of the first Duke, bought five of the colts. He paid 9,100 guineas for Cupbearer, by Orme; 5,700 for Flying Lemur, by Orme out of Vampire; 2,400 for The Gatherer, by Grey Leg; 1,250 for St Benet, by Bend Or; and 440 for Just Cause, by Best Man. Flying Lemur, brother to Flying Fox, was the best of the lot, but even he was only second class. Everybody associated with the young Duke was anxious that he should secure Sceptre, and he would have done but for the determination of one man, Mr Robert S. Sievier.

I think I am justified in describing 'Bob' Sievier as the most picturesque figure we have seen on the Turf during the last thirty years. There was a period when he was constantly in the limelight. His career has been one of wildly fluctuating fortune. Within the space of a few months he would be poor, rich, then poor again; but whatever the state of his finances might be he was invariably optimistic and nonchalant.

At the beginning of the year 1900 Sievier's bank balance was understood to be of minute dimensions, but by the end of March it was once more in a healthy condition, for he took many thousands of pounds from the bookmakers when Sir Geoffrey won the Lincolnshire Handicap. Three weeks later he had a considerable portion of those winnings on The Grafter who was successful in the City and Suburban Handicap at Epsom. It was then reported that he was in command of a capital exceeding £100,000. Early in May a colt called Toddington easily won a two-year-old race at Newmarket. Sievier bought the youngster for £10,000 and a few days later won with him the Woodcote Stakes at Epsom. That race was run on a Tuesday: the next Saturday Toddington won, by a neck, a race at Kempton Park, but went badly lame immediately after passing the winning post, and was never again of much use as a racehorse. Sievier backed the colt heavily both times he won for him, and no doubt recovered his £10,000 with good interest.

When, therefore, the Duke of Westminster's yearlings came up for sale at Newmarket at the beginning of July, Sievier had a lot of money at his disposal. Before leaving London to attend the sale, he went to his bank, drew out twenty £1,000 Bank of England notes, and took them to Newmarket. The night before the sale he called at the Rutland Arms Hotel to see Mr Somerville Tattersall. To quote Sievier's own words: 'I told him that as I had seldom bought anything at auction, and was, in a business sense, comparatively unknown to him, I wished him to take the

£20,000 in notes as security, because I should probably be a bidder for yearlings the following day.'

A year or two ago, when I was lunching with Mr Tattersall, I referred to this incident, and he gave me his side of the story. When Sievier handed over the bank notes Mr Tattersall told him the sum was far too big, adding: 'When the sale is over I shall have to hand you back several of these notes.'

"I'll bet you a bob (a shilling) you will not,' retorted Sievier.

'Very well,' said Mr Tattersall, 'but I did not know you bet in bobs.'

Sievier smiled and departed. He had placed Mr Tattersall in a great difficulty. It was late in the day, and the banks were closed. What was to be done with the £20,000, for Newmarket was full up with racing people, some of whom have unorthodox ideas with regard to other people's property, especially when that property is in the form of bank notes. Eventually, after getting one of his clerks to make a list of the numbers on the notes, Mr Tattersall retired to his bedroom, put the notes in an envelope, and placed it on the top of a wardrobe. First thing the

Sceptre.

following morning the notes were safely deposited at one of the local banks.

Together with his then trainer, Charles Morton, and Mr Peard, the well-known Dublin veterinary surgeon, Sievier made a close examination of the Westminster yearlings. The result of the inspection was that he decided he would buy Sceptre, whether he secured any of the others or not. When the sale took place, Sievier began by giving 700 guineas for a colt by Orme out of Console, and then he paid 5,600 guineas for a colt by Orme out of Gantlet that was subsequently named Duke of Westminster, who will come into this story again later on.

Sceptre was the last but one of the yearlings to enter the ring. Sievier opened the bidding for her by offering 5,000 guineas. Here is a description of what followed that was given to me by the late John Porter, who had been trainer to the old Duke, and was continuing as trainer to the new Duke. As I have explained everyone associated with the latter wanted him to have Sceptre, and none more so than Porter. The famous trainer was accompanied by Mr Cecil Parker, the Duke's land agent at Eaton. 'Mr Parker,' said Porter, 'did the bidding, and began to perspire with excitement when the price rose to 8,000 guineas, then to 9,000, and on further. After Mr Sievier had offered 10,000 guineas, Mr Parker refused to proceed any further, although I urged him to go on. Mr Sievier's good luck was our misfortune. It was, however, more than good luck that came to the buyer's aid that day. He displayed a confident judgment and a fearless determination to beat all opposition. All the same, while I am compelled to give him this credit, I have always regretted that Sceptre did not come to Kingsclere, as she would have done had the old Duke been spared to us a while longer.'

Until that day, the highest price a yearling had realised at auction was the 6,000 guineas Sir Blundell Maple gave for Childwick, with whom he won the Cesarewitch. That 'record' had been eclipsed when, a few minutes before Sceptre came under the hammer, a colt by Orme out of Kissing Cup, subsequently named Cupbearer, was bought for the Duke of Westminster at 9,100 guineas. It is, perhaps, not easy in these days, when the sale of a yearling for 10,000 guineas or more is a frequent occurrence, to understand the tremendous sensation the bidding for Cupbearer and Sceptre created. Mr Sievier has told us: 'I was dubbed by some an ass, by the majority as mad, while a few kindly referred to the proverb about "a fool and his money". I should have gone much higher, for I had determined that Sceptre should be mine.'

The next we saw of Sceptre was when she made her debut on the Turf at Epsom, twelve months later, in the race for the Woodcote Stakes.

Shortly before this Sceptre and the colt Duke of Westminster (another of the yearlings bought at the Westminster sale by Sievier) had been tried with a five-year-old named Leonid, a recent winner of a race at Lincoln. Leonid was giving the two-year-olds 14 lb over five furlongs. They both beat him, and Sceptre finished well in front of Duke of Westminster. It had already been discovered that the youngsters had constitutions which differed greatly. Duke of Westminster was somewhat delicate, and required very light training; Sceptre was robust, full of courage and energy, and could stand, and needed, a lot of work to keep her fit and well.

Sceptre won the Woodcote Stakes easily in fast time. A month later she captured, just as readily, the July Stakes at Newmarket; but at Doncaster, in September, finished third only to Game Chick and Csardas in the Champagne Stakes, beaten a length and a half and a head. This defeat of the daughter of Persimmon and Ornament caused much surprise. She had easily beaten Csardas at Epsom, while Duke of Westminster had twice beaten Game Chick, and Sceptre was known to be superior to Duke of Westminster.

Sceptre did not run again that season, at the end of which Sievier wanted to sell either Duke of Westminster or Sceptre. They were offered to Mr (afterwards Lord) Faber, whose horses were trained by John Porter at Kingsclere, but only one of them was to be taken. As already explained Porter had been very anxious that the young Duke of Westminster should buy Sceptre when she was offered as a yearling. Here, then, was a chance of getting Sceptre into his stable, for Mr Faber left him to decide whether the colt or the filly should be bought. Unfortunately, however, Mr Faber intimated that he himself preferred the colt, who had run twice and won each time. The defeat at Doncaster had rather discredited Sceptre.

It was Sievier's earnest hope that the colt would be selected for purchase. So that matters might shape themselves as he desired, he resorted to the expedient of pricing the colt at 20,000 guineas and the filly at 15,000 guineas, believing that by so doing Mr Faber would jump to the conclusion that Duke of Westminster was regarded as the better of the two. Porter, we may be sure, was not in the least influenced by this stratagem; nevertheless, he finally decided to recommend Mr Faber to buy the colt. When he was giving me material for his autobiography I could see that the recollection of this incident made him feel very unhappy. I could not put all he said into the book, but I may now state that he pointed out to me the awkward position in which he was placed when he had to make his decision. He gave me to understand that if Mr

Faber had expressed no preference, Sceptre, and not Duke of Westminster, would most certainly have gone to Kingsclere; but there was
the fact that Mr Faber had intimated his opinion that the colt was the
better racing proposition. If, therefore, in spite of this, Porter had
selected the filly, and the colt had turned out the better of the two, Porter
would always have been tortured by the thought that he had done his
patron a great disservice. Consequently, he felt bound to decide in favour
of the colt, provided he found, on examination (as he did), that Duke of
Westminster was sound. Once again, therefore, luck favoured Mr
Sievier.

It was about this time that Sievier decided to train his horses himself.
He took a place at Shrewton, in Wiltshire, and engaged an American as
his assistant. Sceptre was entered for the Lincolnshire Handicap, to be
run the following March. It is an event that has rarely been won by a
three-year-old – so rarely, indeed, that of late years few three-year-olds
have been entered. Sceptre was doing well in her training for the race
when, at the end of February, Sievier was called to Paris, and was away
from home two weeks. When he returned to Shrewton he found to his
dismay that Sceptre would hardly look at her food, and was very fretful.
On making inquiries he learned that during his absence she had been
galloped at racing pace over a mile with other horses four mornings in
succession. Sievier's first impulse was to strike her out of the Lincolnshire, but he refrained from doing so because the public had backed her
heavily. He at once took the filly under his sole control, and adopted
every means he could think of to induce her to eat, but she would only
consume a third of her proper ration of oats. It follows, therefore, that
when she ran at Lincoln she was not in a condition to show her best form.
Nevertheless, she had the race won everywhere except at the winning
post. St Maclou caught her in the last two strides and beat her a head.

There is one other fact that should be mentioned. When the jockey got
on Sceptre's back in the paddock before the race, Sievier told him to
ride a waiting race until two furlongs from home, and then come along
as fast as he could. But the American assistant-trainer, who led the filly
from the paddock on to the course, finally instructed the jockey to jump
off in front and keep there if possible. To the consternation of Sievier the
jockey rode in accordance with these latter orders, and no doubt the
filly's failure was due to the adoption of these stupid tactics. When
Sievier learned from the jockey the reason why his own orders had been
disobeyed, he promptly dispensed with the services of his American
assistant.

After a week or two's rest Sceptre began to improve rapidly: she was taking her food normally once more, and putting on 'condition'. At the end of April she was sent to Newmarket to compete for the Two Thousand and the One Thousand Guineas. The day before she left Shrewton she had shown to advantage in a gallop on the training ground, and her owner was confident she would win the two classic races. He, however, did not bet on her, for the simple reason that he had no money to bet with.

In the Two Thousand Sceptre met her former stable companion, Duke of Westminster. The previous week Porter had subjected the latter to a trial in which he was beaten a neck by Flying Lemur, brother to Flying Fox. A note in the Kingsclere 'Trial' book states that Duke of Westminster would have won the trial by two lengths had he not been interfered with by Flying Lemur near the finish. In one of his two races as a two-year-old Duke of Westminster had given Flying Lemur 5 lb, and beaten him two lengths; in the trial the two horses carried equal weights. There is no doubt that Duke of Westminster was sent to Newmarket in the belief that he had a very good chance of winning the Two Thousand Guineas, for which he and Sceptre started equal favourites at 4 to 1.

Sceptre won the Two Thousand by two lengths from Pistol, with Ard Patrick third, another three lengths behind. Duke of Westminster finished a long way back, much to the disgust of John Porter, and, we may be sure, of Mr Faber also. The disappointment caused by the colt's failure in this race was accentuated by his defeats in the Derby and the Cambridgeshire, his only other races that season. As a four-year-old Duke of Westminster won a race at Ascot, but that was only a flicker of the form he had shown as a two-year-old. Porter, in his book, adds: 'His record subsequent to his juvenile days does not bear thinking about, and at the stud he did very little.' Which is sadly true.

With odds of 2 to 1 laid on her, Sceptre also won the One Thousand Guineas very easily. Game Chick, who had beaten her so unexpectedly in the Champagne Stakes the previous year, finished fourth only. As a result of the filly's two classic victories, Mr Sievier was the richer by £10,500, the value of the stakes.

Then came the Derby. With money in his pocket once more, Sievier backed Sceptre for the great race at Epsom to win him £33,000. The bets were lost, for Sceptre came in fourth. She got badly away at the start, and her jockey, Randall, most injudiciously rode her hard up the steep ascent from the starting post to recover the lost ground. The filly was, in consequence, beaten before the race was half over. If Randall had exercised more patience, and drawn up to the leaders more gradually, it is rather more than possible that Sceptre would have won the Derby. She most certainly ought not to have been farther back than second. Ard Patrick won by three lengths from Rising Glass, with Friar Tuck third, another three lengths away. As we shall see later, Sceptre was just about the equal of Ard Patrick as a four-year-old. She had beaten him easily in the Two Thousand Guineas, but Ard Patrick was an improved horse when he ran in the Derby. One is tempted to write that it is hardly conceivable he had, in the course of a month, advanced sufficiently to convert a five-lengths' defeat at Newmarket into a six-lengths' victory at Epsom; yet only this year we saw precisely the same difference between Coronach and Colorado in the Guineas and the Derby. So far as Sceptre is concerned, the Derby was, in fact, a tragedy. If she had won that race she would have held the unique record of having won all our five classic races, for, two days after the Derby, she gained an easy victory in the Oaks, and in the autumn won the St Leger at Doncaster.

From Epsom Sceptre went over to Paris for the Grand Prix. She was beaten at Longchamp, perhaps because her jockey, in order to avoid being interfered with, kept her wide of the other runners all the way round, so that she travelled a much longer distance than her opponents. Sceptre was hurried back to England, and three days later was a competitor for the Coronation Stakes at Ascot. Giving 14 lb or more to her opponents, she ran unplaced; but the following day won the St James's Palace Stakes over twelve furlongs, beating Flying Lemur and Rising Glass – a result that afforded proof that she ought to have been at least second in the Derby. At Goodwood, six weeks later, Sceptre failed by two lengths to give 6 lb to Royal Lancer in the Sussex Stakes, but two days later won the Nassau Stakes over twelve furlongs, giving Elba 17 lb and a four-lengths' beating.

Thus at Epsom, Ascot, and Goodwood Sceptre was first a loser and then a winner, so that some people came to regard her as an inconsistent performer. The fact of the matter probably was that Mr Sievier, still acting as his own trainer, did not quite understand her. There are many people who contend that if Sceptre had from first to last been under the care of a skilled professional trainer she might never have known defeat. At Doncaster the filly departed from habit, for the win came before the loss. She gained a notable triumph in the St Leger the second day of the meeting, and was beaten in the Park Hill Stakes the fourth day, and by none other than Elba, although the latter was receiving 5 lb less weight than when Sceptre beat her so easily at Goodwood. The explanation of this failure at Doncaster is, however, a simple one. When Sceptre was saddled for the St Leger she looked a scarecrow. So severely had she been trained that she appeared to be little more than skin and bone. There was only one gallop left in her, and that she had when she won the St Leger, beating Rising Glass and Friar Tuck three lengths and two lengths. Ard Patrick did not oppose her. This was a pity; but anyway, Sceptre at Doncaster beat Rising Glass and Friar Tuck just as easily as Ard Patrick had done at Epsom.

The Park Hill Stakes was Sceptre's last race as a three-year-old. She had that season won six races worth £28,195. In addition to receiving the valuable stake, Sievier won a substantial sum in bets over the St Leger, but six weeks later he sent Sceptre into the auction ring at Newmarket. He could have sold her in May for £40,000, but refused then to part with her. When he offered her in October he placed a reserve of 20,000 guineas on her. Mr Tattersall could not persuade anyone to bid that sum, so Sceptre remained the property of Sievier. A few weeks later he felt thankful that this was so, because his financial position had improved in the meantime. It may, however, be said that probably he would eventually have been better off if someone had bid the 20,000 guineas and taken the filly from him.

There was one other episode during Sceptre's three-year-old career to which some reference ought to be made. One of the regular contributors to one of the sporting papers had developed the habit of making disparaging comments about the filly whenever he had the opportunity of doing so. After one of these tirades Sievier, metaphorically speaking, took off his coat, and stepped into the ring to defend the filly. He declared his determination to put an end to 'this contemptible nagging', and to that end announced that Sceptre should run any horse at weight-for-age and sex for £10,000 over any distance from ten furlongs to a mile and three-quarters. If either party to the match desired to withdraw a forfeit of £2,000 was to be declared seven days before the date fixed for running. Failing acceptance of that challenge, Sievier said he was willing to run Sceptre against St Maclou on weight-for-sex terms under the same conditions. Neither challenge was accepted. The offer to run against St Maclou at a difference of only 3 lb was certainly a bold one, because when St Maclou beat Sceptre a head in the Lincolnshire Handicap the preceding March he was giving her 19 lb. I have, however, no doubt that if the suggested match had been arranged Sceptre would have defeated him comfortably. St Maclou's owner, Colonel Harry McCalmont probably entertained the same belief, and so ignored the challenge.

We now come to Sceptre's career as a four-year-old in the season of 1903. As in the previous year, the Lincolnshire Handicap was her first race. Naturally enough, as the winner of four classic races, she was at the top of the handicap. With 9 st 1 lb in the saddle, she carried 15 lb more than any of her opponents, started second favourite at 4 to 1, but finished fifth only, the race being won easily by Over Norton, a six-year-old carrying 7 st 6 lb. The previous year Over Norton was third in the Lincolnshire, beaten two heads by St Maclou and Sceptre.

Mr Sievier had taken a big bet about Sceptre, and before the race was run it was an open secret that her success was required to ease his financial position. When it became obvious that Sceptre would not win, many people turned their eyes towards Sievier to see what effect her defeat had on him, but he betrayed no sign of the deep emotion he must have felt. Two days later it was announced that Sceptre was for sale, and within twenty-four hours she became the property of Mr (now Sir) William Bass, a young gentleman who had recently come on the Turf. Writing editorially in his paper, *The Winning Post*, some years after this, Mr Sievier explained: 'We were compelled to sell Sceptre for reasons we are not ashamed of. We had to meet certain financial obligations, and though we hung on to the "old lady", as she was always called at Shrewton, as long as we could, that inevitable day arrived when she had to go. We sold her to Sir William Bass for £25,000. We had originally asked guineas, the shillings to go to Mr Arthur Chetwynd, who negotiated the deal, but he returned them to Sir William.'

During the two seasons she was racing for Mr Sievier, Sceptre won stake money to the value of £25,650. Add the £25,000 paid by Sir William Bass, and we get the total of £50,650 as a return for the 10,000 guineas she cost as a yearling. In other words, Sceptre yielded Sievier a gross profit of £40,000.

Sceptre now went to Manton to be trained by Alec Taylor. The first time she carried her new owner's colours was in the Hardwicke Stakes at Ascot, in June. Much improved in appearance, she simply 'played' with her opponents, and won in a canter, to the accompaniment of great cheering, because long before this she had become a tremendous favourite with the public.

Then came the race for the Eclipse Stakes of £10,000 at Sandown Park, a month after Ascot. This was a never-to-be-forgotten contest. There were only five runners, but, in addition to Sceptre, they included Ard Patrick (the previous year's Derby winner) and the three-year-old Rock Sand, who had recently won the Two Thousand Guineas and the Derby, and astonishing though it now seems, was looked upon as being in a class slightly higher than Sceptre and Ard Patrick. The prospect of seeing these three celebrated horses opposing each other had for two or three weeks been the subject of excited discussions, and the crowd that gathered at Sandown Park was so enormous that the arrangements made for dealing with it completely broke down. Hundreds of men scrambled over the railings into the enclosures without going through the formality of paying.

The race was to decide two issues: (1) the relative merits of the three-year-olds of 1902 and 1903, and (2) the respective claims to supremacy of Sceptre and Ard Patrick. The majority of those able to regard the situation without permitting their judgment to be swayed by sentiment expected to see Rock Sand emerge from the ordeal triumphant, and he started favourite at 5 to 4. As for Sceptre and Ard Patrick, the mare had much the bigger following, and was backed at 7 to 4, whereas odds of 5 to 1 were obtainable about Ard Patrick. The distance to be traversed was ten furlongs, the last four on a sharply ascending gradient. At the foot of this gradient Sceptre, Rock Sand and Ard Patrick were in front, running practically level. There were still two and a half furlongs to go when, to the surprise and dismay of his admirers, Rock Sand began to drop back beaten. The other two, with Ard Patrick next the rails, went on head to head. Presently, for a few strides, Sceptre gained a very slight lead, but a hundred yards from home Ard Patrick had drawn level again, and, amid a scene of tremendous excitement, gained a trifle with every stride. Sceptre was beaten a neck. Her defeat was a sore disappointment to most of the thousands of onlookers. They had gone to Sandown hoping to see her win, and her failure left them so crestfallen that they almost forgot to cheer the fine performance of the winner. There was, however, a numerous contingent of Irishmen in the crowd, and they raised a triumphant shout, for Ard Patrick was an Irish-bred horse, and owned by an Irishman, Mr John Gubbins, who also bred and raced Galtee More. To be strictly accurate, Mr Gubbins did not own Ard Patrick when the race for the Eclipse Stakes was run, though the public were not at the moment aware that there had been a change of ownership. A few hours before the race the horse had, however, been bought by the late Count Lehndorff for the Prussian Government, whose studs he managed. But Mr Gubbins had stipulated that he should not hand Ard Patrick over until the autumn, that he should be allowed to run the horse in the Eclipse Stakes, and the Jockey Club Stakes, and retain the prize money that might accrue as the result of those races.

The Jockey Club Stakes was Sceptre's next race, but, unfortunately, she had not the satisfaction of again meeting Ard Patrick. The latter went lame shortly after the Eclipse Stakes, and Mr Gubbins decided not to risk racing him again, so the horse was forthwith transferred to the

Germans. This premature retirement of Ard Patrick occasioned Alec Taylor one of the greatest disappointments of his long career. When Ard Patrick won at Sandown, Taylor had not yet got Sceptre quite to his liking, but when the filly competed for the Jockey Club Stakes of £10,000 at the end of September she was absolutely fit, and that she would have beaten Ard Patrick is as certain as anything connected with racing can be. She was again opposed by Rock Sand, who, in the meantime, had easily won the St Leger. Owing to his being able to claim a breeding allowance under the conditions governing the Jockey Club Stakes, Rock Sand was meeting Sceptre on terms 7 lb better than weight-for-age and sex. The filly had to carry 10 st and the colt 8 st 13 lb. The distance of the race was a mile and three-quarters. Because of his success in the St Leger, the advantage he had in the matter of weight, and the fact that he was being ridden by Maher, for whom he had always won, Rock Sand, as at Sandown Park, started a slightly better favourite than Sceptre.

Sceptre won, beating Rock Sand four lengths. The astonishing ease with which she gained her victory caused great excitement and enthusiasm. The racing crowds that go to Newmarket are not in the habit of indulging in hysterics, but on this occasion many men became almost crazy, realising that the performance they had just witnessed was one of a most amazing character, and one the like of which they might never see again. No one was more greatly moved than Sievier, the former owner of Sceptre. This man, noted for his imperturbability and sangfroid, a man who had seen fortunes slip through his fingers without betraying his feelings, was now overwhelmed with joy and gladness. This was the culminating point in Sceptre's career. She won, however, three more races that autumn – the Duke of York Handicap at Kempton Park, and the Champion Stakes and the Limekiln Stakes at Newmarket.

Her performance at Kempton demands some attention. That year, 1903, I wrote a book to which the title *The Racing Year* was given. The intention was that a similar volume should appear annually, but the reception given to the one actually issued was so disheartening that the project was abandoned. It may, however, interest many readers to know that that poor book contained the germ of the idea of founding the *Bloodstock Breeders' Review* eight years later.

In order to refresh my memory of Sceptre's achievements in 1903 I turned to *The Racing Year*, and I am going to take the liberty of reproducing a part of what I wrote about the Duke of York Stakes, which produced a very remarkable race. It should be explained that the handicap was made before Sceptre won the Jockey Club Stakes. The weight allotted to her was 9 st 4 lb, and this remained unchanged, because the scale of penalties for the race at Kempton applied only to successes gained in handicaps. After she had 'murdered' Rock Sand at Newmarket, the task awaiting her at Kempton Park looked a very easy one, for at 9 st 4 lb she represented Rock Sand at about 7 st 9 lb. It was feared that she would frighten away opposition, but, as a fact, there were fifteen runners, including the three-year-old fillies Our Lassie and Hammerkop, who had finished first and second in the Oaks. Our Lassie was carrying 7 st 11 lb, and Hammerkop 7 st 3 lb. Now for the quotation. I wrote:

'Some time before the hour fixed for the contest for the Duke of York Stakes there were very disturbing rumours afloat with regard to Sceptre. One report had it that she had been scratched; another that she was very lame. So persistent were these tales that the company generally began to fear there must be some truth in them. Bookmakers were offering 5 to 4 against the mare. You cannot have smoke without fire, and eventually it turned out that there was some foundation for the scare. The soles of Sceptre's feet are unusually thin, and, after her racing plates had been put on that morning, she betrayed unmistakable signs of discomfort. Her trainer passed through a period of keen anxiety. Finally he decided to remove the plates and put on the exercise shoes again. Sceptre appreciated the change at once; all traces of lameness disappeared. In other respects, however, her chance was by no means improved by the step it had been necessary to take. There had been heavy rain the day before, and the ground was sticky, not to say heavy, so that, apart from the extra weight which the substitution of shoes for plates involved, there was increased suction to contend against.

'In due course it became known that Sceptre was all right, and the appearance of her number on the board as a runner had the instant effect of making her an odds-on favourite. Before long the bookmakers were asking 7 to 4, and 13 to 8 was laid just as the race started. Bar the favourite, 10 to 1 was proffered, and at that price Soaraway was befriended. At 20 to 1 Happy Slave was third favourite. Not for a very long time had we seen such a return of betting in connection with a handicap.

'The leader in the first portion of the race was Soaraway, who, on the strength of her runaway victory in the Cleveland Handicap at Doncaster, had been well backed for the Cambridgeshire in the hope that she would follow in the footsteps of her half-sister, Ballantrae. Closely following Soaraway was Happy Slave, who had been beaten by Gourgaud at Newmarket a few days before in a close finish for the October Handicap. Coming round the bend, the negotiation of which has proved fatal to the chances of so many horses in years gone by, Soaraway lost her place, and Happy Slave, on the inside, took up the running, his nearest attendants being Soaraway, Valve and Glass Jug.

'Where was Sceptre? That was a question most people were asking. The light was somewhat poor, and Mr Bass's colours – yellow body and green sleeves – are none too easily discoverable in a *melée* such as the one that occurred at the turn. Apparently the mare had got boxed in. The spectators began to get anxious, for the last thing they desired was to see Sceptre badly beaten, especially through sheer misfortune. No sooner, however, had the main body of competitors entered the line for home than Sceptre emerged from the tangled mass. There was a quarter of a mile still to be traversed. With a clear run that would surely suffice. Taking to the rails, Madden sent the mare along, to the accompaniment of a swelling chorus of cheers from the delighted and thoroughly excited onlookers. When a furlong from the winning post Sceptre had passed all her opponents except Happy Slave. He was still four lengths in front. By the time she was opposite the cheap ring, Sceptre had reduced the gap to one of three lengths. Then, to the consternation of everyone, her store of power seemed suddenly to become exhausted. On every hand one heard the exclamation, in which the tone of poignancy was dominant, 'She's beaten!' A sense of the keenest personal disappointment pervaded the whole assembly.

'Sceptre beaten! Not a bit of it. An instant later the crowd was convulsed with a paroxysm of excitement that no words can adequately describe. Madden had evidently been hoping to see Happy Slave draw away from the rails and allow Sceptre to make her final effort on the inside. But Butchers, who rode Happy Slave, was obdurate. When, therefore, there remained barely a hundred yards to cover, Madden found it necessary to challenge on the outside. The situation was desperate, but the wonderful mare was equal to it. Coming away from the rails, Sceptre put forth an effort that positively staggered all beholders, whose disappointment and chagrin gave way to ecstatic joy. The crowd rose at her as, with each succeeding stride, she drew nearer to Happy Slave. Yet so close were the pair to the winning post, it still seemed well-nigh hopeless to expect the mare to get her head in front soon enough. As they flashed past the judge side by side people held their breath. Only the man in the box could say with certainty what had happened. After a brief suspense that seemed like an age, No. 1 was slipped into the frame. It was greeted with a yell of delight. Sceptre had won. The scene then witnessed cannot be compared with the remarkable outburst of emotion which followed the mare's victory over Rock Sand at Newmarket, but it served to emphasise the magnitude and brilliance of her latest performance. Luck had been all against her in the race, but she had come through the ordeal successfully. That was enough. The crowd had collected to see Sceptre win: they went away more than satisfied, though marvelling that an experienced jockey like Madden should have got himself into such a tangle, and regretting that he had found it necessary to use his whip.

'To Happy Slave, a colt of her own age, Sceptre conceded 40 lb; to Glass Jug, who finished second to her in the Oaks, she gave 26 lb; to Our Lassie (whose last race this was to be) she was allowing 21 lb, or about a stone over and above the weight-for-age provision. . . The circumstance that it was Happy Slave who so nearly defeated Sceptre on this occasion had a peculiarly dramatic significance, for the colt, owned by Mr Sleath Skelton, happens to be trained by Mr Sievier. The latter's feelings, as he beheld the ever-memorable effort which Sceptre made at the finish of the contest, must have been of a strangely mixed order, especially if there was warrant for the statement that he stood to win a big sum if Happy Slave was successful. The chances are, however, that the actual result was the one he preferred, for no man ever held a racehorse in greater reverence than he does Sceptre.'

I hope I have not wearied my readers with that long quotation. When I read the story in my book it revived recollections of one of the most exciting races I ever beheld. Moreover, it conveys a good idea of the adulation which the racing public at that time bestowed on Sceptre whenever a suitable opportunity presented itself. We may now proceed.

As a five-year-old Sceptre took part in three races, but in none of them was she able to reproduce her best form. She was second to Zinfandel in the Coronation Cup at Epsom, third in the Ascot Cup to Throwaway and Zinfandel, and third in the Hardwicke Stakes to Rock Sand and Santry. She might well have been turned out of training at the end of her four-year-old career when her fame was so great that it could not possibly be enhanced. We saw no more of her on the Turf after Ascot in 1904. For Mr Bass she won five races, the total value of which was £12,633½, so that half the money he paid for her had been recovered before she went to the stud. During the four seasons Sceptre was in training she ran twenty-four times. She won thirteen races worth £38,225½, was second in five, third in three, and unplaced in three. Here is the complete record of her performances on the Turf:

Two Years Old (1901)

	£
Won Woodcote Stakes, Epsom, 6 f	925
Won July Stakes, Newmarket, 5½ f	1,530
3rd, Champagne Stakes, Doncaster, 6 f	—

Three Years Old

2nd (beaten a head), Lincolnshire Handicap, 1 m	—
Won Two Thousand Guineas, 1 m	5,050
Won One Thousand Guineas, 1 m	5,450
4th, Derby, 1½ m	—
Won Oaks, 1½ m	4,150
Unplaced, Grand Prix de Paris, 1 m 7 f	—
5th, Coronation Stakes, Ascot, 1 m	—
Won St James's Palace Stakes, Ascot, 1 m	2,500
2nd, Sussex Stakes, Goodwood, 1 m	—
Won Nassau Stakes, Goodwood, 1½ m	770
Won St Leger, Doncaster, 1¾ m	5,217
2nd, Park Hill Stakes, Doncaster, 1¾ m	—

Four Years Old

5th, Lincolnshire Handicap, 1 m	—
Won* Hardwicke Stakes, Ascot, 1½ m	2,463½
2nd (beaten a neck), Eclipse Stakes, Sandown Park, 1¼ m	—
Won Jockey Club Stakes, Newmarket, 1¾ m	7,185
Won Duke of York Stakes (Handicap), Kempton, 1¼ m	1,670
Won Champion Stakes, Newmarket, 1¼ m	900
Won Limekiln Stakes, Newmarket, 1¼ m	415

* In this race she carried Sir William Bass's colours for the first time.

Five Years Old   £

2nd, Coronation Cup, Epsom, 1½ m	—
3rd, Ascot Cup, 2½ m	—
3rd, Hardwicke Stakes, Ascot, 1½ m	—
	38,225½

Here it may be stated that Sceptre was a bay with black points. When a four-year-old she measured 16 hands and half an inch under the standard. She had immensely powerful quarters, a splendid reach in her forehand, with great depth through the heart. Mr Sievier is authority for the statement that during the time he had her she frequently walked as if lame, though there was nothing really the matter, while she was such a high 'blower' that if she was not in continuous work a veterinary surgeon might have certified her broken in her wind. While in training she had a great fondness for apples. In later life her favourite delicacy was chocolate. After she reached Manton she became very fastidious and finnicky about her food. One day she would refuse white oats, but eat black; another day she would prefer the white, while there were occasions when she insisted on black and white mixed. Nor was that all. Some days she would eat oats only if they were placed in her manger, on other days she wanted them in a sieve, and occasionally would not look at them unless they were placed on the ground. It was no easy matter to satisfy her desires and whims.

We now come to Sceptre's career at the stud. It may as well be said right away that as a broodmare her success was a qualified one. Indeed, but for her first-born, Maid of the Mist, we should have had to describe her as a comparative failure. We are not yet able to penetrate the mysteries of breeding far enough to be able to discover the cause or causes of these disappointments. There is, however, one feature of Sceptre's stud record which possibly indicates why she did not realise expectations. She produced eight foals, all but one of them fillies. Two of the foals – the first two – were by Cyllene, then owned by Sir William Bass; two others were by Cicero, a son of Cyllene. Is it unreasonable to assume that these representatives of the Bend Or tail-male line did not suit her? The four other foals were by Isinglass, Carbine, Swynford and Glenesky, and they were all failures, more or less, so far as racing was concerned. One wonders what Sceptre would have accomplished if she had been mated with stallions of the class and character of The Tetrarch or Phalaris. It is extremely likely that she required mates who could be relied upon to impart speed to the offspring, for she herself had a sufficiency of stamina.

Sceptre's first two foals were the sisters Maid of the Mist and Maid of Corinth, by Cyllene. She might have been put to the son of Bona Vista a third time, for it was not until July, 1908, that Cyllene, sold by Sir William Bass for 25,000 guineas to the Ojo de Agua Stud in the Argentine, left England for Buenos Aires. However, in 1907 Sceptre was allied with Isinglass and bred Coronation, while in 1908 she visited Carbine and produced Queen Carbine. In 1910 she was barren to Cicero, and in 1911 to Marco; but to Cicero she produced, in 1912, Curia, her fifth filly, and in 1913, Grosvenor, her one and only son. In 1913 and 1914 she was mated with Swynford, the first year to no purpose, the second year to breed the filly, Sceptre's Daughter. In 1916 she was barren to William Rufus, but in 1917 there came her eighth and last foal, the filly Queen Empress, by Glenesky. Until 1922 fruitless efforts were made every year to get her in foal, and then she went into retirement.

Maid of the Mist, undoubtedly the best of Sceptre's produce, won three races and £1,851; Maid of Corinth won two races worth £1,895 and ran second in the One Thousand Guineas. Coronation won some races in Italy. Queen Carbine a £100 Plate, and Grosvenor one race worth £850. Curia failed to win, and Sceptre's Daughter and Queen Empress never ran. Needless to say, a great deal more than this had been looked forward to.

Now we must retrace our steps a little way. In 1911 circumstances developed which induced Sir William Bass to dispose of all his blood-stock, three of Sceptre's daughters were sold in May as horses in training. Maid of Corinth was bought by Baron Alphonse de Rothschild for 4,000 guineas, and went to Hungary. There, so far as I can learn, she produced only two foals, both fillies, but neither of any use on the Turf, though one of them subsequently bred a winner. Signor Federico Tesio, the highly-successful Italian breeder, bought Coronation for 1,650 guineas. She had raced here several times as a two-year-old, and once as a three-year-old without winning, but in Italy she won races for Signor Tesio, and then bred him some winners. In 1920 she came back to England, and was bought for the National Stud at 3,800 guineas. At the time of the sale she was in foal to Sir Archibald (son of Desmond), who was then in Italy, and the produce was a colt named Corolet, who won a minor race or two; but none of Coronation's later foals has been a winner. Queen Carbine, the third of the fillies sold in May, 1911, was bought by the late Sir Edward Hulton for 4,800 guineas, and for him

won a £100 race. As a broodmare she was a sad failure. After producing
five foals here, not one of which could win a race, she went to France four
years ago.

Maid of the Mist came under the hammer in July, 1911, together with
Sir William Bass's other broodmares. Along with her was sold her first
foal (born that year), a filly by Torpoint. The bidding for mother and
daughter ceased at 4,500 guineas, and Mr Arthur Portman was
announced as the buyer. Presently it leaked out that Mr Portman was
acting for Mr Waldorf Astor (now Lord Astor). It has turned out a most
fortunate deal. The mare's foal by Torpoint (a great stayer by Trenton)
was named Hamoaze, after a district in Plymouth, which town Mr Astor
represented in the House of Commons for many years until he had, on
the death of his father, the first Lord Astor, to go to the House of Lords.
Hamoaze won two races worth £1,355, and has bred the winners
Buchan, Tamar, St Germans (all of whom ran second in the Derby) and
Saltash, winner of the Eclipse Stakes. Those four horses won stakes to the
value of about £40,000. St Germans and Saltash were sold for well over
£30,000, so that from Hamoaze alone Lord Astor has obtained more
than £70,000.

After she came into Lord Astor's possession, Maid of the Mist bred the
winners Skyrocket, Sunny Jane (who won the Oaks in 1917 when it was
run at Newmarket), Craig an Eran (who won the Two Thousand
Guineas and other races worth £15,245, and ran second in the Derby)
and Jura. Sunny Jane is the dam of Bright Knight, who won many good
races, ran second in the Two Thousand Guineas, and was last year sold
at a big price to a breeder in the United States. From first to last Lord
Astor has obtained, one way or another, over £100,000 as a result of his
purchase of Maid of the Mist and Hamoaze for 4,500 guineas.

Sceptre herself came up for sale in July, 1911. Her appearance in the
auction ring once again aroused tremendous interest. Before asking for
bids, Mr Somerville Tattersall made a speech, and I am going to
reproduce the report of it I published in the *Sporting Life*, of which I was,
at that time, the Special Commissioner. Mr Tattersall began by
reminding the great crowd around the auction ring that this was the
third time Sceptre had appeared there. As a yearling she was sold for
10,000 guineas – a record which had not yet been beaten.

> 'At the time I thought she was rather dear, because of her twisted foreleg. I was
> wrong, and Mr Sievier was right. At the end of her three-year-old career, in King
> Edward's Coronation year, she came up for sale again, with a reserve of 20,000 on
> her. I then made some remarks on her value, and advised any rich man present to
> buy her. I said she would be extremely unlucky if she did not win one of the ten

thousand pound races, for she was engaged in three, and came of a stout family, her grandam, Lily Agnes, being an extremely hardy mare, who took part in thirty-two races and won twenty-one of them, several over long distances, and then bred Ormonde, Farewell, and other winners. Sceptre, I went on to say, seemed to have inherited Lily Agnes's disposition. However, she passed out of the ring unsold. Somebody told me afterwards that he did not know how I had the face to make such observations. Well, Sceptre, despite the fact that she had none the best of luck in the Eclipse, as Madden and Martin, who rode in the race, will tell you, won in stakes that year, 13,600 guineas. Her produce have each won something, her three-year-old (Coronation) having been "placed".

'At the Second Spring Meeting here we sold some of her produce for 10,450 guineas, and I calculate that at present Sir William has obtained a profit of about £4,500 before Sceptre and her eldest daughter are sold. There has been a good deal of discussion as to the price Sceptre will make. Some people look at the matter from a commercial point of view. I do not know what she may be worth from that standpoint, but any rich man who can afford to do so should give 5,000 guineas or 6,000 guineas extra for the pleasure of seeing Sceptre each day, just as some people spend thousands on pictures. A mare like Sceptre only comes once in twenty-five years or so. She and her eldest daughter ought not to be allowed to leave the country. Maid of Corinth and the Isinglass filly (who has been happily named Coronation) have both gone abroad. We ought to keep this mare and Maid of the Mist in this country. I shall look upon English racing people as unpatriotic, like some of our politicians, if they let her go. La Flèche was the record-price yearling filly before Sceptre, and she paid her way well. I think she has also paid Sir Tatton Sykes. Her blood has come out in a remarkable way in Swynford. La Flèche very nearly went to France, for there was a certain amount of luck about her going to Sledmere. Had she gone abroad we should have had no Swynford, who throws back to La Flèche in colour.

'It is a great mistake for us to allow all the best mares to leave the country. We have permitted a good many of our best stallions to go. The French people recently tried to buy William the Third, but I am very pleased to hear that the Duke of Portland and the Duchess said he was to live and die at Welbeck. The Duke of Portland and Lord Derby were just too late to save Cyllene from exportation to the Argentine.

'One of the most exciting races we have seen in recent years was that for the Eclipse Stakes, when Rock Sand and Ard Patrick opposed Sceptre. We have lost the two horses. Let us keep the mare, whom Martin considers the best of the three. I do not know whether you are going to act on my advice, but I hope you will do so.'

Reading out the pedigree of Sceptre, Mr Tattersall, at the mention of Persimmon's name, described him as the best Derby winner and the best-looking horse since Ormonde, and in his opinion the best son of St Simon. 'Sceptre,' he added, 'was started at 5,000 guineas when offered as a yearling. Is there anybody who will start her at 5,000 guineas now, though I do not suggest that that is to be her ultimate price.'

Instead of 5,000 there came an offer of 2,000 guineas. There was an immediate challenge from the far side of the ring. Lady James Douglas bid 2,500, and with advances of 500 at a time we quickly got to 5,000. At that point Mr Dalgleish, who had made the first bid, retired. Who came in next I cannot say, but Baron Maurice de Rothschild entered the contest with an offer of 6,600, and he was in front again at 6,800 guineas. Then there was a long halt. Mr Tattersall turned this way and that, and inquired if anyone would go further. Presently came the announcement that 7,000 guineas were bid. The Baron retired, no one else took his place, and the hammer fell. Messrs Tattersall were the buyers. A burst of cheers greeted the news.

For a time there was some speculation as to whether the firm were acting on behalf of some client, but presently it became known that the mare was the joint property of Mr Somerville and Mr Rupert Tattersall, and so we owed it to them that Sceptre remained in England.

Mr Siever's article in *The Winning Post*, from which I quoted earlier, appeared a few days after this sale. The concluding sentences read:

'We refrained from going to the ringside on Monday last, for we had a suspicion that some rich foreigner might buy her, and the last thing we wished to experience was to see her leave the country. Moreover, we had no conception that she would fetch so small an amount as 7,000 guineas. . . When we discovered that Sceptre was bought by that thoroughly sporting firm, Messrs Tattersall, we telegraphed to them asking what they would take, and the reply came back: "Many thanks, Sceptre is not for sale."'

Sceptre was in foal to Cicero when sold, and the produce was Curia. It was, of course, Mr Tattersall who sent her back to Cicero in 1912, with the result that the colt Grosvenor came in 1913. A colt out of Sceptre at last! It was regarded as great news, and I well remember the satisfaction with which I gave it publicity. As a foal the colt was one of the biggest I had ever seen. Nobody realised it at the time, but there can be little doubt that his great size was more of a hindrance than an asset. He proved a difficult horse to train, and, as previously stated, he was successful in only one race, when a three-year-old.

In 1914 Sceptre was barren to Swynford, and again mated with the son of John o' Gaunt. At the end of that year, Mr Tattersall sold her, together with her two-year-old daughter, to Mr John Musker. It was a private deal. Subsequently Mr Musker also bought Grosvenor. The mare was safe in foal when transferred to Mr Musker, who, therefore, ranked as the breeder of Sceptre's Daughter. He put her to his own horse William Rufus in 1915, but there was no produce. In 1917, however, the mare bred Queen Empress to Glenesky, another of the stallions at Mr Musker's stud.

In July of that year, 1917, Mr Musker dispersed his big stud, and so Sceptre, together with her foal, once more came under the hammer. The vendor announced that the sum they fetched would be given to the Red Cross Society. The amount he was able to transmit to that worthy cause was 2,500 guineas. The buyer at that figure was Lord Glanely, and we were at the time given to understand that Sceptre had been sold and bought for the last time – in other words, that Lord Glanely intended to keep her so long as she lived. There was, consequently, a great outcry in 1922 when the public learned that Lord Glanely had sold Sceptre for £500 to Mr F. J. Lundgren, the Brazilian sportsman, who was in England at the time. When reminded of his alleged promise never to part with the mare, Lord Glanely denied that he ever made such a promise, and said that even if he did he was entitled to change his mind seeing that Sceptre had not produced him a foal. It was because Sceptre had been barren for so long a period that Mr Lundgren decided to buy her, in the hope and belief that when transferred to a warmer climate she might be induced to breed.

Sceptre was then twenty-four years old, and many English breeders and sportsmen were anxious that she should spend the brief remainder of her life in her native land. Mr Tattersall offered Mr Lundgren £1,000 for the old mare. Then Lord Glanely said he would try to get the sale to Mr Lundgren cancelled, suggesting at the same time that a fund should be raised to provide a permanent memorial to Sceptre, such as the endowment of a ward in one of the London hospitals. In the end Mr Lundgren gave Lord Glanely a free hand, and the sale was annulled. A Sceptre fund was then raised. Mr Tattersall and Lord Glanely both gave £500, and Lord Astor a subscription to Buchan, which meant 400 guineas. The total eventually obtained was, however, a long way short of the sum that had been expected.

This brings us to the end of the story of Sceptre. In the annals of the Turf her name will ever be prominent and greatly honoured. As a racehorse she has had few equals, and through her first-born daughter, Maid of the Mist, she has established a branch of the Agnes family that seems destined to claim distinction for many generations to come, not only in this country, but in other parts of the world to which some of its representatives have gone.   BBR–1926

In subsequent generations, Sceptre's 'disappointing' daughters. – Curia, Queen Empress, Queen Carbine, Coronation and Maid of Corinth – all became the distaff ancestresses of significant stakes winners throughout the world.

The Death of 'Bob' Sievier

THE NAME of 'Bob' Sievier will always be connected with that wonderful mare Sceptre, winner among other races of the One Thousand and Two Thousand Guineas, Oaks and St Leger. Her story is now ancient history, but the memorable Derby, for which she started favourite but which she failed to win, is still the object of speculation. Those who knew Sievier best, however, are convinced that he would have given everything he had to have won this race. He lived a stormy life, however, and his outspokenness earned him many enemies, and it was perhaps inevitable that rumours detrimental to him regarding this race should have been circulated.

As editor and proprietor of *The Winning Post*, Sievier involved himself in more than one action for libel. Some he lost, but on the whole he was remarkably successful in such litigation. There was never any doubt about his courage, while, whatever else might have been said about him, he always had the reputation among those in a position to know of running his horses straight. The last horse of any merit with which he was associated was Monarch, who now stands in France. During recent years, however, financial difficulties and failing health had made life anything but easy for him. He did a little sporting journalism, and was a familiar figure in the Press stand. He was always spick and span in the clothes of a well-dressed man of an older generation, and his appearance was distinctive in stand or paddock.

'Bob' Sievier had a ready wit, and, though he could be caustic, few people could help liking him in his old age. At Doncaster, in 1938, he remarked to the writer: 'In my day a fellow had to know his business before he trained horses. Nowadays, all a fellow has to do to become a trainer is to walk down St James's Street and buy an umbrella.' For some months before his death his heart had been very bad. He attended the Derby this year, but collapsed in the Press Luncheon room, and was unable to see the race. Most of us guessed then that the end was near, but Sievier's courage never flinched, and he went down with his flag flying.

BBR–1939

'Chasers as Producers

THERE IS a prejudice in many quarters against using steeplechase mares for breeding. The late Count Lehndorff in his *Horse-breeding Recollections* states: 'As far as I know there is in the whole (English) Stud Book not a single steeplechase mare that has made for herself a great name as the dam of winners on the flat.' Apropos of this statement, a Mr J. L. O'Connor, writing to an American journal, draws attention to the case of the mare Forget, who raced for five seasons in the United States, and was the greatest hurdler of her time. At the stud she produced Borrow (winner of the Middle Park Plate), and other good winners in Slumber II, Dreamer, Delirium and Hiatus. Her record does not, of course, vitiate Count Lehndorff's assertion, because she was not in the English Stud Book; but it is worth bearing in mind when a brood-mare is condemned off-hand because she was a performer over obstacles.

How Fairy Gold Came to the US

Fairy Gold, a splendid stakes-winning daughter of Bend Or from Dame Masham, by Galliard, foaled in 1896, was among the most important producers ever imported into the US. Suffice it to say she bred the top-class racehorse and three-time champion American sire Fair Play, he the sire of Man o' War. Fairy Gold also foaled the Belmont Stakes winner Friar Rock. War Relic, the irascible son of Man o' War who saved the Fair Play branch of the Matchem male line importantly in the US, was closely inbred to Fairy Gold through Man o' War and his half-brother Friar Rock. The BBR *of 1930 recites how Fairy Gold got to the US in an item on Goyescas, one of the better two-year-olds of that season and a member of Fairy Gold's distaff family through her daughter Saint Lucre, by St Serf, who founded one of France's most distinguished female families. So Fairy Gold was a famous producer on two different continents.*

IN GOYESCAS we have a colt by Gainsborough, but bred in France by his owner, M. Marcel Boussac. His pedigree will greatly interest readers in the US. His dam, Zariba, is by Sardanapale out of Saint Lucre, by St Serf from Fairy Gold, by Bend Or. Bred by the late Mr Russell Swanwick at his stud on the outskirts of Cirencester, Fairy Gold was, when a yearling, bought for 1,150 guineas by Mr Leonard Cohen, and for him won three races and £1,302, including the Woodcote Stakes at Epsom. Saint Lucre, her first foal, was bred by Mr Cohen in 1901. At the December Sales that year Fairy Gold, covered by Florizel II, was bought by Colonel Harry McCalmont for 2,900 guineas. The foal of 1902 was Golden Measure.

Fairy Gold was barren in 1903, and in July of that year, following the sudden death of Colonel McCalmont, she came up for sale to be bought at 3,600 guineas by Mr August Belmont, to whose stud, near Lexington, Kentucky, she was forthwith sent. Golden Measure was bought, when a yearling, by Mr James Buchanan (Lord Woolavington) for 730 guineas, but subsequently became the property of the late Major J. D. Edwards, who had him for many seasons at his stud in Co. Tipperary. Golden Measure was a fine stayer in a period when good stayers were plentiful. Among other races he won the Ebor Handicap and the Ascot Gold Vase. The most notable of Fairy Gold's produce in America was Fair Play, who three times headed the list of sires of winners in the US. The great horse Man o' War was one of his sons.   BBR–1930

The Death of Pretty Polly

Even today, over eighty-some years after the fact, if a poll were taken as to who was the greatest racemare in English Turf history, it is almost a certainty that Pretty Polly, a foal of 1901, would be the winner over Sceptre, her senior by two years. 'Peerless Pretty Polly' won twenty-two of twenty-four races over four campaigns and was second, with reasonable excuses, in the other two. It was only neglect on the part of her nominator that she wasn't eligible for the Two Thousand Guineas and the Derby, for otherwise she most surely would be the only horse to have won all five English classics. Considering her plebeian heritage, her story is truly as enthralling a romance as the Turf has experienced. Even more so because her name is still a distinguishing presence in the pedigrees of so many elite performers throughout the world.

When Pretty Polly died in 1931 at the age of thirty, still well before her name became such a recognisable treasure in tail-female, the history of her accomplishments, written by Edward Moorhouse, appeared in the BBR. *Considering that most scholars of the Turf consider Mr Moorhouse as peerless in his own field of writing as Pretty Polly was in her field of racing, this article becomes a collector's item which must be saved for posterity and so that Mr Moorhouse and Pretty Polly will continue to be appreciated for what they both did for the Turf.*

IT IS DIFFICULT to realise that to the younger generation the death of Pretty Polly, which occurred in August, was an event of no special interest. She had retired from the Turf before they began to give heed to racing and its celebrities, for it was in 1906, when five years old, that she went back to Ireland to live the life of a broodmare at the stud where she was bred and reared. Those of us who belong to the older generation can, however, recall the great feats she performed during the four years she was in training, feats which led her to becoming known as Peerless Pretty Polly. She just missed being a contemporary of Sceptre, who was the elder by two years. They were, it is true, both racing in 1903 and 1904, but in the former year Pretty Polly was a two-year-old, and in the latter was busy winning classic and kindred races while Sceptre was otherwise engaged. Taken together, their careers lay within the period 1901–06, and it was truly remarkable that during those six years we had the experience of beholding the triumphs, and occasional failures, of two of the greatest mares ever seen on the Turf.

For the past six years Pretty Polly had been an honoured pensioner. Towards the end her teeth were so worn that she could not properly masticate her food, and she rapidly lost condition. When, therefore, it became obvious she could not live much longer, she was painlessly destroyed. The body was buried in the lawn at Eyrefield Lodge, close to the grave of Spearmint. It was a trial with Pretty Polly that revealed the great chance Spearmint had of winning the Derby of 1906.

Bred by the late Major Eustace Loder, Pretty Polly was a big, handsome dark chestnut mare by Gallinule out of Admiration, by Saraband. Apart from the Gallinule side of it, there was little in the pedigree suggesting anything but mediocrity. It was necessary to go back sixty years to arrive at a mare in the tail-female line that could in any way be considered notable – an un-named daughter of Pantaloon, dam of Leamington, who twice won the Chester Cup and then went to the US, where he became a very successful stallion.

Between Pantaloon's daughter and Pretty Polly there were five mares in the direct line. Leamington's half-sister, the fifth dam of Pretty Polly, was Chaperon, foaled in 1885. She was by Touchstone's son Flat-catcher, a winner of the Two Thousand Guineas. Chaperon was first called Sweet Pretty Pet, but was known as Chaperon when, as a two-year-old, she raced twice unplaced at Worcester. Her name had again been changed to Fatty when she won two races as a three-year-old. By the process of induction we may conclude that she was a small, attractive-looking filly who acquired the habit of 'doing' herself too well. When she retired to the stud the name Chaperon was restored to her. She eventually became the property of Lord Scarborough, who mated her with Rataplan in 1868, the produce being Wallflower, a selling plater who won little races at West Drayton and Odiham. On leaving the Turf she became the property of a Mr Lant, and in 1876 he bred from her Pretty Polly's third dam, the mare Eyepleaser. She was by Brown Bread, the inheritor of good stamina from his sire Weatherbit. Eyepleaser did not race and was covered when a two-year-old. Her Stud

Book record reveals a change of ownership nearly every year. When, in 1886, she produced Pretty Polly's grandam, Gaze, she belonged to Mr R. Wright. Gaze was by Thuringian Prince, a half-brother, by Thormanby, to the brilliant sprinter Prince Charlie, and a winner himself of the Royal Hunt Cup at Ascot. She was first named Lady of Beauty, and was so-called when she made her only appearance on the Turf to finish nearly last in a selling race at Warwick. She was subsequently bought by Robert Peck, and so became one of the many mares that roamed the paddocks at the Howbury Hall Stud near Bedford. Her name was then changed to Gaze. In 1890 she produced a colt by Muncaster. That season, and again the following year, she was put to Saraband, then standing at Howbury Hall. The foal of 1891 was Montpensier, who won several races for Mrs Langtry; that of 1892 was a chestnut filly, sent up for sale as a yearling and bought for 510 guineas by Major Eustace Loder, who named her Admiration.

Robert Peck died in 1899, and in December of that year all his mares and foals came under the hammer at Newmarket. Most of them were sold for trifling sums. Gaze, covered by Penzance, made 7 guineas – a somewhat astonishing figure because, though then thirteen years old, she had been a very regular breeder. She was bought by 'Mr Cash', who seems quickly to have rued his bargain, for a few weeks later he sent her to one of Messrs Tattersall's Sales at Knightsbridge, where, offered as a hack, she realised 15 guineas. At the Newmarket sale a filly-foal by Earwig out of Gaze was sold for 6 guineas.

Admiration ran twice as a two-year-old. Her second outing was in the Richmond Stakes at Goodwood, so it would seem that at that time Major Loder had a good opinion of her. The following year the estimate was, however, revised. She raced once more in England, in an unimportant event at Stockbridge, to finish second, beaten half a length, and was then sent to Ireland. There she ran third in a race at Leopardstown, and unplaced in a handicap at The Curragh; but next time out she won, by a short head, a £50 handicap at Baldoyle, run over a mile. Towards the end of that season she was unsuccessful in races at Cork and The Curragh. When four years old Admiration ran eight times for a win, three seconds and two thirds. The win was scored in a handicap at Leopardstown, and one of the 'seconds' was obtained in a run-off after she had dead-heated for first place. The following year she ran unplaced in her only race, an event at The Curragh meeting in April, and was shortly afterwards mated with Red Prince II.

These details may seem tiresome, but they serve to emphasise the fact that when Major Loder put Admiration into his stud at Eyrefield

Lodge, which he had just bought from the Linde family, it was well-nigh impossible to hope, much less to expect, she would become the dam of so remarkable an individual as Pretty Polly. If, however, there had been no Pretty Polly, Admiration would still have gained a considerable reputation as a broodmare. In thirteen years she produced thirteen foals, and nine of them were winners; namely the colts Aderno, Admirable Crichton, Admiral Hawke and Coriander; and the fillies Veneration II, Pretty Polly, Adula, Miranda and Addenda. These daughters and another, Miramonde all 'carried on' at the stud. Veneration II, by Laveno, became the dam of Craganour, Glorvina, Nassovian and The Sybarite. Glorvina, who ran second to Princess Dorrie in the One Thousand Guineas, was for many years in Lord Derby's stud. She bred two winners, but was, nevertheless, a disappointing producer. Major Loder sold Veneration II and her colt-foal by Desmond (Craganour) to Sir Tatton Sykes for £1,700. While at Sledmere she produced foals which, together with Craganour, were sold as yearlings at Doncaster for £30,115.

Adula died after producing three foals, all winners; Miranda also bred several winners, one being King John, who won the Irish Derby and the Manchester November Handicap, and was then sent to New Zealand; and another, Golden Guinea, was sent to the US. Addenda bred Silvius, who won races in Australia and ran second in the Melbourne Cup. It will be seen, therefore, that while Admiration derived much reflected glory from the spectacular achievements of Pretty Polly, her reputation as a broodmare rests on a broad foundation. Her emergence from the humble sphere in which she was born ranks, indeed, among the romances of the Stud and Turf.

In the late autumn of her yearling days Pretty Polly was broken at Eyrefield, and during the process there was an alarming incident, for the details of which I am indebted to Mr Noble Johnson, who has for more than thirty years so ably managed the Loders' Studs at Eyrefield Lodge and Old Connell, near Newbridge. When out on The Curragh one day, being driven in long reins, Pretty Polly got loose, and ran round the top of a sand quarry forty feet deep. She raced along a narrow path, on one side of which was the quarry and on the other a high stone wall, and had been round twice before she allowed herself to be caught. In December, not long after this escapade, Pretty Polly took part of her own free will in a 'rough gallop' over three furlongs with some yearlings that were being got ready for racing early the following season. 'Polly' was merely out for an airing, but Mr Johnson told Anthony, who was riding her, to go down to where the other yearlings were to start their spin and look on.

Pretty Polly.

When 'Polly' saw her stable companions set off, she overpowered
Anthony, and went after them. At the end of the three furlongs, where
Mr Johnson was standing, she was leading, and went on for a considerable distance before Anthony could pull her up, In that, her first 'race',
she carried about 10 st; the others were carrying only 8 st. One of them
was Vervel, who won a race the following April, and ran second in the
'Patriotic' at Baldoyle and in the Grand Prize at The Curragh. Her
performance in the unauthorised gallop caused everyone at Eyrefield to
wonder what manner of filly she was. Shortly after it she was sent to
Newmarket to be trained by Mr Peter Gilpin, who had recently moved
thither from Dorsetshire, and built 'Clarehaven', near the old toll bar on
the Bury Road.

For some time after she had been under his care Mr Gilpin had no
great opinion of Pretty Polly, who 'worked' in a sluggish way. A year or
two later he said to me: 'The first time I saw her in a paddock at Eyrefield Lodge she struck me as being almost too powerful. If anybody had
told me the filly I was looking at was going to develop into a great race

mare I should have laughed.' Nevertheless, Major Loder had taken the precaution of entering Pretty Polly for several important races, including the One Thousand Guineas, the Oaks and the St Leger. The list did not include the Two Thousand or the Derby. This was unfortunate because it is practically certain that, given the opportunity, Pretty Polly would have won all five classic events, and so beaten the record Sceptre had just made by winning four – all but the Derby, in which she finished fourth.* The Two Thousand and Derby of 1904 were won by St Amant, who was beaten by Pretty Polly every time they happened to meet.

In June, 1903, Pretty Polly made her first appearance on the Turf in the British Dominion Two-year-old Race at Sandown Park, and the performance she gave remains a vivid memory with those who witnessed it. She amazed everybody, including her trainer, though he had recently discovered she was not the nonentity he had imagined. The revelation came when, two weeks before the race at Sandown, she took part in a gallop with three stable companions, one being a two-year-old colt by Fortunio out of Pet, subsequently named Delaunay.

The previous February Mr Gilpin went to Ireland to find a horse to lead work. Inquiries led him to the trainer Denis Shanahan, from whom the six-year-old gelding, Wise Alec, was bought for £300. It had also come to Mr Gilpin's knowledge that Shanahan owned a very promising two-year-old – the Pet colt. After the Wise Alec deal had been completed Mr Gilpin, assuming a casual 'air', asked if there were any other horses in the stable worth looking at. Shanahan said there were, and had them led out, one after another. Last of all came the Pet colt, who at once took Mr Gilpin's fancy. Asked to put a price on the youngster, Shanahan said he did not want to sell. Mr Gilpin wrote long afterwards:

> 'We got on to another subject, and walked about the farm inspecting the blood-stock. On returning to the house I again mentioned the Pet colt, and again Shanahan said he did not want to sell; when further pressed he explained that he did not know what to ask. Presently I mounted my hack and Shanahan walked beside me down the road. I was still trying to induce him to name a price, and encouraged him by saying: "You know what you gave for him, you know what he has cost you in the interim, and you know how much profit you want. Tell me, and I will answer Yes or No." As a matter of fact he had paid only 80 guineas for the colt. Then, after further hesitation, he said "£300". I immediately said, "Certainly, Denis, you shall have it." Thereupon he exclaimed, "Oh! Mr Gilpin," as though surprised because I had not attempted to bargain," and wondering whether he was letting the colt go too cheaply.'

---

* Formosa, in 1868, also won all the classic races except the Derby. In the Two Thousand she dead-heated for first place with Moslem. The stakes were divided and Moslem was allowed to walk over.

Shanahan bought the Pet colt at the Dublin Sales from the late Mr
Edward Kennedy. Though he paid only 80 guineas he regretted the
purchase when he got the yearling home, and offered him to a Kildare
publican for the sum he had given. The publican refused to take the colt,
and so missed a wonderful bargain. Carrying Mr Gilpin's colours
Delaunay won many valuable races, and in the autumn of his four-year-
old career was sold to M. E. de Saint-Alary for 7,500 guineas.

A few days before the trial at Newmarket in which Pretty Polly took
part Delaunay had made a successful debut in a race at Manchester,
winning by five lengths. In the trial he was, therefore, carrying 23 lb
more than Pretty Polly. Up to this time the filly had shown her trainer
no form worth attention. As she carried a lot of flesh efforts had
repeatedly been made to cause her to sweat, but they invariably failed.
The boy riding Pretty Polly in the gallop was told to come 'right
through' with her, not that Mr Gilpin expected her to oblige. There was
another two-year-old, Addlestone, in the trial, and the test had, no
doubt, been arranged chiefly for his benefit. Addlestone was receiving
14 lb from Delaunay and giving Pretty Polly 9 lb. Great was the trainer's
astonishment when, shortly after the 'race' had begun, he saw Pretty
Polly coming along with Delaunay, the pair being well ahead of the
others.

The lad riding the colt began to use vigorous methods, but Pretty
Polly still hung on, and at the finish was beaten less than a length. The
result merely showed, of course, that the filly was 'waking up', for a two-
year-old 23 lb and three-quarters of a length behind even the best of her
age could not be expected to achieve great things on the Turf. During
the next few days, however, she continued to show improved form on the
training ground, and Mr Gilpin came to the conclusion that she had a
reasonable chance of winning the British Dominion race run the second
day of the Sandown Park June Meeting.

It happened that Delaunay easily won a race the first day, and after he
had done so tongues began to wag. While many were praising the colt
others were saying: 'Yes, he looks good, but Gilpin is going to show us a
better two-year-old tomorrow, a filly that recently beat this colt in a
trial.' That tale, so greatly at variance with the truth so far as the trial
was concerned, was, in various forms, told all over the course. When the
time arrived for the running of the British Dominion race the big betters
were in the ring watching for an 'inspired' move in favour of Pretty
Polly. No such thing was forthcoming. What about those runners so
freely circulated the previous day? The bookmakers were puzzled, and
treated Pretty Polly like a shuttlecock, offering odds which fluctuated

violently between 12 to 1 and 6 to 1, the latter being the final quotation. At 2 to 1 John o' Gaunt was the favourite of the ten runners. Both Jack Hawthorn and Lanfine, long since forgotten, were also preferred to Pretty Polly.

The horses had been at the starting post barely a minute, when the barrier was raised. Not expecting the start to be effected so quickly many people did not see it. When the customary cry, 'They're off,' brought them to attention they saw one of the runners so far ahead of the rest that they looked for the red flag signalling a false start. But the start had, in fact, been a satisfactory one. The lone leader was Pretty Polly, who had left the 'gate' like a flash. It may be supposed that the jockeys on the other horses were considerably astonished, and assumed, as the onlookers did, that Pretty Polly would presently come back to them. Instead of doing so she increased her advantage with every stride. It was an amazing spectacle, the more so because her jockey, Trigg (affectionately called Hell Fire Jack), was all the time riding vigorously. According to Judge Robinson, who often blundered when estimating distances, Pretty Polly won by ten lengths. Vergia and John o' Gaunt, a neck apart, finished second and third.

There was an amusing sequel in the weighing room, where Trigg plaintively remarked that towards the end of the race Pretty Polly was slowing down of her own accord. 'Slowing down!' exclaimed Mr (now Sir) George Thursby, who had ridden his brother's horse John o'Gaunt; 'as she was leading by a hundred yards it is hardly surprising.' The explanation of Trigg's somewhat eccentric jockeyship is that in the previous race he was beaten on a horse the crowd thought should have won, and he had been hooted. He was, therefore, taking no risks when riding Pretty Polly.

Mr Thursby's statement that Pretty Polly won by a hundred yards was much nearer the truth than the judge's verdict of ten lengths. Be the actual margin what it might, the filly's performance created a tremendous sensation. In some reminiscences he wrote nine years ago, Mr Gilpin, who died in 1928, stated that when the following day Huggins (the American who was training some of Major Loder's horses) called to congratulate him he asked what had been done to produce so remarkable a result. Mr Gilpin assured Huggins he had nothing to tell him because Pretty Polly had been treated in the same way as her stable companions. She differed from them, he said, because she had been born with the gift of 'electric dash', looked for so often and so seldom found. Two years later, when discussing Pretty Polly's debut with me, Mr Gilpin attributed her phenomenal and rapid improvement to the fact that during the long journey from Newmarket to Sandown Park in very hot weather she sweated profusely, a thing she had never done before. It was, he believed, in this way Nature had wrought a wondrous change.

We now have Pretty Polly launched on her career. It cannot be pursued in detail because of an imperative need to economise space. All I can do is to present a summary of her achievements on the Turf, and then briefly refer to the two defeats she suffered, and to one or two other matters.

Pretty Polly's Races

Two Years Old (1903)

	£
Won British Dominion TYO Race (5 f), Sandown Park; 10 ran, including John o' Gaunt (gave 6 lb). Won by about 40 lengths. Betting: 6 to 1 against her	914
Won National Breeders' Produce Stakes (5 f), Sandown Park; 11 ran. Won easily by 2 lengths; 2 to 1 against	4,357
Won Mersey Stakes (5½ f), Liverpool; 2 ran. Won easily by length and a half; 33 to 1 on	680
Won Champagne Stakes (5½ f), Doncaster; 5 ran, including St Amant (3rd). Won easily by length and a half; 11 to 10 against	2,010
Won Autumn Breeders' Foal Plate (5 f), Manchester; 2 ran. Won easily by three-quarters of a length; 25 to 1 on	888
Won Cheveley Park Stakes (6 f), Newmarket; 7 ran. Won, 'hard held', by three-quarters of a length; 100 to 8 on	845
Won Middle Park Plate (6 f), Newmarket; 7 ran, including St Amant (2nd). Won by 3 lengths; 2 to 1 on	2,475
Won Criterion Stakes (6 f), Newmarket; 2 ran. Won cantering by a length and a half; 100 to 7 on	906
Won Moulton Stakes (5 f), Newmarket; 4 ran. Won by 2 lengths; 100 to 7 on	427

Summary: Won 9 races and £13,502

Three Years Old

	£
Won One Thousand Guineas Stakes (1 m), Newmarket; 7 ran, including then unbeaten Fiancée. Won by 3 lengths from Leucadia; 4 to 1 on	3,800
Won Oaks Stales (1½ m), Epsom; 4 ran. Won by 3 lengths; 100 to 8 on	4,950
Won Coronation Stakes (1 m), Ascot; 8 ran. Won by 3 lengths; 5 to 1 on	3,000
Won Nassau Stakes (1½ m), Goodwood; 3 ran. Won by 5 lengths; 33 to 1 on	530
Won St Leger Stakes (1 m 6½ f), Doncaster; 6 ran, including St Amant (6 lb), winner of Two Thousand Guineas and the Derby. Won easily by 3 lengths; 5 to 2 on	4,625
Won Park Hill Stakes (1 m 6½ f), Doncaster; 5 ran. Won easily by 3 lengths; 25 to 1 on	1,085

2nd, Prix du Conseil Municipal (1½ m), Longchamp (Paris); 8 ran, including
Zinfandel, who gave 9 lb and finished third. Beaten easy 2½ lengths by
Presto II (received 9 lb). Zinfandel half a length behind Pretty Polly, and
Macdonald II (fourth) another 4 lengths away. Pretty Polly's share of prize,
£600. Odds of 5 to 2 laid on Pretty Polly; 66 to 1 against Presto II   —

Won Free Handicap Sweepstakes (1¼ m), Newmarket; 4 ran, including St
Amant (received 3 lb). Won by 2 lengths; 7 to 2 on   450

Summary: Won 7 races and £18,440

Four Years Old

Won Coronation Cup (1½ m), Epsom; 3 ran, Zinfandel and Caius being 2nd
and 3rd. Won in a canter by 3 lengths; 9 to 4 on   1,505

Won Champion Stakes (1¼ m), Newmarket; Hackler's Pride only opponent.
Won easily by 2 lengths; 5 to 2 on   900

Won Limekiln Stakes (1¼ m), Newmarket; 2 ran. Won easily by a length;
55 to 1 on   425

Won Jockey Club Cup (2¼ m), Newmarket; 4 ran. Won readily by half a
length from Bachelor's Button; 5 to 1 on   590

Summary: Won 4 races and £3,420

Five Years Old

Won March Stakes (1¼ m), Newmarket; 4 ran. Won by 2 lengths; 1,000 to 35
on   465

Won Coronation Cup (1½ m), Epsom; 3 ran. Won by a length and a half; 11 to
2 on. St Amant finished last   1,470

2nd, Ascot Gold Cup (2½ m); 5 ran. Beaten a length by Bachelor's Button;
11 to 4 on Pretty Polly, whose share of prize was £700   —

Summary: Won 2 races and £1,935

Grand Total (22 races won)   £37,297

If, as in other countries, 'place' money is added, Pretty Polly's total of winnings
becomes £38,597.

Before Pretty Polly resumed racing as a three-year-old her multitude of
admirers were divided into two camps. In one the idea prevailed that she
would be unable to stay much beyond a mile, if so far; in the other the
suggestion that her proved speed was unlikely to be supported by
stamina was summarily rejected. A prominent writer, who shared the
views of those who questioned Pretty Polly's staying power, expressed
his opinions as follows:

'In the first place, she has a heavish top to carry; in the second, the combination of Gallinule and Saraband does not suggest much stamina or hardiness. She may be an exception to all the probabilities of her breeding and conformation, but she is more likely to follow in the footsteps of Ecossais, who was an equally brilliant two-year-old, with tremendous width of quarters, but who could never stay comfortably beyond six furlongs. Pretty Polly may take rank with the most brilliant sprinters we have known, but because of her breeding she cannot be another Sceptre, who is at her best over a distance of ground.'

That is an interesting contemporary estimate of Pretty Polly's abilities and prospects. So experienced a man as John Porter thought the filly might stay twelve furlongs, but could not bring himself to believe she would last the St Leger course.

When Pretty Polly won the St Leger, her fifteenth race, and fifteenth victory, there appeared to be no horse in sight capable of extending her. That she would go through the remainder of her career undefeated was almost taken for granted. There was, however, trouble hiding round the corner. Early in October she was sent to France to compete for the Prix du Conseil Municipal at Longchamp. The race was worth about £4,000. Before it was run Major Loder was asked whether he really thought it worth while sending the filly to Paris to pick up that sum. He replied that the prize was of little or no consequence; his main desire was to see Pretty Polly beat the best horses in France in the way she had accounted for the best in England, 'but,' he added, 'I would rather forfeit £40,000 than see her beaten.' The British public was in complete sympathy with the owner's affection for the filly, and, like him, entertained no fear regarding the outcome of the race.

Major Loder's wish to see Pretty Polly opposed by the best horses in France was not gratified. Several of them were withdrawn from the race. One was La Camargo, who ran third for the Prix du Conseil Municipal as a three-year-old, and won it the two following years, carrying the full penalty each time. Her owner had intended her to meet Pretty Polly, but a leg gave way and she had to be taken out of training. Leg trouble also accounted for the disappearance of Ajax, the best of the French three-year-olds, and M. Edmond Blanc scratched Caius and Gouvernant because he believed neither had the remotest chance of beating the daughter of Gallinule. These withdrawals left Macdonald II France's main hope. He had run Ajax to half a length in the Derby and finished third to him in the Grand Prix de Paris.

There were five other French horses saddled for the Prix du Conseil Municipal. One was Presto II (by Rueil), who was receiving 10 lb from Pretty Polly. He was supposed to have no chance whatever of winning;

indeed, it was only at the last moment that his owner, M. Gaston Dreyfus, decided to allow him to compete. The English four-year-old colt Zinfandel, a son of Persimmon, was sent from Newmarket to oppose Pretty Polly, and was generally believed to be the one horse in the race likely to give her any trouble, if troubled she was to be. Zinfandel was bred by Colonel Harry McCalmont, whose sudden death in 1901 deprived the colt of his classic engagements. Some people thought he was as good as, if not better than, his contemporary, Rock Sand.

Pretty Polly had an unfortunate experience while being transported from Newmarket to Paris. All went well until she reached Boulogne, the French Channel port. Mr Gilpin had hired a special train to convey the filly from Boulogne, and gave her attendant £100 to 'oil the palms' of the railway officials who could facilitate matters. This train should, of course, have run straight through to Paris, but instead of doing so it was held up at frequent intervals and backed into sidings to allow other trains to pass. If, after reaching her destination, Pretty Polly had had a few days in which to throw off the effects of that trying journey all might have been well, but she had only a few hours. Though there seemed to be nothing the matter with her when she was saddled for the Prix du Conseil Municipal the probability is that she was not quite herself. She was an odds-on favourite at 2 to 5. Zinfandel was backed at 6 to 1, and Macdonald II at 8 to 1. The other five runners were all at long odds.

Presto II, against whom 66 to 1 had been laid, went to the front immediately after the start, followed by Frisquet (a 100 to 1 chance), Pretty Polly, Zinfandel and Macdonald II. The distance to be covered was twelve furlongs, and when there remained only three furlongs to go Presto II was still leading, three or four lengths ahead of Pretty Polly and Zinfandel, now second and third. Every moment the onlookers expected to see the two English horses race up to and pass Presto II. Their efforts to do so were, however, futile. They reduced the gap a little, but some way from the winning post it was obvious Pretty Polly was doomed to suffer her first defeat. She finished second, two and a half lengths behind Presto II, and half a length in front of Zinfandel, who came in third. Macdonald II was placed fourth.

This was a staggering result – staggering alike to French sportsmen and to the admirers of Pretty Polly. Nobody believed for one moment the filly had produced anything like her best form. The prevailing idea was that her failure was due to lack of judgment on the part of her jockey, Danny Maher, the suggestion being that, until it was too late, he and Morny Cannon (riding Zinfandel) treated Presto II with contempt and concentrated their attention on each other. Mr

Gilpin, however, refused to countenance that explanation. He attributed the defeat of Pretty Polly wholly and solely to the fact that she was suffering from the effects of her wretched journey from Boulogne. Maher's version of the affair was a very different one. Mr George Lambton, in his book, *Men and Horses I have Met*, says:

> 'Many people who saw the race blamed the jockey, and said he had waited too long, etc. When Danny came back I asked him about the race. He was rather sore about the criticism of his riding, saying that he had no excuse and that the mare was beaten on her merits. He said the course was very heavy, and, as usual, the pace very fast. For more than three parts of the journey he felt he could do what he liked with the field, and that when he first asked Pretty Polly to take her place and win she responded readily, but then gradually began to die away in his hands. Feeling this, like the good jockey he was, he sat still as a mouse, hoping the other horse (Presto II) might crack; but that did not happen, and, when finally he sat down to ride his mare, there was nothing left in her and she was beaten. From that moment he was certain that Pretty Polly, brilliant though she was, was not a true stayer.'

When he made the foregoing statement Maher may have believed he was telling the truth, the whole truth, and nothing but the truth. Nevertheless, it is questionable whether the conclusion at which he arrived was justified by the evidence then available. As we have seen, Pretty Polly had recently won the St Leger in record time, and other of her performances showed that she could stay twelve furlongs with the greatest ease. The fact that she faded out towards the end of her race at Longchamp might well, as her trainer maintained, have been due to the lingering effects of her prolonged and wearisome journey to Paris.

Pretty Polly's first race as a four-year-old was the Coronation Cup, run over the Derby course at Epsom. Zinfandel and Caius were her only opponents. Odds of 9 to 4 were laid on her and she cantered home three lengths ahead of Zinfandel. The previous day, in a hard-run race, Cicero had won the Derby in 2 min 36 4/5 sec, then only one-fifth of a second outside the record time for the event. Now, nearly thirty years later, the Derby time record has been reduced to 2 min 34 2/5 sec, held jointly by Call Boy and Felstead. When, without being pressed, Pretty Polly won the Coronation Cup she covered the twelve furlongs in 2 min 33 4/5 sec. Her performance was recognised as a magnificent one, and her graceful rhythmic action excited great admiration. She looked and behaved like a Queen of the Turf.

A few days later, while cantering up Long Hill at Newmarket Pretty Polly stepped on some slippery ground and strained the muscles of her quarters. This misfortune prevented her competing for the Ascot Cup the following week; indeed, nothing more was seen of her until the autumn when she won the Champion Stakes, the Limekiln Stakes and the Jockey Club Cup. The last-named is a race over 2 miles 2 furlongs (3,600 m). Of her three opponents only Bachelor's Button, a six-year-old son of Winkfield and a pronounced stayer, was seriously regarded. He finished within half a length of the mare, but it seemed to many as if Pretty Polly could have widened the gap very considerably if she had been asked to do so. Bernard Dillon, her jockey, was greatly blamed for riding her too confidently. Maher rode Bachelor's Button; he was not one of Dillon's critics. At the time Pretty Polly won the Coronation Cup Maher had again assured Mr Lambton that she was not a genuine stayer, adding, 'If I meet her in a two-mile race with a good horse I shall beat her.' After the race for the Jockey Club Cup Maher met Mr Lambton in the paddock, and exclaimed, 'What did I tell you? If I had something to help me I should have beaten her, for I am certain she was very tired.' Maher added that if Bachelor's Button and Pretty Polly met in the following year's race for the Ascot Cup the mare would be defeated.

In her last season on the Turf, that of 1906, Pretty Polly ran three times. At the beginning of May she won the March Stakes at Newmarket, and a month later again won the Coronation Cup at Epsom. These races were a part of her preparation for the Ascot Cup. In this event she had four opponents, namely, Cicero, the previous year's Derby winner; Bachelor's Button, who had just won the Manchester Cup; the latter's stable companion, St Denis, started to ensure a good pace all the way, and so probably bring about the defeat of Pretty Polly if, as Maher (who was riding Bachelor's Button) believed, she was not an out-and-out stayer; and a three-year-old named Achilles. The public, unaware of Maher's opinion, took it for granted that Pretty Polly would win, for apparently she only had Bachelor's Button to beat, and had she not defeated him in the contest for the Jockey Club Cup the previous autumn?

It so happened that the Saturday before Ascot I had occasion to pay a call on Mr Gilpin at Newmarket. While we were on his private schooling ground watching a batch of two-year-olds at exercise, the approaching meeting at Ascot came under discussion. I ventured to express the hope that he would have a good time with his horses, and added, 'Needless to say, you will bring back the Cup.'

'Do not be too sure about that,' remarked Mr Gilpin, 'the Bachelor's Button people (the horse was owned by Mr Sol Joel) are cocksure of beating us. He has been doing wonderfully well in his gallops, and from all I hear he won the Manchester Cup the other day in spite of being nearly knocked over in some scrimmaging. We hope to beat him, of course, but he is a formidable opponent.' An hour or two later I was talking to another noted trainer on the same subject, and he said, 'Yes, the combination of Maher and Bachelor's Button will take some beating I can tell you.'

To an ardent admirer of Pretty Polly these expressions of opinion were very disturbing, but they prepared one for the blow that came the following Thursday. Bachelor's Button beat Pretty Polly a length. The strong pace set by St Denis was the undoing of the mare, that plus bad judgment on the part of her jockey, Bernard Dillon, and a temporary physical weakness. There was a large wart on her belly which had recently been lanced. That she was not quite fit for the coming ordeal was revealed by a display of nervousness in the paddock, and by a reluctance to pass from that enclosure on to the course after she had been mounted. Nevertheless, odds of 11 to 4 were laid on Pretty Polly. Bachelor's Button and Cicero were joint second favourites at 7 to 1. Cicero's price rather flattered him, beause it was very doubtful whether he would be able to stay the two miles and a half.

It may safely be asserted that nine-tenths of the onlookers wanted to see Pretty Polly win, whether or not they had backed her. The silence which prevailed when she reached the winning post a length behind Bachelor's Button indicated the regret her failure occasioned. The victor did not get the cheer he deserved. It was as if the public resented the way he had robbed them of the pleasure of seeing the great mare crown her wonderful career by winning the most coveted of the honours to be gained at Ascot. She had made her bid for the trophy a year too late. Writing about the affair in 1922, Mr Gilpin stated that there were too many people hovering around Pretty Polly at the stable where she was quartered at Ascot, and that she was upset before the race by the crowd. 'Yet,' he went on, 'that did not account for her defeat. In my opinion she lost because the jockey did not obey my instructions. Had he done so I feel sure there would have been no defeat for Pretty Polly on an English racecourse to record. I told Dillon this after the race. No doubt he was carried away by excitement.'

From first to last, racing four seasons, Pretty Polly won, as we have seen, twenty-two races worth £37,297 – a splendid total when it is borne in mind that she did not compete for any of the mammoth prizes like the Eclipse and the Jockey Club Stakes. It may be recalled that Sceptre, who also raced till she was a five-year-old, won thirteen races and £38,225½, which included £7,185 gained when she won the Jockey Club Stakes.

Like Sceptre, Pretty Polly did not greatly distinguish herself as a producer of winners. She made an unfortunate start at the stud, for she was barren the first two years and slipped twins to Spearmint the third year. During this period Mr Gilpin actually proposed to Major Loder that the mare should go into training again, but the suggestion was, no doubt wisely, turned down. The much-desired change then occurred. From 1911 to 1920 Pretty Polly produced a foal every year except 1917 – a blank due to the fact that she was not covered in 1916. In the three years 1921–23 she was barren, and in 1924 there came her tenth and last foal, a filly by Spearmint named Baby Polly. Her first three foals were all colts, namely, Polygonum, St Polycarp and Chipilly. The two first-named both died in 1914; Chipilly was shipped by the British Bloodstock Agency to Queensland, where he ran and won twice and then sired winners.

In 1914 Pretty Polly bred the filly Molly Desmond, who, when two years old, was one of the best of her age, but, lacking scope and size, disappointed the following season. As a juvenile she scored in three races. She was beaten a head only for the Middle Park Plate, and in the contest for the Criterion Stakes gave Gay Crusader 8 lb, and ran him to a head. Dutch Mary (1915), by William the Third, and Polly Flinders (1918), by Polymelus, were other daughters of Pretty Polly. Polly Flinders, like her dam, won the National Breeders' Produce Stakes. Three more of the mare's sons were Passchendaele, Clackmannan and Tudor King. Clackmannan (by Lomond) was a useful horse, but the other two were not of much account, though Passchendaele has sired winners.

Just as Maid of the Mist (dam of the Oaks winner Sunny Jane, and of Hamoaze, the dam of Buchan, Tamar and St Germans, all of whom ran second in the Derby), greatly helped to carry on Sceptre's line, so have Molly Desmond, Dutch Mary and Polly Flinders assisted that of Pretty Polly. Molly Desmond is the dam of five winners. One is Spike Island (who became the property of Señor S. J. Unzue), winner of the Irish Two Thousand and Derby. After a season or two in Argentina, Señor Unzue sold Spike Island to an Italian breeder, and the horse returned to Europe. Another was Zodiac, who dead-heated with Haine in the Irish Derby; a third, Strongbow; and a fourth, Golden Silence, who ran second in the Oaks. Dutch Mary, who died in 1927, bred four winners, including Sister Anne (second in the Oaks), and Christopher Robin. Polly Flinders is the dam of the speedy Arabella. It is worth noting that these three daughters of Pretty Polly have produced no fewer than sixteen fillies, so there is every reason to assume that the family will be 'in the news' for many years to come. BBR–1931

How Scapa Flow Remained the Property of Lord Derby

Among the many famous matrons in the ownership of Lord Derby's stud, Chaucer's daughter, Scapa Flow, became a matriarch of inestimable influence. Scapa Flow produced Pharos, the sire of Nearco, and she also produced the classic winner and four-time English sire champion, Fairway. She was a jewel beyond price. But once upon a time there was a price of £50 on her head. This story of how Scapa Flow nearly left Lord Derby's possession appeared in the BBR *of 1935.*

IN A LETTER he sent to the Editor of *Horse and Hound*, John McGuigan, the Ayr trainer, related a story about Scapa Flow, the dam of Fairway. It will surprise most readers to learn that in 1917, then three years old, she ran in a selling race at Stockton, 'winner to be sold for £50'. She finished second, and Wallace Wyllie, who trains at Ayr, was so impressed by the way Scapa Flow ran on towards the finish that he decided to put in a claim for her. On learning this McGuigan told Wyllie that he might be able to obtain the filly at less than the claiming price and approached her trainer, Mr George Lambton. The latter stated that he could do nothing in the matter without Lord Derby's authority. McGuigan then told Mr Lambton that if he wished to keep Scapa Flow he had better get Tom Rintoul, owner of the horse that had finished third, to put in a friendly claim. This advice was acted upon, and Scapa Flow remained in the possession of Lord Derby.

BBR–1935

Scapa Flow – Dam of Pharos and Fairway

IN ALL, Scapa Flow produced nine foals, seven colts and two fillies. Her first was a colt by John o' Gaunt, foaled in 1919, named Spithead. Always difficult to train owing to bad joints, inherited from his sire, he was castrated and proved a fine stayer, despite his disability. Scapa Flow was next sent to Phalaris, during his first stud season, and in due course dropped Pharos, a first-class racehorse and a great sire. After two barren years came Pentland, a moderate racehorse, by Torloisk. After foaling Fairway, in 1925, she was barren once more and then in three successive years she produced, to Phalaris' coverings, the fillies Fair Isle and Fara, and a colt named St Andrews. The latter was a failure both on the race-course and at the stud, but Fair Isle was one of the best two-year-olds of her year, and in 1930 won the One Thousand Guineas. Fair Isle was full of quality, but was never robust, and her stud career was a big disappointment, for she produced but three living foals, and only one, her first, was good enough to win. This was St Magnus, a colt by Sansovino, who won four races, including the Liverpool Spring and Summer Cups, and is now doing well as a sire in Australia.

The other filly, Fara, was quite unlike Fairway or Fair Isle in conformation. She took more after her dam's pattern, being short on the leg and stocky. She won only once, at her first appearance, the Buckenham Stakes at Newmarket, worth £1,950, and was retired to stud, where she did better than her sister, although she did not produce a classic colt. Her best son was Umballa, by Umidwar. Umballa was a good-class middle-distance colt, and he is now at stud in Argentina, where he is getting winners. Another son, Nebris, by Big Game, is at stud in Australia, whilst another, her first colt, named Faroe, sired a few winners in England. Faroe died in March, 1948, whilst on the voyage to Australia.

In 1924 Scapa Flow was mated with Coronach, and the following April produced a grand chestnut colt, considered by many to be the best-looking of all her foals. Named Highlander, great hopes were centred on this colt, but, unfortunately, although he had ability he also had a temperament, and after a number of mulish performances it was decided to castrate him. Subsequently he proved a good servant to Stanley House, winning in all twenty-one races up to 1939, when he was nine years old. In 1931 Scapa Flow produced her last foal, named Pharillon, by Phalaris. By this time the old mare had exhausted her vitality, and although she was covered the following year she did not breed again. Her sons and daughters won sixty-three races, value £85,649, a record for Great Britain and Ireland which still stands.

The Death of Plucky Liège

PLUCKY LIÈGE died at the beginning of March. A week previously she foaled a dead foal, by Casterari. She was bred in England in 1912 by Lord Michelham, and sent to France in 1915. Plucky Liège, who won four races value £1,811, was by Spearmint out of Concertina, by St Simon. She was the dam of ten winners, the chief of which were Sir Gallahad III and Admiral Drake. Sir Gallahad III won the Lincolnshire Handicap, French Two Thousand Guineas and nine other races, and beat Epinard in a match. He was sent to the US and headed the sires' list in 1930, 1933 and 1934 ('place' money included). Admiral Drake won the Grand Prix de Paris and four other races in France, the Grand International d'Ostende, and was second in the Grosser Preis von Berlin and French Two Thousand Guineas, and third in the French Derby. Plucky Liège was also dam of the good winners Bel Aethel and Bull Dog; the latter, sent to the US, has come into prominence as a sire.

BBR–1937

A year after her death, Plucky Liège's son Bois Roussel (by Vatout) won the Epsom Derby. Boir Roussel was the sire of the St Leger winner Tehran (sire of Tulyar); Ridgewood, also winner of the St Leger; and Migoli, who won the Eclipse Stakes, Champion Stakes and Prix de l'Arc de Triomphe. He was also a brilliant sire of broodmares.

Kincsem

Another of the 'unbeaten fourteen' of the celebrated bloodstock writer Dr Platt was that superlative mare Kincsem, a chestnut foaled in 1874. 'This mare,' noted Dr Platt, 'holds a record which is never likely to be beaten. It takes your breath away to mention it.' That was true then and it still is today.

I believe it was Otto Madden's father who rode Kincsem in the Goodwood Cup, and considering he had Tom Cannon and Fred Archer up against him it cannot be said that it was jockeyship that won Kincsem the race. Mr Joseph Butters, formerly jockey and now trainer, wrote, as to the 'best horse of recent times':

'The best horse I have ever seen was Kincsem, by Cambuscan our of Water Nymph. I have ridden in many races behind this famous mare, and the mere fact of her having won fifty-four races (in almost every country on the continent) without ever suffering defeat, stamps her as being the best animal I have ever seen.'

IT IS MOST PROBABLE that the present generation is not familiar with the names of the two outstanding Hungarian-bred horses Kisbér and Kincsem. Therefore, perhaps, it would not be uninteresting to say something about them. Kisbér (by imp. Buccaneer out of imp. Mineral) accomplished the great feat of winning the Epsom Derby and Grand Prix de Paris, which remarkable double was also won by Gladiateur, Cremorne and Spearmint. The chestnut mare Kincsem (by imp. Cambuscan out of Water Nymph, she by imp. Cotswold out of imp. Mermaid, by Melbourne) was foaled in 1874. She was bred by Mr

Ernest de Blaskovich at his Táplószentmárton stud in Hungary. During her four years' racing career she took part in fifty-four races in Austria-Hungary, Germany, England and France, and was never beaten. She won the Austria-Hungary 'Triple Crown', the Baden-Baden Grand Prize thrice, the Goodwood Cup in England, the Grand Prix de Deauville in France. These achievements of the 'Hungarian wonder', as the English named her, will probably never be surpassed.

Not only was she great on the racecourse, but at the stud too. She had five foals. Her first daughter, Budagyöngye (by Buccaneer), won the German Derby. The second daughter, Ollyan Nincs (by Buccaneer), was the winner of the Hungarian St Leger. Her next produce, Talpra Magyar (by Buccaneer), though a moderate performer on the racecourse – a winner, of course – made a name for himself as a stallion, being the sire of Tokio, one of the best Hungarian-bred horses in the last century, winning the Austrian Derby, Hungarian St Leger, Baden-Baden Grand Prize, etc. Talpra Magyar sired later on many good horses in Germany. Kincsem's foal the next year was Kincs-ör (by Doncaster), who won important races and ran second in the Derby. He was a hot favourite for the German Derby, but on the morning of the race he was found dead in his box. It is quite certain that he would have been the winner, for his stable-mate, who was much his inferior, won the race. In 1887, after producing Kincs (by Doncaster), Kincsem died on March 17th, which was her birthday. Kincs never ran, but one of her daughters, Napfény (by Dunure), was an Oaks winner, and in turn produced Miczi, a high-class racehorse. She won the Nemzeti-Hazafi Prize, Hungarian Oaks, Austrian Oaks, Queen Elizabeth Prize, and as a four-year-old the King's Prize, etc.

Kincsem's blood has spread through the whole continent. Kincsem mares are to be found everywhere. From the Kincsem line there were Derby winners in Germany, Italy, Poland, Russia, Yugoslavia, Roumania and Denmark. Though in France there was no Derby winner, there was a high-class descendant of hers named Calandria (by Kircubbin) – the Prix Royal Oak winner in 1929 and beaten by two heads by Hotweed and Buland Bala in the Grand Prix de Paris. Calandria descends from Kincsem through the following female line: Crimea – Ukraine – Bálkirályné – Farsang – Furcsa – Budagyöngye – Kincsem. Bálkirályné (by Jack o' Lantern) was exported as a three-year-old to Germany. Farsang (by Dunure) never ran, but produced, amongst others, Keringö, a very good horse. Furcsa (by Craig Millar), a winner, was the dam of Beregvölgy, a high-class Derby winner.

In the near past there was a very successful broodmare, by name

Rendek, a Tamar mare tracing back to Kincsem. Her son, Kamarás (by Cagliostro), won the Derby in 1941, and her two daughters, Róna (by Mannamead) and Réka (by Cagliostro), were winners of the Oaks and St Leger in 1943 and 1944, respectively. How the Kincsem blood retains its vitality can be seen from the fact that in the last volume of the Hungarian Stud Book there were fifty-five mares descending from Kincsem.   BBR–1947

Part 10

BREEDING THEORIES AND THEORISTS

The Origin of the Term 'Thoroughbred'

Several columns discussing the origin of the term 'thoroughbred' as applied to racehorses eligible to the General Stud Book *appeared in the* New York Herald *in 1917. A Mr John L. O'Connor contended that the term 'thoroughbred' had been used in a New Jersey stallion advertisement as early as 1778 whereas the first time that term was used in England was in 1831. Mr O'Connor's comments, as might be imagined, unleashed some spirited dialogue.*

As the Review *noted in the follow-up article by 'Mankato', a correspondent for the* Sporting Chronicle *and a frequent contributor to the* Review, *Mr O'Connor's 'claim on behalf of America has had a very short run.' 'Mankato' presents evidence proving the term was in popular use in England well before 1756. It all makes for some fascinating historical background on the subject and is well worth repeating.*

It is also worth repeating that 'the British thoroughbred, as is generally known, was in the first instance the outcome of crossing the native running galloways with imported Barbs, Turks and Arabians.'

What is often not remembered is that when these imported horses 'were raced against the best native animals' they made a very 'poor show'. Yet, the best results of this cross between the native and imported strains resulted in an individual 'much superior in racing qualities to either of its parents'. Obviously, a biological mutation of incredible significance had taken place.

THERE HAS BEEN some discussion in the columns of the *New York Herald* concerning the use of the term 'thoroughbred' as applied to a racehorse qualified for admission to the Stud Book. The word is not, we believe, used in this sense in America as universally as it is in the United Kingdom. It is, therefore, all the more interesting to find a claim made that it was so employed in the United States fifty years before its adoption this side of the Atlantic. Mr John L. O'Connor confirms the statement of another authority that the word thoroughbred, applied to a horse, is not to be found in any English publication previous to the year 1830. In a book printed in 1831, bearing the title *The Horse*, and published by the Society for the Diffusion of Useful Knowledge, the 'thoroughbred horse' is, however, used instead of the then familiar 'blood horse'. Again, in *The Chase, the Turf and the Road*, published in 1837, 'Nimrod' wrote: 'Had we no racing, we should not be in possession

of the noblest animal in creation – the thoroughbred horse.' Mr
O'Connor proceeds:

> 'To Americans it seems instinctive to turn to English writers for precedent, so I,
> too, wasted much time in an unsatisfactory hunt through overseas sources before
> turning to home material, but was well repaid, as I found the word
> 'thoroughbred' antedating English application by more than fifty years.
>
> 'As early as 1778 a New Jersey newspaper carried an advertisement worded as
> follows:
>
>> "LIBERTY, four years old this spring. He is a Selim colt out of a Dove mare is
>> full-blooded and THOROUGHBRED."
>
> 'This advertisement was placed by Dr Condit of Orange, NJ. Dr Condit served
> as a surgeon in Heard's Brigade, was a member of the New Jersey legislature, was
> a Representative in Congress from New Jersey, and was assistant collector of the
> port of New York. Since the doctor was held in such high esteem by the public and
> was also a man of undoubted educational advantages, particular stress is laid on
> the fact that the doctor was the first to put into print, either in England or this
> country, the word "thoroughbred".
>
> 'The use of the word by such a man, not only lends the weight of a certain
> authority, but also brings to bear a peculiar and added significance, since it is used
> in a superlative sense and conveys a sense of superiority over other "full-blooded"
> horses. We are curious to know why the doctor drew the fine distinction between
> "full-blooded and thoroughbred".'

BBR–1917

In the last number of the *Review* (p. 277) we referred to a discussion that
had taken place in the columns of the *New York Herald* with regard to the
date when the term 'thoroughbred' was first applied to the racehorse.
One correspondent, Mr John L. O'Connor, maintained that it was so
used in England for the first time in a book called *The Horse*, published in
1831. He, however, produced evidence to show that it was used in
America as far back as 1778 in an advertisement published in a New
Jersey newspaper.

Mr O'Connor's claim on behalf of America has had a very short run.
Our old friend, 'Mankato' of the *Sporting Chronicle*, upbraids us for not
spragging it right away. We confess we had a strong suspicion that there
was something wrong somewhere, but in these days of depleted staffs it is
not possible to pursue every tempting trail. So we were content to quote
Mr O'Connor, feeling sure that if he was mistaken one or other of our
readers would enlighten both him and us. As it happened, we provided
'Mankato' with a peg on which to hang one of his interesting and
informing articles. Without more ado we propose to give our readers the
benefit of his disclosures. He writes:

'It happens that as early as 1756 the term thoroughbred was commonly used in England in reference to the blood horse. I quote from "A Dissertation on Horses", by William Osmer. "Printed for T. Waller in Fleet Street, 1756".'

"Now the attachment of some men to a half-bred, or what is commonly called a good English horse, is, I think, fully as absurd as the opinion of the sportsmen about blood. They object that these cat-legged things (as they are pleased to call bred horses whose legs in general are by the bye a great deal larger than they appear to an injudicious eye) are fit for nothing but the race – that half-bred horses will lose them on some road with a heavy weight, that they go near the ground, are apt to blunder, are long-pasterned, and have an awkward way of going.

"To the first I answer, that if any man be willing to match a horse which he will certify to be half-bred against another certified to be a *thoroughbred*, I will undertake to find him a play-fellow that will entertain him for what sum he pleases, and the owner of the half-bred horse shall choose his ground, length and weight."

'Osmer, who by the way was a veterinary surgeon, makes it clear in this and in other parts of his work that the terms bred horse and thoroughbred horse were used impartially to indicate an animal which was not half-bred, threequarter-bred, etc. He was in point of fact thoroughbred in racing strains.

'In the first edition of Volume I of the Stud Book published 1793 it is stated that the Byerly Turk (who was Captain Byerly's charger in Ireland in King William's Wars, 1689, etc).'

". . . did not cover many bred mares, but was the sire of Jigg, the Duke of Kingston's Sprite, who was thought to be nearly as good as Leedes, the Duke of Rutland's Black Hearty and Archer, the Duke of Devonshire's Basto, Lord Bristol's Grasshopper, and Lord Godolphin's Byerly gelding, all in good forms; Halloway's Jigg, a middling horse; and Knightley's mare, in very good form; and Bowes' mare."

'Again, in referring to Sir J. Williams' Turk, it is stated that "It is not known that this Turk covered any bred mares except the dam of the two True Blues."

'About the beginning of the last century stallion advertisements published in the racing calendars not infrequently stated that such and such a horse would cover thoroughbred mares at a certain fee and half-bred mares on other terms. In fact, the term thoroughbred is used so frequently in the latter half of the eighteenth century and the beginning of the nineteenth in English literature relating to the racehorse that one marvels how it can have escaped the attention of any wideawake American investigator.

'In the *Racing Calendar* for 1795, for example, the advertisement of the stallion Symmetry intimates that the horse would cover "all thoroughbred mares that have won a £50 plate, or that value in matches or sweep-stakes, gratis; other mares at 2gs and a crown the groom". Two years later the Lambton Hunt Sweepstakes was run at Durham, a condition being that the competitors should not be thoroughbred. As in Osmer's day the term "bred" was also used to denote a thoroughbred, and as a qualifying adjective in opposition to half-bred.

'In the beginning of the eighteenth century races were divided into three marked classes – 1: Those open to racehorses proper, this class being sub-divided in a number of ways, *eg*, prizes for horses or mares which have never won a Royal Plate, for such as never won £100, £80, £60, £40, £20, age conditions, and so on; 2: Give-and-take plates open to galloways. These races also were of various values, and certain of them were confined to galloways not exceeding given heights. Thus at Winchester in 1739 ten guineas was given free of entrance fee (which was a general condition in galloway races) for galloways not exceeding 13.0½ hands high. 3: Races for hunters, which generally speaking were not "bred" animals. In 1739 there were races for galloways, and twenty-eight races for hunters, Class 3.

'There is scarcely a shadow of doubt that the early racing galloways of the North were a race apart from the common horses of the country, and that before the importation of the Barb were a perfectly pure strain. They were in other words "thoroughbred". And to these galloways the modern thoroughbred owes many of his best qualities.

'In marked support of this conclusion we have the salient fact that the environment of the United Kingdom had done nothing to evolve from pure imported Barbs or Arabs bred solely *inter se* an individual or a race which for the last hundred and fifty years has been the remotest use when pitted against the British thoroughbred, who, as is generally known, was in the first instance the outcome of crossing the native running galloways with imported Barbs, Turks, and Arabians.

'From the time of James I, and earlier, it occasioned much surprise and disappointment that the imported Barbs and Arabians made such a poor show when raced against the best native animals, and that the best results of a cross between the native and the imported strains should give rise to an individual much superior in racing qualities to either of its parents, though here surprise was accompanied by gratification.

'By the time the eighteenth century was reached the racehorses and their descendants bred in this manner were styled "thoroughbreds". Osmer is very clear on this point. In another part of his work he writes: "Again, we talk just as ridiculously of bad as we do of good blood, and it is a common saying amongst the sportsmen that they would choose to breed from a horse, whose blood they like, though he could not run, rather than from him that could run well, whose blood they did not like, and yet both shall be thoroughbred."

'Reviewing all the circumstances we see then that the writer of the advertisement in the New Jersey paper in 1778 was merely employing a word well established in English racing and breeding lore when he used, or rather misused, the term thoroughbred. I say misused because his colt was not entitled to be so styled, being, in point of fact, half-bred according to the English contemporary method of pedigree valuation.

'It is an interesting fact that the expression thoroughbred is seldom applied to other than the racehorse. Pure bred is generally used when referring to particular varieties of cattle, sheep, swine, dogs, and poultry. Nor do we speak of thoroughbred Shires, Clydesdales, Percherons, Suffolk Punches, etc. In their respective cases the qualification pure is also not infrequently used. Of late years there has been a tendency to review the meaning of the term pure bred.

'The extreme Mendelians would have us limit the expression to given characters, and very truly have pointed out that an animal belonging nominally to a pure-bred race may be pure in one character and impure or hybrid in another. Purity, they claim, is not the result necessarily of a lengthy ancestry, but arises from the union of two germ cells, both of which carry the same character. Thus, chestnut coat colour in the horse is a pure character, and arises from the union of two chestnut-carrying germ cells which contain the determinants for no other coat colour. Hence two chestnut parents invariably give rise to chestnut offspring. But these two chestnuts, as we know, may vary in breed, and if of the same breed may vary in anatomical characters and physiological qualities.

'There is no doubt that when the British thoroughbred was in the making a fixation of characters derived from his Barb, Arab and native ancestors did proceed on Mendelian lines under the powerful and all-important guiding influence of the racecourse test. To this day a large number of individual character combinations are possible, and many frequently take place. Some of these combinations tend to give a higher standard of racing excellence; others make for a deterioration in racing qualities. From this it follows that constant recourse to the racecourse is necessary to maintain the traditions and improve the qualities of the British thoroughbred.'

After perusing the foregoing illuminating essays our readers will, we imagine, be glad that we gave 'Mankato' the opportunity of 'letting himself go' on the subject. Perhaps one of our many American subscribers will make a point of drawing Mr O'Connor's attention to the facts here disclosed. We may mention that Osmer, quoted by 'Mankato', was a veterinary surgeon practising in Blenheim Street, Bond Street, London, and was familiar with many of the South-Country racehorses of his day. He would appear to have had a good working knowledge of anatomy, and may, possibly, have been through one of the medical schools. The Veterinary College in Camden Town was not established until some years after he wrote his work.   BBR–1917

'A First Study of the Correlation Between Racing Performances and Breeding Value in Broodmares' by J. B. Robertson

In its 'Biological Search-light on Racehorse Breeding' by the richly knowledgeable Mr J. B. Robertson, whose learned contributions to the Review *account for some of its finest presentations, perhaps that on 'the correlation between racing performances and breeding value in broodmares' was of the most enduring interest. We say 'enduring' because since the dawn of the thoroughbred, discussions and debates have raged and been waged over 'class in the dam'. It is an accepted fact that 'the best racehorses make the most successful sires'. But just as soon as one suggests that racing performance is a prime requisite in the dam if a classic winner is to result, up pops a classic-producing matron who never raced or who showed dismal form when she did.*

While Mr Robertson's conclusions may not vary one iota from a similar investigation made in this day and age, his research and statistics are so comprehensive and compelling that one can only be convinced of the truth of what he wrote back in 1913.

It is a masterful piece of work which is still invaluable today. One once again – or for the first time – becomes acquainted with the mildewed names of the classic producers of an era too soon gathering the cobwebs of time.

IT IS pretty generally recognised that the modern British racehorse is the product of long-continued natural selection through the racecourse test, and that in males there is a very marked correlation between racing capacity in the individual and the property of reproducing that quality in the offspring. In other words, the best racehorses have made the most successful sires. To this rule there are certain exceptions, but these are too rare to affect the truth of the general axiom. Furthermore, not one of these exceptions – these mediocre turf performers – has stood out from the throng as a progenitor of the race in anything like the same degree as the phenomenal racehorse. Wisdom and Young Melbourne have frequently been cited as well-marked instances of poverty of turf performance being associated with no little ability to beget winners. But was Wisdom in the same street, as a parent of racehorses, as his paternal and maternal grandsires, the brothers Rataplan and Stockwell, or could Young Melbourne be compared with his sire? In parliamentary phraseology, the answer to these questions is in the negative.

When we approach the same problem in its relation to broodmares, there exists no such unanimity of opinion. There are those who hold that there is no association whatever between racing capacity in mares and ability to bring forth offspring possessing turf potentialities. In support of their view they are able to cite numerous instances where dams of good winners were either indifferent performers or never ran at all; whilst they endeavour to strengthen their argument by singling out certain great race mares which were comparative stud failures.

On the other hand there are not a few breeders and judges of blood-stock who pay great attention to a mare's turf career, and consider that ability to go fast and to stay at least moderately well is no less a *sine qua non* for stud success in mares than in horses.

The question has from time to time given rise to spirited discussion. But nothing very tangible has been the outcome. Not infrequently the contending parties have each claimed the day, whilst the large body of interested lookers-on remain *in statu quo* and still open to conviction.

'The Heredity of Racing Stamina', which was reprinted in the December number of the *Bloodstock Breeders' Review*, certainly threw some light on this subject, for I think the evidence then advanced clearly demonstrated that, in the matter of stamina, mares are in the main inferior to horses. It was further shown that this inferiority in many instances is confined to the bodily tissues, and in no way touches a mare's reproductive factor for the staying character. Thus, whilst five furlong sprinters of the male sex do not beget Ascot Cup winners, it is no uncommon thing to find mares who could not stay even the minimum racing distance giving birth to very high-class stayers. In these circum-stances it will be gathered that undue importance should not be attached to the manifestation of stamina by mares. If a mare shows stamina, well and good; but if she fails in this respect it is unwise to jump to the conclusion that she will not transmit the character, at any rate to her male offspring.

But in the present investigation – a first attempt to determine biometrically the relationship of racing merit to a mare's breeding value – attention will be focussed primarily upon the attribute of speed – the most essential consideration in a racehorse. At the same time, whilst sprinters have been given due prominence throughout the various groupings, superior positions have been assigned to mares which showed a measure of stamina in addition to fine speed.

As stated in my opening remarks, it is quite an easy matter to compile a list of high-class racehorses whose dams either never saw a racecourse or, if they started, showed no form whatsoever. Now if it be true, as some have asserted, that there is no correlation between racing merit in mares and the power to produce offspring which can race, then the dams of classic winners will, on the average, come out no better as turf performers than thoroughbred mares in general. On the other hand, if it can be shown that the dams of classic winners are above the mean in regard to racing ability, it must follow that there is a strong tendency for the best performers to give birth to superior racehorses; or, otherwise stated, that there is a correlation between racing capacity in mother and offspring.

The first step towards a solution of the problem was to extract the racing performances of a random sample from the broodmares which appear in Volume XXI of the *General Stud Book*. The investigation embraced the first 300 mares. These were then classified into six groups according to their turf performances. The percentage in each group works out as follows:

Group (1)	Mares which never ran	34%
Group (2)	Mares which ran but showed no form	28%
Group (3)	Mares which ran but showed moderate form	16%
Group (4)	Fair winners	17%
Group (5)	Good winners	4%
Group (6)	High-class race mares	less than 1%

The same procedure was then adopted with the dams of the winners of the Two Thousand Guineas, One Thousand Guineas, Derby, Oaks, and St Leger for the last thirty years.

As a check on the two previous compilations the whole of St Simon's daughters which have gone to the stud in this country were submitted to the same test. These number 146, and as St Simon has figured very prominently as a sire of successful broodmares since 1899, his daughters may be considered to be a selected sample.

The following is the classification of the St Simon broodmares:

Group 1 – Never Ran
Cimiez, Concertina, Catherine Luther, Democracy, Dogmatic, Flete, Lovely Morn, Luscinia, Nadejda, Parisina, Pasquinade, Peschera, Ravensbourne, St Mildred, St Ilma, St Matilda, Santa Nomis, Sigh, St Donatts, St Neophyte, Sesame, Simonia, St Katharine, Vespers, Williamina, Mare by St Simon–Neenah, Mare by St Simon–Tullia, Jersey, Lady Simonetta.
Total 29; Percentage, 20 per cent.

Group 2 – Ran, but No Form
Allumeuse, Atalaya, Columbian, Creme Simon, Cyme, Duchess de Berry, Dame Fortune, Fetish, Intact, Koorali, La Belle, Lady Flippant, Libation, La Tourbie, Miss Simon, Magdala, Mission, Normania, St Bees, Simplicity, Santa Felice, Santa Palma, Ste Adresse, St Mulrose, St Pelagia, Ste Perpetua, Santissima, Santona, Simonella, Sainte Marquise, Valeria, Zaire, Mare by St Simon–Rinovata, Mare by St Simon, dam by Hermit.
Total 34; Percentage, 23 per cent.

Group 3 – Moderate Form
Altnabea, Cot, Dark Duchess, Dramatica, Fleta, Gold Wing, Grand Prix, Lozenge, La Force, L'Ideale, Lady Mischief, Lilla, Madame de Montespan, Osy, Paid Up, Perpetua, St Elizabeth, Saintfield, Simena, St Theodora, Salvaich, St Hylda, Santa Linda, Siphon, Svelte, Simone, Tendril, Veglione, Zobeyde, Witty Girl, Citronella.
Total 31; Percentage, 21 per cent.

Group 4 – Fair Winners
Anna, Cheery, Desdemona, Dusky Queen, Evermore, Festa, Gravitation, Imogene, Lady Frivoles, Lady Susan, Mousme, Mrs Gamp, Perce Neige, Pamflete, Simonetta, Siphonia, St Reine, Sanctissima, Sanderling, Simon's Bay, Santa, Santa Stella, Santhia, Simola, Smean, St Vigila, Styria, Venus.
Total 28; Percentage, 19 per cent.

Group 5 – Good Winners
Charm, Gorgon, Lucy Cross, Roquebrune, Sabra, Saintly, Silene, The Smew, Santa Maura, St Aldegonde, Ste Nitouche, St Nydia, St Windeline, Santa Brigida, Utica, Victoria May.
Total 16; Percentage, 11 per cent.

Group 6 – High-class Race Mares

Amiable, La Flèche, La Roche, Mrs Butterwick, Signorina, Semolina, Winifreda, Memoir.

Total 8; Percentage, 6 per cent.

Adopting the same method of grouping I now present the winners of the five classic races for the last thirty years, with detailed comments concerning the performances of their respective dams. There may be, perhaps, some little difference of opinion in a few instances whether a mare should be placed in Group 4 or 5. But in the end it will be found that a slight rearrangement in no way affects the general issue. Mint Sauce, the dam of The Lambkin and Minthe, I placed in Group 3 since she won a little race, but it is questionable whether she ought not to have been in Group 2. But, on the other hand, Doris, the dam of Sunstar, might by some be considered a fair winner and, accordingly, be elevated to Group 4.

Group 1

Classic Winners whose Dams Never Ran

	Dam
ABOYEUR, Derby 1913	Pawky
SPEARMINT, Derby 1906	Maid of the Mint
ST AMANT, Two Thousand Guineas and Derby, 1904	Lady Loverule
VOLODYOVSKI, Derby 1901	La Reine
ISINGLASS, Two Thousand Guineas, Derby, and St Leger, 1893	Dead Lock
CHALLACOMBE, St Leger 1905	Lady Chancellor
SWEEPER II, Two Thousand Guineas 1912	Ravello
HANDICAPPER, Two Thousand Guineas 1901	Agnes Osborne
DISRAELI, Two Thousand Guineas 1898	Lady Yardley
KIRKCONNEL, Two Thousand Guineas 1895	Sweet Sauce
MERRY HAMPTON, Derby 1887	Doll Tearsheet
ROSEDROP, Oaks 1910	Rosaline
MRS BUTTERWICK, Oaks 1893	Miss Middlewick
GEHEIMNISS, Oaks 1882	Nameless

Group 2

Classic Winners whose Dams Ran but Showed No Form

	Dam	Remarks on Dam's Performances
MINORU, 2,000 Gs and Derby, 1909	Mother Siegel	Did not win. Not run after 2 years.
ARD PATRICK, Derby, 1902	Morganette	Ran once, unplaced. Did not run after 2 years.

	Dam	Remarks on Dam's Performances
GALTEE MORE, 2,000 Gs, Derby and St Leger, 1897	Ditto	Ditto
TROUTBECK, St Leger, 1906	Rydal Mount	Ran once only. Unplaced in the Gimcrack Stakes.
SCEPTRE, 2,000 Gs, 1,000 Gs, Oaks, and St Leger, 1902	Ornament	Ran once only, being easily beaten by Keythorpe as a two-year-old. Only two starters.
SUREFOOT, 2,000 Gs, 1890	Mare by Galopin out of Miss Foote	Unplaced in the Acorn Stakes. Did not run after 2 years.
ST GATIEN, Derby, 1884	St Editha	Did not run after 2 years. Started twice, unplaced.
OSSIAN, St Leger, 1883	Music	Did not run as a two-year-old. Ran 6 times as a three-year-old, but was never placed.
ENTERPRISE, 2,000 Gs, 1887	King Tom mare	Ran 4 times as a two- and three-year-old, unplaced.
GLASS DOLL, Oaks, 1907	Fota	Ran 7 times as a two- and three-year-old at five furlongs. Never placed.
CAP-AND-BELLS II, Oaks, 1901	Ben-my-Chree	Only started once. Ran out in the Croxton Park Stakes, as a two-year-old.
AIRS AND GRACES, Oaks, 1898	Lady Alwyne	Never ran after 2 years. Selling plater. Started 3 times, but showed no form.
AMIABLE, 1,000 Gs and Oaks, 1894	Tact	2 years ran once. Unplaced Maiden TYO plate, Newmarket, July. 3 years. Ran twice. Unplaced, at a mile
L'ABBESSE DE JOUARRE, Oaks, 1889	Festive	Ran up to four years of age. Unplaced in a five-furlong selling at Perth Hunt and in a two-mile selling at Edinburgh.
MIMI, 1,000 Gs and Oaks, 1891	Lord Lyon mare	Ran 3 times as a two-year-old unplaced
BRIAR ROOT, 1,000 Gs,	Eglentyne	2 years. Started 3 times in four-furlong maiden plates. Showed no form. 3 years. Ran 3 times, unplaced, 6 and 8 furlongs.
REVE D'OR, 1,000 Gs and Oaks, 1887	Queen of the Roses	Ran twice. Once at three and once at four years. A very bad mare.

Group 3

Classic Winners whose Dams showed Moderate Form

	Dam	Remarks on Dam's Performances
TAGALIE, 1,000 Gs and Derby, 1912	Tagale	Ran in France. Won one race as a two-year-old, beating a bad lot.

SUNSTAR, 2,000 Gs and Derby, 1911	Doris	Started 9 times as a two-year-old winning five-furlong races value £296. In one, a selling, she was bought in for 300 gns. Did not run after 2 years.
ORBY, Derby, 1907	Rhoda B	Did not run after 2 years. Started 5 times winning one race of £482. Not in the first eight in the Middle Park Plate.
RHODORA, 1,000 Gs, 1908	Ditto	Ditto
CICERO, Derby, 1905	Gas	Ran till 4 years. Started 17 times, but failed to win. Best performances 4th in the New Stakes and 3rd in the 1,000 Gs.
LADAS, Derby and 2,000 Gs, 1894	Illuminata	Did not run after 2 years. Ran 8 times. Won once, the Molyneux Stakes, 4 furlongs, Liverpool, first time out.
CHELANDRY, 1,000 Gs, 1897	Ditto	Ditto
SAINFOIN, Derby, 1890	Sanda	Ran till 5 years. Placed, 5 furlongs, at two and three years, but failed to win. Won a 2-mile hurdle race (£97).
TRACERY, St Leger, 1912	Topiary	2 years. Ran 5 times, placed four. No win. 3 years. Ran 8 times, winning a £10 maiden plate (10 furlongs) at Lanark. Only 3 starters.
YOUR MAJESTY, St Leger, 1908	Yours	Imported from Italy as a three-year-old. Ran 4 times in £100 plates. Placed up to 1½ miles, though failed to win.
OUR LASSIE, Oaks, 1903	Ditto	Ditto
PRETTY POLLY, St Leger, Oaks, and 1,000 Gs, 1904	Admiration	2 years. Ran twice unplaced. Goodwood and Sandown. She then ran in Ireland till 5 years, starting 19 times and winning 3 races, value £257. Maximum course a mile.
WILDFOWLER, St Leger, 1898	Tragedy	Did not run after 2 years. Ran 4 times in Ireland, winning 2 races, value £273.
KILWARLIN, St Leger, 1887	Hasty Girl	2 years. Ran 3 times in Ireland, winning two races, value £323. 3 years. Ran once only; unplaced 1½ miles. Hasty Girl was also the dam of Bendigo.

THE LAMBKIN, St Leger, 1884	Mint Sauce	2 years. Ran once, unplaced in a maiden selling.
		3 years. Ran 7 times. Won a £100 Handicap of a mile at Kelso; 4 ran. Bad race mare.
		Mint Sauce was also the dam of Minting.
MINTHE, 1,000 Gs, 1889	Ditto	Ditto
SLIEVE GALLION, 2,000 Gs, 1907	Reclusion	Did not run after 2 years. Started 5 times (in Ireland), winning 2 races value £195 five and six furlongs.
PARADOX, 2,000 Gs, 1885	Casuistry	Ran 4 times as a two-year-old. Won a maiden plate of half a mile at Epsom in June. Covered as a three-year-old.
CHERIMOYA, Oaks, 1911	Svelte	2 years. Ran once, unplaced.
		3 years. Ran 4 times. Placed at a mile, but failed to win.
KEYSTONE II, Oaks, 1906	Lock and Key	2 years. Ran 8 times, winning 2 races value £296.
		3 years. Ran twice unplaced 6 furlongs.
CHERRY LASS, 1,000 Gs and Oaks, 1905	Black Cherry	Did not run after 2 years. Started 9 times, winning a five-furlong plate (£100) at Thirsk from 10 opponents. Ran unplaced in five-furlong sellings.
LA ROCHE, Oaks, 1900	Miss Mildred	Did not run after 2 years. Showed poor form. Started 3 times, beating Zebra (2 yrs) in a £200 match.
LONELY, Oaks, 1885	Anonyma	Ran till 4 years on 14 occasions. Won 3 races value £300.
BONNY JEAN, Oaks, 1883	Bonnie Agnes	Did not run after 2 years. Started 7 times. Never ran over a greater distance than four furlongs. Won a selling race (£215), being sold to Lord Rosebery for 450 gns. Also won a £390 nursery at Newmarket in October.
WINKIPOP, 1,000 Gs, 1910	Conjure	2 years. Ran 5 times. Won a 5-furlong selling (£100) Alexandra Park. Sold for 200 gns.
		3 years. Ran twice unplaced in 5-furlong sellings.
WITCH ELM, 1,000 Gs, 1907	Cannie Lassie	Ran till 3 years on 8 occasions. Won a 9-furlong maiden plate.
THAIS, 1,000 Gs, 1896	Poetry	Ran 15 times as a two- and three-year-old. Placed second twice, and walked over twice, but failed to win a contested event.

GALEOTTIA, 1,000 Gs, 1895	Agave	Ran 6 times as a two- and three-year-old. Unplaced. Finished fifth in the 1,000 Gs. won by Reve d'Or.
SIFFLEUSE, 1,000 Gs, 1893	Assay	2 years. Ran 6 times, winning 2 races, value £390.
		3 years. Ran 11 times. Failed to win. Maximum course 5 furlongs.
HAUTEUR, 1,000 Gs, 1883	Hawthorndale	Ran up to six years of age. Won 3 races.

Group 4

Classic Winners whose Dams were Fair Winners

	Dam	Remarks on Dam's Performances
BAYARDO, St Leger, 1909	Galicia	2 years. Ran 3 times, winning the Ascot Biennial (£1,232), beating 11 opponents.
		3 years. Ran 5 times, but failed to gain a place.
LEMBERG, Derby, 1910	Ditto	Ditto
FLYING FOX, 2,000 Gs, Derby and St Leger, 1899	Vampire	Ran 12 times as a two- and three-year-old. Won 2 races as a two-year-old, value £825.
SIR HUGO, Derby, 1892	Manœuvre	Ran 11 times up to 4 years of age. Won the Gratwicke Stakes (£900), 1½ miles. Third in the St Leger to Silvio. Third in the City and Suburban to Sefton.
COMMON, 2,000 Gs, Derby and St Leger, 1891	Thistle	2 years. Ran 6 times, winning 4 races, value £1,220.
		3 years. Ran once indifferently.
THROSTLE, St Leger, 1894	Ditto	Ditto
LA FLÈCHE, St Leger, 1,000 Gs. and Oaks, 1892	Quiver	Ran up to four years. A winner as a two-year-old, starting once. At three years won a sprint handicap, and ran second to Lowlander in another. Maximum course 6 furlongs.
MEMOIR, St Leger and Oaks, 1890	Ditto	Ditto
MELTON, Derby and St Leger, 1885	Violet Melrose	2 years. Ran 13 times. Won two four-furlong sellings.
		3 years. Ran 8 times. Won four races, value £685. Maximum course six furlongs.
PRINCE PALATINE, St Leger, 1911	Lady Lightfoot	Ran 9 times as a two-year-old. Won 3 races, value £395.

		Ran 12 times as a three-year-old. Won 3 races value £365. Could stay 1½ miles.
DORICLES, St Leger, 1901	Rosalie	Ran up to 5 years. Started 24 times, winning 8 races, value £1,544. Maximum course six furlongs.
LOUVOIS, 2,000 Gs, 1913	St Louvaine	2 years. Won 4 five-furlong selling plates. 3 years. Unplaced at five and six furlongs.
VEDAS, 2,000 Gs, 1905	Agnostic	2 years. Ran 10 times. Won two nurseries, value £458. 3 years. Ran 12 times. Placed but failed to win. Maximum course five furlongs.
GALLIARD, 2,000 Gs, 1883	Mavis	2 years. Ran 7 times, winning two races, value £790. 3 years. Ran 8 times, winning one race, value £170. Also ran fifth in the Cesarewitch, carried 6 st 6 lb.
HARVESTER, Derby, 1884	Wheatear	2 years. Ran 6 times. Won 3 races. 3 years. Won the Newmarket Oaks and two Biennials at Ascot. 4 years. Won a Biennial at Newmarket.
ENTHUSIAST, 2,000 Gs, 1889	Cherry Duchess	A good two-year-old. Won on four occasions. Unsuccessful at three years. Maximum course five furlongs.
SCOT FREE, 2,000 Gs, 1884	Celibacy	Ran up to five years of age. Won 6 races. Maximum course a mile.
JEST, 1,000 Gs and Oaks, 1913	Absurdity	2 years. Ran once unplaced. 3 years. Ran 4 times, winning two races, value £245. 4 years unplaced. Maximum course a mile.
MUSA, Oaks, 1899	Palmflower	Ran 13 times and till four years of age. As a two-year-old won 4 races, value £2,230. Failed to win after that age, though placed at five furlongs. Best course half a mile.
LA SAGESSE, Oaks, 1895	Saint Mary	2 years. Ran 6 times. Won two races, value £1,567. 3 years. Started three times, unplaced. Maximum course six furlongs.
PEROLA, Oaks, 1909	Edmee	Ran up to six years. Started 31 times. Won 8 races, value £1,429. Maximum course seven furlongs.

MISS JUMMY, 1,000 Gs and Oaks, 1886	Lady Portland	Ran 18 times as a two- and three-year-old. Won 4 races. Course five furlongs.
ST MARGUERITE, 1,000 Gs, 1882	Devotion	Won twice as a three-year-old and twice as a four-year-old. Maximum course a mile.
THEBAIS, 1,000 Gs, 1881	Ditto	Ditto

Group 5

Classic Winners whose Dams were Good Winners

	Dam	Remarks on Dam's Performances
ROCK SAND, 2,000 Gs, Derby and St Leger, 1903	Roquebrune	2 years. Ran once, winning the New Stakes (£1,894) Ascot. 3 years. Ran once, winning the Zetland Stakes (£350), 1½ miles. 4 years. Ran once unplaced. There was considerable difficulty in training Roquebrune.
PERSIMMON, Derby and St Leger, 1896	Perdita II	Ran till five years old. Won seven races, value £3,717, including the Chesterfield Nursery, the Ayr Gold Cup, the Great Cheshire Handicap twice, and dead-heated with Middlethorpe for the Liverpool Summer Cup.
DIAMOND JUBILEE, 2,000 Gs, Derby and St Leger, 1900	Ditto	Ditto
SIR VISTO, Derby and St Leger, 1895	Vista	Ran till five years old. Won the Prince of Wales's Nursery, seven furlongs, Doncaster, the Great Metropolitan Handicap, and the Great Yorkshire Handicap.
BONA VISTA, 2,000 Gs, 1892	Ditto	Ditto
DONOVAN, Derby and St Leger, 1889	Mowerina	Ran till six years old. Won a number of sprint races, including the Portland Plate, Doncaster, carrying 9 st 5 lb. Maximum course, six furlongs.
SEMOLINA, 1,000 Gs, 1890	Ditto	Ditto
AYRSHIRE, 2,000 Gs, and Derby, 1888	Atalanta	Ran up to five years old. Started 37 times. Won 5 races including the Manchester Autumn Handicap, 10 furlongs. Also placed on several occasions.

WOOL WINDER, St Leger, 1907	St Windeline	2 years. Ran four times. Won 3 races, value £1,545.
		3 years. Ran 10 times. Won the Ascot Biennial (£1,115), a mile, and the Lingfield Park Plate (£2,425), 10 furlongs. Walked over twice, and finished second to Sceptre in the 1,000 Gs.
GORGOS, 2,000 Gs, 1906	The Gorgon	2 years. Ran 5 times. Won the New Stakes, Ascot. Second in the Chesterfield Stakes.
		3 years. Ran 4 times. Won the St George Stakes, Liverpool, 11 furlongs.
ST BLAISE, Derby, 1883	Fusee	Ran 9 times as a two-year-old. Won twice.
		3 years. Ran 11 times. Won 9 races, including several Queen's Plates.
ST FRUSQUIN, 2,000 Gs, 1896	Isabel	2 years. Ran 15 times. Won 5 races, value £1,012.
		3 years. Ran 13 times. Won 6 races, value £2,152, including the Ascot High Weight Handicap, 10 furlongs, and the Newmarket Summer Cup, 3 miles 4 furlongs.
LIMASOL, Oaks, 1897	Queen of Cyprus	Ran up to seven years old, winning 5 races, value £1,475, including the Great Northants Handicap, 2 miles, by 30 lengths from 9 opponents. Ran prominently in the Ascot Stakes and Cesarewitch.
FLAIR, 1,000 Gs, 1906	Glare	2 years. Ran 8 times. Won 4 races, including the Brocklesby and Fern Hill Stakes.
		3 years. Ran indifferently.
QUINTESSENCE, 1,000 Gs, 1903	Margarine	2 years. Very speedy. Ran 7 times, winning 5 races, value £2,027.
		3 years. Ran 5 times, but failed to win. Third to Queen's Birthday in the Great Northern Leger, $1\frac{1}{2}$ miles.
AIDA, 1,000 Gs, 1901	Queen Adelaide	Ran up to five years of age.
		2 years. Won the July Stakes and the Dewhurst Plate.
		3 years. Third in the Derby, third in the Oaks, and second in the 1,000 Gs.
NUN NICER, 1,000 Gs, 1898	Priestess	Did not run after two years. Started 7 times, and won 4 races, value £2,535.

| SHOTOVER, 2,000 Gs, and Derby, 1882 | Stray Shot | 2 years. Ran 6 times. Won 3 races. 3 years. Ran 14 times. Won 4 races, in one of which she beat Scamp and Lilian over 2 miles at Newmarket. |
| DUTCH OVEN, St Leger, 1882 | Cantinière | 2 years. Ran 7 times. Won 6 races, including the Woodcote Stakes. Did not run as a three-year-old, and only once as a four-year-old – unplaced in the Stewards' Cup. |

Group 6

Classic Winners Whose Dams were High Class Race Mares

	Dam	*Remarks on Dam's Performances*
SIGNORINETTA, Derby and Oaks, 1908	Signorina	2 years unbeaten. Won 9 races, value £11,724, including the Middle Park Plate. 3 years. Ran 5 times, winning one race of £200. Second to Memoir in the Oaks. 4 years. Ran 4 times. Won the Lancashire Plate (£8,971), beating Orme (2 years), Martagon, etc.
JEDDAH, Derby, 1898	Pilgrimage	2 years. Ran 5 times, winning the Dewhurst Plate and three other races. 3 years. Ran 3 times. Won the 1,000 Gs from Jannette. Won the 2,000 Gs, defeating Insulaire and Sefton, the subsequent Derby winner. Pilgrimage broke down in the Oaks, but nevertheless finished second.
CANTERBURY PILGRIM, Oaks, 1896	Ditto	Ditto
SWYNFORD, St Leger, 1910	Canterbury Pilgrim	2 years. Ran 4 times without winning. 3 years. Ran 6 times, winning the Oaks, the Park Hill Stakes, the Jockey Club Cup, and the Liverpool Cup.
ORMONDE, 2,000 Gs, Derby and St Leger, 1886	Lily Agnes	Ran up to five years of age. Won the Northumberland Plate, the Doncaster Cup, several Queen's Plates, and other races.
FAREWELL, 1,000 Gs, 1885	Ditto	Ditto
SEABREEZE, Oaks and St Leger, 1888	St Marguerite	2 years. Ran 11 times. Won 4 races, including the Chesterfield Stakes. 3 years. Ran 3 times. Won the 1,000 Gs and Nassau Stakes. Second in the Oaks to Geheimniss.

NEIL GOW, 2,000 Gs, 1910	Chelandry	Ran up to four years of age. 2 years won 4 races, value £7,933. 3 years. Won the 1,000 Gs. Second in the St Leger to Galtee More. 4 years. Third in the Jockey Club Stakes, won by Cyllene.
MIRSKA, Oaks, 1912	Musa	2 years. Ran 6 times. Won once (£485). Second in the New Stakes. 3 years. Won the Oaks.
BUSYBODY, 1,000 Gs and Oaks, 1884	Spinaway	Won the 1,000 Gs and the Oaks.
ELECTRA, 1,000 Gs, 1909	Sirenia	Ran up to 6 years of age. Won 9 races, value £7,736, including the Duke of York Stakes and the Jubilee Handicap, at Kempton, and the Lancashire Handicap.
WINIFREDA, 1,000 Gs, 1900	Melody	Ran up to four years of age. Won the Woodcote Stakes, Epsom, and a nursery at Sandown. At three years won the Prince of Wales' Stakes, Ascot. Second in the 1,000 Gs and Newmarket Stakes.

The following is a summary of the foregoing groupings of the dams of the classic winners for the last thirty years. By way of further explanation I should add that a mare is counted once for each classic winner that she breeds. Thus Lily Agnes gains two points as the dam of Ormonde and Farewell. But I wish it to be clearly understood that Lily Agnes gains no extra kudos in the reckoning from the fact that Ormonde won three of the classics. Ormonde counts one point for his dam, and Farewell another point.

Dams of Classic Winners

Group (1)	Never ran	14	12%
Group (2)	Ran, but showed no form	17	14%
Group (3)	Showed moderate form	30	26%
Group (4)	Fair winners	24	21%
Group (5)	Good winners	19	17%
Group (6)	High class race mares	12	10%

We are now in a position to make a comparison between the random sample of mares taken from the Stud Book, the daughters of St Simon which have gone to the stud, and, thirdly, mares which have bred classic winners during the last thirty years. This can only be done in a satisfactory manner by setting out side by side the percentage figures for the various groups. These are embodied in the following table:

General Summary of Results

		Dams of classic winners	St Simon broodmares	Random sample of broodmares GSB Vol. XXI
Group (1)	Never ran	12%	20%	34%
Group (2)	Ran, but showed no form	14%	23%	28%
Group (3)	Showed moderate form	26%	21%	16%
Group (4)	Fair winners	21%	19%	17%
Group (5)	Good winners	17%	11%	4%
Group (6)	High class race mares	10%	6%	Less than 1%

In the above table it will be noted that 62 per cent (approximately) of the mares in the Stud Book either never ran or showed no form; whilst of the dams of classic winners but 26 per cent come in this category. Here, therefore, we have conclusive biometrical evidence that at least a minimum of racing merit is a highly important consideration in broodmares.

Then, again, turning to the other end of the scale, it will be observed that in the random sample of broodmares less than 5 per cent fall in Groups 5 and 6, whereas 27 per cent of the dams of classic winners can, as we have seen, be impartially described as either good winners or high-class racemares, and, therefore, fall in Groups 5 and 6.

Taking these facts in conjunction, we have strong evidence that there is considerable correlation – a high correlation in fact – between racing merit in mares and the power to produce offspring which can not only race, but race with distinction. Or, to state the same conclusion in slightly different terms, biometrical investigation shows that racing performances are a highly important consideration in thoroughbred broodmares.

The circumstances that the daughters of St Simon occupy an intermediate position between broodmares in general and the dams of classic winners is of additional significance. One would naturally expect to find St Simon's daughters ranking higher as turf performers than the general run of mares; and expectation is fulfilled. But, good as are the St Simon mares, they, nevertheless, taken as a whole, fall appreciably below the dams of classic winners, though it should be borne in mind that certain of St Simon's daughters – to wit, Signorina, St Windeline, The Gorgon, Roquebrune, and Svelte – also appear in the tables as dams of classic winners.

Although it is not really germane to the subject of the present inquiry, I would point to a rather important inference which may be drawn from the tables, namely, that training mares has apparently no prejudicial effect whatever on their future value as breeding units. As will be seen from the details given, very many of the dams of classic winners were trained till their fifth year. Further, no one, I take it, would be so bold as to affirm that the dams of classic winners in Group 1 have proved better broodmares than those in Groups 5 and 6.   BBR–1913

Memorative Biography of Mr J. B. Robertson ('Mankato')

A MOST familiar figure at all important race meetings for more than forty years, James Bell Robertson went racing for the last time at Liverpool. It was the first day at Aintree. Too unwell to witness the contest for the Grand National he passed away not many hours afterwards, on April 6th. He was eighty years of age.

Born in Yorkshire of Scottish parents, he lived for a number of years in busy Bradford. He returned to Scotland to complete his education as a Veterinary Surgeon at Edinburgh where he qualified in May, 1889.

To all racing people and bloodstock breeders he was almost affec-

Mr J. B. Robertson

tionately known as 'Professor', a title conferred upon him by numerous friends as for long years he was consulting veterinary surgeon to many of the leading stables.

J. B. Robertson was recognised as about the greatest and probably the leading authority on the breeding of the racehorse in this country [England]. 'Mankato' held a high reputation in the United States. He lived near Minnesota for five years, but decided to return to complete his veterinary qualification as MRCVS. This he did with great success, winning many medals, including the Fitzwagram prize, offered to all the different colleges combined at the end of their student days. The competition for this distinction is very keen. In the US Robertson gained much practical experience. After his return he established himself as a veterinary surgeon at Lancaster. Later, he practically renounced his practice to devote himself to journalism.

As stated he was naturally frequently called in for consultation. It may be truly said that at one time or another every prominent race-horse owner and stud farm manager had desired his professional opinion and advice.

At a public dinner in London a few years ago, a speaker referred to the Aga Khan as 'the greatest living authority on bloodstock breeding'. In reply His Highness paid a remarkable tribute to 'Mankato' – 'nobody, certainly not myself, possesses a tenth of the knowledge of breeding possessed by Mr J. B. Robertson'.

For very many years Professor Robertson was a most popular and justly celebrated writer on topics concerning the thoroughbred, the animal himself, his rearing, and above all his breeding. He first contributed to *The Sporting Chronicle* in 1910.

Naturally opinions usually bluntly expressed and always quite fair were widely appreciated. Now and then he would arouse the ire of people (especially in the United States) who did not agree with him, often because of their inferior knowledge. Then the pen of 'Mankato' was powerfully used to demolish the opinions with which he disagreed or could prove were ill-founded.

It must be admitted, to be just, that Professor Robertson, despite his experience and ability, had not quite grasped the enormous extent racing and breeding conditions in the United States had changed since he was in that country half a century ago.

Unquestionably he was dogmatic in his writings. When 'Mankato' gave his commendation it was usually regarded as proof of the soundness of the view expressed. The pity is, sometimes he could not be convinced he *might* not be absolutely right. Even so, those who had most stoutly criticised him at intervals, paid the highest tribute to his manifold qualities. Yet it must be said there were times when it would have been wise not to have irritated his readers, especially in the US. He would have stoutly disclaimed any intention. It would be due alone to his ardent advocacy of the merits of the British thoroughbred.

He was an indefatigable worker. While he worked he thought only of the paper he represented. He really lived for his work.

Of a kindly nature he was a true friend to hosts of people in the racing and breeding worlds. In his work he was a clean fighter but dearly loved a 'tussle'. Many readers will recall his wordy duels with the late William Allison, the greatest of all 'Special Commissioners'. Robertson's knowledge of the history and development of the thoroughbred was very much deeper than that of his antagonist, who was the more subtle and daring journalist.

When *The Bloodstock Breeders' Review* was founded in 1912 Professor Robertson took keen personal interest in its success. His contributions became world famous. He dealt with such topics as 'Biological Searchlight on Racehorse Breeding'; 'Origin of the Thoroughbred and the History of the Racehorse'. They were the most instructive and practical articles which had ever appeared on these subjects vital to the breeder. Other articles in the *Review* which drew vivid attention to their author were 'Racecourse Performances and Breeding Value in Broodmares'; 'Heredity of Coat Colour', and in particular 'The Heredity of Blood Vessel Breaking in the Thoroughbred'. Such articles have never been equalled in their deep research and practical guidance. Extremely painstaking, he took every care to be accurate.

For many years he was entrusted with the direction of stud farms, in the way of arranging matings for mares and advising as to purchases to be made for the stud. In that way he greatly assisted the late Sir Edward Hulton, then owner of *The Sporting Chronicle*, and whose successes as a breeder are on record. Robertson also advised the late Lord Daresbury (Sir Gilbert Greenall) when he founded the Mount Coote Stud Farm in Co, Limerick. Love-in-Idleness, the Oaks winner, was bred there. He contributed to the *Review* the obituary of Lord Daresbury in 1938. Robertson was also friendly with Winalot's owner, the late Mr J. Shepherd, to whom he rendered much practical advice and help.

Away from journalism he was kindliness itself, and there was none who did not acknowledge his exceptional talent in his field, but in a wordy contest he never spared an opponent, even if a good friend, whose views he challenged.

The last article he contributed to the *Review* was in 1937 – 'The

Determination of Sex and Sex Incidence'. It is masterly. He told the writer he had spent the best part of three months preparing the data for that article. It is an example of his great industry and concentration.

It has been stated that Professor Robertson died from asthma. Probably the real cause of his death was an attack of 'heel-bug' he contracted when examining a horse about two or three years ago, for afterwards his robust constitution appeared to be vitiated. He developed a terrible attack of septicaemia, from which he never really recovered. The cessation of the publication of *The Sporting Chronicle*, due to war conditions, was a grievous blow. He had contributed to that journal over thirty years. His articles were eagerly awaited, for in them he had incorporated many personal features. Ever since the writer first attended bloodstock sales, in 1911, Professor Robertson was to be found in his usual place, on the left of the 'Press Box', quizzing the animals offered and adding comments on them for his article on that day's proceedings, for views expressed were the result of his deep knowledge of the history of the thoroughbred.

His notes on the personal appearance of horses taking part in the important events of the season were of the greatest value to breeders everywhere, and quoted from the United States to Australia.

The last article he penned appeared in *The Sunday Times* the day after his death. He had contributions on racing and breeding topics in that great newspaper for eight years. That article dealt with the Lincolnshire. It is reproduced elsewhere.

In his last years he seems to have discarded any theory he may have enunciated in connection with thoroughbred breeding. He examined all the so-called 'systems' and in the end rejected them all; Parental Ages; Male Line of Classic Winners; Female Line Classic Descent; Principles of Mendelian Heredity; Bruce Lowe's 'Breeding Racehorses by the Figure System'; Galton's Rule of Ancestral Contribution; The Vuillier System of Dosages. His views are crystallised in four short paragraphs. We quote them at the end of this memoir.

In paying our personal tribute to the kindly personality and the vast erudition of Professor Robertson, we feel there will never be another 'Mankato'.

He took his *nom de plume* from the town of that name in Minnesota, US. It was chosen 'on the spur of the moment'. Thus he used it for the first time over thirty years ago. Then was inaugurated his friendship with the late Sir Edward Hulton who personally engaged him for his paper. He commenced to write regularly for *The Sunday Times* on July 17th, 1932, under the name of 'Mankato'.

He left a widow. His only son died during the Great War, due to a tragic accident. Henry Cecil Robertson was a very brilliant young man. Before he was twenty years of age he had worked out the heredity of grey colour according to Mendelian laws. He was a vitally helpful collaborator of his father, preparing the 'graphs' and statistics upon which 'Mankato' could and did rely.

It may not be generally known that about forty years ago J. B. Robertson owned, or was part-owner of, the racehorses Keystone and Athos, on whom he won races. They were half-brothers, being out of Pontillon. The former was by Titterstone; the latter by The Rush.

At Hamilton Park on July 13th, 1901, Robertson won a Welter Handicap with Titterstone, beating the favourite by a head. An objection which followed was over-ruled and the Stewards ordered the deposit money to be forfeited. Four years after, again at Hamilton Park, Robertson on Athos won the Ross Welter Handicap, beating Fred Rickaby on Island Queen. Two months later, on the same course, Athos, with his owner riding, won another Welter Handicap. This time he finished a head in front of J. Priestman on Midshipman, who was a head from Jock Ferguson on Island Queen. This was a notable performance. Priestman was then in the front rank of North country professional jockeys. Ferguson was about the champion gentleman rider of the day. Robertson was also third on Faison d'Or in another Welter Handicap, which was won by a horse ridden by Mr J. M. Bell, the latter being the trainer of that good horse Trespasser.

We believe these winners were prepared by J. B. Robertson, who no doubt had acquired his knowledge of horsemanship in riding his own horses in their work about Carnforth, Lancs.

'Mankato's' Views on Bloodstock Breeding, expressed when eighty years of age

The first rule in the production of racehorses is to make close study of the characters and qualities, abilities and disabilities of the proposed parents. Then to review not less closely the units in the upper ancestry. This cannot be done solely on paper.

First-hand knowledge of at least the male ancestors in the last fifty or sixty years is needful. It is useless to inbreed on paper to a horse or mare unless there are reasonably good grounds for the belief that the parents will be able to transmit the trait or traits desired.

. . . Coat colour is not correlated with other characters, but its behaviour in genetics serves as an important object lesson. . . In like manner it is useless to inbreed to St Simon or Isonomy for stamina unless there is evidence that the factors concerned have been patent in some of the intervening links.

The thoroughbred is the outcome of natural selection through the racecourse test. With very few exceptions horses which have proved well above the mean of ability on the racecourse have become the male parents of the race in general of the future. Variation is always at work, and the phenomenal performers are horses and mares which vary to the greatest degree above the mean. . . St Simon, both in speed and stamina, was vastly above not only the mean but the best horses of his day. . . An idea is current there must be a certain formula in the *Stud Book* and *Racing Calendar* for the production of the highest class winners, and that a diligent search will in the course of time disclose it!

From *Flat Racing* in the Lonsdale Library, published by Seeley Service & Co, Ltd, London, 1940.

BBR–1940

The Duke of Wellington's Charger and The Stud Book

AMONG all the thousands of broodmares whose records are set forth in the twenty-three volumes of the *General Stud Book*, there is only one admittedly a half-bred. This is Lady Catherine, whose name is to be found in Volume II. She is described as 'Bred by General Grosvenor in —, got by John Bull, her dam by Rutland Arabian out of a hunting mare not thoroughbred'. Why did the editors of the Stud Book of that day depart from the rule that only reputed thoroughbred mares should be admitted to its precious pages? Because Lady Catherine produced in 1808 the chestnut colt Copenhagen (by Meteor and bred by General Grosvenor) who was the horse ridden by the Duke of Wellington at the Battle of Waterloo. The exception made in her favour was evidently intended as a compliment to the Iron Duke. Here we have an explanation of the mistake so often made that Copenhagen was a thoroughbred. He is in the Stud Book right enough, but on sufferance only. As the late Mr J. A. Doyle put it, Copenhagen was granted 'a title of nobility for military services'.

An Experiment Doomed to Failure

Mr Rob Bunsow, one of the original members of the Review *crew, had that very happy combination of being extremely knowledgeable and being able to express himself eloquently. This is delightfully exposed in the very first issue of the* Review *in which he deftly warns of 'An*

Amazing Experiment' which is certainly doomed to failure because 'It only shows that it is not sufficient to be an expert in Mendelism' but that 'one must also have a thorough understanding of racing and racehorse breeding in order to be able to apply properly the wonderful Mendelian law'.

The doomed experiment involved jumpers, and people still interested in that phase of the sport will find Mr Bunsow's comments most interesting and exhilarating. Indeed, everyone will.

IT WAS recently announced that Captain D. C. Part, of the 21st Lancers, had bought a few thoroughbred mares and colts, for the purpose of endeavouring to breed from them so-called 'homozygous' jumpers, that is to say horses, who, because of the hereditary qualities of their parents, are bound to develop into 'chasers. The suggestion is that the germ cells of the parents contain only jumping characters, so that they will 'breed true' in the same way that a pure dominant bay or brown, like St Simon, St Serf, Ladas and Missel Thrush can only get bay or brown foals from chestnut mares. We are further told that Mr C. C. Hurst, a well-known student of Mendelism, is associated with Captain Part in this venture. Everybody of course, has the right to make experiments of this sort. But Mr Hurst is, we are told, an adviser on horse breeding to the Board of Agriculture, and therefore occupies an official position. The experiment in which he is participating will be a failure, and unless breeders are at once warned, they will be led into the belief that Mendelism is humbug. It is necessary, therefore, to place this astonishing scheme under a microscope and examine its details.

The following are the animals which Captain Part has acquired for the purpose of the experiment:

> Ballymacarney (Royal Meath–Cinnamon).
> Frigate (Red Prince II–Athela).
> Breemount's Pride (Kendal–Mavourneen).
> Revolving Light (Red Prince II–Revolver).
> Two-year-old filly, by Creangate out of a Hackler mare.
> Yearling colt by Creangate out of a Hackler mare.
> Yearling colt, by Missel Thrush out of Breemount's Pride.

Let it be understood at the outset that there is absolutely nothing new in Mr Hurst's scheme. He is merely following on the lines of all other *fanciers*. There is *not a trace* of Mendelism in it. Mr Hurst thinks that certain characters are present in the tissues of Captain Part's animals, and that there are determinants for those characters in their germ cells. He has, however, no more warranty for his supposition than Mr Bibby had when he tried and failed to breed a decent animal from Breemount's Pride.

Nearly every stallion standing in Ireland sires jumpers, but this is due to the circumstance that the small Irish owner schools all, or nearly all, his horses at jumping. Steeplechasing of a kind goes on in Ireland all through the summer, but many of the horses who take part in the sport are so bad that they would be useless in races of the lowest class in England and in many Continental countries. On the other hand, there are many stallions in England whose stock is never put to jumping, so that its jumping qualities are never discovered. Lord Middleton and his ancestors have bred hunters at Birdsall for over a hundred years, using only flat racers as sires; nevertheless, the Birdsall hunters are the best in England. Many of them are thoroughbreds. The point I wish to emphasise at the very outset is, then, that steeplechasers and hunters can be bred from *all* thoroughbred sires in England and Ireland, provided the offspring undergo proper schooling.

There is no such thing as a Mendelian factor for jumping. A really good jumper is composed of an infinity of Mendelian characters, which, as Mr Hurst knows, are all transmitted to the offspring independently. For every bone, every muscle, every nerve, there are different determinants. There is not among them one that can be called a ''chaser's determinant'. It requires a suitable combination of *all* to make a real jumper. Breeders have not yet the power to bring about this combination.

Skeletal conformation varies greatly in horses which are, or were, proved weight-carriers and good jumpers. Both Cloister and Manifesto had six lumbar vertebræ; Ambush II had five. Why Not was a comparatively small horse; smaller still are Shady Girl and Salmon Fly, now running. The Grand National winners, Emblem and Emblematic, were both mares remarkably light in bone and loin. Eremon presented yet another conformation, being ewe-necked, with an immense 'jumping bump', very long and straight on his hind legs – a feature often seen in good jumpers. Jenkinstown, though by Hackler, bears no resemblance to Salmon Fly, also by Hackler, and the smaller horse is the better 'natural' jumper. So much for skeletal conformation in relation to a supposed ''chaser type'. Steeplechasers 'run in all shapes'.

With regard to the muscles, the gross bulk of the so-called voluntary muscles (those used in locomotion) is to some extent correlated to the size and shape of the bones, but the *specific physiological* properties of muscle fibres (speed and stamina) are absolutely unconnected with the skeletal formation. They are transmitted *quite independently* of variation in the skeleton of the thoroughbred. On the specific physiological properties of the muscles depends the presence or absence of stamina; it does not depend upon the mere bulk of muscle. The muscles of a sprinter are often much more bulky than those of a stayer. A most important factor of a good jumper is his *heart*, which is merely a muscle, and is governed in heredity by the same principles that apply to the voluntary muscles.

True racing stamina is not an essential quality in a 'chaser, as everybody who knows anything about steeplechasers is well aware. Speedy animals on the flat often make the best jumpers. Hundreds of examples could be cited in support of this statement. Many horses have won the Grand National which could not stay a mile on the flat. Old Joe was thought to be a wonderful stayer after he had won the Grand National, and the following autumn was trained for the Cesarewitch, in which race, carrying 6 st 3 lb, he was tailed off after covering six furlongs! In ordinary steeplechases the pace is not fast enough to get the muscles of the non-stayer asphyxiated. During the act of jumping, a horse gets a rest in so far as many of the muscles brought into play when galloping are not for the moment in use, and so get a chance to obtain a fresh dose of oxygen.

This being so – and there is not the slightest doubt that it *is* so – breeding solely from jumpers without recourse to a cross of the high-class stayer on the flat, will give a very low average of true muscle stamina. Yet this is one of the characters Mr Hurst professes to have discovered in his 'homozygous jumpers'. Of course there is a class of 'chasers which may be described as slow plodding hunters, that will run for hours, but which are utterly devoid of all nerve force. The best of them may do for point-to-point races, but not for breeding purposes. The ordinary half-bred mares are slow enough already, and the first consideration should be how to put speed into their offspring. This certainly cannot be done by using slow sires.

Speed depends upon the quality of the nerve cells; but the nerve cells of the animals selected by Mr Hurst or Captain Part, are not, so far as their racing performances indicate, of high class. Breemount's Pride is the best performer of the group, but she is now nineteen years old. Is this a model mare to breed from? How many mares of her age have bred anything of much value?

And what about Breemount's Pride's offspring? Only two, Judina and Hackmount, have faced the starter. Judina was a very moderate hurdler, and was on one occasion beaten by five lengths by San Martino, who was exhibited for a King's Premium this year, and consequently is one of the stallions which Mr Hurst is striving to replace by his 'homozygous 'chaser sires'. Her brother, Hackmount, also by Hackler, the homozygous 'chaser sire (!), is just a moderate Selling 'Chaser, often running in £40 races, winner to be sold for £50, and after winning he has either failed to elicit a bid or changed hands at £70 or £80. If Mr Hurst breeds nothing better than these two animals from Breemount's Pride – and judging from her stud record he may breed something a good deal worse – he is likely to make a laughing stock of Mendelism.

Revolving Light, another of the mares bought for the purposes of this experiment, is a wretchedly bad animal, and has only run once – unplaced in a Maiden Steeplechase. Her dam failed to elicit a bid of 20 guineas as a yearling at Doncaster. She ultimately found her way to Ireland, where she scored in six little steeplechases when five years old. Her produce, two fillies, as yearlings, were sold at Doncaster, for 25 and 170 guineas. One has never run, and the other, as a racehorse, is of little value.

Frigate has been a fair Hunt Steeplechase mare, but is lacking in class. Athela, her dam, has bred two other fillies by Red Prince II, neither of which ran; also a filly by Rays Cross, which never started; and Turco III, a gelding by Red Prince II, which won a little steeplechase in Ireland, and was afterwards used as a hunter. Lord Chatham (by Little John), out of Athela, certainly did manage to win races, but ran a bad third to Moonstruck in the Lancashire Steeplechase at even weights. Moonstruck is a half-bred horse, sired by the *sprinter* Massacre. Strawberry Queen, another of Athela's produce, by Little John, never won a race, nor did Athela herself.

Ballymacarney, the remaining mare in the list, never ran, and is now fifteen years old. She has bred some useful horses by Hackler and Bushey Park. There have, however, been King's Premium winners, which would, I imagine, have had little difficulty in beating, either on the flat or over obstacles, anything bred by Ballymacarney.

There are many mares in the *Stud Book* more suitable for the purposes of this experiment than most of those bought by the Hurst Syndicate. One is apt to lose patience in reviewing such an amateurish attempt to apply the principles of Eugenics. It only shows that it is not sufficient to be an expert in Mendelism, as Mr Hurst undoubtedly is; one must also have a thorough understanding of racing and racehorse breeding in order to be able to apply properly the wonderful Mendelian law. The mention of 'a pure dominant for jumping' almost takes one's breath away. We might as well speak of a homozygous plumber or needleworker.

I am disposed to allow that there are extenuating circumstances for

Mr Hurst's mis-statements so far as racing is concerned. I will not blame him because he is unaware of the fact that *none* of the *best* sires of steeple-chasers were jumpers themselves. Ascetic, the most famous of them all, never jumped a fence in his life; nor did Hackler, St Gris, Esterling, Baliol or Ben Battle. The stock of Red Prince II though he himself was a 'chaser, and out of the Grand National winner, Empress, have fallen far below the offspring of the 'miler' Hackler, who was by the non-staying Petrarch, out of the Cambridgeshire winner, Hackness. There is another point which seems to have escaped the notice of Mr Hurst. He will find that he is unable to keep his colts entire and still make them thoroughly proficient jumpers over a course like that at Aintree. Horses intended for jumping purposes are not cut for the fun of the thing, but because experience shows that with very rare exceptions entire horses, after they are five or six years old, are useless for jumping.

The conclusion to be drawn from the foregoing facts is that an experiment like the one that is about to be made with material so limited, and relatively indifferent, will bring discredit on Mendelian principles by professing to apply them, when, as a matter of fact, the experiment is to be worked only on the most empirical lines. If everything else were satisfactory, the field of operation is too limited, and the resulting *data* will be too meagre to have any scientific value, even assuming there is science in the scheme at all. The inevitable result will be that horses bred on the proposed lines will run at the end of a rein at Agricultural Shows, but never on a racecourse.   BBR–1912

Mr A. F. B. Portman

John Oaksey, in his final article before his retirement after thirty years of writing the 'Audax' column in Horse and Hound, *stated 'I am very proud to have followed Arthur Portman and David Livingstone-Learmonth during such an eventful period of British Racing History.'*

Mr Arthur F. B. Portman was killed together with his wife, following a direct hit by a bomb on his house in the West End of London on September 22nd 1940, at the age of seventy-nine. For the previous fifty years he had been editor of Horse and Hound, *which was founded by his father in 1884.*

He was intolerant of inaccuracy, but he set the same high standards for himself as he did for others. He was always polite, anxious to see the best in people, and a devoted husband to his invalid wife. And it was he who set the high standards of journalism that have become the hallmark of his father's publication.

ON THE night of September 17th Mr Arthur F. B. Portman, editor and senior director of *Horse and Hound* was foully murdered by a German airman, at his home in the West End of London. He had attained the age of seventy-nine years on August 22nd, when many sincere congratulations from staff, readers and friends had greatly touched this fine old sportsman.

Arthur Fitzhardinge Berkeley Portman, together with Mrs Portman, an invalid, as well as their servants, were crushed to death when a direct hit destroyed the beautiful home containing his almost unique library dealing with the thoroughbred.

Approximately fifty years he had been the editor of *Horse and Hound*, which journal had become an institution to bloodstock breeders everywhere. The interesting notes on breeding and racing in most countries were accurately reported by experienced writers.

His own contributions under his famous pen name of 'Audax' were also world famous. An extremely courteous man, very gentle in disposition, kindly in spirit, always desirous of seeing good in any man, next to the companion of his life, he really lived for his journal. His work was so painstaking and accurate, his standard so strict, yet it was typical of his fine nature, whether in the hurly-burly of the racecourse or in quieter moments inspecting mares and foals on a stud. No one could remain a few minutes in his company without feeling reposed and refreshed by his courtesy and kindness for he was never hasty or harsh in his remarks or comments. And the end! – such a drastic and tragic contrast to all that had gone before in that quiet life and noble character.

It was in 1884 that Arthur Portman's father founded *Horse and Hound*. It was due to his parent's illness (which eventually proved fatal) that 'Audax' took over the editorship in September, 1890. He also owned the paper, which was not turned into a company for another twenty-five years, mainly to assure the continuity of the publication.

Mr Portman's family had a long association with racing, for his great-grandfather twice won the Derby, with Sam (1818) and with Sailor (1820), both sons of Scud.

Curiously in the last article 'Audax' penned, he recounted the story of his fifty years' association with *Horse and Hound*. His death came suddenly, before he had revised the final proofs of his reminiscences for the issue of September 20th.

Warm tributes to his great ability and kindly character crowded the pages of *Horse and Hound*. Mr Portman's first visit to a racecourse was as a boy of twelve years old. His vivid memories of contests for the Derby went back to 1877 – Silvio's year. He had seen the race for our greatest classic without a break for over sixty years.

He was an intimate friend of all the leading sportsmen of his time. He wrote of men and horses and racing as he saw them, just as though he were quietly sitting in his chair at the fireside to chat over the day's happenings. He never appeared in a rush, just sauntering in the paddock making notes on the horse running that day in the tiny book he could carry in the palm of his hand. Discreetly retiring to the auctioneer's room in Park Paddocks he would write his comments as the sales proceeded, emerging now and then to witness the disposal of a well-known racehorse or broodmare. His comments on the chief yearlings sold at Doncaster were appealing. He was rarely erroneous in his valuation of the possibilities of any youngster. One felt that Arthur Portman was an integral part of our racing and breeding world. He was steadfastness and thoroughness personified.

There is no doubt the tragic death of 'Audax' has left a gap it will be extremely difficult to fill.

The columns of his paper were used to further best interests of true sport. Possessing such a retentive memory he would never tolerate inaccuracy. He inaugurated in his journal many features of value, especially statistics dealing with various aspects of thoroughbred breeding.

It was the wish of both Mr Portman and his wife that *Horse and Hound* should carry on. He set himself a high standard in life and duty. He was faithful to the end. An intimate friend wrote – one reason for staying in London after war was declared was his devotion to the interests of *Horse and Hound*, as well as his affection for his invalid wife, and his determination not to run away, as he termed it, from the responsibilities of his position.

A memorial service, held on October 2nd at St Mark's, North Audley Street, London, W, was attended by very many friends, who had made long and difficult journeys to pay tribute by their presence to the outstanding personal qualities of an English gentleman and his wife, whose tragic passing they so keenly regretted.

It was in Wellington Street, Strand, that *Horse and Hound* was first produced with a modest staff. In 1923 a removal was made to Bessemer House, Adelphi, London. That building was shattered by a direct hit from a German bomb less than a month after the Nazis had destroyed 'Audax' himself. We learn that the valuable and extensive library of the journal was salvaged, so there has been no break in the weekly appearance of the paper.   BBR – 1940

The 'American Stud Book' in 1912

While Americans were particularly dismayed in 1913 when the English Turf's governing body, seemingly ruthlessly, enacted the Jersey Act, the English, for the most part, were thoroughly convinced they were doing the right thing in keeping the breed pure. The following article, which was entitled ' "Doubtfuls" In the American Stud Book*', appeared in the* Review *of 1912 and suggests the English may have had a point. There are also some fascinating comments on the pedigrees of three of Lexington's most famous sons – Duke of Magenta, Tom Bowling and Joe Daniel.*

WRITING IN *The Thoroughbred Record* (Kentucky), 'Hidalgo', otherwise Captain T. B. Merry, author of *The American Thoroughbred*, has something to say about the inclusion in the *American Stud Book* of mares of doubtful origin. He declares that there are many mares in that book that should have been omitted altogether; or, if given at all, should have been published in an appendix.

'I sent Colonel Bruce two mares, owned by Nathan Coombs, of Nassa, named Becky Rector and Kate Simpson, stating my belief that neither of them was strictly thoroughbred, but he might use his own discretion about inserting them. They both came out in Vol. I, and in Vol. II I found also Minerva Anderson and the Saltram mare, which produced Jenny Cockracy and Timoleon. I have always, however, inclined to a belief that there are several mares in the *American Stud Book* which were really thoroughbred, but could not be definitely traced to any mare imported. These were the following:

1. The "mare owned by Mr T. D. Owings, of Virginia", to which trace such celebrities as Spendthrift, Fellowcraft, Rutherford and Wildidle, and, if I am not mistaken, Macduff also.

2. The "mare from the stud of Harrison of Brandon", to which trace Mollie McCarthy, Winifred, Flood, Hidalgo, Sir John and others.

3. The Fearnought mare, to which traced King Alfonso and Cayuga.

4. The Hoomes mare by imp. Dare Devil, to which trace a dozen of the best horses ever foaled in California, as well as Time Maker (forty-seven wins), Mollie Wood (twenty-eight wins), and others. No attempt was made to trace this mare to imp. Trumpetta till Ansel and Virgil came along.

5. The Janus mare, to which trace Norfolk, Volante, Hermis, and a dozen other cracks, as well as the Maria West or Margaret Woods family, which traces also to that source.

6. The Tristram Shandy mare, to which traces Checkmate, and so many other great winners. I would reject all others.

'The two best sons of Lexington (which outbred all contemporary sires, whether native or imported) were the worst bred of all his many great winners. Duke of Magenta was one of these and his breeding was absolutely rotten. And as for Tom Bowling, his pedigree was a forgery as stupid as it was audacious. Nor was that of Joe Daniel much better, and he was by long odds, the best three-year-old of 1872.

'The fourth dam of Hanover was Ophelia by Wild Medley, son of imp. Mendoza; and old Robert Wooding, as straight a man as ever came to California, always contended that Wild Medley was a myth, and that Grey Eagle's pedigree was cut out of whole cloth.'

Captain Merry assisted Colonel Bruce in the compilation of the *American Stud Book*, the earlier volumes of which made their first appearance in 1869. He was at that time connected with a newspaper in San Francisco, and his offer to compile the records of the thoroughbreds located in California at that time for $50 was accepted. The first edition of the book was a small one, and so quickly sold out that a second edition of Volumes I and II had to be issued in 1873. The *English Stud Book* was started in 1793.   BBR-1912

Scepticism About American Pedigrees

'NORTH COUNTRYMAN', a frequent contributor to *Baily's Magazine* in the 'sixties of last century, wrote as follows in 1864 in the course of an article on stallions of that day:

'The American horses of late years imported into this country, and for which we are much indebted to Mr Ten Broeck, give promise of some day or other doing our breed decided benefit. They certainly possess powers of endurance; their legs are hard, wiry, and bear a deal of hard work; but whether some of them have not a stain on their escutcheon – and that not very far back – is a question which admits of some doubt, so many of them show great coarseness, and a deal of hair about their heels. Charleston is an especially low-bred looking horse, and in a Yorkshire Fair would be taken for a coaching stallion. Prioress, the winner of the Cesarewitch, was also a very vulgar one in appearance; nor can Umpire, though a horse of great bone and substance, and a most valuable and promising hunter sire, be considered but as very coarse and under-bred in his general contour. Not but that this coarseness, as it is decidedly accompanied by great powers of endurance, may eventually be of great service in crossing with the antelope-like tribes of TYC racers which abound; but I look upon the second and third generation as likely to prove, more than the first, what benefits may result from the introduction of the American horse.'

BBR-1930

Towards the Jersey Act

As the previous article shows, British breeders were beginning to look askance at the conformation of many imported American horses. However, the focal point around which the controversy concerning the Jersey Act raged was the conditions under which horses were accepted for registration in the General Stud Book.

Up until the end of the nineteenth century horses who were accepted for the GSB *fell into two categories:*

a) *Horses whose pedigrees could be traced without flaw to progenitors entered in previous editions of the book*

b) *Foreign horses who were registered in the Stud Books of their country of origin.*

As will be shown in the section on the American Stud Book, horses were accepted into this book on terms considerably less stringent than those imposed by the General Stud Book. *This sometimes resulted in the admittance to the* English Stud Book *of American breeding stock of 'impure' blood.*

The chain of events which led to the Jersey Act controversy were set in motion by the passing, between the years 1900 and 1913, of a series of antigambling laws in many states of America. This left a large number of horses in the United States which were surplus to requirements; a considerable number of these were shipped to England and Ireland. Since racing was at a standstill in many parts of America, it seemed likely that these horses would remain in England and go to stud there.

Before the turn of the century there had been a limited number of importations, but they were mostly high-grade stock who returned to their country of origin when their racing days were over. However, in the early years of the century there was a considerable influx of horses of 'impure' blood, who were classified as thoroughbreds by the American Stud Book *rules, which differed from those in England. As they were in the* American Stud Book, *however, they were entitled to entry in the* English Stud Book *under the reciprocal rules then in force. In consequence English breeders became alarmed and feared the results of the wholesale introduction of 'impure' blood into their studs.*

The horse who was almost the centre of the affair was Lexington, whom we have mentioned in a previous article. He was a very fine racehorse and a great stallion, but his pedigree was open to the gravest suspicion. If so great and influential a horse as Lexington was of 'impure' blood, it is not surprising that English breeders were doubtful about other entries.

Messrs Weatherby, therefore, as the owners and publishers of the General Stud Book, *approached the Stewards of the Jockey Club pointing out the discrepancies between American and English pedigrees and asked for guidance. The outcome can be witnessed in the following pages!*

Introduction of the Jersey Act

It was in 1913 that that most disputatious of decisions was made by England's Jockey Club. To be known as 'The Jersey Act' and to remain in force until 1949, it effectively prohibited many horses and mares bred in the US and Australia from being registered in the English Stud Book. *The decision, reviled by those affected and applauded by most English breeders, was to be an on-going sore point between the Americans and the English for some thirty-six years. The decision, as reprehensible as it seemed to American breeders, did not go far enough in purifying the* General Stud Book *in the opinion of most interested Englishmen. The new ruling did not cast out those horses of questionable parentage who had already been accepted. Thus, Americus, perhaps one of the main targets of the Act, remained in the* English Stud Book.

The English Jockey Club was gracious enough and considerate enough to send a full report of its debate on the matter to John E. Madden, the leading American breeder at the time, requesting his comments. He agreed that 'It is to the best interests of all to keep the blood pure as possible at the fountain head (England)'.

THE PREFACE to Volume XXI of the *General Stud Book* contains the following notice:

'The Editors beg to inform subscribers that, since the last volume of the *Stud Book* was published, they have had cause to consider the advisability of admitting into the *Stud Book* horses and mares which cannot be traced to thoroughbred root, but which have fulfilled the requirements given in the preface to Vol. XIX.

'They have decided that, in the interests of the *English Stud Book*, no horse or mare can be admitted unless it can be traced to a strain already accepted in the earlier volumes of the Book. The Editors must, therefore, rescind the Notice published in Vol. XIX.'

On the recommendation of the Jockey Club, who discussed the matter at the instance of Lord Villiers, the Editors have agreed to substitute for the second paragraph the following announcement, which will duly appear in Volume XXII, to be issued during the coming Autumn:

'They have decided that, in the interests of the *English Stud Book*, no horse or mare can, after this date, be considered as eligible for admission unless it can be traced without flaw on both sire's and dam's side of its pedigree to horses and mares themselves already accepted in the earlier volumes of the book.'

The first reference in the *Stud Book* to the registration of imported horses and mares is to be found in Volume XVIII, in the Preface to which we read:

'The importation of a number of horses and mares bred in the United States of America and in Australia, a few of which will remain at studs in this country, may have some effect on stock bred here, but the pedigrees of these horses, though accepted in the Stud Books of their own country, cannot in all cases be traced back to the thoroughbred stock exported from England, from which they all claim to be, and from which, no doubt, they mainly are descended; these animals are therefore, in these cases, marked with reference to their own Stud Books.'

In Vol. XIX, published twelve years ago, there is the following allusion to the subject:

'The increased importation of horses and mares bred in the US and Australia, which, as stated in the last volume, though accepted in the Stud Books of their own country, cannot be traced back in all cases to the thoroughbred stock exported from England, from which, more or less, they all claim to be descended, induced the publishers to refer the question of the admission of such animals into the *Stud Book* to the Stewards of the Jockey Club as the highest authority on all matters connected with the Turf. The Stewards, after kindly consulting most of the principal breeders, came to the conclusion that any animal claiming admission should be able to prove satisfactorily some eight or nine crosses of pure blood, to trace back for at least a century, and to show such performances of its immediate family on the Turf as to warrant the belief in the purity of its blood. Therefore all the imported horses and mares which are included in this volume have been submitted to this test.'

The decision recently arrived at is one of the utmost importance. It means that in future a hard and fast line is to be drawn. It means, further, that there are horses and mares now registered in the stud book who would have no chance of securing admission to its pages under the application of the new rule. As the report of the Jockey Club debate shows, there is, however, no intention of expelling the animals who have already been admitted, though there are purists who would gladly see them excluded.

The whole question was discussed by the Jockey Club at their first Spring meeting. Lord Villiers, who was the chief spokesman, said:

'The importance of the subject became more apparent every year, because more horses were imported from America, and when the owners of doubtfully bred American horses saw horses of similar breeding in the Stud Book they not unnaturally claimed the same privilege for their own horses. It would be better if Messrs Weatherby made it clear once and for all that they could not admit any such claims. The present notice in the Stud Book was somewhat indefinite, and it was sometimes rather difficult for them to refuse admission. "Traced to a strain" was liable to misconstruction. For instance, the May Day breed "traced to a strain" which was already accepted, but could not be traced without flaw, and was quite rightly refused admission. On the other hand, they saw certain more than doubtfully bred horses and sometimes untraceable American horses admitted to the Stud Book, and the inconsistency was obvious.

'Of course, the ideal thing would be to purge the Stud Book of all impurities, but then they would have to remember the hardships that would be inflicted on existing interests. It might be possible in some way to indicate what strains now in the Stud Book had a flaw in their pedigrees, as a warning to breeders who wished for nothing but pure-bred animals; but that was a matter outside the scope of his question, and he would rather leave that for the Stewards to discuss with Messrs Weatherby. He understood that, if the Club was willing to adopt his suggestion, Messrs Weatherby would insert in their Preface words to the effect that they reserved to themselves the sole right, subject to the proposed restrictions, of deciding what animals were eligible for admission. In that way there could be no question of any doubtfully bred animals claiming the right to be admitted in the future.

'The idea of admitting animals of doubtful breeding, such as Colin or Americus, on their own performances, however brilliant, was entirely contrary to the whole principle of the Stud Book. The Stud Book was based on the theory of heredity, and he thought it was not unreasonable to assume that those animals were more likely to transmit to their progeny the weak spots derived from their doubtfully bred ancestors than their own good points. They had an instance of that in Foxhall. In France they were alive to the fact that the time had come to take some steps to purify their Stud Book. They now insisted on eight generations of known pure breeding, and surely, if they had realised that in France, they on the English side ought not to admit any laxity in their own Stud Book.

'When they discussed that question before it had been suggested that if they hermetically sealed the Stud Book its prestige might wane owing to the possible excellence of numbers of horses to whom admittance had been refused. If he might be pardoned for saying so, he thought that was rather a problematical contingency, but if they were to look so far ahead surely there was a far more imminent possibility, which was that if they left their Stud Book open to doubtfully bred horses other countries might lose faith in the purity of the English Stud book, and might look elsewhere for animals which were really purely bred. He thought they owed it to their breeders from a commercial point of view, and they owed it to their own pride in having the very best bred horses in the world, to do all they could to maintain their Stud Book at its present very high level of excellence.'

Mr Lambton (the Senior Steward) said the Stewards welcomed the suggestion Lord Villiers had made and they proposed that the Club should empower them to make this suggestion to Messrs Weatherby. He would like to point out that the Stud Book was absolutely Messrs Weatherby's property. Those who might find fault with Messrs Weatherby for having admitted horses which were not quite pure-bred forgot that without Messrs Weatherby they would not have any Stud Book at all. He believed, as they acknowledged themselves, some horses and mares had been admitted into the book which they would rather were out of the book, but still they must consider the Stud Book as one great book, dating back to the year 1791. The Stewards felt, with Lord Villiers, that it would be quite right to ask Messrs Weatherby not to admit into the book in future any horse with a doubtful pedigree, but they did not feel that they could recommend to the Club, or to Messrs Weatherby, that any horse or mare already entered in the Stud Book, it did not matter in what volume, should now be taken out of that Stud Book. They considered that the vested interests were so great now, and the value of the stock which appeared in the Stud Book so high, that it would be impossible for Messrs Weatherby to withstand, perhaps, claims for compensation, or actions for damages against them, if they attempted to take any horses out of the book. Most of those impure horses came from America, and he thought they would find in the Stud Book the letters 'U.S.A.' were put against them. Messrs Weatherby proposed to rather extend the notice, so that in future the head lines against each mare would trace it back as far as possible, and when it was imported from the United States anyone who cared to work out the pedigree for himself would know.

Lord Londonderry rejoiced very much at the line that had been taken by Lord Villiers, and was glad to think that the Club, as far as he could gather, would support the resolution. However, he himself, as a breeder, would like to have gone very much further than Lord Villiers had done. He would have liked to see the Stud Book, as soon as possible, made as pure as possible and purged of all those animals which he thought at the present moment had no right whatever to be in it. He would like to see nothing in the Stud Book but the descendants of those 40 or 50 mares which were enumerated in Volume I of the Stud Book. For some reason which he could not understand, but which might be explained in the seventies, American animals were admitted into the Stud Book. He could not imagine why it was done, when they saw that Australian horses, which to his mind were far more purely bred than the Americans, were excluded. He himself had two horses by Jack Snipe, a speedy son of Americus, from very good mares. He did not think those animals ought to be allowed to be in the Stud Book, or else if they were there ought to be some mark put against them to show that they were only half-bred. An asterisk or something could be put to show that they were half-bred horses. The mare itself could not be taken out of the *Stud Book*, because in course of time she might have thoroughbred horses, but when she died he maintained that her stock which appeared in the *Stud Book* as half-bred should not be allowed to be in any future *Stud Book*. There were cases where they had very speedy animals bred in this country by half-bred mares. He thought Mr Rothschild once had a speedy mare called Galloping Queen, which ought not to be in the *Stud Book*. They saw at the present moment Shogun running, whose dam was not in the *Stud Book*; that stock ought not to be in the *Stud Book*.

Lord Derby said that he would like to ask one question on what Lord Londonderry had said. Supposing Shogun won the Derby, and became a fashionable stallion. He was not in the *Stud Book*; could animals got by Shogun be included in the *Stud Book* afterwards?

Mr Lambton replied that they could not. Lord Londonderry had asked why American horses were admitted into the *Stud Book* particularly in 1870. He did not think the Jockey Club had anything to do with that. There was no record, as far as he understood, of the Stewards of the Jockey Club having given advice that those horses should be admitted. They were admitted by the proprietors and editors of the *Stud Book*, and he maintained that, having got into the *Stud Book*, it was beyond the power of the Jockey Club to remove them, and that in doing so they would be imposing on Messrs Weatherby a task which it would be impossible for them to fulfil.

The debate having concluded, the members present unanimously decided to recommend Messrs Weatherby to make the alterations in the preface suggested by Lord Villiers.

To Mr John E. Madden, proprietor of the Hamburg Place Stud, Lexington, Kentucky (one of the most important Studs in the United States) and owner of imp. Star Shoot, imp. Ogden, Ballot, Plaudit, and other stallions, we forwarded a full report of the Jockey Club debate, and invited him to send us any comments thereon which he thought it desirable to make. He has favoured us with the following interesting communication:

> Dear Sirs – I thank you for your letter enclosing report of the debate on the subject of Registration. I have read this report with much interest, and think that Lord Villiers has both justly and ably laid before the Jockey Club his objections to admitting to the *Stud Book* any more horses of uncertain lineage. It is to the best interests of all to keep the blood as pure as possible at the fountain head, for breeding studs the world over look to England for the means of replenishing blood lines, and desire that the animals acquired for this purpose be of the purest strains.
>
> My own observation and experience have taught me that though a stallion of uncertain pedigree may command some success in the stud, a horse of pure blood lines will as a rule outclass him in the end; and, therefore, my aim of recent years has been to acquire for stud purposes stallions of pure blood only.
>
> A separate stud book might prove useful in which to enter animals of doubtful pedigree and thus put on record their breeding so far as known. We have frequently seen real virtue in horses of questionable ancestry. This teaches us that purity of breeding does not necessarily indicate a monopoly of excellence. Sometimes the infusion of plebeian blood tends to strengthen and round out the good points of the aristocrat, just as the mental and moral defects of effete nobility, history shows us, have been eliminated by crossing the strain with the middle classes.
>
> I am,
>
> Very sincerely yours,
>
> JOHN E. MADDEN

BBR–1913

Durbar II's Derby Win of 1914

The 1914 Derby, for several reasons, was a historic one. It was to be the last Derby at Epsom until 1919 because of the impending war. It had a big field of thirty runners, the most since Hermit won in 1867, and it was a very restive group of horses as they were under the starter's orders for nearly twenty minutes. Additionally, the winner, Durbar II,

*was a French product, owned by Mr H. B. Duryea, an American, and
the colt's dam, Armenia, had been bred in America.*

Of even more historical significance, however, as the Review *of
1914 explained, is the following:*

DURBAR II has the unique distinction of being the only winner of the
Derby ineligible for admission to the pages of the *General Stud Book*. A few
years ago there would have been no difficulty in securing his enrolment;
indeed, the names of many horses are to be found in the 'thoroughbred
bible', whose claims are no stronger than, if so strong as, those of Mr
Duryea's colt. But in the recently-issued Volume XXII of the *Stud Book*,
it is laid down, with the authority of the Jockey Club, that henceforth
'no horse or mare can be considered as eligible for admission unless it can
be traced without flaw on both sire's and dam's side of its pedigree to
horses and mares themselves already accepted *in the earlier volumes of the
book*'. This edict rules out Durbar II because his eleventh dam was a
mare concerning whose origin and antecedents nothing is known. In the
Sporting Chronicle 'Mankato' suggests that not improbably she belonged
to the same group as Spanish-American bronco and mustang. She was
mated with a grey horse by Gimcrack named Medley, imported into
Virginia. The produce was an unnamed mare who was put to an
imported horse called Stirling. A filly resulted, and she in her turn was
bred to an American horse Pacolet, the produce being Fanny Maria, the
eighth dam of Durbar II. His seventh dam is Lisbon Maid, by Napoleon
(another American-bred stallion); his sixth Sally Ward, by an American
horse called John Grymes; and his fifth, who appears at the foot of the
tabulated pedigree of the Derby winner, Julia, by imported Glencoe,
the sire of Pocahontas. The fourth dam was Minnie Minor, and the fact
that she was by Lexington would, presumably, of itself have been
sufficient to exclude Durbar II from the *General Stud Book*, because
Lexington's pedigree is suspect, great horse though he undoubtedly was.

Armenia, the dam of Durbar II, was for many years the property of
the late Mr William C. Whitney, whose colours were borne to victory in
the Derby by Volodyovski. It was at Mr H. P. Headley's La Belle Farm
near Lexington, Kentucky, that Armenia was foaled. Her dam, Urania,
was bred by Mr J. E. Killson, near Lexington.   BBR-1914

*Of even greater consequence however was the fact that Durbar II was to
become the maternal grandsire of Tourbillon. The last-named horse
was to head the sires' list in France on four occasions. His overwhelming success as a stallion together with that of his son Djebel (who*

was three times champion sire in France), was the principal factor that led to the decision, taken in 1949, to repeal the Jersey Act.

Mr Duryea leading in Durbar II.

Mr William Woodward's Appeal for Rescinding the Jersey Act

Nothing in the history of international thoroughbred racing relations offended a country as much as the onerous 'Jersey Act' of 1913 offended America. Instigated by the Earl of Jersey, then senior steward of the English Jockey Club, the rule effectively made many American horses ineligible for the General Stud Book *in England. Despite the many successes of these 'tainted' horses in English classics and other prestige races, the English stuck by their parochial guns and it was not until 1949 that the rule, so abhorred by Americans, was rescinded.*

During the years it was in force, one of the most persistent and persuasive Americans seeking its repeal was William Woodward, in 1935 Chairman of the New York Jockey Club.

As the honoured guest of the Thoroughbred Club of America that year, Mr Woodward made an eloquent plea for the English to recognise the American Stud Book in its entirety.

It was such a splendid speech and made in such good taste and logic that it seems strange that it took the English, who respected Mr Woodward so highly, another fourteen years to make amends.

The BBR*'s account of that speech is presented here again, not only for the sake of the speech itself, but because of the magnificent aura it casts over Mr Woodward, truly one of the greatest benefactors and shapers in the forward progress of the American Turf. A man to remember.*

THE THOROUGHBRED CLUB of America, which was founded three or four years ago with headquarters at Lexington, Kentucky, the 'capital' of the Blue Grass region, organises annually what is known as a 'testimonial' dinner. It is becoming the US equivalent of the Gimcrack dinner at York. Each year a man prominent in breeding and racing circles is invited to attend as the principal guest. This year the honour was accorded to Mr William Woodward. He succeeded the late Mr Frank K. Sturgis as the Chairman of the New York Jockey Club and in that exalted position has rendered great service to the Turf in his native land. Mr Woodward is also one of the leading breeders and owners in the States, while of late years he has played no small part as a patron of the English Turf. He has a charming personality, and has hosts of friends wherever he pursues his multifarious activities. His testimonial dinner at Lexington was attended by 260 Club members and guests.

Before Mr Woodward was called upon to address the company, Mr S.

H. Strawn, of Chicago, gave an outline of his career, a summary of which will interest many of our readers. After obtaining degrees at Harvard, including that of LL.B., Mr Woodward joined the New York bar in 1901, but two years later went into banking, and succeeded so well that, in 1910, he became the President of the Hanover Bank in New York, a position he held until 1929. He is now its honorary Chairman. About thirty-five years ago Mr Woodward became the owner of the historic Belair estate in Maryland, with which are associated the names of several worthies who were among the early importers of British thoroughbreds, including Governor Samuel Ogle. Mr Woodward began breeding bloodstock at Belair in 1906. In recent years his mares have been located at Mr A. B. Hancock's stud in Kentucky, but when weaned the foals go to Belair to be reared. His best winners have been Gallant Fox and that horse's son, Omaha, both of whom won the Kentucky Derby, Preakness Stakes and Belmont Stakes, three of the chief races for three-year-olds. Other big winners from Mr Woodward's Stud have been Faireno, Gaffsman, Aga Khan, Peanuts, Petee-Wrack, Sir Andrew, The Scout, and Black Devil. We think the 'products' of the Belair Stud must have won close upon £500,000 since 1918.

After a few preliminary remarks, Mr Woodward proceeded:

'The first thing I touch upon is a matter very near my heart. It is a delicate subject. As you know, the Jockey Club has a very pleasant and satisfactory relationship with Messrs Weatherby and Sons, of London, owners and publishers of the *General Stud Book* of Great Britain. Our friendship and relationship in the interchange of information or whatever else may come up, is a very courteous and agreeable one, which I sincerely hope will continue as long as time lasts. I am very anxious to see the day, before I shuffle off this mortal coil, when those gentlemen will recognise our *American Stud Book* in its entirety. I may say that I have taken up the matter informally with them, but have received very small encouragement. I do not want any one line of horses recognised, I want the recognition of our book in its entirety. I have never said this publicly before, but it seems to me that this is a very appropriate time to say it: first, because of the character of this gathering; secondly – and perhaps far more important – because of the signal victories of animals carrying American strains in England in the last few years; and thirdly, because of the ominous results for the thoroughbred of the world if the *English Stud Book* and the *American Stud Book* do not come together.

'The first edition of the *English Stud Book*, Volume I, was published in 1793 and covered a period of about ninety years. The mares on which it was founded were Arab, Barb, and Turkish blood, plus the royal mares, all of which were, so to speak, of cold blood prior to that time. That was, say, two hundred years ago. Since then, of course, they have safeguarded and cherished the development of the thoroughbred, and justly so. There is no one in the world to whom I would bow in safeguarding the merit and purity of the *Stud Book*, and maintenance of its purity must be adhered to.

'Now, what of our book. The first volume was published in 1868, and covered a period of sixty-six years, back to 1802. But we did not start from Barbs and Royal mares; we started almost wholly from English registered stallions, and mares, in so far as Colonel Bruce could ascertain from the prominent horse lovers of the North and South who were greatly interested in the accuracy and publication of the first *Stud Book*. About fourteen Epsom Derby winners amongst many, many other thoroughbreds, have been imported to this country. Our book started as a thoroughbred book. The claim is made that some pedigrees were lost in the old days, but it must be borne in mind that that was long, long ago, and since that time our book has been maintained through many generations, and will be maintained in the future, with the strictest and most careful surveillance.

'Looking backward, and if one has the vision to do so from a period of two hundred years *hence* the two books will be almost of the same period. I am not thinking in terms of years, but in terms of the thoroughbred race of horses of the world in the future and if we do not get together we will grow apart. I want one great breed of thoroughbred the world over, mutually recognised; if this does not result, we will have two breeds, and they will gradually be as far apart as the sun and the moon. The result will be unfortunate, not for you and me, but for the great race of the thoroughbred horse.

'I have felt for a long time that the English blood was pre-eminent in the preservation of certain enduring and fundamental attributes (we constantly need new importations) and I believe that the climate and conditions of the British Isles have an inherent ability to maintain these attributes, but I also believe that the sunlight and electric atmosphere of America produces a condition that gives the sparkle to the diamond of thoroughbred blood.

'I do not want to offend my English friends, of whom I have many. I enjoy racing in their country enormously, but as a sane proposition I hope they can seriously consider the recognition of our *Stud Book* in its *entirety*, not for any selfish reason of our own, but for the sake of the thoroughbred. Our records are open to them; we would welcome a full investigation.

'It is rather amusing to consider the best two-year-olds of England this year. A fair statement of the best includes Abjer, Bala Hissar, Mahmoud, Bossover colt, Sansonnet, and Paul Beg. Four of these six carry American blood. The winner of last year's Doncaster Cup, at two and a quarter miles, carries American blood. These high-class horses will breed on and what will be the result? I leave the result to the future, but when I say that they may be as far apart as the sun and the moon, it reminds me of a negro story. A darkie, asked which was the more important, the sun or the moon, immediately answered, "The moon, because it shines when we need the light." And it may be that our horses would be the moon.'

Mr Woodward's speech aroused tremendous interest in American bloodstock circles, and needless to state, his appeal to Messrs Weatherby (and through them, of course, to the English Jockey Club) was universally approved. The embargo it is desired to remove dates from 1913. In the 'Notice' (preface) in Vol. XXII of the *General Stud Book* occurs the following paragraph:

'. . . the Editors beg to inform Subscribers that to meet a suggestion made at a meeting of the Jockey Club in May last and approved by the members then present, they have, with a view to making the matter more explicit, slightly altered the wording of the qualification for admission to the *General Stud Book*, which was contained in the preface to Vol. XXI. The qualification will now read as follows:

"No horse or mare can, after this date, be considered as eligible for admission unless it can be traced without flaw on both sire's and dam's side of its pedigree to horses and mares themselves already accepted in the earlier volumes of the book." '

This is always referred to in America as the 'Jersey Act' because the late Earl of Jersey, senior Steward of the Jockey Club at the time, was mainly responsible for the tightening up of the regulation. While all breeders in the US strongly resent the way it operates to the exclusion from the *GSB* of a large proportion of the products of their studs, breeders in Great Britain and Ireland are emphatically in favour of the rule remaining undisturbed. The pros and cons of the question have been stated so often during the past twenty years that we need not go over the ground again now. Mr Woodward could justifiably point to the fact that many good horses now bred in Great Britain and Ireland carry American strains which do not comply with the terms of the 'Jersey Act'. These strains come through horses and mares imported before 1909. Rhoda B, the dam of Orby, is a notable example. It was the arrival of shiploads of yearlings, sent to be sold in this country when anti-betting legislation almost put an end to racing in the US, that alarmed Lord Jersey and many others, and led to the imposition of the restriction adopted in 1913. The arguments put forward in the US in favour of its removal can also be applied to several of the so-called half-bred families we have in England and Ireland. As Mr Woodward mentioned, this year's Oaks winner, Quashed, belongs to one of them. Most people are convinced that some of these families are really thoroughbred, but they cannot be proved so and are therefore barred from the *General Stud Book*. The British thoroughbred enjoys the reputation it has throughout the world today mainly, if not solely, because of the records kept in the *Stud Book* from generation to generation. One may sympathise with the anxiety of American breeders to have their bloodstock eligible for registration in its pages, but it is all important to keep the purity of the breed untainted.

BBR–1935

The Rescinding of the Jersey Act

'ESTABLISHED custom is not easily broken,' wrote Dr Samuel Johnson in the account of his journey to the Western Isles, 'till some great event shakes the whole system of things, and life seems to recommence upon new principles.'

During the last ten years the outbreak of the Second World War was the first of many shocks to the people of this country and the other nations of the world. As it moved to its climax so did it appear that the whole scheme of things was broken and that life generally would have to recommence upon new principles.

We have no intention of dilating on a philosophical plane, for such would be beyond our limitations. It is interesting to observe, nevertheless, the effects on the history of the Turf (if we are not too close to history to comment on it) of the cataclysmic events of recent years. During the recent war indeed, many of the organising bodies in the realm of sport have seen fit to take measures to put their houses in order, not least the Jockey Club, who in 1941 appointed a Committee to inquire how racing in this country could best be reorganised.

In parentheses, we may also say that in 1948 the Government decided to establish a Royal Commission on Betting, Gaming and Lotteries, part of whose duties would be to investigate our anomalous betting laws. This Commission is continuing to hear evidence during 1950, and so we propose to wait until the Report of the Committee is published before reproducing any of the points made before it.

Racing, betting and breeding have all been engulfed in this wave of reform. As we reported in last year's *Review*, the Jockey Club announced, in the *Racing Calendar* of July 15th, that the Stewards had been approached by the Owners of the *General Stud Book* on the subject of the conditions of admission to that book. The Club would remember, continued the announcement, that Messrs Weatherby, acting on the advice of the Jockey Club, gave up their attempt to widen the scope of the book which they made when Volume 19 was published in 1901, and in 1913, agreeing with what is known as the Jersey Act, they published a restrictive preface when they brought out Volume 22.

Messrs Weatherby asked whether the Club was in agreement with them that that preface was too restricted, and whether steps should not now be taken to broaden the scope of the book so as to allow for out-crossings with certain strains which were not admissible.

The Jockey Club then set up a small *ad hoc* Committee to discuss the matter. Evidence was taken from interested parties, both at home and overseas, and in December it was indicated that the Committee had reported to the Jockey Club that some modification was advisable in the qualifications then required. Our accounts of events in the 1948 *Review* terminated at December, when nothing definite had been announced.

In the summer of 1949, however, Volume 31 of the *General Stud Book* was published, and contained the following notice rescinding the restrictive preface to Volume 22.

'In July, 1948, the Publishers referred to the Stewards of the Jockey Club the question whether steps should now be taken to broaden the scope of the Book so as to allow for out-crossings with certain strains which at present were not admissible. The stewards appointed a committee to take evidence and report upon the point, and the report given to the Jockey Club at their December Meeting stated that some modification was advisable in the qualifications at present required.

'The Publishers, therefore, give notice that as from this date the conditions which have governed admission continuously since Volume XXII are rescinded.

'Any animal claiming admission from now onwards must be able to prove satisfactorily some eight or nine crosses of pure blood, to trace back for at least a century, and to show such performances of its immediate family on the Turf as to warrant the belief in the purity of its blood.

'All the horses and mares which will appear in Volume XXXII will have been submitted to this test, in which the Publishers reserve to themselves the right of final decision.'

Present-day breeders are all too familiar with the events which caused Messrs Weatherby to have doubts about the preface to Volume 22. It is in the belief that in the years to come reference will be made to these pages for information on this subject that we endeavour briefly to crystallise the points at issue which have provoked such animated world-wide discussion. To this end it will be necessary to quote from the prefaces to various volumes of the *General Stud Book*, with interjected comments, and we trust that the result will not be too wearisome.

The first step in defining a qualification of eligibility for the *General Stud Book* was taken when Volume 19 was published, in May, 1901. The preface to that volume contained this notice:

'The increased importation of horses and mares bred in the US and Australia, which, as stated in the last Volume, though accepted in the stud books of their own country, cannot be traced back in all cases to the thoroughbred stock exported from England, from which, more or less, they all claim to be descended, induced the Publishers to refer the question of the admission of such animals into the *Stud Book* to the Stewards of the Jockey Club as the highest authority on all matters connected with the Turf. The Stewards, after kindly consulting most of the principal breeders, came to the conclusion that any animal claiming admission should be able to prove satisfactorily some eight or nine crosses of pure blood, and to show such performances of its immediate family on the Turf as to warrant the belief in the purity of its blood. Therefore all the imported horses and mares which are included in this Volume have been submitted to this test.'

This preface, published in 1901 (twelve years before the Jersey Act), is also important because it shows that there was no discrimination between Australian- and American-bred animals as such. Further light on this aspect may be obtained from the preface to Volume 18, published in April, 1897, which reads:

'The importation of a number of horses and mares bred in the United States of America and Australia, a few of which will remain at Studs in this country, may have some effect on stock bred here, but the pedigrees of these horses, though accepted in the Stud Books of their own country, cannot in all cases be traced back to the thoroughbred stock exported from England from which they all claim to be, and from which, no doubt, they mainly are descended; these animals are, therefore, in these cases, marked with a reference to their own Stud Books. Some mares, bred in America, Russia, etc., and sent to this country with the view of being bred to English stallions and re-exported, are only given in order that their produce bred in this country may be duly certified.'

This preface of 1897 is more significant than may at first glance be recognised. It shows the unremitting concern of the Editors and Publishers of the *General Stud Book* to maintain its standard as a work of reference and record of pedigrees, and that extra effort, and, necessarily, expense, did not deter them from continuing in the tradition established by the first Weatherbys.

In September, 1909, Volume 21, was published, and contained the following notice:

'The Editors beg to inform Subscribers that, since the last volume of the *Stud Book* was published, they have had cause to consider the advisability of admitting into the *Stud Book* horses and mares which cannot be traced to a thoroughbred root, but which have fulfilled the requirements given in the preface to Vol. XIX. They have decided that, in the interests of the *English Stud Book*, no horse or mare can be admitted unless it can be traced to a strain already accepted in the earlier volumes of the *Book*.

'The Editors must, therefore, rescind the Notice published in Vol. XIX.

'The Stewards of the Jockey Club, who kindly consented to consider the question, fully endorsed the decision arrived at by the Editors.'

In this instance it will be noted that the first step in this further tightening of qualifications for eligibility was taken by Messrs Weatherby themselves, *in the interests of the English Stud Book*. This, we believe, is the first reference, in the prefaces, to the **English** Stud Book, as such. Here we may say that the *General Stud Book* was so named because it was primarily intended to be a publication which collated information on pedigrees and breeding records at studs throughout the country, details of which at that time were kept only in private stud books.

This preface to Volume 21 is, without doubt, the most important, with the exception of that contained in Volume 31. It shows that in 1909, the year before racing ceased in the United States, the Editors of the *General Stud Book* were concerned as to the nature and numbers of animals which were claiming admittance to their book.

The closure applied to racing in America in 1910, which lasted some years, resulted in many animals, rendered useless in that country, being brought to race over here. The situation prompted Lord Villiers (afterwards Lord Jersey), Senior Steward of the Jockey Club in 1912, to bring forward, at a meeting of the Jockey Club held at Newmarket during the First Spring Meeting in 1913, the question of which he had given notice at the Craven Meeting. This was to ask the Stewards:

> 'Whether, in view of the fact that a new volume of the *Stud Book* will be published this year, they will consider the advisability of suggesting to Messrs Weatherby, the Editors, that the last sentence of the first paragraph of the Preface be added to, so as to read as follows:
>
> '"They have decided that, in the interests of the *English Stud Book*, no horse or mare can, *after this date*, be considered as eligible for admission unless it can be traced *without flaw on both sire's and dam's side of its pedigree* to horses and mares themselves already accepted in the earlier volumes of the book."'

According to the official report of that meeting, the Hon. F. W. Lambton, Senior Steward, then said that 'the Stewards had already considered Lord Villiers' question, and were fully prepared to adopt the suggestion it contained, if it was the wish of the Club generally. He understood that the Editors were quite prepared to adopt the suggestion.' On a show of hands, continued the report, the Members present signified their entire approval of Lord Villiers' suggestion.

Volume 22 of the *General Stud Book* was published in November, 1913, and the preface to it was worded as follows:

> 'The twenty-second volume of the *General Stud Book* is now published, and the Editors beg to inform subscribers that to meet a suggestion made at a Meeting of the Jockey Club in May last and approved by the Members then present, they have, with a view to making the matter more explicit, slightly altered the wording of the qualification for admission to the *General Stud Book*, which was contained in the preface to Vol. XXI.
>
> 'The qualification will now read as follows: "No horse or mare can, after this date, be considered as eligible for admission unless it can be traced without flaw on

both sire's and dam's side of its pedigree to horses and mares themselves accepted
in the earlier volumes of the *Book*."

'The Editors reserve to themselves the sole right to decide what horses or mares
can, under the above qualification, be admitted or excluded from the *Book*.'

This, then, was the famous, or infamous (according to the point of view),
Jersey Act. As we said last year, this measure has ever since been the
subject of bitter controversy in racing and breeding circles. It is ironical,
in one sense, to recall that, but for the indiscriminate attitude adopted
by the Jockey Club by which any animal may race under Jockey Club
Rules irrespective of whether it is eligible for the *General Stud Book* or not,
less point would have been given to these heated, indeed acrimonious,
discussions of recent years. By contrast, other important racing countries
are not so indulgent.

With the passing of the years since 1913, it became increasingly clear
that something would have to be done about this restrictive measure.
The Act could not be retrospective in effect, and thus certain lines, not
eligible under the new regulations but which had been previously
accepted, had of necessity to remain qualified. From such lines have
come many famous winners in this country. The dam of Orby, winner of
the Derby in 1907, was Rhoda B., by Hanover, a sire which was not
recognised by the *General Stud Book* after 1913. Orby was the sire of
Grand Parade, winner of the Derby of 1919, whose name is encountered
in numerous pedigrees of good horses today.

From the family of Americus Girl, by the American sire, Americus,
have come such performers as Mahmoud, winner of the Derby in 1936,
and now an outstandingly successful sire in the US; the exceptionally fast
filly Mumtaz Mahal, the grandam of Mahmoud and also of Nasrullah,
the sire of Musidora, winner of the One Thousand Guineas and Oaks
this year; and Tudor Minstrel, winner of the Two Thousand Guineas in
1947. Nasrullah, incidentally, carries another cross of controversial
blood through his sire, Nearco, bred in Italy, whose third dam in direct
female-line was Sibola, imported from America in 1897. Nearco was
leading sire here (England) in 1947 and 1948.

An impartial observer, not altogether acquainted with the background to events, might easily be tempted, as comment on this
apparently illogical situation, to quote Warwick's sporting expression
from *Henry VI*:

> Between two hawks, which flies the higher pitch;
> Between two dogs, which hath the deeper mouth;
> Between two blades, which bears the better temper;

Between two horses, which doth bear him best;
Between two girls, which hath the merrier eye;
I have perhaps some shallow spirit of judgment;
But in these nice sharp quillets of the law,
Good faith, I am no wiser than a daw.

Since the end of the second war, the success of foreign-bred horses, not eligible for the *General Stud Book* because of the Jersey Act, has focused attention on this anomaly. Caracalla II, winner of the Ascot Gold Cup in 1946, and Arbar, winner of the same race in 1948, both bred by Monsieur Boussac, are notable examples. The prominence of Black Tarquin and My Babu during the 1947 season, when they raced as two-year-olds, further accentuated the position, which was given a greater atmosphere of urgency when it was announced by the French authorities, in 1948, that they had decided to keep a special section of the *French Stud Book* for American thoroughbreds, thus affording them a recognition hitherto denied them because of the acceptance in France of the Jersey Act.

My Babu, winner of the Two Thousand Guineas in 1948, is by Djebel, a son of Tourbillon, one of the most famous stallions ever to stand in France. The great-grandam of Tourbillon was Frizette, also the fourth dam in direct tail-female of Black Tarquin, who is by Lord Astor's sire, Rhodes Scholar (exported to the US in 1940), out of Mr William Woodward's great racemare, Vagrancy. Mr Woodward, the owner of Black Tarquin, is also the Chairman of the American Jockey Club, publishers of the *American Stud Book*. Black Tarquin secured classic honours in the St Leger of 1948. His fourth dam, Frizette, being by Hamburg (US), became ineligible under the Act. Black Tarquin also 'merited' disqualification through his grandam, Valkyr, who was by the great American horse, Man o' War, whose ancestry did not survive scrutiny under the requirements.

With two classic winners in 1948, the half-bred tribe could no doubt regard their 'bars sinister' with a certain amount of pride, a practice, we understand, at one time indulged in the earlier days of chivalry. But the possibility of classic winners standing at the stud in this country (England), where they would no doubt enjoy full books was one to be regarded with the utmost concern, for no official record of their progeny would be available. It was only meet and just that such horses as these, not to mention Caracalla II and Arbar, should be made available to breeders who still held the *General Stud Book* in high regard and the improvement of the breed dear to their hearts. And that, we are glad to record, is what has been done.

It may not be inappropriate here to quote from an American journal an article which shows the opinions held on the Jersey Act in that country. The following is taken from the *American Racing Manual* of 1947:

'The Jersey Act, so-called, is a measure which was brought before the English Jockey Club at a meeting held in May, 1913, and passed unanimously by that body. It was introduced by the Earl of Jersey (now dead), then known as Lord Villiers. Its text is as follows:

"No horse or mare can, after this date, be considered as eligible for admission to the *General Stud Book* unless it can be traced without flaw on both sire's and dam's side of its pedigree to horses and mares themselves already accepted in the earlier volumes of the book.

"The Editors reserve to themselves the sole right to decide what horses or mares can, under the above qualification, be admitted or excluded from the book."

'This announcement appeared in Vol. XXII of the *General Stud Book* which appeared almost simultaneously. Its meaning was this: Only animals registered in the *General Stud Book* are thoroughbred, the mere fact that they appear in it making them so. Exclusion from it therefore stigmatises horses thus discriminated against as merely "half-bred". Previous to this enactment, by mutual agreement, horses registered in either the *English* or *American Stud Book* were automatically eligible to the other and had been since 1873, when the two parent volumes of the *American Stud Book* appeared. At that date (1913), ten volumes of it had been published. The *American Stud Book*, originally founded by Colonel S. D. Bruce, was sold by him, with all rights appertaining, to The Jockey Club of New York, by which body it is now owned and published, as have all its volumes since and including Vol. VIII in 1902. As a gesture of courtesy, the chairman of each Jockey Club, English and American, is an honorary member of the other organisation.

The English Jockey Club was founded about 1750. Like the American, it did not originally own the *General* (English) *Stud Book*, which was in the beginning a private venture of James Weatherby, who since about 1771, had been the "keeper of the match books", or secretary, of the Newmarket course. It was an experimental undertaking with him, which he began in 1791 "with a view to correct the increasing evil of false and inaccurate pedigrees". Just when he sold out to the Jockey Club is uncertain, but it was not until several volumes had been published. From the time he founded it the *General Stud Book* has been compiled and published by himself and his family in the later generations, which now does so as "agents for the Jockey Club", which owns and controls it.

'Previous to the passage of the "Jersey Act" in 1913, several similar moves had been made aiming at the exclusion of American horses which were not of purely British blood, from the *General Stud Book*, but their provisions had not proved sufficiently stringent; hence the sweeping nature of Lord Jersey's measure, which was not only absolute in its provisions, but was reinforced by the second paragraph that went still farther by conferring upon the editors the "sole right" to admit, or to reject any horse seeking admission, regardless of its blood.

'The importation of thoroughbreds from England and their breeding and racing in the US had begun as far back as 1730, which was twenty years before the English Jockey Club was formed and over sixty years before Weatherby published the first volume of his *General Stud Book*. During all this time it would have been impossible for American breeders to conform to any standard of blood or pedigree laid down in England, there being none, nor was there ever anything of that kind suggested until about 1897. As was inevitable, during this long period of over a century and a half some strains of blood were introduced into the American thoroughbred breed that were non-English, and these appear today, far back, in the pedigrees of the most modern American racehorses, sires and dams, the proportion of them that are of exclusively English blood being minor.

'By the Jersey Act, the great mass of these horses were declared to be "half-breds". In effect, it was intended to warn breeders of all other countries to beware of them as "impure" and not to use them in their breeding operations. So effective was the operation of the Jersey Act that it at once killed our export trade in thoroughbreds, which, since 1913, has not existed.

'At that time, 1913, conditions in America were the worst ever known. All the New York racetracks had been closed since the spring of 1910, racing had shrunk to a mere skeleton of its normal self the country over, breeding and bloodstock values were at ruinous levels, most of the leaders of sport had deserted the American turf and were racing and breeding in England and France and a condition bordering upon complete despair blanketed the entire US. In consequence, the Jersey Act was received with apathy and without any real opposition, of an organised or unorganised sort, though the sentiment aroused by it was extremely unfavourable.

'During the period of 1913–1920, a revival gradually took place and turf and stud succeeded in regaining much of their lost ground, despite World War I and its very adverse effects. The feeling then began to take shape in America that the Jersey Act was an unjust and oppressive measure, which had affixed an undeserved stigma upon the American thoroughbred, making of him an international outlaw, as well as destroying our foreign market. This has been gaining in strength and today the general body of our breeders and turfmen are a unit in the assumption that fair play and sportsmanship both demand the repeal of the Act.'

The last sentence of the foregoing was omitted in the 1948 Edition of the *American Racing Manual* and the following substituted: *Finally in 1948, the English Jockey Club took under advisement the question of modifying the iniquitous Act. Meanwhile, France has opened its Stud Book to American strains.*

We are not primarily concerned here to correct all the inaccuracies portrayed above, but we may say that the *General Stud Book* is still the property of and is still published by Messrs Weatherby & Sons. We must also point out that impartially restrictive measures were taken long before the acute period of the American Turf, 1910–1913, as we have more than fully demonstrated. American Turf-writers cannot blame the wave of puritanism which hit their country during the early part of the century for the loss of 'purity' occasioned the American thoroughbred by the 'iniquitous Act'.

Many students may wonder why it was decided merely to rescind the Jersey Act, and revert to the qualifications required by the preface to Volume 19, published in 1901. It may appear to future generations that this preface is rather loosely worded. Should some eight or nine crosses (assuming 'generations' is meant) of pure blood be required, surely the necessity to trace back for at least a century could be dispensed with. It may well seem that the repetition of the phrase 'to show such performances of its immediate family on the Turf as to warrant the belief in the purity of its blood' is a particularly courageous move. Once again, let us repeat, we are not concerned with any criticism of the new qualifications. Even to the lay mind it must be obvious that those best qualified to decide, and their decision was taken in no hurry, have closely investigated the position in the light of subsequent events, have heard evidence and views from breeders all over the world, and have elected to revert to the 1901 preface rather than simply recognise the stud books of other countries, a measure advocated by some critics. The qualifications as they now stand are in fact tantamount to such a recognition.

Following the publication of Volume 31 of the *Stud Book* with its new restrictive clauses, there was immediate discussion on whether the family of Quashed, winner of the Oaks in 1935, and of the Ascot Gold Cup the following year, would be accepted. Quashed is by Obliterate out of Verdict, winner of the Cambridgeshire in 1923, by Shogun, who started second-favourite for the Derby in 1913. Shogun was not eligible for the *General Stud Book*, but apart from that, this female line, known as the 'Birdhill Family', is recorded in Miss F. M. Prior's *Half-Bred Stud Book*. Its first records date from about 1850, and the Coventry family were breeding from it from about the 1860's until the last year or so.

The fact that Verdict was ineligible for the *Stud Book* did not deter bidders at the yearling sales when any of her offspring were offered for sale. Between 1928 and 1936, four yearling colts from her, all sired by thoroughbred stallions, realised a total of 16,600 guineas, amongst them Thankerton, who finished third in the Two Thousand Guineas and Derby of 1936.

Between 1940 and 1945, dark days indeed for vendors of bloodstock, five yearlings from Quashed, a daughter of Verdict, aggregated 8,950 guineas. At the December Sales of 1947, Quashed, covered by Court Martial, was one of a consignment offered for sale by the executors of the late Lady Barbara Smith. Quashed was bought by the Hon. D. E. Hely-Hutchinson for 1,100 guineas.

Quashed, now eighteen years old, has yet to breed a winner under

Jockey Club Rules, a fact which is inevitably brought into discussions on her stud book merit, though there are many other instances of good race-mares failing in like manner. It has now been made known officially that her line will have to wait many years before it becomes eligible. We can only commiserate with the new owner of this famous mare, just as the decision may be, and, like Hamlet, reflect that:

> Their virtues else (be they as pure as grace,
>   as infinite as man may undergo),
> Shall in the general censure take corruption
> From that particular fault: The dram of ill
> Doth all the noble substance often doubt,
> To his own scandal.

We cannot close this account of the Jersey Act without quoting the following extracts from the preface to the first edition of Volume 2 of the *General Stud Book*, dated December 31st, 1821, which will not be without interest to present-day breeders:

'If any proof were wanting of the superiority of the English breed of horses over that of every other country, it might be found in the avidity with which they are sought by foreigners. The exportation of them to Russia, France, Germany, etc, for the last five years, has been so considerable as to render it an object of some importance in a commercial point of view. But this advantage, some of our continental neighbours are of opinion, will not long remain with us: they are fully aware of the source whence we derive this superiority, and are in consequence endeavouring to establish Races on the English plan, which, together with a more careful selection of stallions and mares than they observe in England, will very soon, they say, enable them to excel us, and they anticipate a day (not very distant) when the English must send to the Continent, if not for speedy, at least for *sound* horses.

'This hint about soundness may be worth attention, but for the rest, with the advantages this country already possesses, and so long as horse racing continues to be followed up with spirit by her men of rank and opulence, there can be little to apprehend.'

The italics indicated above were Mr Weatherby's. When one remembers the performances since the last war, of such French-bred stayers as Caracalla II, Marsyas II, and Arbar, the Italian-bred Tenerani, the American-bred Black Tarquin, that Pearl Diver and My Love, winners of the Derby in 1947 and 1948, were both by Vatellor, a French stallion who contested thirty-five races from two to five years of age, not to mention the successes of the British Turf of other foreign-bred animals before the war, it must be said that the Editor of the *Stud Book* of nearly 130 years ago was a particularly shrewd observer and reporter of the

events of his time. One may almost detect a hint of prophetic utterance
in his words.   BBR-1949

*In the immediate postwar years it became clear that the case for
rescinding the Jersey Act was overwhelmingly strong.*

In the first instance, the passing of the Act had excluded from the
Stud Book *a very large number of the most successful horses in
Europe. This became particularly evident in 1948 when the Two
Thousand Guineas winner My Babu and the St Leger winner Black
Tarquin were both ineligible. In the second place the 'impurities' which
had formed the original bone of contention, had now become so remote as
to possess little significance.*

*Ironically the principal victims of the controversy were the English
and Irish breeders. For during the 'closed shop' period (1913-1949)
they had cut themselves off from some of the world's most potent
bloodlines.*

The 'American Stud Book'

What Edward Moorhouse was to The Bloodstock Breeders'
Review *from its inception in 1912 until Mr Moorhouse's death in
1939, John Lewis Hervey, who wrote under the pen name 'Salvator',
was to the literature of the American Turf prior to 1900 until his
passing in 1947. Beyond question he was that country's 'most
distinguished scholar and historian' in reference to racing and breeding.
He contributed to many publications, including* Daily Racing Form,
The Blood-Horse, The Thoroughbred Record *and* The
Bloodstock Breeders' Review. *However, his most monumental
work was* Racing in America, *a troika of volumes which The
American Jockey Club commissioned him to write. The first two
covered the history of the sport from the beginning to 1886 and the third
from 1922 to 1937. There is nothing comparable as a reference work
for those years in American racing and breeding and that, along with
Mr Hervey's writing, which is always eloquent without ever being
unfaithful to the facts, makes these books a treasure. He was a true
'knight of the plume'. All this and his extensive knowledge of the
American racing scene is richly exposed in his article, 'The American
Stud Book and Its Founder' which originally appeared in* The
Thoroughbred Record *and then found a second 'home' in the* BBR
of 1928.

REPEATEDLY, of late, I have noted references to, and quotations from, the preface, or the introduction to Vol. I of the *American Stud Book*, with attribution of authorship to Colonel S. D. Bruce, the chief compiler, editor, and publisher of that volume. There have also been repeated references to the *Stud Book* and Colonel Bruce aside from these, which, from time to time, show a lack of familiarity with some of the facts in the case. It will therefore, in the interests of accuracy – I will not say history, for anything dignified by that name is not my object in the present contribution – perhaps be apropos if I endeavour to set forth some of these facts as correctly as possible.

We all know – or, at least, those of us interested in the historic background of the American thoroughbred – that the *American Stud Book*, now in its fourteenth volume, was, one might say, the life work of Colonel Bruce and that his name is indissolubly connected with it. But just how, when, and why it came into existence is apparently known to very few people, and to them, in some details, incorrectly.

There had been various earlier attempts to compile and publish an *American Stud Book* before Colonel Bruce entered the field. Several compilers made starts in that direction early in the nineteenth century, but none of them ever got to press with their results until, in 1833, P. N. Edgar published what was the first and only volume of his *American Race-Turf Register, Sportsman's Herald, and General Stud Book*, which was printed by Henry Mason, 76, Maiden Lane, New York. The second volume was to have completed the work, but was never issued, as the first one was a losing venture. Previous to its appearance the only repository of American pedigrees had been the final sections of the monthly issues of the *American Turf Register*, published by John S. Skinner, who had begun originally to collect and publish them in his earlier, *American Farmer*. In 1834, also, Skinner brought out a large single volume in which he reprinted, *verbatim et literatim*, the three first volumes of the *English Stud Book*, the only ones up to that time issued, and at the back end of the volume appended a few pages of pedigrees of American horses, very hastily thrown together and unsystematically arranged.

For years thereafter there was nothing else available except the pedigree section of the work known as *Mason's Farrier*, of which several different editions appeared, the first, I believe, about 1830. It has been stated that Skinner compiled this collection of pedigrees, and he may have done so, but it is more probable that Theophilus Field and J. J. Harrison were joint authors. Finally, in 1867, John H. Wallace, then living in Muscatine, Ia, published, through Townsend and Adams, of

New York, Vol. I of Wallace's *American Stud Book*, containing by far the largest 'repertoire' of any work of the kind that had yet appeared in America. It represented, however, only about half the data he had collected, but as in the case of Edgar, thirty-four years before, the reception of the volume was so discouraging that he abandoned his enterprise and turned his energies to the compilation of the pedigrees of trotters; subsequently making himself both rich and famous through his *American Trotting Register*, of which the first volume appeared in 1871 and the last compiled and published by him, before his sale of his interests in 1891.

One reason, however, for the failure of Wallace to establish his thoroughbred Stud Book was that when he placed his first volume on the market he came into direct conflict and opposition with Colonel Bruce. Bruce had for over twenty years been collecting pedigrees and planning the publication of a Stud Book that should become official, and he was well on the way towards completion of his first volume when Wallace anticipated him with his venture. However, Wallace had taken the plunge with very little backing and a similarly limited acquaintance of a personal nature with the leading breeders and owners; whereas Bruce and his brother Benjamin, who was closely associated with him, were widely and favourably known in the Turf and breeding world and had succeeded in obtaining the co-operation of a number of leading horsemen in their undertaking. Moreover, Bruce was also the owner and manager of the *Turf, Field and Farm*, a weekly devoted to the Turf and field sports which he had founded and was publishing in New York, and in whose columns a large part of the contents of the first volume of his Stud Book serially appeared.

In a struggle for survival between two such opponents there was no question which would win. Bruce was the sure victor, but his victory was by no means an easy one, and in order to gain it he had to resort to all sorts of deals, 'dickers', wire-pulling, and the like. But first let us take a look at the personality of the man and his antecedents.

Sanders DeWeese Bruce was born at Lexington, Ky, August 16, 1825, and was the son of a Scotch father, John Bruce, and a mother who, while of Scottish ancestry, was born in the fortress of Gibraltar – Margaret Ross Hutton. He became passionately addicted to racing and the blood horse as a mere boy, and the future trend of his existence is said to have been fixed through his having been a witness, when fourteen years old, of the historic match race between Wagner and Grey Eagle, in 1839. It is difficult for us to appreciate the intensity of the excitement attending this contest, during the progress of which it has been written that 'strong men became so wrought up that they fainted'.

While still in the early twenties, the idea of compiling a Stud Book took root in his brain. Racing interests were growing rapidly, north and south, and there was no publication in which the ancestries of American thoroughbreds could be satisfactorily traced. He accordingly began to collect pedigrees from all available sources, and in this way came in contact not only with the Kentucky breeders and owners, but those of Virginia and the Carolinas, Mississippi and the other states of which New Orleans was the focus, and Tennessee, while he also cultivated the northern terrain as best he could. He married early and had a growing family and the practicalities of life became paramount. Among his early business ventures was a crockery store in Lexington. Later he became proprietor and manager of the Phoenix Hotel in that city – the old Phoenix which for nearly a century has been 'horsemen's headquarters' in the Blue Grass, a portion of the old structure being still in use as an annexe to the modern hostelry which bears no resemblance to the one of ante-bellum days over which Colonel Bruce presided. Here his opportunities for contacts, acquaintance and friendship with turfmen and breeders from all parts of the country were naturally unexcelled, and he made the best use of them. By this time he had become one of the leading citizens of that part of Kentucky. Politics attracted him and he entered the field and was elected County Clerk of Fayette County. He was also carrying on continuously, as a very profitable 'side line', the buying and selling of thoroughbreds, was breeding in a small way, and even occasionally starting a horse of his own in a race.

Closely associated with him, as aforesaid, was his brother Benjamin Gratz Bruce, who was two years his junior, born at Lexington, 1827. Like S. D. Bruce, B. G. was a graduate of Transylvania University, at Lexington, which he quitted with the degree of doctor of medicine. He began the practice of that profession but did not like it, and turned to mercantile life, while as he also was passionately fond of the racehorse, he joined hands with his elder brother in both his pedigree work and his activities as a factor. In 1860 the Bruces, backed by M. H. Sanford, then one of America's leading turfmen and breeders, other parties also being interested, formed what was known as the 'Kentucky Importing Co', and Benjamin Bruce, as one of its representatives, visited England and there selected and purchased a group of yearling fillies which were shipped to America and, in several instances, made a deep mark as matrons.

At the outbreak of the Civil War, in 1861, the Bruce Family, like a host of others in the border states, was divided in its allegiance. Despite the bond of blood and business interests, the two brothers espoused different sides in the conflict, Sanders that of the north, Benjamin that of the south, and they parted not to reunite until the long struggle was over. In the service of the Confederacy, B. G. Bruce attained no distinction, but in that of the Union S. D. Bruce won high honours. Enlisting promptly when hostilities began, he raised the 20th Kentucky Volunteer regiment and received the commission of colonel. During the war he built the fortifications at the mouth of the Cumberland river, fortified Bowling Green, Ky, was made commander of the important post at Clarksville, Tenn, and in the battle of Shiloh, one of the most desperately contested of the major actions of the war, commanded the Twenty-second Brigade under General Don Carlos Buell. When peace came in 1865, he was in active service at Louisville, Ky.

No sooner was the war over than the Bruce brothers resumed their old close connection. The south was devastated and their eyes turned northward. The original *Spirit of the Times*, which W. T. Porter had founded in 1831, had gone down with the outbreak of the war, but previous to that time Porter had left it, and in partnership with George Wilkes founded what was known as *Porter's Spirit of the Times*. The latter weekly had outridden the storm, but Wilkes, its ruling spirit, had been so bitterly anti-southern throughout the struggle that he had made enemies of almost all the leading southern breeders and turfmen; the circulation of his journal was wholly northern and its future in Dixie looked doubtful.

In consequence, the Bruces decided that the moment was opportune for establishing a new sporting journal to compete with the *Spirit*. They had some capital of their own, but the 'sinews of war' were furnished liberally by R. A. Alexander, of Woodburn Farm, and M. H. Sanford, the owner of the Preakness Stud, in New Jersey, already mentioned in this sketch. New York was chosen as the base of operations, and there No. 1, Vol. I, of the *Turf, Field and Farm* was issued but a few months after the surrender of Lee at Appomattox. It bore the date of August 5th, 1865, and the editorial page carried the statement: 'S. D. and B. G. Bruce, Editors and Proprietors: Hamilton Busbey, Literary and Associate Editor.' Busbey was a young man S. D. Bruce had come in contact with that spring at Louisville, where he was on the staff of the *Courier Journal*. He swung a fluent and clever pen, a bit inclined to the pomposity of the period (which he never outgrew) but was without any particular knowledge of horses or racing.

On page 5 of the maiden issue of the new journal appeared the following announcement:

American Stud Book

The subscribers, at the earnest solicitation of the turfmen throughout the country, with a view to correct the increasing evil of false and inaccurate pedigrees, were induced to attempt the compilation and publication of an American Stud Book. The unfortunate Civil War, just terminated, suspended for the time being the work, but we now propose to publish the book in the columns of the *Turf, Field and Farm*, believing by so doing we will be able to make our work more valuable and reliable. We will be glad to have our attention called to any and all errors. We will exercise a strict and impartial caution upon the publication of all pedigrees offered, and in order to prevent imposition, we will refuse the publication of all information unless coming from a known and respectable quarter, or which cannot be authenticated from the existing American authorities or the *English Stud Book*. That we shall be able to offer the public a work perfectly free from error is far from our expectations. It will be found to contain, arranged in a more concise form, a greater mass of authentic and reliable information respecting the pedigrees of horses than was ever before collected together in this country. Our object is to convey useful, valuable and necessary information to amateurs and gentlemen who breed and train thoroughbred horses for amusement or profit, and to enable the young adventurer in breeding and racing, who from his avocations and engagements has been denied the opportunity of acquiring a complete knowledge of the genealogies of 'blood horses', to trace them himself. We trust our work will not be unworthy of the attention of those gentlemen thoroughly versed in the pedigrees of racehorses and experienced in breeding.

S. D. & B. G. BRUCE

There followed a list of imported mares with their produce (so far as known) comprising animals whose names began with the letter A, but without effort to arrange them in correct order, they apparently being shovelled in at random – a detail not entirely insignificant as evidence of the fact that while industrious and laborious pedigree compilers, the Bruces were slip-shod in their methods. Upon the editorial page a special paragraph was printed, calling attention to the commencement of publication of the *American Stud Book* in that issue, with a call for information, etc.

This, as stated, was in August, 1865. The *Turf, Field and Farm*, successful from the outset, continued to publish weekly instalments of the *Stud Book* thereafter for about three years when Colonel Bruce at last saw the first volume of his long-dreamed-of and worked-for life's ambition a reality. The effort of publication was, however, a big one and was attended by various expedients, which, had not the Colonel been of characteristic Scotch persistence, also a fighter sternly experienced in actual warfare, might never have been carried to a successful issue.

Wallace's invasion of the field which Bruce had grown to regard as almost his private property, made it imperative to get his work before the public in book form, in some shape, as soon as possible. But the expense attendant, as well as the labour, presented a problem. It was necessary to draw from the financial heavens angels whose golden wings would waft him to the haven he sought – and where and how were they to be allured to his assistance? Once more he turned to R. A. Alexander and once more that amiable and helpful gentleman, who was also a Scot, promised his aid, but still more must be had. Mr Sanford could not be interested, nor any other of the leading breeders. But at the 'psychological moment' the rustle of wings was heard and from an entirely unexpected quarter – to wit, Chicago!

Among the supporters and contributors which the *Turf, Field and Farm* had drawn around it was Joseph Cairn Simpson, who was then living at Atwood Place, Riverside, just outside the Windy City. He had begun writing for the old *Spirit* years before as a young man, and was now actively engaged in the breeding, training and racing of both thoroughbreds and trotters on a large scale, for the time and place of his operations. He at one period owned the great progenitor imported Bonnie Scotland, also that horse's good son Malcolm, and was the breeder of Malcolm's famous daughter Marian, the dam of Emperor of Norfolk, El Rio Rey and Yo Tambien. Mr Simpson was also a Scot and he became so much interested in the *Turf, Field and Farm* that, Colonel Bruce being in urgent need of money, he purchased a half interest in the paper. He was not, however, himself sufficiently wealthy to finance the publication of the Stud Book – but he did succeed in finding the angel who, co-ordinately with Mr Alexander, did so. This was Mr John J. McKinnon, then one of Chicago's leading lawyers who was also much interested in the thoroughbred, he being the owner of Red Eye, son of Boston, and the great broodmare Magenta.

With the co-operation of Messrs Alexander, McKinnon and Simpson, Vol. I of Bruce's *American Stud Book* at last appeared in the summer of 1868. McKinnon had arranged with a firm of Chicago publishers of law books, E. B. Myers and Co, to bring it out, the title-page bearing their imprint. In order to facilitate the work of type-setting, proof-reading, etc, the composition had, however, been done in the East and the plates were made in Albany, NY.

One can in imagination enter into the emotions of Colonel Bruce when at last the book was placed in his hand – he was a man of strong feelings and just at that moment they must have been almost 'too deep for utterance'. Very few copies of this volume are today in existence. As a piece of book-making it is superior to any subsequent volume ever issued. Admirably printed in large, legible type on fine paper and handsomely bound in half-calf, with tooled and panelled backs, it was also embellished with twenty fine steel plates, portraits of the most famous American and English thoroughbreds, male and female. Prominently displayed was the following dedication:

'As an humble mark of respect to the memory of one who laboured long and zealously for the improvement of the blood horse, and who earnestly strove to place the sport of the Turf above reproach; and as a token of friendship and high personal regard, this, the first volume of a work that has required the labour of a lifetime, is dedicated to the late Robert Aitcheson Alexander, of Woodburn, Kentucky, and John J. McKinnon, of Chicago, Illinois, by the Author.'

Mr Alexander, it will be seen, had died before the volume was completed. The dedication of the work, to his memory, has appeared, however, in all subsequent editions of the *Stud Book* – but from all subsequent ones the co-dedication to McKinnon has disappeared. Here is the reason:

Jos. Cairn Simpson had bought a half-interest in the *Turf, Field and Farm*, in 1868 and some little time after, turning his facile pen to fiction, began contributing to the paper a 'continued story' entitled 'The Lady of the Lake'. It ran to melodrama as was the custom with novels in the 'sixties, and Mr Simpson undertook to weave into it not only some stirring Turf episodes but also scenes from Chicago's underworld. Today one would laugh at the idea of anything immoral being attributed to it, but 'them days was different' and one of the dragons who guarded the purity of the press in Gotham decided that the morals of the nation were being endangered by the instalments of 'The Lady of the Lake' in the current issues of the *Turf, Field and Farm*. In consequence he made several visits to the editorial sanctum and the upshot was that Colonel Bruce, who was then engaged in a 'duel to the death' – or its equivalent! – with the *Spirit of the Times* and was not looking for more trouble, notified Mr Simpson that further publication of his romance would have to be excluded from the chaste journal which they owned in partnership. The immediate result was the rupture of the partnership and the re-sale back to Colonel Bruce, by Mr Simpson, of the interest in the paper that the latter had purchased two years before.

With this denouement of the relations, which occurred in 1870, the wings of J. J. McKinnon also ceased to be heard rustling in the vicinity of the *Stud Book*. But Colonel Bruce was gradually getting ahead on his own steam and finally in 1873 he brought out together, in uniform style, the two 'parent volumes, I and II, the former revised and entirely reset, the latter brand new, as they have ever since been known and are today (with slight revisions) current'. It was only natural, therefore, that the Colonel should drop McKinnon's name from his dedication. Although, as we have seen, had it not been for that accommodating gentleman's assistance at the time when its affairs had reached an impasse, it is altogether probable that no volume of the *Stud Book*, of any kind, would have been published for perhaps a decade subsequent to 1868, if at all.

When he brought out the revised Vol. I and new Vol. II of the *Stud Book*, in 1873, Colonel Bruce was confronted by a delicate problem. In default of certain information which I do not possess, it seems altogether probable that the remainder of the edition of Vol. I, published at Chicago in 1868, may have been still in the possession of either McKinnon or Simpson, with whom he was no longer on good terms. He was determined to make these books valueless, partly on that account, partly because in the revised Vol. I many new details appeared. So he solved the enigma in this way. The first edition of Vol. I carried the record of pedigrees through the letters A to K, inclusive. But in the new edition he included also those coming under the letter L, and began the second volume with the letter M. This made it impossible to use Vol. II of the new edition with Vol. I of the original one, as all the L pedigrees would be missing.

Now, Colonel Bruce had sold hundreds of copies of the original Vol. I for $10 per copy and by his new wrinkle in salesmanship he made those volumes worthless to their owners! We might, if severely ethical, term this decidedly sharp practice. But it served its purpose. The 'remainder edition' of the original volume became junk, overnight, and worth to the holders only what it would bring as waste paper; while the new edition, both volumes of it, became indispensable to all turfmen and breeders.

It is for this reason that copies of Vol. I, first edition, are today excessively rare. Not only did those who had bought them discard them; Colonel Bruce made a practice of picking up all copies that he could and destroying them, while, I understand, after the Jockey Club took over the *Stud Book* from Colonel Bruce, it continued to do so, whenever the chance presented itself. In consequence, some of the largest Turf libraries in America do not possess this historic volume, which is invaluable in several respects, especially because it contains versions of many pedigrees that were later on 'reconstructed', as it were, the better to benefit their circulation in 'high society'.

A feature of the original Vol. I that Colonel Bruce did retain, however, was the preface, together with the introduction, which had been written by Jos. Cairn Simpson. Colonel Bruce himself was a man almost totally devoid of the literary gift, whereas Mr Simpson possessed it in an eminent degree. The Colonel's prose was prosaic in the extreme; after wading through a page of it the reader has a sense of ennui and exhaustion. In consequence Mr Simpson undertook to contribute the introductory pages which, in after years, and on down to the present, have been, in part, so often quoted. I know this to be true because he so wrote me, in the spring of 1902, at the time of the death of Colonel Bruce; giving me also the interesting information that if their literary style was faulty, it was in part due to the fact that he wrote them on the train, between New York and Chicago, to fill a hurry-up call, and that the jolting of the train could not but have resulted in some roughness of expression. As a matter of fact, they are couched in arresting, well-phrased prose.

It will be observed that the prospectus for the *American Stud Book*, published in the inaugural issue of the *Turf, Field and Farm*, in 1865, was signed 'S. D. and B. G. Bruce', but that when the work itself came to be issued in book form, upon the title-page S. D. Bruce was given as the sole author. The closing paragraph of the preface was, however, worded as follows: 'The author and compiler takes this opportunity to acknowledge his indebtedness to all who have assisted him, and wishes especially to thank – in this public manner – his brother, B. G. Bruce, of Lexington, Ky, for his most valuable aid.'

Colonel Bruce took up his residence permanently in New York in 1865, but Benjamin had no liking for the metropolis, being a devoted son of 'the Blue Grass' and unwilling to leave it. And this he never did. Living there he assisted his brother in a great deal of the latter's 'field work' as well as in his pedigree compiling, while he also made a speciality of writing memoirs of celebrated thoroughbreds for the *Turf, Field and Farm*, which, with his other contributions, he signed 'Neptunus'. In 1875, when ten years of peace had healed many of the wounds and repaired some of the Southern fortunes that the Civil War had ruined, having withdrawn from his partnership in his brother's journal some years before, he founded at Lexington the *Live Stock Record*, of which he continued as the editor and publisher until his death in 1891, when it passed into other hands and was eventually renamed with the title which it now bears: *The Thoroughbred Record*.

Colonel S. D. Bruce had two sons who were associated with him in business, of which the second, Frank, died while still but a young man, to the great grief of his father. The elder of the two, Leslie C. Bruce, who was born in 1849, became business manager of the *Turf, Field and Farm* and assisted in the compilation of several volumes of the *Stud Book*, subsequent to Vol. II. He was a man of striking personality, extremely social in his tastes, and was a devotee of sports of all kinds. As a rifle shot, he reached the highest pinnacle of fame by winning the world's championship, together with the Leech Cup at Creedmoor, in May, 1881, beside making repeated trips to Europe as one of America's representatives in international tourneys. He also served as an official at many athletic contests. He survived his father nine years, dying in 1911 at Greenwich, Conn.

Owing to the great expense of publication and the limited circulation of the work, the *American Stud Book* was never a paying proposition for Colonel Bruce. It has been seen that the publication of the first volumes was only made possible by the financial assistance of prominent breeders who came to his aid. He enjoyed a period of prosperity in the latter 'eighties and early 'nineties, but lost heavily by a fire which wiped out his offices and most of the contents just as he was about ready to bring out Vol. V, and it was only owing to the assistance of such men as the late Pierre Lorrilard, D. D. Withers, August Belmont, Sr, and others, that he was enabled to maintain publication of the work.

When the great financial depression of the mid 'nineties settled like a blight upon the entire country, both the *Stud Book* and the *Turf, Field and Farm* found continuance a struggle. Moreover, Colonel Bruce became involved with the Jockey Club, in an unfortunate imbroglio, arising from his rights in the *Stud Book*, which merged into a lawsuit, bitterly fought and ruinously expensive to him. The decision in the lower court was in his favour, but the Jockey Club took an appeal to the higher tribunal. Past three-score-and-ten, in the evening of a long and strenuous life throughout whose course he had never spared himself, he was fighting now with his back to the wall for all that he held dearest – the monument which he had been striving to erect for himself, and what he believed to be his rights in a thing of his own creation. Public sentiment throughout the thoroughbred world was on his side and the Jockey Club was discreet enough to sense the situation and escape the opprobrium it might have incurred by carrying the fight to the last ditch. The case was settled out of court by its purchase of the *Stud Book* outright, from Colonel Bruce for a price said to have been $35,000, and thereafter all subsequent volumes of the work have been published under its auspices, and, upon their backs the legend 'Jockey Club' has replaced that of 'Bruce' beneath the title.

The career of S. D. Bruce may be said to have terminated with this episode. He lived on into his seventy-seventh year, dying in New York, January 31st, 1902, but the interim had been in retirement, a mere 'looker on in Vienna', observing, from the sidelines, the activities in which for almost half a century he had borne so earnest and, much of the time, conspicuous a part.

As I have, in the past commented, perhaps with some severity, upon some of the methods of Colonel Bruce in his compilation of the *Stud Book* and his manipulation of various thoroughbred genealogies, it may be well, in conclusion, for me to state the cause for this. It is not at all any such spirit as has sometimes been attributed to me – that of a wanton iconoclasm, which takes a malicious pleasure in attacking things long-established and, upon occasion, even trying to render suspect those which are like unto Caesar's wife. No one could possibly respect Colonel Bruce more understandingly for the worth and value of his labours than do I, for the reason that a large part of my life has been devoted to the tracing and verification of pedigrees and the investigation of Turf history. I can appreciate to the full the gigantic task which he set himself and the extraordinary courage and determination with which he carried it out. He thereby placed the entire thoroughbred Turf and breeding industry eternally in his debt, and if there is any one thing which America today owes him it is greater honour than it has ever paid. We have immense and important Turf events christened for all sorts of nonentities who have 'strutted their brief hour' or are at present doing so. But nobody ever thinks, apparently, of naming one for him which should keep his memory green, after a fashion at least. Nor of doing anything else which might serve that purpose.

But at the same time, in compiling the *Stud Book*, in giving to our official genealogies the forms into which they have crystallised as authentic, he did, in various, if not indeed numerous, instances, high-handed and unwarranted things, things which the facts, the evidence and the testimony extant, stamp as indefensible. To be sure, there were what are known in law as 'extenuating circumstances'. In order to put his *Stud Book* on its feet, and make it a going concern, he was obliged to have the support of the leaders in the realm where he was labouring. He reasoned, and without doubt correctly, that he could not afford to alienate their friendship or jeopardise their assistance in his projects – especially as, for many years, he was actively engaged in practical work for them, holding their sales of yearlings and of breeding and racing stock, buying and selling on commission, both privately and publicly, tabulating pedigrees, compiling catalogues, etc, etc.

'Human nature is human nature,' and it was only human in him, when the pedigree of a great horse, belonging to some prominent patron, came under fire or lacked substantiation, to rush to the defence. This he and his brother did in the cases of Lexington, Longfellow, Tom Bowling, Eolus and numerous others. And as a step of this kind is never anything but the first of an endless trial, he came to 'reconstruct' entire families, of many ramifications like those of imp. Duchess, imp. Trumpetta, etc, etc. He believed in 'letting sleeping dogs lie', unless there were good practical reasons for doing the other thing, in consequence of which he shovelled into the *Stud Book* pedigrees so impossible as to be nothing less than absurd, and thus gave to outrageous fictions the official stamp of veracity. Only at the rarest intervals does he intimate that he is doubtful, and when he does so we may be sure that in doing it he trod upon the toes of nobody whose patronage he felt it a necessity to have.

Now, we should not judge him too severely for doing these things. I believe that had he been in a position to 'hew to the line and let the chips fall where they may', he would have done so. But he was not in any such position at the beginning of his work; and, indeed, never at any time attained it, being to the last dependent for his 'place in the sun' to a greater or lesser extent upon the favour of those who sat in the 'seats of the mighty'. These facts should always be borne in mind and allowed for.

But, in the last analysis, while S. D. Bruce 'heard the call' of the vocation of pedigree compiler early and followed it thereafter throughout his long and active career, in some ways he was temperamentally unfitted for the work, never trained himself to overcome these shortcomings, and shared them also with his brother Benjamin. The two parent volumes of the *Stud Book* are disfigured by innumerable errors of detail; omissions, errors, contradictions and the like, which testify to the slip-shod manner in which their data had been assembled and codified. One needs not be expert readily to perceive them, while to the trained scrutiny they are so obtrusive as to become both exasperating and inexcusable. What increases their offensiveness is the fact that ostensibly these volumes, as now current, are 'revised and corrected', the revision and correction being so superficial as to amount practically to nothing. I do not offer these criticisms as mere personal strictures; they will be confirmed by the men today best equipped to render a disinterested verdict.

I have been moved to contribute to *The Record* the foregoing narrative because it seemed to me an opportune moment for its publication. It assembles facts that few turfmen of the present generation are familiar with, quite a few of which are brought together for the first time. At some future day, when the history of the *American Stud Book* comes to be written, they may be of use to the historian, for they are not gossip, guesswork or improvisation, but will be found susceptible to little correction, in the interests of veracity.   BBR–1928

Views on Racing and Breeding

After his homebred filly Pennycomequick, by Hurry On, had won the Oaks of 1929, Lord Astor was interviewed by the Evening Standard *and the* Review *took the liberty of quoting some extracts from that interview:*

'Frankly,' Lord Astor said, 'I do not know that there is any secret of the success I have had with my fillies. I have a variety of theories. Obviously there must be a certain amount of science in breeding anything, whether it be horses, sheep, cattle or orchids. All my animals can be traced to three mares – Conjure, Maid of the Mist, and Popinjay. Every mare in my stud at present I bred myself, except the twenty-four year old Popinjay. That adds greatly to the interest. I do not believe in buying horses. The pleasure of breeding is that you have always something in anticipation. Till you are beaten you hope that you will win. When you do lose you go into the paddock and there you see prospective winners. But when you see one of your horses win, you have the satisfaction of knowing that you bred it yourself. To my mind that is far better and more satisfying than buying a horse, no matter how successful it may prove. After all, a race is only the culmination of about three or four years' effort on one particular animal. During that time to see the horse develop gives me interest, pleasure and recreation. That is how I regard racing.'

H-B Status of Quashed and Solerina

In 1935, the fillies Quashed and Solerina finished first and fourth, in the English Oaks. They were both 'half-bred' horses and thus ineligible for registration in the General Stud Book. *In the case of Quashed it marked the first time that an 'H-B' had captured an English classic. As for Solerina, who secured the Stewards' Cup and other fixtures, she established herself as a champion sprinter. What a rarity that these tainted champions should both have been bred in the same year – 1932!*

IN THE *Sporting Life* Miss F. M. Prior, the compiler of the *Register of Thoroughbred Stallions* and *H-B Stud Book*, has reviewed the performance of 'half-bred' horses during the past season. Miss Prior recalls that last year a classic race was won for the first time by a member of one of our native 'h-b' families. The winner was, of course, Quashed, who won the Oaks. The following are extracts from the article:

'An occurrence nearly as remarkable stands out in the past season's record, for the champion stayer and champion sprinter are the same two "h.b." fillies who finished first and fourth in the Oaks last year.

'Seldom, indeed, does any mare prove capable of winning nearly £19,000 in stakes, but Quashed did so during the past two seasons.

'Quashed's only defeat of the year in six races was at Goodwood, when the five-year-olds Cecil and Enfield, at a difference of only 2 lb, beat her for the Cup.

'In her different sphere, much the same excellence was exhibited by the beautiful filly Solerina, whose successes comprised the July Handicap at Newmarket, Stewards' Cup at Goodwood, Stewards' Handicap, Nottingham, and Challenge Stakes, Newmarket.

'The performances of Quashed raised agitation in some quarters that the rule regarding admission to the *General Stud Book* should be relaxed in her favour.

'Her dam, Verdict, however, is a "double-dyed" "h-b", coming of an unregistered line on both her sire's and dam's side, in addition to having a cross of native American blood, through Umpire, further back in her pedigree.

'This fact alone would be sufficient to debar her entry to the *Stud Book* at the present day, though it so happens that Umpire was accepted under less stringent conditions which prevailed about seventy years ago.

'If Quashed were admitted, where is the line to be drawn as to which should be accepted and which refused? It would be an illogical position if Quashed were to be entered and her dam rejected.

'Though it is inconvenient that a notable mare should not be eligible for registration, it is far more so where a distinguished horse is concerned.

'Whereas the produce of the mare may not amount to more than half a dozen or so, a stallion may sire a large number of foals, and thus flood the Turf with his "half-bred" offspring, as happened within recent years as regards Prospector.

'Quashed's family history dates back to about the year 1847, when her earliest known ancestress, a Perion mare, made the journey from Dunchurch, near Rugby, into the neighbouring county of Stafford, to be mated with Melbourne, then standing at the Bonehill Stud, near Tamworth, and whose fee to half-bred mares was five guineas.

'The resulting produce was the mare who founded the Birdhill family, which, in course of time, has produced two colts placed in the Derby – Curzon, second to Sir Visto in 1895, and Thankerton, third to Mahmoud and Taj Akbar this year, and also third in the Two Thousand Guineas.

'Such details of Solerina's origin as are available date from about forty years later, and begin with the purchase in about 1890, by Mr R. B. Henry, the well-known North of Ireland sportsman, of a black mare, of whose breeding he could ascertain nothing, beyond that she was by the Lothario horse Piersfield.

'Her descendant Soloptic first brought the breed into prominence.'

BBR–1936

Mr James Weatherby, who compiled the first volume of the General Stud Book, *first used the term 'half-bred' to denote horses who could not be admitted. The term is however misleading. The word 'half' is suggestive of a horse only 50 per cent thoroughbred; the vast majority of horses excluded from the* General Stud Book *have a far higher proportion of thoroughbred blood.*

Non-thoroughbred horses have always been allowed to race against thoroughbreds on equal terms. And in terms of conformation and racing performance many are indistinguishable from registered thoroughbreds. Their non-admission to the GSB *is due to the fact that their pedigrees cannot be traced according to the requirements of that volume.*

The rescinding of the Jersey Act in 1949 regularised the position of Tourbillon and that horse's descendants in the Stud Book, *as well as the position of many American strains which had previously been prohibited. But the status of 'half-bred' families of English and Irish origin was to remain unchanged for a further twenty years. Weatherbys continued to allow members of these families to be registered for racing purposes; but they did not maintain any breeding records. This task continued to be performed by Miss Prior.*

By 1969, however, these non-thoroughbred horses constituted a problem which needed a solution; 12 per cent (1,978 out of 15,506) of the horses whose names were registered for the first time lacked properly authenticated pedigrees. At a time when thoroughbreds were subject to strict methods of documentation and identification, this situation amounted to an anomaly. The Jockey Club accordingly regularised the position by setting up a Register of Non-Thoroughbred Mares, *to which all mares employed in the production of horses for racing should be admitted.*

It was further decided, following intensive research into the histories of the 'half-bred' families, that certain mares from these families should be admitted into the main body of the General Stud Book. *The new rulings stipulated that these mares must possess at least eight crosses of thoroughbred blood and that their racecourse performance (or that of the families to which they belonged) must be of an acceptably high standard.*

Solerina possessed five crosses of thoroughbred blood. Her sire Soldennis and the sires of her first four dams in tail-female line were thoroughbred. However the pedigree of Solerina's fifth dam was unknown. Therefore in spite of her considerable racing ability, she was ineligible for the GSB, *as were her daughters and granddaughters (who possessed respectively six and seven crosses). Her great-granddaughters, however, possessed eight crosses of thoroughbred blood, and could therefore be designated 'thoroughbred'.*

The situation in respect of Quashed, however, was more complicated. Although she was a daughter of the thoroughbred stallion Obliterate, she was out of Verdict, who was doubly 'half-bred'; that is neither her sire nor her dam were thoroughbred in their own right. Verdict therefore possessed no thoroughbred crosses; Quashed possessed only one through her sire. The descendants of Quashed will not be eligible for the General Stud Book *until they have become removed from her by seven generations.*

A new rule was passed which enacted that no foal born after April 1st, 1974 should be registered for racing unless it was entered in the General Stud Book *or the* Register of Non-Thoroughbred Mares.

The Death of William Chismon

William Chismon, who died in 1937, made several significant contributions to British bloodstock breeding. He compiled the first complete Stallion Register *and his book,* Stallion Record, *a dictionary of the stallions of the nineteenth century whose names appeared in modern pedigrees, was a much copied success. Mr Chismon, who worked for Lord Wavertree (Colonel Hall Walker) and collaborated with him in many important areas of breeding, almost assuredly was a meaningful adviser to the Aga Khan. Indeed, Mr Chismon's article on 'The Vullier System of Dosage', which was written in 1916, was the first to explain the intricacies of this method (used so prominently by the Aga Khan) in precise, simple language.*

AFTER BEING in ill-health for a long time, William Chismon died at his home at Soham, Cambridge, on February 26th, about six weeks after he had attained his seventy-fourth birthday. He had been settled near Newmarket since 1921. Chismon commenced his career in the Telegraphic section of the Post Office. In his early days, he was located at Maidstone. In the course of his official duties, he formed a close friendship with the late Thomas Phillips, of the West Malling Stud, where the Two Thousand Guineas winner Galliard was standing. Then, a keen follower of racing, his interest in bloodstock breeding was immediately aroused. Possessing a colossal memory, coupled with unusual powers of appreciation and reception, Chismon quickly acquired almost unrivalled knowledge of our blood lines and the characteristics of the thoroughbred families. After filling further official posts, particularly at Thetford, Norfolk, it was in 1905 that Chismon became secretary to the late Lord Wavertree, then, of course, Colonel Hall Walker. Chismon had been in close touch with the Colonel on breeding subjects for many years previously to the time when the Colonel became so prominent as a breeder. A few years later the Tully Stud was founded near Kildare, to become the 'home' of Prince Palatine, Minoru, Polar Star, Cherry Lass, Night Hawk, Charles O'Malley, White Eagle and Gondolette. Chismon and his master collaborated in working out and testing the many theories of bloodstock breeding, in which Lord Wavertree delighted to indulge. Naturally, there were many conflicts over diverse opinions. Again and again Chismon resigned. Colonel Hall Walker always emphatically refused to sanction his departure, for he had the highest appreciation of Chismon's knowledge and experience. After Tully became the National Stud, and Colonel Hall Walker retired from breeding, Chismon became adviser to many other breeders and owners. It was while he was with Colonel Hall Walker that William Chismon compiled the first complete *Stallion Register*. It was issued in 1900. There was a preface by Lord Wavertree, wherein he expressed one of Chismon's ideas, namely, the official registration of all stallion fees. A second volume of the *Stallion Register* was issued in 1904. Both were for private circulation. In 1901, Chismon compiled, and issued under his own name, his unrivalled *Stallion Record*. It is a dictionary of the stallions of the nineteenth century, whose names appeared in modern pedigrees. The idea was copied in other countries. Chismon's book has been out of print for very many years. It is one of the most helpful books of its kind ever published. The *Stallion Registers* for 1900 and 1904 are also practically unobtainable.

His knowledge of blood lines was profound. He was one of the first men in this country to have a thorough grasp of the intricacies of what is now known as the Dosage System. This is explained in the book entitled *Les Croisements Rationnels*, by the late Colonel J. Vuillier.

After the death of Lord Wavertree, the Aga Khan paid a very great tribute of his respect for Lord Wavertree's judgment as a breeder of thoroughbreds. We are under the impression that for some time Chismon was one of the Aga Khan's advisers on breeding.

BBR–1937

William Chismon on Vuillier's Dosage System

In the 1916 Bloodstock Breeders' Review, *William Chismon had an article which, along with a good word for the Figure System and other comments on research in breeding, discussed, with approbation, the system of breeding advocated by the French writer, Monsieur J. Vuillier, in his book 'Les Croisements Rationnels', a system which was ultimately to be used with considerable success by The Aga Khan.*

Besides this early mention of Dosage and a salute to the much reviled Figure System, Mr Chismon speaks of other matters of breeding which are of interest in this day and age.

THE REASON why breeders select their stallions are often somewhat amazing. We have the owner of high class mares who books subscriptions only to the highest-priced stallions, and turns up his nose at anything less than a hundred guinea fee. His mares are probably very finely bred, and, because, as a rule, the high-priced stallions are just as finely bred a breeder of this type is asking for trouble. He forgets that fine gold will not wear well without an alloy; neither will the progeny of his finely-bred mares be very robust or sturdy if got by stallions whose pedigrees contain too much fine blood.

Then we have the breeder who breeds for sales, who tries to catch the will-o'-the-wisp fashion of the day, or rather the day when his youngsters come up for sale. He is like the man who dabbles on the Stock Exchange and hopes always to get out at the top of the market. He is a very clever or lucky man who can, three years ahead, choose a stallion whose stock will be in demand at the end of that period. We have breeders who send a big batch of mares to one stallion in consideration of a largely reduced fee. These breeders have some 'method in their madness', for, assuming a fair proportion of their mares are winners, or dams of winners, and the stallion used is a horse of merit, the breeder is pretty sure to get something that can go. A certain number of the batch are sure to be misfits, but the average result may be satisfactory. If a breeder of this type selects his mares to suit the stallion, this is probably a fairly good breeding proposition. There is evidence tending to show that it is a method that successful breeders like Sir Joseph Hawley and others practised. Other breeders choose stallions for their mares through propinquity, some through friendship; many a nomination has been booked over the dining table during the December Sale week. Again, there are breeders who go in for any free subscriptions that are to be obtained; and so on, down to the man who gets a free service at the price of an option on the foal, this last being more common in Ireland than in England.

Now it is certain there is no system that will suit all breeders, who have, it is true, the one aim, but different ideas of attaining it. There can be no system guaranteed to be successful in individual cases. Even though the breeding theory may be correct, the animal is frequently wrong – wrong in health and constitution, wrong in make and shape, and only too often in breeding capacity. But there are systems, or rather, forms of systematic action, which will, if judiciously used, lead to success. One such has previously been outlined; another is the much maligned, and much misunderstood Figure System. A third (as to which more follows) is, the system of breeding advocated by the French writer, Monsieur J. Vuillier (Lottery) in his book 'Les Croisements Rationnels'.

It is quite likely that, in mentioning with approval the Figure System, I shall call down upon myself the scientific wrath of my friend 'Mankato'. Nothing he can say, however, will affect my opinion, based on experience, that there are very considerable merits in that system. There are more ways than one to success, as there are roads to Rome, or Heaven. The Figure System is the best index to pedigrees that can be found. I used the theory for my own manuscript stud book at least twelve years prior to Bruce Lowe's book making its appearance. Nothing is more useful in breeding than the knowledge of how some female taproots carry their characteristics along. Some taproots are good, some the contrary; some are jady, others are stout; some are shy breeders, others breed better colts than fillies; and so on. Some families nick better than others; some do not nick at all. All these things, and some of them are very important, can become known through an intelligent study of the Figure System, always remembering that the animal must be there, as well as the figures.

Vuillier's theory is that where a stallion (or brood mare) is lacking, or deficient in, any of the above constituents a mate should be selected who brings into the combination representing the offspring the blood that is missing of deficient in either parent. For practical purposes, it appears to me that if attention is given to the last eight strains, most of which can be pretty easily traced in modern pedigrees, the Herod, Highflyer, and Eclipse proportions will be about right.

It will be recognised that by working on these lines a breeder is always aiming at the 'standard' racehorse as represented by the proportions mentioned; and if, from time to time, the average is corrected by the addition of high-class horses of later times, we shall be making a systematic attempt to breed to the highest standard.

The before-mentioned system of M. Vuillier has not, in my opinion, received the attention it deserves from English breeders. Working somewhat on the same lines as Bruce Lowe, Vuillier selected all the classic winners, and also many other high-class horses; but instead of classifying them under their taproots he analysed the pedigrees into their leading constituent parts. In other words, he found out how the best horses were built up. The work must have been arduous in the extreme, and deserves the greatest appreciation. His researches led him to the conclusion that the average analysis of all the best English horses resolved itself into the following chief strains and proportions thereof:

HEROD	750	)
HIGHFLYER	570	)
ECLIPSE	540	) IN TWELVE
BIRDCATCHER	300	) GENERATIONS
TOUCHSTONE	300	) OF
POCAHONTAS	300	) ANCESTORS
VOLTAIRE	200	) WHO MAKE
PANTALOON	200	) A TOTAL
MELBOURNE	150	) OF 4,096
BAY MIDDLETON	120	)
GLADIATOR	120	)

The Contributions of the Arab

IN A CONTRIBUTION to correspondence in *The Times* regarding the merits of Arab horses, Sir Alfred E. Pease wrote:

'I think there is no doubt that the high caste Arabian, certainly in the case of Darley's Arabian, did contribute stamina and "temperament" (mettle and courage) to the English racehorse, but I agree that he is useless as an "improver" in respect to speed. I have had a varied experience of pure Arabians, and of such branches of the family as Syrian, Egyptian, Dongolese, Sudanese, Somali, and others found in Africa, and to a less extent of Indian. Most of these are remarkable for stamina, courage, and wear and tear qualities. Several of the gamest and cleverest hunters I have had were out of Arabian mares. The late Mr Wilfred Blunt lent me one of his high-caste true Arabians (14.2 hands), and he got a first-class hunter (16 hands) from a pony mare 14.3 hands. To those who are familiar with the "hot blood" yet gentleness of the Oriental, there is no more delightful ride than the Anglo-Arabian, Anglo-Barb, or Arab-Barb.'   BBR–1937

Temperament or Stupidity

IN ONE OF his entertaining and informative articles in *Horse and Hound* Mr J. Fairfax-Blakeborough wrote:

> 'Is there any animal so difficult to deal with in case of fire as a horse? Can their paralysing fear of flames and smoke be traced back to the prairie fires of old, or is it just the nervous temperament of the animal, or is it just stupidity? There have been more farm and stack fires this autumn than ever I remember before, and invariably when there has been any danger of the building housing stock being involved, doors have been opened and cows, bullocks, and pigs have not awaited an invitation to escape. They have smelled the smoke, known that there was danger, and were quite anxious to put some distance between themselves and the cause of their alarm. Not so the horses. Their whole idea of safety seems to be to climb into their mangers, to rush forward. In some cases it has been necessary to blindfold them before they could be induced to leave their stabling, and, even then, so terrified are they that it is no easy matter to lead them away.'

BBR–1937

Index

Time and space do not permit a comprehensive index which, in a book like this, would run to many, many pages. The following is, therefore, a selective index highlighting only those horses, people, places, races etc., which have more than 'a passing mention' in the text. Authors of articles who are also subjects are indexed separately. Photographs are indicated by page numbers in italics.